SCHOOL OF ORIENTAL AND AFRICAN STUDIES
University of London

Please return this book on or before the last date shown

Long loans and One Week loans may be renewed up to 10 times
Short loans & CDs cannot be renewed
Fines are charged on all overdue items

Online: http://lib.soas.ac.uk/patroninfo
Phone: 020-7898 4197 (answerphone)

Dilemmas of Victory

Dilemmas of Victory

THE EARLY YEARS OF THE
PEOPLE'S REPUBLIC OF CHINA

Edited by

JEREMY BROWN

PAUL G. PICKOWICZ

HARVARD UNIVERSITY PRESS

Cambridge, Massachusetts
London, England 2007

Copyright © 2007 by the President and Fellows of Harvard College
Printed in the United States of America

Library of Congress Cataloging-in-Publication Data

Dilemmas of victory : the early years of the People's Republic of China / edited
by Jeremy Brown and Paul G. Pickowicz.
    p. cm.
Includes bibliographical references and index.
ISBN-13: 978-0-674-02616-2 (alk. paper)
ISBN-10: 0-674-02616-0 (alk. paper)
   1. China—History—1949–1976. I. Brown, Jeremy, 1976– II. Pickowicz, Paul.
III. Title: Early years of the People's Republic of China.
DS777.55.D527 2007
951.05'5—dc22   2007014277

In loving memory of Frederic Wakeman Jr.
colleague, teacher, friend

Contents

Acknowledgments

This book is the result of a conference titled "The Early Years of the People's Republic of China: Revisiting the 1949–1953 Transitional Era," convened at the University of California, San Diego, on June 20–23, 2004. Our daily discussions took place in the historic Martin Johnson House, located high on the cliffs overlooking the Pacific Ocean and beautifully maintained by our colleagues at the Scripps Institution of Oceanography.

In addition to the authors contributing to this volume, several other outstanding scholars participated in the conference. We wish to thank Robert Cliver of Humboldt State University and Xu Lanjun of Princeton University for sharing their research findings with us and for serving as effective and insightful discussants. Several doctoral students in the Department of History at the University of California, San Diego, played important supporting roles during the conference. Jeremy Murray served as conference rapporteur, while Brent Haas, Ellen Huang, Dahpon David Ho, Matthew Johnson, Elya J. Zhang, and Xiaowei Zheng provided crucial logistical support. Betty Gunderson and Julia Kwan, staff members of the Program in Chinese Studies at the University of California, San Diego, did much to facilitate conference scheduling, communications, and manuscript preparation.

We wish to thank Kathleen McDermott, our editor at Harvard University Press, for her excellent work on the project, and Susan Badger, our capable copyeditor. We are also extremely grateful for the many useful comments and suggestions made by the expert peer reviewers invited by the press to evaluate the scholarship that appears in this book.

We are pleased to acknowledge the generous financial support for the conference and the editorial phase of the project provided by the following organizations at the University of California, San Diego: Office of the Senior Vice Chancellor—Academic Affairs, the Center for the Humanities, the Hsiu Endowment for Chinese Studies, the Program in Chinese Studies, the Council on East Asian Studies, and the Department of History.

Our late colleague Fred Wakeman inspired many people. Generous and supportive, he was one of the guiding lights of the conference. Fred's marvelous chapter sets the tone for the rest of the book. For these reasons, and much more, we dedicate *Dilemmas of Victory* to this great scholar and respected friend.

Dilemmas of Victory

1

The Early Years of the People's Republic of China: An Introduction

Jeremy Brown and Paul G. Pickowicz

EVER SINCE 1953, when the First Five-Year Plan signaled the close of Mao Zedong's experiment with New Democracy and ushered in the beginning of a transition to socialism, China's early 1950s period has disappeared from the radar screens of successive waves of observers. This is not surprising. As attention turned to explaining dramatic new developments in China, including the Great Leap Forward, the Cultural Revolution, and post-Mao reforms, who was interested in dwelling on the period immediately following the Communist takeover of the mainland in 1949? After all, the first years of the People's Republic of China were transitional, and their direct relevance to the upheavals that followed remained unclear.

Officials and academics in China, many of them personally shaken by the traumas of the period after 1953, have been quicker than their counterparts in the West to assess the early People's Republic. In official histories, the early 1950s appear as a "golden age" of relative stability, economic recovery, and social harmony.[1] Indeed, fostering unity was official party policy during the early 1950s. Mao's principles of New Democracy promised a "national united front" that would make room for capitalists and many other Chinese who did not fit neatly into the revolutionary "worker-peasant alliance."

It is no coincidence that post-Mao reform-era publications promote positive memories of the early 1950s: the two periods share striking similarities. After the founding of the People's Republic in October 1949—and again in the late 1970s after Mao died—a massive wave of rural migrants entered cities, private factories coexisted alongside large state enterprises, nongovernmental and church groups operated next to Communist Party–led organizations, and capitalists and other nonparty figures supported the regime and played a role in shaping its policies.

Yet as anyone who lived through both periods knows, 2001 was not 1951. In the early 1950s, China was recovering from a century of imperialist invasion, civil war, and natural disaster. Governing a country as huge, diverse, fragmented, and poverty-stricken as China was an overwhelming task, especially for a party that had spent the previous two decades in the hinterland. Immediately after taking power, the Communists faced immense challenges. By late 1950, the People's Republic was fighting a war against the United States in Korea, while at the same time vast regions of China, roiled by armed insurrections, were only nominally under Communist control. But this period in the early People's Republic was also a time of hope and enthusiasm. Inclusive new institutions were established. In cities, members of the bourgeoisie were expected to reform themselves and to sacrifice their interests for the greater good; but they were also invited to contribute to building a new society. In villages, landlords had less room to maneuver, especially after late 1950, when moderate land reform policies gave way to more violent class struggle.[2]

The first generation of Western scholarship on China in the early 1950s hinted at the challenges, uncertainties, hopes, and fears of the time. By 1953 most Western journalists, students, and clergy had left China, but just four years earlier many witnessed the Communist takeover of large cities such as Beijing and Shanghai. Their accounts ranged from sympathetic to virulently anti-Communist. All were concerned with the question of whether the Communists had rightfully won the civil war or whether the victors of 1949 had simply filled a political vacuum left by the utter collapse of the Nationalists.

Firsthand accounts confirmed that the Nationalist government had lost popular support and that people from all sectors of society were ready for change. Intellectuals, students, and others not necessarily predisposed to support communism warmly welcomed the disciplined rural troops who marched into China's eastern cities in 1948 and 1949.[3] Yet an undercurrent of fear was also evident in these initial reports, especially those that covered the new regime's efforts to clean up and remake society through reforming intellectuals and suppressing "counterrevolutionaries" in 1950 and 1951.[4]

Scholars also debated whether the Chinese Communist Party was a pawn in a vast international conspiracy masterminded by the Soviet Union. The party had been governing areas of north-central and northeast China for more than ten years, but the outside world knew little about the movement. The growing Red Scare in the United States made it easier to argue that the Chinese Communist movement was dutifully following Moscow's orders. China was certainly cooperating with the Soviet Union in the 1950s, but it was also following its own nationalist path. To Mao, Soviet support may have contributed to the victory of the revolution, but the Chinese people had "stood up" on their own. However, the details of the relationship and the nature of interactions between Chinese citizens and Soviet technicians remained obscure.

Evidence that China's Communist government used violent and coercive methods provided fodder for those predisposed to condemn new China as a "totalitarian" society like the Soviet Union. The first academic books on China in the early 1950s, based mostly on intelligence reports and translations of Chinese newspapers, depicted an all-powerful state whipping citizens into meek obedience. Such works concluded that most Chinese people were living "a life of fearful apathy" and that state terror had "cripple[d] any will which the Chinese people might have to resist."[5]

Close studies of decision making at the top levels of Communist leadership continued in this "know the enemy" vein but differed on whether Chinese leaders were blindly following the orders of the Soviet Union. For example, Allen Whiting argued that China entered the Korean War in response to a genuine threat to its national security, not as a part of a Soviet plot.[6] Even in the context of the cold war, some scholars attempted to analyze China on its own terms. However, source limitations and a top-down approach meant that the important domestic repercussions of the Korean War remained unexplored.

Other works based on personal experience or interviews with exiles in Hong Kong suggested that China's new leaders were interested in more than national security, political control, and economic modernization. The revolution seemed to be unfolding on a personal, psychological, even spiritual level. Robert Jay Lifton's *Thought Reform and the*

Psychology of Totalism and Allyn Rickett and Adele Rickett's *Prisoners of Liberation*, a memoir by two Americans who experienced thought reform in a Chinese prison and came to support the Communist regime, showed a system that instead of indiscriminately killing potential enemies offered them salvation in exchange for complete allegiance.[7]

Taken together, memoirs and academic works written in the 1950s indicated that China's rulers had consolidated power through a mixture of popular enthusiasm for change plus terror and indoctrination. But reliance on refugee interviews and newspaper reports left many questions unanswered. By necessity, these studies mostly focused on large cities where the new regime had concentrated its forces, perhaps over-estimating the party's control over society and obscuring events in the more than 80 percent of China that was still rural in 1950.[8] Were all of China's diverse regions undergoing the same process at the same time? Did the changes of the early 1950s affect villagers and city residents, men and women, and Han people and ethnic minorities in similar ways? Had people's allegiances to family, native place, and professional success completely disappeared?

A new generation of graduate students and young professors in the social sciences began to shed light on these questions in the 1960s and 1970s. New works focused on state-society relations and the balance between old (traditional Chinese culture) and new (communist revolution) in the early People's Republic. Several trends emerged during this second wave of scholarship on China in the early 1950s. First, source constraints meant that scholars still paid more attention to the organization and functions of the party-state than to local society. Second, political scientists and sociologists sought to explain how policies were implemented but not how they were experienced. Third, the outbreak of the Cultural Revolution in 1966 led to a heightened awareness of conflict and divisions within China that had been present throughout the 1950s.[9]

Before the Cultural Revolution shattered images of a cohesive society guided by a united party leadership, Franz Schurmann's *Ideology and Organization in Communist China* detailed the Leninist institutions through which the party managed Chinese society.[10] Schurmann held that in the 1950s the party-state had demolished and replaced traditional networks of authority. But as other social scientists continued to look more closely at individual provinces or cities, it became clear that preexisting patterns and divisions had not disappeared. Even for Communist officials, ties to family and native place coexisted with loyalty to nation and party during the early 1950s. Ezra Vogel's *Canton under Communism* exposed friction between locals and outsiders in Guangdong province. Local cadres who had been active in the Communist underground for years chafed at taking orders from the northerners who entered the province en masse in 1949. Tensions worsened when outsiders criticized and overruled Guangdong natives' mild approach to land reform.[11] Vogel's attention to the wide differences in language and outlook among cadres in a single province provided a more complex picture of the party in the early 1950s.

The Cultural Revolution provided striking evidence of divisions within the party and Chinese society as a whole. Scholars traced disagreements on basic policy back to the 1950s. In his study of Tianjin, political scientist Kenneth Lieberthal distinguished between Mao Zedong's mass mobilization model of governance and the party's top-down organization, championed by second-in-command Liu Shaoqi.[12] Liu had visited Tianjin in spring 1949 and spoke out against radical revolution and confrontational demands directed at the upper strata of urban society. During the three years following Liu's visit, urban cadres pursued a policy of relative moderation and accommodation. Many city residents remained untouched by Communist policy and propaganda. Only individuals in targeted groups, such as "counterrevolutionaries" and members of religious secret societies, felt the strong hand of party rule. For Lieberthal, it was the Korean War and the Three-Anti (*sanfan*) and Five-Anti (*wufan*) campaigns of 1952 and 1953 that finally tightened Communist control over the city and ushered in a "second revolution." Readers learned that these turning points were even more pivotal than the 1949 takeover but still knew little about how individuals experienced the campaigns of the early 1950s.

As long as mainland China remained closed to foreign researchers, reliance on newspapers and exile testimony would limit the scope of works on the early 1950s. This situation changed after Mao died. Access to new sources radically reshaped views of the Mao era. Beginning in the late 1970s, foreign scholars could conduct interviews, though government supervisors were often present. More recently, it became possible, even common, to talk to individuals about the past without any official involvement. And although access and holdings vary widely from place to place, in general Chinese archives have been more forth-coming with documents and reports dating from the early 1950s than from later periods. For instance, county-level archives have allowed scholars to explore how rural women took advantage of the 1950 Marriage Law for their own purposes.[13] Documents from municipal archives have led to much more detailed accounts of the Communist takeover of city institutions and the reordering of urban society.[14]

Recent official publications have also provided a wealth of detail on early 1950s politics, especially at the elite level. While many such works are dedicated to celebrating the "golden age" following "liberation," they often provide specific details about eradicating "counterrevolutionaries" and anti-Communist "bandits."[15] These new sources have led to breakthroughs in understanding the revolutionary and nationalist character of Mao's foreign policy, including his decision to enter the Korean War.[16]

As the source base has changed, so have scholarly perspectives. After class struggle was repudiated following Mao's death, many scholars stopped analyzing the People's Republic through the lens of revolution. Putting revolution on the back burner and thinking about twentieth-century China in terms of a steady process of state-building and modernization led scholars to explore continuities between Nationalist and Communist rule. From this perspective, 1949 no longer seemed like a stark dividing line. William Kirby's pathbreaking studies of technocrats inspired new books that analyzed pre- and post-1949 similarities in family structure and the workplace.[17] When the Communists began governing the mainland, it was argued, necessity and strategy ensured that the institutions, individuals, and social patterns of the pre-1949 period would continue to play a major role in the new society.

The chapters in this volume build upon and complicate this scholarly project of bridging the 1949 divide. In such areas as urban policy, public security, industrial development, education, labor relations, ethnic minorities, and rural health care, the Communists behaved in the early 1950s much like the Nationalists had in the 1930s and 1940s. Like the Nationalists, the Communists were committed to the formation of a strong state, even if accelerated state-building weakened the ability of social groups to express their own will. Hence, even though the Communists were the self-proclaimed party of the urban proletariat, they moved quickly after spring 1949 to impose tight state control of the labor movement, just as the Nationalists had done in the past. However, there were significant differences between the Communists and Nationalists in terms of style, methods, and results. As Frederic Wakeman Jr. writes in Chapter 2, "When it came to mobilization, the Nationalists exhorted, passed down decrees, and herded. The Communists' instinct was to go to the primary or grassroot level and commence organizing there, calling on the 'masses' to participate actively."

In the pages that follow, we ask what happened when the Communists went to the grassroots in the early 1950s. Who were the "masses" targeted by mobilization, and how did they respond to the dilemmas posed by Communist victory? For that matter, who were the "Communists"? Not surprisingly, the answers are complex. This is not a study of elite politics; rather, it is an exploration of what happened when people from a variety of backgrounds interacted with mid- to lower-level representatives of the revolutionary party-state. Mao Zedong, Zhou Enlai, Liu Shaoqi, and Deng Xiaoping are, of course, crucial figures and occasionally appear in the next fourteen chapters. Yet more often, readers will become acquainted with deputy mayors, university deans, battalion commanders, and women's league representatives—in other words, with the non–household names who were charged with carrying out Mao's orders at the local level. During the early 1950s, these officials were far more important than Mao was in the daily lives of the rural midwives, rich industrialists, movie stars, scientists, household heads, comedians, and prisoners of war whose stories are told in this book.

The main aim of this volume is to depict the extraordinary diversity and complexity of how individuals, families, and social groups experienced the 1949–53 years. We argue that it is unwise to generalize about China during the early 1950s. Previous scholarship has provided a useful outline of the era: a relatively swift military takeover in 1949, the party's initially inclusive approach to urban social groups, tightening and repression after the outbreak of the Korean War, movements such as land reform and the Three- and Five-Anti campaigns that consolidated party control in villages and cities, and finally the move toward socialist transformation in 1953. Our reassessment of the period reveals an astonishing degree of variations and exceptions to this general pattern. How one experienced the early 1950s depended on geography, social standing, timing, and chance. For example, the military takeover of Guizhou was not swift—it was not completed until 1951. The Three- and Five-Anti campaigns were jarring, life-changing events for Shanghai charity directors and prominent capitalists but were meaningless to rural Shaanxi women, who were affected most profoundly by changes in childbirth practices.

Such diversity makes it impossible to provide a definitive answer to the question of whether the early 1950s represented a relatively peaceful "honeymoon" or an ominous foreshadowing of disasters to come, a time of dashed promises and betrayed hopes. The era was many different things for different people in different places. For a high-level provincial bureaucrat's rapidly growing family in Shenyang, the period was indeed a golden age. In 1951, soldiers stationed in remote Xinjiang enjoyed quite literal honeymoons when the army arranged for unsuspecting Hunanese girls to become their wives. Yet this was only one side of the coin. Movie stars, *xiangsheng* performers, and paleoanthropologists eager to cooperate with the new regime "had no idea they were about to get kicked in the teeth," as Perry Link observes in Chapter 9. As we shall see, serious tooth-kicking ensued as the party attempted, with mixed success, to eliminate potential enemies, unacceptable satire, and ideologically incorrect scientific viewpoints.

The party was most effective when it focused its full attention and resources on a given task. In the early 1950s, the new regime's juggling act was by turns awe inspiring and comical, as the party prioritized which prized balls to keep in the air and which lesser orbs were allowed to drop and skitter across the floor. Occupying such key cities as Shanghai, restoring industrial production in the northeast, persuading rich capitalists (and their money) to stay in mainland China, and making sure Tibet became a part of the new People's Republic were top priorities. Central leaders worked tirelessly to ensure the success of these ventures, and in the process, the party looked like a well-organized revolutionary force. In contrast, the party postponed, ignored, or bungled less pressing tasks. For example, the new regime seemed surprisingly lax—even incompetent—in occupying Guizhou, sorting out the checkered pasts of labor activists in Shanghai, and allowing Hollywood films and pamphlets on creationism to circulate, especially before 1951. In the complex interaction between "state" and "society" in 1949 and 1950, society often had the upper hand.

Unlike previous studies of the early years of the People's Republic, this volume travels far beyond urban coastal China to explore the Communist takeover of non-Han regions. As chapters on Guizhou, Tibet, and Xinjiang show, before 1949 the party was willing to consider autonomy and national self-determination for ethnic minorities. But as soon as it became clear that victory was at hand, leaders' definition of "China" hardened and largely followed the boundaries of the Republic of China and, interestingly, the Qing empire. Through a mix of military maneuvers and hard-edged diplomacy, the People's Liberation Army (PLA) occupied Tibet by late 1951. Taking control of Xinjiang was a messier process, requiring Joseph Stalin's intervention and Mao's recognition of the independence of Outer Mongolia. In each case, top Communist leaders viewed non-Hans as less civilized people—to be handled with caution, perhaps, but not with respect. In this regard, the Communists looked much like their Nationalist predecessors.

Although Stalin's role in handing Xinjiang to the Chinese Communists comes as a revelation, tension between Mao and the Soviet dictator is better known. This volume goes beyond top-level contacts and generalizations about "emulating the Soviet model" to shed new light on Sino-Soviet cooperation and conflict during the early 1950s.[18] At China's first "new-style" university, in the Soviet-occupied port city of Dalian, and in the world of evolutionary science, Chinese people interacted on a daily basis with Soviet officials, technicians, and ideas. On the ground, Sino-Soviet relations were forged not by Mao and Stalin but rather by such functionaries as Filippov (at Chinese People's University) and Kozlov (head of the Soviet military garrison in Dalian) and the Chinese officials with whom they butted heads. These encounters were characterized by neither wholesale dependence nor constant animosity. Midlevel Chinese cadres knew that the Soviet help was crucial to invigorating urban industry and establishing institutions of higher education. Yet both sides harbored suspicions. Insults and slights angered Chinese officials, who were at least as nationalist as they were communist. They wondered: how could it be possible that the Soviet Union was both a socialist and an imperialist country?

Jaded Soviet advisers chuckled at the Chinese Communist Party's earnest efforts to transform the consciousness and worldview of the nonrevolutionary and antirevolutionary majority in China. But the various campaigns waged in business, education, scholarly, and arts circles in the early 1950s were a major facet of urban life. Many nonrevolutionaries seemed to become "true believers" overnight. But what can be said about the depth and sincerity of these conversions? The case studies in this volume show that profound concerns about personal careers and family trajectories played a major role in the "thought transformation" process of individual citizens. These personal concerns were (and are) rarely acknowledged. Many people were faking it. Many others were opportunistic. The party knew this and did not care much in the early years. What people said in public was more important than what they really thought or what they said at home. From the perspective of the present day, the "thought reform" campaigns of the early 1950s look like superficial solutions that failed to make much of a long-term impact.

Far more important was the climate of fear that was becoming ever more deeply ingrained. If the party was not successful in convincing many people to genuinely "transform their consciousness," it was quite adept at generating fear and getting people to turn on one another instead of acting in concert to express group interests and thus pose a potential threat to the concentration of state power. Philanthropists, labor leaders, businessmen, and artists undoubtedly preferred not to inform on one another. But when the choice was to be an activist in a struggle campaign or a target, many saw the wisdom of becoming a militant.

Fear mixed with hopeful idealism fostered what we call a "culture of accommodation." Instead of resisting or simply fleeing China, many nonparty figures bent over backward to collaborate in their own demise. Capitalists handed over their money, leaders of social welfare organizations gave up their autonomy, and performers and scientists relinquished their artistic and academic freedom. Their hope was that coming to an accommodation with the new regime would, at best, lead to political and material rewards. At the least, those who collaborated hoped to spare themselves and their families unnecessary violence and turbulence. For some the strategy worked: cooperative businessmen were granted official positions, and even if they were no longer filthy rich, they were still guaranteed comfortable lives. By 1953, many people had survived the campaigns of the preceding years. They were perhaps bowed, but they were unbroken. How many could say the same in 1957 or 1966 or 1976? The gradually intensifying atmosphere of paranoia fostered before 1953 did not preordain the later tragedies of the Mao years, but the seeds of catastrophe had been planted.

Our exploration of the early years of the People's Republic begins with chapters in Part I on the takeover of large industrial cities, especially Shanghai. Considering that the Nationalists were unpopular and fled Shanghai without a fight in May 1949, the takeover was surprisingly touch and go, and the ease of victory more apparent than real. In Chapter 2, Frederic Wakeman Jr. subtly probes the complicated ways in which top leaders of both the Communist and Nationalist parties interacted with diverse and shadowy lower-level operatives on the streets of Shanghai on the eve of the takeover, presenting a powerful portrait of the survival strategies of ordinary people, including policemen, cadres, soldiers, spies, neighborhood watch committees, speculators, vagrants, pickpockets, armed robbers, and saboteurs. He observes that people changed sides all the time, just as they had in the aftermath of Chiang Kai-shek's 1927 anti-Communist coup, the Japanese wartime occupation, and the civil war of the late 1940s. Anyone, even a family member, could be a turncoat or a spy. Wakeman shows that these legacies of betrayal and deceit fostered the deeply rooted culture of paranoia mentioned earlier, a culture that fueled subsequent campaigns to track down and eliminate imagined "traitors" and "counterrevolutionaries."

Many industrial workers and communist labor organizers in Shanghai assumed they would be the "masters" of new China. After all, the proletariat did much before and immediately after the party's seizure of power to support the revolution. But as Elizabeth J. Perry argues in Chapter 3, after spring 1949 the party increasingly acted to stifle labor radicalism in the interests of promoting political stability and economic development. Perry shows that the Communist attitude toward labor was quite similar to the old Nationalist approach. Party and state control of unions and factory militias was absolutely required. Indeed, after three decades of mutual imitation and infiltration between the two parties, it was often impossible for the party to distinguish clearly between Nationalist and Communist components of the labor movement. From the beginning, the Communists, like the Nationalists, embraced labor leaders who subordinated the class interests of the proletariat to the party's state-building agenda and rejected labor activists who put the interests of the working class above all else. Many workers and labor leaders felt betrayed. Since almost everyone in the labor movement had a complicated background, many labor leaders were willing and able to demonize their comrades in the high-stakes political environment that followed "liberation."

The social complexity of urban China in the early 1950s becomes even more apparent when we consider the fate of Shanghai's influential philanthropic community. In Chapter 4 Nara Dillon demonstrates that charities were linked in the late 1940s to the Nationalist state and the industrial bourgeoisie but remained in place and did much to serve society and the new regime in 1949 and 1950. The number of charities in Shanghai actually increased after 1949. Beginning with the Campaign to Suppress Counterrevolutionaries in early 1951, however, the party worked slowly but steadily to eliminate charitable organizations, many of which had ties to China's Korean War enemies. Vague charges of corruption were hurled at voluntary associations in order to undermine the legitimacy of the bourgeoisie. Dillon notes that campaign tactics also pitted bourgeois leaders against one another, as prominent members of the charitable community disassociated themselves from their economic and organizational sources of power. The regime was not ready for the kind of open class warfare that many industrial workers unsuccessfully sought in 1952. But its systematic assault on the bourgeoisie in other settings was ultimately just as effective. The philanthropic bourgeoisie not only failed to resist its demise but actually cooperated in it, pursuing individual strategies to prove one's loyalty, transform one's class status, and rejoin the regime's social base in other capacities.

The chapters in Part II point to the profound difference between the takeover of centrally located cities such as Shanghai and the occupation of peripheral areas. The occupation of Guizhou province and other places in the southwest where the party had almost no organizational presence was a low priority and poorly planned. Locals experienced the takeover as an alien occupation by hostile forces. In Chapter 5 Jeremy Brown shows that the PLA raced through Guizhou in late 1949 but was unprepared to rule. The invading armies confiscated grain, left villagers hungry, and placed administration in the hands of ex-Nationalists, local power wielders, and even bandits. The region soon exploded in rebellion. Brown argues that the party finally secured the region by launching a reign of terror in the guise of the Campaign to Suppress Counterrevolutionaries. Thousands were executed, their bodies displayed in public as a warning. Tens of thousands were conscripted into the PLA and became cannon fodder in Korea. Many of these instant inductees were put on trains and misled about their final destination. Not surprisingly, PLA soldiers from the southwest were remarkably overrepresented among the many Chinese who were killed in Korea, who quit the battlefield, who were captured by the UN side, and who defected to Taiwan after the cease-fire.

Tensions of a different sort characterized the long-distance interactions between the Communist Party and Tibetan elites from spring 1949 to fall 1951. As Chen Jian points out in Chapter 6, prior to 1949 the Communists opposed Nationalist policy by insisting that Tibet had the right to be separate from China. But once the Nationalists were defeated, the Communists suddenly adopted the Nationalist policy as their own. Tibet was to be a part of new China. While building up troop strength in the region, the party stressed flexible negotiations. Still, most Tibetan elites stalled or resisted, though some collaborated. In October 1950 the Communists resorted to military force and easily crushed the poorly equipped Tibetan army at Chamdo. Even then the Tibetans continued to balk. But with the United States, Britain, and the United Nations doing almost nothing in response to their desperate appeals, the Tibetans had no alternative but to negotiate a settlement in spring 1951. They were forced to say Tibet was part of China. Chen Jian finds that the takeover of Tibet was experienced by Tibetans as a Han takeover, and Tibetan-Han relations were poisoned. Mao's attitude of Han ethnic superiority, now in socialist disguise, was deeply resented by locals.

Ethnic tensions of a profoundly different sort complicated the Communist takeover of Dalian in present-day Liaoning province close to North Korea. Indeed, as Christian A. Hess shows in Chapter 7, the Dalian region was not "liberated" by Chinese Communists in 1949; it was taken over by the Soviet Union in 1945. The Soviets administered the strategic port well into 1950 and stationed troops there until 1955. Nowhere in China did the Soviet Union and the Chinese Communist Party interact more closely than in the Dalian region from 1945 to 1950. The relationship was problem ridden, foreshadowing greater tensions in Sino-Soviet relations in the decade after 1950. Some Chinese cadres meekly accepted Soviet authority, but many others were infuriated by Soviet behavior. The Soviets seemed more like the imperialists of old than like revolutionaries. For their part, the Soviets, favoring social and political stability, were shocked by the violence of Chinese class struggle campaigns. Overall, Hess shows, the Soviets were a moderating influence on Chinese Communist urban policy after 1949. Relations improved when the new Sino-Soviet treaty was signed in 1950. Upbeat Sino-Soviet friendship associations and summer youth camps seemed to flourish, but the Chinese authorities had to conceal the conflicts of the late 1940s and disseminate misleading propaganda about Soviet "contributions" to the socialist transformation of the region.

Xinjiang, our final case study of the occupation of the periphery, was inhabited by Muslim Uyghurs who were deeply suspicious of Hans. The Communist Party had no organization or military forces in Xinjiang. Indeed, the Soviet Union had more influence in Xinjiang than the Chinese Communists. In Chapter 8 James Z. Gao argues that initially the Soviets wanted to keep the PLA out of Xinjiang, hoping for the formation of a compliant non-Han state. But fearful of the unwelcome rise of an independent Xinjiang hostile to the Soviet Union, Stalin changed course and offered Mao assistance to speed up a Han takeover. Mao accepted. Ethnic Han representatives of the defeated Nationalist regime in Xinjiang soon declared loyalty to the Communists. From November 1949 to March 1950 the PLA pushed through Xinjiang, systematically crushing resistance by Muslim rebels. Heeding Stalin's advice, Gao observes, the party soon began to colonize Xinjiang by creating closed-off oasis compounds farmed by active-duty Han soldiers. The party then brought in Han women, including many daughters of "class enemies," from Gansu, Hunan, and Sichuan. The women were misled about career opportunities, assigned to military units, paired up with Han soldiers, and told to have lots of babies.

Part III takes us back to the Han heartland to explore the ways in which well-known people in the cultural and educational sphere adjusted to the new order. As Perry Link demonstrates in Chapter 9, stand-up comedians known as *xiangsheng* artists were prominent among those who responded with enthusiasm to the vision of a New Democratic society. Their goal was to transform *xiangsheng* from a beloved, if bawdy, regional art form to a "progressive" national one. But it was not clear how the comics should portray the emerging "new" society. Cultural bureaucrats, already a formidable presence in 1950, wanted the comics to praise the new society. But it was difficult to make blanket praise seem funny. The essence of *xiangsheng* was unsparing satire. Party functionaries were happy to see satire directed at "feudal" vestiges, but they were not at all amused by loyal, well-intentioned satire directed at people within the revolutionary camp. It was galling for humorless bureaucrats to discover that some of the satire aimed at the party was being performed by party members, including *xiangsheng* master He Chi.

The party was more successful when it came to getting scientists to conduct politically motivated research on the problem of "human origins." What defines the human condition? And where did human beings come from? In Chapter 10 Sigrid Schmalzer shows that while the creationist view that God created humanity was still being disseminated by Christians in China as late as 1951, Chinese scientists began at once to follow the lead of the Soviet Union by canonizing certain texts by Friedrich Engels on the question of human origins. Humans, they said, evolved from apes, and the act of "labor" played the key role in the evolutionary process. The new regime thus embraced a socialist, internationalist, and materialist doctrine celebrating the historical contributions of laboring people. But Schmalzer notes that lurking just below the surface of these apparently internationalist orthodoxies were some distinctively nationalist ideological preoccupations. By 1952 scholars firmly rejected the foreign theory that the Peking Man fossils discovered in the 1920s were evidence of a dead-end branch of human evolutionary activity. They favored a theory that featured Peking Man as the vibrant ancestor of all the people of the Chinese nation (including ethnic minorities) and perhaps of all the people of Asia.

In Chapter 11, Paul G. Pickowicz looks at the ways in which the glittering film world responded to the revolution. He focuses on a leading private-sector enterprise (the Wenhua Studio) and the painful experiences of Shi Hui, one of the most famous screen stars of the 1940s. Profoundly impressed by the influence of the mass media, but with little experience in this realm, the party needed private-sector filmmakers and matinee idols. Despite their bourgeois backgrounds, stars such as Shi Hui expressed an enthusiastic, even romantic resolve to support the revolution. In 1949 and 1950 they made significant contributions, doing their best to "act like revolutionaries." But even before the Chinese entry into the Korean War in late 1950 and the launching of a destructive crackdown in the arts in early 1951, the state increased control of the cultural sphere, creating a climate of fear and self-censorship. Increasingly, Pickowicz argues, old friends turned on each other to protect themselves and to advance their own careers. The culture of paranoia discussed by Wakeman was taking a serious toll. Shi Hui was an extremely talented actor, but nothing he did was good enough for the party. By 1953 the private film studios were shut down. Many film people made accommodations. Shi Hui was marginalized and denounced. His last performance, a powerful act of protest, was a carefully staged ritual suicide.

To minimize its dependence on "old-style" intellectuals such as Shi Hui, the new regime hoped to train large numbers of "new-style" intellectuals. As Douglas A. Stiffler suggests in Chapter 12, the opening of People's University in Beijing in October 1950 was intended as a step in the right direction. Working closely with Soviet advisers, the party was eager to produce technically competent and politically reliable students. But from the outset there was tension between the Soviet specialists and university leaders on the issue of student recruitment. In this case, the Chinese were the pragmatists, insisting that students be recruited from all quarters, not just the revolutionary camp. This view recognized a harsh reality: the educational level of old cadres, most of them rural people, was shockingly low. Leaders did not want to rule out the recruitment of "young intellectuals," that is, better-educated people who came from bourgeois, merchant, Nationalist, Christian, rich peasant, and landlord backgrounds. The Soviets played a leftist role by complaining that the intellectuals were opportunists who would pollute the revolution. The Chinese responded that urban youth could be transformed ideologically. This tension between Soviet advisers and Chinese leaders, Stiffler points out, was paralleled by serious conflict among the two groups of new student recruits.

The concluding section of this volume, Part IV, investigates the ways in which families experienced and adjusted to the victory of revolution. In urban and coastal China, the family system had been "modernizing" in various ways since the late nineteenth century. The Communist takeover sped up the process, but the family was still eternal. In Chapter 13 Joseph W. Esherick explores these changes by taking a finely textured look at the complicated life of one large family of urban professionals. Ye Chengzhi, a police official in the late Qing era and a businessman in early Republican times, died in 1930, but his children became scientists, entertainers, editors, and journalists in the 1940s and 1950s. Some were active in non-communist politics, and some were members of the Communist Party. The Ye offspring hoped that postings in government units would protect and benefit their branches of the family. After 1949, Esherick points out, the structure of such families differed according to the nature of service roles. The families of party officials were housed in special walled-off compounds guarded by armed sentries. Their children often lived at elite boarding schools. Scientists, scholars, and others lived more simply but had more affectionate relations with their children. All were concerned with discovering ways to deflect unwanted political attention in the "new society."

For rural women and families facing the age-old dangers of childbirth at home, the state was not Mao or the party but the village women's association and officially sponsored midwives. Party rhetoric stressed the dangers of "feudal" superstitions when it came to the delivery of new citizens, but as Gail Hershatter demonstrates in Chapter 14, the Communists had a flexible policy on the thousands of old-style midwives who populated the villages of China. The party had no choice. Countless women and babies suffered or died unnecessarily in the past while in the care of the old-style midwives, but revolutionaries recognized that many midwives had performed very well. So the party condemned unhealthy practices, while local women's organizations worked patiently in the early 1950s to train new-style midwives and retrain old-style practitioners. Despite the scientific reforms, many of the older midwives functioned in more than one cultural sphere. Some of the midwives who were honored by the new state as models of selfless, modern, scientific, socialist dedication also worked effectively in realms inhabited by powerful spirits and ghosts, forces that the modernizing state was incapable of seeing or loath to mention in official reports.

We end *Dilemmas of Victory* by returning to industrial Shanghai and asking why the vast majority of capitalist families, most of whom had close ties to the Nationalists, decided to remain in China after 1949. Communist leaders have always argued that it was because the business families were "patriotic." In Chapter 15, Sherman Cochran challenges this view by providing an intimate look at the case of famous industrialist Liu Hongsheng and his many sons. Aggressively courted by both the Nationalists and Communists in spring 1949, Liu fled to Hong Kong. But in November he returned and made strenuous efforts to bring all his sons back, including one poor soul he tricked into returning. Capitalist Liu was hosted by Zhou Enlai and Mao and was promised that his assets and way of life would not be targeted. He was called a "national capitalist." But Liu questioned this designation: he had functioned as a comprador for a British firm and had worked once as a bureaucratic capitalist in one of Chiang Kai-shek's state-owned industries. Amused, Zhou Enlai explained that a national capitalist is anyone the party says is a national capitalist. Liu worked hard for the regime and benefited personally at a time when the party desperately needed his skills. But the Lius and other capitalist families were cruelly humiliated during the Five-Anti Campaign of early 1952 and lost all their enterprises in the nationalization drive that began in 1953—the end of the transition era examined in this book.

I
Urban Takeover

ॐ *2*

"Cleanup": The New Order in Shanghai

Frederic Wakeman Jr.

> In the past three years owing to the persistent efforts of the people,
> Shanghai has changed from a city dependent on the imperialist
> economy for its existence to a city independent of the imperialist
> economy and which is developing on its own. Shanghai is no longer a
> city serving the imperialists and reactionary elements but a city for
> the people and production. Shanghai has wiped out the dirt and
> poison left behind by the imperialists and their running dogs and has
> started on its way to normal and healthy development.
> *Mayor Chen Yi, Shanghai, May 28, 1952*[1]

IN APRIL 1945 the Chinese Communist Party (CCP) announced its plans to shift from a rural to an urban strategy. The major resolution of the Seventh Plenum of the Sixth Central Committee called for shifting the nub of the War of Resistance against Japan to China's major cities. "This will be a new change of historical significance for our party, which shifted the center of gravity of its work to the countryside with so much difficulty after the defeat of the revolution in 1927."[2] With the growing prospects of victory in the civil war with the Nationalist regime, Mao Zedong's concerns about ruling both urban and rural China deepened. In spring 1947, Hu Zongnan's attack on Yan'an had sent Mao fleeing under a new nom de guerre, Li Desheng. By August, however, Mao's armies had counterattacked at Shajiadian and destroyed Hu's two leading brigades, crushing the remnant twenty-eight thousand soldiers of the Nationalist 26th Army at Yichuan seven months later and opening a path for Mao to cross the Yellow River to spread the revolution all over China.[3]

The Party's New Urban Policy

Even before that victory, Mao had received a message from Bo Yibo reporting the excesses of the Communist occupation of such northern cities as Shijiazhuang, where the People's Liberation Army (PLA) had encouraged urban mobs to attack private households and execute the city's elite. Mao wrote on the margins of the report: "Such an idea [that we destroy urban industry and commerce] is a reflection of rural socialism. Rural socialism by its nature is a reactionary, backward and regressive ideology, and we must oppose it."[4] Mao went on to declare, in February 1948, that the party's policy in the newly liberated cities should be devoted to "developing production, promoting economic prosperity . . . and benefiting both labor and capital."[5]

After Mao crossed the Yellow River, he went to the small village of Boqiang in Fanzhi county (Shanxi), where his communications staff informed him that Luoyang had been captured by the PLA after fierce fighting. On April 8, 1948, he drafted the following telegram to the Luoyang front leaders:

> One, be very prudent in the liquidation of the organs of Nationalist rule. Two, set a clear line of demarcation in defining bureaucratic capital, and do not confiscate all the industrial and commercial enterprises run by Nationalist Party members. Three, forbid peasant organizations to enter the city to seize landlords and settle scores with them. Four, on entering the city do not lightly advance slogans of raising wages and reducing working hours. Five, do not be in a hurry to organize the people of the city to struggle for democratic reforms and improvements in livelihood. Six, in the big cities food and fuel must be handled in a planned way. Seven, members of the Nationalist Party and Three People's Principles Youth League must be screened and registered. Eight, it is strictly forbidden to destroy any means of production, whether publicly or privately owned, and to waste consumer goods.[6]

This telegram became one of two key texts (the other being Mao's instructions "On a Policy for Industry and Commerce") that cadres had to study in preparation for taking over China's cities.

Training Liberation Cadres

The immediate problem facing the party was to train cadres to take over central and south China. In May 1948, Liu Shaoqi told the North China Bureau on behalf of the Central Committee that it must set up a "large party school," "a large military academy," and a university to train intellectuals and young students for urban work. The following November, two months after a Politburo meeting convened by Mao at Xibaipo (the temporary rural headquarters of the party) approved a decision to train thirty thousand to forty thousand cadres for the newly liberated areas, the Central Committee announced plans "to select a large number of promising cadres among industrial workers and clerks in Jinan, Weixian, and Xuzhou, and offer them short-term political training to prepare for the takeover of Nanjing, Shanghai, Hangzhou and other cities."[7] The East China Bureau of the party readily took on that assignment, partly because it wanted to advance some of its more than two hundred thousand veteran cadres who longed for promotion and partly because it had also recruited a large number of industrial workers and young intellectuals who restlessly anticipated a movement south.

By fall 1948, party center had come to realize that it simply did not have the number of cadres needed for taking over the cities. Mao himself sent a telegram to the Second and Third Field armies, ordering their commanders to stop everything "and use the whole month learning how to work in the cities and the new Liberated Areas. . . . All army cadres should learn how to take over and administer cities."[8] On October 28, the Politburo issued a "Notice on the Preparation of 53,000 Cadres." Fifteen thousand of these cadres were to be trained by the East China Bureau and assembled by March 1949. The bureau in turn decided on December 25 that it would recruit all of these cadres from three areas of Shandong. Luzhongnan (southern and central Shandong) was to be responsible for choosing and preparing 4,430 cadres to take over Shanghai, Zhejiang, and Fujian.

When party center announced on New Year's Day 1949 that the preparation work for crossing into Jiangnan was under way, steps were immediately taken to choose individual cadres and rehearse the invasion. The primary criterion for selecting Shandong liberation cadres was to "pick the strong cadres for the south and keep the weaker ones home." The term *nanxiang ganbu* (southbound cadres) quickly became synonymous with *lao geming* (veteran revolutionaries). The southbound cadres were not entranced by the prospect of moving into Jiangnan. Many Shandongese had worked in Shanghai as coolies. When they returned home, they complained about the humidity, the strange dialect, the crafty locals who were prejudiced against rural people, the bad food, and the numerous poisonous snakes in the Yangzi delta.

On February 7, 1949, the Luzhongnan Party Committee issued orders to require all counties to hold a two-day mobilization meeting and put together a final list of southbound cadres. The group mustered at Taierzhuang a week later to learn about the areas to which they were assigned. The deputy director of the Social Affairs Department of the East China Bureau, Yang Fan, led sixty-odd cadres (including a radio transmission team) to Huaiyin to gather intelligence and "incite defection" *(cefan)* in Shanghai. In addition to printing materials to hand out to cadres moving into the city, the Huaiyin team organized a group of cadres to analyze the military and civilian intelligence sent them by Shanghai underground agents and then to prepare highly specific materials on Shanghai, Nanjing, Suzhou, and Hangzhou to be printed up for distribution to "liberation cadres." The Shanghai set of twenty-six volumes, titled *Shanghai Investigation Materials*, was handed out later in April 1949.[9]

Meanwhile, the East China Bureau's Social Affairs Department had also opened up a police officers' school in Jinan, which recruited over one thousand young students. Their task was to take over the Shanghai police force and organize a public security organ. In March these young cadres were addressed by Chen Yi, who stressed the exceptional importance of entering Shanghai in a disciplined fashion that would not allow their "wild" *(ye)* guerrilla side to appear. Rowdiness would squander victory, Chen Yi said, and his young listeners nodded in agreement.[10]

By now the police training group was in Danyang, and name lists were already being prepared for assignments to departments, bureaus, offices, and even specific precincts, once they took over Shanghai. Chen Geng, one of the party's security specialists who knew Shanghai well from his underground days, was appointed shadow head of Shanghai's Department of Public Security. The takeover group was thoroughly briefed (Communist Party members of the Shanghai police were spirited north to Danyang, ostensibly on home leave, to fill in the now-assigned police officials on the specific details of their units), and each cadre knew exactly what his or her post was to be.

Tightening the Noose

Just before Mao left Xibaipo for Beiping on March 23, the party held a meeting of the second session of the Seventh Central Committee. Mao repeated to the plenaries: "The center of gravity of the party's work has shifted from the village to the city."[11] The very morning he left for the capital, where last-minute peace negotiations were taking place between the Communists and the Nanjing regime, the chairman told Zhou Enlai, "Today we are going to the capital to take the imperial exam." Zhou answered, "We should be able to pass it. We cannot step back." Mao smiled and said, "No. We won't be another Li Zicheng."[12]

On April 18, 1949, the Communists officially announced that the Beiping peace parleys would end on Wednesday, April 20.[13] Acting president Li Zongren thus had two more days to accede to the Communists' demand that they be allowed to cross the Yangzi and establish ten bridgeheads on the south bank.[14] Li met with top-level Nationalist leaders on April 19; the group rejected what amounted to a conditional surrender. That same day, the Communists announced that the Third Field Army of General Chen Yi had completed its preparations to cross the Yangzi River.[15]

Mao's strategy was brilliant but daring, reflecting his persistent determination to outflank the enemy with rapid troop movements, forced nighttime marches, and field flexibility. Rejecting the advice of his planners to concentrate forces in a single-minded assault upon Nanjing, Jinjiang, and Jiangyin, he decided to attack along a four hundred-mile front using all four of his field armies—a total of one million troops—to strike simultaneously at the two hundred-mile front between Nanjing and Shanghai and at the two hundred-mile stretch between Nanjing (where the Yangzi turns south) and Anqing. While Tang Enbo prepared to defend Jiangnan against a crossing at Jiangyin, Mao's Western Front Army would breach the Yangzi at Anqing and Dongling before racing across southern Jiangsu to help close the net around the cities of Lake Tai and meet up with Chen Yi's Eastern Front Army somewhere south of Shanghai.[16]

In Shanghai proper, Communist artillery fire began to gather momentum at 5:00 P.M. on April 20, seven hours before the formal expiration of the deadline.[17] On April 20 the Nationalist general at the Jiangyin forts, which commanded the defenses of Nanjing, ordered his men to withhold fire while the Communists crossed the Yangzi. A young officer loyal to Chiang Kai-shek shot the general in the back, but by then it was too late: the PLA was already on the south bank. They now faced the 350,000 Nationalist defenders arrayed in twenty-two corps. All but eight were between Nanjing and Shanghai, "clearly demonstrating Tang En-po's [Tang Enbo's] ultimate intention of conducting an evacuation."[18] While the Communist Eastern Front Army of 350,000 men occupied the area around Jinjiang and Shanghai, another 300,000 troops in the Zhejiang-Anqing sector drove inland along an eighty-mile river front, while 240,000 PLA soldiers crossing between Anqing and Wuhu punched twenty-five miles through to Jingyan.[19] The Nationalist capital of Nanjing fell on the night of April 23–24. By April 25, meanwhile, the Communist armies "snapped shut a trap" on General Tang's 300,000 Nationalist soldiers who had fallen back on the Jiangsu-Zhejiang pocket between Shanghai and Hangzhou. Intentionally bypassing Shanghai for the moment, Chen Yi's army captured Jiaxing, fifty-three miles southwest of the metropolis. Now the Shanghai-Hangzhou Railway and the Suzhou-Jiaxing Railway were in Communist hands, cutting off the last trains south for retreating government troops.[20] Nonplussed, Shanghai garrison commander Qian Dajun insisted that the city would be defended to its death.[21]

Shanghai "Sunk in a Melancholy Stupor"[22]

Uncanny, dead, quiet days; nights that burst aflame with [the sound of shells]. Men's death gasps. Women's screams as unpaid soldiers billeted themselves forcibly on terrified people, yelling, raping, killing in dark alleyways. Half-starved civilians crawling through city-encircling barbed wire to smuggle rice from the country. Jewels and dope and gold bars sewn into corpses for transporting to hideouts. . . . A crescendo of evil mounted until daylight.[23]

Refugees from the countryside packed the roads into the city until they were impassable. Some brought small bags of rice with them; others looted whatever they could find: "a light truck . . . stalled on the Garden Bridge end of the Bund with some small citizen's hoard of five bags of rice. Before [the driver] could get the truck started again, swarming beggars had punctured every sack and carried off his rice in hats, pockets, and hands."[24] On April 23, Shanghai was put under martial law and a 10:00 P.M. curfew declared. Armored cars guarded key bridges. Drivers were stopped at almost every corner by soldiers with fixed bayonets.

The next day, Shanghai urbanites could observe British and U.S. naval vessels casting off their moorings in the Huangpu and heading downstream to the Yangzi River and the open sea. American citizens were boarding the *President Wilson*, while U.S. diplomatic staff left by aircraft for Guangzhou.

> So crowded was the road to Hungjao [Hongqiao] airport that airlines there said the field could not be approached from the city. The airlines were forced to ferry passengers and ground crews from the Lunghwa [Longhua] airport by plane. The road to Lunghwa was . . . jammed. A number of foreign businessmen who live in mansions on the edge of the city have come home to find their servants gone. They had been impressed by the [Nationalist] army to work on pillboxes and tank traps on the city's perimeter.[25]

That Monday, Mao and Zhu De broadcast a proclamation calling on Shanghai government officials at all levels, and especially the police, to stay on the job to prevent industrial sabotage and looting.[26]

Police Subversion

Within the Shanghai police force, underground Communist cadres commenced preparing for the takeover. By then, despite the Nationalists' special system of "policemen putting policemen under strict surveillance," which had led to the arrest of more than fifty officers, at least three of whom were important underground party members, there was a total of nineteen party cells throughout the twenty thousand-member police force.[27]

The Communist Party had organized cells within the Shanghai Municipal Police (International Settlement) and the Shanghai Police (Special Municipality) in the late 1930s. In deep cover, this small group of stalwarts followed the "three diligents" *(san qin):* "diligently study" Mao's "On Protracted War" and other rectification materials, "diligently follow your profession" so as to use your position as a cover for party work, and "diligently befriend" to create a network of supporters and future allies.[28] The War of Resistance against Japan offered an opportunity for expansion, and by the time the Pacific War broke out, there were about forty party members.[29]

From 1942 to 1945 the party's Jiangsu Provincial Committee was moved to the Huai'an base area, where a Central China Bureau was put in charge of Shanghai's underground work. The handful of cadres working within the Shanghai police, such as Shao Jian and Liu Feng, were brought back to the base area one by one, sometimes with their families, to train and study in the Central China Party School before moving back into Shanghai and taking over one of the ten party cells within the police. By then there were about one hundred underground party members heeding the command of a Police Party Committee, which in turn reported to the underground municipal committee represented by Wan Ren.[30]

Wan Ren was originally put in charge of the Sino-French Alumni United Friendship Society, which had a small number of Communists working for the French Concession police as officers and translators. Recruitment was tricky and based entirely upon personal friendships. After conducting a certain amount of propaganda work, a would-be member was treated as an activist and asked to set up a front organization, the key term of which would be Sino-French Alumni United Friendship Society, which instantly evoked the Communist New Fourth Army.

Despite the Communist Party's artfulness, the Japanese Kempeitai occupying Shanghai deeply suspected the reliability of their Chinese collaborators. They mistakenly thought that this was because of lingering loyalty to the Westerners who had led the Shanghai Municipal Police. Consequently, the Japanese frequently enjoined the policemen who collaborated with them to "eradicate English and American thought." By the end of 1944, more than two thousand policemen had been washed out of the collaborationist force. A few of these were Communists, and when they left the police, they also left Shanghai to join the New Fourth or Eighth Route Army. Nonetheless, by the end of the war, one Communist front group still had two hundred members.[31]

The Communists not only recruited new party members; they also worked closely with sympathizers or fellow travelers within the police force but outside the party. Lu Dagong, the inspector general of the Shanghai police, was just such a person. He was not a member of the Nationalist Party, did not participate in gang activities, and had no patron or "mountain to lean upon" *(kao shan)*. This made him vulnerable to leadership changes, so that he had little recourse in 1949 when Yu Shuping became police chief and bumped him upstairs to a position as head of the Police Consumers Cooperative Association. This made him very bitter, especially when he discovered how many Nationalist officers were on the take as inflation raged and as the initiative in the civil war seemed to be shifting to the Communists. Yang Hu, the former head of the Shanghai Garrison Command, had already long been in touch with the Communist underground, and the Revive China Study Society (Xing Zhong xuehui) he led was a prominent front organization for the Communist Party. Lu Dagong became a member of this group, which put him in touch with Xiao Dacheng, a leading Communist agent, who persuaded him to accept the guidance of the Communist Party and "stand on the side of the people."[32]

Working underground with the Nationalist police during the civil war was a harrowing experience, requiring the greatest caution and an extraordinary attention to secrecy. There was always the fear of exposure, especially after Nationalist special services agent Mao Sen became chief of police in December 1948. Yang Hu's connections with the Communists were quickly uncloaked, and he went into hiding. Lu Dagong endured mortal fear of retribution, especially after Mao Sen's secretary told him that "if someone has relations with the Communist Party, then if he confesses a minute before [being discovered], he'll escape punishment. But if he's found out, then a minute later not only will he be shot; his entire family will be killed." Lu Dagong feigned calmness but lived on pins and needles thereafter.[33]

Under the direction of Shao Jian and the central police party committee, each of the five hundred Communist Party members was assigned to link up with local district party committees throughout Shanghai and to prepare to mobilize the more than two thousand "external activist elements" who could back up the Shanghai police force, once the Communists arrived. Their greatest concern was to keep the departing Nationalists from destroying industrial machinery and killing off political prisoners.[34]

By April 1949 the Communists in the Shanghai police force had organized People's Security Teams under a special Preservation Committee. Five officers formed a *zu* and ten a *dui* to protect archives and preserve firearms as the end of the Nationalists' rule drew near. At the same time, they also investigated the locations of secret service units and drew up detailed reports on the crimes of police officers and secret agents. This register was later handed over to PLA officers.[35]

After Mao Zedong and Zhu De issued the April 25 "Yuefa bazhang" (the famed Eight Regulations, which were to become the charter of the new Shanghai municipal government), the Shanghai police party committee instantly went to work under Shao Jian's direction, printing up great quantities of the announcement to be mailed to the homes of Nationalist police and secret agents.[36] Since many of the Nationalist police officials had recently moved in order to slip away from Communist surveillance, even receiving these notices of the fate that they might meet was profoundly unsettling, and there was a great furor and panic within the Shanghai police force in the days that followed.[37]

The diehard secret police element—many of them Mao Sen's followers—within the Shanghai police's Political Investigation Department was determined to round up as many suspected Communists as possible before the city fell. The Communist Party, however, had four underground agents in this unit, and they were able to gain access to reports coming into police headquarters from special service units throughout the city. Whenever they came across detailed arrest plans, they tried to notify the suspects soon enough for them to get away. Many lives were saved as a result.

Lu Dagong remained under suspicion. Zhang Datu, the head of the Intelligence Department of Jiangsu province who had served with Lu in the Shanghai police, told his friend that Mao Sen thought he was a traitor. To help clear his reputation, Zhang took Lu Dagong to see Mao Renfeng, head of the Bureau to Protect Secrets. Mao received them with his bodyguard at his side and asked Lu to write an "autobiography." Lu Dagong realized, somewhat to his own astonishment, that Mao, the head of the Nationalist secret police, was preparing to recruit him for underground work after Shanghai fell. A day later, Lu was given a fund of silver coins for agent payments along with a post office box number to use once the Nationalists pulled out.[38]

The Picket Fence

In a pathetic gesture of defiance, the defense authorities proceeded in mid-May 1949 to build a protective palisade.

> While guns boomed in the western distance, local defense authorities erected a fantastic wooden fence along the southwest and north sides of Shanghai as token of their solemn promise to "fight to the death." Suspected Communists were executed in Shanghai streets and the local economic structure disintegrated at an unprecedented pace. Obviously no one had the slightest confidence in Nationalist capacity.[39]

By then, Chen Yi's forces had taken Hangzhou, and a line of Communist troops was advancing along the Nanjing-Shanghai and Shanghai-Hangzhou highways. Mayor Wu Guozhen (K. C. Wu) had already fled Shanghai, leaving his secretary, General Chen Liang, in charge. Chen Liang, in turn, handed the mayor's seal over to Cornell-trained engineer Zhao Zukang, who directed the Bureau of Public Works. Zhao, a man without party affiliations, reluctantly agreed to become acting mayor because of his strong sense of public responsibility.

Although the military was charged with maintaining social order, the Nationalist army was already unraveling. Chiang Kai-shek had stopped off in Shanghai on his way to Taiwan in his private C-47 (reputedly with $200 million in U.S. gold reserves), blithely entrusting the defense of Shanghai to Premier He Yingqin and General Tang Enbo. But by May 24 the Shanghai newspaper article reiterating He Yingqin's determination to defend the city had a little box in the middle of the story, explaining that the premier had already left by plane for Guangzhou.[40] And though General Tang held a victory rally that morning, marching past posters that announced "we will fight to the last drop of blood, Shanghai will be the Communists' graveyard," he was nowhere to be seen by mid-afternoon.[41]

Endgame

As the endgame approached, Chen Yi, "the scholar general," instructed his Third Field Army to abide by three pledges: observe all regulations and laws issued by the people's governments and the military control committees; respect city policy and protect city property; and uphold hard work and a simple lifestyle as a revolutionary tradition. Chen further instructed his troops, many of them teenagers, to pay attention to ten points:

1. Nobody may shoot without permission.
2. Nobody may live in a store or house owned by a citizen and nobody may visit theaters or places of amusement.
3. Nobody may go to town without permission.
4. Nobody may drive carts or ride horses recklessly in the streets.
5. Nobody may eat in the streets or walk arm-in-arm with anyone in the streets or jostle about in crowds.
6. Do business fairly.
7. Keep the guard stations clean and urinate/defecate in latrines only.
8. Nobody may visit a fortune teller or gamble or visit prostitutes.
9. Nobody may get involved in feudal or superstitious activities.
10. Nobody may write on the walls.[42]

By noon on May 24 Chen Yi's young soldiers had reached the wooden Maginot line—what foreign wags called the "picket fence" or "Great Wall of Shanghai"—between the western suburbs and downtown districts.[43] Long columns of Nationalist troops began to retreat down the avenues into the former French Concession. Trucks drew up in front of police stations, and squads of policemen with families and baggage climbed aboard for Wusong and the fleet of evacuation ships. As the Nationalists marched out, their flag was hanging from every home in accordance with an ordinance designating the day as a "victory celebration." "Touring the streets one got the impression of a dam having been broken. Military vehicles of every description raced down the streets. Soldiers in full field-packs boarded the scheduled city buses. Civilians were ordered off pedicabs to provide other soldiers with quick transport."[44]

Mao Sen, the Nationalist chief of police, seemed determined to stay until the very end. Ever suspicious of Lu Dagong, General Mao had already held a meeting earlier that morning with his own secret service backbone cadres. He proposed that Lu be killed because he knew too much about Nationalist secret police activities. Mao's lieutenants argued that Lu should be kept alive and used as an intermediary with the incoming Communists.[45] Mao acquiesced, dismissing his top agents. The police chief then ordered Lu to report to his office. When Lu appeared, Mao told him that reinforcements from Taiwan had not yet arrived and that the leadership was going to have to retreat. He asked Lu to continue to serve as deputy police chief in order to "maintain local order." Military deserters and local "ruffians" posing as Communists had already appeared in several precincts carrying banners inscribed "Zhong gong dixia jun" (Chinese Communist Underground Army), trying to take over the police stations and their arsenals.[46] Commands were subsequently given to all precinct chiefs to obey Lu Dagong's orders.[47]

As soon as he could excuse himself, Lu left the station and reported the meeting to Communist Party underground headquarters. Communist Party intelligence cadre Xiao Dacheng told Lu that the party approved of his appointment as temporary police chief. At Fuzhou Road, tensions were visibly rising. At 3:00 P.M., Mao Sen's assistant telephoned Lu Dagong at home and told him that the time had come for Lu to take over formally as chief of police. Lu returned to the station with Xiao Dacheng disguised as an ordinary Shanghai constable. Lu expected that Mao Sen would by then have abandoned his post. The Nationalist chief of police, however, tarried, reluctant to leave. Ordering that the police department's household registration registers be destroyed (an order Lu secretly countermanded), Mao Sen was still occupying his office at 7:00 P.M. At that point, Lu told him that PLA units had already reached Zhaofeng Park (present-day Zhongshan Park). Mao panicked, ordering Lu to have the motorized brigade send several armored cars to protect him as he fled. The motorized brigade was already suborned, however, and in the end Mao Sen and his bodyguards had to flee for the docks and the next boat out to Taiwan in two ordinary automobiles.[48]

Now in full charge, Lu Dagong spoke with acting mayor Zhao, who advised him to do all that he could to maintain order in the city. Lu promptly declared a curfew. His second act was to send garrison officers to go along with Xiao Dacheng to the mobile brigade to make certain that the paramilitary units were under control. A handful of Communist

Party agents were brought in that night to police headquarters to coordinate the takeover. The management committees set up by the CCP were also activated in each precinct station, and they lowered their Nationalist flags and prepared to hoist white banners of surrender.[49] Lu also issued orders to his precinct captains to be prepared to receive PLA units with hands in the air, shouting "surrender."

Over the Great Wall of Shanghai

By midnight, under cover of the curfew, Communist scouts slipped into the city. A few hours later, a larger advanced guard of Chen Yi's troops, armed with Thompson submachine guns and Browning automatic rifles, breached the wooden blockade and from the south and southwest began to move, two abreast, down avenue Edouard VII.[50] They stopped briefly at each intersection while squads peeled off to patrol the side streets. Finding nothing but unmanned barricades, some of the young soldiers exhausted by the forced march across Jiangsu quietly dropped to the ground and fell asleep. Behind them, auxiliaries unreeled field telephone wires and marked major crossroads with white arrows, setting up their own machine-gun emplacements.[51] At five minutes past midnight on May 25, Deputy Police Chief Lu was notified by telephone that the PLA had reached the Changshu district police office, which had surrendered. Other stations called in with similar reports in the early hours of that same morning, and Lu Dagong prepared to receive the PLA cadres sure to follow. By 8:00 a.m., as the main body of the Third Field Army marched along tree-lined Avenue Pétain into the French Concession, Chen Yi's vanguard had reached the Bund, defended at both ends by Nationalist machine-gun nests. Two hours later it was over. The center of the city belonged to the Red Army.[52]

> The first wave of invaders was the miraculous "People's Liberation Army," which entered on felt or rubber-soled moccasins, and in orderly fashion: ill-equipped peasants who behaved like well-bred soldiers, infantrymen in jackets the color of grass, who settled down without assaulting the civil population or looting the houses. The second wave consisted of teams of Communist "kan-pu" [ganbu], civilians in uniform, carrying no badge of office, anonymous and

placable, invisible men almost, who moved into the seats of government without disturbing anyone or anything and immediately inaugurated a regime of frantic work and incorruptible morals. It was
indeed, as some wit remarked, a case of "Martians in Shanghai."[53]

The conquerors were an army of adolescents. Sophie Souroujon, a
twelve-year-old girl that day, was warned by her White Russian father
not to look out the window when the troops passed by because these
dreadful Communists might shoot her out of spite or play. She could
not help but sneak a peek through the slightly parted curtains of their
apartment on rue Molière, and to her astonishment she saw a motley
armed column of children marching gravely down the street in their
straw sandals.[54]

Mariano Ezpeleta, the Philippine consul-general, had a similar reaction:

> I had expected to see tough, weathered, fire-eating soldiers, swag-
> gering with assertive sureness of themselves—surly and mean, bel-
> licose in attitude. I'd expected to see them equipped with Holly-
> woodesque fastidiousness, or at least in gangsterial fashion—steel
> helmets at rakish angles, submachine guns under the arms, pistols
> at the hips, hand grenades dangling from their pockets, quills of
> ammo belts around them, and knives between their teeth. I was
> mistaken. Here they were, the Communist soldiers—mostly
> teenagers in the first blush of youth, slightly built boys still awk-
> ward in gait; others almost adult country bumpkins trying to
> steady themselves first on one foot and then on the other. They
> stood on street crossings, casually held their carbines at rest,
> looking around open-eyed, obviously bewildered by the ornate
> and magnificent buildings of the city. One could mistake them for
> curious school cadets from some rural inland town, learning their
> primary lessons in the art of sentinel duty.[55]

None of them appeared the least likely to pillage, rape, requisition
food, or even accept glasses of water from residents—a forbearance
that made a tremendous impression on the population of Shanghai.[56]

Indeed, "Shanghai swung into the Communist camp with a rush and
not by degrees." On May 26, as long lines of Communist soldiers slept

side by side in the streets despite a bright sun and crowds of curious passersby, mile after mile of shops and houses sported red flags, while students plastered posters of welcome on walls, trolley cars, billboards, and windows.[57]

> Communist partisans went wild with enthusiasm. The Great World in the French concession, the city's largest amusement resort, hosted a mammoth picture of Mao Tse-tung [Mao Zedong], which obviously had been weeks in the making. The red flag appeared over buildings and flew outside stores which twenty-two years earlier had quite as enthusiastically flown the Nationalist flag. Sympathizers who found themselves without Communist emblems hastily manufactured them by tearing the blue sky and white sun quarter from the red field of the Nationalist flag. Madly jubilant and easily moved students danced the *yang-ko* [*yangge*] in the streets, welcoming Mao's men with all the fervor another generation had welcomed Chiang's. It was like a Hollywood remake with Marxian inflections.[58]

As a French correspondent put it, "In Shanghai . . . the revolution began to the sound of singing voices."[59] While lorries decked with red banners carried students—many of them young women in white blouses and half-length cotton slacks—through the streets, soldiers' choruses rose from campsites and blared through loudspeakers in city parks.

Fighting continued on the outskirts of the city. Gunfire was still being exchanged in front of the U.S. consulate on the Bund and along Suzhou Creek, which was the defense line covering the continuing Nationalist retreat northeast toward Wusong.[60] That night the northern sky glowed red as the Jiangwan airfield gasoline supplies blazed. Shipping also burned near Point Island. Flames from newly ignited fuel oil flared into the sky.[61] But the surrender of troops holding the American-owned power plant at 3:00 P.M. on May 27 gave the Communists control of virtually all of Shanghai.[62] That evening the radio announced that the Nationalists' last escape route down the Huangpu River had been cut with the PLA controlling both banks of the river after Nationalist vice-commander general Lin Zhangyi surrendered with forty thousand of his men when the final defense line along Suzhou Creek collapsed. Foreigners spoke of a Nationalist "Dunkirk" from Wusong:

Apparently, there was either no room or no time for the Nationalists to take their armored cars, heavy artillery, and trucks, which
had been waiting two and three abreast for loading aboard ship. A
mile-long mass was burned, setting off ammunition and spreading
havoc through the neighboring countryside. Municipal busses lay
helter skelter along the road, some pierced by shell holes. There
were taxicabs, all forms of amphibious vehicles, road scrapers and
other forms of earth moving equipment. . . . At several places the
road was covered with navy life jackets. Much of the equipment
still had "United States Army" on it.[63]

According to Communist authorities, over one hundred thousand Nationalist troops had been captured or had defected during the battle for
Shanghai.[64] In the wake of the old regime's defeat, much remained to
clean up.

Takeover

Whatever public gawkiness the PLA cadres may have displayed, their
organizational takeover was brilliantly executed. At 10:00 A.M. on the
morning of May 25, the PLA vanguard arrived at Shanghai police
headquarters. Lu Dagong was standing outside in plainclothes. He
stepped forward and announced: "I am Lu Dagong, the acting chief of
the Nationalist Shanghai Municipal Police. I have come especially to
welcome the Liberation Army, which is here to occupy our police station, and I will respectfully obey your orders." The PLA commander
instantly ordered him to replace the guard post at the front of the station with a simple PLA soldier. To Lu, deeply moved, this shift represented the moment when power passed from "imperialism and the reactionaries" to the people's government.[65]

The Communist cadres moved swiftly. On May 25–26, the "shadow
police" mustered in Danyang were brought by train to Shanghai, where
they were matched up with the members of the Communist Party underground committee within the police force. The "special personnel
to take over control" (*jieguan zhuanyuan*) then moved into their various positions in the precinct stations and police headquarters.[66] Re-
peating the Eight Regulations, they ordered each person to stay at his
or her post and to carry out the orders of the people's government

while awaiting the "disposal" *(chuli)* of individual cases.[67] That term
had a slightly ominous ring to it, and many officers were considerably
relieved when Zhong Xidong, the political commissar of the PLA's
27th Army, addressed a meeting of police section and bureau chiefs,
saying: "In the past you served the reactionary regime and did some
bad things. This time you were able actually to respond to the PLA's
appeal in the Eight Regulations and not stubbornly resist or destroy
things. You also did a good job of preserving local order and welcomed
liberation. This is your political awakening. You handled this affair
well. You did it correctly."[68] Later, General Chen Yi addressed 2,800 of
Shanghai's police officers during a three-hour meeting on the morning
of June 8, held in the Tianshan theater, asking merely that they compare the behavior of their Communist liberators with the Nationalist
Party's carpetbaggers and draw their own conclusions. The new mayor,
looking like a French peasant in a dark beret, with an unlit cigarette
dangling from his mouth, "exhorted the old personnel to change their
old thoughts and ideas, to understand the meaning of the victory of the
people's democratic revolution, and to support the people's government. They should reform themselves, and at the same time carry on
their work without undue anxieties." Chen Yi also promised that if a
policeman was able to serve the people conscientiously, then he would
be encouraged to continue to serve on the force.[69]

The truth of the matter was that the Communists who now ruled the
city had little choice but to try to reeducate these former Nationalists
and puppet policemen into becoming conscientious security cadres,
committed—in the words of Article Ten of the Common Program—"to
defend the independence, territorial integrity, and sovereignty of
China, and to defend the revolutionary gains and all legitimate rights
and interests of the Chinese people."[70] Throughout all of China, there
were only eighty thousand police officers in 1949–50, so that apart
from certain cities in the northeast, approximately 60 percent of the
Nationalist regime's policemen and women were kept on after being
subjected to "educational reconstruction."[71] This policy was called *chai
wu chong jian* (dismantle the house and build again)—that is, destroy
the old police department but retain the individual policemen themselves after they had been investigated and reassigned.[72] In Shanghai
this meant that "the original personnel of the various police stations . . .
will be given reeducation and taught the principle of New Democracy

from 7 to 8 every morning so that each of them may be trained to be a perfect policeman for serving the people."[73]

The prospect of reeducation was far from reassuring for many "held-over personnel" (liuyong renyuan). When members of the Bureau of Labor Affairs, for example, were told later that fall they were going to be sent to a "study unit for personnel detached from work" (lizhi renyuan xuexiban), they became quite agitated over what they took to be the Communist Party's broken promise to retain them. They were only reassured when Deputy Mayor Pan Hannian explained,

> The Bureau of Labor Affairs has more or less completed the period of transferring [power]. Most of the personnel are basically going to be kept on, which means that you've closed ranks with the party. Many of you have professional skills and can serve the people. If you want to serve well, you have to understand party policy and change old [ways of] thinking in order to meet the new circumstances. This is the purpose of participating in study. We want you to study not because we wish to throw you aside but rather to train you all the better to serve the people.[74]

The model Communist cadre whom these co-opted Nationalist policemen were supposed to emulate was usually a Shandong native, called "Model Thirty-Eight" (sanba shi) by the Shanghainese because he or she arrived in 1949 (minguo 38) and carried a Smith and Wesson .38-caliber pistol. As sketched by Robert Guillain:

> The typical bureaucrat of the regime in his blue or khaki uniform, like a soldier's, topped by a cloth cap which he often wears even in the office, resembles a Soviet commissar much more than a Chinese official. He lives frugally. He takes his meals in a mess, eating (according to his rank) one of the three standard menus—"high-table," "middle," or "low"—that are provided, the best of them little less Spartan than the others, consisting of rice, a few vegetables, noodles and, rarely, of meat. He is a poor man and is clothed, fed and housed by the Party. His tobacco and his soap are given to him on the official ration, and he hardly earns enough in a month to buy himself a pair of shoddy sandals. He sleeps on the floor and in requisitioned European buildings he rejects the soft mattresses

that would prevent him from sleeping. He is distant with strangers and, apart from those few men who are appointed to deal with "foreign relations," he is inaccessible.[75] He insists that other Chinese speak to him in the Peking tongue, now more than ever the official language of the whole country, and not in the local dialect of Shanghai or elsewhere. He is rarely to be seen with a woman, and then only with some hefty country girl dressed in Army or Party uniform, her face innocent of rouge and her black straight hair hanging in a fringe from under her khaki cap.[76]

Behind the benevolent facade of the revolutionary regime and the dogged devotion of its conscientious cadres, however, the authorities were also constructing a new and much stronger urban security system. On May 28, the day Chen Yi took over as mayor, Li Shiying and Yang Fan formally assumed control of police headquarters, renamed the Public Security Bureau (PSB) on May 31.[77] On June 15, 1949, the new unit was reorganized into departments, each with a Communist cadre as its head: secretariat, administration (traffic, peace preservation, marriage examination, business control), criminal police (judicial, fingerprints, ballistics, political, investigation), social affairs, fire brigade, and logistics.[78]

Yang Fan's appointment as chief of police coincided with Pan Hannian's return from his security work in Hong Kong. Now forty-six years old, the distinguished-looking former Comintern representative returned to assume a variety of tasks in 1949 and the early 1950s, including deputy mayor and secretary general of the Shanghai People's Government and chief of the Communist Party Central Committee's Eastern China Bureau. Pan Hannian's prominence—he accompanied his old friend and fellow poet Chen Yi onto the podium on May 28 when the new mayor took over the keys of the city—was reassuring to Shanghai capitalists, who thought him "well educated and always well dressed and well mannered. He lacked that air of cunning and menace which most of the Communists had."[79] His mastery of the Shanghai dialect, his sincere and easy manner, and his ability to socialize familiarly with businessmen and financiers (some of whom were friends of his wife's father, a Cantonese banker) made him seem a perfect choice to head Shanghai's united front and security work; and many thought he might easily go on to become mayor. He was, at the very least, a pleasant contrast to Chen Yi whose "cruel eyes" and grim features made him look like a stocky gangster to many members of the Shanghai bourgeoisie.[80]

As leader of united front work in Shanghai, Pan Hannian took his mandate to be the restoration of "normal" operations to the city's factories and businesses. One week after the PLA took Shanghai, Pan invited the city's most prominent capitalists to a conference presided over by Mayor Chen Yi, who both celebrated the Communists' victory and warned of enemies still at hand. *Jiefang ribao* (Liberation Daily) proclaimed jubilantly, on the one hand: "At this moment of the liberation of Greater Shanghai, standing as we do on the threshold of this great turning point in Chinese history, let us be joyful, let us be triumphant. Look! The history of an old China that had been the object of aggression is now ended, and the history of a new China, independent and free, now begins." But it warned darkly, on the other:

> The enemy political and military forces have been defeated but the enemy is very wily, and he is experienced in his counterrevolutionary activities. He knows how to put on the false mask of democracy. He knows how to undertake secret acts of sabotage. He knows how to utilize "leftist" terms, or to spread rumors to fool those within the revolutionary ranks whose political consciousness has not been awakened to a high degree. And more than all, he knows how to pick out the weaknesses within the revolutionary camp and to attack where there is opportunity and thereby attempt to work havoc.[81]

While the regime assigned itself three great tasks—to destroy remnant Nationalist elements, to safeguard freedom and democracy, and to recover economic production—everyone agreed that the overriding imperative was to maintain order.[82] This mission—which was also, incidentally, the primary assignment of the Nationalist Public Security Bureau in 1927 when it took over Shanghai's Chinese sectors—was assigned to a special Peace Preservation Commission.

Primary responsibility for the maintenance of orderliness fell upon the PSB, which worked closely together with military and civilian authorities through an Army-Police-People's [Government] Joint Office. Under this broad rubric the PSB set its own priorities: to establish social order, to suppress bandit or robber activities, and to eliminate special service elements.[83]

Social Order

Social disorder was epitomized for the Communists—as it was for the Nationalists in 1927 and again in 1945—by Shanghai's turbulent and rowdy traffic. Traffic order simply had to be enforced on streets jammed with hucksters' stalls and along waterways stuffed with boats.[84] New rules and regulations for both land and water traffic were enforced by special traffic control stations under the command of the PSB, the Garrison Command, the Customs, and so forth. In contrast to the Nationalist police takeover, however, the Communists strongly emphasized, first, propaganda and, second, the organization of peddlers into local street associations. On July 11 a meeting of street peddler organizations for the entire municipality was convened in the Tianchan Dancehall. Together, and through voting, the conference decided to register all peddlers (tanfan), to issue permits for peddling in legalized locales, and to organize small groups of vendors to meet and review the situation periodically. At the same time, the total number of peddlers was almost halved to about eighty-four thousand, and plans were initiated—and then fairly rapidly implemented—to regulate and reduce the size of the illegal kiosks on city sidewalks.[85]

This was the key difference between the two sides, which is no surprise to any who study modern China. When it came to mobilization, the Nationalists exhorted, passed down decrees, and herded. The Communists' instinct was to go to the primary or grassroot level and commence organizing there, calling on the "masses" to participate actively.[86] This was the primary significance of the meetings of various "circles" in Shanghai during late May and early June 1949. The stated objective of the meetings was to unite all classes under the banner of the New Democracy so as to study and promote activities for the building of a "new China."

When it came to organization, however, there was much more similarity between the two regimes, connected as they were by mutual responsibility and household registration systems mediated via the hokō system imposed by the Japanese on Shanghai during the wartime occupation.[87] At that time, the collaborationist government issued "citizen cards" (liangmin zheng). After the war, the Nationalist police authorities handed out *shenfen zheng* (identity cards), a practice excoriated by the new government after liberation. In place of individual identity cards, the Communists issued *jumin zheng* (resident cards), which were given to heads of household (*huzhang* or *jiazhang*).[88] But, in fact, we can go so far as to say that the Communist PSB inherited the Nationalists' urban *baojia* system of police-supervised household registration, keeping it intact, while adding two important new ingredients: food ration cards and mass participation. Putting it simply, the new PSB brought foodstuffs together with mobilization.

Initially, the Military Control Commission and PSB were concerned about getting their records straight, and that meant being sure that the census reports of the Nationalists' Civil Affairs Bureau were preserved. As soon as they took over that bureau, they discovered the records to be intact, though there had been an attempt at the last minute to burn them.[89] Using those records as a foundation, the Communist authorities reinstituted the household registers (*hujibu*), which ordinarily had one page for each member of a house (which could be extended to include a collective living unit like a company dormitory, an apartment house, or even a hospital). That page included entries for name, birth date, occupation, place of work, family background (*jiating chushen*), individual status (*geren chengfen*), education level, marital status, religion, and ancestral place of origin. Any time one of these categories changed, the head of household was supposed to note the change in the register and report it to the local PSB station.[90]

As we have noted, the Communists had been so critical of the Nationalists' "fascist" system of control that they did not issue personal identity cards. Instead, individuals were registered as members of households, whether that was a regular residence, a public dormitory, a boat, or a temple. The head of household (*huzhu*)—family head, factory manager, captain, or abbot—was held responsible for reporting all changes in the constitution of the household. However, that did not spare the individual resident from surveillance by the "census police" in the "household registration section" (*hujike*) of each police station.[91]

The registration system entailed a staggering amount of paper work. Each police station's *hujike* had to issue ration tickets two to three times a month to each household while attempting to maintain its registers. After July 21, 1950, new regulations stipulated that applications for all newly built houses or buildings had to be filed with the PSB, along with Shanghai Public Works Bureau building permits and ground plans. Numbers for the buildings would then be scored on enamel plates (the infamous *menpai*) paid for by each tenant.[92]

Though the Shanghai puppet police had supervised the rationing and distribution of food during the war, neither it nor the Nationalist police had ever deployed such an extensive scope of control. The Communist PSB household registration system differed in one other extremely fundamental way as well from its predecessors: even though Neighborhood Committees (Jiedao weiyuanhui), with their "bound-feet police," were not set up in Shanghai until 1954, mass participation in this surveillance system was encouraged from the very beginning and from the bottom up. By December 1951 there were 2,083 street and lane residence committees with a membership of 24,862, representing 239,000 of Shanghai's working-class residents.[93] Especially as the mass campaigns began in 1950–51, additional security defense committees and militia committees helped investigate crimes, reported illegal travel, mediated neighborhood disputes, and supervised people "under control" (*guanzhi*).

It is important to note the voluntary quality of this mass participation. Shanghai's citizens were obsessed with social order while undergoing Nationalist bombing raids (the January–February 1950 air raids that left hundreds dead did much to attract positive support for the new regime) and witnessing the capture of Nationalist secret agents week after week in the pages of *Liberation Daily*. Furthermore, they found on the part of the PSB a degree of responsiveness—in work style, at least—that contrasted sharply with the Nationalist police. The government ostensibly encouraged citizens to write to newspapers with complaints that could be forwarded to the offending authority. Many of these were intended for the police, and they apparently had a beneficial effect.

For example, on June 6, 1949, the PSB issued a public notice that all Shanghai inhabitants, except for those whose homes were destroyed, should remain at their residences unless permitted to move by the police.[94] When the PSB realized how much distress this was causing the populace, it amended the order to require that a person wanting to move get two guarantors and submit a request in writing to the police.[95] Similarly, when a resident complained that a policeman had come to his house and asked his mother how she could afford to eat white rice and salted eggs, the PSB asked the officer in question to write a *jiantao* (apology and self-criticism) for "arousing people's disgust" *(fangan)*.[96] And when people also complained about having to stand in long queues at the police stations in order to get their ration tickets, the public security authorities ordered that rations be issued directly by the commodity companies, once police identification papers had been shown to them.[97]

Policemen apologized in public print for failing to adjust to the new circumstances of Communist rule by "speaking casually and running counter to policies." For instance, Officer Yang Changqin had responded to an eighty-year-old mother's complaint against her "disobedient, swindling" son's "coercive" tone of voice in the following way: "*Lao taitai* (Old lady), think it over. Who do you depend on after all for food?" Her reaction was to send a letter to the editor of *Shenbao*, saying that "I think that today's People's Public Security personnel ought not to preserve this kind of reactionary manner. I hope that Comrade Yang will pay attention to amending [his behavior]." After being reprimanded by his superiors, Officer Yang made a self-criticism: "We have still not eradicated the special privilege mentality." He promised to do away with the "vestiges of authoritarian thinking" he had brought along with him from the old Nationalist police force.[98]

On August 9, 1950, *People's Daily* in Beijing announced that "public security work is the most important single task in the nation." In response, the Shanghai public security authorities launched a public campaign to correct the failings mentioned just above, as well as to expose instances of "pulling the wool over superiors' eyes and perfunctorily handling the case" and of "using one's status for corrupt purposes." Readers were encouraged to send their complaints to *Liberation Daily*, which forwarded them on to the appropriate police authorities and published the results.[99]

An example of "pulling the wool" was an officer who misled his superior at the Xincheng district subbureau into thinking that an ordinary householder was dealing drugs, then using the pretext of household registration to order the man's grown sons to come down to the station for a "chat." The police department subsequently apologized for the "mistake," issued a "self-criticism," turned the detective over to the law court for being of "bad character," and criticized the superior for his negligent "coarse branch and large leaf " *(cuzhi daye)* work-style.[100]

An example of "corrupt purposes" was a plainclothesman from the Penglai subbureau who took a flat iron from a secondhand-goods shop without paying for it. This "holdover from the former regime" was said by the police to have received too much of the "old society's poison" to have been thoroughly reeducated. The year before he had borrowed money from a criminal, but the leadership had been lenient with him then because "liberation had not been [in effect] for long." The detective was simply told to return the money and undergo "serious education" in repentance. Now the "old habits" had cropped up again, and because he had exhibited "corrupt thoughts" the plainclothesman would be punished by the personnel office at PSB headquarters.[101]

I cannot recall reading reports about the Shanghai police from the 1920s, 1930s, and 1940s similar to this practice of inviting and then responding to popular complaints. Thus, even though the Nationalist police were much less invasive than their Communist counterparts, interfering primarily in public life along the streets and in places of entertainment, they seemed to remain much more aloof, feared, and unresponsive to public opinion.[102]

Not that the Communist authorities failed to interfere in public life. Two days after it took power, the Military Control Commission promulgated publication regulations that ostensibly promoted free speech but were actually designed to curtail it. The first article read: "In order to protect the freedom of speech in publications of the people and to suppress all counterrevolutionary speeches and publications, all newspapers and periodicals which will be published or will resume publication, and news agencies which are operating or will start operation or will resume operation, are required to apply to the committee for registration in accordance with these regulations."[103]

By June 1 a cultural and educational control committee had been set up under Chen Yi's chairmanship. On June 15 that committee proceeded to annex National Jiaotong University; and on June 24 it took over Ji'nan University.[104] The Nationalists never went so far so quickly, even at the height of "partification" *(danghua)*; and in no other sphere at this point was there such a contradiction between rhetoric (protect freedom) and reality (seize universities).[105]

Nonetheless, the efficacy of the Shanghai control system was impressive, especially when it came to curbing Shanghai's traditional vices by forcibly educating prostitutes, gamblers, and drug addicts into becoming productive members of society.[106] And the vigorous willingness of the police to intervene effectively in such malodorous manipulations as currency speculation—which had virtually brought down the previous regime despite Chiang Ching-kuo's gold yuan reforms in 1948—also attracted public support.[107] The "silver oxen" (yin niu) of old had reappeared early in June 1949, just after the Communist takeover. Speculators manipulated silver dollar quotations on the currency exchange, pushing up commodity prices threefold and threatening to cause financial panic by loudly announcing that the Communist Party did not have any experience in economic administration.[108] The new government denounced this "evil currency inflation" and the manipulation of the market by financial capitalists, which they associated with Nationalist subversives, but by June 8 one silver yuan dollar had inflated to the value of two thousand renminbi.[109] On June 10, at 10:00 A.M., Chief Li Shiying led PSB plainclothesmen and Garrison Command soldiers to surround the currency exchange, which they sealed off after arresting a large number of speculators. This reportedly won the support of most of Shanghai's populace and rapidly led to a stabilization of prices after the silver yuan deflated by one-half.[110] Another form of currency fraud—counterfeiting—also met with public abomination. The streets were jammed with spectators on December 1, 1949, when six counterfeiters (all said to be Nationalist special agents) were driven by in trucks on their way to the execution grounds.

Controlling Vagrancy and Petty Crime

After liberation the Shanghai police had unfettered power to detain and convict criminals. They could conduct large-scale "administrative" roundups of petty thieves, gamblers, whores, pimps, opium addicts, and vagrants and subject them to "noncriminal" reform measures during the course of a long confinement.[111] Although they began to assert these new powers immediately, the first real wave of roundups took place after a conference of representatives of "all groups" of the people of Shanghai adopted a resolution proposed by the Bureau of Civil Affairs Bureau regarding "taking in and reforming" beggars, pickpockets, and petty thieves as part of the repatriation of refugees in the execution of the "winter relief program."[112] The PSB began to execute the order late in the night of December 12, 1949.

During the next three days, more than five thousand beggars and pickpockets were taken to custody centers in nursery schools and training units.[113] Among these, 3,700 liumang (homeless loafers) fit for labor were selected for "reform training." Most came along willingly because they could get food and a place to sleep. Others came in reluctantly, under coercion and fearful of being sent either to Taiwan to fight or to the northeast for reclamation work. Their captors explained to them: "The People's Liberation Army is a people's armed force of great glory and might. Therefore, we do not need any loafers to take part in the Taiwan campaign. . . . The Northeast is in need of competent workers, but those who are needed there are experts and technicians, not loafers." The inmates, confident of their laggardly incompetence, were reassured.[114]

Pickpockets, petty scourges of the city, were another matter. The new practice of the PSB was to arrest a few pickpockets, take them to the station, record their vital information, and then lecture them on correct behavior in a socialist society. When they said that they were willing to repent, they were given a slip with their name on it and the notation that they were giving up their criminal trade. Invariably, the pickpockets went back to their regular calling. Apparently oblivious, the police checked their repentance slips and quickly built up a list of the most egregious offenders. When the latter were again picked up, they were interrogated and threatened more severely; most cooperated by providing information about the various zones of pickpocket activity, the recruiting and training methods of apprentices, and so on. Now, as repentant "leaders" of the pickpockets' fraternity, these cutpurses were told to summon their colleagues to a meeting. When their followers arrived, a police officer took the microphone and announced that the government had a special training course for them. Most realized this meant prison, but they were surrounded by armed police and had no choice but to march off to a detention center where they were divided into small groups and put through "training": confessions, autobiographies, elementary lessons in socialism, songs, speeches, selfcriticisms, and interrogations. Once the training was completed, they were sent home. Since the police now knew everything about them, most of them gave up pickpocketing. Those who went back to their old profession were arrested and summarily sent to distant labor camps, never to reappear again. As news of this crackdown spread throughout Shanghai, pickpocketing ceased altogether.[115]

Another scam the authorities attacked was conducted by pedicab drivers who preyed upon travelers disembarking from their trains at North Station. The chief hoodlum in that neighborhood was a man named Liu Shouli who, together with two gangster lieutenants, had organized the pedicab men into a gang that swindled "bumpkins" *(tubaozi)* freshly arrived in the city. On July 6, 1950, a visitor from Anhui, Lu Jinting, arrived at North Station with 2.7 million yuan in his pocket to pay for medical treatment for a leg injury. It was his misfortune to select a pedicab driven by Liu Shouli himself. Followed by another pedicab, Liu drove Lu to a lane off of Northern Shanxi Road, where he and his two accomplices jumped and robbed him. The sum was so considerable that the North Station PSB ran the case to the ground and arrested Liu and his two lieutenants a little over two months later. The Pedicab Union thanked the police for their intervention and expressed the relief of its members for being able to go peaceably about their business in the future.[116]

Suppressing Armed Crime

The second priority of the PSB was to deal with serious crime, especially armed robbery. In order to do so, two major problems had to be solved: clogged legal dockets and public disorder associated with refugees, professional criminals, and demobilized Nationalist soldiers. The Communist regime had abrogated all Nationalist laws.[117] There was a national judicial conference in August 1950 to discuss a new set of laws, but there seemed to be no urgency to draft them—an opinion voiced by Peng Zhen the following May.[118] This was in part due to the very active role played by People's Tribunals, whose general organizational rules were promulgated on July 10, 1950. The tribunals were ad hoc institutions to "consolidate" the proletarian dictatorship, to bring agrarian reform to a successful conclusion, and to punish counterrevolutionaries and secret agents.[119]

According to Father André Bonnichon, dean of the law faculty at the Université Aurore, which had trained so many Chinese lawyers since the 1920s, the Communists instilled an entirely new legal culture in Shanghai. Bonnichon, who suffered imprisonment for ten months in 1953–54 and whose judgment should be weighed in that regard, claimed that the urban professionals of Shanghai expected new but familiar legislation after May 1949 and only gradually came to realize that the change to come was of a much more radical nature. There would be no penal code, only regulations. The stated rationale was to supplant unfamiliar "bourgeois" procedures with a system of justice understandable to litigants who before 1949 had not realized the class embeddedness of the law. Judges were no longer to be independent arbiters but rather officials who contacted the appropriate government department before announcing a decision. The decision itself—announced by joint tribunals in place of single judges and endorsed by a party authority—was to be guided by secret circulars not available to the public.[120]

As Bonnichon's own experience attested, along with those of a host of other prisoners both foreign and Chinese, the accused had to wait a long time—often many months—for a first judicial interrogation after being arrested. The judge would then simply state: "You are guilty because the government has not arrested you without considerable investigations and deliberations. Therefore, two ways lie open to you: either you confess and implore the clemency of the government; in which case the government will be lenient. Or you resist and subject yourself to the severest of punishments."[121] Prisoners were then judged by analogous reasoning, being accused of sabotage, feudalism, reactionary tendencies, and counterrevolutionary activities because of their background or current class identity. "Judges rarely say: 'You have committed this or that act.' They say rather, 'You are a reactionary. You are a foreign agent.'"[122]

In that way, under these new legal dispositions, the state prosecutors did not have to name any infraction at all. The arrested person was simply told to yield rather than defend, which effectively displaced Shanghai's many lawyers and made statutes irrelevant. Thinking "right" became, in effect, a juridical obligation throughout China, and this in return enforced the omnipotence of the state and its courts, which no longer defined offenses, judged proof, or legally considered confessions in light of plausibility.

In Shanghai proper, until the new People's Tribunals were established, the PSB handed culprits over to the old courts' detention bureaus.[123] On June 17, 1949, Deputy Mayor Pan Hannian convened a meeting of jurists and lawyers who proposed the organization of a formal people's court for Shanghai that would take place once the legal archives were usable.[124] Legal work would continue to be dominated by the PSB, as was true elsewhere in China, but the Communists' tribunals did succeed—albeit in ways that contravened any contemporary notion of civil rights—in clearing the city's docket, which in February 1950 amounted to 10,962 accumulated cases.[125] The following month, over four thousand male and female inmates of the jails attached to the Shanghai Municipal People's Court were sent to Dongtai (northern Jiangsu) to undergo "reform through labor."[126] By August, the Shanghai, Tianjin, and Beijing police could claim to have solved an average of 95 percent of the robbery cases and 80 percent of the theft cases in their respective jurisdictions.[127] To clear the remaining backlog, the Government Administration Council and the Supreme People's Court in Beijing issued instructions in October 1950 to decide "vicious" cases according to the laws governing suppression of counterrevolutionary activities and to have the remainder determined at various government levels by the People's Government. Thus, by the first half of 1951, the courts in Shanghai, Tianjin, Beijing, Nanjing, Guangzhou, Chongqing, and Wuhan had handled 95,983 cases, of which about 35,000 were criminal and 61,000 were civil.[128]

As dockets were cleared, new cases were brought forward. The East China Military and Political Commission regarded the extirpation of banditry and robbery one of the Shanghai PSB's most important tasks.[129] The Communist cadres brought in from outside, however, had little knowledge of local conditions, and the "former personnel" were often compromised by previous social and economic debts owed to the criminal element in the city. In the seven months between June and December 1949, there were 737 cases of armed robbery: some of the bandits were Western-clothed gunmen who held up cabarets, some were river pirates, and some were former Nationalist soldiers and special agents who pretended to be Communist military officers or PSB personnel. Some of these—such as the group led by Liu Yinqiu in the fens of Lake Tai—were Nationalist secret service elements working with local bandits; many carried machine guns.[130] With the help of the populace, however, the PSB managed to break or solve 665 of the 737 cases by the end of year, arresting 1,667 robbers and seizing a large quantity of guns and ammunition.[131]

It was important, at the same time, to attack the roots of such banditry: demobilized soldiers and refugees. On June 13, 1949, the Garrison Command ordered former Nationalist soldiers and "roving braves" (youyong) to present themselves at several "concentration" (jizhong) points around the city to be registered. Those who refused would be punished. During the next week, 7,832 people, including one general, ten major generals, and seventeen colonels, turned themselves in. Another 3,000 former troops reported also. Their weapons were handed over, and they were sent back to their original place of registry to assume productive roles in society.[132] At the same time, starting on June 29, the first tens of thousands of hut dwellers and refugees were repatriated to their native villages.[133]

Refugees, however, continued to pour into the city, especially after summer rains caused widespread flooding and destroyed crops in northern Jiangsu, northern Anhui, and central Shandong. By mid-September 1949, the six workstations of the Provisional Refugee Relief Association of Shanghai were reporting a total of 454,147 refugees. Many of these were among the 500,000 refugees originally repatriated in June and July who were now returning to the city in desperate search of famine relief.[134] The key to handling the refugee problem, then, was twofold. On the one hand, Shanghainese had to be made aware that they were not economically separated from their own immediate hinterland and that they had to help pay for the cost of assigning refugees to engage in productive activities back in the countryside. And on the other, they had to accept some measure of responsibility for funding public works projects in Shanghai and its immediate suburbs for refugees who could not be guaranteed productive labor back in their own hometowns. On January 31, 1950, the standing committee of the Shanghai Winter Relief Committee launched a work-for-relief movement to dredge Shanghai's three main shipping courses and twenty-one irrigation canals. A total of 4,350 refugees were employed by the dredging project.[135]

Suppressing Counterrevolutionaries

As we have seen, the jubilant announcement of the final liberation of Shanghai was tinged with fearful warnings of Nationalist counterrevolutionary activities. This was neither paranoia nor propaganda: the city was indeed swarming with special service agents left behind by the Bureau to Protect Secrets and other secret police units of Chiang's regime.[136] The new authorities warned of the likelihood of these Nationalist remnants linking up with gangsters and criminals to foment social disorder.[137]

On May 29, 1949, the CCP inaugurated the Wusong Shanghai garrison headquarters to direct mop-up campaigns against bandits, deserters, and stragglers. The threat was real. Xu Tong, Jiang Hanxiong, Chen Datong, and Kang Yijun—all men with Nationalist secret service connections—had already brought together a number of loafers, deserters, and local bullies to conduct counterrevolutionary operations. They were quickly arrested, but other teams were also being formed.[138]

According to Chinese press releases, these units included the former Shanghai Station of the Nationalist Defense Ministry's special services, which was a secret police organization headed by Xiao Jianhe; an underground branch of Dai Li's former paramilitary Traffic Police led by Wu Zibin; Mao Sen's own special agents from the Shanghai police, including a team charged with assassination and demolition activities; and a contingent of the Jiangsu-Zhejiang-Anhui Special Dare to Die Corps, led by Chen Yuqing, the former commander of Chiang Chingkuo's Youth Service Corps of Greater Shanghai.[139] There were also individual spies, such as Fan Qingxi, who were instructed to build new agent networks, gather information on the location of PLA and police units, collect the addresses and license numbers of people's government officials, and pinpoint the location of steel and iron works factories to help in the planning of assassination activities, bombing raids, and industrial sabotage.[140]

As soon as the new PSB was constituted under Communist leadership, the authorities announced, at the behest of the Military Control Committee, that reactionary organizations were against the law, that all special service units were to be dissolved, and that their illegal weapons and radio transmitters were to be seized.[141] During the next six months, vividly documented in *Shenbao*, 1,499 Nationalist spies were captured, along with hundreds of radio sets, guns, and ammunition. Some of these special service elements had been left behind when the Nationalists had decamped. Others were sent in from Taiwan and Zhoushan (Chusan), which the Nationalists still held. Assassins bent upon killing Chen Yi were captured, saboteurs planning to blow up airplanes were arrested, and numerous Nationalist agents carrying out destabilizing missions (robbing banks, killing soldiers and policemen, and so on) were seized.[142]

On June 6, 1949, the Shanghai Military Control Committee issued a public notice dissolving all Nationalist special service organs.[143] Nonetheless, the authorities believed that the Nationalist secret service would continue to try to create a state of confusion in order to further its own plans for "a miracle [that] will come to save them from extinction."[144] Newspapers listed thereafter case after case of arrests of former Nationalist military or secret service officers caught with false documents, arms, and other incriminating material.[145]

At 4:00 A.M. on June 29, therefore, the PSB launched a series of "surprise raids" on suspected safe houses throughout the city "in order to ferret out bandits, special agents, stragglers and deserters." They succeeded in arresting 317 Nationalist soldiers and secret agents, along with a handful of weapons and pistols. The next day more raids were conducted, and another 328 subversives were seized. Interrogations of these led to a further 6,000 seizures of "bandit agents."[146] These arrests, and their attendant publicity, helped establish the sense in Shanghai that the enemy was everywhere, that eternal vigilance was vital, and that your next-door neighbor could easily be a spy. This attitude, of course, persisted well into the Cultural Revolution and led to many of the bizarre accusations of that dreadful period.[147]

Pudong Counterrevolutionaries

Pudong, the poor farming area just across the Huangpu from the Shanghai Bund, remained a hotbed of opposition—as it was for the Japanese during their occupation of Shanghai a few years earlier. The leader of the Pudong resistants was Zhu Shishan, who had been deputy chief of the second section of Dai Li's Military Statistics Bureau. Arrested shortly after liberation, then quickly freed, he had returned to Pudong to organize an anti-Communist resistance. It was a futile effort.[148]

Between early June and mid-August 1949, the PLA sent small units to supervise the surrender of arms by village officials. Cadres were also sent in to help local party organs take over local government and urge resisters to surrender. After mid-July, larger PLA units began mopping-up operations against resistance units in their garrison areas. Even though the army had an imperfect knowledge of local topography and of the special agents' "work style," and although they did not call in more extreme military pressure, the PLA gained discernible results. More than seventy "bandits" and a considerably larger number of local village militia came over, along with Nationalist deserters and stragglers.[149]

Now that the troops and cadres had mastered the coordination of military mopping-up operations with political mobilization of the masses, a unified Bandit Suppression Command was established. Armed work corps were sent to local districts partly to launch a political offensive against the "bandit remnants" and partly to promote the welfare of the peasants by helping collect autumn crops, educate the illiterate, and so forth. This was accompanied by the formation of thirty-three peasant associations in as many *xiang*. At the end of October, a combined police-army task force defeated the Haibei Column of the Popular Anti-Communist and National Salvation Army of the Southeast, which supposedly reported to the Nationalists' Bureau to Protect Secrets and was actually commanded by four Pudong bandit chiefs.[150] By late November, Nationalist army elements had either surrendered or taken to sea along with the local bandits and pirates who sailed between Pudong and Hangzhou.[151]

But other resistance units had to be rooted out as well. On September 3 the Public Safety Bureau of Southern Jiangsu launched an attack on the (Nationalist) Defense Ministry's Youth National Salvation Army, which had been operating in the Wuxi area. The commander, Mao Xin, escaped; but the deputy commander was arrested, and more than twenty clandestine units were smashed.[152] On October 13, Shanghai river police arrested the notorious Subei bandit chief Liu Zhankui, who had served the Nationalists as a secret agent and guerrilla commander attacking the New Fourth Army and who later led a division of Wang Jingwei's puppet army that "perpetrated rapes, arsons and massacres everywhere."[153] In November 1949, the Shanghai PSB uncovered the second column of the Youth Anti-Communist Army, which consisted mainly of remnants of Dai Li's Loyal and Patriotic Army (Zhongyi jiuguo jun), conducting assassination and sabotage operations in Shanghai under the command of Hu Shaomei. Hu was captured along with his deputies, and the column disbanded.[154]

As the government forces tallied up their successes at the end of 1949, they could claim to have crushed three underground special service agencies in the Nanjing and Shanghai areas and all of the Nationalist resistance units in the Suzhou, Changshu, and Wuxi zones.[155] The PLA played the leading role in this campaign. During this mopping-up campaign, the Wusong garrison captured 31 machine guns, 762 rifles and pistols, 13 artillery pieces, more than 70,000 rounds of cartridges, and 7 transponders, plus mimeograph and counterfeiting equipment. More than 432 bandit special agents' cases were broken; 2,273 commanders and deputy commanders and 18,541 bandits, deserters, and stragglers had been taken prisoner.[156]

Public Enemies

The public's wariness was dramatically intensified by the Korean War, which "stimulated a series of political and social revolutions in China that would have been otherwise inconceivable during the early stage of the new republic." After China entered the Korean War, as Mao Zedong had anticipated, "the Communist regime found itself in a powerful position to penetrate into almost every cell of Chinese society through intense mass mobilization."[157] The government announced that it was "imperative to rely upon the people to raise their ardor in opposing special agents and spies to heighten their sense of political vigilance and to turn the work of guarding against special agents and spies into an integral, regular, and important part of the every-day life of the people so that the interests of the country and the people can be effectively protected, and the vicious schemes of the counterrevolutionary beasts thoroughly smashed."[158]

On July 23, 1950, Premier Zhou Enlai issued general instructions to suppress counterrevolutionaries by life imprisonment or execution.[159] These instructions were bolstered during a conference in October 1950 that declared that policy toward counterrevolutionary elements had been too magnanimous. On February 20, 1951, the Central People's Government Council approved "regulations of the People's Republic of China for punishment of counterrevolutionaries," which were formally promulgated by the Central People's Government on February 21.[160] The campaign that followed was intensely formative. It introduced Shanghai's populace to "the processes of institutionalized violence, both physical and mental, which are essential components of the political style of the regime." Like later campaigns, the Campaign to Suppress Counterrevolutionaries weakened primary allegiances and introduced the urban population to "struggle."[161] According to Pan Hannian, who spoke on December 14, 1951, after orchestrating the campaign in Shanghai, over 3,200 accusation meetings had been held, and investigation committee members had collected material on more than 40,000 individuals.[162] Hundreds of these were subsequently killed and thousands jailed.[163]

A prime agent in these mass campaigns was the residents committee, colloquially called *lilong weiyuanhui* (neighborhood committee). By 1952, the Shanghai neighborhood committees had organized newspaper reading groups to publicize party policies, explain foreign affairs, broaden residents' horizons, and mobilize political enthusiasm. In the Resist America Aid Korea Campaign *(Kang Mei yuan Chao)*, residents donated 16.5 billion yuan for airplanes and artillery. And in the Campaign to Suppress Counterrevolutionaries, and the Three-Anti (against corruption, waste, and bureaucratism) and Five-Anti (against bribery, tax evasion, theft of state assets, cheating on labor or materials, and stealing state economic intelligence) campaigns, members of residents committees were called on to conduct patriotic spying on neighbors and even to publicly denounce their own parents.[164] By the mid-1950s, "the ordering of political and social life in Shanghai *lilong* was accomplished through the efficient work of residents committees."[165]

That "ordering," of course, could be presented as a benignly democratic reconstruction of society, once the public's enemies had been removed.[166] "Cleaning up" Meifeng Alley, a *lilong* in the poor working-class district of Putuo in the southwest quarter of Shanghai, meant first of all getting rid of the "number one crook and despot" Xu Youliang, who terrorized the neighborhood. "Backed by the reactionary Nationalist regime, the despot, who was the head of the *baojia* system, pressed one young man into the Nationalist army, which finally forced the father to die of grief. The despot was at the head of many gangs under which the people groaned. But not long ago Xu was brought to book at a mass accusation meeting attended by over a thousand people and was given due punishment by the people's government in accordance with popular demand."[167] Before liberation, the residents tried to install garbage boxes and latrines, but Xu Youliang pocketed the money for himself. Now the alley "wears a completely new look. The roadway is now paved with flagstone, the walls have been whitewashed. Many alleyway lamps have been installed along with hydrants, garbage boxes, and latrines." The children were said to be the happiest of all. Before only twenty attended school; now more than a hundred are in class.

The residents run their own affairs, and their residents committee solves their own safety and health problems. "Democracy has certainly done wonders, and the residents in this alleyway are now living as one big happy family." The story of Meifeng Alley, we are told, is "indicative of the progress made by the Shanghai people towards a better, happier life."[168]

It is also a history of modern Jacobinism—of the belief in the possibility of transforming society through totalistic actions.[169] The Shanghai "cleanup" struck at the nub of the tension between liberty and equality, or, as S. N. Eisenstadt puts it, the tension "between emphasis on a vision of the good social order and the narrow interests of different sectors of the society, between the conception of the individual as an autonomous sovereign and emphasis on the community, between the utopian and the procedural components of this program, and the closely related tensions between revolutionary and normal politics."[170] Should we then simply fall back upon the comforting tension in Jean-Jacques Rousseau's social contract between the "general will" and the "will of all"? I think not. The price for cleaning up Meifeng Alley's latrines turned out to be too much to bear.

✑ 3

Masters of the Country?
Shanghai Workers in the
Early People's Republic

Elizabeth J. Perry

CHINA'S ESTABLISHMENT OF a Communist regime in 1949
was accompanied by extravagant pro-labor rhetoric that promised a dramatically improved political status for the proletariat. Workers were
heralded in official pronouncements as "masters of the country" (*guojia
de zhuren*), the "leading class" (*lingdao jieji*) that should rightfully "take
charge" (*dangjia zuozhu*). Looking back on this period more than a half
century later, one may be inclined to disregard such declarations of
proletarian hegemony as little more than empty verbiage manufac-
tured by a cynical state. But there is evidence that at the time many
workers, as well as many union cadres, took these pledges quite seriously. With tens of thousands of Shanghai workers having just participated in Communist-sponsored militias that played a key part in protecting their factories from enemy sabotage and delivering them safely
into the hands of the revolutionary regime, workers naturally expected
an influential voice in the new order.[1] The militancy of the Shanghai
proletariat in the initial years of the People's Republic bespoke a heady
sense of political prowess and entitlement—encouraged both by official propaganda and by their own recent history of struggle.

This chapter will explore the effort by Shanghai workers and unions
alike to seize the opportunities for expanded activism afforded by the
young Communist regime. While studies of labor in the People's Republic have usually focused on managerial relations within industrial

workplaces, here our attention will be directed toward labor activism
that occurred (for the most part) beyond the shop floor.[2] First I will
consider the remarkable wave of labor protests that swept across
Shanghai in the months following the Communist victory, examining
several incidents for which detailed information is available. Then I will
turn to the reestablishment of worker militias, a union-sponsored
initiative—drawing upon revolutionary precedents—that deployed tens
of thousands of Shanghai workers as factory and neighborhood patrols
in the early years of the People's Republic. Both of these developments
gained momentum soon after the city's takeover by the New Fourth
Army in May 1949; and both came to an abrupt halt four years later
with Mao Zedong's fateful decision to abandon "New Democracy" in
favor of a Stalinist mode of rapid industrialization.

Labor Unrest

In just the six months from June through December 1949, Shanghai
experienced—according to official union statistics—a total of 3,324
strikes and other major labor disturbances.[3] These figures are extraordinary even by comparison with the Republican period, when the May
Fourth Movement of 1919, the May Thirtieth Movement of 1925, the
Shanghai Workers' Three Armed Uprisings of 1926–27, and the
protests of the civil war years gave rise to one of the most impressive
labor movements in world history.[4] The year of greatest strike activity
in Republican-era Shanghai, 1946, saw a total of 280 strikes. By contrast, in the second half of 1949 the new authorities were confronted
with an average of more than 500 disturbances each month.[5]

This outpouring of labor unrest was clearly a response to the economic hardships of the time. The civil war and attendant departure of
many Shanghai capitalists for Hong Kong, Taipei, Tokyo, and other des-
tinations contributed to massive factory closures and cutbacks. Most of
the labor disputes that took place in this period revolved around bread-
and-butter issues: demands for factory reopenings, a return to work, and
the payment of back wages. But the protesters were also emboldened by
the new regime's avowed commitment to the political supremacy of the
working class.

In some cases, official unions (whose leadership was drawn from
members of the Communist underground who had been responsible

for organizing strikes and militias during the civil war period) promoted contentious behavior as an appropriate expression of proletarian
prerogative. A report by the preparatory committee for the Shanghai
Federation of Trade Unions (SFTU) in September 1949 commented
sympathetically on the burgeoning protest movement: "Shanghai has
just been liberated. The working masses of Shanghai for a long time
were oppressed by imperialism, the Nationalist Party, and the capitalists. Having suddenly gained liberation, they naturally are swept up in
a widespread mass movement. With most workers having participated
in the campaign to protect their factories, followed by the policies and
proclamations of the government, demands to reopen the factories and
return to work have developed swiftly and broadly."[6] The union appreciated that workers' revolutionary enthusiasm, reinforced by official
government pronouncements, fueled the upsurge in labor activism.
The report went on, however, to sound a note of caution:

> Because some benighted capitalists treated the workers with cruel
> exploitation and unrestrained oppression before liberation, added
> to the fact that some of the working masses have a simple "stand
> up" *(fanshen)* mentality, at some factories demands have devel-
> oped for settle-accounts struggles. For example, at the Yihe Cotton
> Mill, workers who were fired twenty years ago for participating in
> mass struggles now want to vent their pent-up anger on manage-
> ment. At the same time, due to the agitation of a few secret agents,
> at places like the Yizhong Tobacco Factory more than 600 unem-
> ployed workers, dismissed for various reasons, have raised ultra-
> leftist demands for a return to work. These factors account for the
> escalating number of disputes.[7]

In the eyes of the SFTU, then, revolutionary (and counterrevolutionary) legacies and rivalries presented a serious challenge, radical-
izing the labor movement in potentially dangerous directions.

The torrent of labor disturbances that burst forth in the latter half of
1949 was concentrated at small- and medium-size enterprises, particularly in the textile and tobacco sectors, which had been especially hard-
hit by the economic downturn. For the most part, these protests were
scattered and defensive expressions of severe worker distress. But in
those enterprises that boasted a long history of labor agitation (including

the Yihe Cotton Mill and the Yizhong Tobacco Factory singled out in
the union's report), a more politicized pattern could be discerned. Sites
of intense competition between Nationalist and Communist labor organizers from the 1920s through the civil war years, these factories continued to attract rival partisan activity—including armed militia
formation—even after the Communist victory. Union ambivalence about
the propriety of strikes and other forms of labor struggle under the new
regime only heightened such tensions.

Take the case of the Shenxin Number Seven cotton mill, part of the
Rong family's industrial empire, where a Nationalist-sponsored union
remained basically intact for nearly a year following the Communist
takeover.[8] With general manager Rong Hongyuan having fled to Hong
Kong on the eve of liberation, his successor decided to reduce the
workweek—and the wages—of the hard-pressed labor force. In January 1950, hundreds of angry workers twice surrounded the general
headquarters of the Shenxin Textile Company to demand redress for
withheld wages. When these initiatives did not resolve the problem,
the disappointed workers marched to the home of the new manager,
Rong Heqing. A group of the protesters, under the pretext of looking
for cotton magnate Rong Yiren, broke into Rong Heqing's house and
proceeded to confiscate, cook, and consume chicken, ham, and cakes.
Having dined without the company of Rong Yiren, they then marched
to *his* home to continue the movable feast. Follow-up investigations by
the SFTU determined that much of the blame for this unseemly "eat-
in" lay with the factory union, which had taken a passive stance during
the incident, permitting former Nationalist activists to assume a leadership role. These remnant elements, according to the SFTU investigation, were seeking to take advantage of current opportunities by acting
as "heroes" intent upon improving worker welfare. The result, however,
was the inappropriate continuation of "old methods of struggle dating
from the period of reactionary Nationalist rule." In an effort to squelch
such "outmoded" patterns of behavior, the SFTU instructed Shenxin
Seven to establish an armed militia known as a workers' picket team
(*gongren jiuchadui*), with more than a hundred members, to patrol the
premises.

The Zhengtai Rubber Plant offered an even more worrisome example of labor unrest instigated in part by Nationalist loyalists.[9] With
a labor force of 1,600 workers, half of whom were women and nearly

all of whom retained close ties to peasant families in the neighboring Jiangsu countryside, Zhengtai had proved an inhospitable setting for underground Communist organizers during the revolutionary years. After liberation, efforts to develop an effective party presence at the factory made little immediate headway. Cadres' bland pronouncements against "economistic struggles" and in favor of developing production fell on deaf ears.

Only days after the New Fourth Army's advance on Shanghai, workers at the Zhengtai Rubber Plant demanded a travel subsidy of seven yuan to enable them to return home for the Dragon Boat Festival. This had been the standard travel subsidy issued in previous years, but the abstemious Communist Party cadres assigned to the factory estimated that three or four yuan should be sufficient to cover the travel expenses of returning workers—most of whom hailed from nearby villages. With the new union indicating only halfhearted support for the workers' request, management decided to dig in its heels and refused to provide any travel subsidy at all.

On the day of the festival, the factory officially closed for the holiday, and none of the Communist cadres went to work. Taking advantage of their absence, remnant Nationalist unionists called on the entire workforce (which presumably lived on the factory premises) to surround the general manager's office. When party cadres rushed to the factory to try to defuse the protest, they too were surrounded. With emotions running high, the workers—egged on by the ringleaders—now demanded payment of a fourteen-yuan subsidy as a precondition for dispersing. To complicate matters still further, a number of party cadres also joined the demonstration—clamoring for the inflated subsidy.

In negotiations with management, the party representatives at the factory reversed their previous stance and demanded a minimum subsidy payment of ten yuan. When the case was taken to the municipal union, however, the SFTU—afraid that payment of the subsidy would encourage workers across the city to demand similar handouts—took the side of management. The union's diffidence disappointed the workers and created a further pretext for protest. Calling themselves the New Youth Association (Xin qing tuan), Nationalist partisans at the rubber plant attacked and injured some of the Communist cadres and locked the general manager's brother in the lavatory. Only when he promised his captors that they would all be issued expensive new

athletic shoes was the prisoner released. Exasperated by these developments, Zhengtai's management responded by deploying a militia of
more than two hundred workers, armed with iron bars, to restore order.
Led by a pistol-toting "Nationalist Party agent," however, this "Industry
Defense Corps" (*hugong dui*) actually tried to expand the protest rather
than extinguish it. Not until threatened by armed Communist cadres did
the team leaders back down from their attempt to widen the struggle by
force. Changing tactics, the New Youth Association—claiming that the
party had established the new factory union undemocratically—announced
the inauguration of its own "reformed" union to negotiate with management over a new minimum wage. Municipal authorities refused to recognize the rival union, of course, but the illegal body nevertheless vied with
its Communist-sponsored counterpart for the allegiance of the Zhengtai
workforce.

After more than two weeks of unrest at the rubber plant, the SFTU
sent a work team to the factory to investigate. The armed, uniformed
pickets who operated as part of the work team frightened the workers,
however, and as a consequence the workers were reluctant to interact
with them. Moreover, several work team members—veterans of the
land reform movement in the north—spoke with a heavy Shandong dialect that was unintelligible to the locals. When they convened meetings for the workers to air grievances, these northerners were also at a
loss to understand the local patois of the workers. Finally, a few of the
staff did open up to the work team, confiding that they were terrified of
the workers because "since liberation workers have status." The work
team reported that although the staff "look down on the workers as
backward," still they were "petrified of worker struggles directed
against them."

Further investigation revealed that the heart of the trouble could be
traced to the Nationalist-influenced organization at the rubber plant:
the New Youth Association. Some thirty workers at the factory had
joined the group, which—despite its "leftist demeanor"—was deemed
to be the creation of "secret agents" intent upon preventing Communist control of the factory. Claiming a close connection to the mayor of
Wuxi (the hometown of many of the Zhengtai workers), members of
the New Youth Association allegedly spread rumors that Communists
were being assassinated in Wuxi and that a similar fate would soon be-
fall them in Shanghai. New Youth Association members were found to

have infiltrated and assumed the leadership of study groups and other political and recreational organizations at the factory, using this mass foundation to foment protest and isolate the Communist cadres. Only when the work team finally gained access to the name list of the association was it able to seize the upper hand.

Although the SFTU work team managed to defuse this particular protest by exposing and disbanding the New Youth Association, problems at the Zhengtai Rubber Plant continued.[10] In 1951, around the time of the lunar new year festival, a string of industrial sabotage incidents was reported at the factory. Coming just at the moment when Shanghai was starting to register "reactionary associations" in conjunction with the Campaign to Suppress Counterrevolutionaries, the incidents raised suspicions of renewed "secret agent" activities at the rubber plant. Public security authorities were called in to investigate and, assisted by informers among the workforce, fingered twelve "counterrevolutionaries" at the factory. Workers testified that some of these individuals had predicted the imminent return of the Nationalists, warning that anyone caught wearing a "Lenin suit" would soon be killed.

Subsequent interrogation among the detainees led to the arrests of seven individuals outside the factory who were charged with masterminding the sabotage at Zhengtai and inciting similar incidents at a number of other factories around the city where Nationalist loyalists remained in place. One of those arrested, Cao Ajin, had served in the Shanghai Garrison under the previous regime and retained ties to former members of the Nationalist-sponsored Industry Defense Corps—a workers' militia that had been responsible for ferreting out suspected Communist labor organizers during the days of Nationalist rule.[11] Cao had allegedly called together more than twenty of his contacts at various factories for a secret meeting in October 1950 at which he was said to have encouraged the ex-militiamen by predicting the impending return of the Nationalists in quasi-millenarian terms: "The Nationalist Party is coming. Platoon captains and higher-level cadres will all be issued guns. We will recover the factories and then we won't have to work anymore. We will live in foreign-style houses and ride in cars. Those without cars will ride the busses for free. We will be the bosses."

Despite the well-publicized arrests of "secret agents" like Cao Ajin, similar cases of labor unrest continued throughout the first several years of the People's Republic. In the single month of May 1952, for example, Shanghai's Labor Bureau reported a total of 1,153 labor disputes in the city.[12] Among the many industrial protests that occurred that year, one of the most influential took place at the Dadong Tobacco Factory, an enterprise that—owing to insufficient business—had suspended operations (with Labor Bureau approval) for a year and a half, starting in May 1950.[13] As soon as the suspension period had expired, the factory union, at the request of the workers, initiated negotiations with management aimed at resuming production. Five rounds of talks resulted in no agreement, however, and in January 1952 management— pleading a lack of funds—petitioned the district industry and commerce department for authorization to remain closed. This was just at the time of the Three-Anti Campaign, however, when the government had called a temporary halt to factory closures. The matter remained unsettled for months, until finally in mid-June the municipal Bureau of Industry and Commerce approved management's request to shut down the factory. By this point it was clear that the Shanghai tobacco industry was in dire straits; only fourteen of the ninety-eight tobacco factories that had been in operation at the time of liberation were still functioning, and the workforce had dwindled by more than 40 percent. Workers from Dadong were to be issued severance pay, and the Labor Bureau was instructed to find alternative employment for them at other foodstuffs or textile factories.

After numerous meetings convened by the Labor Bureau to inform Dadong's union cadres and worker representatives about the serious problems of the tobacco industry and the government's commitment to make other arrangements to guarantee the workers' livelihood, most workers went along with the decision to close down their factory. However, one woman worker—who had played a leading role in her factory union during the Nationalist era and had recently been expelled from the reconstituted union—was less compliant. Together with the husband of a fellow worker, she submitted a petition in the name of "worker representatives" to the Shanghai Labor Bureau and the East China Office of the All-China Federation of Trade Unions. Upon learning that the woman's confederate was not a worker at the factory, and that he had moreover served previously as an officer in the Nationalist military, the Labor Bureau notified Public Security and refused to consider their petition. The two were not deterred, however, and on July 29 they led a group of eighteen Dadong workers to Beijing to present their grievances to the central authorities. To elicit maximum sympathy in the capital, the protest leaders reportedly instructed their followers to wear old clothes and leave their hair unkempt. Armed with images of Chairman Mao, they would parade through the streets, claiming to have been wronged and threatening to commit suicide by jumping into the lake at Beihai Park. When a cadre from the SFTU rushed to Beijing to try to persuade the complainants to return to Shanghai, he was surrounded and attacked by the petitioners.

At this point, the Dadong dispute took a surprising turn. In Beijing, the All-China Federation of Trade Unions, without consulting their subordinates in Shanghai, reported the case directly to Mao Zedong. Upon receiving this report of unemployed workers marching desperately in his name, Mao flew into a rage, charging that the Shanghai authorities "don't care whether the workers live or die." Blasting Shanghai's handling of the Dadong case as exhibiting "serious bureaucratism along with serious anarchy and lack of discipline," Mao authorized an urgent cable ordering the Shanghai Party Committee to reopen the Dadong Tobacco Factory and to dismiss the cadres who had previously approved the factory closure. The Shanghai government scurried to comply with these instructions, but Dadong's management still refused to accede to the demand that the factory resume production. Only once it became clear that the municipal authorities were prepared to provide significant financial incentives in order to fulfill Mao's instructions did management relent.

On September 15, 1952, Dadong formally reopened. A group of cadres from the Labor Bureau, the Bureau of Industry and Commerce, the SFTU, and the Foodstuffs Union were duly disciplined for having recommended the factory's closure, two all-city meetings of party cadres were convened to publicize the case, and for more than a month municipal agencies at all levels carried out an "anti-bureaucratism" campaign focused on the Dadong affair. In the long run, however, the hefty subsidies that the city was paying Dadong to resume production were unsustainable. Three years later, when labor protest was no longer an option for disgruntled workers in Shanghai, Dadong was quietly merged with three other tobacco factories; in 1958, tobacco production at the amalgamated factory ceased altogether, and remaining operations were folded into the Shanghai Instruments Factory.

Extreme though these particular disputes may have been, they nevertheless suggest the tumultuous nature of labor relations in the early years of the People's Republic. Emboldened by the promise of a new political status, yet faced with severe economic hardship, workers protested their plight in dramatic actions ranging from "eat-ins" and sieges at the homes and offices of factory managers to petitions and demonstrations directed at government officials. Caught in the middle, union cadres vacillated between supporting the workers (for which they risked criticism for committing the errors of "economism" and "syndicalism") and attempting to restore order (for which they might just as easily be accused of "bureaucratism"). With official unions thus stymied, rival groups—often organized by individuals with lingering ties to the ancien régime—fanned the flames of worker discontent.

Labor relations under the previous Nationalist regime had also been highly contentious, of course. Strikes had been frequent, and tensions were often exacerbated by workers' participation in rival armed militias sponsored by competing Nationalist and Communist forces. Perpetuating this tradition of militancy, confrontations in the initial years of the new regime were frequently violent affairs. And leadership by former militiamen—some of whom retained allegiance to the Nationalist Party—was a common feature.[14] The ambivalence and indecisiveness of official unions, combined with objective economic duress, afforded an opening for "counterrevolutionaries" to make common cause with disgruntled workers—all in the name of the proletarian privileges promised by the new revolutionary regime.

This complicated situation created a serious dilemma for labor. Li Lisan, who headed the first Shanghai General Labor Union back in 1925 and later lost his party leadership post for continuing to instigate proletarian insurrections at a time when Mao and his colleagues were concentrating on the countryside, by the time of liberation had returned from a fifteen-year exile in the Soviet Union to take charge of both the All-China Federation of Trade Unions and the Ministry of Labor. Li tried to walk a fine line between advocating workers' rights and yet admonishing workers against the exercise of those very rights: "Are strikes prohibited? That would be impossible and improper. Strikes are the workers' right, but today the workers don't need this method. In the past, they had no choice but to strike; today, however, they can use rational methods to settle things. If negotiations fail, they can go to the Labor Bureau ... The old method is not only non-beneficial, but harmful. This is a new form of class struggle. To deny class struggle would be fallacious, but class struggle takes many forms."[15] As Li and his fellow unionists grappled with the question of what forms of "class struggle" to encourage under the changed circumstances of a new Communist regime, they were drawn toward an institution with an established revolutionary pedigree: worker militias.

Worker Militias

Worker militias (known as "worker pickets") were the very first organization that the Chinese Communist Party, after its establishment in July 1921, had employed to conduct armed insurrection. In fact, Li Lisan himself had mobilized a cohort of Communist-sponsored pickets during the historic Anyuan coal miners' strike in 1922.[16] Until the Nationalists launched their White Terror five years later (precipitated, in no small measure, by fear of armed Communist pickets in Shanghai and other cities), worker pickets were the principal means by which the Communist Party attempted to realize its revolutionary ambitions.

Although Nationalist repression decimated the ranks of the Communist pickets in 1927, the Nationalists established their own armed worker militias immediately upon taking power. These Industry Defense Corps, operating in tandem with Nationalist security agencies, were important in obstructing Communist attempts at labor organizing during the Nanjing decade. The Japanese invasion afforded the Communists a second chance at mobilizing a revolutionary labor movement, however, and throughout the 1940s Communist and Nationalist militias competed—often violently—for the allegiance of the workers. In Shanghai, both parties relied heavily upon secret-society participation in recruiting worker militias. And both sides actively encouraged their militiamen to infiltrate the opposition. These practices contributed to notoriously mercurial militias, which further fueled mutual hostilities and suspicion between the two parties.

On the eve of Shanghai's liberation, the underground Communist Party committee established a clandestine organization—named the People's Peace Preservation Corps (Renmin baoandui)—to coordinate the activities of the various Communist-affiliated militias in the city. By the time of the takeover, the People's Corps numbered more than sixty thousand semi-armed workers drawn from most of Shanghai's major factories. Their vigilance helped forestall any attempt by the fleeing Nationalists to destroy or dismantle industrial materiel on their way out.[17]

During the liberation of Shanghai, the People's Corps not only assisted the People's Liberation Army (PLA) in preventing industrial sabotage and keeping public order; its members also made the rounds of the city's factories in search of the six thousand people whom the Communist Party suspected of serving as "secret agents" for the Nationalists. At one cotton mill, eight hundred of the more than one thousand People's Corps militiamen active at this time later received special commendation for their work in smoking out enemy agents.[18] Despite the impressive achievements of the People's Corps in securing the city and its factories for the new Communist regime, the organization was disbanded on orders from the Military Control Commission within days of the New Fourth Army's assumption of effective control.[19] Military authorities were suspicious of an armed workers' militia operating under civilian auspices. Moreover, the composition of the People's Corps was a matter of some concern inasmuch as many former members of the Nationalists' Industry Defense Corps had surreptitiously enlisted under the banner of the People's Corps once it became clear which way the political winds were blowing.[20]

Although the military disbanded the People's Corps, interest in a workers' militia—under union rather than PLA control—remained strong. With labor unrest sweeping Shanghai factories, the SFTU argued for reviving the workers' pickets as a means of restoring order. Stressing that Nationalist agents were inciting strikes and spreading anti-Communist rumors among the workers, the union called for rearming the proletariat.[21] While military and public security authorities were less than enthusiastic about the prospect of putting guns in the hands of ordinary workers, the party gave its blessing. The revival of union-sponsored armed worker pickets was publicly announced on May 31, at a workers' congress to commemorate the May Thirtieth Movement, and was implemented immediately afterward.[22]

Under the provisions of "New Democracy," the trade unions enjoyed a (temporary) position of considerable prestige and influence as the official representative of the working class.[23] In the eyes of other bureaucratic agencies, particularly those charged with maintaining public order, the idea of arming potentially unruly workers was a matter of some concern.[24] For the moment, however, there was little they could do to challenge the situation in light of the proletariat's special political status.

The SFTU's newly established Picket Department (Jiucha bu) issued a report in July 1949 in which it noted that Nationalist agents had been particularly active the previous month—even infiltrating the ranks of the fledgling pickets as a smokescreen for their own efforts to mobilize the workers. The solution, according to the union, was an expanded and better-trained and -commanded picket force that would prove capable of resisting such challenges.[25] Although it was implausible to imply that the explosion of labor unrest—coming as it did during a time of extreme economic duress—was primarily the result of enemy agents, the union's call for a beefed-up picket force would soon gain decisive support from other events.

On February 6, 1950, Shanghai was bombed by Nationalist planes from Taiwan. There had been a few smaller attacks prior to this date, but the February 6 incident brought the first serious industrial damage. On that day two B-29s piloted by Nationalist air force personnel flew four sorties over the city, targeting power companies.[26] According to official Chinese statistics, the assault resulted in more than five hundred fatalities, more than six hundred injuries, and more than fifty thousand refugees.[27] This ugly reminder of the continuing civil war between the Nationalists and the Communists provided a persuasive justification for the revival of the worker pickets, which were, after all, a key element in China's revolutionary tradition. The raid triggered an emergency bulletin that called upon all unions in the city to organize armed worker pickets within forty-eight hours in order to strengthen defenses against enemy air attacks. The Shanghai Power Company, where twenty-eight workers died and thirty-two were seriously wounded in the February 6 assault, took the lead in forming picket units. On the night of February 7, braving heavy rains, pickets began patrolling the power plant. A former member of the Nationalists' Industry Defense Corps at the company was apprehended by pickets after spreading rumors that more airplanes were on the way from Taipei.[28]

An internal-circulation SFTU memorandum underscored the importance of this February Sixth Incident, as it was soon known, in converting the mission of the pickets from mundane factory inspections to major public security responsibilities:

The Shanghai worker pickets were established on the foundation of the Shanghai People's Peace Preservation Corps. After the liberation of Shanghai, because we didn't have a good grip on the situation, the activities of the Corps were converted into ordinary inspection work at factories and enterprises. . . . Most of those who held the title of pickets had no real work. They simply maintained order at marches and demonstrations or when mass meetings were convened, or else they mediated conflicts among workers in the factories or handled petty thefts and other minor problems. In some factories they even took the place of management in keeping tabs on the workers, conducting body searches and thereby becoming divorced from the masses. . . .

In the February Sixth anti-bombing struggle, virtually every factory revived and consolidated a picket organization, to stand guard and carry out patrols, protecting the factory in round-the-clock shifts, assisting military and police forces in conducting air defense work. They now made a major contribution.[29]

In the aftermath of the February Sixth Incident, an expanded Picket Office was set up under the aegis of the SFTU, and more than twenty thousand pickets were mobilized within the space of a couple of weeks. Rifles and bullets were issued to the recruits, who received a brief stint of military training.[30]

The combination of proletarian prestige, vigorous union leadership, and a new national campaign against "counterrevolutionaries" soon permitted the pickets to enlarge their political role still further. In October 1950, a few months after the outbreak of the Korean War, Party Central issued instructions on suppressing counterrevolutionaries. The international battle raging just beyond China's northeast border heightened fears of hidden enemies at home. In Shanghai, the SFTU took the lead in carrying out the movement in the industrial arena—expanding picket membership to some forty-five thousand by the spring of 1951.[31]

The SFTU convened a five-person special task force, headed by former underground labor leader and union vice-chair Zhang Qi, to oversee the campaign. Within a year, the SFTU had organized thousands of accusation meetings against counterrevolutionaries with the active participation of nearly half the city's workers. Tens of thousands of pickets underwent special training in how to capture and forcibly restrain victims. Issued flashlights, handcuffs, ropes, and the like, they set up dragnets at factories around the city. Suspects were seized by surprise when they went to work, then handed over to the police.[32] By early May, the number of arrests in Shanghai had topped nine thousand.[33] A picket at Shanghai's Number Five China Textile Mill, deemed exceptionally meritorious in capturing counterrevolutionaries, was praised as a national model in press reports across the country.[34]

In some cases, however, the sudden arrests generated a backlash. After the detention of more than thirty alleged counterrevolutionaries at the Shanghai Power Company (the city's pacesetter in picket activism), workers raised questions about one of the detainees. The captain of the pickets in the machinery repair workshop, Chen Jinfu, had been accused by the SFTU of being a Nationalist Party member posing as a Communist activist. On the day after Chen's arrest, the union organized mass meetings to explain its actions. Chen's co-workers expressed support for the policy of suppressing counterrevolutionaries in this time of national crisis, but they questioned whether Chen Jinfu fell into the targeted category.[35] Thinking that the problem could be defused by appointing another mechanic to assume Chen's role as picket captain, the union turned to a skilled worker with considerable standing. But their nominee—noting the similarities between Nationalist and Communist modi operandi—refused the offer: "In the past, the [Nationalist] authorities first nabbed people and then held a meeting afterwards to settle things. Now the people's government nabs people and then holds meetings afterwards. What's the difference?" When the union leaders criticized his outburst, the nominee fell silent but refused to recant. His workmates were equally unmoved. The mechanics recalled that Chen had been unjustly imprisoned by the Nationalists and had served as a diligent worker throughout his career. Although Chen had openly admitted to past connections with the Nationalists, he had also expressed interest in joining the Communist Party. Seeing that further persuasion was required, the union cadres tapped some activists to convey their message to the workforce at large. Chen Jinfu, they insisted, was a highly placed officer in the Nationalists' Industry Defense Corps who had only pretended to be arrested in order to mask his true identity. The union's nominee for Chen's replacement was sternly rebuked: "Although we know that you were just letting off steam, what if the people's government were to decide to execute you because of your intemperate remarks? Wouldn't that be an injustice!" Thus reprimanded, the nominee publicly confessed his errors.[36]

The Campaign to Suppress Counterrevolutionaries led to a general expansion in the pickets' responsibilities. New duties ranged from encouraging political activism in the factories to detaining suspected counterrevolutionaries outside the factories. When the designated leaders of the political study groups at Shanghai's Huaming Tobacco Factory decided to skip out on the weekly indoctrination sessions, for example, pickets were dispatched to round up the truants and return them to the factory. Thereafter, we are told, participation in political study at the factory was not an issue![37] In December 1951, pickets at the Yihe Cotton Mill captured a counterrevolutionary who had escaped from prison and was seeking to change his household registration in order to move out of the neighborhood. With the blessing of their union and local police station, militiamen acted swiftly to detain the escaped convict.[38]

The union obviously welcomed proletarian activism, but the pickets came under increasing criticism for several reasons. For one thing, lingering links to their Nationalist forerunners raised suspicions about the political reliability of the pickets. For another, as the union's star began to wane, so too did its ability to lead and discipline an armed militia.

The matter of Nationalist connections was a particularly troubling concern. A confidential report on an investigation at the Number Ten Cotton Mill revealed that "the masses are not happy that so many former Nationalist Party types are in the pickets. Some of them behave arrogantly toward the ordinary workers."[39] Although the Industry Defense Corps was an important target of the Campaign to Suppress Counterrevolutionaries, with many of its members sentenced to execution or labor reform as a result of the movement, by no means were all former participants eliminated.[40] At the Number Ten Cotton Mill, for example, the postcampaign investigation found that forty-five of the factory's ninety-five pickets had once enjoyed close connections to the Nationalists; of these, thirteen had participated in the Industry Defense Corps.[41]

Drawing clear lines between Communists and Nationalists was seldom simple. A worker accused of reactionary connections explained how the party's long-standing policy of infiltrating enemy forces had

blurred political identities: "There was nothing unusual about participating in the Industry Defense Corps. Didn't the Communist underground comrades also participate? I joined some of those reactionary
organizations in order to protect workers' interests. In the past, the
Nationalists said I was Communist; today the Communists say I'm Nationalist."[42]

Even so, the pressure to reveal past connections was intense. And
such admissions could have serious ramifications; those considered too
compromised by past liaisons were excluded from the generous labor
welfare provisions *(laobao)* for state workers, which had been drawn up
by Li Lisan and promulgated by the Ministry of Labor in March
1950.[43] These coveted benefits—of medical insurance, job security,
housing allocation, decent wages, pensions, and the like—were extended to only a minority of the workforce: politically approved
workers permanently employed at state enterprises.[44] The munificent
(and expensive) provisions of *laobao* were withheld from many of the
neediest workers—temporary and contract laborers, apprentices, and
people employed in nonstate enterprises—in addition to those tainted
by "reactionary" backgrounds. Workers who were denied the fruits of
revolutionary struggle often found the situation unbearable. Shut out
of the advantages of the emerging socialist system, many of them
turned to suicide.[45]

In October 1951, a registration of the more than fifty thousand
pickets in the city was carried out to clarify the situation and distinguish between those with redeemable and irredeemable records.[46] At
the Guangzhong Dye Factory, the registration drive revealed that
fourteen workers had served as "backbones" in the Industry Defense
Corps. Of these, twelve had been dealt with in the Campaign to Suppress Counterrevolutionaries; two had been shot and ten sentenced to
prison terms. One other had already died, and the remaining backbone, who had just been discovered, was slated to be expelled. Nevertheless, the fifty ordinary members of the Industry Defense Corps,
many of whom had switched over to the Communists' People's Peace
Preservation Corps in the spring of 1949 and some of whom had subsequently joined the Communist Youth League or Communist Party,
were permitted to remain in place.[47]

Even after the registration drive had been completed, disciplinary
problems persisted. Symptomatic of the troubles was the fact that

lower-level picket offices had given up submitting the required work
reports on pickets' mentality, training, and the like.[48] Such shortcomings strengthened the hand of bureaucratic competitors, most notably
the PLA and the Public Security Bureau, who had long bristled at the
union's maintenance of a separate armed force. Whereas previously
these critics had been unable to challenge union prerogatives, now the
tide was turning in their favor. It was just at this juncture that the national union leadership—Li Lisan in particular—came under attack for
having strayed too far from party supervision.[49]

With Li Lisan's union accused of "syndicalism," it was increasingly
difficult to justify the maintenance of a large, armed, and sometimes
unruly force operating under its aegis. Although the SFTU was reluctant to relinquish this visible symbol of proletarian power, its repeated requests for clarification from higher levels met with little response. The paralysis of union administration that accompanied Li
Lisan's demise had taken its toll. By fall 1952, the SFTU was exasperated with the lack of central direction: "Despite our countless memo-
randa about the pickets, we've received no guidance. We don't yet
know whether our municipal-level pickets department has actually
been abolished or not. . . . What is to be done with the more than
fifty thousand pickets? In the past, when leadership was unclear the
masses wavered. What happens now? The basic picket members are
grumbling, 'When the leadership has problems they call on us; when
they don't have problems they forget about us.' "[50] The following
year the SFTU followed up with a letter to the Shanghai Party Committee, requesting that the pickets not be dissolved in light of their
past achievements and a membership numbering more than fifty
thousand that included many party and league activists.[51] This time a
clear response was forthcoming, but it was not the one the union
wanted. After three and a half years of service under the new regime,
the worker pickets were disbanded.[52]

The disbandment of the worker pickets was part of a broader shift in
national policy that eschewed "New Democracy" and embraced a Stalinist five-year-plan of industrial development.[53] Although workers
themselves would organize illegal picket units during the strike wave
that rolled across urban China in the spring of 1957 in tandem with the
Hundred Flowers Movement and the socialization of industry, not until

the Cultural Revolution were worker patrols again officially promoted as an appropriate appurtenance of the "masters of the country."[54] Operating under the sponsorship of the "Gang of Four," the notorious Shanghai Militia would prove a formidable successor to its revolutionary forerunners.[55]

Masters of the Country?

The problems surrounding the pickets fed into a larger controversy about the role of the trade union, and indeed the proletariat, in the new political order. At the September 1949 meeting of the People's Political Consultative Conference in Beijing, at which Chairman Mao famously declared that the Chinese people had at last "stood up," Li Lisan's remarks highlighted the special role that the proletariat would assume: "Our working class, as the most conscious masters of the country, will carry forward the revolutionary spirit of heroic struggle, shouldering the arduous burden of constructing a new nation and a new society."[56] As minister of labor and head of the All-China Federation of Trade Unions, Li drafted the bold labor insurance law, founded and edited the influential *Workers' Daily* newspaper, and generally championed the role of the union in the new political order.[57]

Two years later, however, Li Lisan was criticized for "representing backward workers" and promoting "narrow economism" and "syndicalism" by regarding the union as above party supervision.[58] Several local union constitutions promulgated with Li's blessing in 1950–51 had in fact neglected to mention that the trade unions operated under party leadership.[59] An articulate advocate of worker interests, Li Lisan insisted on the need for union independence. His unceremonious dismissal from the All-China Federation of Trade Unions in early 1952 on grounds of having encouraged worker welfare and autonomy at the expense of party leadership plunged unions across the country into a state of pandemonium.[60] The Shanghai union's initial mishandling of the Five-Anti Campaign (detailed by Nara Dillon in Chapter 4 of this volume) was a symptom of this general disarray.

The early years of the People's Republic were a time of mixed signals for Chinese workers. On the one hand, Mao presented his New

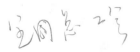

Democracy as being under "the leadership of the proletariat." By this formula, workers were granted a paramount place in the new order—a political role that extended well beyond the factory gates. On the other hand, Mao also characterized New Democracy as a "people's democratic dictatorship." Here the stress shifted from the special prerogatives of the revolutionary vanguard to the unity and power of the nation-state. The ambiguity reflected, among other things, the challenge of trying to blend revolutionary practices and prescriptions with the imperatives of state-building. In this respect, although Mao and his comrades took pains to underscore the differences between their mode of governance and that of their Nationalist predecessors, the similarities were also unmistakable.

As China's first Leninist party-state, the Nationalists had established important precedents for their successors. Party-controlled unions and militias were a small piece of a much larger pattern of rule that the Nationalists bequeathed to the Communists.[61] Such continuities, strengthened by three decades of mutual imitation and infiltration between the two parties, help to explain the ease with which "counterrevolutionaries" navigated the familiar terrain of the early People's Republic. Although one must treat the ubiquitous allegations of secret agent activities at this time with caution, there is no doubt that the fear—and often the reality—of involvement by forces with Nationalist connections (at least in the past if not necessarily the present) weighed heavily on the minds of the new Communist rulers. As Frederic Wakeman Jr. observes in Chapter 2, "This was neither paranoia nor propaganda: the city was indeed swarming with special service agents left behind" by the Nationalists. In this atmosphere of high suspicion, intensified by the hostilities of the Korean War, it was hardly surprising that "New Democracy" was often honored in the breach. Moreover, neither the Communists' own revolutionary traditions nor the state-building methods of their predecessors were particularly conducive to democratic governance.

Had the international environment appeared less threatening to the Chinese leadership, perhaps the possibilities for an expanded and more humane form of labor politics could have gained further headway. In the tense cold war climate that prevailed, however, "reactionary" leanings and worker indiscipline came to be viewed as greater concerns than workplace injustice. Fearing military escalation across both the Taiwan Straits and the Yalu River, Mao and his colleagues backpedaled on revolutionary promises in an urgent drive toward state power. Labor militancy and trade union autonomy were but two of the many casualties of this process.

ॐ *4*

New Democracy and the Demise of Private Charity in Shanghai

Nara Dillon

MORE AND MORE scholars now question the 1949 revolutionary divide in Chinese history and search for continuities across what was long seen as a chasm between the Republican and Communist periods.[1] The end of the cold war, newly available sources, and theoretical questions about the nature of revolutionary change have all contributed to shifting perspectives on the meaning of 1949. Armed with archival documents and oral histories that reveal the messiness and contingency of the Communist project at the local level, scholars have begun to uncover strong continuities in personnel, institutions, and practices through the 1940s and 1950s.[2] As a result, in the last ten to fifteen years the 1949 revolution has been looking less and less revolutionary—and correspondingly more evolutionary.

The New Democracy period from 1949 to 1953 occupies an awkward position in this emerging debate over the nature of the Chinese Communist revolution. During these first years of the regime, the Chinese Communist Party (hereafter the party) pursued a populist cross-class coalition, established semidemocratic political institutions, and fostered a mixed public/private economy. The "revolutionists" explained these apparent continuities with Nationalist rule as a deliberate ruse that allowed the Communist leadership to lull their opponents into accepting and even supporting them while they consolidated their hold on power. Beyond achieving that goal, the revolutionists claim that the period had no lasting importance, and indeed its many internal contradictions ensured that it could not last very long. In contrast, the "evolutionists" offer a more straightforward explanation by arguing that the continuities of New Democracy were real, rather than a strategic gambit, and they left a mark on both the regime and Chinese society that ultimately proved to be longer lasting than the radical experiments of the later Maoist period.

While we still lack the sources to gauge the intentions of the top party leadership, exploring the political campaigns carried out in the charity sector in the early 1950s can contribute to this debate over the place of New Democracy in the Chinese Communist revolution. Although private charity may seem marginal as an arena of state-society interaction in comparison to industry, it offers insight into the surprising behavior of China's urban elite during the New Democracy period. Why did so many members of the old elite support the very regime that destroyed them? Why did some go so far as to cooperate in their own demise? Unraveling this puzzling behavior provides an entry point into the forces of change and continuity during the New Democracy period.

Shanghai's large and vital Republican-era voluntary sector offers a promising starting point for a local case study of state-society relations since the resources, organizations, and expertise of Shanghai's elite were important to even the top levels of the fledgling Communist regime. The New Democracy campaigns against private charity were important to the larger Communist revolution in several ways. Accusations of corruption in private philanthropy helped to destroy the legitimacy of the old elite, tainting a key source of its social power. In addition, repeated rounds of narrowly targeted struggle campaigns steadily undermined the old elite's capacity for collective resistance over the New Democracy period. Finally, the end result of these campaigns was the elimination of all voluntary associations and public organizations with any degree of autonomy from the party-state. Regardless of whether these organizations qualified as a true civil society in the Republican period, their elimination in the early 1950s represents one of the most fundamental differences between the Chinese Nationalist and Communist regimes. Thus, revolutionary change did take place in the cities during the New Democracy period, but it happened more gradually and more peacefully than anyone expected.

New Democracy and State Corporatism in Shanghai

While the official New Democracy period only lasted a little longer than three years, from 1949 to 1953, its origins lay in war against Japan in the late 1930s. In addition to providing a framework for an anti-Japanese alliance with the Nationalists, Mao Zedong sought to use New Democracy to broaden the party's appeal and build a cross-class coalition of workers, peasants, and elements of the bourgeoisie.[3] By framing New Democracy as a bourgeois-democratic revolution, and therefore a necessary first step toward a socialist revolution, Mao Zedong sought to portray the party's moderate wartime political and socioeconomic policies as a transitional stage rather than a tactical retreat.

The New Democracy agenda included a more tolerant attitude toward private charity. Following Marxist critiques, the party had long derided private charity as a deception that obscured the reality of bourgeois exploitation, but the pressure of war and the strategy of mobilizing a cross-class coalition quickly led to a turnaround. The first policy shift came in response to the 1937 Japanese invasion, when the party actively participated in the bourgeois-led relief effort mounted in response to Shanghai's massive refugee crisis.[4] In 1938, the party took a step further and encouraged Song Qingling to establish the China Welfare Foundation (Zhongguo fuli hui) to raise funds abroad for the Communist war effort. At the end of the war, the party also established the Chinese Liberated Areas Relief Commission (Zhongguo jiefang qu jiuji zonghui) to lobby the United Nations Relief and Reconstruction Administration for a share of the postwar aid slated for China.[5]

New Democracy proved to be a successful political strategy, even if it did not sustain an effective military alliance. Indeed, well after the United Front with the Nationalists had disintegrated beyond repair, the party ratified New Democracy as the basis of its postwar strategy for returning to the cities at the Seventh Party Congress in 1945.[6] At that point, Communist leaders envisioned the bourgeois-democratic revolution as requiring ten to twenty years to complete.[7] Indeed, as late as 1948 they thought the civil war alone would take another five years to win.[8] Just as the sudden collapse of the Nationalist regime was not foreseen, the short life span of New Democracy was not expected, much less planned.

While the party repudiated its call for a coalition government, once it gained military dominance in the civil war, most other elements of the New Democracy agenda remained in place. Even as the Nationalists were turning against Shanghai's capitalists in Chiang Ching-kuo's failed attempt to regain control over hyperinflation in 1948, the Communists stepped up their efforts to woo the same constituency. Before, during, and after the takeover of Shanghai in 1949, the party made a concerted effort to convince the city's elite to stay on, rather than flee to Hong Kong or Taiwan. The symbolism of the decision to stay or flee was considered vitally important by the party—an all-too-literal vote of confidence in the new regime. Furthermore, the party's goals of quickly reviving and advancing economic production left the party quite dependent on capitalists' resources and expertise.

Before liberation, the Shanghai underground met with businessmen individually and entertained them at large dinner parties to try to win their confidence in the party. While most of the city's leading financiers left Shanghai, many other businessmen chose to stay. Guo Linshang, owner and manager of the Yong An Department Store, one of Shanghai's largest and most successful, chose to stay, as did Rong Yiren, owner of multiple textile and flour mills. The party heavily publicized their decisions.[9] Even after the takeover, the party effort to woo businessmen back to Shanghai continued in Hong Kong. As Sherman Cochran shows in Chapter 15 of this volume, well-known industrialist Liu Hongsheng was enticed to return home after just six months, even though he had gone to considerable lengths to move family members and assets out of Shanghai in the event of a revolution.

Incorporating Capitalists

New Democracy extended far beyond recruiting wealthy individuals to the Communist cause. In the realm of civil society, for example, continuity with Republican-era policies, if not personnel, prevailed. The party replaced Nationalist-sponsored corporatist organizations (such as the chambers of commerce and labor unions) with its own mass associations, but these were very similar to their predecessors in their internal structure and in their privileged relationship to the party-state.

Upon establishing control over Shanghai, the party moved immediately to take over and replace the Nationalists' official business

associations, sending takeover teams to the Shanghai Chamber of
Commerce and its 337-member trade associations. Following the First
Shanghai People's Representative Congress in August 1949, the new
Preparatory Committee of the Shanghai Municipal Business Federation was established. The preparatory committee spent the following
year reorganizing the constituent trade associations, as well as reviewing and replacing their leadership and staff. By September 1950,
there were 269 trade associations with approximately eighty thousand
member businesses, estimated to be more than half of the total number
in Shanghai. The new business association was officially established in
February 1951 at the first Shanghai Municipal Business Representative
Congress.[10]

Although the party sought to promote continuity, capitalists with
close ties to the Nationalist regime soon found themselves eclipsed by
a new group of businessmen who had been peace activists in the civil
war. Sheng Pihua, leader of the Shanghai Federation of People's Associations (Shanghai renmin tuanti lianhehui) and head of the 1946 peace
delegation to Nanjing, proved to be the biggest beneficiary of this
turnabout. Sheng became deputy mayor of Shanghai and chairman of
the Shanghai Business Federation.[11] Kui Yanfang, another bourgeois
member of the 1946 peace delegation, was also rewarded with a
prominent position in the new business federation.[12] Although the
Nationalist-era chairman of the Shanghai Chamber of Commerce,
Wang Xiaolai, was persuaded to return to Shanghai in 1950, he played
no role in the new business federation.[13]

Beyond reforming the official labor and business associations, the
party did not attempt to exert much control over the more than 1,300
other nongovernmental organizations in Shanghai during the takeover.[14]
District takeover teams visited and collected information on all the
formal organizations in their districts, and municipal agencies such as
the Bureau of Civil Affairs attempted to survey all of the organizations
registered with the previous government.[15] Private charities continued
to function and helped the Communists establish order in the city.
Their activities ranged from taking care of the injured and dead during
the brief battle for Shanghai to helping care for typhoon victims in the
summer of 1949. After the February 1950 Nationalist bombing raid on
Shanghai, private charities such as the Tongren Fuyuan Benevolent
Hall (Tongren fuyuan shantang) and the Pushan Charitable Cemetery

(Pushan shanzhuang) took on the work of collecting and burying the dead and providing relief to fire victims.[16]

Early party tolerance of most nonofficial voluntary associations reflected more than their low political priority. Private charities were even successful in gaining tax-exempt status from the new regime.[17] To place these policies in comparative perspective, this treatment of the voluntary sector was far closer to the state corporatism of the Nationalists than the revolutionary monism pioneered by the Soviet Union. In the Russian Revolution, for example, the attack on bourgeois civil society began almost immediately in the wake of the Bolshevik seizure of power.[18]

Incorporating Philanthropists and Private Charities

The party also sought to incorporate philanthropists in much the same way as the Nationalists had tried in the 1940s. For example, the party continued long-standing practices such as establishing winter relief committees and engaging philanthropists in fund-raising efforts. A new Shanghai Municipal Winter Relief Commission was established on December 29, 1949, followed by a fund-raising subcommittee dominated by members of Shanghai's elite.[19] The Winter Relief Commission opened forty-four temporary shelters, which housed more than nine thousand homeless people until the end of March 1950, when the commission ended its operations.[20] In addition to the winter relief fund-raising drive, philanthropists actively participated in fund-raising efforts for refugees and unemployed workers through separate committees set up by the municipal government.[21]

The Communists also continued the Nationalist project of incorporating private charities into an official federation.[22] Song Qingling, director of the China Welfare Foundation, chaired the first national People's Welfare Congress in April 1950 in Beijing. The Congress transformed the party's existing relief organization, the Liberated Areas Relief Commission of China, into the People's Welfare League of China (Zhongguo renmin jiuji zonghui) and laid out plans to create branches of the national league in every province, city, and county in the country.[23] In his speech at the National People's Welfare Congress, senior party leader Dong Biwu articulated party policy toward private charity in the following terms: "Under New Democracy, social welfare and relief work is under the leadership of the people's government. Individuals and organizations should be encouraged to participate, as long as they are engaged in real welfare work [and] respect our regulations and policies."[24] Dong also tried to set new priorities for charitable work, asserting that unemployed workers and the victims of natural disasters should be given top priority for receiving goods and services.[25]

Although the People's Welfare League was a top-down initiative, it elicited active participation from members of the urban elite. Respected philanthropists and charity directors were given important roles in the key preparatory committees that arranged the representative congresses and set up the new organization. Philanthropists such as Wu Yaoshi, director of the Shanghai YMCA, and Yan Fuqing, director of the Shanghai Red Cross hospitals, were given leadership roles in the national organization.[26] The man chosen to head the Shanghai branch of the People's Welfare League, Zhao Puchu, was the director of a prominent lay Buddhist organization and had risen to prominence in Shanghai's wartime refugee shelter movement.[27] This new position was a reward for Zhao's assistance to the party underground during the war against Japan, as well as his subsequent opposition to the civil war.

The Shanghai People's Welfare Representative Congress was held in October 1950 with 198 representatives from private charities, official mass associations, and the city government. In a departure from Nationalist practice, the congress also included a few representatives of the poor—three refugees, three unemployed workers, and two soldiers' dependents. The elite, however, had far greater representation than the poor and included some of the most prominent businessmen of the Republican era, people such as Wang Xiaolai and Liu Hongsheng. Leadership roles in the Welfare Congress, however, were reserved for elite men like Zhao Puchu and Kui Yanfang, who broke with the Nationalists during the civil war.[28]

The speeches and group discussions that took place over the four-day meeting served to educate Shanghai's philanthropists and charity workers on the party's welfare and relief policies. Wu Yaoshi, the director of the Shanghai YMCA, gave a speech showing how much Communist rhetoric he had absorbed at the national congress: "In the past, imperialism, feudalism, and bureaucratism oppressed and slaughtered the masses, and at the same time 'charity' was used as a pretext to cheat and fool them. From now on, Shanghai's social welfare organizations will not be divided by category or religion; instead they will all be guided by the city government and the People's Welfare League of China."[29] Cao Manzhi, the director of the Shanghai Bureau of Civil Affairs, announced the Shanghai League's priorities for the upcoming year, including plans to expand private institutions for orphans, the elderly, the disabled, and refugees.[30] These plans clearly indicated that Shanghai's party leaders thought private charity would play an important role in the city for some time to come.

The Welfare Congress officially established the Shanghai branch of the national People's Welfare League. The Shanghai Welfare League became a major bureaucracy almost overnight, since the Nationalist-sponsored Provisional Shanghai Relief Federation was folded into the new branch league, including its staff, ongoing programs, and fund-raising committees.[31] Like its predecessor, the Shanghai Welfare League set out to centralize private fund-raising and exert control over the planning and services of individual organizations. In keeping with Communist practices, member organizations were also required to organize political study groups among their staff to read and discuss the new policies endorsed at the national Welfare Congress. While it is unclear how much control the league actually exerted over fund-raising, it did succeed in changing long-standing charitable practices. One of the biggest changes engineered by the Welfare League was to convince native-place organizations to serve the poor without regard to native place. For example, the Ningbo Guild (Siming gongsuo), one of the oldest and most prestigious native-place organizations in the city, opened its burial services, hospital, and schools to all Shanghai residents.[32]

Furthermore, autonomous organizing efforts to establish new private charities came to a halt after the Shanghai People's Welfare League was established. Although on paper the party's Welfare League had no greater authority than its predecessor, it managed to end the flurry of organizing activity that had been characteristic of the Republican period. A new orphanage established at the Longhua temple early in 1950 was the last independently established charitable organization in the city.[33] One reason the party had more success in limiting autonomous organizing was that it did not register voluntary associations, thus withholding the legal sanction that registration had provided under the Nationalist regime.[34] Although the central government issued regulations on registering voluntary associations in September 1950, their implementation was repeatedly delayed.[35]

Even with these important shifts, through late 1950 continuity rather than change was the dominant experience of Communist rule for Shanghai's elite. The party implemented state corporatism far more quickly and effectively than the Nationalists, but it remained essentially the same project. They incorporated the same classes, created very similar institutions, and to a surprising degree, followed the same policies. This evolutionary process of change, however, encountered a new dynamic in 1951, when the party launched the first mass struggle campaigns to affect Shanghai's elite.

New Democracy Mass Campaigns

In Shanghai, the Campaign to Suppress Counterrevolutionaries was launched in January 1951 as the Korean War was heating up. The campaign targeted the Nationalist underground, as well as other banned organizations, including the Green Gang and heterodox religious groups.[36] As Frederic Wakeman Jr. shows in Chapter 2 of this volume, at the city level the campaign was largely a police action, accompanied by propaganda efforts, mass rallies, and public executions intended to intimidate enemies and inspire patriotic support for the war. The campaign began with an order for all counterrevolutionaries to register with the police. Arrests followed soon after, culminating in a midnight raid on April 27, when 8,359 people were arrested. On April 29, the chairman of the Shanghai Federation of Trade Unions, Liu Changsheng, led a mass rally in a local park with more than 10,000 participants. The event was broadcast live on radio, and tens of thousands more people were gathered together to listen to the event at work and other places around the city. The rally consisted of a mass struggle meeting against nine of the most notorious counterrevolutionaries arrested in the midnight raid, introducing this signature political practice to the Shanghai public. After hours of angry denunciations, the rally endorsed death sentences for the nine struggle targets, who were immediately executed. The following day another 285 counterrevolutionaries were publicly executed.[37]

In the workplace, the campaign was largely waged by the labor unions against labor racketeers and former Nationalist labor organizers.

The bourgeois owners and managers of Shanghai's factories and shops were largely untouched by the campaign—neither classified as counter-revolutionaries nor targeted for mobilization. Elite charity leaders were much more actively involved in the Resist America Aid Korea Campaign that followed quickly on the heels of the Campaign to Suppress Counterrevolutionaries. The goal of this campaign was to eliminate American influence in China, consolidating domestic support for the Korean War. The central government ordered all charitable, educational, and cultural organizations that received any American funding or had any American staff members to register with the government in preparation for being reorganized, taken over, or disbanded.[38]

In response to the new orders, the Shanghai municipal government established a registration office to lead the anti-American campaign on January 19, 1951. As director of the Shanghai Welfare League, Zhao Puchu was put in charge of the registration office's daily operations, even though he was not a party member.[39] Zhao divided the office staff into six divisions, one each for higher education, lower education, health care, social welfare, religious, and cultural organizations.[40] Registration staff held roundtable discussions with the staff of both Chinese and foreign organizations to explain the new anti-American policy and discuss the Korean War.[41] Despite the fact that charity leaders like Zhao Puchu had considerable experience working with foreign charities and Christian missionaries, wartime patriotism helped them elicit enthusiastic participation from Chinese philanthropists and charity workers in the attack on their former colleagues. By the end of March 1951, 660 organizations in Shanghai registered for receiving donations from the United States or for employing American staff. Once the registration process was completed, the campaign office established investigation committees, which then held struggle meetings against American staff members and Chinese collaborators with close ties to Americans.[42]

By the end of the campaign, most registered organizations were disbanded, while fifty-one were taken over by the Welfare League and various government agencies. The survivors included hospitals, schools, and orphanages that continued to operate largely as before but under government supervision. Only a few groups survived as autonomous organizations—several Catholic charities with predominantly Chinese staff and funding were allowed to continue operations after being reorganized to exclude foreign priests and nuns.[43] In the wake of the campaign, the Bureau of Civil Affairs conducted a survey that found 904 voluntary associations remaining in the city, including 261 charitable organizations.[44]

At the same time that Chinese philanthropists and charity leaders got their first taste of campaign politics in the anti-American movement, the Campaign to Suppress Counterrevolutionaries brought their central role in winter relief to an end in the winter of 1951. Just as in previous years, the Shanghai municipal government established a winter relief committee, although it was given a new wartime name, the Winter Protection Committee (Shanghai shi dongfang weiyuanhui).[45] The membership of the new committee was restricted to party leaders and government officials, without any of the elite philanthropists who had dominated the previous winter relief committees. Winter relief was explicitly tied to the Suppression of Counterrevolutionaries Campaign and given an additional mandate to prevent sabotage, spying, and banditry.[46] The new committee mobilized workers, rather than the elite, to participate in this protection effort. Each enterprise and industrial union was ordered to establish its own Winter Protection Committee to patrol the factories and neighborhoods.[47]

Although charity leaders cooperated with the party's corporatist project and actively participated in the new mass campaigns, their cooperation served to divide a social group capable of rivaling the regime in social prestige and financial and organizational resources. Even as Shanghai's charities and bourgeois leaders helped the new regime to overcome the city's unemployment and refugee problems, they began to split along political fault lines separating those who actively supported the Communist regime and those tarnished by close ties to the former Nationalist regime. The Resist America Aid Korea Campaign created new divisions and reinforced this polarization process by co-opting patriotic Chinese charity leaders to lead and carry out the attack on foreign and Chinese Christian organizations. Even with these tensions, however, most members of Shanghai's elite could still claim a central position in the New Democratic coalition.

The Three-Anti and Five-Anti Campaigns against Corruption

The Three-Anti and Five-Anti campaigns began to undermine the elite and its place in society. The campaigns started as a response to the economic difficulties posed by the Korean War. In fall 1951, Mao called for troop reductions and budget cuts in an effort to curb inflation, which was being fueled by heavy military procurement. A campaign to cut government spending in Manchuria uncovered serious problems with corruption in military procurement, spreading alarm over the state of party discipline to the highest levels of the party. On December 1, 1951, the Communist Party Central Committee ordered the rest of the country to conduct a nationwide party rectification campaign to ferret out corruption.[48] The Shanghai Party Committee responded to this call quickly, creating a special committee to carry out this Three-Anti Campaign (against corruption, waste, and bureaucracy). Led by Deputy Mayor Pan Hannian, with Shanghai Federation of Trade Unions chairman Liu Changsheng and Shanghai Business Federation chairman Shen Pihua as deputy directors, the committee's forty-six members included several members of Shanghai's elite, including Shanghai Welfare League director Zhao Puchu and industrialist Rong Yiren.[49]

The Three-Anti Campaign was extended to the voluntary sector in January 1952 when the municipal Three-Anti Committee chaired by Pan Hannian worked with the Bureau of Civil Affairs to form a Shanghai Municipal Welfare Organization Investigation Committee. The new committee included representatives from a variety of government agencies and the Shanghai Welfare League.[50] As with the Resist America Aid Korea Campaign, Zhao Puchu organized the campaign within the Welfare League. This early phase of the movement was apparently a tepid affair, without any effort to mobilize accusations or stage struggle meetings.[51]

The Three-Anti Campaign uncovered serious corruption in the municipal party and government, including officials as highly placed as Li Yu, the secretary *(mishuzhang)* of the Shanghai Party Committee.[52] The extent of official corruption in Shanghai and other major urban centers such as Tianjin frightened an already alarmist central leadership. Viewing corruption as a more serious threat to the party than the Korean War itself, Mao identified the urban bourgeoisie as the main source of temptation for Communist cadres. As a result, party center ordered that the anticorruption campaign be extended to the bourgeoisie in January 1952 in what came to be known as the Five-Anti Campaign (against bribery, tax evasion, theft of state assets, cheating on labor or materials, and stealing state economic intelligence).[53]

In Shanghai, these orders allowed Liu Changsheng and the Shanghai Federation of Trade Unions to take control of the mild Three-Anti Campaign then being conducted in the Shanghai Business Federation and transform it into a struggle campaign. To kick off the new campaign, the municipal trade union convened a Five-Anti Congress with more than four thousand union members, who were exhorted to investigate their employers and struggle against any corrupt behavior they uncovered. In addition to their fiery speeches, union leaders set a martial tone for class struggle by beating drums and parading with wooden cannons. The union organized "tiger-beating" teams to spearhead the campaign, adopting the same terminology employed by the Nationalists in the 1948 crackdown on Shanghai's bourgeoisie. The tiger-beating teams went into factories and stores to teach union cadres and workers how to investigate their companies' accounts, solicit confessions and accusations, and stage struggle meetings. The party supplemented these efforts by setting up dozens of broadcast stations on busy street corners to announce propaganda and accusations over loudspeakers.[54]

Shanghai's workers responded to this call to arms with alacrity, and their enthusiasm for struggle soon went far beyond the five illegal practices targeted by the regime. Some workers began struggling against decadent lifestyles, the profit principle, and capitalism in general. Workers were soon exacting wage hikes and improved benefits from their frightened employers, then going on to demand the immediate nationalization of their enterprises. In parallel to these escalating demands, the conduct of struggle meetings also frequently spiraled out of control. More than two hundred businessmen were imprisoned in their offices by their employees, and many were beaten or forced to undergo painful and humiliating punishments, such as kneeling for hours or wearing dunce caps. Under the pressure of these psychological and physical assaults, forty-eight businessmen attempted suicide and thirty-four succeeded.[55]

The charity campaign also took a decisive turn when a joint work team from the national Welfare League and the Shanghai Federation of Trade Unions arrived on February 8 and took over the leadership of the movement. In addition to investigating the Welfare League, they organized six tiger-beating teams to take the campaign to private associations: two for native-place and trade guilds, two for charities, one for native-place associations, and one for orphanages and rest homes.

The teams began organizing a struggle campaign to carry out their investigations. Their basic campaign protocol was to start by convening a meeting of all the employees (and in residential facilities such as orphanages, the clients as well) to explain the party's policies regarding corruption and to solicit confessions and accusations. Following this initial meeting, cadres were sent to talk to staff one on one and to encourage them to make accusations. At the same time, they began to lay the groundwork to organize an employee union. After collecting and investigating the accusations and confessions generated through this process, the tiger-beating teams staged a struggle meeting against a "model" corrupt person to liberate the organization from feudal practices. These struggle targets were usually punished on the spot by meeting participants. Punishments varied widely, ranging from fines to arrests, beatings, and other forms of corporal punishment. Two charity workers responded by attempting suicide.[56]

By late February 1952, the Five-Anti Campaign was severely disrupting the economy, both in Shanghai and across the nation. Production stalled and unemployment surged as private factories and stores were shut down by the campaign. In addition, government economic ministries, state-owned enterprises, and construction projects were disrupted and delayed by the ongoing Three-Anti Campaign in the public sector. What had started as an effort to cut government spending and curb inflation turned into a sharp economic recession, revealing the regime's continued dependence on its bourgeois rivals to help maintain social and economic order in the cities. Central party leaders moved quickly to suspend the Five-Anti Campaign in Shanghai and to postpone it in all cities and towns where it was not yet under way. They also adopted emergency tax, purchasing, and contracting measures to try to revive production quickly.[57]

Bo Yibo, minister of finance and director of the national campaign, was dispatched to Shanghai to assert central party control over the movement. He ordered immediate suspension of all campaign activities and the release of all the businessmen being held in custody. He reported back to Beijing that Shanghai's leaders were in disarray and blamed them for losing control of the campaign.[58] Liu Changsheng was suspended from his position as party secretary of the Shanghai Federation of Trade Unions and replaced by Zhong Min from the All-China Federation of Trade Unions.[59]

During the suspension, Bo Yibo sought to impose top-down control over the conduct of the campaign. New regulations were issued prohibiting workers from taking any direct action in the campaign beyond reporting crimes to the campaign authorities. Instead, twelve thousand party and union cadres were quickly trained to review financial records and organized into inspection teams. After successfully carrying out trial inspections of seventy-four firms, a campaign protocol for the new work teams was fine-tuned and a crash-training program put in place. On March 25, the Shanghai Party Committee convened another Five-Anti assembly. In place of the martial flourishes of the first rally, Mayor Chen Yi emphasized the limits of the campaign and reiterated the regime's commitment to New Democracy: "The measures adopted by the People's Government are in no way an indication that it has changed its policy towards the bourgeois class."[60]

This restrained phase of the Five-Anti Campaign was brought to a conclusion in summer 1952 with the announcement that fines of more than 10 billion yuan had been levied against Shanghai's capitalists. But at that point the party leadership was still more concerned with economic recovery than with punishing corruption. The fines were discounted, payments were postponed, and price controls for government contracts were eased in an effort to revive economic production. The party's leading bourgeois supporters were treated especially leniently, at the recommendation of the top leadership in Beijing.[61]

While the demobilization of Shanghai's workers at the behest of party center seemed to restore New Democracy, the long-term impact on the urban elite was profound. The workers' unrestrained assault not only undermined the authority of their employers; the Communist tactic of promising leniency to those who informed on others further undermined any basis for collective resistance against the regime.[62] State takeover of industry began to accelerate during the 1952–55 period, at least in part owing to the pressure of paying off the fines levied in the Five-Anti Campaign.[63]

A further indication that these anticorruption campaigns represented more significant change than the official rhetoric admitted was the fact that the voluntary sector campaign was never suspended. While the regime was still dependent on private industrialists as producers and employers, the social protection provided by private charity was no longer as high a priority. The impact on the Shanghai Welfare

League and private charities was severe. By the time the Three-Anti Campaign was wrapped up in late June 1952, 151 of the Welfare League's 435 staff members had been labeled as corrupt. Most of the actual charges, however, involved violating Communist welfare policies or administrative practices rather than corruption per se; only 45 of these "corrupt" employees received criminal punishments or were removed from their posts.[64]

Zhao Puchu was the most prominent Welfare League employee to be labeled as corrupt, and he was fired as punishment. Multiple charges were levied against him, few of which could be construed as criminal acts. The charge that came closest was the accusation that a series of currency conversions and commodity purchases that Zhao made on behalf of the Nationalist-era Provisional Relief Commission on the eve of liberation resulted in major financial losses. But these transactions had taken place before the Communists seized control of Shanghai and took over the Relief Commission, and the Three-Anti investigations were supposed to be limited to post-1949 activities. Furthermore, these transactions were made in an attempt to protect the value of the commission's assets from hyperinflation, rather than for personal gain.[65]

The charge of corruption ultimately boiled down to the accusation that Zhao Puchu promoted the autonomy of the Shanghai Welfare League from party and government control. The most serious charge was that Zhao displayed a negative attitude toward party and government supervision, describing it as interference rather than guidance. He was quoted as publicly declaring that "the Bureau of Civil Affairs is an organization of equal rank, [so we] do not have to report to it."[66] Zhao was also accused of distributing relief goods to Shanghai's charities without regard for political considerations, as well as sending relief to disaster areas outside Shanghai. Thus, the same kind of independence that led Zhao to hire underground Communists as shelter directors and teachers in the 1937 refugee relief effort had become a political liability in the People's Welfare League in 1952.

Most of the other corruption charges were violations of Communist administrative practices. For example, Zhao was accused of bureaucratism for overemphasizing hierarchy in the league staff and failing to conduct regular criticism and self-criticism in the organization. Similarly, he was charged with paternalism because he hired "feudal elements," such as former charity managers with bourgeois class backgrounds or previous connections to the Nationalists. In addition, Zhao failed to favor party cadres in making work assignments.[67]

As can be seen in Zhao Puchu's case, the Three-Anti Campaign redefined long-standing charitable practices and the everyday politics of corporatism as corruption. Labeling these actions and attitudes as immoral behavior not only decisively altered the relationship between the Welfare League and the party-state but also tarnished the image of elite philanthropists in the eyes of the public. The damage to the Shanghai Welfare League was permanent. The 1952 representative congress called for in the league's bylaws was never convened (nor were any subsequent congresses), and its leadership was not replaced. Instead, staff from the Bureau of Civil Affairs took over the commission's day-to-day operations, moving its administrative offices into the bureau headquarters.[68] Corporatism in the charity sector effectively came to an end in 1952.

Although this broad and ambiguous redefinition of corruption strains understanding of the term, its use was strategic. Philanthropists and charity leaders were pilloried in front of their employees and clients in struggle meetings, and in front of the broader public through the press. Whether the basis of the campaign accusations was personal gain or some more esoteric violation of Communist policy, framing them all as corruption was critical in damaging the high social prestige that philanthropists had enjoyed up to this point. The party attacked private charity at its foundations, deeply undermining a key source of elite legitimacy.

When the Three-Anti Campaign was brought to a close in the summer of 1952, investigations of private voluntary associations were still under way, and the Bureau of Civil Affairs was allowed to continue them under guise of the "New Three-Anti" Campaign. The new campaign went far beyond the goals of the original. It was a comprehensive review of every private organization's programs, services, administration, and staff that was portrayed as a preparatory step toward legal registration. Only those organizations that could prove that they benefited society and had undergone thorough reform would be allowed to register; all others were to be taken over by the municipal government or disbanded. Any organization deemed counterrevolutionary was to be banned outright.[69] The welfare services and programs the party considered beneficial to society included hospitals, midwife services, orphanages, and homes for the elderly and disabled.[70]

For the most part, the New Three-Anti investigations were conducted in the same manner as the original campaign. Work teams were sent to each voluntary association to organize employee unions and mobilize the staff against their managers and boards of directors. For example, at the Ningbo Guild, cadres organized the carpenters and painters employed in the coffin-building workshops into an enterprise union. While some workers participated enthusiastically, the managers and directors of the once-powerful guild offered little resistance to the campaign. The guild quickly stopped functioning, so the workers only struggled themselves out of a job. In the meantime, however, they helped the work teams inventory the guild's extensive landholdings and other property. The Ningbo Guild turned over its hospital to the Shanghai Public Health Bureau in 1953, when it became the Number Ten People's Hospital. The guild itself was officially dissolved in 1954 when the city took control of its land, rental housing, and guildhall.[71]

The New Three-Anti movement lasted until the end of 1954. Over the two years of the campaign, 223 charitable voluntary associations were investigated. Twelve were banned as counterrevolutionary, while another 162 were shut down and their property taken over by the municipal government. Altogether, the city government confiscated more than 3,000 mu (200 hectares) of land, eight large office buildings, and more than six thousand apartments and houses from private voluntary associations during the campaign.[72]

Most of the forty-nine organizations that "survived" the campaign bore no resemblance to the originals. For example, one of these forty-nine ostensibly private organizations was the Number Two Rest Home for the Elderly and Disabled (Di er canlaoyuan), which was created by merging the property and some of the staff of five native-place guilds, none of which had operated a rest home prior to the merger. The legal status of the Number Two Rest Home and other organizations similar to it was ambiguous. Despite the official-sounding name, it was not taken over by the municipal government. It continued to rely on property rentals from the holdings of the original voluntary associations for funding, but a new board of directors was never established, and no charter or organizational bylaws were drafted.[73] Furthermore, it was still not allowed to register.[74]

A few charities survived the New Three-Anti Campaign largely intact, but their relationship to the party-state was irrevocably transformed, no matter how ambiguous that relationship continued to be. For example, the Xinpu Orphanage (Xinpu yuyingtang) operated by the Catholic Church was one of the first charities targeted in the original Three-Anti Campaign. After the investigation was completed in 1953, the orphanage was allowed to continue operations as a "privately operated and publicly assisted" organization. The public assistance consisted of a work team from the Shanghai Religious Affairs Committee continuing to investigate the orphanage's Catholic connections, as well as a work team from the Bureau of Civil Affairs helping to reduce its infant mortality rate, which had surged during the original Three-Anti Campaign. The work teams replaced staff, reorganized the infant care department, and upgraded its health-care and nutritional services.[75]

Most organizations that escaped becoming targets in the New Three-Anti Campaign quietly ceased to function and were abandoned by their staff and boards without going through the procedures to formally disband.[76] Among those organizations that escaped the campaign, the main group of survivors included sixty private hospitals, which benefited from the immense surge in demand for health-care services created by the implementation of labor insurance in 1951. In 1953 the Ministry of Health addressed the shortage of health-care providers by reclassifying private hospitals as charitable social welfare organizations rather than capitalist enterprises. This regulation freed the way for firms with labor insurance to contract with private hospitals to provide health-care services. At the same time, however, the Public Health Bureau began regulating the staffing, services, and fees of private hospitals.[77]

The other main survivors were the Red Cross and the China Welfare Foundation. As national associations with close ties to the Communist regime, they escaped the rigors of the Three-Anti Campaign. The Red Cross was valued for its international connections and prestige, while the China Welfare Foundation was protected by its founder, Song Qingling, and her status as vice-premier of the national government.[78]

The New Three-Anti Campaign marked the effective end of Shanghai's once-vibrant voluntary sector. While these voluntary associations rarely had the autonomy from the state to qualify as a true civil society, they had long provided Shanghai's elite with a vehicle for public engagement and for enhancing their social prestige. The elimination of this sector represents one of the most decisive institutional changes the Communists wrought during their revolution.

Denouement: The Socialization of Industry and the Elimination of the Bourgeoisie

Although the 1952 anticorruption campaigns clearly transformed the regime's relationship to the urban elite, the party kept New Democracy as its official policy until June 1953.[79] The change was publicized in December 1953, when the "General Line for the Transitional Period" declared that the shift from New Democracy to socialism was under way and made the Communists' goal of eventually eliminating the bourgeoisie official. The timetable, however, remained ambiguous, and businessmen continued to be told that socialization would not occur until capitalist development had run its course, perhaps as long as ten to fifteen years.[80]

An economic recession and the sudden rush to complete the collectivization of agriculture in 1955 vastly increased the pressure to speed up the socialization of industry. Mao advocated shortening the transition period considerably at the Sixth Party Plenum in October 1955 and a subsequent conference of the All-China Business Federation.[81] Mao and other party leaders discussed various timetables ranging from two to five years, before settling on a two-year transition in 1956–57 to coincide with the end of the First Five-Year Plan. They planned to carry out the socialization of industry through a major struggle campaign, mobilizing workers against the bourgeoisie to force them into government buyouts. Liu Shaoqi predicted that the struggle campaign to socialize industry would dwarf all previous struggle campaigns.[82]

Before planning for the campaign even got under way, however, Beijing mayor Peng Zhen held a major rally on January 15, 1956, to announce that the city had already completed the entire socialization process. As soon as Shanghai's leaders realized what was happening in Beijing, they raced to catch up. With the active cooperation and participation of the bourgeoisie, socialization of the private sector was reduced to a matter of filling out paperwork. Rather than face the massive struggle campaign envisioned by Communist leaders, the Beijing and Shanghai business federations seized the initiative and orchestrated their own demise. Hasty valuations were carried out, most of which drastically undervalued the worth of private enterprises. Then owners, managers, and their families marched through the streets of Shanghai, holding aloft their government buyout applications in festive paperwork parades.

These displays culminated in a major rally on January 20, when city officials ceremoniously approved the applications for state ownership en masse.[83]

The status of Shanghai's few remaining voluntary associations was quite ambiguous after the New Three-Anti Campaign, with some officially sanctioned but unregistered charities continuing to function under close state regulation, while hundreds of nonfunctioning organizations existed in name only. This ambiguity was resolved during the "high tide" of socialization in January 1956. The furious pace at which private businesses were turned over to state control put pressure on the municipal Civil Affairs and Public Health bureaus to rush to catch up and completely eliminate the private voluntary sector.

Charities were pressed into quickly submitting applications to be disbanded or taken over by the municipal government. The Xinpu Orphanage applied to be taken over soon thereafter and became the Shanghai Children's Welfare Institute under the Bureau of Civil Affairs.[84] The remaining private hospitals were all taken over by the Public Health Bureau on February 7, 1956.[85] The hundreds of non-functioning organizations that had not applied to be officially disbanded were assigned to different government agencies to take over any abandoned property and officially dissolve them. This process basically put the finishing touches on what the New Three-Anti Campaign had already accomplished since 1952. Out of the 904 voluntary associations operating in Shanghai at the beginning of 1952, only 287 remained by 1956. Most of these 287 organizations were officially sanctioned mass associations. All that remained of Shanghai's once-vibrant charity sector were the Red Cross and the China Welfare Foundation.[86]

While the festive atmosphere during the socialization of industry gave every appearance that the urban elite welcomed its opportunity to contribute to the revolution, the Hundred Flowers Movement in 1957 soon revealed a very different picture. Some of the same men who had celebrated turning over their businesses to the state in 1956 then turned around a year later to attack the buyout scheme for drastically undervaluing their assets. Others complained that their new positions as salaried managers lacked any real authority or responsibilities within the enterprise.[87] Complaints about injustices in the Suppression of Counterrevolutionaries, Three-Anti, and Five-Anti campaigns led to a proposal to create a multiparty commission to hear and investigate the appeals of struggle campaign verdicts.[88]

These after-the-fact complaints only reinforce the point that the socialization of industry had been achieved almost overnight without any coercion, much less the mobilization of the working class. Even though it was cut short, one struggle campaign appeared to be enough to convince Shanghai's elite to join the revolution. Instead of collectively resisting the Communist regime, they pursued individual strategies to prove their loyalty and transform their class status.

In the realm of private charity, the "high tide" of socialization proved to be even more anticlimactic than it was for private industry. Repeated rounds of narrowly targeted struggle campaigns increasingly divided the regime's potential opponents against one another. Furthermore, after the delegitimizing Three-Anti Campaign against the Shanghai Welfare League and Shanghai's leading charities, there was little or no resistance to the party's methodical dismantling of the voluntary sector. Instead, the erstwhile leaders of these organizations sought to disassociate themselves from a mission now labeled as feudal and exploitative. The genius of the Communist political strategy against the former elite was to attack its legitimacy first. That blow to social prestige, combined with campaign tactics designed to pit people against one another, led philanthropists to try to disassociate themselves from their economic and organizational sources of power, rather than use those resources to resist their repression.

The party also effectively exploited ambiguity. Registration of voluntary associations was repeatedly promised and repeatedly postponed, withholding legal sanction from all nonofficial voluntary associations. The Three-Anti Campaign used ambiguity strategically, as the purpose of the campaign shifted from rooting out corruption to questioning the very purpose and political basis of private charity. Communists began categorically referring to private charities as "feudal" organizations, and the accusations of exploitation that were earlier directed at foreign charity were now extended to all private charities.

Rather than viewing the Five-Anti Campaign as a temporary loss of control over the working class or a deliberate ruse to instill fear in the bourgeoisie, this analysis of the charity sector suggests that it should be viewed in conjunction with the Three-Anti Campaign as a comprehensive but subtle attack on the former urban elite.[89] The Communist regime may not have been ready for the kind of open class warfare that the workers sought in 1952, but its systematic assault on elite power was ultimately more effective. These anticorruption campaigns were not only intended to distinguish the fledgling Communist regime from the scandal-ridden Nationalist Party it replaced; they also served to undermine the social prestige of the elite. Corruption was not so much a criminal charge as a political effort to redefine the basis of legitimacy. The fact that the Three-Anti Campaign resulted in lasting institutional change with the elimination of civil society is another indication that the anticorruption campaigns were more than a temporary aberration from a moderate policy of continuity. New Democracy had its own revolutionary logic.

The tension between change and continuity in the 1949 revolution is thus extremely complex. The Communists took over and continued to operate many of the corporatist institutions created by the Nationalists—and proved to be much more effective in gaining the support of the urban elite than their supposedly conservative predecessors. Yet this continuity became a tool for radical change: the elimination of civil society and then of corporatism itself. The fact that Shanghai's elite not only failed to resist its demise but actually cooperated in it should not obscure the extent of the change wrought in the early 1950s.

II
Occupying the Periphery

✌ 5

From Resisting Communists to Resisting America: Civil War and Korean War in Southwest China, 1950–51

Jeremy Brown

IN LATE 1952, prisoner-of-war Li Huaguo spilled his guts to U.S. military intelligence officers at a camp in South Korea.[1] Li was a soldier in the Chinese People's Volunteer Army, a force of more than a million men and women sent to "resist America and aid Korea" by the leaders of the recently founded People's Republic of China. As Li sat across a table from his interrogator, he must have marveled at the incredible road he had taken over the past three years. Li was a thirty-one-year-old farmer from a village in the far southwest corner of Guizhou, a province in southwest China more than 1,600 miles away from Korea. Li had farmed for his entire working life, and he continued to work the fields at home after the People's Liberation Army (PLA) occupied Xingyi county in late 1949. But by January 1950, Li had had enough of the new regime. He quit farming and joined a guerrilla army to resist the occupying Communist forces.

Reports of Guizhou's successful "liberation" in November 1949 were premature, to say the least. All across Guizhou and the rest of southwest China, people like Li Huaguo took up arms against the occupying army. Upset by the new regime's onerous taxation policies, some locals joined village militia groups, while others connected with Nationalist Army units. For a time, the anti-Communist resistance was shockingly successful. In late March 1950, the new leaders of Guizhou completely withdrew their besieged soldiers and cadres from twenty-eight counties, including Xingyi.[2] The battle for Guizhou and China's south-west raged on well into 1951.

Li Huaguo's resistance ended in January 1951, when Communist soldiers captured him and 142 of his comrades in a mountain hideout. Twelve guerrilla leaders were executed, but the others spent a month in jail before being conscripted into the PLA. Li received political training and worked on army construction projects in Xingyi for a year before being sent to fight in the Korean War, a conflict known in Chinese as the "Resist America Aid Korea War." In February 1952 Li crossed the Yalu River and marched to the front lines in central Korea. There he underwent infantry training and built bunkers. One day in May, Li removed the firing pin from a hand grenade hanging on his bunker wall. The blast killed two of his fellow soldiers and se-verely wounded another. After the incident, Li was detained, but he escaped two nights later and surrendered to a South Korean marine division.

Li told his U.S. Army interrogator, Mr. Kiyabu, that he had "acci-dentally" detonated the grenade. He also told Kiyabu everything he knew about Communist rule in Xingyi. Li drew maps of the county seat, helpfully identifying the jail, security barracks, Communist Party headquarters, schools, bridges, a post office, and a livestock market. In a report for his commanding officer, Kiyabu wrote that Li Huaguo "lacked common sense," suffered from an "inability to comprehend questions," and "needed to talk excessively to express his thoughts." However, Li seemed cooperative enough, "possessed a great deal of in-formation," was "friendly," and "had a good sense of humor." Kiyabu deemed Li's intelligence information fairly reliable, noting that Li op-posed communism and "would refuse to return to his homeland" in the event of a prisoner-of-war exchange. Given Li's attitude, it is extremely likely that after the cease-fire in July 1953 he went to Taiwan as one of more than fourteen thousand Chinese prisoners of war who refused repatriation to mainland China.[3]

Judging from Mr. Kiyabu's commentary, Li had trouble making sense of the course of events that had changed his life since 1949. How are we to comprehend Li's whirlwind journey from Guizhou to Korea, from resisting Communists to resisting America? By putting the expe-riences of people in southwest China at the center of analysis, the his-tory of China's early 1950s looks different from the standard narrative

of a quick Communist victory and smooth takeover, followed by an inclusive "honeymoon period."[4] When we consider the Communist
takeover from the vantage point of Guizhou, rather than from Beijing
or the "old liberated areas" of north China, Joseph Esherick's assertion
that the new regime was "accepted with remarkable ease and strikingly
little active resistance" deserves reconsideration.[5] In the southwest,
armed resistance against Communist military occupation dominated
life for several years.

In rugged Guizhou, the civil war did not come to a clean end with the
founding of the People's Republic on October 1, 1949. Civil war continued through 1950 and 1951 and was closely linked to China's involvement in the Korean War. U.S. Army archives and recently published Chinese sources indicate that thousands of people like Li Huaguo
battled against the PLA in southwest China before ending up on the
Chinese side in the Korean War. Thousands more were members of
PLA units who collected taxes, established local government offices,
and suppressed anti-Communist rebels before joining their former adversaries on the front lines in Korea. In one sense, these journeys from
Guizhou to Korea reveal a time of fluidity, as people switched sides with
bewildering rapidity. In the immediate aftermath of the military occupation of the southwest, people shed and assumed labels such as "bandit,"
"hero," "martyr," "Communist," and "Nationalist" with relative ease.
Yet this was also an extremely dangerous time when one's identity as a
"bandit" could condemn families and communities to death at the
hands of the revolutionary party-state.

Frederic Wakeman's chapter in this volume (Chapter 2) and James
Gao's work on Hangzhou reveal the meticulous planning that preceded
the occupation of Jiangnan.[6] In contrast, the Communists were unprepared to take over the southwest. Leaders such as Deng Xiaoping and
Mao Zedong underestimated the degree to which people would refuse
to acquiesce to a new government in faraway Beijing. Former power
holders, members of ethnic minorities, farmers, and Nationalist soldiers who had originally surrendered or were simply bypassed during
the initial PLA march through Guizhou all contested the occupation.
To make matters worse, the new regime bungled its chance to make a
good first impression by immediately dispatching armed grain tax collection teams. In some areas, impoverished farmers who might have
been inclined to support the new regime fiercely resisted paying taxes

in early 1950 on their 1949 harvest, a crop that had already been taxed once by the Nationalist government.

After the toll of the spring 1950 uprising in Guizhou became evident—tens of counties lost, thousands of cadres and soldiers killed—the new regime responded methodically with military encirclement campaigns and what Julia Strauss has called "paternalist terror."[7] In Guizhou, this terror took the form of the PLA and local militias incarcerating family members of resistance fighters and publicly displaying corpses of dead "bandits." It was paternalistic in that former resisters were allowed to repent and then fight against the world's most powerful army in Korea. Ultimately the Communist response to resistance in the southwest was successful. By late 1951, the PLA had defeated most guerrilla groups. But the legacy of a military occupation in southwest China that was first bungling, then terroristic, reverberated well beyond the early 1950s.

This chapter details the first several years of Communist rule in Guizhou and surrounding areas in southwest China. I discuss who opposed the new government and why they resisted, and I explore the connection between the military occupation of the southwest and the Korean War. Two main source bases inform this study. First, I draw from U.S. Army interrogation records of Chinese prisoners in Korea. These documents, held at the National Archives at College Park, Maryland, chronicle the life histories of Chinese prisoners and provide remarkable local detail about changes in China between 1949 and 1952. I collected 147 interrogation records of prisoners who lived through the first years of Communist rule in southwest China, including Guizhou, west Hunan, Sichuan, Guangxi, and Yunnan. Second, I use official Chinese documents from the 1950s, along with recently published Chinese sources, including county gazetteers and memoirs.

Each set of sources presents unique problems. Initially, I expected the interrogation records to demonize the Communist regime. Likewise, I assumed that the Chinese sources would prettify the takeover in the southwest. Surprisingly, the opposite is true. Military interrogations always reflect a power imbalance between interviewer and prisoner. In Korea, many prisoners of war undoubtedly lied or exaggerated their roles in resisting the new regime in order to curry favor with their captors. However, a number of prisoners pledged allegiance to the Communists. Overall the interrogation reports reflect American military concerns about China, right down to the location of schools in Guizhou. Interestingly, the Chinese-language sources are open about the initial mistakes of the occupation and the broad scale of resistance. Of course, mainland Chinese sources claim that farmers such as Li Huaguo were "forced" into armed resistance by landlords. But in order to appropriately glorify the "bandit suppression" (*jiao fei*) battles of 1950 and 1951, gazetteers explicitly state how many enemies faced the Communists—and how they were disposed of. Taken together, the sources show ordinary people swept up in a confluence of civil and international war.

The Occupation of the Southwest

In 1949, national reunification loomed as a real possibility much sooner than Mao Zedong had expected. By mid-1949, Mao and other leaders faced the prospect of suddenly assuming control of vast regions that were worlds apart from rural north China, where the party had gradually gained popular support through years of trial and error. Communist leaders scrambled to find reliable people with expertise on the southwest.

In August 1949, Guizhou native and Communist Party cadre Fang Shixin headed for the northeast Chinese city of Changchun. Party center had ordered natives of south and southwest China who were stationed in the northeast to assemble in Changchun and prepare for the takeover of their home region. Some of the officials who formed the Guizhou Cadre Team (Guizhou ganbu dui) with Fang had joined the Red Army in late 1934 and early 1935 as it moved through Guizhou during the Long March. Others arrived in Yan'an during the war against Japan or had been underground party members in Guizhou.[8] The group departed for Nanjing and reported to the Second Field Army, led by Commander Liu Bocheng and political commissar Deng Xiaoping (a Sichuan native who had been named top secretary of the party's new Southwest Bureau in May).

At a meeting in Nanjing on September 20, 1949, Deng Xiaoping told Fang Shixin and his comrades that the Second Field Army would liberate the southwest, including Yunnan, Guizhou, Sichuan, and Xikang provinces. Deng said that the southwest's future was bright but cautioned the cadres about the feudal forces they were about to confront.

Portentously, Deng also said that the first obstacle the army would face in the southwest would be finding enough to eat *(di yi guan shi chifan guan)*.[9] The Second Field Army ordered a number of enthusiastic youngsters from the recently founded Southwest Service Corps (Xinan fuwu tuan) to join the Guizhou Cadre Team. The Southwest Service Corps, primarily composed of over ten thousand high school and university students from the Shanghai-Zhejiang region, would accompany the PLA and assist with propaganda and tax collection.

A week after receiving orders from Deng Xiaoping, the group of approximately 1,400 cadres and students departed for Hunan, where they reported to commanders Yang Yong and Su Zhenhua.[10] There, the two Hunanese generals established a shadow administration for Guizhou, with Yang as chair of the provincial government and commander of the Guizhou military region, Su as party secretary, and Xu Yunbei as vice-secretary.[11] The newly appointed leaders of Guizhou planned to occupy large cities such as Guiyang and Zunyi before attending to villages. Beginning on November 1, PLA soldiers, with the Guizhou Cadre Team and members of the Southwest Service Corps following close behind, moved into Guizhou from Hunan. Resistance was slight. Advance units and underground agents had persuaded many Nationalist officials and secret society leaders to surrender. On November 15 the PLA occupied the provincial capital of Guiyang.

Buoyed by their advance through the main arteries of Guizhou, the province's new leaders pursued a policy of cooperation. Deng Xiaoping and Mao Zedong explicitly approved of this approach. Neither Deng, Mao, Yang Yong, or Su Zhenhua suspected that their leniency would come back to haunt them several months later. On November 12, 1949, Deng Xiaoping sent a telegram to Yang, Su, and Xu Yunbei, urging them to include Nationalists in the takeover process. Between one-third and one-half of all posts in provincial, regional, and county governments were to be reserved for non–Communist Party members. This strategy, Deng wrote, would "definitely make things easier and will at the least decrease resistance somewhat." Deng urged the Guizhou leadership not to classify too many people as enemies and to "avoid the mistake of hastiness" when dealing with armed groups, especially ethnic minorities.[12] Mao liked this emphasis on patient inclusion. On November 19 he circulated Deng's telegram to party leaders throughout China and asked them to distribute copies of the telegram to subordinate units.[13]

On the ground in Guizhou, there were few alternatives to Mao and Deng's leniency. The PLA had only taken over Guiyang, Anshun, Zunyi, and the towns along the highways linking Guizhou to Sichuan and Hunan. The rest of the mountainous province remained unoccupied, and most army units had departed Guizhou for Sichuan and Yunnan by the end of 1949.[14] Along the highway between west Hunan and Guiyang, people who had no intention of willingly ceding authority to Communists—local power holders such as Yang Fengchi and Wei Demao—made a show of surrendering to the PLA and were rewarded with official posts. Yang Fengchi, who served as the Nationalist head of public security in Guizhou's Cengong county from 1935 until 1949, immediately surrendered in November 1949. He was appointed to posts in two new county organizations: vice chair of the "Support the Front Committee" (Zhiqian weiyuanhui) and vice commander of bandit suppression headquarters.[15] Wei Demao, a bona fide bandit leader, proffered an obsequious welcome to the PLA in his home county of Zhenyuan and received a position in the district people's government.[16] Both Yang and Wei were waiting for an opportune moment to rebel against the occupying army.

The occupiers' policy of indiscriminately handing out official posts would backfire a few months later. But it was their taking away, not their giving, that hurt them most. Excessive grain collection eventually pushed many people toward secret rebel leaders such as Yang Fengchi and Wei Demao. As Deng Xiaoping had predicted, the problem of finding enough to eat became the primary activity of soldiers, cadres, and students in late 1949 and 1950. Ren Xiwen, a member of the Southwest Service Corps, remembered the message conveyed by a Communist finance official in Chongqing in January 1951: "Upon entering a new area, race against time to dispose of grain and tax collection." Three weeks later, Ren traveled to southwest Guizhou. There, Song Renqiong, Yunnan provincial party secretary and vice political commissar of the Second Field Army, told a group of cadres about to advance into Yunnan that "you must get the grain into your hands."[17]

As early as December 27, 1949, Song Renqiong had been pressuring his underlings to collect taxes on the 1949 harvest immediately after arriving in Yunnan.[18] This levy on a harvest that had already been taxed by the Nationalists in the fall of 1949 became a source of anger throughout the southwest. According to G. William Skinner, who was living near Chengdu, the tax collected there in February and March 1950 "was about twenty-five percent larger than that which the Nationalists had already collected on the same crop in the previous autumn."[19] A February 1950 report written by Deng Xiaoping reveals that Skinner's numbers were overly conservative. Deng, writing to Liu Shaoqi and the party center, noted that in Sichuan the new government had already collected over a million tons of grain, more than twice what the Nationalists took in. Deng acknowledged that cadres ignored the pleas of overburdened "small landlords" in Sichuan and failed to give credit for taxes already paid to the Nationalists. Even so, widespread resistance to the double levy meant that the Communists missed their grain target by at least 60 percent.[20]

Skinner writes that zealous grain collection in the rich Chengdu plain was meant to feed PLA units on their way to Tibet. Yet evidence suggests that heavy taxation occurred even in the barren hills of the Yunnan-Guizhou plateau, where high transportation costs made opium a far more profitable cash crop than grain.[21] It is clear that troops throughout the southwest, and not just those headed for Tibet, needed more grain than the region could realistically provide. Nor was this problem limited to the southwest. As James Z. Gao shows in Chapter 8, PLA troops' inability to provide for themselves in Xinjiang led to the establishment of exclusive military farms.

The extra tax burden in the southwest was enough to shove people teetering on the edge of subsistence over the precipice. In Guizhou's Sinan county, Sun Xiuhe's two-acre plot was also taxed twice. The Communist tax was five times the amount charged by the Nationalists. As a prisoner in Korea, Sun complained to his U.S. Army interrogator that the new regime pushed many families into poverty by assessing taxes solely on the basis of acreage, without taking into account land quality or the number of dependents in a family. Sun claimed that throughout 1950 only the richest families in Sinan ate rice. His family ate two meals a day consisting of 60 percent potatoes, 30 percent corn, and 10 percent "grass, leaves, roots, etc." Poorer families survived on a diet of 70 percent potatoes and 30 percent wild vegetation, Sun said. He joined the PLA in October 1950 because his family did not have enough food to go around. Sun was transferred to Korea in early 1951. He quickly deserted and surrendered to American troops.[22]

We have seen that the occupiers of Guizhou made several miscalcu-lations. First, Communist soldiers and cadres moved through the province quickly and banked on mass surrenders of Nationalist Army units. In the few regions where the PLA maintained a strong presence, former power holders were allowed to infiltrate the new government. Onerous tax collection was even worse. This obsession with gathering grain ruined poor farmers' first interaction with their ostensible libera-tors. Opposing heavy taxes collected at gunpoint was something that well-off local power holders and poor farmers could agree on. This al-liance, plus the second thoughts of many Nationalist Army units that had initially surrendered, spelled trouble for Guizhou's new regime during the spring of 1950.

Resisting the Occupation

In November 1949, the PLA entered a province that had seen consid-erable change in the past fifteen years. The war against Japan had brought new roads and communication networks to Guizhou. Yet as Dorothy Solinger has shown, the province was not truly integrated with the rest of China before 1949. Throughout the 1940s, locals viewed outsiders with extreme suspicion. Secret societies organized resistance against Nationalist conscription and tax collection.[23] In 1942, a violent anti-Nationalist uprising in eastern Guizhou issued three curt demands: "Do not recruit soldiers, do not request grain, let us openly plant opium."[24] Local farmers loathed the extractive tendencies of any outside army, while people who had benefited from Nationalist rule felt espe-cially threatened by the Communists.

In January 1949, Guizhou's Nationalist governor Gu Zhenglun and provincial public security chief Han Wenhuan flew to Nanjing and re-ceived orders to make Guizhou the last bastion of anti-Communist resistance in the southwest. In addition to intensifying anti-Communist propaganda upon their return to the province, Gu and Han esta-blished an "Anti-Communist guerrilla cadre training class" in Guiyang. There they armed and trained over 1,600 Guizhou residents before sending the trainees out to link up with other sympathizers. In late August, when it became clear that the PLA would soon enter the province, Gu and Han made plans to flee but first distributed radio transmitters to Nationalist agents and opened the doors of the

Guiyang jail, releasing more than eight hundred "habitual bandits and petty thieves."[25]

This network lay low in late 1949 and took advantage of the new regime's leniency. But as Commander Yang Yong remembered it, the Communists' adversaries were emboldened by the departure of many PLA troops for Sichuan and Yunnan. In March 1950, Nationalist Army units that had surrendered in late 1949 suddenly revolted. Simultaneously, armed groups in villages turned against the new regime "one after the other."[26] An estimated 130,000 armed people in over 460 groups began resisting the Communists. Pan Yan, a top military official in Guizhou, wrote that the resisters "robbed, destroyed, murdered, led insurrections, pillaged business transport, besieged army vehicles, encircled and attacked regional governments and county seats and harmed people's government workers."[27] By mid-1950 "bandits" held thirty-one of Guizhou's seventy-nine county seats. According to the new regime's own figures, more than forty thousand government workers and members of the "masses" had been killed, including several newly installed county leaders.[28] Grain collection teams were hit especially hard, and provincial leaders themselves had to fend off ambushes on their way to meet with superiors in Chongqing.[29] In a confidential report, Guizhou provincial leaders revealed that the situation was so miserable for PLA troops on the ground that some soldiers celebrated when they heard in June that hostilities had broken out in Korea. The troops hoped that the Korean War would give them an excuse to leave Guizhou.[30] This was no honeymoon. It was civil war.

Resistance against the occupation of southwest China brought together a diverse array of groups, including local power holders, Nationalist troops, farmers, and ethnic minorities. Individual experiences suggest that in spite of the continuing civil war, labels like "Communist" and "Nationalist" were not necessarily at the forefront of people's minds. Survival, fear, and family trumped political labels and ideologies.

Local Power Holders

Not surprisingly, former local officials, landlords, and secret society leaders feared the revolutionary regime. Many in this category accepted positions in the new bureaucracy. Secret society leaders also encouraged members to join local militias organized by the Communists.

Cadres in west Sichuan complained that militias were "not pure," noting that in one district around 40 percent of the militia belonged to the Paoge hui.[31] When outsider troops stated their intention to heavily tax the richest sectors of society, subterfuge morphed into open resistance. After Nationalist security leader Yang Fengchi received several positions in the Cengong county government, he made his move. On March 10, 1950, Yang left the county seat, assuring colleagues he was going into villages to "convince bandit leaders to surrender." Instead, he persuaded members of a self-defense unit to turn against the new local government. The rebels promptly killed nine cadres, including a district party secretary. Yang then joined up with former county magistrates from neighboring Yuping and Jiangkou counties to form the "Hunan-Guizhou Border Region Anti-Communist National Salvation Army." In late March and early April, three thousand fighters under Yang's command twice laid siege to the Cengong county seat but failed to defeat the PLA soldiers holding the town. After this setback, Yang and his followers remained in the countryside and continued to organize resistance. His forces seized one thousand tons of grain and killed twenty more cadres and peasant association members.[32]

In nearby Zhenyuan, bandit leader Wei Demao also gained a position in the new local government but continued to organize his armed followers. In early 1950, Wei openly declared war against the Communists. He pledged allegiance to a Nationalist resistance force in the area and laid siege to government offices. After killing three PLA soldiers in June, he held a banquet to celebrate his victory and vowed to "drive the Communist Party out of Zhenyuan in three months."[33]

Local power holders fought to protect the status quo and yet recognized that the terms of debate had shifted. Double taxation of the 1949 harvest was enough to turn many farmers against the Communists, but Wei Demao still had to combat tantalizing rumors of impending rent reduction and land reform. According to one PLA soldier who battled against Wei's forces, the bandit attempted to implement his own rent and interest reduction (*jianzu jianxi*) and mass discipline (*qunzhong jilü*) movements.[34] In offering material benefits and stressing discipline, Wei was borrowing from the Communist playbook. And he was not alone in suggesting that his way was better than Communist alternatives. Yang Yong remembered that resistance groups in Guizhou posted such slogans as "refuse to turn in grain" (*kang liang*), "it's better to die in battle than to die of hunger" *(e si bu ru zhan si)*, "open the granary to relieve the poor" *(kai cang ji pin)*, and "keep your gun and keep your life" *(bao qiang bao ming)*.[35] In his February 1950 report, Deng Xiaoping acknowledged that these slogans—along with a call to "only attack northerners, don't attack locals" *(zhuan da beifangren, bu da bendiren)*—had even convinced some "poor people" to join the resistance.[36] Local power holders portrayed themselves as Guizhou's genuine protectors.

People with ties to Nationalist authority in Guizhou before late 1949 were typical resisters in 1950. Yet the uprisings of early 1950 would have been far less serious had entire Nationalist Army units not picked up the guns they had laid down several months earlier.

Nationalist Army Resistance

Hu Zhengming was a prize catch for American intelligence officers in Korea—so much so that he was interrogated at least four times.[37] Hu was a quite forthcoming source. His interrogator approvingly called him "violently anti-communist" and "intelligent." Hu was born in Sichuan, attended two years of primary school, and enlisted in a Nationalist youth battalion at the age of fifteen. He worked his way up the ranks over the next nine years and completed a joint Sino-American training course in Jiangxi during the war against Japan. After V-J Day, Hu returned to Sichuan and commanded a local security unit in Gulin county, which borders Guizhou and Yunnan provinces. As the PLA advanced through the southwest, he prepared for a fight.

Many Nationalist units in the southwest had surrendered en masse in late 1949, while others were bypassed completely. A force of 8,000 Nationalist soldiers commanded by General Tian Dongyun remained intact and retreated to the Sichuan-Yunnan-Guizhou border region. According to Hu Zhengming, General Tian maintained radio contact with superiors in Taiwan and coordinated guerrilla resistance in the border area. Hu linked up with Tian and commanded 1,500 soldiers in Gulin. Hu's forces controlled the entire county through late 1950, save the county seat, which remained in the hands of the PLA. Hu claimed that his troops inflicted two thousand casualties on the PLA. His unit's main activities were to harass the new administration, destroy communication lines and warehouses, ambush PLA troops, and block tax collection.

Again, the issue of grain requisition fueled resistance. Most of the people in Hu's guerrilla army were former Nationalist soldiers, members of local security forces, or local power holders. But after the PLA began collecting taxes, Hu said, many "enraged farmers" joined the ranks. Hu told his interrogator that the new regime's land tax quota for all of Gulin county was more than seven times the old number. Remnants of the Nationalist Army throughout southwest China encouraged this alliance with angry farmers by focusing their attacks on tax collectors and warehouses. In April 1950, a guerrilla group that operated between Guizhou and Guangxi provinces overpowered about fifty men who were guarding recently collected rice. The guerrillas, mostly Nationalist troops, seized the rice and immediately redistributed it to local farmers.[38]

Farmers with Guns

Given that the new regime seized crops while the guerrilla resistance returned them, we should not be surprised by the choices of local farmers like Li Huaguo, the talkative grenade-pin-puller from Guizhou. Across southwest China, farmers joined Nationalist Army–led resistance groups. In Guangxi, just south of Guizhou, eighteen-year-old Li Yu farmed at home until January 1951, when he fled to the mountains to avoid being drafted into the PLA. There, he met up with a force organized by Nationalist officers and enlisted men. Of the 425 fighters, Li Yu estimated that 40 percent were former Nationalist soldiers and the rest were civilian sympathizers.[39] Li Yu's resistance only lasted one month. In March 1951 his group engaged PLA soldiers but found themselves severely outnumbered. In the melee, Li and 70 others were captured and immediately impressed into the unit they had just fought against.

Other farmers organized small, local resistance groups that had no direct connection with the Nationalist Army. Tang Hanlin, a farmer and razor maker from Sichuan, was not well traveled before the PLA captured him in 1951. Tang told his American interrogators in South Korea that until 1951 he had never left his native village except to visit a couple of neighboring towns. "As a result," interrogator Mr. Ng wrote, Tang "lacked common knowledge and appeared to be of the rustic type. [He] spoke a peculiar dialect and was unable to write sensibly or legibly."[40] Yet Tang found it sensible to join a small guerrilla force and

attack the PLA garrison in his village. He said that in late 1949 most of
the poor people in his village approved of the new administration. Soon
thereafter, heavy taxes, the prohibition of the opium trade, and the
change of currency from silver dollars to renminbi gave locals second
thoughts. Throughout the southwest, these issues, along with the
PLA's efforts to confiscate privately held guns, spurred resistance.[41] Li
Zhibang, a local elite and acquaintance of Tang Hanlin, urged townspeople to act on their grievances. For Li, this act of rebellion was personal. His son, an officer in the Nationalist Army, had been killed in action in the civil war.[42] Li and Tang planned a raid together. In March
1950, their group of sixty men collected guns from local townspeople
and besieged PLA troops for a day before reinforcements arrived to
help defend the garrison. Tang claimed that the rebels killed ten troops
before fleeing, but shortly thereafter Li Zhibang and Tang's uncle were
captured and executed.

Ethnic Minorities

When the occupation threatened people's status and survival, a cross-
class alliance united local power holders and poor farmers against the
new regime. Some locals teamed up with remnants of the Nationalist
Army, while others organized on their own. A similar dynamic un-
folded among the southwest's many ethnic minority groups after late
1949. Some minority leaders, afraid that their positions would be
threatened under Communist rule, encouraged members of their tribes
to resist the occupation by cooperating with Nationalist guerrilla
groups. This kind of alliance was exactly what leaders like Deng Xiaoping hoped to forestall.

Deng and Liu Bocheng had passed through minority areas in
Guizhou and west Sichuan during the Long March. In a famous bit of
Long March lore, Liu Bocheng once drank a bowl of chicken blood
and swore brotherhood to a Yi chief, who then promised safe passage
to the Red Army. But the marchers also suffered costly raids at the
hands of ethnic minorities. Liu and Deng knew that cooperation with
minority chiefs was crucial to a smooth takeover in the southwest. It
was official policy to treat minorities in the southwest with extreme
caution. In addition to advocating patience when dealing with armed
minority groups, Deng Xiaoping inveighed against Han chauvinism

and ordered cadres to carry out reforms only when minorities themselves wanted change. In a July 1950 speech, Deng spoke about the need to avoid acting rashly in minority areas. "If we act impetuously," Deng said, "always thinking about quickly collecting grain and organizing the masses to produce results, trouble will definitely arise, just like in Han districts."[43]

This cautious approach prevented large-scale rebellions by ethnic minorities. However, it did not eliminate resistance entirely. Yang Yong recalled that resisters in Guizhou "incited a few upper level people from minority nationalities to oppose us."[44] Hu Zhengming confirmed Yang's account. Hu told interrogators in Korea that about twenty Yi chiefs feared Communist interference and decided to cooperate with Nationalist general Tian Dongyun. Each Yi leader commanded several hundred fighters. The Yi chiefs also provided crops to resisters in the mountainous border region.[45]

The continuing civil war in southwest China pitted ethnic groups, local power holders, farmers, and Nationalist troops against the PLA. The occupying army's initial strategy of a rapid military advance, leniency, and massive grain collection efforts was a recipe for resistance. Deng Xiaoping was not pleased. "Some comrades think that the revolution has been won, we can sleep, become arrogant, enjoy a life of comfort, and not have to work anymore," he said in a June 1950 speech. "This is extremely dangerous. In the war, we have achieved basic victory but still have many enemies. Currently, the bandit problem is very serious, feudal forces remain intact, and the completion of grain and tax collection has fallen way short. Our tasks are formidable and troubles are many. Just what is it that we have to be arrogant about?"[46] Deng's remarks presaged a shift in course that would allow the new regime to quash resistance. China's involvement in the Korean War beginning in October 1950 would prove to be a convenient safety valve in the battle for the southwest. Shipping domestic resisters to Korea to resist America was one way for the new regime to neutralize its foes. Terrorizing them at home was another.

Quelling Resistance in the Southwest

A combination of military might, relaxed grain requisition, and terror allowed the new regime to prevail in the southwest during 1950 and

1951. After the outbreak of the Korean War, these strategies connected the civil war in the southwest to hostilities in Korea and consistently conflated domestic enemies with foreign threats.

The early 1950 withdrawal of cadres and soldiers from around thirty Guizhou counties signaled high-level recognition that occupying forces were spread too thinly. PLA soldiers who had retreated from the abandoned Guizhou counties merged with reinforcements sent from Sichuan and Yunnan and began a methodical "iron encirclement" campaign against resisters. The PLA concentrated its forces, sealed off guerrilla areas, and wore down its enemies group by group.[47] By the PLA's own account of the battles in Guizhou, by the end of 1950 a total of 125,515 resisters in 447 separate groups had been "annihilated" in over four thousand engagements.[48]

Incognito scout groups had the unenviable task of first entering areas to find resistance groups. Li Shulin was an Anhui native stationed in Guizhou and Sichuan during the battles of 1950. He served in the Nationalist Army for three years before being captured and conscripted into the PLA. Li's PLA regiment dispatched scouts disguised as civilians into guerrilla areas for intelligence gathering. The scouts, posing as salt or farm tool peddlers, secretly contacted leaders of Communist-sponsored farmer associations and learned what they could about local resistance. Li described one engagement on the Guizhou-Sichuan border where his regiment surrounded an area and advanced on one hundred guerrillas. The resisters found themselves pinned against a cliff with no escape route. After their food and ammunition ran out, they surrendered in small groups. Li estimated that between June and December 1950, his regiment captured around one thousand anti-Communist fighters in this manner. After December, Li and his comrades moved to Chongqing and boarded steamers headed for Hankou. From there they traveled by rail to Hebei and then Liaodong, finally crossing into Korea and marching south on foot in March 1951. This was a common route to Korea for many soldiers and former resisters in the southwest. Apparently, soldiers were only informed that they were being transferred to "reserve positions" in Hebei, near "where Mao lives."[49] As they left the southwest, people such as Li Shulin did not know that they would soon be fighting in a foreign country. Several months after entering Korea, Li came down with dysentery and was unable to keep up with his retreating unit after a battle. He hid in a village and was captured by South Korean troops.[50]

At times, undercover scouting in southwest China was even more dangerous than catching dysentery in Korea. Xue Yuchao, a Zhejiang farmer and former Nationalist soldier, also battled anti-Communist guerrillas on the Guizhou-Sichuan border after being captured by the PLA. Troops from Xue's regiment worked in groups of twelve and pretended to be woodcutters or peddlers as they collected intelligence on resistance groups. In June 1950, disguises failed three scouts, who were killed by local guerrillas during a foray into enemy territory. But Xue's regiment eventually dispensed of resistance in the area. After ten months, Xue was transferred to Hankou by boat in November 1950, headed north by train, and entered Korea in March 1951. His U.S. Army interrogator wrote that "because of his unwillingness to fight," Xue Yuchao "straggled" and was captured by American troops.[51]

Capturing surplus grain in southwest China remained a priority for PLA soldiers before they shipped out to Korea. However, the disastrous aftermath of the new regime's emphasis on huge grain collection quotas gave way to a more flexible approach. G. William Skinner observed that by mid-1950 party workers had begun to compromise on tax collection. Tax rates were reduced for everyone, even landlords. Collection was postponed in impoverished areas until after the spring harvest, and people could pay with wheat instead of rice. According to Skinner, this allowed for more effective propagandizing about upcoming rent reduction and land reform campaigns. Writing in early 1951, Skinner noted that "the average farmer feels happier about the Communists now than he did at the time of liberation."[52]

The decision to suspend overzealous tax collection was a wise one. Had the new regime not relaxed its grain quotas, it is likely that farmers would have continued to support resistance forces. Nationalist officer Hu Zhengming told American interrogators that by mid-1950 softened grain collection policies had undermined his resistance efforts. Hu and his guerrilla troops needed to eat, too. By postponing tax collection and providing relief grain to certain areas, the PLA made Hu look bad every time he had to confiscate food from local farmers, he said. Popular support for Hu's resisters faded, and the group became more susceptible to encirclement.[53]

Flexible grain collection policies were not carried out uniformly. In some cases, soldiers and cadres wielded grain seizures as a weapon against districts where resistance was particularly recalcitrant. Two PLA soldiers who served in Sichuan in 1950 mentioned the practice of removing all surplus grain from guerrilla areas.[54] Starving out resisters became an integral component of encirclement campaigns. The strategy gave resistance groups little hope of mounting a sustained fight.

One soldier, Zhu Daiquan, said that failure to surrender grain was taken as evidence of collusion with bandits. Zhu's PLA unit collected taxes in northwest Guizhou during the latter half of 1950. Zhu served in the Nationalist Army in Guangdong but was captured in late 1949 and integrated into the PLA. In Guizhou, Zhu visited villages every day as part of a tax collection team. His team carried a list of village households and collected ten times more grain from rich households than from poor ones. But he responded harshly when farmers—rich or poor—were unable or unwilling to pay up. If a family had not handed over any grain after three or four visits from the armed tax collectors, the household head would be classified as a bandit and arrested. Zhu estimated that his regiment arrested around seven hundred tax-delinquent farmers during his time in Guizhou. In February 1951 he was reassigned to Korea. He deserted his unit and hid in the Korean mountains for a month before finally surrendering to American forces.[55]

It is ironic that Zhu sought refuge in the mountains of Korea just months after he saw Guizhou farmers fleeing into the hills at the sight of his tax collection team. The mass arrests noted by Zhu Daiquan were but one part of the new regime's larger strategy to scare resisters into submission. Terror became a brutally effective weapon in the southwest, especially after China entered the Korean War in October 1950. Approval for this strategy came from the top echelons of Communist leadership. Julia Strauss has shown that party leaders such as Peng Zhen explicitly endorsed "shaking and terrorizing" (zhendong konghuang) during the Campaign to Suppress Counterrevolutionaries, which began in late 1950 and escalated during the spring and summer of 1951. Strauss notes that the crackdown on purported domestic enemies coincided with and regularly evoked China's military action in Korea.[56] This connection between disposing of resisters and the Korean War was particularly salient in southwest China.

In November 1950, Mao Zedong enthusiastically supported two of Southwest Bureau secretary Deng Xiaoping's proposals: first, to transfer soldiers from the southwest to fight in Korea, and second, to kill bandit leaders. Mao praised Deng's suggestion of transferring a total of six armies from the southwest to Korea and forwarded Deng's report to other regional leaders.[57] Mao also liked Deng's firmness in handling resisters in the southwest. A November 10 report from the Southwest Bureau criticized the lenient treatment of counterrevolutionaries and blamed insufficient jail space and food for the "casual release of prisoners." Deng proposed a tougher approach: "as for those guilty of the most heinous crimes who should be killed, execute them resolutely, do not appease and hesitate." He also suggested killing "local despots guilty of the most heinous crimes" and executing "a few drug dealers and secret society leaders." Deng even provided specific numbers. He wrote that of the 4,210 criminals being held in west Sichuan "around 1,120 need to be executed" and ordered that each county produce a list of "no more than 20 or 30" people to be executed during the upcoming anti-despot campaign.[58] Mao deemed this plan "very good" and had Deng's ideas circulated widely.[59]

Regional leaders took this message seriously. In west Hunan, just over the border from Guizhou (but not under the jurisdiction of Deng's Southwest Bureau), the death toll reached into the thousands. Mao was pleased and called for more executions. "In 21 counties in west Hunan more than 4,600 bandit leaders, bullies, and spies were killed and this year [the 47th Army] is preparing to let localities kill another group," Mao wrote in a January 1951 telegram to regional party leaders; "I think this punishment is very necessary." In case anyone still doubted his intent, Mao ordered that "especially in those areas where local bandits, bullies and spies are rampant, kill a good many groups" *(yao da sha ji pi)*.[60]

Guizhou guerrilla leaders Yang Fengchi and Wei Demao, who had accepted government positions before rebelling and killing soldiers and cadres, were likely candidates for harsh treatment. Bandit leader Wei Demao felt the pressure of encirclement around Zhenyuan and Sansui counties in late 1950. He escaped one surrounded area but was finally captured in an isolated mountain village in December 1950. He had entered the village in order to ask locals for food. Wei was executed several months later in Sansui.[61] Yang Fengchi held out slightly longer. Yang managed to evade his pursuers until February 1951, when he was trapped in a cave and asphyxiated by smoke from a fire set by Cengong county militia troops. His corpse was transported to the county seat and displayed for three days in a pavilion on the main bridge, "in order to calm the people's indignation."[62]

Public executions and displays of corpses reverberated throughout the southwest in 1951. Nationalist Army officers who had led resistance groups were among the most likely to face execution. Chen Lingyun, a Nationalist soldier from Guangdong, fought the PLA as a guerrilla in Guizhou. In December 1950, the PLA captured Chen and about three hundred other resisters in Songtao county. Chen told an interrogator in Korea that sixty men in his group who had served as officers in the Nationalist Army were executed at the foot of a hill. On the day of the executions, around one hundred resisters under the age of fifteen were released, while Chen and the rest of the prisoners went to Chengdu for political training and eventual integration into the PLA. Chen's unit entered Korea in March 1951. In May, several days after arriving at the front lines, Chen deserted his unit with two fellow soldiers and was captured by U.S. forces.[63]

One PLA soldier who fought against resistance forces in Sichuan confirmed that former Nationalist Army officers of battalion commander or above were executed after being captured.[64] Resistance leaders were clearly aware of this practice and sought to conceal their identities in the event of capture. This is exactly what Nationalist officer Hu Zhengming did after softened grain collection policies and encirclement weakened the force he led along the Guizhou-Sichuan border. The PLA caught Hu in January 1951. Hu told interrogators in Korea that he evaded execution by pretending to be a lowly follower in the resistance group. His strategy worked. Hu was assigned to a mess squad in the Second Field Army and never advanced beyond the rank of private during his brief stint in the PLA. He deserted his unit in Korea and surrendered to American troops in May 1952.[65]

Rumors spread about mass executions of resisters. Prisoner-of-war Liu Zegao's interrogator noted Liu's claim that around July 1951 he heard that 40,600 former Nationalists were executed in Guiyang. Someone also told Liu that 400,000 had been executed in Chongqing and Chengdu. His interrogator may have mistranslated or exaggerated Liu's statement, but Liu's numbers are not incompatible with the death toll of bandit suppression and the campaign against counterrevolutionaries. The estimates of Western scholars, who base their figures on statements by Chinese leaders or Chinese press reports of public executions, range from a low of 700,000 to a high of 14 million deaths nationwide. Most place the number around 2 or 3 million dead.[66]

More terrifying than hearing about mass executions was seeing family members arrested and killed. Shen Jianxun, a former Nationalist soldier who had served in the PLA since being captured in 1948, recounted how the PLA made quelling resistance a family affair. Shen's unit battled rebels in Guizhou during late 1950. PLA soldiers inspected the homes of suspected guerrillas and issued harsh warnings to relatives. If the resister failed to turn up after ten days, a family member would be detained, interrogated, and given political training. If this routine had not produced results after ten additional days, the relative would be imprisoned and treated as a resister himself. Shen told his U.S. Army interrogator that threats against family members worked even better than encirclement campaigns. In early 1951 he was transferred out of the southwest en route to Korea, where he was eventually captured by South Korean forces.[67]

Villagers knew the cost of resistance because death had touched them directly. Liao Zeyuan was nineteen when his father, brother, grandfather, and uncle were executed in late 1950. Liao belonged to a prominent family that owned forty acres in west Hunan. He evaded capture after his relatives were killed and reckoned that joining the PLA under a false name would give him a decent chance at survival. After basic training, Liao was sent to Korea, where he helped to build an airfield. His unit then marched into battle, straight into a fierce artillery barrage. After two days under siege, Liao could not take any more. He deserted and surrendered to an American tank column.[68] In west Hunan, Liao had narrowly escaped death in a civil war that decimated his family. But in fleeing terror at home, Liao did not leave terror behind. The ravages of civil war in southwest China bled into terrifying battles in Korea.

Civil War, Korean War

The new regime used the Korean War to consolidate control in the southwest. Anti-American diatribes conflated domestic resisters with international threats. Bandit suppression and the Campaign to Suppress Counterrevolutionaries became central components of the official home front movement to resist America and aid Korea in southwest China. At a December 1950 meeting in Guiyang celebrating the formation of the provincial Resist America Aid Korea coordination committee, city party secretary Wu Jiamo announced three specific tasks.[69] The first two items, spreading patriotic propaganda and encouraging young people to sign up for military cadre schools, were identical to nationwide policies. But the third task, the organization of greeting teams to express gratitude to PLA units fighting against local resisters, was specific to the southwest.

A *New Guizhou Daily* commentary explained the connection between resisting America and assisting bandit suppression forces in Guizhou: "Our provincial victory over bandits is inseparable from China's peace enterprise and opposing the American invasion. Bandit suppression has greatly strengthened our interior, rooted out the claws and teeth of the American invaders, overthrown the evil reactionary regime, and expanded and strengthened our national power. Henceforth, in the course of the Resist America Aid Korea Protect Home and Country Campaign, bandit suppression is still an important practical action."[70] In rhetorically linking bandits to American invaders, provincial officials attempted to bring the Korean conflict home to people in Guizhou. As we have seen from the stories of Li Huaguo, Hu Zhengming, and many others, this association between domestic resistance and the Korean War went beyond pure rhetoric.

Memoirs published in Guizhou confirm that the Korean War allowed the new regime to neutralize domestic foes. In March 1951, PLA troops in Guizhou's Zhenyuan county who had fought against forces led by Wei Demao held a "bandit training class" *(tufei xunlian ban)* in an elementary school. Wang Jue recalled that his PLA unit ordered peasant associations in surrounding villages to round up anyone who had participated in a wide range of resistance activities, including armed uprisings, blockading army vehicles, opposing the new government, or "running wild in villages and harming common people." All offenders were to bring their own food and belongings and report to the school within two days.[71] Convinced by public executions and threats, 308 "bandits" ranging in age from seventeen to fifty-four showed up for the class. After three weeks of political classes, discussion and criticism sessions, singing, and basketball, the program ended. Some participants returned home, but 25 joined the army and went to fight in Korea and 9 were executed.[72]

A similar phenomenon occurred in the hills of west Hunan, where more than ten thousand "bandits who went through reform and education" became part of the PLA's 47th Army and fought in Korea.[73] Some of these soldiers ended up in American prisoner-of-war camps, but at least two returned to China as official war heroes, including Mayang county's Chen Qiyao. He joined a local armed group in 1946, ostensibly in order to avoid being drafted into the Nationalist Army. Chen participated in a training class after surrendering to the PLA in late 1949 and entered Korea in February 1951.

Chen had several disciplinary problems in Korea before proving himself on the battlefield. First, he was locked up after getting in a fist-fight with a Chinese soldier from another unit. This dispute arose when Chen noticed at mealtime that retreating troops were eating white rice, while his unit only had coarse grains such as sorghum and corn. When Chen pointed out the discrepancy, a rice-eating soldier criticized Chen's unit for being "redesignated bandit ragtag troops" (*tufei gaibian guolai de zapaijun*) who could only eat coarse grains.[74] That others mocked Chen's unit for being reformed bandits suggests that the bandit label failed to fade away, even in Korea.

U.S. Army interrogation reports of Chinese prisoners also indicate that entire units of former resisters against Communist rule remained intact in Korea. Liang Liyuan, like Chen Qiyao, was a former resister from west Hunan who became part of the 47th Army in Korea. Liang engaged in guerrilla attacks against the PLA until his capture in mid-1950. He told his interrogator that his battalion's morale in Korea was low because about 80 percent of the soldiers were former anti-Communist guerrillas. Many of the men's families had been killed in 1950, Liang said, and their misery continued in Korea. Eleven soldiers from Liang's company were killed by air attacks or artillery fire, while nineteen deserted in mid-1951. Liang was among the deserters.[75] Chen Qiyao was not.

After Chen defended the honor of his corn-eating comrades against the insults of rice eaters, his problems continued. Chen punched another soldier during a basketball game and later accidentally shot and severely wounded a fellow Chinese soldier while playing around with his gun. All was forgiven for Chen when in September 1951 he overcame shrapnel wounds to his head and unleashed a flurry of grenades at the enemy, helping to hold the Chinese position during an American counteroffensive. Chen's superiors requested official recognition for his meritorious deeds.[76] Chen returned to China in 1953 and met with

Mao Zedong, Zhou Enlai, and Marshal He Long in Beijing before going home. When He Long noticed that Chen's trembling left hand made eating difficult, he presented Chen with a special silver pair of chopsticks. But the injured veteran had a difficult time back in Hunan. His wife had remarried in his absence, and at the end of 1953, he was committed to a mental institution in Changsha.

Civil war and terror at home coupled with battle and injury in Korea were too much for Chen Qiyao to handle. Scholars have shown that many other Korean War veterans, especially former prisoners of war who chose to return to the mainland, had equally difficult experiences.[77] For the individuals swept up in civil and international war, rapid identity switches and the real dangers attached to changing labels were overwhelming.

War and the Early 1950s

Injury, fear, and struggles for survival cut across diverse groups in southwest China during the early 1950s. In some cases, the struggle continued even after former "bandits" and bandit suppressors found themselves fighting side by side in Korea. Most analytical frameworks and descriptors fail to do justice to the human stories of talkative Guizhou farmer Li Huaguo, wounded hero Chen Qiyao, or the countless others caught up in the wars that bound southwest China to far-away Korea. Zooming in on Guizhou means that we cannot fall back on generalizations about a smooth takeover or honeymoon period to describe China's early 1950s. The merging of China's civil and Korean wars in the southwest canceled the possibility of idyllic honeymoons.

Conceptions of totalitarianism, unintended consequences, and comparative revolution all contribute to our understanding of what happened in Guizhou but fall short in explaining diverse and complex realities. The totalitarian model's focus on repression in the early 1950s reminds us not to forget the desiccating repercussions of state-coordinated terror.[78] Yet we know that Communist control in the southwest was far from total in 1950 and 1951. It was tenuous, threatened, and in the case of grain collection, poorly conceived. Here, Neil Diamant's idea of a "bumbling" Communist party-state beset by the unintended consequences of its policies seems more appropriate than a totalitarian model.[79]

Yet in spite of its initial bumbling, the new regime ultimately occupied the southwest and suppressed armed resistance. It relied on the army, members of local militias, and public security agents to do so. In his treatment of early 1950s China, Maurice Meisner views terror as the unavoidable by-product of revolution but also notes that the Nationalists were not averse to employing terror.[80] Indeed, in southwest China the new regime did not have a monopoly on terror. Because the leaders of the Communist party-state were committed to fundamentally reshaping existing local power relations, elites in Guizhou, especially those involved in secret societies and the opium trade, could be counted on to ferociously protect their interests. Assassinating Communist cadres and grain collection teams was part of the modus operandi of local power holders turned rebel leaders. Armed resistance groups in the southwest played by the same rules as Deng Xiaoping, who called for "resolutely" killing enemies without "appeasing and hesitating." One messenger in a resistance group that operated along the Guizhou-Guangxi border recalled a June 1950 battle in which his regiment of 1,000 troops overwhelmed 150 isolated PLA soldiers. The guerrillas captured 70 PLA prisoners and executed all of them three days later.[81]

Without a harsh crackdown on the resisters who controlled parts of Guizhou in early 1950, the party-state could not govern the province and advance its redistributive agenda. Resistance groups fed off fear and survival concerns but offered no coherent alternative vision. Yet when the new regime responded to resisters by threatening families, displaying corpses, and shipping men to Korea, it could only claim a hollow victory in southwest China. Judging by events in the southwest, terror was indeed "built into the foundations of the revolutionary regime," as Julia Strauss has argued.[82] Fear did not simply dissipate after the last resistance fighter in southwest China surrendered or hostilities ceased in Korea. The legacy of terror and war in the southwest would reverberate for years to come.

6

The Chinese Communist "Liberation" of Tibet, 1949–51

Chen Jian

BY EARLY 1949, Mao Zedong and his Chinese Communist Party comrades already knew that defeating Chiang Kai-shek and the Nationalist regime was no longer a major challenge for them. The main task facing them was how to build a "new China." This was an issue with multiple meanings, including how to establish a new Communist government; how to rebuild China's war-torn economy; and how, as Mao had long envisioned, to carry the revolution to its higher, postvictory stage. At a more basic level, in order to build a "new" China, there was the question of how to define "China"—and the boundaries of China and the composition of the "Chinese nation" in particular. In a practical political sense, this meant that Mao and his comrades would have to determine the relationship between "China proper" and such outlying regions as Xinjiang, Mongolia, and Tibet, which were inhabited mainly by non-Han minority ethnic groups.

During the process of the Communist revolution up to the 1940s, the party at times had favored a program of "China federation" as a way to deal with the future relationship between China proper and the minority-inhabited outlying regions. According to the program, the people of Muslim Xinjiang, Mongolia (both Inner and Outer Mongolia), and Tibet would first be given "full autonomy" and then, in accordance with the principle of "national self-determination," would decide whether to form a federation with China proper and the Han people.[1] Yet the "China federation" program disappeared completely in the party's official discourse in 1949. Replacing it was a grand plan of pursuing a unified socialist China incorporating Xinjiang, Inner Mongolia, and Tibet. The foundation of the plan was the notion of "a republic based on the unity of five nationalities" *(wuzu gonghe)*—Hans, Manchus, Mongolians, Hui Muslims, and Tibetans—which had been the backbone of the Nationalist Party's nation-building efforts. Despite the party's persistent claim that its revolution would destroy the "old" China and create a "new" one, in terms of how to define "China," its leadership's ways of thinking demonstrated a remarkable continuity with those of the Nationalists, the political reigning force of the "old China" that the party had strived to overthrow.

As an important component of their efforts to create a unified new China, Mao and his comrades formulated and carried out plans to "liberate" Tibet in 1949–51. From the beginning, they acted on the assumption that Tibet had to be made a part of China—not only for the purpose of claiming Chinese sovereignty over Tibet but also, and more important, for supporting Mao's proclamation at the formation of the People's Republic of China that "we the Chinese people have stood up." In retrospect, this is one of the most important statements that Mao had ever made—it would play a central role in legitimating the Chinese Communist state then and now, more than a half century after the People's Republic's formation.

This chapter provides a historical survey of the Chinese Communist "liberation" of Tibet. It first reviews the party's attitudes toward "national self-determination" in general and the Tibet issue in particular before 1949. It then examines how the party made the decision to liberate Tibet and how the decision translated into political, diplomatic, and military strategies. It further narrates the process that finally led to the signing of the Seventeen-Point Agreement between Beijing and Lhasa in May 1951. It concludes with some general discussion about how the Chinese experience in dealing with the Tibet issue in 1949–51 has influenced not only Beijing's policies toward Tibet but also the party's efforts to build a new China since the early 1950s.

Tibet did not occupy an important position in the Chinese Communist Party's strategic thinking and policymaking until 1949. During the early years of the Communist movement, the party approached the ethnicity/nationality issue in general and Tibet's status in particular in accordance with a broad yet vague understanding of the Marxist-Leninist theory of "national self-determination." In order to distinguish the party's nationality policies from those of the "reactionary forces" of China, the party argued that "while China proper . . . should be unified as a genuine democratic republic . . . Mongolia, Tibet, and Muslim Xinjiang should become autonomous, as democratic autonomies of freedom (*minzhu ziyoubang*)."[2] In 1932, in a statement targeting the Tibetans and other ethnic minorities in Sichuan and Xikang, the party claimed that the Nationalist Party's notion of "unity between five nationalities" had been designed to "conceal its policy of national oppression" and "to oppose the independence and autonomy" of the minority nationalities. In comparison, the Communists "acknowledged the rights of national self-determination of all minority nationalities, including acknowledging their rights of self-determination, even leading to their separation from China."[3]

The party's first major encounter with the Tibetans occurred during the "Long March" in 1935–36. Under the dramatic pressure of Nationalist troops, the Red Army was forced to pass through Tibetan-inhabited areas in Sichuan and Xikang, which caused conflicts between the Red Army and the local Tibetans and resulted in a major controversy concerning the party's general strategy (whether to move north toward the Chinese-Mongolian borders or to stay south to establish base areas in Sichuan and Xikang). In a debate with Zhang Guotao, Mao argued for the need of quickly moving away from the Tibetan areas since the Red Army's relationship with the Tibetans (*fanmin*) had been "very bad" and since remaining in Tibetan areas would isolate the Red Army from the rest of China. These arguments led to Zhang's criticism of Mao's "great Han chauvinism."[4] In order for the Red Army to pass through Tibetan-inhabited areas, the party tried hard to pursue a temporary "united front" with local Tibetan elites, especially by promising them that the Red Army had no intention of seizing permanent bases in the Tibetan areas.[5] The party leadership further emphasized that "the national liberation movement of the Tibetans in Xikang is for achieving independence by thoroughly splitting with Britain and China and for realizing national self-determination; only by thoroughly splitting from Britain and China will the Tibetans in Xikang achieve genuine independence and liberation."[6]

Even after the Red Army established new base areas in northern Shaanxi, the party continuously favored the notion of a China federation. In an interview with American journalist Edgar Snow in July 1936, for example, Mao said that Tibet, together with Outer Mongolia and Xinjiang, "will form autonomous republics attached to the China federation" after "the People's Revolution has been victorious."[7]

However, when the Communist revolution approached nationwide victory in 1949, the notions of "China federation" and "national self-determination" lost their appeal in the party's design of a new China. Instead, Mao and his comrades began to argue that both the Han Chinese and other "minority nationalities" belonged to a unified "Chinese nation" and that it was unity between the Hans and other nationalities, rather than "national self-determination," that should become the foundation of the party's nationality policies. In meeting in early 1949 with Anastas Mikoyan, a Soviet party Politburo member, Mao revealed some of his basic considerations on this issue. Mao said that China, as a multinational country, was composed of dozens of nationalities with the Hans as the majority and with such minority nationalities as the Mongols, Muslims, Tibetans, and Uyghurs living in outlying regions. Mao stated that although the Hans were usually equated with the Chinese, in reality "Chinese" should also include "all of those who live in the territory of China." He further contended that while the party should oppose Han nationalism, it should make it clear simultaneously that "in history the Hans were also enslaved and dominated by other nationalities, despite the fact the Han nationality was the large one." Therefore, emphasized Mao, the party should abolish national oppression while favoring "unity, friendship, and mutual cooperation between different nationalities, so that all nationalities will unite to construct our country."[8]

Mao's statement is of utmost importance. He defined "China" as a "multinational country" and "Chinese" as including "all of those who live in the territory of China." He also emphasized that it was the party's political and social revolutions aimed at eliminating all oppressions—including racial oppression—that made its nation-building plans justified. Indeed, it was the adjective "new" that provided the "new China" with basic legitimacy while, at the same time, offering the "Chinese nation" the right to claim itself a nation of multinationalities.

On the eve of the People's Republic's establishment, Zhou Enlai, the designated premier of the new government, further clarified the party's attitude toward the nationality issue. He emphasized the importance of "uniting all nationalities into a big family" in the new China. He particularly pointed out that although in a general sense the party continuously favored the principle of national self-determination, "we must also prevent the imperialists from sabotaging China's unification by utilizing the nationality issue." Thus Zhou made it clear that the "new China" would not become a federation, although it would allow "autonomy in [minority] nationality regions."[9]

Many party members, including high-ranking cadres, seemed unable to catch the party leadership's changing attitude toward the "national self-determination" issue. In a speech meant to provide direction on the party's nationality policy for lower-ranking cadres, Cao Diqiu, a leading party official in Chengdu, continuously stated that the party would follow the principle of national self-determination to the extent of "acknowledging the rights of various nationalities within a country to determine their own political fate and establish their own independent states." Cao even predicted that "we will see some of the minority nationalities establish independent states, and (as in such regions as Tibet, Xinjiang, and Outer Mongolia) they will join the new Democratic Republic of China, and thus making it a new democratic republic of federation."[10] Confusing statements like this one must have alarmed top party leaders, and they decided to use explicit language to clarify the party's attitude toward "national self-determination." An inner-party instruction in October 1949 stated:

> Concerning the question of the "self-determination" of various minority nationalities, we should not emphasize it any more. In the past, in order to win the minority nationalities to the side of our party, and to oppose the Nationalist Party's reactionary rule (demonstrated as big Han nationalism toward the minority nationalities), it was completely correct that we emphasized this slogan under the circumstances of the civil war. But the situation today has changed fundamentally. The reactionary reign of the Nationalist Party has already been overthrown, and the new China led by our party has been established. For the purpose of completing the great cause of unifying our country, and for opposing the plots by the imperialists and their lackeys to divide China's national unity, we should not emphasize this slogan on domestic nationality issues any more, so as not to allow the imperialists and the reactionary el-

ements among minority nationalities to use it to put us on the defensive.[11]

The importance of this statement cannot be overemphasized. While demonstrating full confidence in their mission as the "liberators" of a China of multinationalities, party leaders had virtually reversed their attitude on the "national self-determination" issue. Mao and his comrades now made it very clear that, in spite of the party's loud rhetoric about destroying the old China, on the key question of how to define China, China's boundaries, and the composition of the Chinese nation, they were more than willing to embrace the historical legacies in these aspects of the old China (and largely the legacies of the Qing). It was within this context that the party leadership formulated and carried out plans to "liberate" Tibet.

Mao and the party leadership started deliberations on taking over Tibet as a practical strategic and political issue early in 1949. In meeting Mikoyan in early 1949, Mao equated the importance of liberating Tibet with occupying Nationalist-controlled Taiwan, contending that these were the last two main tasks that the People's Liberation Army (PLA) would have to fulfill in order to unify China. However, compared with the more difficult question of occupying Taiwan, "the settlement of the Tibet problem should not be as difficult." Mao predicted that in dealing with Tibet the party would encounter two challenges: "First, the challenge involved in transportation will make the movement of a large army inconvenient and will create problems in logistical supply; second, we might face the nationality problem, especially in areas with strong religious influence." Mao thus concluded that "it will take much time to solve the problem, and we need to be patient and advance steadily."[12]

In June–August 1949, when the party's second in command Liu Shaoqi visited the Soviet Union, Tibet was again a topic of discussion between Liu and Soviet leaders. In a report to Joseph Stalin summarizing the party's policies and strategies, Liu listed Tibet, Taiwan, Hainan, and Xinjiang as the areas that remained to be liberated. He speculated that "the Tibet question must be settled in political ways, rather than by military means."[13]

The party openly announced its plans to liberate Tibet in the wake of the "Chinese expulsion" incident in Lhasa. On July 8, 1949, the Tibetan government, in an effort to demonstrate "neutrality" in the Communist-Nationalist civil war, closed the mission of the Nationalist government in Lhasa and expelled all Han officials from Tibet.[14] When Mao and his comrades learned of this incident, they immediately decided to make public the party's policy toward Tibet. On September 2, Xinhua News Agency announced that the expulsion of Chinese officials from Tibet had been "planned and initiated by British and U.S. imperialists and their follower, the Nehru government of India . . . and carried out by the reactionary local authorities of Tibet." Xinhua stated: "The PLA must liberate all of China's territories, including Tibet, Xinjiang, Hainan Island, and Taiwan, and will never allow a single inch of Chinese land to be left beyond the rule of the People's Republic of China. Tibet is China's territory, and we will never allow it to be invaded by foreign forces; the Tibetan people are an integral part of the Chinese, and we will never allow them to be separated from the Chinese nation."[15]

With the PLA approaching areas neighboring Tibet in the civil war, Mao and the party leadership included Tibet in the PLA's operation plans and viewed the Tibet issue from both political and military perspectives. On August 6, 1949, Mao instructed Peng Dehuai, commander of the PLA's First Field Army: "When you attack Lanzhou you should pay special attention to protecting the Panchen [Lama] and the Tibetans living in Gansu and Qinghai, so that you will be prepared for settling the Tibet issue."[16] When the PLA defeated Nationalist forces in several northwestern and southwestern provinces, Mao established "the fall or winter of next year" as the target date for "the completion of the settlement of the Tibet issue." He calculated that since the military operations against Nationalist forces in the northwest would be completed earlier than those in the southwest, and since "reportedly the roads to enter Tibet from Qinghai are easier to go through" and "Panchen and his group are also in Qinghai," the party's Northwest Bureau should be assigned with the main duty to settle the Tibet issue, with the Southwest Bureau playing a supporting role.[17]

Following Mao's instructions, the Northwest Bureau and the First Field Army acted immediately to prepare for the troops to enter Tibet. But they quickly discovered that approaching Tibet from the northwest was no easy matter. On December 30, Peng reported to Mao several insurmountable difficulties involved in entering Tibet from the northwest through three possible routes. The one from southern Xinjiang was composed of impassable roads most times of the year, and the one from northern Xinjiang, though easier to go through, cut through Indian territory and was thus "impossible due to political restraints." The route from Qinghai was "barred by the great snowy mountains" and thus presented difficulties "next to impossible to overcome." To prepare conditions for the entry, estimated Peng, it would require about two years. In comparison, it was less difficult to enter Tibet from the direction of Sichuan and Xikang. Therefore, Peng suggested that the Second Field Army and, accordingly, the Southwest Bureau be assigned with the main task of entering Tibet, whereas the First Field Army should play a supporting role in the northwest.[18]

Although Mao was then in Moscow for a formal visit to the Soviet Union, he wasted no time in reviewing Peng's report and quickly approved Peng's suggestions. In a telegram to leaders of the Northwest and Southwest bureaus on January 2, 1950, Mao stated that "since huge difficulties exist in marching into Tibet from Qinghai and Xinjiang, it is decided to let the Southwest Bureau take up the task of marching into Tibet and then managing Tibet." Mao acknowledged the difficulties involved in entering Tibet, but he still came up with an extremely ambitious timetable. He contended that since only the months between May and mid-September would be suitable for the troops' entry into Tibet, it was desirable that "the march into Tibet should begin in mid-April, and that all of Tibet should be occupied by October." Mao instructed Liu Bocheng and Deng Xiaoping, who headed the party's Southwest Bureau and commanded the Second Field Army, "to meet in the near future . . . and to arrange everything immediately."[19]

Following Mao's order, Deng and Liu organized a series of discussions about the feasibility of entering Tibet from Sichuan and Xikang in the shortest possible time. In a telegram to Mao on January 7, they expressed "complete agreement to occupying the entirety of Tibet this year, namely, by the coming September." In order to fulfill this task, they would dispatch the 18th Army, with Zhang Guohua as its commander, to enter Tibet, while assigning another division to serve as the reserve force.[20]

Mao was pleased with Deng and Liu's response. In a telegram on January 10, he stated that he "completely agreed to the plans on marching into Tibet as outlined in Liu and Deng's January 7 telegram." He again emphasized that "so long as Liu and Deng enhance supervision of and continuously push Zhang Guohua and the 18th Army, there should be sufficient time" to begin the march into Tibet by mid-May. He further instructed the Southwest Bureau to act immediately to establish the "leading authority of the party" for "controlling and handling everything" related to the Tibet mission. As the first step, Mao gave the Southwest Bureau three and a half months to "complete the investigation, train the cadres, rectify and train the troops, build roads, and move the troops to the border area between Xikang and Tibet." Once again setting up a highly aggressive timetable, Mao stressed that "the areas bordering Xikang and Tibet must be occupied by mid-May."[21]

Mao's eagerness to settle the Tibet issue in the shortest possible time was based on several key assumptions and considerations. First, in formulating strategies toward Tibet, Mao and his comrades acted on the assumption that "liberating" Tibet was a decisive step that they must take for completing China's unification. This issue became even more crucial with Mao proclaiming to the whole world that the People's Republic's formation meant that "we the Chinese people have stood up." In the vision of Mao and his comrades, whether they were able to claim China's sovereignty in Tibet represented a critical test case for the new Communist regime's credibility and legitimacy in front of the Chinese people and the whole world.

Mao and his comrades pursued a quick solution of the Tibet question also because they understood the region's strategic importance to China. In inner party discussions, the party leaders consistently demonstrated an appreciation of Tibet's strategic value. A PLA internal document emphasized that "Tibet is located in China's southwest border area, neighboring India, Nepal and Bhutan and serving as China's strategic gate in the southwest direction. . . . Both the British and U.S. imperialists have long cast greedy eyes on Tibet, so Tibet's position in [China's] national defense is extremely important."[22] Mao used explicit language to argue that "although Tibet does not have a large population, its international [strategic] position is extremely important. Therefore, we must occupy it, and transform it into a people's democratic Tibet."[23]

Party leaders also believed that the international environment was favorable to them. Despite Tibet's de facto independent status in the first half of the twentieth century, it had never received the recognition of the international community as an independent state. Following the People's Republic's establishment, several nonsocialist countries had recognized it by early 1950. Therefore, in discussing the PLA's plans for marching into Tibet, Mao told his comrades that "since now Britain, India and Pakistan have all recognized us, it is favorable for [our] military march into Tibet."[24] Mao and his comrades believed that if they were able to combine shrewd political and diplomatic actions with the backing of carefully planned military operations, they would not face serious international repercussions, let alone encounter any foreign military intervention in Tibet.[25]

Party leaders and PLA planners also believed that militarily they held an overwhelmingly superior position vis-à-vis the Tibetans. A detailed report on "The situation in Tibet" by the PLA's Southwest Military Region pointed out that Tibetan troops were not well trained, and their military equipment was largely outdated.[26] When party leaders and PLA planners considered military strategies and tactics, their main concern was how to maintain logistical supplies for the troops, not how to crush the resistance of the Tibetans.[27] These political, diplomatic, and military factors combined together to make Mao and his comrades firmly believe it necessary and possible to settle the Tibet issue in a relatively short time.

Telegraph exchanges in early January 1950 between Mao and his lieutenants in the Southwest and Northwest bureaus marked the beginning of the party's operation to "liberate" Tibet. In the next two years, the party leadership would have to repeatedly revise its plans and change the timetable, but it would persist in one thing that was most important—Tibet would have to be brought under the sovereignty of the People's Republic.

The Southwest Bureau moved forward quickly after receiving Mao's January 10 telegram. In one week's time, a party "Tibet Work Committee," headed by Zhang Guohua, was established; among committee members was Tian Bao (Sangye Yeshe), an ethnic Tibetan who was born in Sichuan and joined the Red Army in 1934.[28] The Southwest Bureau also presented a more detailed timetable and a military operation–centered plan for conquering Tibet. The 18th Army would complete preparations by the end of February and begin moving toward Tibet in early March; by the end of March the army's main force would complete concentration in the Ganzi area, the gate leading to Chamdo (in Chinese, Changdu), and would occupy Chamdo in May. The plan calculated that the main force of the Tibet army was stationed in Chamdo, so if Chamdo was occupied, "the entirety of Tibet would feel the shock wave, which would in turn cause deeper and broader internal division [among] the Tibetans." If the 18th Army were to fulfill the above tasks as scheduled here, PLA planners predicted, "in another month, namely in June, we would be able to occupy such central regions as Lhasa or even Rikaze, and the Tibet question would be settled basically through military means."[29]

On January 24, the party leadership approved the establishment of the Tibet Work Committee, as well as designating the 18th Army as the main force to enter Tibet. In addition to regarding Chamdo as the main direction to enter Tibet, party leaders also instructed the Southwest and Northwest bureaus to explore the feasibility of simultaneously entering Tibet from Xinjiang, Qinghai, and Yunnan, so that the march into Tibet would be carried out from several directions. In the meantime, Mao and his comrades did not regard invading Tibet purely as a military matter. Obviously for the purpose of justifying the PLA's military invasion of Tibet, the party leadership instructed the two bureaus to study "whether Panchen [Lama] should also follow the troops to enter Tibet, and how the question of Panchen should be managed in the future."[30]

The 18th Army, with the backing of the entire Second Field Army, began mobilization for the Tibet campaign in early February. However, it soon turned out that owing to such factors as poor road conditions, it was impossible for the 18th Army to complete the preparation by late spring. Further, rebellions by Nationalist remnants spread quickly in Sichuan and other areas under the jurisdiction of the Southwest Military Region, making it difficult for the Communist government to maintain normal food supply in these areas. In order to crush the rebellions, in late February the Southwest Bureau decided to put some units of the 18th Army into "suppressing bandit activities." Consequently, the bureau had to propose to Beijing that the operations for Tibet be postponed.[31] In response, the Central Military Commission approved using units of the 18th Army to deal with "the harassing activities of the bandits as well as the difficulties in food supply." Meanwhile, the party leadership also emphasized that "the 18th Army's plan to enter Tibet" should not be postponed indefinitely; instead, "our determination of entering Tibet this year should not be compromised."[32]

Despite Beijing's push, however, neither the 18th Army nor other units of the PLA (including those commanded by the Northwest Military Region, formerly the First Field Army) were able to follow the schedule as established by party leaders. By late spring, it had become evident that the timetable set up by the Southwest Bureau and approved by the party leadership would have to be abandoned. Consequently, party leaders and PLA planners had to reconsider the overall strategies to settle the Tibet question.

The party never regarded "liberating Tibet" purely as a military mission. On the one hand, Mao and his colleagues, with the conviction that "political power grows out of the barrel of a gun," believed that "it is impossible to settle the Tibet question without using military force."[33] On the other, they also believed that "although liberating Tibet is a military issue and, therefore, a certain number of military forces should be used, this is primarily a political issue."[34] Realizing the complexity of Tibet's internal conditions and external environment, Mao and his comrades found it necessary to combine military operations with diplomatic and "united front" work, especially toward Tibet's political and monastic elites.[35] In late 1949 and early 1950, when the party leaders concentrated on preparing the military march into Tibet, they also regarded this as a way to force the Tibetans to yield to Beijing's terms. When the PLA's military mobilization encountered difficulties, the party leadership naturally turned more attention to exploring how the Tibet question might be solved by peaceful means.

In this respect, Mao and his comrades were fully aware that within the Tibetan elites historically there existed rifts between the Dalai Lama and the Panchen Lama. More recently, because of the controversy in the selection of the Tenth Panchen Lama, the Panchen Lama (twelve years old at that time) and his group had been forced to stay in Qinghai.[36] Viewing this situation, the party leadership adopted a strategy of first attracting cooperation and support from the Panchen Lama's group. Panchen and his followers demonstrated a cooperative attitude toward the party. Right after the People's Republic's establishment, reportedly the Panchen Lama immediately sent his greetings, acknowledging that Tibet was part of China and inviting the PLA to liberate Tibet.[37] This gesture by the second most important political and religious leader in Tibet greatly enhanced the legitimacy of the party's policy toward Tibet. On November 23, 1949, Mao and Zhu De, commander in chief of the PLA, responded to the Panchen Lama that "the Central People's Government and the PLA certainly will satisfy the Tibetan people's will . . . to become a member of the great family of new China."[38]

On January 20, 1950, the Chinese Foreign Ministry issued a statement on Tibet, inviting the "local government of Tibet" to dispatch representatives to Beijing for negotiations leading to the "peaceful liberation of Tibet."[39] In late February, the Southwest Bureau reported to Beijing that Zhiqing Fashi, a renowned Han Buddhist monk who had had "close connections with political and religious leaders in Tibet," was willing to travel to Lhasa to "persuade the Dalai clique to shake the influence of the British imperialists and return to the motherland." The Southwest Bureau was in favor of the plan, reasoning this would "help Dalai himself or his representatives to come to Beijing to negotiate ways to settle the Tibet question, or to negotiate during [the PLA's] march [into Tibet], which may prevent Dalai from becoming held by the British imperialists or creating more barriers for us by escaping to India."[40] The party leadership approved the plan immediately, emphasizing that "while our plan of dispatching troops into Tibet is firm and unshakeable, we should try every possible channel to negotiate with the Dalai clique, so that he will stay in Tibet and favor a peaceful settlement with us."[41]

The slow progress of the PLA's military preparations made it more necessary for Beijing's leaders to emphasize settling the Tibet question in peaceful ways. While approving the Southwest Bureau's plan of sending Zhiqing Fashi to Tibet, the party leadership also instructed the Northwest Bureau to explore the possibility of asking Taktse Rimpoche, the Dalai Lama's brother who was then in Qinghai, to "persuade members of the Dalai clique."[42] Taktse Rimpoche accepted the mission and would leave Qinghai for Tibet in early May.

In the face of the prospect of a major Chinese invasion, the government in Lhasa (Kashag) tried to resort to international diplomacy to stop the invasion. In a series of statements in late 1949 to early 1950, the Kashag argued that Tibet had become independent in history, that the relationship between Tibet and China was one of priest and patron, and that there had existed no influence of foreign imperialism in Tibet and so Tibet did not need liberation. They thus asked for the Communists to promise "not to attack Tibet."[43] When Beijing completely ignored these "strangely naïve" requests—as Melvyn Goldstein puts it—by the Tibetans, the Kashag started appealing to Washington and London for support, including helping Tibet to become a member state of the United Nations. In December 1949, after going through the procedure of divine lottery, the Kashag decided to form missions to be sent to China, the United States, India, Britain, and Nepal.[44]

But neither Washington nor London was willing to receive the Tibetans at the moment, and New Delhi was also dubious. Washington, still experiencing the impact of "losing China" to the Communists, was worried that an American policy encouraging the Tibetans would be viewed as "indecent" by the Nationalists (who also firmly claimed China's sovereignty over Tibet) and "provocative" by the Communists. Furthermore, American policymakers feared that U.S. support for Tibet "might hasten Chinese Communist action against Tibet."[45] London, already in active pursuit of establishing diplomatic relations with Beijing, realized that there was little it could do to influence developments in Tibet. In addition, British policymakers were unwilling to see their interests in China harmed because of Tibet.[46]

Although both Washington and London would have liked to see New Delhi play a more active role in supporting the Tibetans, the Indians demonstrated no interest in doing so. For Jawaharlal Nehru, India's prime minister, it was important for a cooperative relationship to be established between New Delhi and Beijing, and he saw little benefit in offending the Chinese Communists through providing support to the Tibetans. The most Nehru would do was to use India's diplomatic influence to persuade Beijing to allow Tibet to remain as autonomous as possible.

Beijing's response was one of anger after learning of the formation of the Tibetan missions, especially the ones to Britain and the United States. Chinese media immediately used this as evidence to claim that the Tibetan local government indeed had been under the strong impact of Western imperialism.[47] Consequently, the Kashag had no other choice but to abandon the plan of dispatching missions to Washington and London.

Only the mission designated for China continued its activities. The mission was composed of three representatives and headed by Shakabpa, a high-ranking lay official of the Kashag. The delegation left Lhasa on February 10, 1950, and arrived in Kalimpong, India, on

March 7. In the assignment for the delegation, there were such tasks as "securing an assurance that the territorial integrity of Tibet will not be violated" and defending the principle that "the people and government of Tibet will not tolerate any interference in the successive rule of the Dalai Lama, and they will maintain their independence."[48] On April 2, 1950, Shakabpa's delegation forwarded these terms to the Chinese officials in India preparing for the establishment of the Chinese embassy there, asking to hold negotiations in Hong Kong with representatives from Beijing.[49]

Beijing made no immediate response to Shakabpa. Not until early May 1950, when it had become evident that the PLA would need more time for getting ready to enter Tibet, did the party leadership start actively pursuing negotiations with the Tibetan authorities. On May 3, after months of delay, the party leadership finally approved the Northwest Bureau's plan of sending Taktse Rimpoche (the Dalai Lama's elder brother) to Lhasa to help "persuade members of the Dalai clique" and to deliver the request that "the Tibetan government should immediately dispatch its representatives to Xikang to hold negotiations with the PLA there."[50]

It was against this background that the party leaders found the need to work out the guidelines and specific terms for negotiations with the Tibetans. Thus discussions were held within the party leadership and between Beijing and party regional bureaus in May–June 1950. On May 11, the Southwest Bureau reported to Beijing that "while continuously enhancing our military preparations for marching [into Tibet], we also plan specifically to strengthen the work of winning the other side over to us through political maneuvering." The bureau proposed that the negotiations with the Tibetans "should be held in Xikang, so that the interference of the Britons and Americans would be averted." The bureau also presented four conditions as the "foundation of negotiation" for the party leadership's examination and approval:

1. Eliminating the influence of British and U.S. imperialism in Tibet, and returning the Tibetan people to the great family of the motherland of the People's Republic.
2. Implementing autonomy in the region of the Tibetan nationality.
3. Temporarily maintaining the various existing systems and institutions in Tibet; and leaving the question of carrying out reforms in

Tibet to the future in accordance with the will of the Tibetan people.

4. Allowing religious freedom, protecting [Buddhist] temples, and respecting the religious beliefs as well as the customs of the Tibetan people.[51]

The party leadership's response came on May 17, which stated, "We must stick to the established policy of liberating Tibet and must resort to military means, but at the same time it is also necessary to do everything possible to strengthen the work of winning the other side to us through political means." The party leadership pointed out that "there existed deep division among the Tibetan elites; therefore, to a certain extent it is possible for the Dalai Lama to turn [toward us]." "Liberating Tibet in peaceful ways" was advantageous in several senses, the party leadership emphasized, because it would help "avoid damaging other nationalities' feelings, minimize estrangements between different nationalities, and enhance the great unity between the Hans and the Tibetans." The key question involved here, as party leaders viewed it, was under what conditions could peaceful settlement be achieved. They emphasized that "the basic condition is that the Tibetan side must eliminate the influence of British and U.S. imperialism in Tibet and must assist the PLA to enter Tibet." In exchange for these concessions, the telegram continued, "our side may recognize Tibet's political and religious systems, including the Dalai Lama's position, as well as maintain Tibet's current military forces and customs—we will not change them, but will protect them." The party leadership asked the Southwest and Northwest bureaus to "conduct further studies about these issues, and, respectively, draft several terms that may be used as the foundation of negotiation, and report them for the central leadership's examination and approval—this should be done the sooner the better." These terms, continued the telegram, would "also be used . . . as the party's promise to the Tibetans if marching into Tibet must be conducted through fighting (and if efforts for a peaceful settlement have failed)."[52]

In accordance with Beijing's instructions, the Southwest Bureau conducted a series of discussions in the next two weeks. On May 27, the bureau proposed ten terms to Beijing for approval. Mao personally reviewed these terms.[53] With Beijing's approval, on June 2, the Southwest

Bureau formally conveyed them to the Tibet Work Committee as the guideline for handling the Tibet issue:

1. The people of Tibet unite to expel the forces of aggression of British and U.S. imperialism from Tibet, and the people of Tibet return to the great family of the motherland of the People's Republic of China.

2. Autonomy will be implemented in the Tibetan nationality region.

3. Tibet's existing political systems will be maintained, the Dalai Lama's position and power will not be changed, and Tibetan officials at all levels will serve as usual.

4. Religious freedom will be implemented, lama temples will be protected, and the Tibetan people's religious beliefs and customs will be respected.

5. Tibet's existing military institutions will be maintained and will not change; Tibet's existing army will become part of the national armed forces of the People's Republic.

6. The language and education of the Tibetan nationality will be developed.

7. Agriculture, industry, and commerce in Tibet will be developed, and people's life will be improved.

8. All matters concerning reforms in Tibet will [be carried out] in accordance with the will of the Tibetan people, and will be solved through consultation with the Tibetan people, as well as with the leading personnel in Tibet.

9. As for those pro-British/American and pro-Nationalist officials, so long as they cut off connections with British/U.S. imperialism and the Nationalist Party, and do not carry out sabotage or resistance, their positions will all be maintained and they will not be retaliated against.

10. The PLA will enter Tibet for enhancing national defense, and will observe the above policies. The PLA's budget will be completely supplied by the Central People's Government. The PLA will conduct fair trading [in Tibet].[54]

While approving these ten terms, Beijing's leaders had in mind three channels of communication with Lhasa. The first one, as discussed earlier, was the delegation that Taktse Rimpoche, the Dalai Lama's brother, had been persuaded to lead. However, it soon turned out that

Taktse Rimposche was not willing to bridge the gap between Beijing and Lhasa. The delegation's trip to Lhasa was repeatedly delayed en route. When the delegation arrived in the Tibetan areas, Taktse Rimposche, after having the two other Tibetan members and the Chinese assistants of the delegation detained, traveled to Lhasa by himself. When in Lhasa, instead of promoting negotiation with Beijing, he advised the Dalai Lama not to do so.[55]

The second channel was through Geda Trulku, a distinguished, incarnate lama from the Beri monastery near Ganzi. As early as 1936, when the Red Army passed through Ganzi, the Geda Lama established contacts with the Red Army and provided it with help. Zhu De signed a letter to the effect that Geda and his monastery had assisted the Communists, and so they would be protected by Communist troops.[56] When the PLA arrived in Sichuan in late 1949, Geda took up the position as vice chairman of the People's Government of Xikang province. On May 5, 1950, he proposed to Zhu De that he could serve as a peace messenger between Beijing and Lhasa, a plan that the party leadership gave full support.[57] The Geda Lama left the Beri monastery on July 10 for Lhasa. Two weeks later, he stopped in Chamdo. On August 22, he suddenly died, with many believing that he was murdered.[58]

Consequently, there was only one channel left—the delegation headed by Shakabpa in New Dehli. Since early April, the delegation had explored ways to establish contacts with the Chinese government. On April 8, Shakabpa received an informal letter from Zhu Shouguang, father-in-law of the Dalai Lama's brother Gyalo Dundrup (who was married to a Chinese woman). According to the letter, the Tibetan representatives were asked to meet with a representative from the Chinese government in Hong Kong.[59] However, the Tibetans were unable to obtain visas from the British government to travel to Hong Kong. In the meantime, the attitude of Beijing also changed. Mao now believed that "the representatives from Tibet must come to Beijing for the negotiation, and the negotiation should not be held in Hong Kong."[60] On May 28, in a much delayed response to the inquiry from Shakabpa's delegation of April 2, the Tibetans were informed that they "must come to Beijing to hold negotiations concerning the peaceful liberation of Tibet in the capacity of representatives of the Tibetan local government" and that if they were willing to do so, they would "be welcomed in Beijing."[61]

But Shakabpa was confined by the instructions from the Kashag, which defined the negotiation's goals as "to secure an assurance that the territorial integrity of Tibet will not be violated, and . . . to inform the government of China that the people and government of Tibet will not tolerate any interference in the successive rule of the Dalai Lama, and they will maintain their independence."[62] The situation became more complicated when, after failing to obtain visas to travel to Hong Kong, Shakabpa and his mission chose to stay in India and wait for the arrival of the Chinese ambassador to hold negotiations. After the establishment of the Chinese embassy in New Delhi, the Tibetans wrote letters to and visited the embassy to request that negotiations be held in New Delhi.

The Chinese government responded by pushing Shakabpa and his colleagues to come to Beijing as "representatives of the Tibet local government." Shen Jian, Chinese chargé d'affaires in India, informed the Tibetans that "as Tibet is part of Chinese territory, we cannot recognize the delegation as Tibet's diplomatic representative." Shen insisted that Shakabpa's mission "must come to Beijing to discuss matters related to the peaceful liberation of Tibet in the capacity of representatives of the Tibetan local government." Shen also made it clear that the Chinese diplomats would only meet the Tibetans in New Dehli for holding "the preliminary talks for formal negotiations in Beijing."[63] On August 21, Zhou Enlai informed P. M. Panikkar, Indian ambassador to China, that "since the Tibetan delegation is a local and nationality delegation, they should come to Beijing to discuss ways by which Tibet will be liberated peacefully."[64]

Even though Beijing's leaders seemed willing to settle the Tibet issue peacefully, they never stopped pushing for the PLA's military mobilization. Mao and his comrades, as masters at alternating between using force and conducting diplomacy, would not put all their eggs in one basket. They knew clearly that the true value of negotiation lay in enhancing the legitimacy of Chinese "liberation" of Tibet. They also understood that even in the event that the Tibetans willingly came to the negotiation table, still they might have to use military means to make sure that the Kashag would accept the party's main terms. Therefore, getting the PLA militarily ready was always a top priority in the party leadership's management of the Tibet issue.

In this respect, the key challenge facing PLA planners was how to transport troops and equipment to Tibet and how to guarantee logistical support to the troops. They knew that before any major military action could be taken, they must first construct roads. Beginning on April 13, as a crucial step for preparing for the attack on Chamdo, the Southwest Military Region mobilized more than eighteen thousand soldiers to work on rebuilding the road between Ya'an and Ganzi. The new road, with a total distance of 603 kilometers, was ready for use in late August.[65] In early August, the Southwest Military Region and the 18th Army held a series of planning meetings, which finalized the operation plans of occupying Chamdo by the end of 1950.[66]

Mao quickly approved the plans, emphasizing that the campaign for Chamdo was more than a military operation. He pointed out that "now India has issued a statement to acknowledge that Tibet is a part of Chinese territory, but is still hoping that the issue can be solved in a peaceful way rather than through military means." He also noticed that "originally Britain did not allow the Tibetan delegation to come to Beijing, and now it has allowed the delegation to do so." Mao further reasoned that if at this moment the PLA could destroy the Tibetan army's main force and, on the basis of it, occupy Chamdo, "it is possible that the Tibetan delegation would come to Beijing to pursue a peaceful solution [of the Tibet issue] through negotiation."[67] Following Mao's instructions, the headquarters of the Southwest Military Region issued "The Order for the Chamdo Campaign" on August 26, which set the goals for the campaign as "eliminating the main force of the Tibetan army in Chamdo and the surrounding area . . . laying down the foundation for marching toward Lhasa and liberating Tibet next year."[68]

In order to further justify the PLA's forthcoming military actions, as well as to place greater pressure on the Kashag, Yuan Zhongxian, Chinese ambassador to India, sent an ultimatum-style message to Shakabpa on September 17, demanding that the Tibetan negotiators "must arrive in Beijing by September 20."[69] When the Tibetans failed to take any action, Yuan sent Shakabpa another warning message on September 23, emphasizing that "the September 20 deadline has passed," that "the PLA will take action as planned," and that the Tibetans "will have to bear the responsibility for the consequences . . . unless they travel to Beijing immediately."[70] When Shakabpa and his group replied that they had to wait for Lhasa's instructions, Beijing's leaders determined that the time for resorting to force had come. On September 30, the party's Tibet Work Committee issued "Instructions for Liberating

Chamdo." Three days later, the Southwest Military Region issued the order for final military mobilization.[71]

The bloody conflict in Chamdo began on October 6 and lasted for two weeks. The PLA's attack was waged from three directions, with forces from the north (the Ganzi area) and the south (Batang) encircling the Tibetan units and cutting off their routes of escape, and the force from the center (Gangtuo) pushing directly into Chamdo. Before the attack began, the PLA units had experienced intensive training for longer than six months. In comparison, the Tibetan troops were ineptly commanded and poorly prepared. On October 19, the PLA occupied Chamdo. When the fighting ended on October 24, the PLA won a clear-cut victory. According to Chinese statistics, a total of 180 Tibetans were either killed or wounded, about 900 were captured, and another 4,300 surrendered.[72] The person who ordered the surrender was Ngabo Ngawang Jigme, the highest Tibetan political and military officer in Chamdo, and this would become the beginning of Ngabo's lifelong cooperation with the Communists.[73]

The PLA's victory in Chamdo placed Beijing's leaders in a more favorable position in managing the Tibet issue. Knowing that the Tibetans were no longer able to wage any effective military resistance, Mao and his comrades believed that the time had come again to shift the emphasis of their strategy to negotiating with the Dalai Lama and the Kashag.

When the battles in Chamdo were still under way, Mao instructed Yuan to inform the Tibetan negotiators that it was their failure to come to Beijing in a timely manner that had caused the Chamdo battle. Yet the door to negotiation remained open, and "if the Tibetans are willing to negotiate, they should come to Beijing immediately."[74] Then, in an open statement on November 10, Beijing continuously stressed that any peaceful solution of the Tibet issue had to include Lhasa's acceptance of Tibet being an integral part of China. Beijing also emphasized that in the long run and as an ultimate goal, Tibet would be transformed into a "people's democratic" society, which, in Maoist discourse, meant the destruction of Tibet's traditional political, economic, and social structures and replacing them with socialist ones. In order for a peaceful settlement in Tibet to be achieved, however, the party was willing to make such key compromises as acknowledging the Dalai Lama's status and power and not changing Tibet's religious and political systems in a given period, so that the Tibetans would accept China's sovereignty over Tibet.[75]

In the meantime, the PLA continued preparations for marching toward Lhasa. Immediately after the Chamdo campaign, the 18th Army followed Beijing's order to begin mobilizing the cadres and soldiers for "liberating Tibet as the first step in constructing a socialist Tibet." The Southwest Military Region carried out logistical preparations and road construction, so that troops could "move into Tibet the next spring."[76]

The PLA's victory in Chamdo also created deeper division and even panic among the Tibetan elites. While the Chamdo campaign crushed any hope on the part of the Tibetans that they might have the military capacity to shut the Chinese out of Tibet, many among the Tibetan elites remained unwilling to subject Tibet to China's sovereignty.[77] The inability on the part of Taktra, the seventy-five-year-old regent in Lhasa, to come up with an effective strategy to cope with the situation led to a movement to support the Dalai Lama to take power. On November 17, the Dalai Lama, who was sixteen years old at that time, ascended to the throne. Traditionally the Dalai Lama took over actual leadership at eighteen.

Since they controlled no other means to stop the Communist entry into Tibet, the Tibetan leaders again decided to appeal to the United Nations. On November 7, Shakabpa, who was still in India, received an order from Lhasa to present an urgent appeal to the United Nations, the United States, Britain, and India, asking them to help "restrain Chinese aggression."[78] The Tibetan appeal came at the time of a massive Chinese military intervention in Korea, so Washington was willing to provide some support to the Tibetans as a way to distract Chinese attention and check Chinese influence. However, largely because Britain was reluctant to take any leadership role (London hoped that India would play the role), the United Nations finally decided not to consider the Tibet issue.[79]

For geopolitical reasons, India demonstrated serious concerns over the PLA's military operations at Chamdo. On October 26, New Delhi expressed its "great regret" regarding the "official statement made in Peiping [Beijing] to the effect that People's Army units have been ordered to advance into Tibet."[80] Then, in another note, the Indian government claimed that "recent developments in Tibet have affected the friendly relations [between India and China] and the interest of peace all over the world." New Delhi also reasoned that the PLA's military operations in Tibet would worsen international tensions, especially in south Asia, produce a negative impact on the friendly relationship between China and India, and create an excuse for those countries to deny the People's Republic its seat at the United Nations.[81]

Beijing firmly rebuffed the protest from New Delhi. Fully realizing how important India's attitude toward Tibet could be, Mao personally dictated the Chinese Foreign Ministry's reactions to the Indian government. When K. P. S. Menon, India's deputy foreign minister, expressed New Delhi's concern over the PLA's entry into Tibet on October 11, Mao drafted Beijing's response for the Chinese Foreign Ministry, stating that "Tibet is Chinese territory, and the Tibet issue belongs to China's internal affairs. The PLA must enter Tibet, but in the first place [we] hope to enter Tibet without fighting a war."[82] When, on October 21, Panikkar mentioned that the PLA's military action in Tibet could produce a negative impact on Beijing's efforts to be accepted by the United Nations, Mao instructed the Chinese Foreign Ministry to "simply reply [to him] that Tibet is China's internal issue and no foreign country has the right to interfere."[83] On October 31, when Menon expressed "regret" upon the PLA's entry into Tibet, Mao instructed Zhou and the Foreign Ministry: "Our attitude [toward India] should be even tougher. We should say that Chinese troops will arrive in any part of Tibet they want, regardless of whether the Tibetan local government is willing to negotiate [with the central government] and what the result of the negotiation might be."[84]

Following Mao's instructions, the Chinese Foreign Ministry firmly rebutted New Delhi's "concerns" over and "regret" about the PLA's entry into Tibet. On November 16, the Chinese Foreign Ministry informed India that the People's Republic "has repeatedly made it clear that Tibet is an integral part of Chinese territory" and that "the Tibet issue is entirely one belonging to China's domestic affairs." Therefore, the Chinese government was "greatly surprised" at New Delhi's attempt to "influence and obstruct the exercise of its sovereign rights in Tibet."[85]

In retrospect, Beijing's unyielding approach toward New Dehli's concerns about Tibet could have caused serious animosity. But, largely because of Nehru's reconciliatory attitude, this did not happen. Although Nehru, like many of his colleagues, worried that the PLA's military presence in Tibet would change its function as a buffer between

China and India, he believed that "it is reasonable to assume that given the very nature of Tibetan geography, terrain and climate, a large measure of autonomy is almost inevitable."[86] Consequently, New Delhi did not take any action beyond expressing "regrets and concerns."

The absence of support and interference from the international community left Lhasa with no other choice but to come back to the negotiating table. Voices favoring a peaceful solution with Beijing increasingly gained influence among the Tibetan elites. Ngabo, who remained in Chamdo after it was occupied by the Chinese, strongly urged the Kashag to negotiate with the Communists. In his reports to Lhasa, Ngabo used his own experience in dealing with the PLA to emphasize that the Communist soldiers were well disciplined, that a peaceful solution would save the people and land of Tibet from the destructive impact of war, and that to negotiate with Beijing represented Tibet's "only chance of preserving a degree of autonomous status."[87] The Dalai Lama responded with cautious approval. In early December, the Dalai Lama left Lhasa and moved to Yadong, a town on the Tibetan-Indian border. On January 27, 1951, the Dalai Lama wrote to Yuan, expressing his intention to negotiate with Beijing. On February 1, Yuan followed Beijing's instruction to "convey Chairman Mao's warm regards to the Dalai Lama" and to "welcome him to send representatives to Beijing to discuss questions concerning the peaceful liberation of Tibet."[88]

Before leaving Lhasa, the Dalai Lama and the Kashag already decided "to give Ngabo full power to proceed with negotiations with the Chinese."[89] After learning that the United Nations had decided not to include Tibet on the General Assembly's agenda, the Dalai Lama and Kashag decided that a group of negotiators headed by Ngabo would travel to Beijing to hold negotiations there. The instructions that Ngabo had received, however, seemed contradictory. On the one hand, he was given "full power" to negotiate with the Chinese; on the other, he was told that he had no authority to make decisions without further consulting with the Kashag and the Dalai Lama.[90]

Ngabo and other Tibetan delegates arrived in Beijing on April 22. Five days later, with the arrangement of the party leadership, the Panchen Lama also came to Beijing. Negotiations between the Tibetans and the representatives of the Chinese government began on April 29.

In the next three weeks, the two sides held seven meetings. Substantial discussions began with the second meeting on May 2. Three issues dominated the agenda: the PLA's position and role in Tibet, the status and power of the Dalai Lama, and the question of recognizing the Panchen Lama. Although Ngabo and his colleagues followed the Kashag's instructions and tried to argue that there was no need for the PLA to enter Tibet, chief Chinese negotiator Li Weihan and his comrades were unwilling to make concessions on this issue. But the Chinese promised that after the PLA's entry into Tibet, the Dalai Lama's status and power, as well as the religious and political systems of Tibet, would be maintained. Therefore, the two sides reached agreements on these issues without prolonged debate.

Negotiations almost deadlocked on the question of recognizing the Panchen Lama. Chinese negotiators insisted upon including cooperation between the Dalai Lama and the Panchen Lama in the agreement (this would also mean that the Dalai Lama had recognized the Panchen Lama). At first Ngabo firmly refused to accept this term, contending that the agreement was one designated for defining the relationship between the central government in Beijing and the Kashag in Lhasa, not for defining the relationship between Tibetans. But Li argued that this was an important issue for the central government, especially because "the Panchen Lama and his group had not done anything against the motherland in twentieth century history" and that right after the establishment of the People's Republic, the Panchen Lama had expressed his firm support to the Central People's Government. Not willing to allow the negotiation to fail on this issue, Ngabo telegraphed the Kashag, proposing that the Panchen Lama should be recognized, to which the Dalai Lama and the Kashag agreed.[91]

On May 23, 1951, the "Seventeen-Point Agreement for the Peaceful Liberation of Tibet" was signed in Beijing. The most important term of the agreement is undoubtedly point one, which stated that "the Tibetan people shall unite and drive imperialist forces from Tibet, and shall return to the big family of the Motherland—the People's Republic of China." In exchange for the most crucial concession by the Tibetans, the Chinese government agreed that it would maintain "the established status, functions, and powers of the Dalai Lama"; would for the time being not alter Tibet's political, economic, and social systems that were by nature feudal and theocratic; and would not push "various reforms" in Tibet unless the Tibetan people so demanded and consultation had been conducted with "the leading personnel of Tibet."[92]

Attached to the Seventeen-Point Agreement were two secret agreements. The first one was titled "Regulations on Several Matters Concerning the PLA's Entry of Tibet," which contained seven points.[93] The most important terms stated that the PLA would enter Tibet and be stationed in "important locations of national defense and transportation," that Tibetan troops would be transformed into units of the PLA, that the Tibetan militia would be gradually demobilized, that all troops in Tibet would be commanded by the PLA's Tibet Military Region, that the commanders of the military region would be appointed by the central government, and that the budget of the PLA units in Tibet would be provided by the central government.[94]

The second secret agreement was about the Dalai Lama. Since the Dalai Lama was then still in Yadong and since it was unclear when (or whether) he would return to Lhasa, the document established that the Seventeen-Point Agreement would be implemented by Tibet's local government and that "during the first year after the signing of the agreement, the Dalai Lama may choose to live in a place of his own choice, and if he returns to his position, his status and power will not be changed."[95]

The signing of the Seventeen-Point Agreement represented a major victory for Beijing. However, until the agreement had been approved by the Dalai Lama himself, it would not have the influence the party leadership wanted it to have over the fate of Tibet. Indeed, if the Dalai Lama had decided not to recognize the agreements that Ngabo and the other Tibetan negotiators had signed in Beijing, the Seventeen-Point Agreement would have lost its very legitimacy as the foundational document defining Tibet as part of the People's Republic.

Mao and the party leadership fully understood the importance involved in achieving the Dalai Lama's endorsement of the agreements. Therefore, immediately after the signing of the agreement, Mao decided to dispatch Zhang Jingwu as his representative to travel to Yadong to persuade the Dalai Lama to return to Lhasa.[96] In order not to create any barrier to the Dalai Lama's return, the party leadership asked the Panchen Lama and his group not to begin the journey to Tibet (Lhasa) until the Dalai Lama had issued an invitation for them to return.[97]

The Tibetan elites around the Dalai Lama were divided on whether he should accept the Seventeen-Point Agreement and return to Lhasa or reject the agreement and go into exile. After a lengthy and heated debate, the National Assembly in Yadong proposed to the Kashag that the Dalai Lama should return to Tibet. The Kashag approved the proposal on July 10 or 11.[98] On July 14, Zhang arrived at Yadong. Two days later, he submitted to the Dalai Lama a letter signed by Mao. The chairman praised the Dalai Lama's appointment of Ngabo to hold negotiations with the central government in Beijing and urged the Dalai Lama and Tibet's local government to "carefully carry out the agreement on peaceful liberation of Tibet, and to try their best to assist the PLA to peacefully enter Tibet."[99] When Zhang asked when the Dalai Lama would return to Lhasa, the Dalai Lama replied, "Soon."[100]

The Dalai Lama left Yadong for Lhasa on July 21, and Zhang left Yadong two days later. On August 18, the party leadership telegraphed Zhang, instructing him to use every opportunity to approach members of the Tibetan elite, including "officials of autocratic background" and "high level religious figures," and explain to them the "spirit of leniency" in Beijing's policy toward Tibet as reflected in the Seventeen-Point Agreement.[101]

However, resistance to accepting the agreement still existed among officials within the Kashag, especially from Lukhang and Lobsang Tashi, the two acting Lonchens. Under these circumstances, Ngabo requested that a meeting of the National Assembly be called in Lhasa, so that he and the other Tibetan representatives who signed the Seventeen-Point Agreement could provide an explanation of the terms of the agreement. With the Dalai Lama's support, the Kashag agreed to the request.[102]

The meeting was held on September 28. Ngabo stated that he had only received a photo of Mao and a box of black tea as a negotiation representative in Beijing. He also emphasized that he had acted in accordance with the instructions from Lhasa. In particular, he explained that the Seventeen-Point Agreement would neither harm the status and power of the Dalai Lama nor threaten Tibet's political system and religious institutions. While asking the assembly to approve the agreement, he also said that if the assembly found the agreement wrong, he was willing to accept any punishment to his "body, life, or property." After heated debate, the assembly decided to recommend to the Dalai Lama that the agreement be approved.[103]

On October 24, 1951, the Dalai Lama dispatched a telegram to Beijing, formally expressing his confirmation of the Seventeen-Point

Agreement: "The local government of Tibet and the Tibetans, lamas, and the entire Tibetan people unanimously support this agreement. Under the leadership of Chairman Mao Zedong and of the Central People's Government they are actively helping units of the PLA that have entered Tibet for the strengthening of the national defense, the expulsion of imperialist forces from Tibet, and the guaranteeing of the sovereignty of the entire territory of the motherland."[104]

Two days later, on October 26, 1951, Mao sent his reply to the Dalai Lama: "Your telegram of October 24, 1951 has been received. I thank you for the efforts of translating into reality the agreement regarding the peaceful liberation of Tibet, and I send you my sincere greetings."[105]

Following the telegrams between Mao and the Dalai Lama, the Panchen Lama also issued a public statement to endorse the Seventeen-Point Agreement, applauding "Tibet's returning to the Motherland."[106] The approval of the two most influential leaders of Tibet brought huge legitimacy to the Seventeen-Point Agreement. Tibet formally became a part of the People's Republic.

The Seventeen-Point Agreement opened a new era in Chinese history as well as in the history of Tibet. The agreement seemed to set up a series of mutually agreed-upon principles that clearly defined Tibet's relationship with the central government. On the one hand, the Tibetans would embrace China's sovereign claim to the "Land of Snows," thus wedding them to the "great family" of the Chinese motherland; on the other hand, Beijing would treat Tibet in ways that were very different from its policies toward other "minority regions," including Xinjiang. Most important, the party would not wage the social and political revolutions that it was determined to carry out in Tibet for a certain period, and during this period, it would respect and coexist with Tibet's existing political, social, and monastic systems.

In reality, however, the commitments by the two sides in the Seventeen-Point Agreement were highly unequal. While the commitment of the Tibetans—accepting that Tibet was an integral part of the People's Republic—was *permanent* and *irreversible*, the commitment of the party—respecting and coexisting with Tibet's existing political, social, and monarchic systems—was *conditional* and *provisional*. By using "liberation" in describing and defining the exertion of the sovereignty of the Communist state over Tibet, the party already made it clear that its programs of political and social revolutions had placed it in a morally superior position to destroy the "old" Tibet and build a "new" one. All of this, on another level, formed a crucial component of the party's nation-building project aimed at creating a "new" China.

Indeed, behind the Communists' plans to "liberate" Tibet was a profound confidence that history was on their side. The support for this confidence was both ideological and cultural. As communists, Mao and his comrades firmly believed that only through the political and social revolutions directed by the party would Tibet's oppressive and feudal society be destroyed and replaced by a new society.[107] Underlying this belief, though, was a hidden sentiment of cultural superiority. Although Mao and his comrades acknowledged the importance of pursuing "ethnic equality" and avoiding "big Han nationalism," when they presented themselves as the "liberators" of Tibet, and when they talked about the necessity of transforming Tibet's "backward" political, economic, and social systems and institutions, they already placed themselves—as *Chinese* Communists—in a culturally superior position vis-à-vis the Tibetans.

Many factors contributed to the failure of the efforts by the Kashag to pursue Tibet's independence. In military confrontations, the Tibetans simply were too weak and too poorly prepared to resist the mighty Communist forces. In the diplomatic sphere, Lhasa had tried but failed to obtain substantial international support. In a deeper sense, though, it was the profound division among the Tibetans themselves that had facilitated the party's plans to occupy Tibet. The Tibetan story of encountering the Chinese Communists in 1949–51 was not only one of resistance but also, as revealed by this study, one of collaboration. Many Tibetans (such as Ngabo) chose to cooperate with the Communists—often because they had been overwhelmed by China's power as well as the apparently superior moral strength of the Communists. This, in turn, provided legitimacy to the claim by the Communists that their takeover of Tibet was not conquest but liberation.

The party's management of the Tibet issue in 1949–51 was highly successful in military, political, and diplomatic senses. The "liberation" of Tibet symbolized the completion of the Communist regime's unification of the Chinese mainland. From a long-range perspective, however, the party's victory over Tibet in 1949–51 also presented new challenges for Mao and the party in terms of ethnicity, religion, and culture. As history's later development would reveal, Mao and his comrades were far from ready to deal with these challenges. The "new

China," with Tibet incorporated into it, became a country more complicated and difficult for Mao and the party leadership to manage. The party's political strategy and military power allowed it to "liberate" Tibet in 1949–51, yet they did not enable Beijing to finally settle the Tibet issue. More than half a century after the Communists occupied Tibet, two fundamental—and closely interrelated—challenges continue to face the Communist state: how to define Tibet's position in China and how to define "China."

ᔖ 7

Big Brother Is Watching:
Local Sino-Soviet Relations
and the Building of New Dalian,
1945–55

Christian A. Hess

THROUGHOUT THE SPRING of 1955, the city of Dalian, located at the tip of the Liaodong peninsula in northeast China, was
ground zero for massive celebrations of Sino-Soviet friendship. In
Stalin square, the city's largest public space, huge rallies were held to
commemorate local Sino-Soviet relations and to thank the Soviet army
for liberating and protecting Dalian. Images of smiling Soviet troops
splashed the front pages of the *Dalian People's Daily* newspaper. Depicted more as superstars than soldiers, some are shown being hoisted
into the air by a jubilant crowd of Chinese people; other images show
them signing autographs for excited young Chinese students.[1] Three
major commemorative statues were unveiled that month, including a
large bronze statue of a Soviet soldier on top of a marble foundation,
part of a commemoration of Soviet martyrs who died helping to liberate
the northeast.[2] On guard for eternity, the bronze soldier firmly grasps a
machine gun as he stares out at the offices of the Dalian government.

Given the fact that the mid-1950s are viewed by many scholars as the
high point in Sino-Soviet relations, such scenes might not seem so out of
the ordinary. The Soviet presence in Dalian was, however, far from ordinary. On August 22, 1945, Soviet air force and tank divisions first rolled
into Dalian and nearby Lüshun, ending forty years of Japanese colonial
rule over the area. However, the city's liberators had no intention of
leaving soon. In fact, it would be ten years before the last batch of Soviet

troops and military officials departed in May 1955. The celebrations of 1955 were a sendoff and marked the closure of a unique chapter in the history of Sino-Soviet relations from the late 1940s to the mid-1950s.

The public portrayals of friendship in 1955 are more surprising when contrasted with the situation a decade earlier, when the Soviet military's looting of factories, rape of Chinese women, and violence against locals fostered negative images among the population. Common sayings among locals even likened the arrival of the Soviets to that of the Japanese: "the small noses [Japanese] have gone, but the big noses [Soviets] have arrived" *(zou le xiao bizi, lai le da bizi).*[3] At the peak of their military rule over the former Japanese colonial territory known as the Guandong Leased Territory (Kantō shū) in the late 1940s, the Soviets had stationed up to three hundred thousand troops in the area.[4] The Yalta agreement of the final days of World War II, and the subsequent "Sino-Soviet Treaty of Friendship and Alliance" of August 14, 1945, between the Nationalists and the Soviet Union, granted the Soviets a thirty-year lease to develop and maintain a naval base at Lüshun (Port Arthur), the boundaries of which extended northward to the town of Shihe. Half of the harbor facilities in Dalian were also leased to the Soviets, while the city was, in theory, to be administered by a "civilian" Chinese government. Importantly, the agreement promised to keep Dalian open as an international port, but only after a peace treaty had been settled with Japan.[5]

The Soviets' postwar prize had the potential to be a flashpoint in the emerging civil war and cold war conflicts. Both the Nationalists and the Chinese Communist Party (hereafter referred to as the party) intended to establish and control Dalian's civilian administration. The Nationalists, the internationally recognized government of China, had signed the "Sino-Soviet Treaty of Alliance" on August 14, 1945, and in September and October of that year their representatives began arriving in Dalian.[6] Expecting the port to be open to international shipping as stipulated in the Yalta agreement of February 11, 1945, the United States attempted to land navy officials in the city in 1946.[7] The party, expecting support from the Soviets, began rushing cadres from Yan'an, Shandong, and northeast China to Dalian in order to forge its own governing structure in the area.

Recent publications of internal documents and cadre memoirs reveal that problems and conflicts arose between Soviet military authorities and party cadres in Dalian over a host of issues, including questions of urban administration, industrial recovery, mass mobilization, and trade. Newly available sources, often firsthand accounts from those sent to work in Dalian, reveal that the "advantages" of Soviet military stability and expertise were not always so clear to the newly arrived cadres whose task it was to rebuild the society and economy of the territory. Some party cadres sent to Dalian even went so far as to characterize Soviet authority there as imperialistic. At stake were two of the key issues that the party confronted after 1945: how to govern cities and manage their resources and how to work with the Soviet Union in doing so.

Party cadres sent to Dalian came from rural revolutionary base areas throughout China. From their perspective, the city and surrounding rural suburbs must have seemed like fertile ground on which to sow the seeds of revolution. It had been under Japanese domination for forty years and was full of oppressed workers, traitorous landlords, and big business collaborators. Soviet military leaders, however, had a different agenda. The postwar Soviet Union had its own pressing needs, ones that Dalian's shipbuilding facilities, chemical industries, salt fields, and tax-free port facilities could help fulfill. Bound by international treaties that called for a nonmilitary Chinese civilian administration to be established in the area, the last thing the Soviets wanted was party-orchestrated mass political rallies, struggle sessions, and violent class struggle. For leaders in Moscow, such action would give the Nationalists, and their U.S. backers, the excuse to try to take away their postwar prize. Soviet authorities, acting in accordance with the complex political environment set up by the Yalta agreement, did not permit the party to openly operate in the Dalian area. It was not until April 1949 that the party was able to reveal its local administrative apparatus publicly.[8]

Sino-Soviet relations were a key facet of the post-1945 history of Dalian. Much of the existing scholarship on Sino-Soviet relations deals with the high politics surrounding the origins and decline of the relationship.[9] This chapter builds on such work by examining Sino-Soviet relations in Dalian and its outlying areas, from 1945 to 1955. It focuses on the Chinese side of the relationship and draws exclusively from Chinese source materials. Memoirs and official histories on politically sensitive subjects such as Sino-Soviet relations must be used carefully. In the late 1950s through the 1960s, when Sino-Soviet relations turned hostile, close ties to the Soviets were a political liability for party cadres.

Thus, many memoirs, while acknowledging certain benefits of the Soviet presence, tend to highlight friction and confrontation. When read together with official documents, however, these sources provide significant detail about the nature of the conflicts that existed between party cadres and Soviet authorities in Dalian, providing a stark contrast to public portrayals of solidarity and friendship. Further research is necessary in the archives of the former Soviet Union to adequately present the Soviet side.

The "Lüda Incident" and Sino-Soviet Political Relations in Occupied Dalian, 1945–50

As hundreds of party cadres poured into Dalian from rural liberated areas in late 1945, a key question was how their vision of governing a former Japanese colonial urban center might clash with that of the Soviet Union. Dalian may have been fertile ground for the party, but it was also an environment ripe for conflict. The political and social problems that lay ahead would test the early relations between the party and the Soviet Union. The "Lüda Incident" and its aftermath, in which several top-ranking party cadres in Dalian were ordered to step down by the Soviet military authorities, provide an important window through which to view local Sino-Soviet political relations in an understudied episode of modern Chinese history.[10]

Buildup to a Crisis: Street-Level Conflicts and Limitations to Communist Party Operations

The Soviet occupation army's mistreatment of Chinese civilians, particularly sexual assaults on Chinese women, put strains on Sino-Soviet relations soon after the arrival of party cadres in October 1945. Liu Yuquan was one of seven cadres from the Northeast Anti-Japanese Allied Army who were sent to Dalian by Soviet authorities to form a district police force. These men had spent time in the Soviet Union, wore Soviet military uniforms, and were among the first wave of party personnel sent to the area, often arriving alongside Soviet forces.[11] One day Liu discovered that two Soviet air force officers were raping a Chinese woman. Liu arrived on the scene and angrily refused to let the two men leave. During the heat of the argument, one of the officers unholstered his firearm and put a round in the chamber. Liu responded by firing at the man, killing him. The Soviet officer who Liu killed was a decorated war hero, a fact that prompted a full-scale investigation by Soviet authorities. Liu was eventually released on the grounds of self-defense and because the men had indeed raped the woman, but he was forced to leave Dalian. Dong Chongbin, also a Northeast Anti-Japanese Allied Army officer, likewise recalls having to forcibly stop a Soviet soldier from sexually assaulting a Chinese woman. Dong disarmed the man and brought him to a local police station.[12]

Less violent problems also lurked in the complicated task of building some sort of political order to govern the residents of Dalian. The Soviet Union, in accordance with the stipulations of the Yalta agreement, appointed a civilian mayor for Dalian. Mayor Chi Zixiang was a rich businessman from the colonial era who, together with Zhang Benzheng, the wealthiest Chinese entrepreneur in Dalian, had taken control of the city for several months after Japan's defeat.[13] Although Chi Zixiang was technically a figurehead, his presence at all official functions was a constant source of annoyance for the party. Han Guang, the party secretary in Dalian from October 1945 to July 1948, recalls the countless times he called on Soviet authorities to remove Chi, only to be rebuffed.[14] When meeting with Kozlov, the head of the Soviet military garrison in Dalian, Han asked whether he could appoint a party mayor and was bluntly informed that "Moscow had already made its decision."[15] In April 1947, when the Soviets established a civil administration for the whole of the Dalian area, Chi was again tabbed as the visible leader.

Troop misconduct and issues of unpopular political appointments began to subside by the middle of 1946, when a new problem arose, one with more damaging consequences for local party authority. As more and more cadres arrived from Shandong and north China, they began to go about their work using the tactics honed in rural base areas during the war against Japan. In both rural and urban areas of Dalian, businessmen, landlords, labor bosses, and former colonial police collaborators were all likely targets for the party's "settling of accounts" movement.

No sooner had these cadres started their operations than Soviet authorities began to restrict and, in some cases, violently stop them. Indeed, the years 1946 and 1947 may be viewed as a period of political contestation and conflict, where the different operating styles of party cadres and local Soviet military leaders clashed. With party urban policy still in its infancy, cadres found themselves not only on the front lines of forging a game plan for urban governance; they also had to deal on a daily basis with Soviet military authorities who attempted to restrain their efforts. Eventually, an emphasis on strengthening Sino-Soviet relations emerged as a dominant theme in political work. However, the strength of Soviet authority in Dalian had yet to be tested, and the attractiveness of Soviet guidance and models for urban management were, for many of the cadres sent here, secondary to their own tactics and needs. Even in Dalian's outlying rural areas, many of the party's standard tactics for developing mass support came under fire from Soviet military authorities.

The Soviets initially had no specific orders about activities in the countryside. That began to change, however, as cadres started to conduct "settling of accounts" movements and land reform in February and March 1946.[16] After witnessing a mass meeting in Jinxian, a rural area north of Dalian, Soviet authorities called for such activity to stop, for it seemed to them to be a disorderly, destabilizing attempt at social reordering. Party cadres believed that the Soviets simply did not understand their intentions and tactics.[17] Miscommunication had dire consequences for land reform activities in rural areas near Dalian. Cadres in a village southwest of Dalian organized a mass rally to denounce a local landlord. Informed that the meeting was a cover for armed bandits preparing to go on a looting spree, Soviet troops arrived and fired on the sizable crowd. The cadres in charge of the meeting were arrested, and it was only after Wang Qiren, the party secretary for Lüshun, urged an investigation into the matter that the men were released. Wang, a cadre sent from Shandong in November 1945, refused to accept Soviet interference in mass mobilization efforts. He openly confronted the Soviet officers, saying "Chiang Kai-shek doesn't grant the common people the freedom to assemble and now you Soviets won't allow them to hold meetings either!"[18]

But it was Jinxian that became a hotbed of conflict over land reform. In 1947, major problems erupted in Meijiacun village. Village cadres, defying Soviet orders, had been carrying out land reform "secretly." Soviet authorities soon discovered this and immediately called on Jinxian's party secretary, Chen Shaojing. Chen was told that the cadres involved would be jailed. The head of the Soviet garrison in the area reportedly even told the landlords involved not to worry, that this sort of trouble would soon stop.[19] A party work report also mentions problems in Jinxian. It describes an episode in which Soviet authorities, upon discovering land reform activities in an unnamed village, actually ordered cadres to return confiscated land to a landlord![20] The more their efforts were blocked, the more the cadres began to grumble that Soviets were against all agrarian work and were meddling in China's internal political issues.[21] Cadres such as Wang Lizhi, sent from Shandong to serve as a district head in Jinxian, were so despondent that they actually used a variety of excuses to leave. In Wang's case, he said he had to return home to look after his family. Actually he returned to work in his original base area.[22]

Efforts to hold mass meetings denouncing traitors and labor bosses within Dalian city limits likewise met with Soviet disapproval. In one incident, Soviet military forces broke up a mass rally led by cadres to denounce several Japanese accused of murdering Chinese. Fearing a major insurrection, Soviet commanders went as far as sending in tanks to disperse the crowd.[23] Liu Yunguang, a labor leader sent to Dalian in November 1945 from Shandong, recalls in his memoirs how critical such public activity was for the party's legitimacy. "We wanted to root out traitors, counterrevolutionaries, and landlords. Especially in 'the Red Building' (Hong fangzi), people there had started struggling against traitors and colonial-era henchmen. How could we stop them? We had to guide them. The Soviets did not allow us to hold these kinds of meetings. They said Moscow doesn't have these policies, and told us to stop them, and if we had carried them out, we were to correct our ways."[24] Han Guang, bowing to Soviet pressure, called for an end to this type of activity by late 1946.

The party's most successful programs in urban areas throughout 1946 and early 1947 aimed at alleviating the most pressing issues facing the urban poor. When these efforts did not include open struggle, or the forcible seizure of land and property, Soviet authorities were willing to grant the party some flexibility and assistance. One program involved a citywide movement to relocate poor families from outlying shantytown areas into the apartments and houses formerly occupied by Dalian's Japanese residents.[25]

While these measures ensured temporary social stability, the party in Dalian faced the greater challenge of how to manage and mold a more permanent urban society and how to bring factories back on line while providing for an urban workforce. Moreover, they had to do so in ways that did not conflict with Soviet authorities, who had their own agenda, to say nothing of greater experience in governing cities and managing labor in large-scale industries. These unique political conditions led cadres in Dalian to confront early on what would be one of the key themes in the history of the early People's Republic: to what extent, and in what capacity, would they follow the Soviet Union? Some cadres found the limitations placed on them to be too great. Others developed a distrust of Soviet officials and a disdain for their policies in Dalian. Matters came to a boiling point in 1947, as several of Dalian's top cadres began to speak out openly and aggressively against Soviet control and began refusing to follow Soviet policies.

Growing Pains: Local Cadres Revolt

One of the first things that party cadres did after they arrived in Dalian was to change their wardrobe. Quite literally, a fashion makeover was mandated by Soviet authorities for officials serving in the Guandong administration, the civilian government established by the Soviets in April 1947. Cadres in Dalian were expected to wear Western-style suits, a necktie, and leather shoes, not the military-style uniforms and clothing common in other base areas. Han Guang recalls, "[W]e called this the 'watermelon policy' *(xigua zhengci)*, green on the outside, red on the inside."[26] Other top party cadres were less willing to adapt to such conditions. Liu Shunyuan, vice party secretary of Dalian, despised this regulation. Born and raised a farmer in Shandong, he was never comfortable in a suit and tie. Liu even received jabs from Soviet officers for his grooming habits. One Soviet official reportedly commented to Han Guang about Liu, "Your man Liu, doesn't he have enough money for a haircut? Tell him to come in (to Soviet army headquarters) and we can loan him some."[27]

The issue of proper attire was but one of the policies and regulations in Dalian that were a difficult fit for many cadres. Throughout the late 1940s, the local party makeup could best be described as a diverse mix of revolutionary base area cadres, seasoned local underground operatives, and those like Han Guang, head of the party in Dalian, who had studied in the Soviet Union and had proficient Russian-language ability. They came to Dalian with different agendas. Some were sent from neighboring Shandong to purchase clothing, medicine, and even munitions for the party's civil war efforts. These people had little permanent stake in local politics; they were there to get what they needed and leave. Others were sent to establish all sorts of trade and small manufacturing companies to raise funds for their respective base areas.[28] Cadres such as Tang Yunchao, who headed the labor union after 1945, were born in the area and had been working as underground operatives for years. Others, such as Liu Shunyuan, arrived from Shandong to serve in the local government. This diversity made forging a single road for urban management difficult. It also led cadres to view Soviet authority through a variety of lenses based on their own background and experience.

In 1947, divisions among this diverse cast of party leaders emerged at the crucial moment when the party's mission grew from controlling rural areas to include larger urban centers, particularly in the northeast. Those in charge of Dalian were on the forefront of a trend culminating in Mao's 1949 proclamation that the city was to lead the countryside.[29] The party's political mission was shifting, and many cadres in charge of urban work found themselves criticized throughout 1947–48 for their continued attempt to transfer rural-based policies to urban environments. Yet in Dalian, one must also take into account conflicts between party cadres and Soviet authorities as part of this political picture. Serious rifts began emerging between local cadres in positions of authority and their Soviet counterparts as the latter's way of doing things began to be widely implemented. This conflict led to a major Soviet-initiated shakeup of local leadership in late 1947 that highlights the extent of Soviet power and the centrality of the Sino-Soviet relationship in local politics in Dalian.

To best explain what happened between party leaders and Soviet authorities, it is worth briefly examining the backgrounds and actions of two of the main cadres involved in the "Lüda Incident" of 1947. Tang Yunchao arrived in Dalian in 1945 from neighboring Jinzhou, where he had worked in an underground capacity during the final year of the War of Resistance. Tang was a local man, born in Jinzhou. He had spent his career organizing workers in Dalian throughout the 1920s and had served three jail terms for his activities there.[30] Armed with the task of organizing workers and building the foundations for a massive labor union, Tang's main charge in August 1945 was to create teams to protect factories and industrial equipment from being stolen or destroyed. By early September 1945, Tang's union attracted two hundred members representing fifty-two different small factories. It continued to grow exponentially within a matter of months.[31] His reputation for looking out for workers and his fiery confrontational tactics earned him the respect of his constituents but also garnered disdain from his targets, including wealthy colonial-era businessmen such as Zhang Benzheng, from whom Tang regularly demanded cash donations for his union.[32]

It was, however, his attitude toward the Soviet occupation forces that would have the most profound effect on Tang's career. As efforts to revive production picked up steam in late 1946 and early 1947, Tang's clashes with Soviet authorities escalated. This was particularly true in factories under Soviet control.[33] His distrust and eventual rejection of Soviet guidance stemmed from several specific incidents. The first issue involved a loss of face for Tang. Soviet factory leaders at the Dalian locomotive factory, a former Japanese industry under Soviet control, told Chinese workers that they were safeguarding equipment and new uniforms in the factory storehouse. Tang negotiated a purchase price for the goods, and upon delivery of the cash, the items were to be distributed to his workers. It turned out that what he had negotiated to buy were nothing but piles of rags and used uniforms. When Tang demanded the money be returned, his requests were denied.[34] He had been cheated, and his workers knew it.

Conflicts lurked in the area of wages as well. Through 1946 and 1947, workers in Dalian's factories were frequently paid in grain. Promised that his workers in Soviet-controlled factories would have comparable salaries to those in Chinese enterprises (which had higher wages as part of the party's policy for developing the support of the working class), Tang found that in fact workers at the Soviet enterprises were receiving between five and ten kilograms less grain than those at Chinese factories. According to Soviet authorities, Tang reported this through his union publications and even allowed his workers to refer to the Soviet Union as "an imperialist country." In spring 1947 Tang complained openly about these issues at a welcoming meeting for a general from the Soviet Far East Military division. For the Soviets, Tang's behavior crossed the line. In a summary of their indictment against him, Soviet authorities highlighted the following incidents. Tang's union routinely ignored Soviet proclamations and failed to carry articles lauding the Soviet's liberation of the northeast in their publications. His popularity led workers to "praise him for helping them, for liberating them," while no mention was made of Soviet assistance.[35] Concerned primarily with the immediate welfare of his workers, Tang, according to the Soviets, saw little future in his trade union's relationship with them. In one of the few references made to Northeast Bureau Party Secretary Gao Gang in available sources, Tang mentions in his memoir that Gao had pronounced him guilty of being "anti-Soviet" *(fan Su)*. Tang's days in Dalian were numbered.

Liu Shunyuan was one of the top cadres in Dalian. He was the city's vice–party secretary and also the vice-chair of the visible "civilian" government, the "Guandong Administrative Office" (Guandong xingzheng gongshu) set up by the Soviets in April 1947.[36] Liu was also one of the most outspoken critics of Soviet authority, and it was his contestation of several key policies that set in motion a major purge of party leadership in Dalian. To be sure, even before his protests arose over specific policies, Liu had problems with the Soviets' way of doing things. In his memoirs, he recalls what he considered to be the oppressive presence of Soviet liaison officers in all party organizations. "Every office, no matter how big or small, had a Soviet military representative, and for all affairs, big or small, you had to have his support to do anything," he complained. "When they wanted something done it was handed down like an order. If you argued, or refused to act you would be reprimanded." Particularly disturbing for Liu was the Soviet presence at party meetings, even at those where cadres were criticized. "When, in our meetings, the discussion heated up, they [Soviets] were there, watching and listening. I never grew accustomed to this."[37]

The first of Liu's major confrontations involved his outright criticism and mistrust of Soviet authorities in carrying out currency reforms in 1947. The Soviet military had been issuing its own currency since arriving in the northeast in August 1945. The party feared that the Nationalists might use the Soviet military notes they collected in other parts of the northeast to flood the Dalian market, severely affecting prices and causing even more economic instability. To solve the problem, Soviet authorities initiated a plan to revalue the notes in circulation. Residents could exchange their old Soviet military dollars for new ones at the set rate of ten to one. A limit of $300 (of old notes) per person could be exchanged.[38] Liu and other top cadres had little or no knowledge of the plan until it was ready to be implemented and had no say in the exchange rates. Liu was fearful of the effects the switch might have on the average resident's standard of living, and he vehemently protested the idea. He even ordered subordinates to disregard the policy. Soviet authorities, trying to ease the situation, explained to Liu and other skeptics that they had conducted research into the matter, and the situation would only hurt rich people, not average workers.[39] Liu simply did not trust Soviets or their policies.

Liu's protests hit crisis level, however, when he began to openly denounce and ignore his posting in the Soviet-installed civilian government. Criticizing the organization for being composed of capitalist big businessmen, he refused to participate in any of its important activities. When the head of the Soviet Civil Administration Office (Minzheng ju) in Lüshun ordered Liu to act in his capacity as a vice-chair by participating in a meeting in Jinzhou organized to commemorate the Soviet army's liberation of the northeast, he simply refused to show up.[40] Liu was also noticeably absent from later high-profile meetings commemorating the liberation of Dalian.

His refusal to sign an agreement setting up Sino-Soviet joint enterprises was the final straw for Soviet authorities. In his own words, Liu recalls his interpretation of the Sino-Soviet companies. "The Soviets were afraid the Nationalists would regain control of Dalian and all of its industrial capacity," he wrote. "So they set up these 'Sino-Soviet' industries in the event that even if the Nationalists came, the Soviets could maintain control over them. Actually we [the party] were merely hanging our name on such industries, while in reality the Soviets were in complete control." When called to Lüshun to sign the agreement, Liu flatly refused. He was informed that the treaty must be signed that day, and he remembers waiting for hours well after nightfall until finally being allowed to see the document. He refused to sign, saying that he and other party cadres must first adequately review the agreement. The presence of an eager-to-sign Chi Zixiang, the colonial-era industrialist then serving as the figurehead chairman of the Guandong government, made Liu even angrier.[41]

With top cadres such as Liu and Tang openly confronting Soviet policy, issues of authority and of the nature of the role of the party in rebuilding Dalian came to a boiling point in 1947. By September the

Soviets had had enough. On September 17, Soviet military authorities vented their criticisms and frustrations in a meeting with Du Ping, a leading cadre in the Northeast Democratic Allied Army (Dongbei minzhu lianjun) on an inspection trip to the area. For Du and other party leaders such as Han Guang it became apparent that both the party's own goals in the area and its relationship with the Soviets needed to be clarified. Tang and Liu's behavior would no longer be tolerated. Soviet authorities told Du that "when your comrades engage with us [Soviets] they should not be so arrogant. Please believe us, if you follow us, then the area's economic problems will surely be fixed and we can help with your plans." Addressing the issue of Liu Shenyuan, Du was informed that "Liu simply doesn't get it. This place is under Soviet military control. He thinks it shouldn't be. He thinks that it should be just like other liberated areas, under the control of the party." The critique continues: "Liu thinks capitalists and landlords should have their money taken from them. We feel that economic recovery needs the cooperation of all, including capitalists, workers, and the common people." Liu and others were accused of taking tactics and policies from other liberated areas and applying them in Dalian and of disregarding Soviet authority.[42]

In Du's view, something had to be done, or conflicts would continue. In response to the criticisms put forth by the Soviets, Han Guang called for a meeting of top cadres in October 1947 in order to spell out what was now becoming the "correct line" on the role of local Sino-Soviet relations and to lay to rest what lingering conflicts remained between the party and the Soviet authorities in Dalian. A policy of "Putting Soviets First" (yi Su wei zhu), which called for the strengthening of Sino-Soviet relations across the board in Dalian, became a central feature of the political landscape.[43] Top local cadres such as Han Guang were now caught in the middle. The main issue for leaders like Han was how to carry out this new line in a context of ongoing Sino-Soviet conflict that continued to damage the party's relations with the local populace.

Picking Up the Pieces: "Putting Soviets First"

When the smoke had cleared from the political conflicts and meetings held in late 1947, the Soviets had successfully demanded the removal of three of the five top-ranking party cadres in Dalian. The leadership core in Dalian had been purged. The party lost the popular head of the area's largest labor organization in Tang Yunchao, and it lost a vice–party secretary in Liu Shunyuan. Also ousted was the head of police, Bian Zhangwu, and several other labor organizers.[44] Bian Zhangwu was removed for "secretly increasing production without notifying Soviet authorities."[45] This incident illuminates the extent of the Soviets' power in Dalian. It is clear that openly criticizing Soviet policy and authority had disastrous political consequences for party cadres.

It must be pointed out that these meetings came at a time when the party was starting its anti-leftist campaign, when much of what cadres such as Liu Shunyuan and Tang Yunchao believed in would come under attack.[46] However, the initial impetus for removing Liu and Tang stemmed from their refusal to recognize Soviet authority. Top cadres in the northeast believed that these cadres had stepped out of line in their critique of the Soviets. In other words, the party's relationship with Soviet authorities was a major factor in local politics. The new political line for governing urban centers was swinging to the right, toward more Soviet-style policies and reforms. For local cadres in Dalian this meant acceptance of Soviet authority. Would cadres like Tang and Liu have been removed as leftists regardless of their conflicts with Soviets? According to internal documents and minutes from party meetings that aim to explain to other cadres just why these men were banished, Liu and Tang's main fault was their insolence toward Soviet authority. Liu recalls in his memoirs being briefed by top party cadres, such as Liu Shaoqi, about why he needed to understand the new line and to work with the Soviets. Despite their removal from Dalian, Tang and Liu continued to hold top positions in other areas.[47]

One of the first points Han Guang put forth at the October 1947 meeting was that "the main responsibility of our work in Guandong is to act in accordance with the needs of this Soviet controlled base area." Another was to "uphold the Soviets and propagate their policies."[48] The meeting also pointed out the urgent need to develop better communication between Soviet and party authorities, particularly with regard to policy implementation. Han was clear that although top cadres had erred in their rejection of Soviet authority and in their assumption that Dalian was like other liberated areas, Soviet military officials were also to blame for their attitudes toward party cadres. "As for incidents of Soviet chauvinism, we are not to blindly tolerate and accommodate this," he ordered. "Rather, you should criticize such behavior like you would criticize that of a fellow comrade."[49] To conclude, Han spelled out why there were so many problems: "We have no plan for the management of economic and social life. We have no concrete plan for economic development." The task of the party was now twofold: to push its new slogan of "develop production, stabilize the people's lives" and to do so by following the Soviets.[50] The irony of this, from the view of a local leader such as Han Guang, was that doing the latter seemed to interfere with the former.

The party's own rectification movement in 1948 would further cement the new line. The mistakes of Liu and Tang brought top cadres in charge of the northeast to Dalian in order to resolve past mistakes and lay out future plans. Zhang Wentian, a leading cadre from the Northeast Bureau in charge of organizational work, held one such meeting for top cadres in Dalian. In his opening remarks, Zhang noted that "those comrades with responsibility here have had some shortcomings, for example, their work style had problems in terms of dealing with relations among classes. Fortunately we have the Soviets to help us, and if we follow their basic policies, we can avoid much turmoil. The Soviets are wiser than we."[51]

Yet what did putting Soviets first mean in Dalian? It meant foremost that class struggle in both urban and rural areas was to take a backseat to increasing production, which became the main shared goal between the party and the Soviet authorities. Following the Soviets also meant developing and using a system of courts to take care of social problems and crime. In liberated areas throughout China, the party had grown accustomed to handing out punishments at mass meetings. Soviets wanted such sentencing to take place behind closed doors, within the confines of a courtroom. Thus they instructed the party to build up legal, police, and surveillance systems to manage society.[52] Cadres were also urged to "take this opportunity to study our Soviet comrades' management of factories, industries, trade, anti-espionage tactics, and propaganda efforts."[53]

All this was consistent with a well-known shift in party policy in late 1947 through 1948.[54] The situation in Dalian, like in the rest of party-held urban centers, was in part a conflict between two party lines, one pro-Soviet and the other favoring more indigenous policies. What complicates Dalian's experience even more, however, was the reality of local Soviet military authority. Despite the call to follow and learn from the Soviets, many cadres in Dalian still had qualms about following Soviet policy when their firsthand experience working with Soviets had been so strained. A wry slogan circulated among doubtful cadres at the time reflects this apprehension: "Putting the Soviets first is to make us their slaves" *(yi Su wei zhu, yi women wei nu)*.[55] Bowing to Soviet authority not only meant learning from foreign expertise; it also put local cadres on the spot in terms of how to deal with new and ongoing conflicts.

Local party leaders such as Han Guang were in the difficult situation of having to implement the policy shift while at the same time resolving ongoing conflicts with Soviet authorities. To this end, Han Guang and other top cadres sent a carefully crafted six thousand-character letter to the head of the Soviet military command in Lüshun on March 15, 1948, outlining problem areas in party-Soviet relations. This document provides valuable insight into the party's perception of Soviet attitudes toward local cadres at the time. It also gives us a glimpse of what the Soviets expected to gain from their control of Dalian. The document mentions several problem areas, including issues of taxation and trade, continued Soviet interference in the party's work with the "masses," and communication breakdowns between the public Guandong civil authorities and the Soviets' own civil administration office.[56]

Conflicts over trade and taxation reveal the extent of Soviet control over Dalian's economy. The Soviet military, in full control of Dalian's sizable port facilities, exported goods tax free to the Soviet Union using its military ships. However, civilian vessels had their cargoes taxed. In spring of 1948, however, a nonmilitary Soviet trading vessel docked at a pier in Dalian and ordered the Chinese dockworkers to begin loading the ship with salt. The captain refused to pay any taxes on his cargo. Upon hearing this news, Han Guang ordered the dockworkers to strike. They were not to load this ship until the matter was resolved. After some consultation with Soviet military authorities, the issue was resolved, and the Soviets promised such a situation would not happen again.[57] For Han, there was more at stake than just tax revenues on salt shipments. How could local cadres be expected to learn from the Soviet Union when its local representatives were trying to cheat them?

Han's letter also illuminates other ways in which the Soviets intended to gain and protect economic advantages in Dalian, even if it resulted in damaging the party's ability to carry out its programs and promises to the local population. Han's major complaint involved the Soviets' manipulation of trade and falsification of export records. One such instance involved trading salt (a local product) for valuable fertilizer, no doubt part of the party's promises to aid local farmers. The Soviets were to receive the salt in exchange for a preset amount of fertilizer. Yet the Soviets, who accepted the salt, failed to deliver the promised amount of fertilizer, causing, as Han notes, considerable damage to the party's agricultural planning in the region. He also discusses conflicts arising over the manipulation of the prices of important local crops such as peanuts, with the Soviets demanding that peanuts be traded on the "free market" at lower prices.[58]

The emphasis on production led Soviets to order a decrease in holiday time in Dalian. This became an issue for the party, which had promised workers certain rest days and holidays. Han Guang's letter cites a specific example of how this caused a significant loss of face for party officials, who actually had to cancel a holiday that they had already promised to hold. The case involved a planned day off for International Women's Day, March 8, 1948. The party, after highly publicizing the plan, was ordered by the Soviet authorities to cancel the holiday. Han notes this was a major dent to the legitimacy of the party-led women's federation and the Guandong government. Even Chi Zixiang, who owed his political position to the Soviets, complained, "See, I approved of it [the holiday], the vice chair approved it, county leaders approved of it, city leaders approved of it, but in the end without Soviet approval, we cannot do anything."[59]

In April 1949, the party in Dalian finally went public. This move in and of itself was of great benefit to local Sino-Soviet relations, particularly for the party, which could now take a more active, open role in governing the area. Moreover, in September of that year the work of both party cadres and Soviet military authorities in Dalian went on display for all of new China to see, as Dalian played host to a major industrial exhibition that drew over three hundred thousand visitors to the city. Showcasing the fruits of Dalian's reinvigorated industrial base was one objective of the exhibition, but the city itself was also on display. Sino-Soviet relations were a highly visible part of the definition of new Dalian. Articles in magazines published throughout China praised Dalian as "new China's model city," marked by "vitality, order, a city where everyone is laboring and sharing in production."[60] The final hall of the industrial exhibition, "the hall of Sino-Soviet friendship," featured the history of the party's relationship with the Soviet Union, Soviet military heroics in the liberation of the northeast, and exhibitions of local industry, education, and culture, all of which pointed out the great assistance of the Soviets in building new Dalian.[61] One group of journalists even proclaimed Dalian to be "a workers' paradise."[62]

Governing Dalian was, for many party cadres, a painful learning experience, as their strategies were questioned and blocked by Soviet authorities. In their desire to maintain order and reap economic and trade advantages in the area, Soviet interests often ignored or even damaged the party's needs and plans. Tang Yunchao, the labor leader expelled from Dalian, must have had his doubts when he read that the city had become a paradise for workers. But there were indeed changes, and Sino-Soviet ties were strengthened between the conflicts of 1947 and the emergence of Dalian as a "model city" in 1949. The real difference came after 1950, when a treaty was signed with the newly established People's Republic government formally ending Soviet military rule over Dalian. At Mao's request, Soviet troops remained in Dalian throughout the Korean War to better protect the area from possible attack from the United States, but they did not hold the governing powers they once had.[63]

From "Big Noses" to "Big Brothers": Sino-Soviet Cultural Relations in Dalian, 1945–52

There is, of course, another side to the Sino-Soviet relationship in Dalian. How did ordinary people experience the ten-year Soviet military presence there? Equally important, in what ways did the party mobilize residents there in support of its own agenda while operating in accordance with Soviet authority? The local population, with little or no knowledge of the Soviet Union or its brand of socialism, likewise harbored doubts about why the Soviet military was in charge in Dalian. They viewed Soviets as foreigners. Stories of Soviet troops raping, looting, and removing industrial equipment were well known. Locals often used racial slurs to describe Soviet troops. In some cases the attitude and behavior of individual Soviet commanders could rouse local condemnation.[64] Popular religious groups took advantage of the fear and anger some locals felt at having another foreign occupying army in town and spread anti-Soviet, antiparty messages.[65]

How to change negative perceptions of Soviet authorities was one of the major challenges confronting local party cadres in Dalian. They faced the difficult task of having to explain the Soviet military presence in the area while at the same time establishing their own authority and organizations among the local population. Movies, newspapers, social organizations, and even summer camps modeled after those held for Soviet children were all highly visible efforts used by the party to accomplish this multifaceted goal and reinforce an internationalist image that China was on the verge of enjoying the fruits of socialism just like the Soviet Union was. These examples are representative of widespread efforts to reach large segments of society and spread the message that acceptance of Soviet authority was the only acceptable political option in Dalian.

Sino-Soviet Friendship Associations

By far the most prevalent organization in Dalian for promoting Soviet culture was the Sino-Soviet Friendship Association. Originally formed in late 1945, the first such organization was used largely as a front for party operations in Dalian.[66] After 1947, in accordance with the party's new push to strengthen Sino-Soviet relations in Dalian, the role of friendship associations grew, and by 1949 one-quarter of the area's population claimed membership in one of more than 800 branches. The Sino-Soviet Friendship Association served to propagate Soviet culture through films, newspapers, magazines, lectures, and discussions. They were also important forums for cadres to discuss and listen to what people felt about the Soviets.[67] By 1949, the Guandong Sino-Soviet Friendship Association claimed to have held over 180 photography exhibitions and 3,000 discussion sessions and to have shown 700 Soviet films.[68]

Several articles in the main publication of the Guandong Sino-Soviet Friendship Association (Guandong Zhong-Su youhao xiehui), the journal *Friendship (Youyi)*, highlight the activities of the association's discussion groups. These were designed to teach people about the Soviet Union and about the role of the Soviet military in liberating and helping to build a new society in Dalian. One such article describes a Friendship Association meeting in Siergou, one of the poorest neighborhoods in Dalian. Early on, cadres held meetings and lectured to neighborhood residents about Soviet socialism, only to find out that people had no idea what they were talking about. Eventually residents got the message that the Soviet Union was good. However, in the words of an oil mill worker attending one such lecture, "I knew the Soviet Union was good, and that it was a socialist country, but I didn't really understand how it was good, was it the same as socialism?"[69]

Other workers had their doubts about Soviet intentions on the peninsula. After listening to a lecture on the history of colonial oppression in Dalian, one worker asked the highly charged question, "How is it that this used to be a Russian concession, and now it has been liberated by the Soviets? Aren't the Soviets Russian people after all? What is going on?"[70] Addressing the need to provide more specifics about the Soviet experience and the role of the Soviet military in Dalian, cadres at subsequent meetings spent more time introducing various aspects of Soviet society and culture. This included discussions of Soviet labor conditions, factory worker life, family life, and the role of women in Soviet society. Cadres also paid significant attention to explaining Soviet foreign policy, the Sino-Soviet Friendship Agreement, and the role of the Soviet military in the "liberation" of Dalian.[71]

One way the party tried to generate a good image of the Soviet troops stationed in Dalian was through storytelling at such meetings. Usually this involved inviting a speaker to talk about heroic deeds performed by Soviet soldiers for the benefit of local Chinese. These stories were collected and frequently circulated at meetings and in newspapers. Interestingly, their messages contributed to conflicting images of just what the relationship with the Soviet Union was. On one hand, the Soviet Union was presented in films and newspapers as a socialist paradise, a status to be attained by China some day; on the other hand, we see cases where people in slum neighborhoods such as Siergou were identifying with Soviets because they understood them to be like themselves: poor. For example Mr. Li, an employee at a tobacco plant, upon hearing a friendship story, exclaimed, "See, our Soviet big brothers are really great; this just goes to show you that all poor people under heaven are one family."[72]

Regardless of these mixed messages, Sino-Soviet friendship stories spread through the Friendship Association and local newspapers were heavily used tools in propagating Sino-Soviet relations to the general public. By the early 1950s in Dalian, these stories consisted of several main themes. Some recounted heroic efforts on the part of Soviet soldiers to aid local Chinese, which often involved saving the life of a child or an elderly person.[73] Stories with an emphasis on the family were another major theme. In Dalian, these went beyond the standard familial references to Soviets as "Soviet elder brother" *(Sulian lao dage)*. Here, it is the Soviet military that is brought into the family, as stories tell of Chinese children professing their love for Soviet soldier "uncles" *(Su jun shushu)* and Soviet mothers.[74] The maternal theme was a particularly potent way to propagate an image of Soviets in Dalian as protecting and helping Chinese people.

Some stories combated negative images of Soviet troops as "foreigners." For example, Song Fengchou, a sixth grader, wrote an article titled "I love my Soviet army uncle" *(Wo ai Su jun shushu)* in which he learns that his "uncle," a Soviet officer in his neighborhood, is really not like other foreigners. He asks, "In the past, when we lived under Chiang Kai-shek's bandit regime in Nanjing, I used to see American soldiers and fear for my life. Why is it that when I see Soviet soldiers I am not only not afraid, but I find it easy to be around them?" The answer, provided by Song's mother, is of course that "Americans are an imperialist country," while "Soviets are socialists like us."[75] Here the message is that it was the common bond of socialism that transformed the foreign soldier into someone more familiar, in this case part of the family.

The theme of motherhood was another feature of friendship stories, and those involving Soviet women adopting Chinese children were not uncommon. Many of these surfaced in 1955, when Soviet troops and their families finally pulled out of Dalian. These usually build up to a tearful parting at a train station, where a Chinese individual is left to watch his or her Soviet family return home. Yan Shouming, for example, lived with a Soviet family for nine years, and her story was publicized in a daily newspaper. In her column, Yan remembers that her Soviet mom "loved me just as much as my birth mother loved me. I believe that all Soviet mothers love all Chinese children." Yan wrote of her sorrow upon her family's departure, "My most beloved mother, my dearest brothers and sisters finally departed from me, how could I be anything but sad?"[76]

These stories contrast greatly with the very real political tensions between party cadres and Soviet authorities during the late 1940s. It is difficult to imagine how popular indifference and outright resentment and resistance to Soviet military authority had been so quickly transformed into familial love. Obviously these stories did not reflect reality for most people in Dalian. Friendship stories were designed to humanize Soviet troops, often through familial rhetoric, and to present an image of them as helpful and caring toward Chinese residents. They reached their peak during the Korean War and during the months leading up to the Soviet military withdrawal from Dalian in 1955, after most of the political conflict had ended and acceptance of a Soviet presence became the only political option. These stories were one way of driving this point home to people. How could one despise the Soviets in Dalian when they were presented as such caring mothers and heroic soldiers? Likewise, cadres at Friendship Association meetings were bombarding workers, housewives, and students with images and information about the Soviet Union, all of which made criticism of Soviet policy in Dalian increasingly difficult.

The work of Sino-Soviet Friendship Associations was thus twofold. The main tasks of this organization in the aftermath of the Dalian incident were to disseminate information about Soviet culture, to popularize the Soviet Union's style of socialism, and to build positive images of the Soviets' presence in Dalian. These associations also represent one of the ways that the party adapted to unique political conditions set up by Soviet authorities. Unable to openly present their agenda to key social groups such as workers before 1949, party cadres were able to use these meetings to increase people's knowledge and acceptance of socialism and carry out important groundwork for the day when the party would govern Dalian free of Soviet interference. In this way the associations represent an important compromise, satisfying the need to smooth out relations with Soviets while also serving as an environment for the party to organize key social groups and educate them about the socialist cause. The Sino-Soviet Friendship Association's highly publicized efforts to praise the Soviet military, and to humanize Soviet troops and their families, aimed to demonstrate that Soviet troops were there to help people. They rescued children, they protected Dalian from American imperialist invasion, and they were shown to be loved by Chinese as "family." In other words, Soviet troops belonged here.

Such institutions likewise helped to integrate Dalian into the newly formed People's Republic by characterizing it as a Sino-Soviet city, a place that was shown to have benefited from the presence of Soviet troops and had used the experience to model urban society after that of the Soviet Union. Cadres had lost the political battle to carry out reforms in the late 1940s the way they had in other liberated areas. Forced into a compromise, much of their work was done through institutions and organizations that were designed to propagate Sino-Soviet messages of friendship and solidarity and to make promises that a Soviet-style socialist society was at hand. Socialism was introduced to residents of Dalian in a Sino-Soviet package with methods and messages borrowed from the Soviet Union.

Dalian's experience highlights the differences in Chinese and Soviet approaches to the process of making revolution and constructing a socialist state. For those cadres sent to Dalian, Soviet actions and regulations there were often viewed as restrictive and foreign, compared with strategies used in rural base areas. Soviet authorities, like many conquest regimes, emphasized keeping order, particularly in the early years of their occupation. In contrast, the rural party's strategies for building mass social revolution from below took a backseat to stabilizing the economy and rebuilding industry. As the political winds shifted toward appeasing Soviets locally, the emerging position of the party itself toward urban governance placed great emphasis on the Soviet model. Party cadres in Dalian struggled to operate under Soviet authority, which often meant promoting Sino-Soviet relations and a Soviet model for China's future.

This chapter crosses the 1949 barrier and views the early 1950s as part of a process for rebuilding and reordering society in Dalian that began in August 1945. Thus to understand the early 1950s, we must recognize a longer takeover period that stretched back to 1945. The case of Dalian can also add to our understanding of urban change during the early years of the People's Republic, and it raises important questions for comparison with other cities. How did Dalian's experience, heavily influenced by the Soviet Union, differ from that of later liberated cities such as Shanghai, in which the Soviet presence was not as strong? Dalian's postwar experience provides an important baseline for comparing the process of building socialism in China's major cities during the formative years of the People's Republic.

Dalian emerged from forty years of Japanese colonial rule to become a central place in the industrial recovery of the People's Republic in the early 1950s. A visitor to the city during the 1949 industrial exhibition, which served as Dalian's highly publicized introduction to new China, praised this model city. But his report also contained a hint of uncertainty. The author mentions the necessity of making sure that Dalian "faced" *(miandui)* the whole country in the future and that the benefits that the city was sure to reap were not limited to Dalian itself.[77] Probably the author was concerned about the sharing of the city's wealth with the Soviet Union—hence the need to "face" China. For the time being, ideological and economic realities pointed toward greater contact between the two nations. Yet from the perspective of the party cadres who had survived the political conflicts of the late 1940s, it must have been ironic that the bronze statue of a Soviet soldier grasping his machine gun, atop a marble tower in Dalian built to commemorate the Soviet military's liberation of the region, stared directly through the office windows of the Dalian municipal government, as if watching everything.

✥ 8

The Call of the Oases: The "Peaceful Liberation" of Xinjiang, 1949–53

James Z. Gao

IN 1949, after a protracted trial of strength with the Nationalists, the Communist Party completed its triumph over all of mainland China. The Communists stepped into different political and cultural landscapes and designed diverse approaches to control and transform the country's local societies. To no one's surprise, the new rulers encountered very different challenges in China's frontier areas, where non-Han people constituted the majority of the local population. Recent literature on the Communist takeover, however, only tells the story of areas where residents were overwhelmingly Han Chinese. It does not disclose the implications of the 1949 revolution for China's ethnic minorities.[1] To bridge this gap, this chapter explores the Communist movement in China's northwestern frontier region, an event that came to be known as the "peaceful liberation" of Xinjiang.

This chapter examines the Communist takeover of Xinjiang from the perspective of frontier history, treating it as a political transformation as well as a sociocultural process. It begins by examining the interaction of different political and cultural forces (including Han and non-Han, Chinese and foreign) in the frontier area, then moves to the various circumstances that led to the Communist takeover, and finally concludes with the arrival and settlement of the women soldiers of the People's Liberation Army (PLA) in Xinjiang. The presence of women in the newly developed oases finally completed the "peaceful liberation" of Xinjiang.

Frontier Politics

The Xinjiang frontier was opened up by Manchu military expansion during the seventeenth century. This occurred in a situation in which the indigenous people, the Kazakhs and Uyghurs, were living in small groups isolated from one another. Xinjiang's capital Dihua (today Urumqi) was built in 1763. The first group of Han merchants came with the Manchu army, who soon discovered a good opportunity for barter and exchange. The shipment of agricultural produce to the city of Dihua opened a new frontier on which Han and non-Han people made their early contacts. As the Manchu emperor Qianlong assigned the city the name Dihua (*qidi jiaohua*, meaning "enlighten and educate"), he hoped that the municipal government not only would rule over the land but would also educate and assimilate these indigenous populations. For a long time, Dihua had remained a frontier zone where indigenous culture met and clashed with intruders, while the majority of the indigenous people continued to live in the numerous isolated oases of the Tarim Basin.

Justin Jon Rudelson has noted that the "historical focus of the Xinjiang oases was not inward, toward each other, but outward, across borders."[2] It was true that communication among the desert oases was less than the contacts between the oasis dwellers and outside people. The southern Tarim Basin was mostly influenced by Indian culture, while the northern basin was influenced by the western Turkestan region. The northwest part of Xinjiang was oriented to central Asian countries, and the eastern part was tied closely to China proper.[3]

China has long been characterized by a center-periphery dichotomy, where China proper dominated such peripheral areas as Xinjiang, Tibet, and Inner Mongolia. From the perspective of people in Xinjiang, however, China proper constituted their peripheral area, and everything that happened in China proper had only a marginal meaning for them. Neither the 1911 Revolution nor the Sino-Japanese War (1937–45) directly affected Xinjiang. Most of its residents expressed a cynical attitude toward regime changes in China proper. The first Republican governor of Xinjiang, Yang Zengxin, looked down on all the warlord governments in Beijing, but he recognized every central authority in light of the principle "worship the temple but not the gods inside." Following this tenet, his successors were always ready to deal with any new government that came to power in Nanjing or Beijing.[4] This was because most government officials in the frontier area were Han Chinese. Recognition from the central government bolstered their authority over the indigenous non-Han people and legitimized the persecution of their rivals as well as of political dissidents.[5] Also, since the Qing dynasty the local military supply and government budget had mainly depended on financial support from the central government. "Worship the temple but not the gods inside" proved to be a successful strategy for confirming the legitimacy of the local government and avoiding conflicts with China proper.

In the Republican years, inadequate transportation, insufficient communication, and decreasing fiscal support from the Nanjing government set the "new dominion" apart from China proper, making it into "an autonomous appendage of the Chinese state."[6] Sheng Shicai, a Han warlord, ruled Xinjiang for eleven years and built his own despotic kingdom. In 1934, Chiang Kai-shek planned a military expedition against Sheng, devoting 15 million yuan and mobilizing 150,000 troops, but he was informed that it would still be impossible to guarantee the troops adequate food, water, fuel, and other supplies.[7] When Chiang canceled the campaign, Sheng commented, "Chiang Kai-shek does not like my policies but he cannot do anything to me. I am too far away from his reach."[8] After Sheng Shicai finally left office, Chiang Kai-shek appointed him minister of agriculture and forestry, arguing that despite his cruelty and dictatorship, "Sheng did not declare independence from Nanjing nor did he permit the Russians to annex Xinjiang."[9] The departure of Sheng Shicai saw the replacement of one Han warlord by another, which did not change the conditions for mistrust, resentment, and rebellion among non-Han people. It remained difficult for Han provincial governments in Xinjiang to penetrate rural areas. Heavy taxation and forced labor service provoked several revolts among the Uyghurs and Kazakhs. The term "Han" became a synonym for oppression and corruption. "To compete with the Han," the oasis dwellers developed a "new Uyghur ethnic identity."[10]

Nonetheless, frontier history was also a process of collaboration and assimilation. Although Dihua became a more sinicized city, an increasing number of Uyghurs went to the city to receive their education, to conduct business, and to engage in politics. To rule the frontier city, the Han rulers had to seek indigenous allies, a strategy designed to "control the situation by using Islamic imams."[11] In the 1940s, the Nationalists began to recruit young urban intellectuals to join the administration. Burhan Shahidi was regarded as a man with a "strong sense of the motherland [China]" and was appointed governor of the province.[12] Saifudin Azizi, a pro-China Uyghur, became the provincial commissioner of education. These appointments, however, did not change the Nationalist view that real power always had to remain in the hands of the Han military leaders.

The frontier history of Xinjiang during the first half of the twentieth century was marked by warlordism and the growth of foreign influence. As with all frontiers, there were multiple intrusive forces in Xinjiang—Turkish, Russian, and British. In constant competition with one another, no single external power succeeded in establishing its hegemony. Sheng Shicai allied with Moscow to consolidate his dictatorship, while Zhang Zhizhong used the Pan-Turkish leader Masud Sabri to restrain Russian influence. Fluid frontier politics took place under the shadows cast by foreign powers.

As Tsarist Russia focused on political and economic expansion, the Ottoman Empire initiated its cultural penetration of Xinjiang. As early as 1915, several elementary schools were opened at Kashgar (Kashi) to teach children Islam and Pan-Turkish ideology, and "some Turks often sent pamphlets and other mail to Islamic imams and our military officers in order to propagandize Islam and pan-Turkism."[13] After the Bolshevik Revolution, the Russians built schools in Dihua; exported books, newspapers, and films to Xinjiang; and developed special broadcasting programs for local people.

The growth of Russian influence in Xinjiang resulted from two contradictory policy thrusts of the Soviet Union. One was its policy of supporting Han-dominated governments in order to secure political and commercial privileges in treaty negotiations with them; the other was instigation of anti-Han revolts among Kazakhs or Uyghurs in order to establish Russian power bases. In 1944, they initiated and sponsored the Yili Uprising, known as the "Three Districts Revolution," in an attempt to turn an anti-Han and anti–Chiang Kai-shek rebellion into a socialist revolution. The Russians, however, soon discovered a strong Pan-Islamic and Pan-Turkish tendency among the rebels. An unintended consequence was that the Muslim independence movement in the "three districts" posed challenges to the legitimacy of Soviet domination over Russia's own Muslim minorities.

During the first half of 1949, the PLA swiftly advanced along various fronts, and the Nationalist government in the northwest was near collapse. In Dihua, students and intellectuals were divided into pro- and anti-Soviet groups. I interviewed Abdurahim Amin, who was a new student at Xinjiang College in 1949. He tells how antagonistic student associations struggled to recruit freshmen at the college. Amin recalled the showing one evening of *Admiral Usakof*, a Soviet movie that described several wars between Tsarist Russia and the Ottoman Empire. When this movie showed the Turks defeating the Russians, the pro-Turkish students reacted vociferously. When the movie showed the Russian destruction of the Ottoman navy, the pro-Soviet students jumped for joy. The showing of this movie was finally interrupted by fighting between two groups of students.[14]

Isa Yusuf Alptekin was a popular professor at Xinjiang College, where he expounded his dream of an independent Islamic state in Xinjiang, arguing that "Xinjiang is the home of Uyghurs and all other nationalities are foreigners."[15] Moreover, Isa stressed the ethnic and cultural unity of the various Turkic-speaking Muslim peoples of Central Asia, which infuriated the Soviets.[16] As Burhan openly advocated a pro-Soviet policy, Isa became more anti-Soviet than anti-Han or anti-Nationalist. The Russian consulate reported that Isa had discussed the possibility of an independent Islamic state in the northwest with Ma Bufang, the warlord leader of Qinghai, and Mehmed Emin's wife had traveled to southern Xinjiang to prepare for its establishment.[17] According to these reports, the situation was serious because "American imperialism was very active among the Uyghur people. . . . The British consul has very close connections with Masud and Isa."[18] The Russian leaders calculated that a policy reorientation was necessary at this crucial moment.

A striking change occurred in Soviet policy toward relations between the Chinese Communist Party and the Yili regime. A couple of years earlier, Moscow had purged Abdul Kerim Abasoff, who tried to establish contact with the Chinese Communist Party.[19] In June 1949, however, Moscow suddenly demanded that the Chinese Communists send a representative with a radio transmitter-receiver to Yining in order to establish effective communications between the Yili regime and Beijing. Furthermore, in September, Moscow asked the Chinese Communists to incorporate the Yili regime's military force, the National Revolutionary Army, into the PLA.[20]

According to Allen Whiting and Sheng Shicai, the Soviet consul-general in Dihua repeatedly met with Tao Zhiyue and suggested that he declare independence, using the case of Outer Mongolia as a precedent. The Soviet consul-general promised Tao that the Soviet Union would stop the PLA from marching toward Xinjiang.[21] This message obviously contradicted Joseph Stalin's conversation with Liu Shaoqi on June 27, 1949, in which Stalin urged an early march of the PLA to Xinjiang. If Whiting's information is correct, a reasonable explanation of this discrepancy can only be that Stalin had redirected Soviet policy vis-à-vis Xinjiang by June.

The shift in Soviet policy was related to Stalin's judgment of Xinjiang's political prospects. The Uyghur separatist movement in 1949 increased Western influence and threatened the Russian presence. Moscow would not tolerate the emergence of Xinjiang as an anti-Soviet base, but it was unable to use the Yili regime or military intervention to stifle it. In negotiating future relations between the Soviet Union and Communist China, Mao expressed his respect for the independence of Outer Mongolia, while Stalin made a few compromises on the issue of China's Manchuria.[22] Newly accessible archival documents show that the main Russian goal was to hand over the frontier's complex political and ethnic problems to Chinese Communists. The PLA's military progress in China proper convinced Moscow of its capacity to take over this hot potato. Dieter Heinzig points out that Russian nationalism and Moscow's security concerns were the driving forces in its foreign policy making.[23] In the case of Xinjiang, a Muslim area controlled by Han-Chinese Communists meant following the Soviet model of a multinational state to suppress any Pan-Turkish and anti-Soviet revolts, thus ensuring Chinese and Soviet territorial security.

The Xinjiang Uprising

In the first half of 1949, Mao Zedong's plan was not to launch a military offensive against Xinjiang before spring 1950.[24] From July 10 through July 14, 1949, a decisive battle took place in western Shaanxi in which the PLA destroyed forty-four thousand troops.[25] On July 23, Mao ordered Peng Dehuai to change the original plan and "occupy Dihua in winter [1949]."[26] A month later, when the Communists defeated Muslim cavalry and stormed the city of Lanzhou, Mao urged the PLA

Second Army commanded by Wang Zhen to stop moving toward the provinces of Ningxia and Qinghai and to quickly turn westward to block the path to Xinjiang.[27] Du Pengcheng, a Communist war correspondent, wrote that the soldiers were so tired from the uninterrupted rapid marches that they would fall asleep in heavy rain.[28]

Mao's impetuosity was stimulated by Stalin, who criticized Mao for overestimating the fighting capacity of the Muslim cavalry and for hesitating to march on Xinjiang. To encourage Mao, Stalin promised to offer the PLA military support including the use of its air force. Moreover, he suggested that the Chinese Communist Party not only advance into Xinjiang but also radically alter the demographic landscape of the frontier. In order to consolidate Communist control, Stalin argued, the percentage of Han Chinese in Xinjiang should be raised from 5 percent to 30 percent by means of a massive emigration.[29]

In subsequent weeks, the PLA's operations tore the heart out of Nationalist forces and assured final victory on the northwest front. On August 6, Mao sent Peng Dehuai a telegraph, expressing his hope for a peaceful settlement of the Xinjiang issue by "using Zhang Zhizhong to organize a Xinjiang Military-Political Committee as a transitional institution."[30] However, the Nationalist government in Xinjiang had been divided into one group that advocated negotiations and a second group that advocated fighting. It was not as easy for the parties to reach the peaceful solution suggested by Mao.

A year earlier, Zhang Zhizhong had foreseen the inevitable defeat of the Nationalists and planned "to retreat to the northwest."[31] He did not construct any fortifications along the Xinjiang-Gansu border, assuming that the PLA would not advance to the frontier. As military crises loomed larger in 1949, Liang Kexun, director of the Political Division of the Xinjiang Garrison Headquarters, suggested that the Xinjiang government make a deal with the Communists, following the old model of "worship the temple but not the gods inside."[32] This was in accord with Zhang's early suggestion for making peace with the Communists while, at the same time, leaving the Xinjiang government intact.[33] Some months later, Zhang clarified his stance by broadcasting a statement calling on the Nationalists in Xinjiang "officially to declare a break with the Nationalist government in Guangzhou and a shift to the democratic people's camp."[34]

Encouraged by Moscow, the Yili regime expressed its desire to join the Chinese revolution and have its army incorporated into the PLA.[35] Mao Zedong replied that "[the Yili regime's] many years of struggle were part of our Chinese people's democratic revolution," and he invited its representatives to Beijing for the national political consultative conference.[36] Nationalist leader Tao Zhiyue wanted to cross over to the Communists but worried about the Russian-sponsored Yili regime. Burhan, who had close connections with Russians and the Communist Party, told Tao that as long as Tao supported the anti-Nationalist Xinjiang Uprising, "I will guarantee your safety in the name of my eighty-year-old mother."[37]

On September 19, Zhang Zhizhong telegraphed Tao from Beijing, stressing that the best time to launch the uprising was "prior to the establishment of the people's central government." Tao felt pressure to take immediate action, but he understood that the key to a peaceful solution was to persuade the hardliners, who controlled three-quarters of the armies in Xinjiang, including Ye Cheng, the commander of the 78th Division, Luo Shuren, the commander of the 179th Brigade, and Ma Chengxiang, the commander of the 5th Rivalry Army. Within two months, Tao held several talks with Ye, Luo, and Ma, telling them that if they insisted on fighting, "thousands of officers and soldiers would be victimized for nothing, people in Xinjiang would lose their homes, different ethnic groups would begin to kill one another, and we would then be able neither to fight nor ask for peace."[38] Tao suggested that they hand over their troops, leaving Xinjiang with their money. Tao would guarantee their safety.

Two incidents made Tao's words even more persuasive. One was the brutal murder of Sheng Shicai's family in Lanzhou. Eleven family members were killed, including Sheng's seven-year-old nephew and five-year-old niece. According to the police investigation, the murders were all committed by Sheng's former subordinates who desired to avenge their friends and relatives whom Sheng had killed in Xinjiang. As soon as this news reached Dihua, Uyghurs organized a thirty-six-member delegation headed by Isa to greet and defend the murderers.[39] Isa argued that Sheng killed many innocent people in Xinjiang and deserved this punishment, which suggested that killings for purposes of revenge would also occur in Xinjiang. The other incident was the rape of Yinchuan by Ma Hongkui's cavalry. As the troops were defeated by the Communist army and re-treated to the province of Ningxia, Ma could no longer control his Muslim soldiers, who had begun to loot stores, rape women, and burn houses in Ningxia's Muslim capital of Yinchuan.[40]

Moreover, both Tao and the Nationalist diehards recognized that they could no longer ask their soldiers to fight since military supplies from the central government had been entirely cut off and the soldiers had not been paid for months.[41] Inflation and currency devaluation in Xinjiang were beyond their control. A monthly salary of a low-ranking officer in the Nationalist Party army could only buy a couple of packs of cigarettes.[42] To make matters worse, after his troops were defeated in Lanzhou, Ma Bufang took military funds worth $50,000 and fled to Hong Kong. Reports from neighboring provinces told of the surrender of Nationalist troops. On September 19, the 81st Army announced that it would join the PLA. Four days later the Nationalist armies and government in the Ningxia region signed an Agreement of Peaceful Settlement to welcome the Communist takeover. On September 24, thirty thousand Nationalist troops surrendered at Jiuquan. The door to Xinjiang was now wide open.

As Tao Zhiyue and Burhan decided to launch a "peaceful uprising," the Dihua Chamber of Commerce, the Islamic Chamber of Commerce, and the Municipal Congress held meetings to support them. Afterward, a Uyghur delegation went to Lanzhou to welcome the PLA. At this crucial moment, the Nationalist hardliners split. Ma Cheng-xiang's family left Qinghai for Hong Kong. Ma wanted to join them as soon as possible. Ye Cheng's wife was opposed to her husband going into battle and urged him to sell their properties at a good price. Luo Shuren might have wanted a final battle, but he definitely did not want to fight alone. At the last minute, Tao Zhiyue managed to dissuade Ma, Ye, and Luo from fighting and escorted them from Dihua.[43]

On September 25 and 26, 1949, first Tao and then Burhan sent open telegraphs announcing that "[the army and government in Xinjiang] had cut off all relations with the Nationalist government in Guangzhou and accepted Chairman Mao's eight-point peace statement. They would re-main at their original stations, maintain local social order, and await or-ders from the People's Revolutionary Military Committee and the PLA Headquarters."[44] This became known as the "Xinjiang peaceful uprising." On September 28, martial law was proclaimed, and social order in Dihua was quickly restored.

The success of the peaceful uprising bolstered Tao's confidence in his ability to rule Dihua and the entire province. He sent his representative, General Zeng Zhenwu, to Lanzhou to confer with Peng Dehuai and suggested that the PLA not enter Xinjiang during the winter of 1949–50. On September 26, Mao instructed Peng Dehuai "not to argue with him [Zeng Zhenwu], i.e., do not tell him that the PLA will advance into Xinjiang this winter. But you have to make all preparations by November 1 or November 10 in order to set off in early or mid-November."[45] Meanwhile, emphasizing that every military action had to be approved by Beijing, the party's Central Committee rejected the demand of the old Yili regime that its army "take control of the places that the Nationalist Party evacuated."[46] It was obvious that the Yili regime, a Soviet-supported "state within a state," would be dismissed and that Xinjiang had to be put under the direct control of the Chinese Communist Party. Having inherited the historical legacy of the Qing dynasty and the Nationalist government to establish a Chinese Xinjiang province, Mao Zedong would not allow "relative independence" of any part of the frontier, much less a government that "worshipped the temple but not the gods inside."

The Magnificent March

The PLA troops Wang Zhen took to Xinjiang included the Second Army, Sixth Army, and Fifth Mechanized Regiment, totaling 90,000 men. The force included 760 trucks, 589 camels, and great amounts of food, cloth, gasoline, medicine, and other supplies. The Soviet Union provided 40 transport planes to ship part of the military force. On November 10, 1949, the first group of 555 PLA soldiers advanced toward Xinjiang. They took 45 armored cars and 37 trucks, crossed the deserts and snow-covered mountains, traveled 779 miles (1,253 kilometers), and after a 10-day rapid march, arrived in Dihua, where they met 50,000 urban residents lining the streets for 3 miles, greeting the Communist troops.

The PLA's march across a wild frontier area was beset by unusual difficulties that most of the soldiers from China proper could never have imagined. The headquarters of the First Front Army of the PLA reprinted a pamphlet, *Introduction to Xinjiang's Transportation*, edited by the Association of Northwest Studies under the Nationalist government, and distributed it to all of the troops advancing into Xinjiang. The pamphlet began by offering the useful suggestion that "while marching in the desert, every stop should be planned in accordance with how much water and forage are available, not in terms of how far you can go in one day."[47] It listed all of the rivers, streams, and wells en route from Dihua to the major townships. It described all of the villages—even ones that were populated by only five to ten households—and described all visible natural and artificial landmarks. The pamphlet became a guidebook for the Communists. The PLA's 15th Regiment began its march from Aksu to Hotan on December 5, with plans to walk 247 miles along the dry riverbed and to cross the Taklamakan Desert, where supposedly no human being had previously set foot. The troops studied all available road instructions in the pamphlet, including the following legend about mysterious pigeons:

> Pigeon Dike. The dike is on the western edge of the desert. Numerous dunes shift and confuse. During the Qianlong period, General Zhou Wen became lost here while leading his troops. A pigeon led him out. Afterwards, he ordered the soldiers to open the land, plant millet, and dig a well to feed the pigeons. . . . In the early years of Emperor Guangxu, General Dong's army moved towards Hotan and passed this place. His soldiers had dug a dozen wells but found only bitter water. Suddenly, Dong saw pigeons flying above his head. Believing that wherever there is a pigeon there is a spring, he ordered his troops to follow the pigeons and at last they found fresh water.[48]

In 1932, a revolt by Uyghur peasants in this area was suppressed. The Nationalist soldiers torched the towns and villages, but no one touched the pigeons.[49] These Han Chinese accounts reflected their fear of this inhospitable non-Han area, believing that nobody could survive Taklamakan without the blessing of gods or mysterious pigeons. In 1949, this area continued to be a terrible place for travelers. Soldiers were tortured by bone-chilling cold and piercing winds as they sought to continue their journey; their supply of water was nearly exhausted, and life-threatening sandstorms could occur at any moment. To cross the "death desert," the Communists believed that not pigeons but good Uyghur guides could help them. Yet a good guide was hard to find.

In its early days, the PLA was happy to meet friendly indigenous people. It was the first time for most Uyghurs to hear about communism. Because of their intense hatred of the Nationalists, they welcomed the troops who drove out the Han Chinese government. They were quickly disappointed, however, to find that the Communists were Han Chinese, too. When the PLA desperately looked for a guide, very few Uyghurs were willing to serve. They did not trust any Han soldier.[50] Now, it was time for the Communists to show that they were different.

Every time the Nationalist troops arrived at a new place, they asked the local residents for food, housing, money, and labor. As the PLA passed through the villages, the residents were not disturbed but instead were pleasantly surprised to see that the soldiers ate their own food and slept along the roadside. Moreover, wherever they went, the PLA paved roads or constructed bridges for military as well as local use.

Abdurahim Amin recalled that when he was a small child living in Dihua before 1949, he was never permitted to go outdoors during May and June. As the snow that had accumulated during the winter melted, the city streets became a morass, and a child who fell down might be unable to stand up and could easily die. The PLA came to Dihua in the winter, and they immediately began preparing stones for road construction. When spring came, the project commenced. Many streets soon turned into cobbled roads. The children were happy to play in the streets, and the urban residents were delighted to find that the soldiers were city builders.[51]

In March 1950, the last troops reached their outposts at Altay on the northern border. The PLA soon launched a military campaign against the rebellion of Masud Sabri and Janimhan. An estimated 20,000 Kazakh herdsmen had joined the rebels. The PLA assembled one division and several regiments to launch the offensive and held mass rallies among the Kazakhs to denounce Masud and Janimhan as "Muslim traitors and American spies."[52] The campaign concluded by destroying the rebel forces and capturing Masud on July 15, then sending 16,400 Kazakh herdsmen back to civilian life.[53]

It was part of the PLA's task to get involved in political and cultural activities during the military occupation. For example, the PLA successfully conducted language programs in Kashgar to teach Chinese to the Uyghurs and to teach the Han Chinese cadres Uyghur. These language-study workshops produced the first group of Uyghur cadres.[54] The Communists also began to recruit new party members among the indigenous people. The recruitment was to follow a "top-down approach": begin with cities and then move to the countryside; admit revolutionary intellectuals first and then workers and peasants. On December 23, 1949, with the recommendation of Wang Zhen and Deng Liqun, fifteen local leaders, including Burhan and Saifudin, joined the Communist Party and became junior members of the party's leading institutions.[55] Communist leadership was quickly established at provincial, municipal, and grassroots levels.

The Communist rent reduction campaign and land reform were not much different from their counterparts in China proper. And these campaigns produced a considerable number of non-Han people who supported the primarily Han Chinese Communists. When the PLA troops finally departed, they left some of their officers, including a few women, to stay on to help the local government.[56] In the early days, the Communists were very cautious in dealing with indigenous people and their religious practices. However, guided by class struggle theory, some later military and political campaigns victimized a considerable number of innocent Uyghur people, ruined their traditional ways of life, and created new tensions in the frontier's ethnic relations.[57]

The PLA was proud of its accomplishment during this "magnificent" march. In 1874, the Qing court had initiated a military expedition to control Xinjiang, and more than two years elapsed before its commander could occupy the province. By contrast, within six months, ninety thousand PLA troops had successfully reached all of their military posts and had gained effective control over the entire province.[58] Nonetheless, logistical supply remained the decisive factor in the military operation. As a poor frontier province, Xinjiang could not afford to feed the suddenly increased military forces, and local governments began to complain.[59] PLA troops had to support themselves by producing food and cloth, which led to the decision to develop PLA farms.

This policy was designed not only to resolve the economic problems of the PLA but also to ensure the security and development of the frontier. This reflected the long-standing Chinese practice of "stationing troops to develop wasteland and defend the frontier" (tunken shubian). Inspired by this "farming and defending" strategy, Wang

Zhen and other Communist leaders in Xinjiang began to investigate the most appropriate sizes for PLA farms. Wang emphasized that the PLA should not "scramble for land with the indigenous people" and required that his troops create new oases in the desert. According to Wang's blueprint, the farms would begin with agriculture and then develop industry, commerce, various services, and education.[60] This plan required tremendous efforts by men and women alike.

New Oases

Many studies have portrayed the Communist takeover of Xinjiang as a men's story, while the participation of women has remained invisible. More recently, however, the experiences of the women soldiers who accompanied or followed the PLA troops to the frontier have begun to attract attention. The memoirs of individual women soldiers have been published in various journals, and interviews with these female pioneers have been televised. In addition, newly released archival materials have facilitated an assessment of the contribution made by women to the frontier.

According to government reports, the first group of women soldiers came from Linyao county in Gansu. In August and September 1949, the PLA enlisted 1,350 male and 150 female students there for its First School of Military and Civilian Cadres. The students signed up with enthusiasm but were not aware where they would be sent. One of the female students recalled that the "army school" greatly intrigued her, but she would not have joined it if she had known they would be sent to Xinjiang. She very quickly became ashamed of that admission because she and her classmates had been taught to be proud of their glorious tasks and determined in their efforts to "liberate and develop" Xinjiang.[61] After brief training, they were shipped by train to Turpan, in eastern Xinjiang, where the "school" was dismissed and the female students were sent to different military posts as regular soldiers. From Turpan, the first oasis city of Xinjiang, the women set off by foot on a long trek, marching into the desert and experiencing the same hardships, dangers, and missions as their male comrades.[62] Forty-nine years later, photographs of this march were published along with the women soldiers' memoirs. Wearing men's uniforms, they marched in three columns and sang and danced in the rest areas as if there was nothing in the world that scared them.[63] Nonetheless, since the women soldiers had experienced hardship on the march, none of them arrived at the frontier expecting things to go easily.

The second and largest group of women soldiers was recruited from Hunan province. It was Wang Zhen's belief that the PLA could not really settle down in the frontier unless the party assisted the soldiers in establishing families. There had previously been one hundred thousand Nationalist troops in Xinjiang, and almost one hundred thousand PLA troops had just recently arrived there. In a male-only world, the soldiers would likely become bandits, he worried. In addition, to avoid ethnic conflict, the party prohibited Han Chinese men from marrying non-Han women.[64] In 1950, Wang Zhen addressed a letter to his friends, the governor and the party secretary of Hunan, asking for help: "Please recruit a large number of women soldiers for us. We welcome all 18–19 year olds, educated, unmarried girls, regardless of their family backgrounds. We want them to come here to be good workers, good wives, and good mothers."[65] An unpublished government document offered a further explanation of Wang Zhen's requirements for female recruits. First, the girls had to be unmarried or legally divorced. Second, the girls had to be in good health and have regular features (*wuguan duanzheng*). Third, girls from the families of landlords and rich peasants or girls whose relatives had been suppressed by the Communist government could also be recruited.[66] These requirements indicate that for the new women soldiers being "good wives and good mothers" was more important than being "good workers."

On February 10, 1951, *New Hunan Daily* published an advertisement recruiting some two hundred professionals, skilled workers, and women students.[67] In fact, the work team intended to recruit women soldiers only. The team enticed people in Hunan by offering glorious opportunities in Xinjiang: going to the Soviet Union to study, learning advanced technology and skills, building Soviet-style mechanized farms, becoming actresses in the PLA, and enjoying delicious fruits that the people in China proper had never tasted.

Three groups of girls responded with particular enthusiasm. The first was composed of idealistic students who wished to redirect their lives in ways that differed from their classmates and the majority of women. The PLA promised that middle school graduates would be appointed as platoon leaders and college graduates as company commanders. In fact, as soon as these students reached Xinjiang, most of them became teachers and secretaries, enjoying treatment equivalent to the ranks of platoon leaders or company commanders.[68]

The second group was made up of girls from poor families with little brothers and sisters. Poverty and disease still plagued most rural areas in 1950–51. Girls could find few opportunities for education or decent jobs. In the belief that the women of poor families could bear greater hardships and could better handle hard work, recruitment efforts after 1951 were shifted from the cities and towns to poor and undeveloped villages.[69]

The third group consisted of girls from the families of landlords, rich peasants, or other "exploiting classes," and girls whose fathers served in the Nationalist Army or government. Because of their "shameful" family background, these girls experienced discrimination in employment and a sense of inferiority in public settings. When they heard that they could forget their families and join the army, they took this as an opportunity to "cast off their old selves" and to change the social status of their families. As Liu Sixiang's mother recalled, her entire family celebrated when she joined the troops to Xinjiang since her "bourgeois family now became a revolutionary soldier's family," which would be treated favorably by the local government.[70]

Nevertheless, even before their arrival in Xinjiang, these Hunanese girls became suspicious of the recruitment. Why did the team recruit only women soldiers? At every stop, the local leaders came to visit the girls and asked about marriage. Why? A rumor began to spread that the girls would be distributed to wounded and disabled soldiers or that they would be forced to marry and be shared by several husbands.

The reality was not that bad. They were expected to marry the soldiers, and the marriages were arranged by the party, but no overt violence was involved. They were told that the guiding principle was "the party assigns and the woman agrees," although they did not have many choices. According to the PLA's marriage regulations, in order to get married, a man had to meet one of the following criteria: a battalion commander or officer of the equivalent rank; a platoon leader or company commander with five years of service in the army and at least twenty-six years of age; a Red Army soldier who had joined the army before July 7, 1937; a veteran soldier with six years of revolutionary experience and at least thirty years old.[71] Since most of the newly recruited women soldiers were seventeen to eighteen years old, it was not uncommon for their husbands to be ten to twenty years older. In the 1990s, looking back on their lives, some women said that their marriages turned out well because their husbands treated them as little sisters, while others complained that the differences in their age and education caused their marriages to fail.[72]

Since most urban and young girls did not want to marry in a hurry, the PLA began to recruit more rural women or widows between the ages of twenty and thirty from the poor provinces of Sichuan, Henan, Shandong, and Gansu.[73] The PLA even allowed divorced women or young widows to bring their children with them to Xinjiang.[74] In 1954, the Xinjiang Women's Work Division decided "not to accept any girls between the ages of eighteen and nineteen."[75] Meanwhile, it relaxed its limitations on the man's age, rank, and service year to enable more middle-aged men and women to get married.

The first group of female students to arrive engaged in various jobs, the foremost of which were teaching and nursing. The first nursing school was organized during the PLA's westward movement, and it recruited female students in Shaanxi who followed the troops to Xinjiang and served in various armies and farms. On August 1, 1950, the first kindergarten was opened up for military children, and all child-care workers were young women from Shandong. In that year, the PLA initiated a cultural campaign requiring every soldier to learn to read and write. All the women soldiers with middle school education became full-time teachers. Gradually, a considerable number of elementary and middle schools were built up and began to employ both male and female teachers.

Despite the small number of women soldiers on each oasis farm, their educational and medical work provided significant civilizing influences in a frontier community. The young women assisted the male soldiers in doing laundry and advocated personal hygiene at home. The women provided crucial services, lessening the community's dependence on the outside world. Each oasis farm became a self-sufficient society and had limited contact with Uyghur farmers. Conflicts occasionally broke out with their neighbors over the issue of water, but environmental pollution was not a major concern during the 1950s. The PLA farms grew by leaps and bounds and took pride in the women soldiers. A Han female named Li recalled that the Uyghurs came to her farm, asking to exchange four hundred sheep for a few women soldiers. The Uyghurs wanted to marry these hardworking girls, but the Communist farms would not allow their women to marry anyone who was not one of their "own people."[76]

Although the Communist Party required the employment of more women in government offices and encouraged women to participate in society, the family was the focus of a woman's life, and the ideology of "domesticity" predominated on the frontier as well as in China proper.[77] The age, education, urban origins, and revolutionary ideals of the women soldiers did not substantially alter their gender roles and the expectations of women. Homemaking and child rearing were the primary purposes for bringing them to Xinjiang. Wang Zhen and Tao Zhiyue issued an order stipulating that pregnant women not do any heavy manual work and that various vacations be given to them: a short vacation during the first couple of months of pregnancy, part-time work release beginning in the seventh month of pregnancy, and a full two-month vacation following childbirth.[78] The headquarters of the Production Corps demanded that the workloads of young mothers be reduced and promised that any nonmilitary mother would receive all of the benefits of PLA soldiers as long as she gave birth to and reared three or more children.[79]

The women who arrived after 1952 engaged primarily in agricultural labor. They shared all of the hard work with the men. This included chopping wood, plowing the fields, sowing, and harvesting crops. In June 1952, 150 girls from Hunan were assigned to the 25th Division, and 476 more girls from Shandong joined them in July. As soon as they arrived at the farm of the 25th Division at Laopaotai, they met a horrible plague of locusts. Locusts came in black clouds that shut out the sky and attacked every green crop. When they were gone, 133,333 square hectares (515 square miles) of land at the farm were as bare as scorched earth. The women soldiers had to fight alongside their male partners day and night. They swept up locusts, cleaned new land, channeled water from the Manas River into the fields, and developed a new rice plantation. At the end of that year, they finally could celebrate the harvest, the growth of the farm population, and new families.[80]

At first, several young married couples at Laopaotai and other farms had to share one bedroom, curtaining off each bed with sheets. Later they lived in crude homes and had children born on the frontier. With the expansion of new oases in the margin of the desert, the young women aged quickly. Preoccupied with caring for their families and their children, the women did not have opportunities to continue their education or obtain technical training. When the farms were mechanized and the men became skilled workers, most women continued to engage in manual labor. The deserts prevented women from returning to their former homes in China proper, while the frontier both expanded and constrained their lives. But most survived the physical hardships, the loneliness, the family quarrels, ethnic conflicts, and homesickness. The women substantially contributed to the growth of the numerous oasis farms that quickly emerged all over the frontier. As wives, mothers, homesteaders, teachers, nurses, shopkeepers, and laborers, the women constituted an ever-growing proportion of the population of the frontier and helped to settle, shape, and develop it.

In 1953, the party's Central Military Commission set a high value on the recruitment of women soldiers and worked out a five-year plan for bringing another 99,300 women from China proper to Xinjiang in an effort to resolve once and for all the problem of gender imbalance on the PLA farms.[81] The central government assigned responsibilities for recruitment to each province, while the provinces assigned enlistment quotas to each county and subdistrict.[82] The continued arrival and settlement of women stabilized frontier life and helped the PLA attain its goal of the "peaceful liberation" of Xinjiang.

Dominating the Frontier

Marxist theory does not explain the changes that took place in Xinjiang between 1949 and 1953. It was neither a class struggle in Dihua nor an uprising in Yili that culminated in the Communist victory. The PLA's advance into Xinjiang was more of a contingency than a simple extension of the PLA's military progress in China proper. In early 1949 Xinjiang remained remote from the main battlegrounds of the civil war, and people there believed that the military defeat of the Nationalist Party in north China suggested different possibilities for its future. The indigenous and intrusive forces were powerful yet vulnerable in the frontier zone. Communications, competition, and negotiations among the distinct segments of society in the following months reshaped the complex frontier politics.

The Han-dominated Nationalist government in Xinjiang was too weak to resist the new central government. It also lacked a legitimate claim to independence and had no serious chance of depending on a foreign state for survival. Russian culture was highly influential in the urban areas, but when competing with Pan-Islamism and Pan-Turkism, it was less appealing to Uyghur peasants and Kazakh herdsmen. Although Islamic tradition was deeply rooted, the "oasis populations remained isolated from one another" and therefore did not form a unified polity.[83] The Pan-Islamic and Pan-Turkish rhetoric was emotional, but its political program appealed only to some urban intellectuals and members of the rural elite. The peaceful solution of the Xinjiang problem was not due to the wisdom of a few politicians but resulted from negotiations among different political forces. Historians should not ignore the roles played by Zhang Zhizhong, Burhan, Tao Zhiyue, Wang Zhen, and the Nationalist hardliners. It was not their personal character but the frontier situation that shaped their ways of thinking, their policy orientations, and their negotiations.

The "peaceful liberation" of Xinjiang replaced the Nationalist regime with a more effective form of domination. More so than in many other places, the PLA functioned as "an armed body for carrying out the political tasks of the revolution," expanding state control to areas that the Manchus and the Nationalist Party had never reached.[84] The PLA farms were scattered throughout the province, contributing to political stability and economic development. The Communists promoted *tunken shubian* (stationing troops to develop wasteland and defend the frontier), which in reality was an imperial policy of holding on to the newly conquered territory through military settlement. The migration of women from China proper made it possible for the soldiers to enjoy family life and enabled *tunken shubian* to become a permanent undertaking.

Mao Zedong accepted Stalin's military aid and suggestions on domestic migration but did not entirely follow the Russian model in dealing with Xinjiang. Soon after the Communist takeover of Xinjiang, the Yili regime no longer existed and its military forces were ordered to withdraw from the National Defense Army (Guofang jun) and join the Production Corps (Shengchan jianshe bingtuan). This arrangement reflected Mao Zedong's vigilance regarding ethnic tension and Russian influence.[85]

The success of PLA farms led to an influx of people from China proper and changed Xinjiang's demographic landscape. They set the pattern for population relocation in the following years: as the state relocated factories from China proper or exploited oil fields in Xin-jiang, it transferred workers and their families together. When the party called on educated youth to go to the frontier, it recruited both males and females. As a result, Han people now constitute 43.02 per-cent of the population of the province, while the Uyghurs make up 43.35 percent and Kazakhs 6.47 percent.[86] The proportion of Han would be even higher if researchers counted the large number of mi-grant seasonal laborers from Henan and Sichuan working on cotton farms and merchants from Zhejiang and Jiangsu doing business with local people and the central Asian republics.

The Communist takeover, however, also fueled ethnic divisions be-tween the indigenous and the intrusive peoples. First, the PLA created new self-sufficient and isolated oases, in which the presence of Han women made the farms a more exclusive world of Han Chinese. The new oases did not successfully incorporate Uyghur agriculture into the regional economy. "Do not scramble for land with indigenous people" was a smart idea for avoiding conflicts, but it also reflected an ethno-centric attitude, which assumed that the PLA would not deprive the non-Han peoples of anything as long as it occupied uncultivated land and used it more efficiently. Second, earlier governments ruled the frontier using the approach of "cooperating with the non-Han but keeping real power in the hands of the Han." This approach was fol-lowed by the Communists within the framework of "peaceful revolu-tion." The veteran Han Communists led the junior non-Han party workers; the seniority principles of the Communist Party enabled its leaders to suppress any moral outcry about Han chauvinism.[87] Nonetheless, indigenous people showed great capacity to accommo-date and survive the impact of an intrusive culture. Striking differences in physical appearance, clothing, speech, and food were enforced by in-digenous attitudes toward religion. The Communist takeover of Xin-jiang established a new political hegemony but did not end the socio-cultural processes that began in a frontier context.[88] Since 1949 Xinjiang has remained a frontier area where Han-minority interaction continues to be a predominant theme.

ॐ III

The Culture of
Accommodation

The Crocodile Bird: Xiangsheng *in the Early 1950s*

Perry Link

HINDSIGHT CAN BE tricky. We often say that we "benefit" from it, and no doubt we do. But the benefits may be easier to see than the costs. To the serious historian, one cost of hindsight is that impressions of a past time are inevitably colored by what we know came later. We need to remind ourselves that people living at any past time did not know what came later. If we really want to appreciate their position, to "get inside" their feelings and outlooks, we need to attempt a feat of imagination: we need to sweep from our memories certain obvious and important latter-day facts. Beyond that, we must try to weed from our minds all of the associations and implications, conscious and unconscious, that have grown up as a result of our knowing those facts. This is not easy. Indeed, I think we must acknowledge that perfection in the matter is impossible and that the best we can do is to minimize the problem.

The matter is especially difficult when the later events were cataclysmic. What, for example, did the morning of August 6, 1945, feel like for a citizen of Hiroshima ten minutes before the atom bomb? Ōe Kenzaburō, John Hersey, and others have tried to imagine that moment, have sought valiantly to recapture its ordinariness, and have failed. How could one not fail? One can, yes, reconstruct an image of morning toothbrushing: sink, mirror, brush, glass of water. We can "see" these things in our mind's eye. But we cannot, try as we might, get rid of another element in our reconstructed mental image of that Hiroshima morning—a horrible foreboding, that feverish sense that the imagined scene is about to explode. It seems to inhere in the very sink and mirror. Yet that foreboding was not there for people at the time. For us to sense it as inhering the mirror is not historically accurate.

China's Anti-Rightist Movement of 1957 and Cultural Revolution beginning in 1966 were not as abrupt as the Hiroshima bomb, and of course there are many other differences between these events and the bomb. But the challenge that the historian faces in trying to imagine a status quo ante is in principle similar. To understand Chinese writers and artists in the early 1950s, we need to try to imagine their outlook before anyone knew what was in store for them. Many of them (not all, to be sure) were enthusiastic about the Communist project. They saw and felt a new day for China; they wanted to help and wanted to be part of figuring out the best ways to help; they had good intentions and assumed that others did, too; they were optimistic about the likely results; they had no idea they were about to get kicked in the teeth.

This chapter looks at performers and writers of the popular performing art called *xiangsheng*, literally "face and voice," often mistranslated as "crosstalk."[1] The term might best be rendered simply as "comedians' routines." In a very rough sense *xiangsheng* resembles American vaudeville. Its stock-in-trade is humor, especially satire, but singing, imitation of sounds, and other kinds of oral antics are also involved. Its traditions in China are several hundred years old, but because it is an oral art that has been passed from master to disciple largely without written records, its history before the Communist period is not very well known. In the 1930s and 1940s it was performed mostly in marketplaces, where performers would pass a bowl among onlookers to collect donations; since the 1950s it has migrated to auditoriums and to radio and television broadcasts where the opportunity for live interaction with an audience has been sharply curtailed even as the size of the audience has grown immensely.

Performances are normally done by two comedians, a *dougende*, or "funny man," and a *penggende*, or "straight man." (Pieces for a single performer—or for three, four, or five—also exist but are not very common.) The essential relationship between *dougende* and *penggende* is well captured in a sketch by the distinguished cartoonist Fang Cheng (see the accompanying figure). Here the *dougende*, on the left, is appar-

Two *xiangsheng* comedians: the *dougende* (funny man, left) presents a crock of baloney to the *penggende* (straight man, right). Drawing by Fang Cheng, in Xue Baokun, *Zhongguo de xiangsheng* (China's *xiangsheng*) (Beijing: Renmin chubanshe, 1985), 176.

ently presenting a crock of baloney to the *penggende*, whose role is to represent the common sense of the audience and whose combination of indulgence of the *dougende* and skepticism about his baloney is well captured by the straight lines of the eyes and mouth.

Traditionally all *xiangsheng* routines were set, and performers memorized them by rote. Audiences did not look for creativity. As in listening to opera, they were attracted by the prospect of hearing the best possible renditions of well-known pieces. Only seasoned performers would dare to make ad lib revisions, then only occasionally. In recent decades the emphasis has gradually shifted from rote performance to the creation of new works. Audiences now come to hear new satire more than to enjoy old favorites. I have written elsewhere about the history and structure of *xiangsheng* and will not address these questions in detail here.[2]

The fate of *xiangsheng* artists in the 1950s—wanting to help the revolution and then being crushed—was perhaps even more poignant than it was for other writers and artists because of the sprightly nature of their art. Writers of history, poetry, and fiction in China were accustomed to society's assumptions about the moral weight of their work. They inherited notions about "bearing responsibility for all under heaven" (yi tianxia wei ji ren) and "being first in the world to assume its worries." More recently, Mao Zedong, borrowing a phrase from Joseph Stalin, had told them to become "engineers of the soul." But xiangsheng performers were newcomers to such ponderous phrases and were generally as thrilled as they were stunned to see their whimsical art be promoted anywhere near that level. They embraced the idea that their satiric vision could help to cleanse the new society by picking out its flaws. Why not?

In several ways their self-conception suggests the African plover known as the "crocodile bird" (Pluvianus aegyptius). This species feeds on parasites that infest the bodies of crocodiles. By legend, the bird sometimes even ventures inside a crocodile's open mouth to scavenge between the teeth. For their part, crocodiles (or so, at least, it is said) leave their jaws agape in respect for the symbiosis involved. How often have crocodile jaws come down on plovers? The question is beyond my scope here, but the perceptions and intentions of the plover at time "T minus one" provide a good metaphor for what I will try to do in the rest of this chapter. I will try to set aside what we know happened in China after 1956 and to re-create the outlook of the xiangsheng world from 1950 to 1955.

The Legacy

Xiangsheng in the 1940s was performed in open areas of market towns or in urban entertainment quarters such as Tianqiao in Beijing. Tianjin and Shenyang were also major xiangsheng centers, but the art had not yet spread much in the rest of China. Performers wore long gowns (dagua) and used folding fans to fan themselves or—more important— to slam shut and use as miniclubs in mock attack on the other performer. They would begin by using a white powder to write on the ground a menu of their offerings. Then they used singing or a short comic piece (called a "cushion" [dianhua]) to try to attract a crowd who, once captured, would be ethically obliged to address the question of how many coppers to put into their bowl after the performance. Disciples learned the *xiangsheng* art by living with their masters and serving them in daily life (presenting tea, washing feet, and so on) while memorizing and imitating the masters' performances in every detail. Master-disciple chains formed *pai*, which I will translate as "schools." Relations among the schools were competitive and sometimes bitterly adversarial.

The content of traditional *xiangsheng* pieces was not very "politically correct," if I may use this term anachronistically. Country bumpkins were a favorite object of satire: they stank of garlic, spoke in funny accents, and were hopelessly lost when they showed up in cities. Cripples, mutes, and idiots also made for good fun—as did the deranged logic of the *dougende* himself, whose nonsense, like Archie Bunker's, obeyed its own rules even if no one else's. (Caught in a blatant self-contradiction, a *dougende* can squirm out of it by saying, "You find that strange? . . . Right! Even I find it strange!")[3]

Pornographic pieces were prominent. Such works were called *hun* (meat-eating) to distinguish them from the *su* (vegetarian) pieces that steered clear of sex. Meat-eating pieces were common, and women and children were not welcome at their performances. If a woman happened by during an open performance, according to one eyewitness, the performers would stop, bow in her direction, fall silent, and wait for her to leave.[4] But this ban on women had the interesting exception that nonvegetarian *xiangsheng* were often played by female performers. In most contexts, most of the time, only men performed. But—probably because it sharpened the salacious edge—women often played one of the two roles in the meat-eating pieces.

By standards today, nonvegetarian *xiangsheng* are tame. The descriptions are indirect, subtle, and sometimes indeed very funny. A piece called "The Birdie Won't Chirp" *(Qiaor bujiao)* relies on a double entendre in which "birdie" is code for "penis."[5] The audience knows this, and so does the *dougende*, whose own penis is being discussed. But the *penggende*, played by a female, thinks that birdie only means birdie. She wants to know what the *dougende*'s birdie looks like.

"Got feathers?"

"Nope, he's smooth and bare all the way to the tail, where there's a bunch of hair."

"You mean *feathers*, right?"

"No, hair."

"Hair? That's a new one! . . . What about the eyes? Pigeon eyes
or phoenix eyes?"

"Mm . . . only one eye, up top."

And so on. In north China it was customary to take caged birds on
walks *(liu niao)* and, arriving in a teahouse, to hook the cage up on a
wall or rafter while having tea. The female *penggende* wants to know if
the *dougende* does this service for his bird.

"Hang him up? No way!"

"Why not?"

"Get dizzy from the height."

"Nonsense. Birds don't get dizzy."

"No, *I* would get dizzy."

"What's it got to do with you?"

"It's *my bird!*"

"So? You hang him up, then sit down."

"Hang him up and I *can't* sit down."

This passage neatly illustrates a feature of *xiangsheng* humor that is
common in nonpornographic pieces as well—the multiple cracking of
a single joke to build an atmosphere. Having to hang one's penis from
a teahouse rafter might seem funny enough the first time around, but
in the art of *xiangsheng* essentially the same joke is cracked several
times by unpacking further implications (it could make you dizzy, it
would make it hard to sit back down, etc.). The re-cracking of the joke
builds a cumulative effect—an atmosphere—that magnifies the enjoy-
ment beyond what any of the punch lines taken singly could produce.

The published studies of *xiangsheng* as it was practiced before 1949 are
generally dull.[6] Some offer speculative comments on cryptic references
that appear in texts as early as *Zuozhuan.* Others look at the oral tradition
of the last two centuries or so but are fairly dry accounts of schools and
groupings. No one has tried in print to capture and describe the life of
the art. It was also exactly that task—to capture the life of the art—that
faced the *xiangsheng* world in 1950 when the new government turned to
it for help. The "life" and "art" of *xiangsheng* had to be winnowed out
from the politically incorrect dross in which they were embedded.

The Reform Effort

The distinguished writer Lao She, famous for *Camel Xiangzi* and other fiction, was a longtime aficionado of China's oral performing arts. He had already experimented in trying to "reform" them for modern uses during the war with Japan, when he himself wrote several *xiangsheng* pieces aimed at stimulating popular resistance to the Japanese invasion.[7] In 1946 he traveled to the United States on a program sponsored by the U.S. State Department and was visiting the American West Coast when the Communist victory arrived in 1949. He decided to return home to help.

A number of Beijing's *xiangsheng* performers—Hou Baolin, Hou Yichen, Yu Shide, and others—learned of Lao She's return to Beijing in December 1949 and went directly to "pay their respects" one evening. According to Yu Shide's memoirs, Lao She was enthusiastic about the prospects of *xiangsheng*.[8] "Let's reform it!" he is reported to have said, volunteering to get things started by personally rewriting some traditional pieces.

The next day a headline in *People's Daily* read "*Xiangsheng* Artists Pay a Visit to Lao She." This report in the Communist Party's central newspaper gave a major boost to *xiangsheng* prestige and also shows that the new government must have been behind the approach to Lao She, because such quick publication could not have happened otherwise. It seems likely, although I cannot prove it, that Mao Zedong himself was behind the initiative. Mao was a *xiangsheng* fan, and during the early 1950s he regularly invited Hou Baolin to his residence in Zhongnanhai for private performances. Hou recalls some of the details of these visits in a 1982 essay in which he also notes that Mao was a moving force in the establishment of "The Small Group for the Improvement of *Xiangsheng*" (Xiangsheng gaijin xiaozu).[9] This committee, which I will refer to as the "Small Group," played a big role.

It was formally founded on January 19, 1950, at Beijing's Qianmen, just north of the Tianqiao entertainment area. The group's members, in addition to Lao She and a few leading performers, included distinguished scholars such as the linguists Luo Changpei and Lü Shuxiang and literary scholar Wu Xiaoling. Lao She and Wu Xiaoling, in different ways, played especially active roles. Yu Shide recalls that for *xiangsheng* performers the willingness of famous scholars and writers to descend to the level of the *xialibaren*—the common folk—was deeply gratifying and motivating.[10] Until then, some performers apparently had feared that the revolution might choose to weed *xiangsheng* out and were actually considering career shifts. But now the government had decided to honor them with the title "cultural workers" *(wenyi gongzuozhe)*.

Lao She notes that one drawback of lending his prestige to *xiangsheng* was that performers, apparently in awe of his reputation, were reluctant to criticize his own efforts at writing *xiangsheng*. On the other hand an advantage of his prestige, as both he and others noted, was that he could pull performers together.[11] Factions and jealousies tended to soften under the warm, unifying gaze of great writers and scholars who were backed by the new government.

The Small Group formally existed for two years, after which two larger groups, the Beijing Work Group for Popular Performing Arts and a Great Assembly of *Xiangsheng* inherited its mission.[12] The work of reform began in 1950 with the drawing up of an ambitious list of tasks: *xiangsheng*'s importance would be consecrated through a study of *xiangsheng* history; *xiangsheng* would be transformed from a regional art to a national one; this expansion of scope would benefit China not only by spreading new ideas of the revolution but by helping speakers of dialects to master northern Mandarin, which was now called *putonghua*. (In an interesting exception to the latter goal, the Small Group also favored creation of *xiangsheng* in non-Mandarin dialects and even in national minority languages such as Tibetan and Mongolian. This shows that the goal of spreading social and political ideas took precedence over the goal of promoting Mandarin.) The Small Group even took on the task of setting up "literacy classes" *(shizi ban)*. This may seem an odd activity for practitioners of what was, until then, a purely oral art, but it shows again how deeply the Small Group had embraced the broader social goals of the new government.

All of these tasks were secondary to the Small Group's main work, which was to produce *xiangsheng* whose content would be appropriate to the new society. This job in turn was divided into two: the overhaul of existing pieces and the creation of new ones. Lao She began the overhaul work by rewriting pieces called "Phony Dr. Jia" *(Jia boshi)* and "Vitamins" *(Weishengsu)*. These works relied heavily on "word-fountains" *(guankou)*, a technique of sustained, rapid-fire speech that is reminiscent of auctioneers in the American Midwest a generation or two ago. Word fountains were relatively easy to "revise," because it did not much matter which syllables spewed forth, so long as there were a lot of them. In "Phony Dr. Jia," for example, Lao She strings together the names of sixty-six party-approved literary works in one long sentence—and there it was: a piece that was politically correct, had "educational value," and was all set for delivery by the nimble tongue of a performer.

Lao She also began writing new pieces, but only reluctantly, because he felt that *xiangsheng* performers were better positioned than he to do this. Writers could have ideas, Lao She later wrote, but only performers produced the best work.[13] This was because they had closer contact with audiences. Traditionally a *xiangsheng* piece evolved as it was passed around among performers, each of whom put it to the test in front of live audiences.[14] By a sort of Darwinian logic, only works that adapted and improved could endure.

Understanding this principle, the Small Group set up a honing process for its creation of *xiangsheng*. After a writer produced a text, the Small Group reviewed it and suggested revisions. Then the piece was put before an audience while experienced performers watched the performance from backstage and took notes. The audience itself was invited to contribute opinions. There is anecdotal evidence that political correctness was not just something that the party was pushing in the early 1950s; performers also sometimes felt pressure "from below" to make their content more socially healthful. Yu Shide tells of audience jeers when performers sometimes reverted to smut.[15] In any case, a piece was published only after revisions that followed live audience testing. In its first ten months, the Small Group released thirty-two new or substantially revised pieces.[16]

These works were very uneven in length, artistic quality, and sophistication of message. But an enthusiastic idealism runs through all of them, as it does the clappertales, drum songs, and other "popular performing arts" (*quyi*) produced at the time. "Let's help make China a better place!" seems to leap forth from page after page of the early 1950s issues of the government's new *quyi* magazine *Telling and Singing* (*Shuoshuo changchang*).

When the official Resist America Aid Korea Campaign got under way in fall 1950, the Small Group moved quickly to put *xiangsheng* to the task. In March 1951 a delegation of *xiangsheng* performers traveled to Korea to cheer Chinese troops. I suspect, but cannot prove, that the trip was in part a response to the United States' having sent comedian Bob Hope, a few months earlier, to cheer American troops in Korea.[17] *Xiangsheng* performer Chang Baokun, whose stage name was "Little Mushroom" (*xiao mogu*) and who was a favorite in the Tianjin school of *xiangsheng*, was killed during the visit. This horrible fact only fueled further dedication in the *xiangsheng* world to "resist America." In June 1951 *xiangsheng* performers traveled the length and breadth of China, spreading the message. This was the first issue that brought *xiangsheng* truly nationwide. Pieces were translated into dialects and minority languages, and performances were broadcast over the radio.

Three signature pieces of the campaign were produced very quickly in late summer of 1950 under the aegis of the Small Group. They were called "Paper Tiger" (*Zhi laohu*), about the cowardice of U.S. soldiers; "This Is America" (*Ruci Meiguo*), about the gap between rich and poor in the United States; and "Uphold Peace" (*Yonghu heping*), about the international struggle against U.S. hegemonism.[18] As experiments in the adaptation of *xiangsheng* they are almost disastrously bad and certainly would have gone nowhere, had it not been for the cause that animated them. They insert utterly humorless political jargon, as when "The Soviet Union long ago applied its atomic energy to industrial uses!" comes from the mouth of the ostensibly "funny" man.[19] A "word fountain" gives numbers for all the standing armies of the world.[20] As if to leaven the preachiness, some not-very-subtle smut is dropped in from time to time: U.S. soldiers in Korea write to their girlfriends asking them to send toilet paper, a high priority because "as soon as they hear the People's Army coming, they shit in their pants."[21] But the most interesting flaw in these pieces was that many of the images of America were ones that could cut both ways with Chinese listeners. How high are American skyscrapers? Somebody was in an elevator for three hours and still didn't reach the top! (Wow! Impressive!) But, we then learn, that was only because the elevator workers were on strike.[22] The joke works, but the impression lingers that U.S. skyscrapers are unimaginably tall. The same ambiguity attends the debunking—and yet underscoring—of U.S. military power, technological capability, and opulent daily life. The two-edged nature of these messages does not seem to have been intentional. It seems, rather, that the writing was done in haste, before the creators had time to think very much about possible complexities in audience response.

The best of the "resist America" pieces were the work of Lao She, whose experience in the United States gave him firsthand impressions to work from. Lao She commented that *xiangsheng* was an especially good medium for satirizing America because of its "unreliable" *(bu laoshi)* nature: more than other art forms, *xiangsheng* could get away with turning things upside down.[23] It is not clear whether this meant that *xiangsheng* (1) can invert the Chinese people's positive impressions of America and still be believed or (2) display the U.S. government's tendency to turn things upside down. He may have meant both. Let us consider an example of each.

In a piece called "Matching Couplets" *(dui duilian)*, the *dougende*, who is a virtuoso of verbal parallelism and a feisty critic of capitalism, travels to America.[24] As soon as he arrives he pastes up a couplet (A = *dougende*; B = *penggende*):

A: And on it I wrote: "I speculate, I get rich, I live it up, my life is good; pleasure's all I seek."

B: How come everything's "I . . ."?

A: Because the matching line is all "You . . ."

B: How does it go?

A: "You're honest, you're poor, you're hungry, your life is shot; death serves you right!"

B: *(pretending to misinterpret the "you" as referring to himself)* Death would serve *you* right!

A: I don't mean you! This is about the gap between rich and poor in America!

The funny man then goes in succession to a dance hall, a hospital, a draft board, the Supreme Court, the FBI, Hollywood, and a few other places. At each he writes his satiric parallelisms while cleverly avoiding capture by the police. The piece is much more successful than "Paper Tiger" and "This Is America" in "turning around" positive impressions of the United States.

A piece that shows the other use of *xiangsheng*'s "unreliability"—to reflect upside-down U.S. government rhetoric—is a "cushion" piece called "Interviewing Dulles" *(Fangwen Dulesi)*:[25]

A: Mr. Secretary of State, why do you think it is that the Soviet Union keeps reducing the size of its military?

B: Because the more it cuts the bigger it gets—and the scarier!

A: Is the U.S. also planning to reduce its military, Mr. Secretary?

B: No, we are expanding the military!

A: Why, may I ask?

B: The more we grow the smaller we get—and the more peaceful!

A: Pardon me, but I'm a bit confused: why do Soviet troop numbers go up the more they are cut and U.S. troop numbers go down the more they grow?

B: Numbers sometimes go down as they grow and go up as they shrink.

The contrast here between smoothness of delivery and utter nonsense in content is a standard technique in traditional *xiangsheng*. The rhythm, parallelism, and confidence in Mr. Dulles's lines implicitly claim a "legitimacy" that is simultaneously undermined by his ridiculous logic—and the contrast is funny.

Despite Lao She's expectation that *xiangsheng* performers would be best positioned to create new pieces, the record shows that professional writers did better after all. The weakest of the new work, such as the "Resist America" pieces noted above, were the creations of performers. A few pieces by the performer Hou Baolin were strong on *xiangsheng* technique but not very good at including reformist content. A piece called "The Miracle Worker Pulls a Disaster" (*Miaoshou chenghuan*), for example, tells of a surgeon who works in a hospital that has a department of *xiangsheng*, because laughter helps in healing, but who keeps sewing up the bodies of his patients with operating tools left inside.[26]

The combination of art and thought was made most successfully by three writers who adored *xiangsheng* but did not perform. Lao She was one. He produced more than thirty new or reworked pieces in the early 1950s,[27] and in matters of rhythm, word choice, and authenticity of dialogue, no sensibility was finer than his. The only blemish in his work was a tendency to overuse political phrases such as "We all love the Soviet Union!" or "The greatness of Stalin blankets the landscape."[28] (I view these awkwardnesses more as signs of Lao She's sincere wish to help the party than as flaws in his talent.) He Chi, another highly successful writer of *xiangsheng*, had a background very different from Lao She's. Lao She knew English, had gone to a Christian Sunday school as a boy, and had lived in both England and America. He needed to prove his loyalty to the Communists. He Chi, a party member and veteran of guerrilla struggles in both the Jin-Cha-Ji and Shaan-Gan-Ning border areas, had no such burden. He had been on the side of the revolution from the start. The new society was "his" as much as anyone else's and hence was his to criticize as he saw fit.[29] Gifted with a marvelously dry sense of humor, He produced works like "Buying Monkeys" *(Mai hou)* and "Hooked on Meetings" *(Kaihui mi)* that were among the most successful and controversial social and political satire of the early 1950s. A third notable writer was Wang Guoxiang, a worker, apparently, and author of "The Flying Oilcan" *(Fei youhu)* and a few other *xiangsheng* pieces that display true artistic genius. Wu Xiaoling, the literary scholar and member of the Small Group, wrote an article in 1955 singling out Wang's work for possessing exactly the right combination of new thinking and authentic *xiangsheng* art.[30] We will return to He Chi's and Wang Guoxiang's work after a closer look at the problems that they and others confronted.

Problems of Reform

Communist Party guidelines on *xiangsheng* reform appeared in the early 1950s from the new government's Ministry of Culture. Although perhaps good as moral support for writers and performers, they were not very helpful in practice. They said that new works should avoid all that is "brutal, terrorizing, obscene, enslaving, abominable . . . and unpatriotic" and substitute "healthy, progressive, and beautiful elements."[31] This was fine in principle but not much of a guide for practice. Writers had to imagine for themselves what actually to do.

The easiest changes had to do with oral mimicry, word fountains, and other verbal acrobatics in which the meanings of words did not much matter. One set of words could substitute for another. But these easy substitutions did not get to the heart of *xiangsheng*. They were only peripheral aspects of the art. And even if successful, they did little to promote progressive thought. A string of syllables listing the names of fraternal countries in the socialist camp sounded funny, and was amusing, but did not bring listeners much closer to the principles of socialism.

For that goal, meaning mattered. *Xiangsheng* would somehow have to communicate new thinking. Party guidelines said that "praise" *(gesong)* of the new society was the key. Writers and performers of *xiangsheng* were generally happy to embrace this guideline, but it led to an intractable dilemma that dominated the *xiangsheng* world for several years.

The problem was that the essence of *xiangsheng* is satire. The very conception of the *dougende* on stage is grounded in a premise of self-mockery. So how could a fundamentally satiric art begin to "praise" things? And how could "praise" cause an audience to laugh? It was a technical challenge *xiangsheng* performers had never faced before.

Certain early attempts to incorporate "praise" foundered when satire, like an unwanted guest, tended to seep back in. Lao She tells of a Korean War piece (author unnamed) in which a man has donned a uniform, a helmet, and a gas mask and holds a machine gun, a rifle, and a bayonet.[32] Someone asks him:

> "What are you doing?"
> "Helping the army to move!"
> "Going to the front?"
> "No."
> "Why not?"
> "I was so afraid that I forgot to wear my pants."

Ostensibly in "praise" of the Korean war effort, this joke (aside from its intrinsic weakness, which is a different question) feeds on satire of exactly what it is supposed to be praising. Another piece, Xi Xiangyuan's "Notes on Travel to the West" (*Xixing manji*), tells about building a highway from Xikang to Tibet.[33] It is supposed to praise the building of ties between Han and Tibetan compatriots. But the finer texture of the joke-cracking belittles Tibetans. Their language sounds odd, and they wash cars for the Han Chinese while ignorantly referring to the cars as yaks.[34] Yet another piece, designed to discourage grain thievery, in the end generates considerable sympathy for the thief, whose clever methods the audience cannot but admire.[35] A piece ostensibly promoting equality of the sexes, on close reading, in fact depends on satire of pushy women:[36]

> *A*: In the old society women were oppressed, and in the new society women control men.
> *B*: Right . . . (*then realizing*) Hunh? No, men and women are supposed to be *equal* in the new society.
> *A*: Equal? I don't think so.

B: What's your evidence?

A: Just come visit our production team: female team leader, female deputy team leader, female work-point officer, female director of the militia. . . .

B: All *women?*

A: Only the accountant is a man, but he's a traitor to the cause.

B: What do you mean?

A: He's still married to a female!

A is meant to be ridiculous here. His whole point of view is "incorrect." Yet it was all too possible for an audience to laugh with him, not at him. Satire could support exactly the things it was designed to discredit. To ask performers to deliver lines in such a way that only "correct" laughter could result was to ask far too much.

If people might laugh at something that is supposed to be praised, so might they be indirectly impressed by something that was supposed to be discredited. For example, in response to Lao She's piece "Matching Couplets" (which satirized American institutions; see above), one party theorist wrote: "The audience of *xiangsheng* is, for the most part, the broad masses, and one must not assume that all of them are clear about the basic nature of American imperialism and its internal conflicts. There are bound to be misunderstandings if one uses the satiric mode exclusively. The ironic use of a string of phrases like 'democracy,' 'freedom of speech,' 'due process,' 'scientific civilization,' 'full supply of soldiers,' and 'a million crack troops' is bound to create a certain amount of confusion in the realm of thought."[37] In short, the problem of "how can *xiangsheng* praise?" resolved into "how can such a slippery art be controlled?"

Between 1951 and 1955 the *xiangsheng* world came up with a series of attempted answers. Some performers reserved real satire for the "cushion" pieces that preceded formal dialogues. These cushions did not have to be preapproved and thus were more flexible. In one of his cushions, a storyteller named Zhang Yiming warned listeners against buying state bonds. Zhang joked that the character *guo* in *guozhai* (state debt) looks like a crying face—and said that is just what you will look like if you buy state bonds. Probably not for this reason alone, Zhang was eventually sent to a labor camp.[38]

Another technique, called "flowers inserted from the outside" (*waicha hua*), was useful in several ways. It allowed one to insert jokes into what was essentially a political monologue or, the other way around, to stick political points into something whose main theme lay elsewhere. An early example was a revision of the traditional piece called "Major Job Shift" (Da gaihang). A charming piece that had broad popularity before 1949, it tells about opera singers in the Qing period who were obliged to stop performing for three years in respect for the death of an emperor; in search of work, they convert their opera voices to hawkers' calls and ply the streets. In the early 1950s someone thought of putting it on the radio with the occasional insertion of lines such as "Just look at how disgusting feudal society was!"[39] The insertions were mechanical, and the political messages were poorly integrated.

Better integration was achieved in a work called "New Lantern Riddles" (Xin deng mi) by Zhao Peiru and Chang Baokun. Here "new society" content is inserted into traditional word games. The performers play a game in which A tries to get B to say the word "good" (hao) and B tries to avoid it:

> A: How are you?
> B: Not bad.
> A: And your family?
> B: Depends on whom you ask.

B remains clever. Then the theme shifts to politics:

> A: To join the army these days is . . .
> B: Glorious.
> A: Discipline in the PLA is . . .
> B: Strict.
> A: When an army has strict discipline the people support it, and that's why this war is going so . . .
> B: Courageously.
> A: The ordinary people think the PLA is . . .
> B: Adorable.[40]

The drawback of Zhao's and Chang's approach was that although lively and natural sounding it provided only a superficial analysis of the new society. There remained a need to go deeper.

But early attempts to go deeper often resulted in preachiness. "Notes on Travel to the West," about a highway to Tibet, starts off briskly enough but then drops the following:[41]

A: Traffic on the Xikang-Lhasa Highway commenced on December 25, 1954, and this link has had a major effect on economic construction and solidarity among the nationalities in our motherland. It has also brought great development to the politics, economy, and culture of the Tibetan people. You and I are literary and art workers—if we do not come here in person, and experience life for ourselves, how can we bring this great engineering accomplishment to the broad masses of the entire country?

B: Right. What are some of the other good points?

A: There are too many! The highway was constructed on the Tibetan plateau, known as the rooftop of the world, and is a total of 2,255 kilometers in length. In the few years since 1950, our PLA road-construction troops, together with civilian workers, have brought into play the high level of their spirit of patriotism and of revolutionary heroism to engage with mother nature in stubborn stalwart struggle, day and night, and in bitter cold of 30 degrees below zero. They have vanquished glaciers and quicksand, snowy mountains and grassy plains, and primeval forests. They have built more than 230 bridges across towering cliffs and raging torrents, have drilled more than 2,860 culverts through rock, and have moved more than 29 million cubic meters of earth and stone. Taking a walk along the Xikang-Lhasa Highway is excellent political study!

Such detail could suffocate *xiangsheng*, as could excessive solemnity. When the new government sought to suppress *yiguandao*—a folk religion that it could not control, and hence feared—Hou Baolin and Sun Yukui in 1950 created a piece that told how *yiguandao* "superstition" leads to many ills, including a daughter's carving off bits of her own flesh to feed to her ill mother, and so on.[42] This was hardly *xiangsheng* material. In short, "flowers inserted from without" had its limits. If the flowers were too small, they seemed merely distracting; if too heavy, they were counterproductive.

Another approach to the dilemma of how to combine satire and reform held more hope. This was to release the spirit of satire in a friendly way toward people who are basically good but have flaws. *Xiangsheng* can help such people to overcome their flaws, and this helps the revolution. Good people who put too much stock in old-style thinking are satirized in Hou

Baolin's 1949 piece "Marriage and Superstition" *(Hunyin yu mixin)*.[43] A 1954 piece called "Traveling at Night" *(Ye xing ji)* tells of a man who jay-walks, will not line up for busses, disobeys traffic rules on his bicycle, and so on.[44] He is flamboyantly miscreant but not evil. From *xiangsheng* he receives "benevolent admonition" *(shanyi de guiquan)*, whose aim, in the words of *xiangsheng* historian Xue Baokun, was to "wash the face, not chop off the head."[45] Wu Xiaoling spelled out the rationale more explicitly: "Satirical works are especially well suited to highlighting the struggle between progressive and backward forces in vivid and concrete ways. By contrast with the strong, indomitable new forces, the laughable, disgusting, and ultimately futile aspects of the decaying patterns stand out all the more clearly. That is why satire not only can hasten the demise of the backward, rotting things, but also can encourage the growth of new, progressive ones."[46] But in practice the strategy had mixed results. "Superstition and Marriage" is dull, and "Traveling at Night" descends into slapstick. Only a few pieces achieved true success with the new formula. Three such pieces were "Buying Monkeys" and "Hooked on Meetings" by He Chi, and "The Flying Oilcan" by Wang Guoxiang.

"Buying Monkeys" criticizes a department store copy clerk whose carelessness leads to big problems. His name is Ma Daha, where Ma is from *mamahuhu*, Da means *dadalielie*, and ha is from *xixihaha*—to translate freely, "what the heck?," "this'll do," and "who cares?"[47] Ma Daha is supposed to put labels on canisters of sesame oil and tung oil, and does—except that, distracted by a phone call from his girlfriend, he reverses the labels. A few days later the bakeries in town are outraged that their cakes stink of tung oil, and the furniture shops complain that sesame oil has ruined their tables. But this is just warm-up. Ma Daha's biggest gaffe is his copying of an instruction that reads, "Comrade So-and-So: Proceed immediately to the northeast quarter to purchase fifty crates of Monkey Brand soap." Again distracted, Ma Daha scrawls, "Proceed immediately to the northeast to purchase fifty monkeys." The recipient of this order, Comrade So-and-So, also displays indifference to common sense by accepting it without question and immediately setting out for Manchuria (i.e., the northeast) in quest of monkeys. The funniest passages occur when he arrives in Shenyang trying to explain himself:[48]

> "I am from the Tianjin Department Store. The leadership has sent me here to pick up some commodities. I hope you can help."

"No problem. What's on your list?"

"My company wants to buy fifty monkeys."

"Buy what?"

"Buy monkeys."

"*What?*"

"Monkeys."

"What monkeys?"

"You know, the kind that's covered with hair from top to bottom."

The Shenyang supply official, startled but obliging, refers Comrade So-and-So to Changbai Village in the foothills of the mountains, a place where monkeys are more accessible. The mayor of Changbai, equally bemused by the odd purchase order, suggests that they convene a general meeting of the local Hunters' Cooperative that evening so that Comrade So-and-So can explain his errand directly. Now finding himself up on stage and obliged to give a formal speech—but still with no idea of why he is buying monkeys—Comrade So-and-So does his best:

"Countrymen!"

(*Applause*)

"Comrades!"

(*Applause*)

(*Coughs*) "I . . ." (*coughs*) "I . . ." (*coughs*) [in an aside to the *penggende*] "What am I going to *say?*"

"Comrades! The leadership has sent me to your village. My mission is to buy monkeys. And what use are monkeys? Monkeys . . ." [to the *penggende*] "What do you think I should say?"

After further floundering, Comrade So-and-So comes up with "monkeys make definite contributions to our country," which, upon further pressing, turns out to mean that monkeys can guard a house, can act in plays, and can provide hair for making thread. What's more, says Comrade So-and-So, humans evolved from them.

Author He Chi tells us that the piece was based on an actual reported incident in Tianjin in which "buy Monkey Brand soap" was inadvertently shortened to "buy monkey."[49] That single spark, falling upon the tinder of He's mischievous imagination, apparently led him to write out the whole piece during one night in 1953. It was adopted for performance by the famous master Ma Sanli and his partner Zhang Qingsen, and in November 1954 it was published in *Shenyang Daily*. Its popularity in society reached the point where the term "Ma Daha" came to be used in ordinary language. People said, "I pulled another Ma Daha" or "that guy's a complete Ma Daha."[50]

The success of the piece clearly sprang from its resonance with daily life. The idea of buying monkeys in Manchuria was of course utterly far-fetched, but the general problems reflected in the piece—indifference to sloppy work, unquestioning obedience of orders from above, and the stuffiness of official language—were all too familiar. The generality of the problems was also implied by the fact that Ma Daha was not the only character in the piece to exhibit the problems. Comrade So-and-So, the Shenyang officials, Ma Daha's girlfriend, and others are all imperfect. At the same time, none is an "enemy of the people." Ma Daha is irresponsible but hardly ill-willed. He is human, funny, and in an odd sense even lovable.

He Chi's "Hooked on Meetings" satirizes the long-winded, self-important official who thinks that the sound of his or her voice, droning interminably at meetings, is in itself worthwhile. On "the question of washbasins," the manager of an opera troupe says:[51]

Comrades! The washbasins of our opera troupe are cracking. If they crack, of course, we should solder them. But now the cracking is so bad that soldering probably will not work. Accordingly we have decided to purchase two new washbasins. Now of course, these two washbasins will also, sooner or later, become cracked. But we will need to pass through a fairly extended period of time before the onset of cracking, and so, accordingly, we have determined to proceed with the purchase of the two basins. However, because our opera troupe includes male comrades and also includes female comrades, and because, under normal circumstances, male comrades favor the use of plain washbasins while female comrades, for a variety of reasons, tend to prefer washbasins bearing flowery designs, while, at the same time, a minority among the male comrades are willing to use flowery washbasins and a minority among female comrades are ready to use plain washbasins, we need, therefore, to unify our thinking. If we do not, and should we proceed with the purchase of plain washbasins only, then our female comrades will object; if, on the other hand, we buy only the patterned basins, then male comrades may be unhappy. Accordingly, we must look for unanimity to emerge from contradiction, and for unity to replace confrontation. In order to guarantee unanimity of action, we should first achieve unity in thought; otherwise the washbasin issue could lead to splits in our opera troupe.

The pomposity heads toward even higher levels of theory, but, as with Ma Daha, the satire is still fundamentally friendly. This official is self-absorbed and even a bit stupid (he wonders, for example, if workers should line up to go home or just wander out individually); but he is not a villain. His concern for the male and female comrades and their differing preferences in washbasins might be silly—but it is egalitarian, after all, and his faith that holding a meeting to talk things out does suggest a certain respect for group opinion even if he dominates. He wears a constant smile, which can seem phony, but at least it is a smile, not a scowl. He is always "positive" (*jiji*). He does not smoke or drink.

"The Flying Oilcan" by Wang Guoxiang is not as famous as He Chi's works but is even more successful at combining natural satire with support of reformist thinking. It is about a slothful and negligent worker who shows up late, holds up the work of others, and neglects to oil a machine, thereby causing a serious accident and sending himself—"gloriously," in his own view—to the hospital. The language of the piece is especially lively, natural, and clean. It is no-nonsense "worker idiom" that shows little influence from political language, Westernized grammar, or the Sino-Japanese compounds of modern *baihua*. When the injured hero counts himself "glorious," the *dougende* snaps at him, *"bie bu xian hanchen"*—roughly, "Try not to find yourself undisgraceful!"—thus packing two or three levels of sarcasm into five pungent syllables. In *xiangsheng* pieces by Lao She and He Chi, there is always at least some sense of the literatus writing "down" to a worker audience; such a seam is not visible in Wang Guoxiang's work.

Wang also structures his work for excellent artistic effect. He makes the troublesome worker utterly unaware of the bad impressions he is leaving with others. When people criticize him, he cannot figure out why they would do such a thing and so indignantly repeats their criticisms

("They say I come late to work!" "They think I'm not careful!"). Hence, deliciously, we learn all the details of his misbehavior directly from his own mouth. The political lessons fit in naturally, with no sense of "flowers inserted from without." For example, when the lax worker complains, "They're making me look bad!" the *dougende* snaps, "No, they're helping you!"—thus making an up-to-date political point without any need for jargon about "criticism and self-criticism."

These three *xiangsheng* pieces are unusual in their quality but not in their general approach to reform. Many other pieces of the early 1950s showed the same sincere, almost naive, zest for the new experiment in *xiangsheng*. They showed as well a generosity of spirit toward the objects of satire whether they were workers, officials, clerks, or anyone else. The foreign imperialists, to be sure, were enemies; but we Chinese people, flaws and all, were pulling together to make the new society work. To compare these *xiangsheng* pieces with what had been standard only ten years earlier—that is, ridicule of bumpkins and cripples, and "nonvegetarian" innuendo—a fair-minded person would have to say the changes had been remarkable. But not everyone in China saw it that way.

Crocodile Jaws

Without intending to (or even knowing that they were doing it), the creators of the new *xiangsheng* began giving offense to party ideologues who were watching from inside the Department of Propaganda and the Ministry of Culture. These people had no objection to satire of the old society, but when the problems of the new society began to appear in *xiangsheng*, they took notice.

"Buying Monkeys" had become a huge popular success by the end of 1954, but in 1955 the party leadership instructed Central Broadcasting to cut back its broadcasts of the piece.[52] Then some "different opinions," including "negative views," began to appear in the controlled press. Editors of the journal *Plays* must have received specific instructions from above, because in 1955 they opened a "letters to the editor" forum in which, quite counter to public sentiment, they published more criticism than support for "Buying Monkeys." They followed this with a conference on "satirical plays" that took aim at "Buying Monkeys" and other pieces that had gone too far.[53]

If we put ourselves in the position of the authorities, it is possible to imagine why they had become leery. The humor in "Buying Monkeys" does rest heavily on the vulnerabilities of the new society—on problems either that did not exist in the old society or that did exist but now seemed to grow worse. Ma Daha seems alienated from public property; Comrade So-and-So seems a pawn in an authoritarian order; political meetings look a bit like charades. When the *dougende* turns in an aside to the audience and wails, "What am I going to *do?*" he strikes a chord that resonates with the daily life of the audience a bit too much.

Occasionally the implied criticisms are put into concrete words. (The published criticisms do not cite such lines, presumably because to cite them might only draw more attention to them and make things worse.) In a piece called "Unity-itis" *(Tongyi bing)*, He Chi wonders why everybody in a certain family has to wear the same kind of clothing "just because the family head likes it."[54] In "Hooked on Meetings," one of the topics that appeals to the long-winded official, and on which he would like to hold a meeting, is "Workers' Welfare 100 Years from Now." This follows:

> *B*: A hundred years hence? Then why do we have to discuss it now?
> *A*: We need to lay out the beautiful destiny of Communism!
> *B*: Beautiful it may be, but we don't have to start the talk so soon!

I do not find it plausible, in context, to read these words as subversive. He Chi, who had grown up in the Communist movement, still meant them as friendly satire. But nervous bureaucrats may well have seen the passage as a poisonous weed.

And that, I believe, is the essential mistake that party ideologues made during the *xiangsheng* reform. They were too suspicious and insecure. They should have trusted *xiangsheng* writers and performers to ply their trade—and to do it with basically good intentions; and they should have trusted the Chinese people to laugh in normal, healthy ways, without any need for their micromanagement. They should have relaxed. The crocodile bird was there to help.

The error on the side of the *xiangsheng* artists was their naiveté. They might have noticed the crocodile jaw looming above them somewhat sooner than they did. Intermingled with their first efforts at new *xiangsheng* in magazines such as *Shuoshuo changchang,* they might have noticed the confessions of "bourgeois thought" by a senior left-wing writer[55] and "self-criticisms" by magazine editors for "mistaken views" and insufficient attention to the "thought-character" of performance literature.[56] Political jargon like "Mao Zedong Thought" and "a tiny handful of trouble-makers" (*yi xiaocuo*, used many times since and featured even as late as the 1989 Beijing Massacre) were also popping up here and there.[57] In the larger cultural world, criticisms of "Between Husband and Wife" by Xiao Yemu and the film *The Story of Wu Xun* had been elevated to national object lessons. But the *xiangsheng* world did not see these signs—or, if it did notice, assumed that they did not apply to *xiangsheng*.

It is clear from He Chi's autobiography that he had no idea he might be labeled a "rightist" in 1957. When he was paraded up on stage and taunted for "hating socialism," "organizing an anti-party clique," and "pursuing fame and profit," he kept cooperating with his tormentors in an apparent confidence that, with the next turn, they would certainly perceive his innocence and leave him alone.[58] He agreed to come back for a second struggle session even after the first was a disaster. He "admitted" to pursuing fame and lucre even while he felt, inside, that "the question simply did not exist." He agreed to hand over his personal letters, confident that these would exonerate him, and then watched as the letters turned into "ironclad evidence" against him. In short he was squeezed between two unmovable articles of faith: (1) that he was innocent of any ill will toward the party and (2) that the party could not be incorrect, so there must have been something, somewhere, that indeed was wrong with him. In any case, the "rightist" hat did fall on his head and stayed there as he moved in and out of labor camps for the next twenty-two years.

He emerged in 1979, was officially "exonerated," and the next year published a long self-exculpatory article in *Quyi*, the major national magazine for the popular performing arts. In it he continues to insist that "I wasn't anti-party" and, borrowing a phrase that Mao Zedong had made famous in 1957, said that he was writing only about "contradictions among the people." But he also gives considerable ground to the attacks against him. He writes, for example, that Ma Daha's behavior "was not a product of socialism, but an individualist thing that had been left over from the old society."[59] In fact, the very opposite had clearly been the case in 1954: the popularity of Ma Daha had sprung largely, if not entirely, from its comment on the new society. Had He Chi forgotten this? Had twenty-two years of pressure permanently warped his views? Or was he just protecting himself, in case political storms should return? I do not know but guess the third. Elsewhere in his 1980 article he writes that "to portray characters like Ma Daha in 1953 or 1954 was accurate realism. To write about this kind of character today would not be right."[60] This seems like patent self-protection. He Chi must have been aware that the Ma Daha phenomenon in Chinese society was, if anything, even more salient in 1980 than in 1954. The term "Ma Daha" was still alive in daily-life language, as it is even today.

Still, He Chi did survive the Cultural Revolution, while others in the *xiangsheng* world, most poignantly Lao She, did not. Lao She's suicide in 1966 was not over *xiangsheng* in particular, but his *xiangsheng* activities are as good an emblem as any for the unforeseen disaster that befell him. In 1949 he could have remained in the United States, or could have gone to Taiwan, where he had been invited. Instead, he returned to Beijing, wrote satire about America, supported Chinese troops in Korea, praised the Soviet Union, extolled Stalin, penned the phrase "Long Live Chairman Mao" as early as 1951 (long before it was fashionable),[61] and when political troubles began to arise, simply could not, as He Chi could not, imagine that his goodwill and hard work would go unappreciated. Trapped, as He Chi had been, between wanting to help and trying to comprehend the attacks that came from precisely those whom he thought he was helping, Lao She gave up.

But let us try, one more time, to banish this latter-day bad news from our memories and re-imagine the situation and mood of the early 1950s. Programs of social reform were under way, and the *xiangsheng* world, recently elevated to a higher social status, was ready and willing to help. It got organized. It tried various things, some of which worked better than others. It learned from its mistakes and by 1954 was closing in on a pretty good answer to the question of how to make satire fit the goals of the revolution. The popular audience of *xiangsheng* was following along and was expanding rapidly. Things looked fairly good. The question whose answer we will never know is: *could it have worked?* If no crackdown had come, if a more secure and tolerant political regime had been in charge, might the *xiangsheng* experiment have succeeded? The question is not as narrow as it may seem. It has, I believe, parallels in other aspects of the early 1950s.

🌿 10

"The Very First Lesson": Teaching about Human Evolution in Early 1950s China

Sigrid Schmalzer

A CATHOLIC BISHOP, Cuthbert O'Gara was assigned to missionary work in China in 1924 and remained there throughout the communist revolution. He continued to preside over his cathedral until June 1951, when he was imprisoned during a massive crackdown on Christianity. In 1953, he was deported. Years later, he wrote about the seminars organized throughout the Chinese population upon the Communists' assumption of control: "Now what, I ask, was the first lesson given to the indoctrinees? One might have supposed that this would have been some pearl of wisdom let drop by Marx, Lenin or Stalin. Such however was not the case. The very first, the *fundamental*, lesson given was man's descent from the ape—Darwinism!"[1]

The story "from ape to human" was indeed the "first lesson" in study groups and political lectures. It was also, beginning already in 1950 and 1951, the subject of a great many exhibits, slide shows, magazine articles, and books for all reading levels. With everything else that the new state had to worry about—from finishing the revolution in the hinterlands to establishing control over cultural institutions to fighting the Korean War—why was teaching about human evolution such a priority?

The answer lies in the critical importance the new state placed on ideology—that is, on transforming people's consciousness as a means to the larger end of creating a socialist country. Perhaps ironically, an important focus of such early efforts was the eradication of "idealism" and installation of "materialism" in its place. Propaganda based on key Marxist texts urged people to see natural and social phenomena alike as products of material forces. The irony was that the very notion that teaching people to think as materialists would drive social and political change was itself an idealist position—thought preceded substance; superstructure drove structure. Early 1950s propagandists did not, however, appear troubled by this contradiction. They seem largely to have understood "idealism" as virtually synonymous with religion and superstition, while "materialism" represented science and objectivity. Instilling materialism throughout the population was, they hoped, an expedient way to bring the country quickly onto a socialist track. In the story of human evolution, they found an extraordinarily powerful medium for teaching people—even those with limited education—the basic principles of the materialist worldview.

It was powerful in large part thanks to the existence of the perfect text. In 1876, the great Marxist authority Frederick Engels had written a pithy and elegant essay titled "The Part Played by Labor in the Transition from Ape to Human." Together with a short piece from his *Dialectics of Nature*, this essay was published in China again and again in the form of a thin volume called simply *From Ape to Human (Cong yuan dao ren)*. The text came to serve as a prologue to the Marxist stages of social development—namely, primitive society, slaveholding society, feudalism, capitalism, and socialism—that formed the skeleton of history as studied in the Soviet Union and in socialist China. As an origin story, it effectively challenged and replaced religious accounts of the world. On June 6, 1950, Mao proclaimed that while some "idealists" held that God created humans, "we say, from ape to human."[2]

The political utility of paleoanthropology—the study of human origins and evolution—determined its domination by Engels's theory. Nonetheless, and especially in those first few years, there was considerable room in dissemination materials for diversity in content and approach. In 1950 and early 1951, the inclusive politics of New Democracy encouraged intellectuals and even religious leaders to believe their perspectives would be valued, or at least tolerated. Moreover, while most intellectuals did attempt to adapt to the new paradigm of dialectical materialism, the adjustment process took time. Paleoanthropologists brought with them across the 1949 divide the knowledge they had gained in nonsocialist contexts, including work with foreign scientists.

Finally, unresolved questions within the field of paleoanthropology itself added to the diversity of opinion represented. For example, the
problem of whether humans had originally emerged in Africa or in
Asia added the spice of uncertainty to many popular texts. Even more
important, in the early 1950s the ancestral status of the Peking Man
fossils was unclear. These human fossils, dating to approximately five
hundred thousand years before present, had been unearthed in the late
1920s and 1930s at Zhoukoudian (just outside Beijing) by Chinese and
foreign scientists working collaboratively. At the time, Zhoukoudian
represented the richest trove of fossil human evidence in the world, but
the precise relationship of those fossils to modern humans had not
been resolved.

Over the course of the first years of the People's Republic of China,
several key issues became much more sharply defined, thus contributing
to the crystallization of what might be thought of as an orthodoxy on
human origins. The process of publishing and criticism was of critical
importance in distinguishing welcome interpretations from unwelcome ones. In 1951 we see the ironing out of creationism, and of idealism in general, from the literature on human origins. In addition, the
Korean War acted as a catalyst in identifying political opponents and
solidifying opposition to the ideologies they represented. The Resist
America Aid Korea Campaign (the domestic front of Chinese participation in the Korean War) not only spurred an attack on foreign
churches but also gave added significance to two of the most important
themes in the emerging orthodoxy: international socialism and nationalism. At the same time, events in paleoanthropology taking place in
New York transformed the very shape of the human family tree, which
in turn had enormous consequences for the interpretation of the
Peking Man fossils.

Tracing these processes reveals the enormous significance of science
in ideological foundation work in the early People's Republic of China.
Science dissemination—particularly on the potent question of human
origins—served the state well. Yet we must resist a simplistic account of
science shaped by and in the service of politics. Science was not merely
a political charade employed cynically by party leaders for ulterior purposes. While theories that flew in the face of Marxist authorities were
restricted, questions generated from within paleoanthropology significantly shaped discourse. Moreover, encouraging people to think criti-

cally and scientifically was itself a state priority. This was clear in the empirical evidence displayed in science dissemination materials and in the willingness to let open questions remain open until the necessary evidence accumulated.

A Paleolithic Revolution

The first years of the People's Republic saw an explosion of attention paid to another, earlier beginning: the dawn of humanity itself. Paleoanthropologist Jia Lanpo linked these two transformative events in the preface to a 1951 serial picture book titled *Our Ancestors 500,000 Years Ago*. "Actually," he wrote, "not only have we been transformed in revolution *(fan le shen)*, but following the victory of liberation, so has our ancestor—Peking Man." Jia referred specifically to the attention the new state had begun paying to Peking Man with the purpose of teaching the "broad masses" about human evolution. His statement, however, also had metaphorical significance: Peking Man was to begin a new life with new meaning as an icon of revolution.[3] The story "from ape to human" was one of liberation and transformation that resonated with the political triumph of the day.

In 1950 and 1951, government officials and scientists produced a profusion of materials designed to familiarize "the masses" with the socialist interpretation of "human origins and development" and with the fossil evidence for human evolution in China. These materials included books written for all levels of education, articles printed in popular science and general-interest magazines, political lectures and cadre classes, exhibits in museums and other arenas, and lectures and slide shows presented in factories and other places of work. After this initial burst of activity, new materials continued to appear at a slower pace until the beginning of the Cultural Revolution in 1966.

Virtually all of these dissemination materials were based on Engels's thesis that "labor created humanity." Engels's 1876 essay on human origins, "The Part Played by Labor in the Transition from Ape to Human," was translated into Chinese and published in China by 1928.[4] Immediately after 1949, it became the basis for an extraordinary number of books and for articles in popular science magazines. Some of these materials were translations of Soviet texts, but the majority were original, and the authors were often paleoanthropologists—such as Pei Wenzhong (credited with the discovery of the first Peking Man skullcap in 1929), Jia Lanpo, and Liu Xian—who had studied in Europe or had worked on the Peking Man site excavations alongside foreign scientists. These men had a wealth of knowledge and diverse experiences to integrate into the new framework Engels supplied. While Engels was new to many of them, the importance of spreading scientific knowledge was not. On the question of eradicating "superstition," scientists and officials were allies.

The new state did not rely on people to read books and magazine articles on human evolution on their own. Rather, "political lectures" (*zhengzhi dake*) given by such important party intellectuals as Ai Siqi introduced many to Engels's interpretation of human evolution.[5] Many more learned about it through participation in the "small study groups" (*xuexi xiaozu*) that cadres, workers, peasants, and soldiers attended.[6] Based on interviews conducted in Hong Kong with recent refugees, A. Doak Barnett reported that in early 1950s small groups "one of the most universally used texts is a book called *The History of Social Development* . . . [and] everyone reads *From Monkey to Man [From Ape to Human]*."[7] One of Robert Lifton's Chinese interviewees similarly recalled a "memorable," five-hour lecture on biological evolution and social development, the beginning of which was based on "a popular pamphlet" titled "From monkey to man, through labor."[8]

Engels's essential thesis was that the "liberation" (*jiefang*) of the hands through the adoption of an erect gait made possible labor, and labor in turn promoted complex social interactions, language, the development of the brain, and all the other attributes that separate humans from the apes. Engels insisted that labor itself had "perfected" the hand: "the hand is not only the organ of labor, *it is also the product of labor*."[9] The development of the hand made possible more complex forms of labor, which encouraged "mutual assistance and joint cooperation," which in turn required language. It was only under these conditions that the early human brain was stimulated to grow in size and "perfection."[10]

This is important: although Engels posited a type of positive feedback loop in which labor and social stimulus encouraged brain development, and a larger brain encouraged more complex forms of labor and social interaction, there was no question for him that labor and not brain growth initiated the loop.[11] For Engels, this followed directly from a materialist—as opposed to an idealist—understanding of natural phenomena. The brain-first theory was idealist both in its failure to provide a material cause for brain growth and in its understanding of intellectual development as an evolutionary force. While Engels's contemporaries did not necessarily share his philosophical perspective or the terms in which he defined the issue, they did actively debate whether the development of the brain or erect posture emerged first. Indeed, this question remained at the center of debates about human evolution in the nonsocialist West at least until the mid-twentieth-century theoretical revolution in Darwinism and debunking of the Piltdown Man fossils. "Discovered" in 1912, for forty-one years these fossils provided evidence for the popular view that development of the brain preceded other morphological changes in human evolution. When in 1953 they were proven fraudulent—an orangutan jaw and two human skulls doctored to appear ancient—the consensus settled on the position Engels had taken, although apparently none of the scientists involved interpreted this precisely as labor having created humanity.

Engels stood behind every popular depiction in early socialist China of the life and times of Peking Man and other early humans. A 1950 picture book written in verse offered this concise ditty emphasizing Engels's thesis:

> Only through labor did the body become straight,
> Able to run, able to flee; using hands and using brain,
> Then they had fire to burn, and words to speak,
> In several tens of millennia, apes became human,
> All these were, day after day and week after week,
> Created by labor.[12]

In another book, readers learned, "Because they were able to use tools, make tools, and engage in labor, ape-humans *(yuanren)* were able to become humans and savages were able to become civilized people."[13] Moreover, nearly every popular representation of human origins at least included the phrase "labor created humanity." In this way was science used to define humans as laborers and social animals, to naturalize labor as a category fundamental to the human experience. Science dissemination writings thus joined such cultural productions as the film *Ideological Problems* (*Sixiang wenti,* discussed in Paul G. Pickowicz's chapter in this volume [Chapter 11]), in labeling those who did not labor as not quite human. Through such discourse, the politically privileged position of the laboring classes became further cemented.

This primary concept easily expanded to encompass other core elements of historical materialism. In the era of "primitive communism," humans forming small communities were characterized by harmony within and danger without. Toolmaking, foraging, hunting, and other activities required communal labor, for only by working together could the early humans scrape together a meager existence and protect themselves from ferocious predators. In another 1950 picture book, the artist depicted a group working together to make tools, next to which Jia Lanpo wrote, "The first person from the left is searching for stone tool materials from the river bank; the second is making flakes; the third is refining a stone flake tool; the fourth is learning from their construction experience; through this kind of cooperative labor, they are exchanging collective experience."[14] A book written a few years later for more advanced reading levels contrasted socialist and capitalist anthropologists on this point. While the "ruling classes" believed that people were naturally competitive and combative, early human society actually worked through cultural exchange and peaceful interaction.[15] Moreover, no one was exempt from labor; no class divisions existed, and all members of society contributed to production.[16] As attractive as such a society might have seemed, one author warned that it was no use wishing to return to an earlier historical time. But, no matter, he continued, for there was the "even more beautiful, fortunate, free, and happy society" of communism itself.[17]

From "God Created Humanity" to "Labor Created Humanity"

The story of ape to human was thus an elegant lesson in historical materialism and in socialist organization. Many authors of dissemination materials, however, took no chances that the larger point would be lost. Instead, they stepped back and placed Engels's theory into a larger narrative of the triumph of materialist explanations of the world over idealist ones. Soviet and Chinese books used Darwin and Engels as a one-two materialist punch: Darwin, to demonstrate the commonality of humans and animals; and Engels, to assert the primacy of labor. The chief target in this program was idealism, specifically religious idealism, and it was therefore religious creation stories that served as antagonists in these narratives.

The title of the opening chapter of the Soviet book *How Humans Developed* asked bluntly, "Do You Believe in the Bible or in Science?"[18] Chinese writers largely adopted the anti-Christian crusade of the Soviet materials, and they sometimes added references to Chinese creation stories—most commonly of the male Pangu who created the world by splitting heaven and earth and the female Nüwa who created humans out of mud.[19] Following the Soviet popular science writer Mikhail Ilin, Chinese authors also called attention to the 1925 Scopes trial in the United States in which a schoolteacher in Tennessee challenged a law against teaching evolution in the classroom, and the local inhabitants protested that they were "not monkeys" and "would not be made monkeys of."[20] The story helped reinforce the political message that the supposedly advanced United States was actually held back by religious belief.

In general, authors offered a sympathetic interpretation of the origins of religious explanations for natural phenomena. Jia Lanpo said in one of his picture books that superstitions arose out of early humans' fear and misunderstanding of natural phenomena such as thunder and lightning.[21] Chinese books published in later years further noted a common theme in ancient Christian, Egyptian, and Chinese origin stories: all described humans as having been created out of dust, clay, or mud and thus likely were invented when pottery became an important technology in these societies.[22]

Most materials, however, focused on the later use of religion on the part of the ruling classes to deceive and exploit the workers. Soviet writer M. S. Plisetskii dedicated an entire chapter of his *How Humans Were Produced and Developed* to the question "Why Capitalism Supports Religion," with substantial discussion also of the relationship between religion and imperialism.[23] In China, the 1950 *From Ape to Human: A Simple Account* proclaimed, "This kind of religious superstitious thought is very damaging to workers . . . making them think they have no ability to conquer oppression."[24] Some Chinese books further referred to religious accounts of human origins derisively as "ghost stories," in this way linking them to other forms of superstition slated for eradication under socialism.[25]

While some materials on human origins also addressed native beliefs—most commonly about Nüwa but also sometimes from the Buddhist tradition—the chief "superstition" targeted was Christian creationism. This was somewhat strange in a country with only a few million Christians out of a total population of more than five hundred million.[26] It was partly due, no doubt, to the sheer power of the Soviet example. In the early years, it likely also resulted from the party's concern about the influence of Republican-era missionary education on intellectuals and other urbanites. At least with respect to biology, scientists educated during the Republican era had almost always attended a missionary school at some point.[27] As time went on and such reasons faded, continued bashing of Christian "idealism" was a way of reminding people of the superiority of socialism, especially as practiced in China.

Accounts of creation stories in these materials were in all cases set up to be torn down by science. Darwin was usually given first honors, and he was always credited with "conquering religion" and acclaimed as a "great scientist" who showed that humans are a part of the natural world and were not created by God.[28] This was very much in line with the views of Karl Marx and Engels. For example, Marx wrote in an 1860 letter to Engels that Darwin's *The Origin of Species* was "the book which, in the field of natural history, provides the basis for our views."[29] And in another letter Marx elaborated that "it is here that, for the first time, 'teleology' in natural science [i.e., the idea that nature is guided by a purpose and unfolds according to design] is not only dealt a mortal blow but its rational meaning is empirically explained."[30]

This is not to say, however, that Marx and Engels were entirely satisfied with Darwinism. Rather, they considered Darwin to have been overly influenced by the intellectually idealist and socially capitalist environment in which he lived. In an often-quoted letter to Engels, written in 1862, Marx said, "It is remarkable how Darwin rediscovers, among the beasts and plants, his English society, with its division of labour, competition, opening up of new markets, 'inventions,' and Malthusian 'struggle for existence.' "[31]

Chinese and Soviet authors of books on human evolution sometimes echoed Marx's criticism. For example, a 1950 Chinese book noted that Darwin's idealist perspective caused him to see only the effects of competition and not of cooperation.[32] A Soviet writer whose book was published in China in 1951 further linked Darwin's emphasis on competition to the influence of Malthus's theories of population.[33] Most commonly, however, such writings portrayed Darwin's theory of evolution as merely incomplete, rather than philosophically flawed. As another Soviet writer put it, Darwin "did not completely resolve the question of human origins . . . [because] he did not completely resolve how humans separated from the biological world."[34] Pei Wenzhong and Jia Lanpo's 1954 book *Labor Created Humanity* similarly explained that Darwinism had a "fundamental gap" because Darwin "had not yet realized the basic difference between humans and the animal world, and so was unable to point out the differences in the causes for human evolution and the causes for animal evolution."[35] According to these materials, Engels himself had filled this gap. Later, another Chinese paleoanthropologist would neatly summarize it thus: "If we say that Darwin liberated humans from the hands of God and returned us to the animal world, then Engels separated us from the animal world, allowing people to see clearly that humans are laborers and the transformers of nature."[36]

Ironing out Idealism

Engels's thesis that "labor created humanity" was thus a compelling and efficient means of educating people about historical materialism, while delivering the desired "mortal blow" to idealism and particularly to Christianity. Yet it took some time for the new orthodoxy to solidify and for published materials to fall into line. There were several reasons for the initial diversity of materials on human evolution. One of the most important was the inclusive politics to which the new state professed commitment.

In the earliest years of the People's Republic, the party maintained an allegiance to the goals of "New Democracy," as established in the revolutionary base of Yan'an in 1939–40. Part of the purpose of New Democracy, according to Mao's article by that name, was to provide for the "possibility . . . of a united front against imperialism, feudalism and superstition" in which progressive members of the bourgeoisie and, significantly, "natural scientists" could participate alongside the Chinese proletariat, so long as they were free of "reactionary idealism."[37] Such relatively inclusive language continued in the first few years of the People's Republic to encourage intellectuals to believe that their contributions to social and national reconstruction would be valued. That New Democracy politics were of significance to early 1950s writers on human evolution is evidenced in the frequent and deliberate connections they made between New Democracy and their own acts of writing and publishing.[38]

Mao's "On New Democracy" further promised that "some idealists and even religious people" could join the proletariat in a united front against imperialism and feudalism, even though the party would "never approve of their idealism or religious doctrines."[39] In 1950 and early 1951, Protestants and Catholics had productive meetings with Premier Zhou Enlai in which Zhou even gave provisional assurance that ties between Chinese Catholic churches and the Vatican could be maintained.[40] Given the enormous emphasis placed on disseminating a scientific explanation of human origins, the publication of a creationist account in January 1951 can be understood only if we fully appreciate this initially inclusive political atmosphere.

The book—titled *The Question of Human Origins* and published by the Catholic Education Joint Committee—attempted through persuasive argument to deny the validity (or at least the certainty) of scientific claims about human evolution. In a manner similar to that employed by creationists today, the author cited famous scientists including Pei Wenzhong and Henry Fairfield Osborn to reveal that scientists themselves recognized the spottiness of the fossil record and the difficulty interpreting what existed. He then noted, "Usually when we read about evolutionary theory, we come across the sentence [referring to Darwin's contribution]: 'And so the ghost story that God created humans was toppled.' What we have seen above is that the question of human evolution is an unproven theory."[41] After raising a few "problems" with evolutionary theory, he concluded that human evolution required a designer *(jihua zhe)*.[42] Had the author delayed a few months, his book would never have been published. By summer 1951, the Resist America Aid Korea Campaign began to target Protestant and Catholic churches in China: religious leaders were persecuted, and government oversight of all church-related activities tightened dramatically.[43]

I have found no other examples of creationist publications in the first years of the People's Republic. The foggier specter of idealism, however, haunted some early works on human evolution. This is partly attributable to the tolerance of New Democracy politics. It was also, however, a consequence of the time needed for scientists to adjust their old ways of thinking.

The process through which intellectuals adapted to the new order is most vividly seen in the experiences of Liu Xian. Liu had studied in London with the notable Sir Arthur Keith. Keith was among those who focused most heavily on the role of the brain in human evolution and who saw the development of the human brain as the result of a latent tendency in this direction.[44] This, as we saw earlier, was precisely the opposite of Engels's position that the development of the brain had followed the liberation of the hands and the beginning of labor and that the causes for these changes lay in the material world. In Marxist terms, Keith's perspective reflected his idealist philosophy. With respect to evolutionary theory, he subscribed to orthogenesis—the notion that evolution proceeds through the realization of inherent trends.

After his return from England, Liu became one of China's most influential anthropologists. He founded China's first anthropology department at Jinan University in 1947.[45] As with many others, Liu Xian's prospects under the new state initially looked promising, and he published a book in 1950 for a general audience titled *The History of Development from Ape to Human*. His colleague Lu Yudao wrote a preface to the book in which he optimistically stated that humans had been developing at an astonishing rate since the stone age of Peking Man, and "having entered the era of 'New Democracy,' we must all use our hands and our brains in order to create."[46]

Eight months later, Liu Xian's book fell under attack in a review published in *People's Daily* by a reader named Han Wenli (he is not otherwise identified).[47] According to Liu's own recollections, bookstores quickly responded by removing the book from their shelves.[48] Han's main line of criticism centered on Liu's idealism. Liu portrayed our ape ancestors as having succeeded in making the transition from the trees to the ground through their bravery in accumulating new experiences and their ability to use these experiences to think of a plan of action. Indeed, Liu's narrative was marked by a strongly voluntarist interpretation of evolution reminiscent of the brain-first theories of his teacher Arthur Keith. The apes in his account seemed to map out their own evolutionary trajectory.[49]

Yet it was not precisely voluntarism that Han opposed. Voluntarism was, after all, a core element of Chinese Marxism, beginning with its founder Li Dazhao and continuing with Mao Zedong.[50] What bothered Han was the suggestion that such voluntarism had existed *before* the necessary first step of engaging in labor. After quoting a relevant passage of Liu's book, Han demanded, "Is this not equivalent to saying that ancient anthropoid apes who had not yet begun to labor were already able to think?" Several paragraphs later, he concluded, "What we must realize is that the ancient apes' transformation into humans did not depend . . . on 'bravery' or 'determination,' but rather on the long and slow [process of] learning how to labor."[51]

Liu, however, was no rebel. His ambition was not to challenge Engels. Rather, he took great pains to showcase Engels's theory in his work. Nor is it likely that he intended to write a book that changed the conventional understanding of labor's role in human evolution. The most probable explanation is that Liu simply failed in his attempt to incorporate Engels's theory that "labor created humanity" into his preexisting understanding of human origins. He sandwiched his own narrative within thick slices of "labor created humanity," but between meat and bread lay real philosophical differences.

In 1950, some books on human evolution were published that did not mention Engels or his theory that "labor created humanity."[52] In January 1951, it was even possible to publish a creationist account of human origins. Criticism of Liu in May 1951—along with at least one other similarly negative review of another popular book about human origins in June—suggests that this initial slack had begun to be taken up.[53] Early hopes for New Democracy faded quickly as the Korean War heightened the political stakes of being associated with foreign idealism and capitalism and as critics got around to reading recently published materials and identifying politically inappropriate content therein. One could now be attacked, as Liu Xian was, for failing to interpret Engels correctly, despite apparently earnest efforts in this direction.

This incident did not spell the end of Liu's career. In 1952, he helped found China's most important post-1949 anthropology department at Fudan University. Han's critique, however, provided a foundation for years of subsequent criticism and interference in Liu's research and teaching activities. In 1955, he was again targeted during a Chinese Academy of Sciences campaign against idealism, and though the editors of *Science Bulletin (Kexue tongbao)* solicited his opinion as part of a forum the journal was to print, they deemed his contribution insufficiently self-critical and declined to publish it. Liu recalled that in 1956 he was made to "wear many hats" (the expression used for political labeling), including "idealism" and "anthropomorphism" *(niren lun)* and that his book was again denounced, this time for promoting "reactionary political thought" and "harming the study movement."[54] When Mao Zedong launched his Hundred Flowers Movement in 1957, Liu Xian was among many intellectuals who took the opportunity to voice their frustrations, and he joined several others in writing his experiences in a short article in the *Guangming Daily*—the source of the recollections cited here. During the subsequent Anti-Rightist Movement, however, Liu was criticized again. Students then in the anthropology department of Fudan University recall that Liu was banished to library work because of his "rightist" label, although he was at some point (probably during the early 1960s) allowed to teach a few classes on the use of classical texts in the study of anthropology.[55]

"Our Ancestor, Peking Man"

The unifying principle of the New Democracy was one reason for the ideological looseness of writings on human evolution in 1950 and 1951; the time it took for intellectuals to adapt to materialist perspectives was another. A third cause can be found in the historical context of the international science of paleoanthropology. The year 1950 marked a turning point in the field; before that point the jury was still largely out on some questions that had not arisen in Engels's time—for example, the ancestral status of Peking Man. Two related but contradictory issues were at stake for Chinese socialists in the resolution of this question. One was the usefulness of certain theories of human evolution as exemplars of racism and imperialism; the other was the usefulness of Peking Man as a national symbol. The coalescing of an orthodoxy (albeit a somewhat contradictory one) on these questions involved such disparate factors as the "modern synthesis" in paleoanthropology and the Korean War.

Peking Man was not widely embraced as a human ancestor during the Republican era in China or abroad. Beginning in the second decade of the twentieth century and lasting through World War II, the tendency among scientists was to notice the differences among fossil hominids rather than the similarities and so to place them not only in separate species but in separate genera.[56] Thus *Pithecanthropus erectus* (Java Man), *Sinanthropus pekinensis* (Peking Man), and the Neanderthals, among others, were all understood to have been side branches on the human tree. They had become extinct, replaced by our direct ancestors who were typically missing from the fossil record.[57]

Franz Weidenreich was an exception to this pattern. Weidenreich had taken over as director of research at the Peking Man site of Zhou-koudian after Davidson Black's death in 1934. He held to a linear model of human evolution in which human populations in any single evolutionary period represented different races of only one species. There were thus no "replacements" and no "dead ends" but only continuous evolution from one form into another. Weidenreich identified key apparent morphological similarities between Peking Man and modern Mongoloid peoples, and between other fossils and the modern peoples among whom they were found. Each of these populations retained specific racial characteristics while following the basic, shared "trends" of human evolution—an orthogenetic model somewhat similar to that of Arthur Keith. For Weidenreich, Peking Man was not only a human ancestor but specifically an ancestor of the Chinese people.[58]

In 1950, scientists at a series of symposia at Cold Spring Harbor in New York brought the "modern synthesis" in evolutionary biology to bear on paleoanthropology. Participating scientists radically simplified the human family tree, placing Peking Man within the species *Homo erectus*, held to be directly ancestral to *Homo sapiens*.[59] While Weidenreich's theory of racial continuity was sidestepped, the "single species" thesis to which he was committed became the theoretical foundation for paleoanthropology for years to come.[60] Significantly, the modern synthesis also cemented the opposition to the kind of orthogenetic theories to which Keith and Weidenreich subscribed. Unlike Han Wenli in his critique of Liu Xian, however, scientists at Cold Spring Harbor were not interested in the evolutionary role of labor; natural selection was their focus.

The transition to this linear view of human evolution, in which Peking Man and other fossils lay on the main trunk of the family tree, occurred in China during the first few years of socialist rule. There is no direct evidence that Chinese scientists changed their positions based on the new international consensus. The coincidence, however, is striking.

Since Chinese scientists were still in contact with their foreign colleagues during these years, it would be difficult to argue that the transformations in China bore no relation to those occurring abroad.[61]

While some materials published in 1950 and 1951 portrayed Peking Man as a direct ancestor, others continued to consider her an offshoot or insisted that the evidence was not yet sufficient to determine the matter conclusively. For example, in 1950 Pei Wenzhong wrote, "We still have no way of knowing which of the ape-humans (*yuanren*) is a human ancestor. Perhaps none of them is a human ancestor, and he [our ancestor] is still waiting for us to discover him."[62] One important work from 1940, republished in 1950, even suggested that Peking Man in some ways resembled modern Europeans more than modern Asians.[63]

Jia Lanpo's *Peking Man*, also published in 1950, argued that Peking Man was a direct ancestor of modern humans, and he specifically cited Weidenreich's evidence to prove it. Nonetheless, he took issue with Weidenreich's theories on racial continuity. He noted Weidenreich's identification of features shared by Peking Man and modern "Mongoloids" (the major racial group that includes peoples of East Asia) and his conclusion of racial continuity between these two forms. Jia then explicitly disagreed with this formulation, saying that the modern races were too similar to have such ancient roots and that the split must have occurred after the Neanderthal period.[64]

The uncertainty over Peking Man's ancestral status disappeared from published accounts around 1952. After this point, Chinese authors increasingly referred specifically and repeatedly to "our ancestor, Peking Man." In one book with particularly flowery language, the phrase "our ancestors" appeared twenty-four times in fewer than one hundred sentences, and ten of these cases specified "our ancestor, Peking Man."[65] Although Jia Lanpo had apparently been convinced otherwise, at least two books from the 1950s further pointed to the apparent similarities in bone structure between Peking Man and her purported modern progeny (in one case identified as "Mongoloids" and in the other as "Northern Chinese people").[66]

While the transformation of the human family tree made it much easier to call Peking Man an ancestor in scientific terms, other factors were responsible for Peking Man's becoming celebrated as such in materials produced for general audiences. Part of what was at stake in the question of Peking Man's ancestral status was the antiquity of Chinese people's roots in China. One author perceived a threat to national pride in earlier theories about Chinese people originally coming from Babylon, Central Asia, Japan, and other places.[67] With Peking Man, "the Chinese people finally found their own ancestors, proving that Chinese people and Chinese culture have been born and raised in Chinese soil and are not imported goods."[68] Once accepted as an ancestor, Peking Man extended China's claim to be China back half a million years and thus supported Chinese national identity.[69]

Another way the story of human evolution was made more "Chinese" was in the interweaving of paleoanthropological evidence and allusions to the Chinese classics. Ancient texts traced human society back to early figures such as Nest Builder (Youchao shi), Flint Maker (Suiren shi), and the Divine Husbandman (Shennong), all of whom contributed important inventions to the creation of civilization. History textbooks from 1950 and 1951 presented the Peking Man fossils together with these legendary figures.[70] The legends served to put flesh on the bones—to give an idea of what life was like for "our ancestors." Such texts also emphasized that the sequence of legendary figures conformed substantially with modern knowledge of the past. "According to general laws of evolution, humans first lived in the trees, then invented fire, then fishing and hunting, then animal husbandry, and finally agriculture. This generally corresponds to the sequence of Nest Dweller, Flint Maker, Paoxi [also known as Fuxi, inventor of snares for trapping fish and game], and the Divine Husbandman."[71]

Popular books on human evolution joined textbooks in drawing on the classics to create a *Chinese* history for China. A 1952 book on human evolution used Nest Dweller, Flint Maker, and Fuxi to illustrate changes in early human social organization based on the work of Lewis Henry Morgan and Frederick Engels. Nest Dweller lived an egalitarian life in which all members shared the fruits of their labor with all the others. In Flint Maker's time, males hunted and females gathered, and each group shared with the other. With Fuxi came matrilineal society and more complex production relationships, but still no private property.[72] Another book devoted considerable space to a description in the ancient *Book of Rites* of the earliest people, who lived in nests and ate uncooked grasses and meats.[73]

Nothing did more to make human evolution a nationalist concern than excitement and frustration over the Peking Man fossils' whereabouts. The fossils had gone missing in 1941 while en route to the United States for safe keeping. In a book published in 1950, one author wrote of the fossils' disappearance as "a great loss for our nation's most precious 'people's property' *(zui baogui de renmin caichan)*" and suggested that Americans had concocted "nefarious plots" and harbored "wild ambitions" to plunder this treasure.[74] Newspaper articles printed in 1950 and 1951 brought more specific charges. *People's Daily*, the Hong Kong paper *Dagong bao*, the *New York Times*, and other newspapers around the world detailed allegations, attributed to Pei Wenzhong, that the missing Peking Man fossils were being secretly held at the American Museum of Natural History in New York.[75] These claims found ready believers in China. The Chinese public was already angry about illegal American acquisition of many valuable cultural relics.[76] The Resist America campaign provided a political context in which such sentiments could gain sustained fury.

Years after the Korean War, charges against Americans continued to find widespread appeal in the People's Republic. In 1956, visitors to the Peking Man site exhibition hall at Zhoukoudian (built in 1953) often highlighted this issue in the comments they wrote in the guest book. One member of the Institute of Architectural Science fumed, "We saw many fossils, but none of them are the original, real fossils. The Japanese and American imperialists used despicable methods to steal all the original, real fossils. These [fossils] all belong to Chinese people; we should demand payment of this debt from the imperialists."[77] Another, from the People's Liberation Army, contributed, "During my visit, one thing that I regretted was that in many cases we can see only models and cannot see the real items because they were plundered by the Americans. This gives me an even deeper understanding of American imperialism. It's true, we should denounce their criminal stealing of cultural relics in front of the entire world."[78] A screenplay published in 1961 that took the "stolen" fossils as its theme bore the title *Nation's Vengefulness, Family's Enmity*.[79]

The loss of the Peking Man fossils was sorely felt by scientists around the world. Yet it was not nearly as damaging to science as it was bolstering of Chinese nationalism. The excellent casts made at Peking Union Medical College in the 1930s and the meticulous descriptions by Weidenreich have largely sufficed for research purposes, as a Chinese science magazine predicted in 1946.[80] One Chinese paleoanthropologist explains today, "The loss of the Peking Man fossils are a spiritual loss, a loss of the heart," rather than a scientific loss, "because they had already been studied very carefully and are not likely to give any new, very important information."[81] The enormous attention paid to missing fossils, and particularly the alleged role of the United States in their disappearance, arose from a very specific spin on this "spiritual loss": a nationalist feeling of attachment inspired by the notion that the fossils represented the ancestors of the Chinese people.

International Socialism: "All the World Is One Human Family"

People who produced popular materials on human evolution in the early People's Republic juggled many conflicting influences and priorities. Not least of these were the competing paradigms of nationalism and internationalism. A century of struggle against imperialism, culminating in the Korean War, had created a widespread conviction that nationalism and national identity were necessary for the preservation of the country and people. On the other hand, China was now, by virtue of its Communist leadership and relationship to the Soviet Union, a member of a larger community that privileged internationalism, specifically in the form of international socialism. In discourse on international socialism the Chinese nation as such took a backseat to the global struggle between the capitalist countries bent on oppressing the "colored races," on one hand, and the socialist countries engaged in spreading the liberating force of international socialism, on the other.

Educational materials on human origins offered an excellent venue for this core theme of the new ideology. Anthropology in the nonsocialist West was replete with explicit justifications for imperialism on the grounds that the races were inherently separate and unequal. Moreover, Marx and especially Vladimir Lenin had written extensively and persuasively on the connections between capitalism and imperialism. With such easy targets and ready ammunition, Soviet and Chinese writers had little trouble foregrounding the struggle against imperialism in their narratives of human origins.

The anti-American politics of the Korean War contributed to the force with which early writers on human evolution in the People's Republic attacked imperialist strains in anthropology. Materials on human evolution sometimes singled out American anthropological writings as especially egregious examples of racism and imperialism. For example, one author pointed in 1950 to the American book *The Negro a Beast*, published in 1900, along with the American Earnest A. Hooton's more recent publications on human origins and race, as illustrations of anthropology at its worst.[82] It was ironic—perhaps even paradoxical—that one of the chief targets of these criticisms was none other than Franz Weidenreich. Even as Peking Man was gaining the status of ancestor of the Chinese people for which Weidenreich had so vociferously argued, Weidenreich's theories of racial continuity were slammed as emblematic of American imperialism.

It was further ironic inasmuch as Weidenreich was a German Jew who had fled the Nazis and who thus had every reason to believe himself different from the kind of racist and imperialist anthropology of which he was accused. He had lived in America for only a short time after escaping Germany, and he had returned to America after war had driven him from China. Weidenreich's theory of racial continuity was not the same as the notorious polygenism. He had explicitly rejected earlier polygenic theories that suggested, for example, that the modern races had originated from different anthropoid apes ("Negroes from the gorilla, Mongolians from the orangutan, and whites from the chimpanzee").[83] In Weidenreich's account, all humans had emerged from one kind of ape, and the human races had remained a single species throughout evolutionary history because of interbreeding. Given the politically sensitive character of the race issue, however, the two theories were easy to conflate.

Weidenreich had had a strong mentoring relationship with Jia Lanpo, which likely explains Jia's acceptance of his conclusion that Peking Man was an ancestor of modern humans. Nonetheless, as we saw earlier, in 1950 even Jia rejected Weidenreich's theory of racial continuity. Despite this critique, however, Pei Wenzhong wrote a preface to Jia's book in which he professed to be concerned that Jia had assimilated ideas from Weidenreich and had thus been tainted with idealism. Pei suggested tactfully that Jia should read more Marxist philosophy before revising the book for a second edition.[84] By 1952, Jia had come to understand the importance of explicitly distancing himself from his foreign teacher. In an article titled "A Look at American Imperialist Methods of Aggression from the Viewpoint of Anthropology," Jia blasted Weidenreich as a representative of the idea that the modern races have different evolutionary origins.[85]

Fang Qie, the author of the 1950 book *From Ape to Human*, further tied criticism of Weidenreich to the domestic issue of Han chauvinism in a 1951 book titled *Sons and Daughters of the Chinese Nationality*. According to Fang, Weidenreich's claim that Peking Man was "the direct ancestor of the Chinese people" bore striking resemblance to an idea popular among Chinese people in the past that they were the "descendants of the Yellow Emperor" (a legendary Chinese ruler). Fang Qie charged that the appeal of this notion lay in the Yellow Emperor's reputed conquering of the Miao nationality leader Chiyou, thus glorifying the majority Han people. In actuality, Fang went on, the notion that the Chinese people were descendants of the Yellow Emperor was "a narrow-minded, nationalistic type of defensiveness, a mistaken, high-and-mighty stele [erected to glorify] Han chauvinists." He then cited Mao Zedong on the long history of interaction among the many ethnic groups *(minzu)* currently living in China and quoted Stalin to the effect that "[n]ationalities are not communities made up of a single race *(zhongzu)*."[86] This vehement insistence on incorporating China's many "minority nationalities" into a larger definition of the "Chinese people" *(Zhonghua minzu)* reflected the state's effort to attain the loyalty of those nationalities and thus maintain as closely as possible the territories of the former Chinese empire.[87] Interestingly, this new Chinese nationalist project gained strength from attacks on the "chauvinistic" Han nationalism of old.

The attacks on Weidenreich and on racist and imperialist trends in paleoanthropology as a whole served as a foundation for what was to become one of the defining features of science dissemination materials on human evolution in socialist China. Chinese authors did not confine themselves to exposing racism in the works of their politically unsavory colleagues overseas; they also had a positive message. The chapters in which such attacks occurred were usually the concluding chapters and were optimistically titled "All the World Is One Human Family" or some other variation on this theme.[88] A movie produced in 1959 to accompany the Peking Man site exhibition hall at Zhoukoudian concluded with a charming painting of a group of young people of different races all happily and resolutely holding hands over which a voice narrated, "All the world's humans—no matter the color of their skin, no matter their race—went through the same process of development."[89] A 1954 book written for youth approached this concept from another direction. While the movie highlighted the sameness of all peoples' past development, this book concluded with a prediction about their present and future development. Before the October Revolution, the author explained, the Soviet Union's many minority nationalities had suffered from oppression that kept their lives simple and their cultures backward. Under socialism, however, they had developed quickly and were now on the same level as the most advanced nationalities. This was the promise, he implied, that international socialism held for the rest of the world.[90]

Books incorporating such themes thus often emphasized a vehemently internationalist and antiracist interpretation of human origins. At the same time, however, the use of such quintessentially Chinese sources as the *Book of Rites*, together with the increasing identification of Peking Man as a Chinese ancestor, served a strongly nationalist purpose. The authors of such materials expressed no discomfort with this apparent contradiction. A likely explanation for this peculiar situation is that authors held different peoples to different standards based on their power relations. Thus, nationalism in the hands of Western imperialists was bad from the perspective of Chinese people, and nationalism in the hands of Han Chinese was bad when considering China's minority nationalities, but nationalism on the part of Chinese people as a whole, given their sufferings at the hands of imperialist nations, was acceptable and even desirable.

Science and Ideology in Early 1950s China

It should no longer be surprising that the "very first lesson" in the very first years of socialist rule in China should have been the story "from ape to human." Not only was human evolution a tale of liberation and transformation strikingly appropriate to the time of revolutionary triumph; it was also deeply important to the new leaders that the entire Chinese population understand and accept the basic principles of the materialist ideology. Engels's thesis on human evolution was an accessible and engaging prologue to the Marxist stages of history. It moreover proved an excellent weapon in combating idealism, particularly in the form of creationist explanations of human origins. Engels threw out "God created humanity" and offered instead "labor created humanity." In its effort to replace religious worldviews with a scientific one, the state found ready allies among scientists, who combined "labor created humanity" with fossil evidence to produce a wide variety of educational materials for diverse audiences.

Engels's take on human evolution provided further opportunities to highlight concepts the state considered important as propaganda. Defining labor as the essence of the human, the politically privileged laboring classes themselves were exalted. In addition, the existence in the past of a harmonious and class-free society and the partly contradictory twin priorities of nationalism and international socialism each found a place in disseminated materials on human origins.

Science was a powerful instrument in the hands of the state. The political utility of paleoanthropology in particular can be seen in the commitment of large amounts of time and resources to its dissemination immediately after the 1949 revolution. The state, moreover, viewed human evolution as too important to be left open to all interpretations. The first years of the People's Republic witnessed a hardening of the orthodoxy on human evolution, and theories and narratives deemed out of line suffered criticism and censorship. Specifically, creationist, idealist, and imperialist accounts of human evolution became targets for eradication. The kinds of censorship and political harassment employed in this endeavor are explicitly rejected in societies that identify as democratic. Nonetheless, it should be noted that all of these strains in paleoanthropology have been vigorously criticized and discredited by mid- and late-twentieth-century scientists throughout the world.[91] Participants in the modern synthesis would have agreed that Liu Xian's model of evolution suffered from a lack of attention to material forces.

The Chinese socialist state's use of science for propaganda, moreover, was not a disregard for science itself as an empirical mode of inquiry. Propagandists cared about science because it was useful as a means of turning political truths into "natural" ones, and they typically favored scientific theories that supported the state's political priorities. They also, however, thought of science as a mode of thought that liberated people from ideological authorities and allowed them to think critically. Here again, scientists and party officials had a common interest. Science dissemination materials highlighted the importance of empirical evidence in proving the evolutionary relationship between humans and apes. While Engels was indisputably an authority figure in such texts, he was rarely left to proclaim his theory alone. Fossils together with anatomical, embryological, and behavioral comparisons of humans and apes were conspicuously presented as the evidence required to convince audiences of the fact of human evolution. In many cases, moreover, scientific questions were explicitly declared still open for lack of evidence. This was even true when clear political interests were at stake. For example, while Chinese authors favored Asian origins for humanity over African origins, they typically insisted that the issue could not be resolved without further evidence.[92]

The early People's Republic looks different when science dissemination is a part of the picture. That ideology was a key priority of the new state is not a new finding. Early contributions to scholarship on socialist China by Doak Barnett, Robert Lifton, Franz Schurmann, Martin King Whyte, and others all foregrounded ideology, and often ideological "indoctrination" in particular.[93] But what is typically missing in such accounts are the details of the ideological content imparted. Engels's essay on human origins was for many Chinese people a rich source of exciting and thought-provoking new ideas. While it was certainly used as a club to mete out blows on rival modes of thought, "labor created humanity" also helped expose millions to evolutionary theory and to the value of empirical evidence in the resolution of questions about the world. A member of the Writers' Association (Zuojia xiehui) who visited the Peking Man site at Zhoukoudian in 1956 will have the last words on this first lesson. Bishop O'Gara would undoubtedly, and understandably, have read the visitor's comments as evidence of ideological indoctrination. I think, however, we can also discern genuine inspiration about socialism and about science:

> This visit has been extraordinarily meaningful. In 1949 at a cadre class I heard a professor lecture on "humans' evolution from apes" *(ren shi yuanhou biancheng de)*. At that time, I was full of doubt. How could humans have evolved from apes? The history of social development is not convincing in theory. Only with the facts have I come to admire *(peifu)* it within my heart. The ironclad evidence of our ancestors' fossils has taught me that "labor created humanity." I have no doubts whatsoever anymore. From now on I will participate even more positively in every kind of labor and dedicate myself entirely to constructing our communist society and making the most of the precious property passed down to us from our ancestors.[94]

Acting Like Revolutionaries: Shi Hui, the Wenhua Studio, and Private-Sector Filmmaking, 1949–52

Paul G. Pickowicz

Shi Hui as "Son of a Bitch"

I FIRST SAW Shi Hui on screen in 1977 at Hong Kong screenings of *Jia feng xu huang* (Fake bride, phony bridegroom, 1947) and *Ai le zhongnian* (Sorrows and joys of middle age, 1948), important civil war–era productions. Both films are marvelous comedies made by the Wenhua Film Studio in Shanghai, the best in China in the postwar years. Shi Hui starred as an impish but lovable con artist in the first and as a wise and caring school principal in the second. I jumped to the conclusion that Shi Hui was the most versatile actor in Chinese film history. It was clear, though, that whenever Shi Hui and Wenhua were mentioned, other key names were almost always linked to their success. With respect to *Jia feng xu huang*, the screenwriter was Sang Hu (a rising talent in the wartime and postwar theater and films worlds and a close associate of Shi Hui's), the director was Huang Zuolin (a former Cambridge student who had served as Shi Hui's mentor in wartime Shanghai), and the cinematographer was Huang Shaofen (whose legendary camera work dominated Chinese cinema).[1] In the case of *Ai le zhongnian*, Sang Hu was both the screenwriter and director.

In an effort to learn more about Shi Hui and Wenhua, I began an oral history project that included interviews with Sang Hu, Huang Zuolin, and Li Lihua (who played opposite Shi Hui in *Jia feng xu huang*). The most interesting remarks about Shi Hui came from his old friend Huang Zongjiang:

> Shi Hui had a huge chip on his shoulder. If I made 600 [yuan] a month in the 1940s, he wanted to make 601. When he was young he had worked at a lot of odd jobs—such as service worker on a train—where he was pushed around. People with money and position abused him, and he never forgot it. He hated the world and he was incredibly cynical. He had no interest in politics. He didn't believe in anything. But he hated rich people nevertheless. He felt no pity for the Nationalists when they fell.
>
> Among his friends he was very haughty with his nose up in the air. But at the same time, he had lots of experience mingling with low-life [people], including prostitutes, people in bars, and so forth. So, when he had trouble once the Anti-Rightist Movement began [in 1957], no one felt sorry for him or was willing to come to his rescue. In 1980 when Li Lihua [came back to China and] saw me, she was still referring to Shi Hui as a "son of a bitch."
>
> Shi Hui was quite irreverent. One time he sat down at a fancy piano in a nice home and mockingly began to play some classical music, punctuating it every so often with a loud fart.
>
> Just before he fell in the Anti-Rightist Movement, he and I were leaving a screening of Chaplin's *The Great Dictator*. Shi Hui said, in dejected tones, "We haven't laughed like that in eight years." He was always making comments like that—which later got him into trouble. If others made the same kinds of remarks, no one cared. But when Shi Hui did it, people reported his words.
>
> After 1949 Shi Hui was an outsider. There was a new system and political structure. To get into the mainstream, you had to join the Communist Party. It was for this reason that Shi Hui showed some interest. He wasn't used to life out in the cold. But his chances of being admitted to the party were just about zero.

Shi Hui as "King of the Stage" in Occupied Shanghai

Sanitized official biographies of Shi Hui offer more systematic, but much less colorful, accounts of his life.[2] Shi Hui was born in 1916 near Tianjin. Though he achieved fame in Shanghai, he never lost his strong northern accent or his affection for northern culture, including old-style theater and other popular art forms such as *xiangsheng*. When Shi Hui was one, his father moved the family to Beijing. When he was in middle school, his father was out of work, and Shi Hui had to quit school and enter a Beijing-Shenyang railway training program in 1930. He worked on a train and in the Shanhaiguan station until late 1931 when he returned to Beijing, where he ended up selling odds and ends at the Zhenguang Cinema. This provided him with an opportunity to see many foreign and domestic films. He studied English in an extension class and pursued his amateur interests in Beijing opera and the *erhu* (a two-stringed Chinese musical instrument). Thanks to a friend, Shi Hui got his start as an actor in the China Traveling Theater Troupe (Zhongguo lüxing jutuan), and this led to work in Chen Mian's prewar Salon Troupe (Shalong jutuan).[3] His early performances included parts in such famous Cao Yu plays as *Lei yu* (Thunderstorm) and *Richu* (Sunrise).

In 1940 when Shi Hui was twenty-five years old, Chen Mian introduced him to theater contacts in Shanghai, where Shi Hui worked throughout the wartime occupation. His passionate performances were soon noticed. The wartime flight of many leading Shanghai actors created opportunities for newcomers such as Shi Hui. He performed in *Jia* (Family) and other "progressive" plays put on by the Shanghai Theater Art Society (Shanghai ju yi she), said to have loose affiliations with the Communist Party underground, but moved on in summer 1941 with Huang Zuolin (his new mentor), Wu Renzhi, and others to launch the Shanghai Professional Theater Troupe (Shanghai zhiye jutuan).

In December 1941, Japanese occupation forces in Shanghai took control of the International Settlement, and Huang Zuolin's new group was shut down. In early autumn 1942 Huang and others formed the famous Kugan Players (Kugan jutuan), a group that brought Shi Hui to the very pinnacle of the Shanghai theater world. Under the careful patronage of both Huang and Fei Mu, Shi Hui soon emerged as the most popular actor in wartime Shanghai. He got leading roles in *Da maxituan* (The big circus), which enjoyed a spectacular 40-day run in October and November, and *Qiu haitang* (Begonia), which broke all records by running for 135 days between December 1942 and May 1943.[4] Theater fans began heralding Shi Hui as "King of the Stage" (*huaju huangdi*) at the tender age of twenty-eight.

After the war Shi Hui remained in Shanghai. He continued to perform onstage, but like many others, he became increasingly involved in the film world. In 1947 he joined his old friends Huang Zuolin and Sang Hu in forming the Wenhua Film Studio, a private company that specialized in decidedly humanistic film projects that had more than the usual amount of artistic value. Four roles that propelled Shi Hui to postwar film stardom deserve special mention. In the delightful comedy *Jia feng xu huang*, written by Sang Hu and directed by Huang Zuolin, Shi Hui played a struggling Shanghai barber. In both *Taitai wansui* (Long live the missus, 1947), written by Zhang Ailing and directed by Sang Hu, and *Ye dian* (Night lodging, 1947), written by Ke Ling and directed by Huang Zuolin, he played nasty old men.[5] In *Yan yang tian* (Bright sunny days, 1948), written and directed by Cao Yu, Shi Hui played a lawyer. Things were going so well during the filming of *Jia feng xu huang* that the American periodical *Life* magazine published an attractive photo spread on Shi Hui and the postwar Chinese film scene.

In late 1948, on the eve of the collapse of the Nationalist regime in Shanghai, Shi Hui began writing and directing for the first time. The movie was titled *Muqin* (Mother, 1949). But he remained best known for his acting, nevertheless, and his unique box-office appeal was indisputable. In early 1949 Sang Hu recruited him to play the lead in *Ai le zhongnian*, a heartwarming comedy written and directed by Sang Hu about a gentle primary school principal who finds love late in life. Both *Muqin* and *Ai le zhongnian* revealed that there were problems in contemporary Chinese society, but both films adopted a light, optimistic tone. Outside the gates of the Wenhua Studio in April 1949, however, society was unraveling, and the revolutionary forces of the Communist Party were poised to enter Shanghai.

Shi Hui as Liberation Celebrant

When Luo Xueqian, head of the leading state-owned film studios in Shanghai, fled on May 3, 1949, it was clear to most in the film world that the days of Nationalist rule were almost over.[6] Few in Shanghai's glittering movie industry had much sympathy for the departing Nationalists. Film personalities had ample opportunity to flee, but almost none made the move. Still, few moviemakers had knowledge of the Communists or working relations with their representatives.

There was widespread agreement in film circles on the sad state of the domestic film industry. Many believed that the Nationalists had done far too little to protect the postwar film industry from the aggressive marketing strategies of the American movie industry. Hollywood competition, many felt, threatened to destroy the domestic industry. There were calls throughout the late 1940s to control the number of American films imported to China. Actors, actresses, screenwriters, and directors called for government intervention and protectionism. The Nationalist response had been disappointing, but there was reason to believe that the Communists would be more assertive. Shanghai filmmakers had their own reasons for embracing the anti-American position associated with the Communist Party.

Communist forces occupied Shanghai on May 25, 1949. Six days later, on May 31, film and theater people held a hastily convened conference as part of the "liberation" celebrations taking place throughout the city. The next day movie and stage personalities took to the street in a colorful parade. Closed down for two weeks beginning in mid-May, Wenhua, Kunlun, and Guotai, three of the most important private studios in Shanghai, reopened for business on June 2.[7]

The Communist Party, for its part, made it clear that the political support of theater and film people was welcome. Indeed, in sharp contrast to the behavior of the Nationalists, the Communists actively recruited film professionals to their cause. This does not mean that the party did not harbor suspicions about the ideological orientation of bourgeois film stars, many of whom, like Shi Hui, had remained in occupied Shanghai throughout the Japanese occupation and had continued with their glamorous careers during the bloody civil war. But given its often expressed interest in the cultural and intellectual spheres and its strong desire to consolidate its rule in urban centers, the party was in desperate need of the mass media expertise of urban filmmakers.

The party formally took over the Nationalists' two major film studios in Shanghai on June 2, 1949, putting veteran party member Yu Ling in charge of these state filmmaking units, now merged and renamed the Shanghai Film Studio (Shangying).[8] But the message went out that, especially in Shanghai, the heart of China's prerevolution film industry, the new state studio would need time to gear up and that the private studios, including Wenhua, were needed.

To better control the Shanghai arts world, the Shanghai Theater and Film Association (Shanghai xiju dianying xiehui) was set up on June 18. An election was held to determine its leadership. It is not clear precisely how the election was organized, but the number of votes received by the top twenty-seven candidates was published.[9] The leading vote-getters, with 586 and 554 ballots, respectively, were veteran party members Yu Ling and Xia Yan. The rest of the list was composed primarily of famous nonparty figures who clearly wanted to cooperate with the party and play a leading role in the postrevolution art world of Shanghai. Shi Hui's mentor Huang Zuolin came in fifth with 450 votes, the popular actor Zhao Dan came in seventh with 356, followed by director Chen Liting (ninth with 342), director Ying Yunwei (tenth with 287), director Wu Yonggang (eleventh with 274), actor Lan Ma (twelfth with 252), and director Zheng Junli (fourteenth with 235). Shi Hui ranked sixteenth with 215 votes.

The tally was good news for Shi Hui because his strong desire to be acknowledged as an enthusiast of "liberation" was recognized by his appointment to the executive committee of the association. But it was disappointing news because many of the people higher on the list were not his equals, and only a few votes separated him from relatively unknown figures such as the politically ambitious twenty-four-year-old actress Huang Zongying (who came in twenty-first with 180 votes).

The Nationalists had done little to cultivate the support of theater and film people, thus perpetuating the caricature of actors and actresses as empty-headed and oversexed prima donnas. Shanghai film personalities were flattered to be courted by the Communists. In summer and fall 1949 many in the film world, acutely aware of an important opportunity, worked very hard to be noticed by the new authorities and perceived as revolutionary activists. This competitive jockeying for position had practical implications. It was assumed that those who could establish revolutionary credentials would be in a position to play a leading role in the postrevolution film world, while those who failed to attract political attention would be pushed aside. In the early months, this high-energy climate gave rise to a mood of optimism. It was widely known that all the film stars had unconventional personal histories and a poor track record of political activity. But none of that seemed to matter in mid-1949. What mattered was acting revolutionary. Thus, one of the first major activities supported by the new theater and film association was a massive parade of performing artists held on July 4 to honor the People's Liberation Army (PLA).[10] Almost all the big stars were there.

A few days later the association promptly announced that its members were determined to clean up the film world by preventing unhealthy Chinese films from being screened. Calling for both censorship and self-discipline, Xia Yan urged veteran film workers to sign a pledge to maintain high standards. *Qingqing dianying* published photos of both Shi Hui and Huang Zongying signing the pledge.[11] A few movies were subsequently banned, but in fact, despite the solemn pledges, in the two-year period from April 1949 through May 1951 many hundreds of prerevolution Chinese films were shown in Shanghai, along with a very small number of new, postrevolution works. Films from the prewar 1930s, the controversial Japanese occupation period, and the civil war period were widely shown, along with movies from Hong Kong. There were approximately fourty-eight movie theaters in Shanghai in 1949, twenty-two of them higher-quality, first-run venues.[12] Virtually all of them were privately owned and operated. In the two-year period mentioned above, these theaters scheduled over forty-six thousand screenings of Chinese films for more than twenty-four million customers.[13]

Shanghai film veterans actively supported the various movements that were launched in late summer 1949 and later against "poisonous" Hollywood films.[14] In their youth, many of them were addicted to Hollywood film culture; now it was in their artistic, economic, and political interest to denounce films from capitalist countries. But in 1949 and most of 1950 it was still necessary to show American and British films in order to satisfy public demand for movies and to ease the transition to the postrevolution era. In the eighteen months from April 1949 to October 1950 when Chinese forces entered Korea, there were more than 33,000 screenings of 646 American and British films (virtually all of them pre-1949 titles) to a total Shanghai audience of more than 14 million.[15] Western film culture was still very much a part of the immediate postrevolutionary scene.

Shi Hui was especially active in mid- and late 1949 in showing enthusiastic support for the new regime. On August 1, celebrated as the founding day of the PLA, Shi Hui and a friend performed a *xiangsheng* comedy routine as part of a radio fund-raising event to benefit army veterans. Five days later he sold autographed paper fans *(shanzi)* to help raise funds for veterans who had helped disaster victims. On October 1 he and the popular silent screen matinee idol Jin Yan led the largest march ever of stage and screen personalities, this time in support of the formal establishment of the People's Republic.[16]

Other stars, with better political connections to the new regime, engaged in higher-profile public activities. In late July, Zhao Dan went to Beijing to participate in the first meeting of the China Film and Theater Workers' Association (Zhongguo dianying xiju gongzuozhe xiehui), an organization that was to help coordinate filmmaking nationwide. Bai Yang (who had traveled to Beijing from Hong Kong with politically active director Zhang Junxiang to pay homage to the party even before the fall of Shanghai) was included in a Chinese delegation that went to Moscow in late October to celebrate the anniversary of the October Revolution. Only two years earlier, in 1947, she had been honored as the first recipient of the Chiang Kai-shek Best Actress Award! Now she was one of the most visible film world supporters of the Communist Party. Back from Moscow in December, she was assigned to work at the state-run Shanghai Film Studio, where she presented a glowing report of her visit to the Soviet Union. On December 21, 1949, she even recited a poem in honor of Joseph Stalin's seventieth birthday at a public gathering in Shanghai.[17]

Beginning in July 1949 the newly established Shanghai Literature and Arts Office (Shanghai wenyi chu), a state organ led by Yu Ling and Xia Yan, convened several conferences and meetings attended by both state and private-sector filmmakers, including representatives of the four leading private film studios.[18] The new ground rules were spelled out in general terms, but many questions went unasked. Who, among the ranks of the prerevolution Shanghai film veterans, would be able to enter the party and the government? How would they prove themselves?

In early November 1949, Shi Hui raced off to Beijing to plan Wenhua's first postrevolution film. The relationship between the new government and the private-sector filmmakers of Shanghai was far from clear, but movie production leaped ahead anyway.

Shi Hui as Kindly Cop

Wu Xingcai, Wenhua's principal financial backer, was still in Hong Kong in fall 1949. But he was soon convinced by the new Film Bureau in Beijing to renew his interest in the company. The first Wenhua picture initiated after the occupation of Shanghai by PLA forces was a grand film adaptation of Lao She's novella *Wo zhei yi beizi* (This life of mine), originally published in 1939.[19] Production began in late fall 1949 with an eye to completing the project in time for the lunar New Year holiday season in early 1950. *Wo zhei yi beizi* was directed by Shi Hui and starred Shi Hui in the title role of an old-fashioned Beijing policeman.[20]

This undertaking provided Wenhua with an excellent chance to get off to a good start in the new postrevolution era. *Wo zhei yi beizi* had several advantages. It was an important piece of May Fourth–type fiction crafted by a highly respected non-Communist writer, Lao She, who had returned to China after the revolution and showed initial enthusiasm for the new order. Very few works of May Fourth fiction had been adapted for the screen prior to 1949. Wenhua would be doing the regime a favor by demonstrating that the new society was the legitimate heir to the May Fourth cultural legacy. The film would highlight the softer, flexible side of the new order.

Wo zhei yi beizi was also promising because it had an epic quality. Rather than taking a microscopic look at a particular moment in time (as most films did), it showed dramatic changes in Beijing over a long period. Lao She's original novel covered the period from 1909 to 1921. To make the film even more sweeping in historical terms, screenwriter Yang Liuqing, working closely with Shi Hui, extended the story all the way to 1949 and the Communist victory.

Most scholars regard *Wo zhei yi beizi* as a directorial and performance tour de force for Shi Hui. Filled with rich details of local life in Lao She's beloved Beijing, the movie traces the life of an ordinary neighborhood cop. The film is especially effective in conveying in a strikingly sentimental way the colorful language and street customs of Beijing folk. The hero of the story is a decent, morally upright, gentle, unassuming man who spends most of his time mediating minor disputes. People trust and respect him. As a twenty-two-year-old cop, he takes great pride in his work and is full of enthusiasm. But he is naive and knows nothing about politics. He is confused when the Qing dynasty suddenly collapses in 1911.

Our hero stays on the job during the warlord regime that follows. But he and his partners are given degrading jobs (such as guarding the

entrance to the homes of corrupt government officials) or forced to harass patriotic students who take to the streets first to protest the
Twenty-one Demands in 1915 and later to advance the May Fourth
Movement in 1919. Our cop, still naive, sympathizes with the students
and cannot understand why the government suppresses them. Meanwhile, the local economy stagnates, and policemen struggle to hold
their families together. The first half of the film covers the material
contained in Lao She's original novella and takes considerable pains to
remain faithful to the text.

The second half of the film picks up where Lao She left off and is
quite disappointing in that there is less Beijing local color and more
politics—politics consistent with the late 1940s party perspective on
the recent history of China. Thus, Beijing is shown to be in decline
in the Nanjing decade after the capital is moved south by the Nationalists. Our hero's wife has died and his daughter has married into
the family of another policeman. Only his son, who also becomes a
cop, remains behind. Like his father, he is a decent person, but he is
more politically conscious and befriends a number of revolutionary
students.

The Japanese occupation of Beijing is treated in a highly emotional
but predictable manner, highlighted by an episode of popular outrage
in response to a sexual assault (a familiar trope found in both pre- and
postrevolution Chinese films). The cop's son is engaged to a sweet local
girl. Monstrous-looking Japanese arrive at the home one day in the
company of Chinese collaborators looking for any "Chinese girl" who
can be pressed into service as a sex slave for Japanese troops. The cop
and his son do their best to trick the villains but are reduced to looking
on in horror as the lass is dragged away, kicking and screaming. The
son then resolves to leave Beijing to join the guerrilla fighters. The father allows him to do so but points out that without the son he will be
alone in the world with no one to help in his old age.

The final sequence involves the civil war period and the return of the
Nationalists. The regime, not surprisingly, is shown to be totally corrupt. A former traitor, who now works for the Nationalists, mercilessly
tortures the old man to get information about his son's Eighth Route
Army activities. In prison, the old cop meets a young revolutionary
who was once a friend of his son. He watches helplessly as the young
man is executed.

The old cop is then forced into a labor gang before being tossed away like a piece of trash. He is reduced to begging, wanders the streets of Beijing trying to find shelter and food, and finally dies one night in a back alley. Images of his son in a PLA uniform, fighting to win national victory, appear briefly on the screen, but it is too late for the old man.

Wo zhei yi beizi is both predictable and propagandistic in the second half, but it must be acknowledged that the film did a credible job of fusing the prerevolution Wenhua legacy of soft, humanistic, highly aesthetic filmmaking with the postrevolution demand for harder, overtly political narratives that reinforced the party's version of history. If the point was to make a united front film that contained a little of the old and a little of the new, then *Wo zhei yi beizi* and Shi Hui were certainly successful. The only minor concern involved the final scene. Should the old man be allowed to die alone on the street without seeing his son and the happiness of the new society? Or should he be shown welcoming his son and joining in the victory parades? The original screenplay contains the happy ending. But Shi Hui came up with a variety of excuses for his decision to end the film on a tragic note. At a conference convened in Shanghai on February 13, 1950, and attended by numerous film world luminaries, Shi Hui explained rather defensively that he wanted very much to do the shot according to the script, but a mass scene involving troops entering the city would be too expensive for a private film company. He said he tried to rent an airstrip in Shanghai to shoot the last mass scene, but Nationalist pilots were still dropping bombs in the region.[21] To this day, summaries of the film invariably contain the rosy ending that was never filmed.[22]

Reviews were quite favorable, and the audience clearly regarded it as a wonderful gift for the 1950 lunar New Year. The film was screened in Shanghai 575 times before a total audience of 314,389 in 1950, a record that Wenhua's subsequent efforts in 1950 would not be able to match.[23] The new government was so pleased with the film that it decided to send it to a film festival in socialist Czechoslovakia.

Shi Hui expressed only one reservation in public about the artistry of the film. He told a number of film insiders that the character of the revolutionary youth who appears throughout—and who is executed in the end—was not present in Lao She's original novel. Shi Hui expressed some regrets about imposing this character on the narrative because the representation was stiff and unconvincing in his view.[24]

Shi Hui as Good-Hearted, Small-Town Tailor

The second postrevolution film produced by Wenhua was *Taiping chun* (Peaceful spring). Released in late spring 1950, it brought together many pivotal members of the old Wenhua team, including director Sang Hu and master cinematographer Huang Shaofen. It starred Shi Hui in the complicated role of Liu Jinfa, a kind-hearted old-style tailor in a small town in eastern Zhejiang in the years from the Japanese occupation to the arrival of the PLA.

Meticulously photographed, expertly edited, and nicely performed, the movie was simple and compelling, reminiscent in many respects of late-1940s Wenhua productions. The main character is tailor Liu, played by Shi Hui in a highly nuanced manner. Liu is a decent, good-hearted, kindly, nonconfrontational figure who does not want to hurt anyone's feelings. Indeed, he does what he can to please everyone around him. The portrait of the tailor is vintage Wenhua humanism: Liu is a profoundly sympathetic character whose gentle disposition is viewed in a positive light.

Early in the film, Liu takes in a poor rural boy, Genbao, as a long-term apprentice. As time goes by it becomes obvious that the hard-working Genbao is a perfect match for Liu's daughter, Fengying, played nicely by the legendary postwar actress Shangguan Yunzhu (who failed to gain entry to the party in the 1950s and ended up committing suicide in the Cultural Revolution by jumping from a building in Shanghai).[25] Tailor Liu thinks the best of everyone, but the two young people are more politically astute.

The only other main characters are Zhao Laoye and his wife, prosperous local elites who have been good customers of Liu's for many years. Liu appreciates their patronage, but his daughter and Genbao are vividly aware that Zhao collaborated with the Japanese and then worked closely with local Nationalists after the war. Liu values his old-style relationship with the Zhaos, while the young people remain suspicious. Nevertheless, Fengying and Genbao are extremely respectful of the old tailor and do nothing to question his authority. In brief, they love and admire the kind old man in ways consistent with Confucian codes, though they worry that ill-intentioned people might take advantage of him.

Two crises are featured toward the end of the picture. First, since Zhao Laoye still has no son, he wants to take tailor Liu's daughter as a second wife. Liu has no alternative but to decline on the grounds that the girl is already committed to apprentice Genbao. Zhao then secretly arranges to have Genbao drafted into the army and jailed when the lad refuses to serve. Zhao, a wily manipulator, knows Liu will come to him for help, at which point a deal is arranged. Zhao will "use his influence" to get Genbao released if Liu agrees to give over his daughter to Zhao in marriage. Liu goes along in order to save the young man. But before the marriage takes place, the two young people, without Liu's knowledge, run away.

Denying knowledge of the escape plan, Liu is jailed. Before long, however, PLA forces arrive on the outskirts of the town. Zhao Laoye's wife shows up at the jail to tell Liu that she feels sorry for him and will pull some strings to get him released. Once Liu is out, however, Zhao's wife asks for a favor. She pressures Liu to store several boxes of valuables "for safe keeping" and pays him for his assistance. Given their long-term business relationship and his belief that Mrs. Zhao "saved his life," Liu foolishly agrees.

The second crisis occurs after the PLA arrives. At first, things go well when Liu's daughter and Genbao return to the house and everyone in the joyous community welcomes the advent of the "new society." But then Fengying discovers by accident that her father is hiding valuables that belong to the Zhaos. In a fascinating sequence toward the end of the film, Fengying confronts her father, but the old man asserts he has done nothing wrong. The Zhaos helped him in the past, and they were good customers. He gave his word, and his word must mean something. Defying her father, Fengying tells Genbao the story. Genbao is still very respectful of his future father-in-law, but he has become politically involved in the community and argues that the only moral thing to do is to hand in the valuables to the new government. Tailor Liu strenuously objects, clinging to the notion that his word and customary human relations stand for something.

The rejoinder of the young people contains both moral and practical components. First, they say there is a new morality. The Zhaos were exploiters and collaborators, so turning their property over to the "people" is morally justified. Second, since the Zhaos are "reactionaries," anyone who helps them will also be branded a reactionary. The young people understand what this means, but old Liu sticks to his ethical guns.

When a family friend who was drafted by the Nationalists shows up at the shop missing a leg, tailor Liu is deeply troubled. His daughter tells him he must turn over the valuables. But Liu continues to balk. It is only when Genbao gets a letter from his home village saying his dear mother has been killed in a Nationalist air raid that old Liu becomes enraged and turns over the valuables. Liu says he now knows what an inhuman reactionary is and that he wants to be a "human." A local government cadre tells Liu he is entitled to a reward, but he says he will not take it. The cadre insists. In the final shot, Liu is praised at a large public meeting for buying government bonds with his reward money.

In many respects *Taiping chun* was a notable success in that, like *Wo zhei yi beizi*, it almost seamlessly bridged the gap between the prerevolution and postrevolution Shanghai cultural scene. The film stands in clear political opposition to both Japanese wartime aggression and Nationalist postwar bungling. It also reveals the class structure of society and shows the class enemy (the Zhaos) to be in league with foreign and domestic oppressors. The victory of the revolution and the masses of laboring people is explicitly applauded. From this point of view, there is little difference between *Taiping chun* and Wenhua's first postrevolution film, *Wo zhei yi beizi*.

All of this was accomplished in *Taiping chun* without Wenhua sacrificing its artistic integrity. Shi Hui, director and screenwriter Sang Hu, and cinematographer Huang Shaofen dominate the show in almost exactly the ways they did in prerevolution Wenhua films. The film's overt praise for the revolution notwithstanding, *Taiping chun* looks and feels a lot like *Ai le zhongnian*. This film, also written and directed by Sang Hu and starring Shi Hui, was released by Wenhua in early 1949 in the final days of the old regime. Indeed, *Ai le zhongnian* was screened in Shanghai for many months after the arrival of revolutionary forces in May 1949 (including 322 postrevolution screenings in 1949 and 14 screenings in 1950).[26]

The humanism of *Taiping chun* overshadows the attention it pays to human conflict, including class tensions and international conflict. *Taiping chun* tries very hard to be revolutionary but ends up a humanistic work. The most interesting characterization is Shi Hui's portrayal of Liu Jinfa, the kindly tailor. Thanks to Shi Hui's brilliant acting, Liu is utterly convincing and sympathetic. The audience likes him, even though he seems oblivious to the evil that swirls around him. Not only does he not resist abusive people; he completely fails to recognize injustice when it stares him in the face. The issue is not simply that Liu is naive and entirely too trusting; it is that he remains attractive as a character in spite of his sentimentality. The young people are far more aware of harsh realities that the old man consistently fails to grasp, but they too are clearly paralyzed by their Confucian devotion to the patriarch. They defer to his authority throughout the film and thereby reveal the extent to which they too are invested in "old" social relationships.

Given the popularity of *Taiping chun* (188,577 people viewed 467 screenings in Shanghai alone in 1950), Shi Hui and his old friend, writer-director Sang Hu, must have been shocked by the hostility party critics expressed toward the work.[27] In its June 24, 1950, edition, *Wenhui bao* carried two blistering attacks on the film. One critic said that director Sang Hu had ignored warnings about the need to make changes. Much of this fanciful story, he charged, would be misinterpreted by the film audience. The class enemies slipped away quite easily without being made to suffer for their crimes. And the reward given by the revolutionary cadre to the old tailor at the end was totally inappropriate. Conduct like his should not be rewarded.[28]

A more serious attack was offered by Mei Duo, the editor of *Wenhui bao*'s biweekly theater and film supplement. She argued that the problems with the film centered on the backward nature of screenwriter Sang Hu's mind. It was ideologically misguided to have the film revolve around the life of a hopelessly "empty" character like the old tailor. The relationship between the tailor and the local class enemies is illogical, Mei said, and the film does not do nearly enough to expose the exploitative nature of Zhao Laoye, the local elite. Sang Hu had an "attitude" problem, she wrote, and was in urgent need of thought reform.[29]

Sang Hu knew there was trouble even before these attacks were published. His response was printed in the second issue of the new journal *Dazhong dianying*.[30] Assuming a humiliating posture, Sang Hu simply surrendered without a fight. In line after line of self-flagellating prose, he confessed that his mentality was indeed petit bourgeois to the core and that the whole story was an irresponsible fabrication. All the criticisms of *Taiping chun* were on target, he stated. In fact, he wrote, the film was "a total failure." The criticism was devastating: the film was pulled from distribution and rarely mentioned thereafter.

Shi Hui as Cultural Revolutionary

In July 1950, not long after the appearance of the stern criticisms of *Taiping chun*, Shi Hui published a highly political and self-congratulatory article titled "The Shanghai Film and Theater Worlds in the Year since Liberation."[31] Nowhere in the essay did he mention the *Taiping chun* debacle or his connection to it. Referring instead to general developments between June 1949 and June 1950, he began by saying that the film and theater world wanted to "thank the Communist Party and thank the People's Liberation Army" for the chance to start a new life. Using the new political jargon, Shi Hui said that in the past the film and theater scene served relatively few people because Shanghai was controlled by imperialists and reactionary Nationalist bureaucratic capitalists who squeezed out the "sweat and blood of the laboring people." True, Shanghai was rich in dance halls, restaurants, and theaters, but, upon reflection, he could now see that people in the film and theater worlds got little more than leftover scraps.

In the year following liberation, Shi Hui proclaimed, artists had abandoned a misguided sense of pride in their privileged positions in Shanghai society. Given new life, the stars of old worked hard to accomplish as much as possible. "Within three days of liberation," he wrote, "we formed scores of performance troupes" that went out to the factories to put on shows for "worker brothers." Moreover, he reminded readers, theater and film people also participated enthusiastically together with soldiers and ordinary citizens in a grand victory parade. Even though it rained that day, the "stars" still went out "to dance in the streets." According to Shi Hui, soldiers said that "what you've done is just as heroic as what we do at the front."

Organizationally speaking, Shi Hui observed, the formation of the Shanghai Theater and Film Association was an unprecedented event because it united the performing arts world for the first time and thereby allowed for the "collectivization" of cultural activity. The association sponsored a massive liberation parade for performing arts workers and organized a spectacular six-day fund-raising event held outdoors during summer 1949. Tens of thousands of people mobbed the park to see their favorite stars. Owing to this direct contact between entertainers and the masses, the theater and film world was able to make ideological progress, Shi Hui claimed. This gala was followed by a successful radio fund-raising marathon to benefit old soldiers and disaster victims. Shi Hui describes such events as "miracles" that could never have happened in the old society. The "petty bourgeois feeling of superiority" that had caused so many artists to behave in "self-indulgent ways" had disappeared.

The transformation of the arts world was so profound, Shi Hui reported, that "many comrades, including all types of artists, joined the army, went to the countryside, and enrolled in revolutionary universities" that offered crash courses in the new politics. Artists no longer wanted to be admired as a privileged class; they wanted to be "good revolutionary workers" who "wholeheartedly served the people." They did this in the first year, he said, by turning out several short, public service films urging patriotic citizens to buy government bonds. Ironically, buying bonds is exactly what old Liu Jinfa did in the now-discredited film *Taiping chun*.

At the end of his article, Shi Hui paid homage to theater workers who had turned out two new plays, *Hongqi ge* (Song of the red flag) and *Sixiang wenti* (Ideological problems). The first of these, he said, dealt with the working class and required stage people to become familiar with proletarian life. The second play, *Sixiang wenti*, was for educated people. Shi Hui concluded by saying that the film and theater world would undoubtedly face many challenges and problems in the future. But, he insisted, a good start had been made in the first year. The important thing was that people in the cultural arena wanted to "transform" *(fanshen)*, had merged with the "people," and were willing to use "criticism and self-criticism" to make further progress.[32]

It is notable that Shi Hui's self-promotional article referred to the alleged contributions of the heavy-handed play *Sixiang wenti*. The third feature film produced by Wenhua after the revolution (and the first after the *Taiping chun* controversy) was in fact a movie version of *Sixiang wenti*. Released in August 1950 (with 446 screenings and an audience in Shanghai of 220,516 in 1950), this frightening work had almost nothing in common with *Wo zhei yi beizi*, *Taiping chun*, or the humanistic Wenhua tradition.[33] Shi Hui himself was totally uninvolved in the production.

No doubt it made political sense for Wenhua to be associated with the filming of *Sixiang wenti*, especially in the aftermath of the criticism of *Taiping chun*. Shi Hui's mentor, Huang Zuolin, the leading figure at

Wenhua, oversaw the production but is designated in the credits as one of eight people in a direction "collective" that linked Wenhua to the Shanghai People's Art and Theater Institute (Shanghai renmin yishu ju yuan). Huang's artistic genius notwithstanding, *Sixiang wenti* is quite simply a disaster, though a disaster with very sharp teeth. The acting and cinematography are terrible, the characterizations are wooden, and the story line is quite mechanical. Worse still, it featured an unprecedented orgy of intellectual bashing.

Sixiang wenti deals with one of the many "revolutionary universities" set up in China in 1949, in this case East China People's Revolutionary University on the outskirts of Shanghai. Ostensibly, the university provided non-Communist educated people with an opportunity to reorient their "thinking" in preparation for a suitable job assignment in the new society. Owing to their shaky class backgrounds and cultural bearings, all the students have an attitude problem. The school functions as a thought reform camp. Indeed, in some respects it resembles a prison for ideological sinners. All the internees are spiritual transgressors who require cleansing before they can be returned to society. Indeed, conditions at the school strongly resemble the circumstances of penal detention in the early 1950s described in Allyn and Adele Rickett's classic book *Prisoners of Liberation*.[34]

A few students are zealots determined to prove to the authorities that they are pure and ready for leadership positions in the new society. One such activist is also motivated by the fact that he has a serious case of venereal disease and thus is obsessed with getting the party to notice his "clean" ideological disposition. These unsparing activists spend most of their time bullying the other backward students and threatening to mount "struggle meetings" against them.

Most students are people who have been contaminated by feudal or bourgeois values, the most important of which is selfish individualism. They are sinners who do not yet understand the extent to which they are in serious need of redemption. They include such stock characters as the American-style bourgeois intellectual, the party girl, and the landlord's son.

The progress of this study class is overseen by yet another stock character, a masculinized, slightly plump, ever-smirking, always calm, self-righteous, middle-aged, female party cadre who wears baggy Maoist unisex fatigues and a worker's cap in every scene. The movie consists primarily of one criticism/self-criticism meeting after another in which the actors and actresses, standing stiff and straight, appear to be reading their lines from posters held to the side of the camera.

At the outset of *Sixiang wenti*, one gets the impression that the dual problems of harsh zealotry and bourgeois backwardness will be given equal attention by the wise party cadre, so that both issues can be resolved at the same time. But as the picture progresses, the problem of ultra-leftism is neglected, and all the emphasis is placed on the bourgeois backwardness of nonparty intellectuals. One never gets to see the sort of "struggle session" that the zealots threaten at the beginning because the party cadre prefers to advance the thought transformation process in a more congenial way, but the option of resorting to a struggle meeting, once mentioned at the outset, is never repudiated. The transgressing students are fully aware that "struggle" is still an option.

Most students are in denial about the full extent of their ideological sins. But long sermons and longer meetings make it clear that confession is the only way to salvation. One by one, all the students see the error of their ways and willingly "convert" to the new morality.

Given the thrust of Sigrid Schmalzer's chapter (Chapter 10) on Chinese interest in the early 1950s in the issue of human origins and the criteria that define the "human" condition, it is useful to note that *Sixiang wenti* definitely addresses this topic.[35] The logic of the film builds on the basic idea that there is no middle path. Either you are with the revolution and the people or you are opposed to the revolution. Furthermore, a concerted effort is made in the film to "dehumanize" those who are not clearly inside the revolutionary camp. By this logic, a nonrevolutionary is a counterrevolutionary, and a counterrevolutionary is nonhuman. Since no one wants to be seen as inhuman, it is essential to position oneself solidly within the revolutionary camp. When the students at the revolutionary university recognize that they do indeed want to be saved by reforming their "thought," what they are really saying is that they want to be included in the "human" category.

Understanding the politics of *Sixiang wenti* makes it easier to comprehend the shrill criticism directed in mid-1950 at Shi Hui's vivid portrayal of Liu Jinfa, the kind-hearted tailor. Sang Hu's script and Shi Hui's acting, not to mention Huang Shaofen's deft cinematography, humanized a nonrevolutionary. By contrast, the viewer of *Sixiang wenti* is given no way to admire the ugly people who have "thought" problems. Tailor Liu has just as many problems as they do but remains attractive and respected nonetheless, even in the eyes of the progressive young people in his life. *Taiping chun*, unlike *Sixiang wenti*, pays attention to the ways in which a decent man like tailor Liu can be full of contradictions but still thoroughly human.

Sixiang wenti states quite explicitly that it is not just "thought reform" that makes a person human. Thought reform cannot be achieved without labor—hard physical labor. One of the bourgeois intellectuals in the film protests to the masculinized female cadre that he already has his mind right and that there is no need for him to work in the fields since he can make a better contribution elsewhere. This remark prompts another long-winded lecture by Baggy Pants about the sacred nature of labor.

Sixiang wenti and its Wenhua producers received rave reviews in the press. The Ministry of Culture organized a symposium and stated that it was extremely satisfying to know that a private film studio had turned out a work of such enormous "educational significance."[36] Much was made of the seemingly impressive attendance figures nationwide and in Shanghai. For example, in the last three months of 1950, *Sixiang wenti* was screened 446 times in Shanghai to an audience of more than 220,000. But these totals are misleading. The numbers were high because a serious effort had been made to orchestrate group attendance. Huge discounts of up to 80 percent were offered to units that applied for collective admission three to four days in advance.[37] When the campaign was over, screenings and attendance plummeted—18 screenings in Shanghai in 1951 for 6,500 viewers.[38]

Shi Hui as Pimp

Wenhua's willingness to help with the filming of *Sixiang wenti* was rewarded. In late summer and early fall 1950, just before the entry of Chinese forces into the Korean War, Wenhua began production on a relatively soft film that was more in keeping not only with *Wo zhei yi beizi* and *Taiping chun* but also with the longer-term Wenhua artistic legacy. Based on a May Fourth–type novel titled *Fushi* (Corruption), originally published in 1941 by the celebrated writer Mao Dun, this film was adapted for the screen by the respected Shanghai literary figure Ke Ling and directed by Huang Zuolin, who had recently worked so hard on the *Sixiang wenti* disaster.[39] *Fushi*, identified by the Wenhua leadership as a "priority" *(zhongdian)* project closely tied to its desire to emulate "the filmmaking experiences of the Soviet Union," was released on December 15, 1950.[40]

Set in 1940, the story deals with a self-centered young bourgeois woman in wartime Chongqing who breaks with her socially responsible husband to pursue a life of adventure. She falls in with the wrong crowd and ends up functioning as a spy for the dark forces of Nationalist reaction linked to American intelligence agencies. Her ex-husband, a Communist, is played by Shi Hui in his first role since *Taiping chun*. Throughout his career Shi Hui specialized in playing a variety of colorful ordinary people, including low-life characters. Playing the part of a clean-cut revolutionary youth was new to Shi Hui. His performance was credible but lackluster.

In the story, the young, corrupted woman provides information about her former husband. After he is arrested, the authorities ask her to help make him talk. But she admires his resolve and refuses to cooperate. She soon befriends a young woman who is trapped in a situation quite like her own. Later, the protagonist is shocked to learn that her ex-husband has been executed. Reading a farewell letter from him that begs her to get out of her dreadful circumstances, she sees the light and runs away to the liberated areas, taking the younger woman with her. Mao Dun seems to have expressed no objections to the screen adaptation of his novel, though the original work is more introspective than political and contains no final sequence about the two women heading off to a Communist Party base area.

Shi Hui played a much more memorable part in the fifth Wenhua production since the party's victory in Shanghai, a gut-wrenching movie titled *Jiejie meimei zhanqilai* (Sisters stand up) that explored the unsavory subject of prostitution in Republican China. Filmed in late fall and early winter 1950 and released in early 1951, *Jiejie meimei zhanqilai* was written and directed by newcomer Chen Xihe, who had researched the topic by visiting a Women's Labor Training Institute in Beijing to which former prostitutes had been assigned. To provide himself with political cover, Chen also convened a number of "discussion sessions" in which he respectfully requested the "advice" of various political and cultural authorities.[41]

Set in Beijing in 1947, the first half of the film takes a highly dramatized, but still strikingly ethnographic, approach to the sordid business of prostitution. Focusing on the sad story of Daxiang, an illiterate peasant girl whose mother was tricked into selling her into prostitution, the audience is offered an extremely detailed look at the ways in which prostitutes were recruited, bought and sold, trained, controlled, and marketed in late Republican Beijing. In addition to being introduced to the various personal stories of seven prostitutes, the audience gets a close look at a number of specialists in the industry, including terrifying procurers of young women, older men who handle the finances, older women who take responsibility for disciplining the prostitutes, and heartless young men who actually run the brothels. Equally important, the film offers portraits of male customers, parents, and loved ones of the prostitutes, as well as corrupt policemen who are paid for their support.

Though the first half is fascinating, the film still must be regarded as one-dimensional in that it presents few of the nuances and gray areas of the industry discussed by Gail Hershatter in her study of prostitution in China.[42] In the movie, the people who run the industry are monsters, and the prostitutes are ruthlessly oppressed victims. There is little middle ground. The picture is graphic, disgusting, and powerful. But, given these distortions, one is surprised in the first half to see at least some prostitutes who appear to adjust to their fate and bond to some degree with "Mother," the controlling older woman who feeds them carefully selected bits of information about the outside world. For instance, when word circulates that the PLA is on the outskirts of the city, the older woman has no trouble convincing the women under her control that the Communists regard prostitutes as inhuman trash. The Communists will round them up and murder them.

Shi Hui, a man who by some accounts was personally familiar with the pre-1949 world of prostitution, gives a brilliant performance as the loathsome Ma San, a thoroughly despicable procurer of innocent young women. As he did so successfully in *Wo zhei yi beizi*, Shi Hui speaks in the rich and colorful Beijing dialect in order to allow the distinctively local character of Beijing to surface. The image of Ma San is genuinely bone chilling.

The second part of the film, which coincides chronologically with the early weeks and months of the Communist occupation of Beijing, is quite disappointing and rather predictable—and Shi Hui plays almost no part in this portion of the film. Indeed, the second part is a lot like *Sixiang wenti.* In fact, the *very same* always smirking, always correct, masculin-ized, baggy pants, Mao-capped woman cadre who appears in *Sixiang wenti* shows up in *Jiejie meimei zhanqilai* to reeducate the prostitutes.

The women, scared to death, are sent to a reeducation center (one that, like the "revolutionary university" in *Sixiang wenti,* has the look and feel of a prison) where they are cleaned up and organized in study groups. Baggy Pants guides them every step of the way. Gradually, after countless meetings and lectures, the women tell their horrible stories and come to understand the exploitative nature of the old so-ciety. Daxiang, our heroine, becomes an activist and is appointed head of her group.

Once again, the issues of "humanity" and "labor" come into play. The party repeatedly tells the women that prostitution work was "not their fault" but, rather, the fault of the evil class enemies. Yet there is no es-caping the conclusion that they are in a detention center and that their status is something less than human. Otherwise, why is there a need for reeducation? Baggy Pants makes it clear that thought reform cannot be achieved without participation in labor. Naturally, she does not regard prostitution as real labor. And, of course, the ex-prostitutes want to be-come "human" by participating in honest work. In fact, many of them, including Daxiang, "volunteer" for prostitute reeducation work in Subei (and forsake reunification with families and loved ones, including, in Daxiang's case, a fiance), once their own course of study is complete. The film audience is Shanghai could not have missed the less-than-flattering reference to Subei, the region believed by many to have been the native place of most lower-class Shanghai prostitutes.[43]

Jiejie meimei zhanqilai was shown widely in Shanghai in early 1951. Surpassing the standard set by *Wo zhei yi beizi* one year earlier, it was screened 657 times in 1951 to an audience totaling 344,521 people in Shanghai alone.[44] Even though the virtuoso performances by Shi Hui as the dastardly Ma San completely overshadowed the uninspired per-formance of Ding Wen as Baggy Pants, the film was warmly received by critics.[45]

One explanation for this reception is that Wenhua had learned its lesson with *Taiping chun.* That is to say, it was necessary to show the militancy of the aroused masses and the suffering of the class enemies before the film could end. Thus, *Jiejie meimei zhanqilai* has what *Taiping chun* did not have: a large-scale struggle meeting. A stage is set up, the masses of prostitutes in the camp are gathered together, the class enemies are dragged forward, and Baggy Pants orchestrates the struggle session. Emboldened by their new consciousness, the former prostitutes denounce and spit on the old brothel owners. The prostitutes then charge the stage in an attempt to beat the class enemies to death. Baggy Pants intervenes, saying that the new society requires that these cases be handled "according to the law." But then she asks the enraged throng, "What do you think their punishment should be?" The women scream out, "Execution!" Baggy Pants shouts back, "OK!" Scenes of this sort made *Jiejie meimei zhanqilai* immune to criticism.[46]

Shi Hui as Peasant Soldier

Wars require war movies, and the Korean War was no exception. Veteran film personalities wasted no time in showing enthusiastic support for the war effort. In mid-December 1950, shortly after Chinese forces entered Korea, a photo appeared in a popular film magazine featuring the famous actresses Bai Yang and Shangguan Yunzhu singing anti-American songs at a troop support rally.[47]

Immediately following the filming of *Jiejie meimei zhanqilai*, Wenhua and Shi Hui quickly began work on *Guan lianzhang* (Platoon Commander Guan), a war film based on a propaganda novel by Zhu Dingyuan. This effort reunited the creative team that completed *Wo zhei yi beizi* in early 1950, including Yang Liuqing as screenwriter and Shi Hui as both director and lead actor in the title role. *Guan lianzhang* was released in spring 1951. It was Shi Hui's first attempt to play the part of a peasant soldier. Huang Zuolin and other leaders of Wenhua undoubtedly concluded that it was good for the studio to do its patriotic bit. It would be a "safe" and noncontroversial agit-prop (agitation-propaganda) film. They were wrong.

Guan lianzhang was one of the unfortunate political casualties of the aggressive campaign launched by the party press in May 1951 against another film, *Wu Xun zhuan* (The life of Wu Xun), a private-sector Shanghai movie involving two film world icons, veteran director Sun Yu and leftist actor Zhao Dan.[48] In superficial terms, criticism of the film was directed at the wrongheaded, and thus counterrevolutionary, mass education activities of a mid-nineteenth-century intellectual. In reality, the attack was part of a frightening, nationwide "rectification" campaign targeting the alleged "bourgeois" ideological orientation of writers and artists in mid-1951—a campaign entirely in keeping with the political agenda spelled out in Huang Zuolin's disturbing film *Sixiang wenti*, released the previous summer. This time, however, the party's critique of bourgeois intellectuals could not be ignored, blunted, or circumvented: the *Renmin ribao* (People's Daily) editorial spearheading the campaign was written by Mao Zedong himself.[49]

At one level, *Guan lianzhang* was, indeed, unproblematic. Set in rural Jiangsu in the weeks leading up to the final PLA march on Shanghai, the movie tells the simple story of Commander Guan, a poor peasant from Shandong who had risen through the ranks during the civil war. Guan has the common touch and is respected by his troops and the higher-ups.

All of this is established in a number of extremely interesting opening scenes in which a highly educated "college student," now on active duty in the military, is sent to Guan's unit to offer "cultural instruction" to rank-and-file peasant soldiers, many of whom are illiterate. In addition to "raising the cultural level" of the troopers, the student is expected to be modest and learn about the hard life of those who have been sacrificing at the front.

The student gets off to a bad start by speaking in ways that are highly abstract and thus cannot be comprehended by the common soldiers. But this tension is worked out early in the film, and the student goes on to have cordial relationships with the troops. In the second part of the film, the entire focus is on the heroism of Guan's unit as they take a key Nationalist position just west of Shanghai. The cowardly Nationalists are holding up in a building that contains women and orphans, so Guan must figure out a way to vanquish the enemy without putting the innocents at risk. The unit is successful, but Guan loses his own life in the final showdown.

Guan lianzhang was shown widely in Shanghai in 1951 (347 screenings and a total audience of almost two hundred thousand people), but, much to Shi Hui's dismay, the film was not at all appreciated by urban, intellectual party critics in the immediate wake of the Wu Xun campaign.[50] The problem was that Shi Hui's portrayal of peasant soldier Guan was too vivid for its own good. When playing the roles of local cop, old tailor, and pimp, Shi Hui tried his best to bring out the color and complicated truth of these memorable characters. The same was true of his rendition of the peasant soldier. Guan and his men are shown to be peasant soldiers from the north (Shandong) fighting in the unfamiliar environs of the south. Their Shandong accents are extremely heavy, they employ exotic Shandong colloquialisms when they speak, and they use vulgar curses. In short, Guan and his men have a strong local identity. This was unacceptable to critics at the time of the Korean War who wanted to see China and Chinese troops presented as unified and culturally sanitized "national" subjects who spoke perfect *putonghua*.

Urban ideologues were embarrassed by the colorful, rough-and-tumble representation of peasant warriors in *Guan lianzhang*. Their criticisms of the film reveal a complex love-hate relationship with peasants. On the one hand, according to the official party line, peasants were heroes of the revolution worthy of deep respect. But it was embarrassing to show peasants as they really were. It was fine to represent peasants in folksy ways, but it was dangerous for characterizations to get too close to reality. As Jeremy Brown has shown in his research on the late-Mao era, urban, intellectual contempt for peasants, it is often the case that profound disgust and revulsion lurked just below the surface of patronizing party images of the peasantry.[51] From this urban, intellectual perspective, the peasant soldiers in *Guan lianzhang*, and especially Guan himself, look and act like a bunch of ignorant yahoos and yokels. This was not the image of heroic Chinese fighters the leadership wanted the world or even the nation to see. Shi Hui thought he was doing his job, but the critics made it clear that he was taking his job much too seriously.[52]

Another problem with *Guan lianzhang* was that it failed to adhere to Leninist notions of hierarchy and discipline. In one of the earliest scenes, Guan cannot be located by the urban student because he is rolling in the dirt, playing with local children who have stolen his cap. To make matters worse, Guan's relationship with his troopers seems much too casual. From the party's point of view, Guan does not behave like an official with power, and his underlings are insufficiently respectful of his "authority." There is not enough "structure" in the unit.

In one particularly interesting scene, a major battle commences, and senior officers tell Guan to hold his troops in a rear area and wait for instructions. Guan is repeatedly seen complaining to his superiors and urging them to send the unit into battle. Critics pointed out that it was totally inappropriate for a junior officer to be raising questions about the wisdom of those higher in the chain of command. One critic went so far as to say that it was not clear whether Guan's troops were fighting for the nation or fighting out of loyalty to Guan himself.[53] In effect, the critics were charging that the ignorant and undisciplined peasants from Shandong under Guan's personal command looked more like an old-fashioned bandit gang than a unit in the national army.

Rather than straighten out the peasants, the urban intellectual in their midst adjusts to the situation by "joining" the primitive gang. Films such as *Sixiang wenti* made it clear that it was fine for party elites (like Baggy Pants) to bash bourgeois urban intellectuals, but it was not fine for urban intellectuals (like the "university student" in *Guan lianzhang*) to lose their identity by merging with an undisciplined and uncultured band of crude illiterates.

As he had in his previous roles, Shi Hui worked hard to "humanize" his multifaceted character. Once again, the problem was that he succeeded. That is, he created a sympathetic, likable, flesh-and-blood human character complete with warts at a time when the party's definition of humanity called for homogenized and disciplined uniformity. The party's hypersensitivity to characterizations like Shi Hui's Commander Guan revealed serious insecurities within the ruling elite. The victors in the civil war, including Mao himself, spoke with very heavy regional accents, a fact that was often concealed from the public. They had regional identities and were linked to regional networks and regional power bases, but they wanted ordinary citizens to think in terms of national unity. They talked about the organic and open relationship between the revolutionary leadership and the masses but very much demanded the respect and deference that came along with strict Leninist hierarchies of power.

Shi Hui as American Capitalist

By the end of 1951, following the problematic reception of *Guan lianzhang*, it became clear that Wenhua's days were numbered. A plan was in the works to integrate all private-sector studios into the state sector. Wenhua's final attempt to serve the new society was a rather remarkable movie titled *Meiguo zhi chuang* (Window on America), another anti-American, Korean War–era work that has been systemati-

cally ignored by film scholars in China, many of whom find it embarrassing. The film was shot in winter 1951–52 and released in early 1952
as yet another expression of film world political support for the Chinese war effort.

Adapted for the screen by Huang Zuolin from an original Soviet
text, codirected by Huang Zuolin, Shi Hui, and Ye Ming, and filmed by
Huang Shaofen, all of them important members of the Wenhua team,
Meiguo zhi chuang is the only movie in Chinese film history set entirely
in the United States and featuring Chinese actors and actresses in the
roles of white and black Americans.[54] Shi Hui, complete with fake
nose, plays the lead role of Mr. Butler, a New York capitalist whose
business is in trouble owing to economic disruptions caused by the Korean War. This long-forgotten movie is a work of wartime propaganda,
but it is unusually memorable nonetheless, in part because it is a surprisingly effective comedy and in part because Shi Hui is masterful in
the challenging role of Butler.

The entire film takes place during a two- to three-hour period on
the forty-second floor of a Manhattan skyscraper. Butler and his volup-
tuous secretary fret because the stock market news is alarming. Business is bad because the economy had shifted to a wartime footing.
Their deliberations are interrupted by the sudden appearance of a
lowly thirty-two-year-old window washer named Charley Kent, who
enters their office through an open window. Startled, Butler offers the
young man a fancy cigarette and listens attentively to his story.

Recently laid off from a factory job owing to the restructuring of the
wartime economy, Charley asks a favor. Deeply depressed, he has decided to commit suicide by jumping out the window. But he wants his
final pay packet, meager as it is, to be handed over to his mother. The
hilarious Shi Hui character, Butler, agrees to help, saying that since
"America is a free country," Charley certainly has the freedom to kill
himself. But he argues that Charley is missing a great moneymaking
opportunity. For instance, if Charley agreed to make a public statement to the effect that his final wish before jumping was to enjoy a famous brand-name cigarette one last time, he could earn $300, which of
course would be passed along to his poor mother.

When Charley agrees to the scheme, Butler becomes quite excited
and offers to serve as Charley's agent. The poor worker, whose brother
was drafted to fight in Korea, is then asked to wait for a couple of hours

before jumping. Butler explains that Charley's reasons for committing suicide have absolutely no market value and sound like "commie propaganda." He needs to think like a Hollywood filmmaker and tell a romantic story about an unhappy love affair. When a confused Charley agrees to the new plan, Butler scrambles to line up sponsors of the suicide: a men's clothing dealer wants Charley to wear one of its fine suits, a famous whiskey distillery wants him to take a final gulp of its product before jumping, and a manufacturer of "unbreakable" sunglasses (who looks exactly like American president Harry Truman!) wants him to put on the glasses before leaping.

Butler, now thinking of starting a new business as a "suicide agent," writes up a formal contract for Charley and makes arrangements for the big event to be broadcast on radio. When Charley notices that Butler gets three-quarters of the profits, Butler responds indignantly by saying that Charley has the easy part. All he has to do is jump.

The riotous fun continues when a team of workers (including a "black" man) arrives to set up the broadcast equipment. All belong to a trade union. Once the workers learn what is happening, they do verbal battle with Butler and slowly convince Charley that he is being exploited. Indeed, Charley soon discovers that the capitalists need him more than he needs them. Insisting now on being called "Mr. Kent," Charley begins making various demands. In the end, he decides to cancel the suicide altogether. With the suicide scheme in ruins, Charley and the workers depart in victory.

The film ends with Butler being hounded by all the sponsors he had lined up and with the workers standing on a hill outside the city, pointing to the horizon and referring to the good society that exists in "another country" (the Soviet Union) far away.

It would be a mistake to dismiss *Meiguo zhi chuang* as a low-budget propaganda film. Its significance resides in the fact that it was successful and that it could not have been made in state studios that lacked directors such as Huang Zuolin, multitalented actors such as Shi Hui, and top cinematographers such as Huang Shaofen. With the Wu Xun campaign still unfolding, Shi Hui and Huang Zuolin were asked to make an anti-American film based on an original Soviet text, and they did so with enthusiasm. Indeed, looking at the entire Wenhua postrevolution production record, one wonders what more these filmmakers could have done to serve the new society. To win the favor of the new political elites, and to seek entrance to the party, Shi Hui had played a humble cop, an old-fashioned tailor, a patriotic youth, a sadistic pimp, a revolutionary soldier, and finally, a New York capitalist.

But his work always fell short of party standards. His characters, including Butler, were never mere cardboard caricatures of good or evil. The positive characters, like Commander Guan, always exhibited character flaws. The "middle characters," like the Beijing cop and the Zhejiang tailor, were often befuddled and confused. The negative characters, like Ma San the pimp and Butler the New York capitalist, consistently revealed an undeniable humanity. Nothing that Shi Hui did was good enough for party critics.

By the time *Meiguo zhi chuang* was released, the party had already given up on Shi Hui. In the end, the party was incapable of distinguishing between Shi Hui the man and Shi Hui the Shanghai film-world bad boy. It was incapable of seeing the difference between Shi Hui and the colorful characters he played. In the end, the verdict was that Shi Hui, only thirty-seven years old in 1952, could not be trusted and had outlived his usefulness.

Shi Hui as Rightist

After Wenhua released *Meiguo zhi chuang*, the eight private film studios still functioning in Shanghai were shut down and their staffs integrated into the expanding web of state-sector filmmaking. Shi Hui, officially categorized as a director and an actor, was placed at first in the Shanghai Film Studio.[55] But in the state sector, the studio heads made all the decisions. It was no longer a matter of directors and screenwriters coming up with their own ideas. It was a command economy. From the outset, Shi Hui was marginalized at Shangying, and his career rapidly deteriorated. After *Meiguo zhi chuang* he was never again invited to participate in a movie that had anything to do with the serious topic of revolution.

His work—when he got any—took him out of the world of contemporary society (where he had been a dominating force since 1942) and into a world of fantasy and retreat. In 1952 and 1953 he had no work at all. In 1954 he directed a charming children's movie for Shangying called *Jimao xin* (Feathers with a letter) about a cute little boy who used his wits to help the Red Army during the resistance war. In 1954 he made a cameo appearance in a mediocre historical film titled *Song*

Jingshi, about a Qing-era peasant rebellion. In 1955 he directed an exotic fairy-tale opera titled *Tian xian pei* (A heavenly match) that had been written by his old friend Sang Hu. Shi Hui, the most accomplished actor of his time, was only forty years old in 1955. No doubt he felt underappreciated and wondered whether his celebrated career was over. After a four-year engagement, Shi Hui married actress Tong Baoling in 1955. They had no children.

The Hundred Flowers liberalization campaign launched in 1956 raised Shi Hui's hopes. In an effort to shake up the film world, directors at Shangying were encouraged to form small creative collectives. Shi Hui immediately led a group that included the noted young director Xie Jin, veterans Xu Changlin and Chen Baichen, and screenwriter Shen Ji. Qu Baiyin, the deputy head of Shangying, dubbed the group the Five Flowers (Wu hua she). They became affiliated with a smaller state-sector film studio in Shanghai called Tianma.

Xie Jin and Chen Baichen worked on the screenplay for *Nü lan wu hao* (Woman basketball player number five). Xu Changlin produced a script called *Qing chang yi shen* (Endless passion, deep friendship). To support his old colleague, Shi Hui agreed to make a cameo appearance in the film. He played the role of a worker who gradually "loses his sight." No one knew it at the time, but the sightless worker would be Shi Hui's final role.

Shi Hui's own project was a daring screenplay titled *Wu hai ye hang* (Night voyage on a foggy sea). Thanks to the Hundred Flowers cultural opening, filming on this thinly veiled piece of political criticism was approved. The story involved the fate of a group on a boat trip from Shanghai to Ningbo. The ship was called *Democracy No. 3* *(Minzhu san hao)*. When the ship runs into a dense fog, the people on board are required to work together to save themselves. The political message was not hard to figure out: to avoid a "shipwreck" the Chinese people had to swing into action, bypassing incompetent leaders.

Just as the filming of *Wu hai ye hang* was completed, Shi Hui, veteran director Wu Yonggang, and actress Wu Yin were summoned to Beijing in late spring 1957 and criticized as rightists. Chen Baichen, another member of the Five Flowers group, was also identified as a rightist. The enormously destructive Anti-Rightist Movement was under way.

Back in Shanghai, Shi Hui was ordered to attend a "big criticism meeting" *(pipan da hui)* organized for the special purpose of "examining his thought" *(sixiang jiancha)*. Shi Hui had always loved the spotlight, but the struggle meeting directed at him was not the sort of attention he was accustomed to in his days as a big star. It was pointed out that one of the negative characters in *Wu hai ye hang* was explicitly identified as a "party member." This character was said to be selfish and doing things only for personal gain. The appearance of this character, the attackers said, was proof that Shi Hui was putting the party down. No one, especially friends from the late 1940s who had finally made it into the party or still had hopes of winning party membership, stepped forward in his defense.

Shi Hui was ordered to appear at a second criticism meeting. But after returning home, he disappeared the next day. In a final and carefully planned performance that can be regarded as either a case of "life imitating art" or an instance of "art imitating life"—the distinction was now entirely unclear—Shi Hui boarded the same ship (*Democracy No. 3*) featured in his "rightist" movie and began the trip from Shanghai to Ningbo. Many of the sailors knew Shi Hui because he had taken the trip many times as a way of better understanding life at sea. Right on cue, one of the deck hands recognized him as the ship pulled away on that fateful day. "Are you here again to experience life?" he asked. Shi Hui nodded. Yes, indeed, he was there to experience Chinese life in mid-1957.

Not long after this encounter, the forty-three-year-old Shi Hui committed suicide by jumping overboard and drowning.

Days later Public Security officers were summoned to Wusongkou, south of Shanghai, to examine the body of an adult male that had washed up on the beach. The face of the corpse had deteriorated beyond recognition, but a subsequent inquiry identified the body as Shi Hui's.

To this day, no published source in the People's Republic has acknowledged that Shi Hui committed suicide.[56] His final performance was ingenious. Suicides committed by prominent people were not reported because they made the party look bad. Shi Hui, finding a way to silence the critics, got the last word. It would not be easy for the party to explain why Charley Kent chose life in capitalist America, while Shi Hui chose death in socialist China.

Huang Zuolin and Sang Hu survived the Anti-Rightist Movement but were among the many prerevolution film luminaries who were kept outside the party for the remainder of their careers. A few eventually got what they wanted. Huang Zongying was admitted to the Communist Party in 1956, Zhao Dan in 1957, and Bai Yang in 1958.[57]

ꙮ 12

Creating "New China's First New-Style Regular University," 1949–50

Douglas A. Stiffler

ON OCTOBER 3, 1950, one year and two days after the establishment of the People's Republic of China, four thousand people gathered in Beijing to hear speeches by Vice-Premier Liu Shaoqi and other dignitaries celebrating the formal establishment of "New China's first new-style regular university": Chinese People's University (Zhongguo renmin daxue, abbreviated as Renda).[1] Liu told the assembled crowd of dignitaries, school officials, Soviet experts, teachers, and students that they not only were engaged in the creation of a single "new-style" university but were in fact establishing the basis for reform of the entire Chinese system of higher education: "Comrades! Renda begins classes today. This university is the first new-style university ever run in China and is unprecedented in the history of our country. In the future in China, many universities will study the experiences of our Renda and [we] will copy the example of Renda in starting other universities."[2] The new university, created by a decree of the State Council in December 1949, was charged with the task of "combining the advanced experience of the Soviet Union and China's concrete conditions." The university would thus play a key role in establishing a Soviet-style state and economy in China during the first decade of the Communist Party's rule.[3]

The establishment of a new "red" university in the People's Republic harkens back to the founding of "red universities" in the Soviet Union of the 1920s. "Red universities were to solve a serious problem for revolutionary regimes: the university systems inherited from the old regime were absolutely necessary for modernization, but these same universities were largely the preserve of the bourgeoisie. The new Communist leaders intended to transform such universities—to "open the doors"—to workers and peasants but knew that such transformations could not be undertaken overnight without serious harm to the existing universities.[4] The immediate creation of a red university on the Soviet pattern was an important stopgap measure for the Chinese leaders.

The creation of a red university in the People's Republic turned out to be far more difficult than originally envisioned, however, in large part due to the social heterogeneity of party cadres and low educational levels. Party leaders faced a dilemma: if length of party service and party loyalty became the main criteria for admission to the new red university, the great majority of the cadre students would have only a year or two of elementary school–level education. They would be politically qualified but educationally unqualified and incapable of doing university work. The leadership's modernization goals would be threatened. If the leaders made educational qualifications the standard for admission, the ranks of the new university would be filled by cadres who had attended Nationalist-era high schools and universities and had joined the Communist Party after 1942. This would serve the leadership's modernization goals but risked alienating the regime's most loyal (pre-1942) cadres.[5]

In the case of Renda, the compromise worked out was to recruit both regime loyalists ("old cadres" [*lao ganbu*] with low educational levels) and the better-educated but less-experienced (and presumably less loyal) "young intellectuals" (*qingnian zhishifenzi*). This meant a student body divided into two competing groups by age, background, and educational level. Old cadres and young intellectuals were in conflict with one another for power and position in the new China of the 1950s. An educational opportunity and choice job assignment for one group would likely mean the loss of power and position for the other. It would take years to produce red and expert cadres. In the interim the regime had to choose who would advance.

This study of Renda shows that in the early years of the People's Republic it was the young intellectuals who held an overwhelming advantage. In a regime committed to rapid modernization with the assistance of the Soviet Union, young intellectuals were best positioned to make use of the new Soviet knowledge to turn themselves into a red and expert elite. Old cadres, on the other hand, were at a sharp disadvantage in this new phase of China's modern history: they faced being left behind by an increasingly urbanized, modernizing society.

The Founding of the New University

The party's creation of the new red university in October 1950 can be traced back to Sino-Soviet discussions of 1949–50 over the scope of aid that Joseph Stalin's Soviet Union would be prepared to offer the new Chinese regime. This negotiating process began when Anastas Mikoyan visited the Communist Party leadership's base camp at Xibaipo village in February 1949 and continued when Liu Shaoqi secretly traveled to Moscow and spent July–August 1949 working out the practicalities of the new Sino-Soviet relationship. All of this culminated in Mao's visit to Moscow from December 1949 to February 1950 for negotiations that produced the Sino-Soviet Treaty of Friendship, Alliance and Mutual Assistance and formalized the relationship.[6]

One little-known aspect of these negotiations was Liu Shaoqi's proposal to Stalin in the summer of 1949 that a Soviet-staffed university for Chinese cadres be established in the Soviet Union. Liu proposed that the Soviets set up a school "similar to the former Chinese Workers' University" in Moscow that could train one thousand or so Chinese Communist cadres in "industry, trade, banking, law, teacher training" and other fields.[7] Stalin did not like the idea of locating the school in Moscow, however, possibly because he did not wish to provoke the West by training thousands of Chinese cadres in the capital. Instead, he countered with the suggestion of locating the school in Alma Ata, Kazakhstan. Such a remote provincial location did not appeal to the Chinese side. The issue was resolved when the Chinese apparently decided that it would be more convenient to have the university established in Beijing and to have the Soviet Union send the teachers there.[8]

In the aftermath of Liu's summer trip to Moscow, two Soviet educational advisers, P. I. Fesenko and V. F. Filippov, were assigned by the Soviets to assist the Chinese in drawing up plans for the new university. Fesenko was an educational official in Moscow in the late 1940s but was in rather poor health and left Beijing within a few months of his arrival. Filippov was a Siberian who spoke some Chinese: he may have been an intelligence agent.[9] Filippov authored and signed most of the reports sent back to Moscow in 1949–50 on progress in the creation of the new university.

The two Soviet advisers joined members of a commission (led by propaganda chief Lu Dingyi) charged with preparatory work for the establishment of the new university.[10] The commission visited a number of existing universities in Tianjin and Beijing in fall 1949 with an eye toward taking over one of the institutions as a base for the new red university. Lu Dingyi cautioned that the bourgeoisie should not be antagonized, however, and plans to take over Beijing Normal University were abandoned in favor of basing the new university at the already existing cadre training school North China University (Huabei daxue). This also happened to be the base for most of the party's central-level education specialists serving on the preparatory commission.[11]

In the process of seeking a site for the new university, the Soviet experts noticed many things about Chinese higher education that disturbed them. The advisers reported that the university faculty who were foreign trained had received their training in America or Western Europe; that their libraries had few, if any, Russian books; and that their student bodies were largely composed of the children of the national bourgeoisie, the big bourgeoisie, landowners, and intellectuals, with few, if any, students from the peasantry and poor laboring classes. They also noted that many of the institutions received large parts of their budgets from the United States or the Vatican. The advisers did report that Beijing University, founded in 1898, was "widely known for its tradition of democratic student protest," but they did not comment further on the recent activism of university students in Beijing, activism that had done much to undermine the Nationalist regime in the civil war years.[12] The Communist Party organization at Beijing University was noted only to be "small in numbers."[13] It would seem that, in the eyes of the Soviet advisers, universities such as Beijing and Qinghua were culturally alien territory.

The advisers expanded on their views of American influence in the conclusion to their report:

1. The United States of America exerts a very strong influence among higher education institutions in general and in those

educational institutions supported by American funding, for example, at Qinghua and Yanjing, both in the ranks of the faculty and in the student body. This can be clearly observed not only in the structure of the institutions, but also in the course materials used by the students, in the ideology of the professors and students, and even in their clothing which is cut and sewn in the American style.

2. The professors and teachers in higher education institutions are taking a wait-and-see attitude and are quite worried about the reorganization of higher education institutions and whether they will keep their positions in the universities and institutes. Part of the professorate is inclined to hostility to the new social order and is particularly unhappy about the introduction in the universities and institutes of compulsory courses in the social-economic disciplines and in Russian language.

3. The higher education institutions are full of the sons and daughters of Chinese landowners, the national bourgeoisie, and the kulaks. The higher schools are essentially out of the reach of the workers and the peasantry in view of the fact that the great masses in the countryside like the workers in the cities are either completely illiterate or in the best case, semi-literate.

To deal with these problems, the advisers recommended that worker-peasant divisions be added at the various higher education institutions and that the sons and daughters of the laboring classes be educated in three- to four-year courses.[14] This recommendation recalls the worker's faculties (*rabfaks*) set up in higher education institutions in the Soviet Union in the 1920s.

Shortly after the Chinese Communists entered Beijing, the party's top cadre education specialists scouted about for a location for North China University, the leading cadre training (and ideological retraining) school. The school's new rector, the seventy-year-old veteran of the 1911 Revolution, Wu Yuzhang, used his considerable influence with the leadership to obtain a choice piece of property for the school: the old Duan Qirui mansion near the Forbidden City.[15] The leaders of the planning commission for the new red university decided to rename North China University, calling it the Chinese People's University. Thus, the school's administrative and teaching personnel, and some of its students, remained at the "new" university (which was really the old cadre training school).

While Wu Yuzhang served as rector of the new university, daily leadership at Renda was exercised by first vice-rector and school party secretary Hu Xikui, a tough underground commander in the "White Areas" of north China.[16] Cheng Fangwu, a veteran party literatus, served as second vice-rector.[17] Two factions predominated in the school's leadership: the "underground" faction under Hu Xikui composed of party guerrilla leaders and the "cadre school faction" composed of people who had worked for years in party cadre training institutions alongside Wu Yuzhang and Cheng Fangwu.

In a 1959 summary description prepared for foreign visitors, the leaders of Renda described the school's faculty as being composed of 10 percent "old cadres," 80 percent young teachers trained by Soviet experts during the period of "half-study, half-teach," and the remaining 10 percent "old bourgeois intellectuals."[18] In the 1949–52 period, the heads of academic departments were either associates of Hu Xikui from underground struggle days or of Wu Yuzhang and Cheng Fangwu from the north China cadre training schools. Some of the more promising students from the cadre training schools were then appointed as trainee teachers in the departments. None of the Chinese departmental administrators or teacher trainees had any experience in the Soviet managerial fields: many professed total befuddlement as to how to run an academic program in their specialty and could only await the arrival of the Soviet experts.[19]

The initial eight departments at Renda were Economic Planning, Factory Management, Finance-Credit, Cooperatives, Trade, Law, Diplomacy, and Russian. These departments remained in place from 1950 to 1954, with only a few changes. A Statistics Department was added in August 1952 and an Agricultural Economics Department in June 1954. The departments corresponded to the Soviet faculties (*fakultety*) and, unlike the American system, were not the fundamental academic units. The fundamental academic units were instead the sub-departmental *kafedra* in the Soviet system, which Cheng Fangwu translated into Chinese as *jiaoyanshi*, or Teaching-Research Section.[20]

The most important *jiaoyanshi* taught courses required of either all students or students in various departments. The most important of these were the ideological *jiaoyanshi* responsible for teaching the required ideological courses (Foundations of Marxism-Leninism, Dialectical and Historical Materialism, and Political Economy). These supradepartmental *jiaoyanshi* played a key role at Renda and, outside of the Russian department, had the largest number of Soviet experts assigned to them in the early 1950s: Marxism-Leninism (five Soviet experts in 1950–52), Political Economy (three Soviet experts in 1950–52), and Dialectical and Historical Materialism (one Soviet expert in 1951–56). The eight departments each had from two to five *jiaoyanshi*, with most of the latter having one (or sometimes two) Soviet experts assigned. The Finance and Credit Department, for example, was composed of four *jiaoyanshi:* (1) Finance, (2) Banking, (3) Product and Money Circulation, and Credit, and (4) Accounting.[21]

In keeping with Liu Shaoqi's vision for the school, in its first years Renda emphasized the training of economic, legal, and diplomatic personnel. Six of the eight departments were devoted to economic management, and the subjects of study were the Stalinist economic-management fields. One way to look at Renda in the early years would be as a Stalinist Harvard Business School, Yale Law School, and Georgetown School of Foreign Service rolled into one. The goal of Renda, stemming from Liu's plans but embraced by all the party leadership, was for Renda to serve as the key institution for the party's cadres to learn how to manage a Soviet-style state and economy. Although it would be several years before Mao proclaimed the beginning of the transition to socialism, it is absolutely clear that in 1949 the party's leaders were already committed to training the personnel needed to run an economy "more or less exactly similar to the present economy of the Soviet Union," in the words of Liu Shaoqi spoken at the school's opening ceremony.[22]

Students at Renda would mostly be party cadres, with at least middle school–level education, who in the Regular Course Division would study in programs of two to four years. Most would then go on to become factory managers, statisticians, accountants, teachers, and economic specialists of one kind or another. In its early years the school also included a Short Course Division in which in-service cadres, that is, teachers and managers currently on the job, could come to Renda for up to six months of training in their field. The Short Course Division proved to be one key way that Renda exerted its influence over schools and government institutions nationwide.

The "new-style regular" university was the product of negotiations and interactions between the Chinese and Soviet leaderships and their respective education specialists. One great irony of this interaction was that the Soviet experts on the scene urged a rapid transformation of higher education through the recruitment of ideological loyalists (i.e., workers and peasants) when it had taken the Soviets themselves more than ten years to transform their own higher education system.[23] The Chinese Communists' moderate line toward the bourgeoisie in 1949–50 irked the Soviet advisers. Since Liu had little confidence that workers and peasants could become university students overnight, the compromise solution would be recruiting both poorly educated old cadres of proper red background and better-educated young intellectuals of more heterogeneous backgrounds and bringing them together in the urban atmosphere of the new, red university.

Social Heterogeneity at the New University

Both the Soviet and Chinese reports from 1950 show leaders struggling to create a proper "Sovietized" student body from party cadres of confusingly heterogeneous social origins. In reports sent back to Moscow at several points in 1950, the Soviet advisers complained of the poor social backgrounds of the students and reported that these backgrounds explained anti-Soviet attitudes on the part of some in the student body.[24] The Chinese administrators, for their part, reported difficulties with the "old cadres" of worker-peasant background who seemed unaccustomed and unwilling to study.[25] Many students of "young intellectual" background, in contrast, seemed intent on making careers for themselves but unwilling to take ideological study seriously.

The human material that party educators and Soviet advisers had to work with at first consisted of the "ideological retrainees" of North China University. Under the leadership of Cheng Fangwu, thousands of "young intellectuals" and former Nationalist government employees were retrained in short, ideological retraining classes. The Soviet advisers Filippov and Fesenko did not like what they found in the party's "thought reform" schools in 1949–50:

> Now the Chinese comrades are paying great attention to the reeducation of the old intelligentsia, who served in former Nationalist

institutions, the police and local security organs. In Beijing there are three institutions engaged in this reeducation: Revolutionary University, Administration and Law University, and North China University. North China University, on the basis of which Renda is being organized, has alone reformed more than ten thousand people in the course of the year. The process of reform: the students study Marxism-Leninism for four months, thereby forming a new world-view, in light of which they critique their past incorrect views and mistakes. They announce that they are now done with the past, and wholly and completely share the new ideas and that they are ready honestly to serve the revolution to the end. The leading communist directors of these institutions seriously believe in this reeducation, and in the way of proof offer up a number of examples in which students, undergoing reform, have—as though suddenly becoming conscious—offered up secret radio sets and weapons.[26]

These Soviet advisers viewed the party's "thought reform" efforts as misguided, at best. Certainly, the Soviet experts were rejecting the Chinese party's apparent "soft" approach to intellectuals and Nationalist government employees in favor, perhaps, of a more typically Stalinist approach, which would have been to arrest, exile, or shoot those suspected of counterrevolutionary sympathies and to train an entirely new, "red" cadre to take the place of the "old" specialists.[27]

These efforts wound up in December 1949 with the graduation of the last class of retrainees from North China University, after which the remaining personnel of the school were assigned to Renda.[28] Not all students were graduated from the retraining school and sent south, however. Hundreds of students were kept on from North China University in the form of the Russian Brigade, a large Russian-language teaching unit that had been established in mid-September 1949. It was exactly at this time that North China University's leaders learned that the school would serve as the basis for the "new style, regular university."[29] Soviet-nationality teachers of Russian who originally were proposed for work in the Communist Party Central Committee happened to arrive early and were assigned to Renda. For most of the 1949–50 academic year, the students of the Russian Brigade and newly selected students who began arriving occupied themselves with the study of Russian under the guidance of the Soviet Russian-language teachers.

In this transitional period, the Soviet advisers looked with suspicion upon the social origins and political reliability of the 466 students of the Russian Brigade, in much the same way that they had disparaged the "political thought" retraining schools. In fact, students in the Russian Brigade were largely drawn from the "political retrainee" groups, so it is not surprising that the Soviet advisers found them just as problematic. In a February 27, 1950, report sent to E. F. Kovalev of the Central Committee, the Soviet adviser Filippov reported on the status of Russian-language teaching at the school and on the nature of the student body.[30] Filippov reported that the Russian Brigade aimed to produce, in the course of two years, students who could serve as Russian-language translators and teachers. He observed great enthusiasm for Russian on the part of the Chinese: "After a month of lessons, it is clear that there is a huge interest in the study of Russian. It is not only the students who are studying Russian with great enthusiasm, but also almost all the employees and service personnel of the university, from the rector to the tea peddler."[31]

While Filippov was greatly cheered by the enthusiasm for Russian study, he was troubled by the nature of the student body. "The political background of these students," he wrote, "leaves much to be desired."[32] The data showed students with few, if any, "natural" inclinations to support the party. The majority in the Russian Brigade were students by social position, with no party affiliation, and came from the nonrevolutionary family backgrounds of petty trader, intelligentsia, free professions, and landowner.[33] In the context of the party's entry into the cities and recruitment of educated urban youth, this made perfect sense, but to the Soviets, it was about as distant as one can imagine from a "worker-peasant" ideal. The best that Filippov could say was that the social and political backgrounds of the students being recruited for the regular courses at Renda "would, in any case, definitely be better [than this]."[34]

Filippov reported that the poor social and political backgrounds of these political retraining-era students explained something very troubling: the anti-Soviet attitudes of many of them. These passages from Filippov's February 1950 report are worth quoting at length, as they demonstrate the deep suspicion with which the Soviets regarded the

Chinese intellectuals, the very people whom the Chinese party was trying to win over in 1949–50:

> A majority of the students with higher education come from Shanghai and Nanjing, and many of them have graduated from religious colleges. A portion of these are fluent in English and Japanese. Of 466 students, 100 profess religious belief. Some of these say that there is no difference at all between Christianity and communism: "Communism aims at the elimination of poverty, and Christianity does, also." "Communism means peace and general prosperity, and Christianity does, also." Some students voice reactionary opinions, such as the following: "America is stronger in technology than the Soviet Union," and, prior to the signing of the Soviet-Chinese Treaty of Friendship and Mutual Aid, said that Port Arthur and Dalian were going to belong to the Soviet Union. After the signing of the Treaty, they are asking questions like the following: "Why is it that the Changchun railway, Dalian and Port Arthur will be returned to China in 1952, and not right now?" "Why will the Changchun railway be turned over [to China] free of charge, while the facilities in Dalian and Port Arthur must be paid for?" "Why was Outer Mongolia granted independence?" "In 1945 the Soviet army in Manchuria took advantage of the situation and looted extensively." "Tell me, how is the USSR going to help China concretely?" These opinions and questions testify not only to political illiteracy, but to a reactionary disposition among some sections of the student body.[35]

The Soviet advisers found these "political retraining" students suspect and objectionable. This was further confirmed, in the Soviets' view, by the students' frankly careerist aspirations, their disdain for political education courses, and their concern for their landlord fathers. The Soviet advisers painted a very ugly picture of what they were up against in the capital of new China.[36]

While the Soviet advisers clearly felt that the party should be recruiting students with worker and peasant backgrounds, Liu Shaoqi himself held a quite different view. Liu was pessimistic about the educational potential of factory workers, and he told the planners of the new university that it would take two to three years to bring such workers up to a level at which they could handle university-type academic work. Wu Yuzhang, Cheng Fangwu, and Vice-Minister of Education Zhang Cunru agreed with Liu, saying that the questions of establishing *rabfaks*, or remedial-type "workers' faculties" attached to universities, was a question that would be taken up sometime in the future.[37] The message to the Soviet advisers was that, considering China's special conditions, higher education for workers and peasants would not be a reality anytime soon. Given the Soviet advisers' dissatisfaction with the human material that the Chinese party was "reforging" in its political retraining schools, this must have come as discouraging news.

Plans for the recruitment of students for the new university moved forward in November and December 1949. The party directed that the school would recruit three types of students: old revolutionary cadres, young intellectuals having at least middle school–level educations, and old intellectuals who had undergone thought reform (a category the Soviets on the scene found most objectionable).[38] Old revolutionary cadres were those who had joined the party before 1942. Regulations stipulated that students of the young intellectual category should be eighteen to thirty years old and graduates of senior middle school or young intellectual party cadres who had graduated from junior middle school or the equivalent and had at least three years of experience in party revolutionary work or specialized organs.[39] These students would be enrolled in the Regular Course Division. Students from the "reformed old intellectual" category were not actively sought because Renda stood to inherit a large number of this type already present at North China University, at the Administration and Law University, and in the Russian Brigade.

In January 1950 the university sent out recruiting teams to each of the five military-administrative regions of China, and these teams contacted party organizations, government bureaus, labor unions, peasant, women's, and youth organizations, and People's Liberation Army units in search of suitable candidates.[40] By the end of February 1950, a total of 965 students had been signed up, 10 percent more than had been planned. Together with 300 political retrainees from North China University, and 300 from the Administration and Law University, the regular-course student body of the school totaled 1,565.[41]

The data on social origins, social positions, and political backgrounds of these 1,565 students do show an "improvement" over the data on the members of the Russian Brigade. Those classified middle peasant comprised 29.1 percent of the student body. Poor peasants and industrial workers together made up 20.3 percent. School authorities could thus claim that admitted students from these favored social categories made up about half of the student body. Despite this, a combined total of 428 students still came from the politically suspect categories of landlord, kulak (rich peasant), and petty trader, for a combined total of 27.6 percent.[42]

Most striking, however, are the differences in party membership and education level between the newly recruited 965 students and the approximately 600 students who were transferred from the political retraining center North China University and from the Administration and Law University. Recruitment data suggest that nearly all the 965 students recruited in January 1950 were party or Youth League members. The new recruits had been recommended by party, government, and military committees, and they were the "party's own" in ways that the political retrainees of 1949 were not. In terms of education level, most newly recruited party and Youth League members had only junior high or elementary school educations, while those transferred from North China University and the Administration and Law University, few of whom were party or Youth League members, comprised the great majority of those having higher-middle or university-level educations.[43] What the data show, then, are two social groups brought together in the new university in Beijing. One social group consisted of party cadres with little formal education, almost all of whom were party members, most probably from rural backgrounds. The other consisted of more highly educated "young intellectuals," many with urban backgrounds.

In spring 1950, as the new students arrived in Beijing to take up their studies at the new university, the Soviet advisers and Chinese administrators of the school reported trouble in the ranks. In February 1950, Filippov warned of anti-Soviet, careerist, and pro-landlord moods among students in the Russian-language courses.[44] The adviser further reported that the Chinese comrades were defending their efforts to retrain the students and cited in particular a February 9, 1950, school administration meeting at which Wu Yuzhang explained that such students, whose attitudes so disturbed the Soviet advisers, were simply "sick" and needed first to be cured, then taught. This, of course, is the familiar Maoist formula from the rectification campaign of 1942–44 in Yan'an, but the Soviets seemed highly skeptical of this "soft" approach to dissent: "The Chinese comrades, leaders of the university, are convinced that a Marxist worldview can be inculcated in every student, regardless of his class inclinations."[45] Filippov, evidently, did not agree.

Filippov reported that the school administrators decided to strengthen the political courses among the 400 students of the Regular Course Division already present and, in the Russian-language courses, to teach political topics in place of most of the Russian-language lessons.[46] Interim classes started at the university on February 13, 1950, to keep the students busy until the Soviet teachers arrived. Courses included Russian language, New People's Democracy, History of the Chinese Revolution, Mathematics, and Physical Culture.[47] Most of the 1,565 students of the Regular Course Division arrived at the new university by the end of March 1950.

What view did the Soviet advisers, who had objected so strenuously to the earlier group of political retrainees, have of these new students? In his final report on work at the school, dated December 18, 1950,[48] Filippov declared the social positions of the students in the Preparatory Course, in which 63 percent were classified as workers and peasants, to be "better" than those of the Regular Course and Short Course divisions, where genuine workers and peasants were relatively scarce.[49] This indicated displeasure, on the Soviet part, with the social composition of the student body.

Indeed, after the students arrived, and some were reclassified as to social origins and positions, the reality looked worse than the optimistic projections of the spring. For example, those of poor and middle peasant origins had been reported to comprise 44.5 percent of the student body in the spring. In December 1950, they were down to 31 percent. The proportion classified as workers by social position, never great to begin with, had declined dramatically from 14 percent in the spring to under 7 percent in December. Those with undesirable backgrounds, such as "landlord" and "capitalist," had increased in number. Party membership decreased from almost 55 percent to approximately 37 percent. Finally, while more were classified as having some higher education than had been the case in the spring, the proportion of the student body having had only elementary-level education increased from 27.5 percent to 36.5 percent, over one-third of the student body in the Regular Course Division. In the Short Course Division, the situation was clear-cut: party members comprised 83 percent, but a whopping 75 percent had only elementary school–level educations.

From the Soviet perspective, the only real bright spot was the Preparatory Course, which was majority worker-peasant in composition and 89 percent party members. However, Filippov did not even include educational levels for this group in his report, suggesting that a large number may have had little or no formal schooling and may have been barely literate in Chinese. Hence, they were placed in the remedial Preparatory Course.

From the Chinese perspective, Liu Shaoqi's goal of producing competent, technically trained specialists in six-month short courses must have seemed nearly impossible ("dead on arrival"). The plans for recruitment of Short Course Division students had called for recruiting experienced party cadres with educational levels equivalent, at a minimum, to the lower middle school level. The plan for the short courses had also called for the recruitment of at least some retrained intellectuals to these courses.[50] In practice, however, these educational requirements for admission were waived, and party membership plus work experience became the most important criteria for admission. The short courses, then, were monopolized by party members with only elementary school–level educations, people likely to be in positions of functional authority in their home areas but of limited academic abilities.

Friction between Old Cadres and Young Intellectuals

The bifurcation between old cadres with low educational levels and young intellectuals at Renda was most severe in the school's early years, when the short courses still enrolled large numbers of in-service cadres. In his 1960 Draft History of Chinese People's University, Hu Xikui described the situation with the student body in the early years as follows: "The approximately 72 percent [of the student body] who were cadres or worker-students had good quality politics, but low cultural levels; the approximately 28 percent who were young students had relatively high cultural levels, but lacked revolutionary tempering. That the students' political and cultural levels were so different undoubtedly created a whole host of new problems in academics, and led to quite a few new problems."[51] In reports written in 1950, Hu described the myriad problems that poorly educated old cadres faced at the new university, and he referred to problems in their relationship with the young intellectuals.

In his report to the Central Committee in spring 1950, Hu Xikui divided the new intake of 865 party cadre-students at the university into two groups by length of party service. Those who had served as party cadres for three to eight years were overwhelmingly the better-educated "young intellectuals," and most had probably joined the party in the civil war period. They comprised 45 percent of the group of 865, or roughly 390 students. Of these cadres, Hu Xikui recorded the following:

> The majority of cadres with three years of revolutionary experience are from the intelligentsia or from people who are close to the intelligentsia. In ideological terms, these people do not have the slightest shortcomings, working without becoming conceited. Having the chance to study, they throw themselves into it with happiness and resolution. However, some of them, in the pursuit of personal glory, try to be admitted to the Diplomatic Department or the Factory Management Department. They try to be admitted to those faculties where, in their opinions, they will not have to study mathematics or economics and where they will not have to work too hard.[52]

"Young intellectuals" who had already served as party cadres for three years were, at this point, irreproachable from the ideological standpoint, but their obvious enthusiasm, relatively high levels of education, and abilities left them open to charges of careerism. Those who had more difficulty adjusting to the new order charged these young intellectual party cadres with trying to "get ahead" and make names for themselves.

Ambition and careerism among well-qualified cadres were the least of Hu's worries. Hu Xikui revealed that the serious problems were not with the young intellectual party cadres but with the hundreds of poorly educated or even semiliterate "old cadres" who had been recommended to the university by regional party and military committees. Of the 865 cadre-students, 30 percent had eight years or more of revolutionary experience: approximately 260.[53] They were cadres who joined the party-led struggle before 1942 and are likely to have been rural base-area cadres. Introducing them, Hu Xikui wrote:

The portion of the student body who are cadres with eight years or more of revolutionary experience study with the greatest enthusiasm. For example, the Diplomatic Department student Yu Taohe has 17 years of revolutionary experience, conducts himself modestly, and studies enthusiastically. Another portion of the student body were decorated members of the PLA before entering the university. Only recently have they undertaken independent work. These students have a cultural level that is not too high, but they are tempered politically and have a great desire to study.[54]

Having introduced these "old cadres" in rather positive terms, however, the report goes on to narrate a litany of problems with them. From the tone of these complaints, it is clear that Yu Taohe was the positive exception used to introduce the negative rule: many "old cadre" students seemed inordinately proud of their long terms of service and looked down on those who had joined the revolutionary ranks more recently.[55]

Reading between the lines of Hu Xikui's report, it is evident that the basic problem with old cadres in 1949–50 was a "victors' mentality" combined with a wide cultural gap between the rural cadres and the new, urban environment in which they found themselves. The old cadres had fought for years in the rural areas, undergoing immense hardships and making huge sacrifices: it is only natural that they would have expected better lives upon entering the cities as the justly earned fruits of their struggle. Instead, many of these cadres found that the deprivations continued and had, in fact, been compounded by the new social and psychological pressures of the city:

A portion of the student body is dissatisfied with living conditions at the university. Students say that the food at the university is poor: constant *gaoliang*, sometimes spoiled food is served, there isn't enough boiled water, and water for drinking is boiled in the same kettle in which food is prepared. Among the students are quite a few who, before entering the university, enjoyed relatively good rations/living conditions, and they complain that now they do not receive anything, that their stipends are not always paid regularly, and that they have to sleep on bunk beds when they want real beds. The students do not want to clean up their rooms, or perform various chores. They are not used to physical exercises in the morning and to observance of the daily routine.[56]

There is a sense here of unmet expectations. City living conditions should mean, at a minimum, decent food and sleeping in real beds. Some students found the situation so discouraging that they sought to return home: "Some students want to go home and have demanded travel expenses for the return trip. The university cannot provide this, and so there are grounds for dissatisfaction among them. Some say: 'I took part in the revolution for ten years, and now I can't even get travel money.' 'If something isn't done to improve material conditions at the university, we are not going to be able to study for a whole year, much less four.'"[57] These may have been minority views. Given that Hu Xikui was writing to the Central Committee, and had in mind the center's material support for his institution, he would have had ample incentive to portray the situation at the school as particularly grave. It nonetheless seems likely that the expectations of some students would be disappointed amid the hardships of 1949–50. Evidence from Hu's report suggests that the students most disappointed were those who had been with the revolution the longest, such as the cadre who wanted travel money to go home.

"Young intellectuals" from urban backgrounds were not as vocal about material conditions at the university.[58] Most young intellectuals were not inclined to complain about material hardships, as they were continually reminded that the hardships in rural areas were much worse. They thus felt relatively privileged, and poor food and lodgings in the cities to them signified a sharing of the hardships of party and army. For rural cadres who had themselves experienced these hardships for years, the feeling was different: victory and entry into the cities deserved reward in the form of material improvements in their lives.

Hu Xikui reported that the old cadres' academic difficulties were extremely serious and contributed to their low morale. Here, Hu was describing a much broader group than the "old cadres" with eight years or more of experience. It should be recalled that 36.5 percent, or some 470 of the Regular Course students, had only elementary school–level educations. Fully one-half of the student body was taking remedial courses in Chinese and mathematics, indicating that the problem extended even beyond the ranks of those with elementary school–level educations.[59] A comment of one student enrolled in the Short Course Division, where educational levels were even lower overall than in the regular departments, illustrates the psychological difficulties these students faced: "[a] student from the city of Shijiazhuang, a former secretary of a supply organization, thirty-two years of age, of elementary-school level education, revealed that when he was called up by the local party committee for study in the Short Course, and heard that he would have to study Russian, he became upset, got a headache, and his spirits fell."

This kind of extreme reaction to the prospect of having to study in a higher education institution, and to study something as unfamiliar as Russian, was apparently quite common: "Students with poor general education preparation, who see subjects like higher mathematics in the schedule, become frightened. They feel that they are not up to the task, are afraid of studying Russian, and become discouraged. They are afraid of quizzes, evaluations, and exams, and start to say that they cannot understand the subjects they are taught. They voice their dissatisfactions and lose interest in studying."[60] The prospect of studying for long periods of time also inclined older, less educated cadres to try to win transfer to the two year regular course in factory management. Older cadre-students often had families back home, and the prospect of long years of study in an unfamiliar environment seemed daunting.

Simple fear of having to study difficult subjects and family concerns were heightened by the perceived alienness of the urban environment. Poorly educated cadre-students of rural backgrounds adopted hostile attitudes, in some cases, to their surroundings and to their fellow students: "Students with more than eight years of revolutionary experience are proud of their pasts, but worried about their families, and about their futures after they finish university. Material difficulties, fear of studying foreign languages and mathematics inclines these students to pessimism, and they say: 'What I was before, at the start of the revolution, is still what I am today. For whom did we carry out the revolution? Was it really for the intelligentsia?' Because of this, they do not have the will to study."[61] It is obvious that the morale of such students was low and that they viewed as troubling the ease with which intellectuals seemed to be recreating an alien world. These attitudes extended further, to a general fear that the cultural order at the university and, by extension, in the party in the cities was morally corrupt: "Some students from the countryside are against dancing and are against male and female students walking arm-in-arm and talking. When they see something like this, they say: 'What a university!' 'This university was not created by communists: something has changed!' "[62] All of these attitudes were not limited to rural cadres at Renda but were a general phenomenon attendant upon the party's entry into the cities in 1949.[63]

One immediate and practical problem created by the differences between "young intellectual" cadres and "old cadres" was that of cooperation between the two groups. Hu Xikui noted that the "young intellectuals" were none too impressed by the old cadres:

> Before meeting the old cadres, young cadres think of them with respect. As [the former] have a long history of revolutionary work, [the latter] have [at first] a high opinion of them. After meeting them, however, the young cadres were disappointed as the old cadres in fact turned out to be completely different from what they had thought. These old workers, in their opinion, seemed disorganized, without any particular inclination to work, and are haughty while being inadequately prepared in theory.[64]

The most common complaint about the old cadres was that they trumpeted their long revolutionary records, while in fact being of only marginal competence. For their part, the old cadres viewed the younger ones as "quite activist" but as disrespectful of their elders. Old cadres complained that younger ones "did not take them seriously enough."[65] Old cadres craved respect but were at a severe disadvantage at the new university in a new era in which academic and technical competence could be expected to take priority over length of revolutionary service.

The regime experimented with higher education for workers and peasants at Renda as well as in other places, but with even such an authority as Liu Shaoqi quite dubious about its potential success, it is not surprising that the regime abandoned all experiments with worker-peasant education by 1955 and chose the path of academic "regularization."[66] By 1956–57, Renda's Soviet-trained "young intellectual" students were poised to make themselves into a new elite, dominating in the Stalinist economic-managerial specialties, in the training of Marxist-Leninist theory teachers, and in other state-oriented technical fields such as archival administration.

In the Hundred Flowers Campaign of May–June 1957, however, Renda would be attacked as a "great beehive of dogmatism." For the next two decades—owing in part to the deterioration and then collapse of Sino-Soviet relations—Renda with its elitist and technocratic values would be on the defensive as Maoist old cadres turned the tables on the temporarily ascendant young intellectuals of the new regime.

IV

Family Strategies

↬ *13*

The Ye Family in New China

Joseph W. Esherick

YE DUZHENG WAS no leftist, but—like Liu Hongsheng, the prominent businessman discussed in Sherman Cochran's chapter (Chapter 15)—he returned to China within a year of the Communist takeover. As Chiang Kai-shek's Nationalist armies collapsed in the final year of the civil war, Duzheng was completing his doctoral degree in atmospheric physics at the University of Chicago. He had followed the Communist victories in the U.S. papers, discussing the course of the civil war with his Chinese classmates. If the Communists had not emerged victorious, he might never have returned: he viewed China under the Nationalists as just too corrupt and chaotic. The founding of the People's Republic in 1949 promised peace and order and hope for the future. It was time for Duzheng to go home.

Ye Duzheng was the seventh son in a large and distinguished Tianjin family. The family's origins lay in Anqing, the Qing dynasty capital of Anhui province and a port on the Yangzi River. A surviving genealogy traces ancestors back to the fourteenth century, when the family moved to Anqing during the warfare that expelled the Mongols and established the Ming dynasty. In the mid-nineteenth century, the Taiping rebels attacked Anqing, and Ye Duzheng's great-great-grandfather gained prominence aiding the Anhui Army in its fight against the insurgents. His son, Ye Boying, had an even more distinguished career, culminating in a term as governor of Shaanxi province in the 1880s. By the early twentieth century, this branch of the family had moved to the north China treaty port of Tianjin. Duzheng's father, Ye Chongzhi, was a police *daotai* in Tianjin in the final years of the Qing dynasty, then abandoned politics after the 1911 Revolution for a career in banking and industry.[1]

In the early years of the republic, Ye Chongzhi presided over a large family in a spacious compound behind the Anhui guildhall (*huiguan*). His wife and two concubines bore him ten sons and five daughters. Only the youngest of these daughters received more than a minimal education in the female arts, but the sons were given a classical education by a father-son pair of Confucian scholars, then sent off to the renowned Nankai Middle School and a variety of colleges in north China. The three eldest brothers had arranged marriages and settled down to family life and business in Tianjin; the younger ones—especially after their father's death in 1930—were active in student politics, protesting the advance of Japanese imperialism in the 1930s. Following the Japanese invasion the family scattered, the older brothers staying in Japanese-occupied China, two of the younger ones joining the Communist Party (CCP), two ending up in the wartime capital in Chongqing, and Duzheng finishing his college education in China before earning a fellowship to study in America. (See the accompanying table.)

The years after 1949 marked the beginning of a new life for the Ye family, as they did for the Chinese nation. The surviving eight brothers and four sisters were no longer part of a single large household. Gone was the spacious compound that housed dozens of servants and assorted relatives in addition to the immediate family. Now the siblings each had families of their own, as the new China put an end to the old "feudal" patriarchal family system and ushered in an era of nuclear families for all.[2] The nature of these new families differed, with Communist Party cadres living in large government compounds forming one distinctive type. This chapter will explore some of those differences and the various ways in which politics slowly worked its way into family life.

The educated Ye brothers represented the sort of urban elite talent and expertise that the party wished to attract to its new regime. In order to revive the urban economy, the Communists sought the cooperation of the "national bourgeoisie"; and many businessmen, both to test the bona fides of the new regime and to earn the coveted "national bourgeois" label, were prepared to work with their new Communist over-

Children of Ye Chongzhi

Name	Birth Order	Dates	Mother	Marriage Date	Career
Unknown	1st sister	1906?–9?	Cang	—	Dies as child
Dushi	2nd sister	1907?–29?	Chen	?	Marries landlord
Duren	1st brother	1908–80	Liu	1931	Banker
Duzhi	2nd brother	1909?–15	Chen	—	Dies as child
Duya	3rd sister	1910?–79?	Chen	?	Marries official's son—a heroin addict
Duyi	3rd brother	1912–2004	Chen	1934	Democratic League
Duxin	4th brother	1912–81	Liu	1935	Businessman
Duzhuang	5th brother	1914–2000	Liu	1946	Agronomist/ translator
Ye Fang	6th brother	1914–	Chen	1945	CCP cadre
Duzheng	7th brother	1915–	Chen	1942	Scientist
Dusong	4th sister	1916?–79?	Liu	?	Marries Cornell graduate/ businessman
Fang Shi	9th brother	1916–	Chen	1939	CCP journalist
Duquan	10th brother	1919?–29?	Liu	—	Dies as child
Durou	5th sister	1921–	Liu	?	Teacher; marries translator
Dushen	12th brother	1924–99	Liu	1957	Entertainer

Sources: Ye shi zupu (Ye family genealogy), 6th ed. (n.p.: 1944), 7:17a–b, 42a–44a; Ye Duzhuang, untitled 1991 ms., 84–114; interviews: Ye Duzheng, Ye Durou, Chen Cheng.

Notes: There was no eighth brother: the second son was moved to that spot in an unsuccessful attempt to save him from a youthful illness. The eleventh "brother" was a grandson of the late president Yuan Shikai, whose family hoped to benefit from the Ye family's success in bearing sons by staging an "adoption" into the family.

lords. In the spring of 1949, the eldest Ye brother, a banker in Tianjin, was present when Liu Shaoqi, the party's second-ranking leader, met with businessmen in north China's most important port and industrial city. Liu's purpose was to persuade business leaders to keep their capital in China and assist in reviving the urban economy. The businessmen complained that despite the employment they provided to thousands of workers, they were still being treated as "exploiters." Liu would not deny the Marxist precept that capitalist profits derived from exploiting the labor of others, but he admitted that there was "merit" in their efforts (a line for which he was much reviled during the Cultural Revolution) and promised to allow private enterprises to keep and reinvest their profits.[3] Eldest brother was sufficiently impressed by the message that when his wife's wealthy friends spoke of fleeing to Hong Kong, he urged them to stay and do business with the Communists.[4]

Among the Ye brothers, the American-trained Duzheng's return was the most dramatic evidence of Communist Party success in attracting the support of "petty bourgeois" professionals and of patriotic Chinese intellectuals' hope for the new order. With a University of Chicago doctorate earned under Carl G. Rossy, the world's leading atmospheric scientist, he had forsaken a promising career in the United States to return to an uncertain future in China. By the time he arrived in China, the cold war had turned hot in Korea. But the boat on which Duzheng and his wife returned was filled with young Chinese who, like them, were drawn back to their homeland not by communism but by patriotism and who longed for the opportunity to serve their country and make it great again. When they crossed into China from Hong Kong, they were greeted like returning heroes. Touched by the officially organized welcome, Duzheng's eyes filled with tears.

Soon he was on a train to Nanjing, where he joined the Institute of Geophysics of the Chinese Academy of Sciences. Once facilities were arranged in Beijing, the Academy of Sciences moved to the new capital. Duzheng helped to organize the Meteorology Bureau to coordinate China's weather forecasting—a critical enterprise in a largely agricultural country plagued by persistent floods and drought. He rose to the rank of research scientist (yanjiuyuan) and became a leading member of the Institute of Atmospheric Physics when it was established within the academy.[5]

Like all the Ye brothers, Ye Duzheng was in the prime of life in the early years of the Communist regime. The eldest brother, in Tianjin, had just turned forty when the People's Republic was founded; the youngest, staying in Sichuan to pursue his career as an entertainer, was just twenty-five. The others were all in their thirties and eager to get to work. The third brother, Ye Duyi, was the only one of the group, besides Duzheng, who had finished his college education, having gradu-

ated from the American-supported Yanjing (Yenching) University in
political science in 1934. During and after the war he had been active
in the Democratic League, a party of liberal intellectuals who became
increasingly critical of Chiang Kai-shek's Nationalist dictatorship in
the postwar years.[6] As his politics moved left, Ye Duyi had extensive
contacts with Communist united front operatives. In September 1949,
he was named an alternate member of the Chinese People's Political
Consultative Conference. This was the Communist-dominated united
front organization that proclaimed the founding of the People's Republic on October 1, 1949; passed the Organic Law, which served as a
constitution for the first years of the People's Republic; and gave the
new regime something more than revolutionary legitimacy. In a sense,
Ye Duyi was present at the creation of the new government—but he
was dissatisfied with his "alternate" status. He brought up the issue
with Li Weihan, who headed the party's United Front Department. Li
assured him that the "alternate" label was unimportant: it only meant
that Ye could not vote. As Li candidly explained, voting rights were in-
consequential, since the party would decide all important issues before
the meeting anyway. It was Duyi's first lesson in the politics of the new
regime.[7]

With his degree in political science, Ye Duyi was recruited to serve on
the Politics and Law Commission (Zhengzhi falü weiyuanhui). This
commission, headed by party elder and Politburo member Dong Biwu,
was charged with overseeing the ministries concerned with domestic,
legal, and internal security affairs, an organ of considerable importance.[8] Duyi was a diligent official, the only member of the commission
for whom it was a full-time job, and he was soon named its executive
secretary. Later his duties came under the jurisdiction of the Ministry of
Justice, and he was provided an old-style courtyard house in a choice
neighborhood, a regular salary, and quite comfortable working conditions. He was also a leader of the Democratic League, which was permitted to continue in the People's Republic, having accepted the leading
role of the Communist Party. He was becoming one of the group of
Western-educated liberal intellectuals co-opted into an uneasy working
relation with the new Communist state.[9] It was a significant group in
the early People's Republic. Eleven of the twenty-four ministers of the
new government were members of the Democratic League or other
minor parties, or independent "democratic personages."[10]

The fifth Ye brother, Ye Duzhuang, an agronomist educated in Japan, had also been active in the Democratic League, though not at the national level like his third brother Duyi. When the Communist forces surrounded Beiping early in 1949, he had no intention of leaving and worked to persuade others to remain at the agriculture institute in the city's suburbs. With his expertise in agriculture and progressive politics, he too had hopes for an official position—perhaps in the administration of the institute. But he was too independent minded for the new Communist leadership. During the war, he had briefly joined the Communists' Eighth Route Army, using his Japanese to interrogate prisoners, but he chafed under the rigors and political discipline of army life. In 1949, he was put off by the superior attitude of the cadre appointed to head the institute. In his first meeting, the new head addressed his subordinates striding across the stage in a gray People's Liberation Army (PLA) uniform, avoiding all eye contact and conveying a simple message—"stay if you wish, go if you want"—which made the assembled agronomists feel like prisoners. But Duzhuang's public stance in the Beijing Democratic League was consistently supportive of the new regime. In spring 1951, *People's Daily* printed a statement he drafted praising the "awesome power" of recently issued laws for dealing with counterrevolutionaries.[11]

Duzhuang felt underused in his job as head of the institute's editorial committee, but he put out a newsletter and a journal whose main theme was learning from Soviet science, especially the theories of the peasant-agronomist Ivan Michurin. Michurin's ideas would be championed by Trofim Lysenko, a favorite of Joseph Stalin's, in a theory (now discredited) arguing that acquired characteristics could be inherited independently of any genetic mechanism. The embrace of these "advanced discoveries" of Soviet science did nothing to improve Chinese agricultural practice, but Duzhuang dutifully joined in translating Michurin's works from an English edition and, for a while, found them fresh and exciting. *People's Daily* hailed his translation for transmitting Michurin's important message that one should not simply accept natural phenomena as given but "struggle with nature . . . transforming nature."[12] It was this optimistic transformative message of Michurin and Lysenkoism that made it so attractive.

When Ye Duyi returned to Tianjin after the war, he had persuaded his eldest brother to join the Democratic League. In theory, this eldest son, Ye Duren, should have been the most vulnerable of the Ye brothers facing a communist revolution. A banker living in his wife's mansion in the former concession area—a house left by her uncle, the warlord and onetime president of the Republic, Xu Shichang—the eldest brother was far and away the richest of the lot. He had stayed in Tianjin during the Japanese occupation and was accordingly open to the charge of collaboration with the enemy. But this brother was nothing if not cautious, exceptionally effective at avoiding attention, and just as successful at collaborating with the Communists as with every other regime that Tianjin had seen. He liquidated most of his property during the 1940s. He quit his job at the bank, took up a salaried position with the Democratic League, cooperated with every party campaign that came along, and taught his children to live simply and without display— once insisting that his daughter, who wanted a foreign watch like her friends, content herself with a cheap domestic brand. His approach worked perfectly: he and his family led an uneventful life, accomplishing little but suffering less.[13]

The other Tianjin businessman of the family, the fourth brother, Duxin, had been living off stock dividends for some time. After 1949, he taught briefly at a night school, but he suffered from tuberculosis and was unable to continue. His cheerful and outgoing wife was active in the local neighborhood committee, looking after public hygiene and social order, doing propaganda work for the government, reading the newspaper aloud to illiterate women (she was quite good at transforming dull official accounts into lively stories that entertained her audience), and serving as one of the commoner-judges on the local court. She was effective and popular at her job, even daring to complain against petty officials who abused their privileges, and was probably less the intrusive busybody than many other women in that position. The couple had no children, and after private enterprises were socialized, Duxin received fixed monthly interest payments that were enough for their simple needs.[14]

Staying in western China after the war was Ye Dushen, the youngest brother and black sheep of the family, who had defied his eldest brother by becoming a comic entertainer *(xiangsheng)* during the war.[15] For the scion of an elite family to become an entertainer was regarded as something of a disgrace, but this youngest Ye brother, without paternal discipline from age six, was rebel enough to take to the stage.

Fleeing west during the war, he worked in tea houses and with small theater troupes, finally settling in Chongqing. One day late in 1949, the Nationalist police simply lined up and marched out of town, and the PLA entered behind them. For Dushen, the new China brought an end to much of the discrimination against actors that he had felt in the old society; and within a year he held a regular salaried job as a member of the Great Masses Performing Arts Troupe. He learned the new revolutionary songs and stories and performed with his usual gusto. He did not marry until 1957, but his transition to the new China was very smooth. Nonetheless, still smarting from his 1940s expulsion from the family by his eldest brother, he would not contact his brothers in Beijing and Tianjin until the 1980s.[16]

Of course the two brothers for whom 1949 brought the least change were the sixth (now known as Ye Fang) and ninth (who even changed his surname to become Fang Shi), the two members of the Communist Party. They had been working for the revolution for some years, and now they simply moved to a new stage of that project. Ye Fang had joined the Communist New Fourth Army during the war, then was sent to Manchuria in 1945. After several years fighting bandits as a magistrate in the northeast, he was appointed vice president of a provincial party school. This began a long period of service in such institutions, which were designed to provide local party cadres with basic political instruction in Marxist doctrine, the history of the Chinese revolution, and party policies. Ye Fang's years at Nankai Middle School and Qinghua University, where he had first gotten involved in leftist politics during the December Ninth Movement of 1935, made him unusually well educated for a party member. (The party included only about forty thousand college graduates in 1949—less than 1 percent of its 4.4 million members.)[17] His calm intellectual demeanor and capacity for guarded circumspection on sensitive political matters suited him for an administrative role in party education. In 1948, when Shenyang was taken, he was sent to organize the party school for the entire northeast region and headed its education department until 1955.[18]

Fang Shi, the ninth brother, had joined the December Ninth Movement in 1935, then traveled to the Communist base areas in north China when the war broke out. During the war, he married a young comrade, and the couple endured terrible hardships in those years. They lost their first child, who was born in a freezing cave during a retreat from a Japanese offensive, and his wife was left permanently crippled by the ordeal. During the Rectification Movement, Fang Shi was imprisoned for two years on vague suspicions of working for the Nationalists, but on his release his talents were well utilized in the New China News Agency. The civil war years were perhaps his most rewarding, as he worked at the Communist headquarters, putting out the daily bulletins on PLA victories on the battlefield. In 1949, he followed the party center to Beijing. It was August before housing could be arranged in the city, but when the news agency found an appropriate space, it turned out to be the same Beijing College of Law and Commerce that he had attended as a student. His responsibility was now political reporting, including the activities of the Communist leadership. Thus he covered the meeting of the Political Consultative Conference that led to the founding of the People's Republic. There he got a taste of some of the changes that were coming over the revolutionary leadership. He ran into an old friend from his days in the student movement, who was now a governor in the northeast. They greeted each other in the warmest manner and quickly sought to catch up on their respective revolutionary careers. But when his friend discovered that Fang Shi was neither a high official nor a delegate to the conference but only a lowly reporter, his manner became abruptly formal and cold, and he turned to seek a more important partner for conversation. The casual relations that Fang Shi had enjoyed with China's highest leaders at the Xibaipo headquarters—where he had interacted with Zhou Enlai, Liu Shaoqi, and even Mao Zedong while editing dispatches for the New China News Agency—were a thing of the past. Hierarchy, rank, and official airs would find a place in new China too.

Of the three sisters who survived to 1949, only the third, Duya, lived in Beijing and interacted much with the rest of the family. Her husband had worked in a tax bureau under the Nationalists and accumulated enough money to buy a house for his family. To protect his job in the postwar era, he had entertained his superiors at brothels or with drugs. Third sister suffered greatly from his whoring, and she once attempted suicide. After 1949, he managed to escape punishment for his work for the Nationalists and worked for a time at a local handicraft workshop. But eventually his unsavory past and penchant for speaking too freely got him arrested, and he died in prison in 1960. Third sister, meanwhile, became an activist in her neighborhood committee, seeing to the peace, order, cleanliness, and political correctness of her neighbors. She raised three sons, all of whom went to college and became her primary consolation in an otherwise bitter life.

The fourth sister, Dusong, had a similarly grievous life in the southwest, where she and her husband had fled during the war. He was a Cornell-trained engineer with no sense of marital fidelity. In Yunnan he brought his mistress into the household, where they lived in bigamous disharmony until the woman left him. Dusong had three children with him: two had distinguished technical careers, and one became a high official. Meanwhile, the fifth sister, Durou, ended up in Shanghai. Her husband, Yao Zengyi, with whom she had fallen in love and married during the war, became a prominent official in the Nationalist government, fleeing to Hong Kong in 1949. The Nationalists promised him a high position in Taiwan, but his wife refused to leave China while her mother was still in Tianjin. So he returned, and they stayed on in Shanghai. She (the one sister with any formal education) became a biology teacher, while her husband, fearful that his past would be held against him, worked at home as a private translator. Living away from their brothers in Beijing, these two sisters had little interaction with the rest of the family, and at this point, we allow them to drop from our story.[19]

With the exception of the childless and mostly unemployed fourth brother, Duxin, all of the Ye brothers found a role contributing to the new China, whether it be in science (number seven, Duzheng) or entertainment (number twelve, Dushen), in government (number three, Duyi) or party (number six, Ye Fang) or with the Democratic League (number one, Duren), as editor of a technical journal (number five, Duzhuang) or journalist in the official news agency (number nine, Fang Shi). They were also all raising families—but families very different from the one in which they themselves had grown up. The large "feudal" family—with wives and concubines and dozens of servants living under one roof, with children confined to the household compound, and boys attending school at home under a private tutor—was a thing of the past. The nuclear family, perhaps with the addition of a surviving grandparent, had long been the norm in ordinary peasant or small merchant families; but now even elite families conformed to this pattern.

Among the Ye siblings, the same divide that had separated older and younger brothers in the Republican era was evident in the demography of their families under the People's Republic. The three eldest brothers, all of whom had arranged marriages, had wed before the war at the age of twenty-two or twenty-three, very close to the norm for Chinese males. Beginning with the fifth brother, Duzhuang, however, all the others married during or after the war, usually when they were near or past the age of thirty, to women of their own choosing.[20] All but one of the seven children of the three elder brothers were born before or during the war, while all but two of the eighteen children of the younger brothers were born after the war. Indeed, when we consider that the sixth brother, Ye Fang, was living in "liberated" Communist-controlled areas of the northeast from 1946, fifteen of these children were born under the new regime. As such, they were very much part of the Chinese population boom that came with the peace and order of the new regime.

It is the families of these younger brothers that most interest us, for they brought a new type of child rearing, characteristic of the early years of the People's Republic. Not all of these families were alike, of course. The most distinctive new type was the sixth brother Ye Fang's large family, for his was a privileged provincial-level cadre family. It was distinctive in part by being very large. In the early 1950s, the party's policy was clearly natalist, following the anti-Malthusian theories of the Soviet Union that held that class oppression and imperialist aggression, not overpopulation, were responsible for poverty in countries such as China. One of the duties of a residence committee activist like Duxin's wife or third sister Duya was to encourage young couples to have more children.[21] Ye Fang and his wife certainly heeded this injunction. They had eight children (six in their first ten years in the northeast), and the party did everything necessary to accommodate their large family, providing a large Japanese-built house with a separate bedroom for each child and a nanny until the child was two years old and ready to begin nursery school.

The family lived in a compound reserved for leading cadres of the provincial party apparatus. One can see such compounds in any provincial capital, surrounded by high walls usually topped with barbed wire or broken glass and guarded by a PLA sentry at the gate. Inside, the grounds were spacious, with plenty of trees and open space and room for children to play. The children's nursery school was within the walls. There they boarded, in dormitories with about ten beds to a room, from Monday through Saturday, returning home only on Sundays for a noisy meal with the family. The children spent so little time together at home that they all agree that family ties were not that important when they were young. Their personalities were quite different, and during vacations they were more likely to play with schoolmates than siblings. In their games, the elite status of the peer group was easily seen, as the boys' make-believe world was filled with generals and ministers and party secretaries—the posts of their fathers to which the new generation naturally aspired.

At nursery school, they learned revolutionary songs and dances—resisting American imperialism and aiding North Korea being particularly popular themes during the early 1950s. At home, their father reinforced this message, urging the children to develop a revolutionary spirit and devote their lives to China and the party. They attended the Cultivating Talent Primary School (Yucai xiaoxue), headed for a time by the wife of Gao Gang, powerful party boss of the northeast region. The talent to be cultivated at such schools belonged to the children of party and army leaders—and the best teachers and facilities were provided to train this next generation of the revolutionary vanguard. Even during the worst years of shortages, the food was always adequate, with steamed wheat buns and noodles instead of the corn meal that many ate, vegetables for most meals, and meat several times a week. In general, it was better food than they got at home. On the weekends, a great line of black sedans would queue up outside the school gate, sent by the fathers' units to take the kids home for a brief visit with their families. The Ye children, however, lived only a few blocks away and walked home on the weekend.

In the early 1950s, party and government cadres' compensation remained on the supply system inherited from the revolutionary era. In lieu of a salary, each family was provided housing, food, clothing, and other necessities. At New Year, two new suits of clothing were issued—the younger children receiving theirs through the nursery school. They were just the colorless basics: tee shirts and pants for summer, cotton-padded jackets and pants for winter. Invariably, the younger children's simple wardrobe was supplemented by hand-me-downs from their older siblings. Until the 1960s, when rubber-soled canvas shoes became available, the Ye children wore cotton shoes made at home by their mother and maid.

The big annual holiday was always Chinese New Year. Everybody got at least a week off from school and work, and the party supplied food for a major feast. Invariably there was fish (required for any New Year's celebration), and Ye Fang's large family usually got half a pig as well. With no refrigeration (except the northern winter), these unprecedented provisions were quickly consumed. There were free tickets for New Year's entertainment, usually a dubbed Soviet-bloc movie or revolutionary Chinese film. Each summer, Ye Fang was given the opportunity to take a vacation at a party retreat on the beach near Dalian. There was not room for the whole family, so he would take one or two children, usually the younger ones, leaving his wife to care for the rest. One of his youngest sons fondly remembered these vacations and the fancy white bread he was allowed to eat. By the time they reached middle school, the kids would go on school-organized holidays, with special buses and food and lodging provided. Such comprehensive care could breed a psychology of dependence in the children, which would make it difficult for them to fend for themselves later on. One remembers with embarrassment that as teenagers, when they went to take a public bus, they did not know how to buy tickets.

A curious and somewhat contradictory spirit prevailed in this privileged party family. On the one hand, with spacious housing, maids and nannies, special schools, and ample supplies from the party, Ye Fang's children led a privileged, pampered life. Their friends all came from similar circumstances, and it was assumed that they would pursue the same party, government, or military careers as their fathers. There was almost a sense of entitlement in this fledgling party aristocracy. On the other hand, their father (and their teachers) lectured them on the hard times the party had gone through to reach this point and the need to emulate that spirit of hard work and simple living. Thus, for example, when one daughter brought her dirty clothes home from school for the maid to wash, she was sharply rebuked and told to wash her own laundry. Ye Fang was perhaps more strict with his family than many of his colleagues, only rarely using an official car to take the children to a movie, sometimes allowing his free movie or theater tickets to expire unused (one boy recalls his dismay at discovering a pair of tickets in the wastebasket), and strictly prohibiting his children from reading his copies of such sensitive internal party publications as *Reference News,* whose excerpted reports from foreign publications were often made available to other high cadres' children.[22]

The family of the fifth brother, Ye Duzhuang, provides a contrast to this provincial cadre lifestyle and was similar to most of the others in the Beijing area. For Duzhuang and his wife, the Japanese-educated artist Sun Song, children and family life were much more important—and sending their daughters to be raised by the state was unthinkable. When the couple was courting, they talked of owning a farm in the Western Hills outside of Beijing, where Duzhuang would carry out agronomy experiments and Sun Song would raise the children, paint, and (in her romantic imaginings) raise horses. The revolution put an end to Sun Song's dreams of horseback riding on the family farm, but she eagerly welcomed Duzhuang's assignment to the agricultural institute in the suburbs. The Chinese Academy of Agricultural Sciences, the successor to the institute Duzhuang joined in 1948, was surrounded by open fields, and Sun Song loved the fresh air and closeness to nature. This was the healthy environment in which she wished to raise her children, and she would take the girls into the corn fields and strip them to their undergarments to romp about exposed to the sun.

They lived in a simple apartment in a two-story compound of about twenty units, built by the Japanese during the war. Their ground floor unit had a kitchen, bathroom, bedroom for the children, living room in which the parents had their bed, and a room with a tatami floor (made, at some expense, to suit Sun Song's Japan-derived taste) where the nanny slept and the children would play. In the early 1950s, the girls all lived at home with their mother, who had turned down an offer to work in the film business. Soon, however, her professional ambitions returned, but the only convenient job she could find was as an underpaid illustrator for the journals that Duzhuang edited at the agriculture institute. Duzhuang wanted another child, hoping for a son, but she was unwilling, even terminating one pregnancy—though in this natalist period of the early 1950s, the abortion required ministerial approval.

The family lived comfortably on Duzhuang's salary plus royalties he earned from his own publications. Housing was essentially free and deducted from his pay. Accounts in his wife's diary from 1955 show a monthly income of 144 yuan plus 108 yuan in royalties. From this, 20 yuan went to the nanny, 15 yuan to help support Duzhuang's mother, and 12 yuan to repay some unspecified loan. In a typical month, he spent 16.40 on books and 28 yuan for transport into the city, both business or educational expenses that came to 21 percent of the total. Food was clearly the biggest expense, 81.63 yuan, or 35 percent of the total, with the remainder spent on clothes, heating, toys, and 3.80 for the one clear luxury: cigarettes.[23] This bought a very comfortable standard of living, with meat, fish, and even shrimp frequently on the table. Sun Song insisted on a healthy diet that included an unvarying daily breakfast of warm milk, an egg, and toasted *mantou* (steamed buns) with butter and jam. The girls grew so tired of this regimen that one once sneaked off to school without eating her portion—only to have it served again for lunch. They went to a special new pediatric dentist for their teeth, and the middle daughter even had orthodontics—a very new practice at the time. There were colorful clothes for the girls, often designed by their artistic mother and specially made. Books were very much part of family life, and Duzhuang bought so many children's books for his daughters that the house became a lending library for the entire neighborhood.

At school, the girls were model students. With intellectual parents and plenty of books at home, they excelled at their studies. Their father was also a strong supporter of the agriculture academy's primary school, his editorial office generating income from which he provided supplementary funds for the school. This helped to make his daughters favorites of the teachers. Indeed, when his second daughter began primary school, she was selected to represent the new students and give a short speech, for which her mother made a special pleated white dress of silk.

Family memories from this period are uniformly happy. Their father would take the girls to parks, the zoo, or the popular Soviet industrial exhibition hall. They would take the bus into the city to listen to storytellers with their father or watch movies with their mother—once a memorable special showing of the 1924 Douglas Fairbanks silent classic *The Thief of Baghdad*. Its flying carpet and magic rope provided a welcome contrast to the usual fare of Russian spy movies. On special occasions, a birthday, for example, they would eat at the Moscow Restaurant, a cavernous facility near the exhibition hall that served Russian food, an exotic if not always tasty treat. Duzhuang had enough money to buy toys—blocks, puzzles, and a red fire engine—and he started the girls on stamp collecting. As the girls grew older, they spent summer days swimming in the muddy pool in the academy yard. The second became quite a good swimmer, while the eldest had a clear voice and sang in a local choir.[24]

The other Ye brothers in Beijing, Duyi of the Justice Ministry, Duzheng at the Academy of Sciences, and Fang Shi at the New China News Agency, enjoyed a family life not so different from this, though they all lived in the city, and their wives did not share Sun Song's romantic notions about pastoral life. Duzheng and Fang Shi had three children not so different in ages from Duzhuang's, and they would occasionally visit and let the cousins play together. As a party member, Fang Shi shared many of Ye Fang's ideas about child rearing. When both he and his wife were working and had meetings in the evening, they found it convenient to leave their children in boarding schools. They also wanted their offspring to develop good socialist values of cooperating and getting along with their peers at school. The children of Duyi and Duzhuang, by contrast, were exposed to a great deal more Western culture. Duyi loved to tell stories to his children, and this Western-educated intellectual's favorites were Victor Hugo and Charles Dickens. So for days and weeks on end, with great energy and emotion, he would recount serialized versions of *Les Misérables*, *The Hunchback of Notre Dâme*, or *A Tale of Two Cities*. For Duzhuang's children, the art books that his wife had brought back from Japan introduced them to the masters of the Renaissance and modernist painters. In the astrophysicist Duzheng's family, a scientific culture dominated: one of the cousins remembers a blackboard on which was written the incomprehensible truth: "The universe has no end." There were, then, important differences in the culture and values of these different families, but all lived quite comfortably, put great stress on education, and brought up their children to contribute to the new China.[25]

Relations among the Ye siblings were handled with some care under the new regime. They had grown up together in Tianjin; most had studied at Nankai; the younger had all been engaged in progressive politics as students; and they had corresponded and occasionally seen each other during the long years of the war. But the Communists were wary of excessive concern for family (*jiating guannian*) among their cadres, and the Ye party members were particularly circumspect about reestablishing connections with their siblings. Fang Shi, for example, had left his inheritance with his third sister when he went off to join the revolution in 1937. They had corresponded occasionally, and she had sent him such scarce necessities as toothpaste when communication with Yan'an became easier in the immediate postwar period. But after arriving back in Beijing, he waited several months before visiting his sister. Even then, he made the mistake of taking a rickshaw to save time and was criticized for this forbidden bourgeois luxury. When his first child was born in 1950, he was still being compensated on the supply system and received no salary to cover extra expenses. His sister sent him 300 yuan from his own money. This was still a significant sum of money, and when it became known, a colleague accused him of using capitalist profits and thus allowing bourgeois consciousness to creep into the party. It was a serious threat to his budding career, a predicament only resolved by extensive and sincere self-criticism for bourgeois failings and the donation of the money to the party.[26]

As time went on and families grew, it became more common for the brothers to visit each other, often with their wives and children. When no political campaigns were going on, ordinary communication about family matters was easy enough; but since Fang Shi at the news agency was a party member, and Duyi held an important post in the Justice Ministry, there were many sensitive matters about which they could not speak. So family gatherings involved delicate avoidance of certain (especially political) topics, though these might actually be the areas of greatest concern.

If sibling interactions were sometimes complicated, gender relations and their impact on conjugal life in the new China were even more complex. The party's rhetoric supported the liberation of women from the shackles of patriarchy and promoted the notion that women "held up half the sky." The party itself, however, was a male-dominated institution. With most of its members recruited from the socially conservative countryside, any feminist agenda of gender equality was inevitably subordinated to the cause of building socialism.[27] As a result, gender relations in the early People's Republic were a contested terrain in which no one was quite sure of the rules, and the potential for conflict and domestic discord was substantial.

In the Ye family, most of the wives had some education, many had served in the revolution, and they hoped for and expected to play a role in the new China. Male domination of the institutions of power and employment often frustrated them, and when their husbands (fearful of criticism for nepotism or corruption) were unwilling or unable to assist their search for a suitable job, some marital tension was inevitable.[28] In most cases, these difficulties were overcome with time. Fang Shi's wife, for example, had joined the party even before he did and served in the guerrilla bases. Then her first pregnancy and childbirth, alone in that cold cave in the winter of 1940–41, left her crippled for life. By 1949 she had recovered enough to walk with a limp, but she was offered no job and felt held back by her husband's position. So she left Beijing for Shenyang, where a friend gave her a job in a rubber factory. This move toward independence forced a resolution of her problem: several months later Fang Shi went to Shenyang and brought her back to an editorial job in the New China News Agency where he worked. Domestic harmony was restored and lasted for the rest of her life.[29]

When Ye Duzhuang's first child was born, his wife wanted to stay home with the baby. But she soon grew restless, especially when Duzhuang was away in the evenings for political meetings. The problem was made worse when a young lady started pursuing him, writing love letters that Sun Song found in his desk. He professed innocence of any dalliance with the woman and vowed to have nothing more to do with her, but things only settled down when Duzhuang found his wife work doing illustrations for the journals he edited. She was grossly underpaid, and when in the course of criticizing Duzhuang for alleged corruption colleagues targeted her as the "boss's wife," she was furious. Fortunately, a job at the film studio soon became available, and she was able to achieve a professional recognition consistent with her extensive art training in Japan.[30] Duzheng's wife, with graduate training in the United States, quickly found work in the Academy of Science's Biology Institute, and their happy marriage was never affected by problems over jobs.

The wives of these three brothers all made the transition to a new order in which women of professional families would have jobs—though none as prominent as their husband's. While the women were responsible for most domestic duties, they were helped by nannies who did much of the child care, cooking, and cleaning. All-day schools for the children helped, and with schools and small shops located within the compounds where the family lived, parents could rest assured of the children's safety while they were at work. In addition, husbands were certainly more involved in child rearing than had been the case in previous generations.

In the early years of the People's Republic, Duyi in the Justice Ministry and Ye Fang in the northeast party school were politically the most successful of the Ye brothers, and in part for that reason, their marriages ended up being the most troubled. Ye Fang's wife was a pretty, young, outgoing actress when he met her with the New Fourth Army. They were married on the road to the northeast, and she immediately started having children at a remarkable rate. Though she longed to resume a performing career, her children's security was her first priority. In the fall of 1950, soon after the Korean War broke out, she fled to Harbin to give birth to her fourth child. Ye Fang's wife always insisted that the party had authorized this move, but the Organization Department denied any such approval and accused her of harming morale by fleeing to the north when Shenyang was threatened by American bombing across the Manchurian frontier. In 1951, she was expelled from the party. She bore the scars of this perceived injustice for the rest of her life—complaining to any who would listen (and many who would not) that she was a loyal and dedicated Communist hounded out of the party for no good reason.

Eventually she accepted any work she could get, at a nursery school or later as a file clerk. But she appealed her verdict endlessly, seemed incapable of accepting any form of party discipline, and blamed her husband for failing to clear her record. As a result, her obvious gifts as a social person with a talent for performing never found an outlet. Frustrated outside the home, she asserted her authority as boss of the domestic sphere. Her husband responded by maintaining a deep silence to her endless complaints. Despite the tensions between them, the two managed to keep having children, and their large family was the favorite of the kids' grandmother, who liked to visit from Tianjin and enjoy the noise and activity of a large family. The domestic quarrels of husband and wife did not bother her, and the old lady shared the party's idea that big families were a good thing.[31]

Ye Duyi's marriage was perhaps the unhappiest of all, though the dynamic was quite different from Ye Fang's. His wife came from a very wealthy family, and during the war, her dowry had supported her husband and children. Duyi was in Shanghai on Democratic League business when the time came for the oldest children to start school. His wife wrote to ask if they should begin their studies, and with no money of his own, he replied saying, "This is like asking a beggar if he wants

to eat . . . If you can help them go to school, I will be forever grateful."
She put them in the local primary school—and kept the letter to remind
him of his debt. After 1949, Duyi thought that his wife, like other
women in her position, should get a job. Despite a lack of formal education, her classical Chinese was excellent, and he thought she would
make a fine teacher. She adamantly refused. She had supported the
family during the war; now it was his turn to support her.

As a result, she stayed home as a housewife. But Duyi's position required frequent evenings out, and in the early 1950s, these events often
included dancing. Duyi felt he had to go; but his wife had grown up in
a conservative official family, lacked formal schooling, and felt quite
unprepared for such modern customs. She refused to go. However,
fearful that he would be dancing with other women, she sent her eldest
daughter in her place, to watch her husband's behavior and report back.
If she heard anything the least bit suspicious, she would hound him all
night so that he could not sleep. Always troubled by insomnia, this became unbearable, and eventually Duyi moved out to live in the Democratic League compound, eating in the cafeteria. His wife became increasingly despondent, three times swallowing pills in attempts to take
her own life. Much later she would be committed to a mental institution, where she was so heavily medicated that on her release she was a
completely different person: quiet and often depressed, while she had
been active and sociable before, and extremely frugal with money,
though she was once an avid shopper. At that heavy price, a measure of
domestic peace was achieved.

Compared to what would come later, the early years of the People's
Republic were relatively calm on the political front. But there were still
a number of political movements that had a substantial impact. For
Duyi, as a leading member of the Democratic League, the experiences
became part of his political education. In early 1950, he led a team to inspect natural disaster conditions in northern Jiangsu and later spent
eight months in Guangdong, observing land reform.[32] It was Duyi's first
experience in the countryside, and in this area of extensive landlordism,
he saw for the first time the poverty and suffering of the peasantry. He
was also impressed by the violence and cruelty of villagers mobilized to
overcome their oppression. Landlords were driven to suicide, and on
one occasion he watched painfully as a young activist viciously beat his
own landlord father. Duyi knew that such violence was a violation of

party policy and that his team was expected to report its assessment of the land reform experience. He also understood that any objection to this violent treatment would invite accusations of protecting the exploiting landlord class—so he said nothing. As he watched the party orchestrate the land reform process, he learned just how tough and brutal the Communists could be.[33]

Back in Beijing, he experienced another side of the party: its skill at manipulating the democratic party leaders. His first taste came in late 1949, just after the founding of the People's Republic. A Democratic League congress devoted much of its energy to criticizing the "pro-American" views of some of its leaders. Ye Duyi felt targeted by the attacks and withdrew. Several days later, as Zhou Enlai was about to leave for the Soviet Union to negotiate a Treaty of Friendship and Mutual Assistance, Duyi and other Western-educated Democratic League leaders were summoned to meet with him. The party was fearful that such men might oppose the alliance with the Soviet Union. Meeting through the night, Zhou told them that he would feel uneasy going abroad if he could not close ranks with the league. Such a personal appeal by the revered Zhou Enlai was extremely effective. Duyi made his first public self-criticism, for having walked out of the congress, and when Zhou complimented his speech, he was much encouraged.[34]

Western-educated intellectuals were under great pressure to demonstrate that their sympathies were on the right side in the cold war. Duyi watched as one after the other league leaders failed this test. For one it was a matter of criticizing the behavior of Russian troops in the northeast after the war. (See Chapter 7 by Christian A. Hess.) Another thought of urging Mao to abandon the policy of "lean to one side" (i.e., the Soviet side), but the outbreak of the Korean War made this notion unthinkable. Duyi saw those who held such views slowly fall from grace in the party's eyes, and he was careful to hew closely to the party line. When the Democratic League issued a declaration supporting China's entry into the Korean War, condemning "ninety years of American imperialist ambition to invade China" and comparing the U.S. advance in Korea to the Japanese aggression in World War II, Duyi's name was prominently listed in the *People's Daily* announcement.[35]

Journalist Fang Shi's job at the New China News Agency was to articulate this party line and to produce the reports to support it. An interesting episode came in 1952, when he was called upon to travel to

Korea to document charges that the United States was carrying out
bacterial warfare against China's troops by dropping rats carrying fleas
infected with bubonic plague. The scholarly consensus now holds that
these charges were false, but the American postwar harboring of the
Japanese Unit 731, which had carried out bacterial warfare experiments on Chinese prisoners during World War II, led many to give the
charges credence.[36] The New China News Agency produced many reports on this alleged American perfidy, with articles on strange insects
discovered by peasants and scientists' testimony on bacterial agents
identified in their labs. In 1952, Fang Shi was the Chinese head of a
joint Chinese-Korean delegation sent to interview two American prisoner-of-war (POW) airmen who had confessed to dropping germ-
warfare bombs. He led a group of experts and journalists to the northeast by train, then by truck at night across the Korean border until they
reached the POW camp. In six days of interviews, they found the
airmen friendly and cooperative. While Fang Shi recalls no clear confession from the two, the published account says they admitted to
having dropped special bombs at low altitude that were allegedly bacterial warfare weapons and were officially reported as "duds." The men
may have been aware of an inherent weakness of their testimony: Chinese accusations of germ warfare attacks quite uniformly date them
from January 28, 1952, but the two airmen were shot down on January
13. Despite such problems, Fang Shi's team produced a long article and
newsreel footage on the interviews. They never visited the crash site or
examined any of the physical evidence (though other Chinese scientists
had), but the will to believe was strong enough that their reports were
added to the evidence of U.S. crimes in Korea.[37]

By 1955, Fang Shi had acquitted himself so well that he was due a
promotion. As part of the preparations, he was sent for a year of study
at the Central Party School. There he was given systematic training in
Marxist philosophy, political economy, social development (which
meant the inescapable historical transition from feudalism to capitalism to socialism), and contemporary domestic and international affairs. When his training was over, he was returned to the New China
headquarters in Beijing as deputy head of the domestic bureau. This
was also the time at which the supply system was replaced by salary
grades in the bureaucracy, and he was assigned to grade 11 out of 24.
Since the top grades were reserved for the highest party leaders, and

even a minister was only grade 8, this was a very high rank and earned him the generous monthly salary of 195 yuan.[38]

The Ye brother who had the greatest difficulty conforming to the political demands of the new China was the agronomist Duzhuang, the fifth of the Ye brothers. His experience is a telling case study in how the successive political movements could end up trapping a person in their fearsome logic. The process of political transformation began innocently enough (or so it seemed at the time) with a "loyal and sincere study movement" in 1950–51. Small groups of colleagues gathered to review each person's background, help each other overcome his prior class background, and prepare to contribute to the new society. Duzhuang told his entire life history from the family school in Tianjin through Nankai, his study in Japan, service with the Eighth Route Army during the war, and then with the Nationalists and Americans, and his American friends in Beijing after the war. Naturally there were questions about his American connections, but the Americans were allies when he worked with them during the war, and his postwar American friends were all liberals and leftists generally sympathetic to the revolution. There was no doubt in Duzhuang's mind that everything he did in the 1940s was on behalf of the struggle to defeat Japan and then the Nationalists and to build a strong, progressive, and democratic China. But his dossier indicates intense questioning, especially on his American connections, and a verdict that he was not sufficiently humble *(xuxin)* and demonstrated a superior attitude, thinking he was above politics *(qinggao sixiang)*. He himself confessed to the sins of "individualism and liberalism."[39]

The first major political campaign of the early years of the People's Republic was the patriotic Resist America Aid Korea Campaign following China's entry into the Korean War in October 1950.[40] Duzhuang had no hesitation in signing the Democratic League declaration condemning American imperialism in Korea and its threat to China.[41] Whatever friendships he had with progressive American journalists did not weaken his instinct to defend China against any aggressive threat. The Three-Anti Campaign of 1952 was the first movement that really affected work at the academy, with its attack on corruption, waste, and bureaucratism. The Ministry of Agriculture sent a representative to oversee the movement at the institute, and he encouraged people to criticize the director. When he got little response, he called on Duzhuang, who was known for his forthright views. The young agronomist noted problems with the director's temper and authoritarian style but praised him as uncorrupt and knowledgeable of agriculture. The ministry representative was unhappy with this mild criticism (Duzhuang thinks because he coveted the director's job), so he turned to other targets and induced one of Duzhuang's own subordinates in the editorial department to criticize his boss for bureaucratism. In a fit of pique, Duzhuang countered, "You can find all the little bureaucratic flaws in me that you want, but you won't find a hint of corruption!" The ministry representative took this as a challenge, replying, "Fine! Then we'll check your corruption problems." They first found problems with the financial manager of Duzhuang's editorial office, and then, starting with a gift of the selected works of Michurin to a colleague, they uncovered a series of minor transgressions on his part, including one questionable business dinner and a long-distance phone call to Shanghai in which, at the end of a discussion of some editorial matter, he asked his colleague to send milk powder for the children. That made the phone call a private matter, and together with the dinner, the total of cases judged "close to corruption" came to 45.65 yuan. The fact that he had never pocketed any public funds proved an inadequate defense. He had not clearly separated public and private affairs, a sure sign of bourgeois thinking. He made matters worse when, under criticism, he withdrew from the study sessions and sought solace reading the eighteenth-century novel of official hypocrisy and misgovernment, *Rulin waishi* (The Scholars). In the end he was forced to make two self-criticisms before meetings of the institute's employees, swallowing his "stinky pride" and coming to "recognize more concretely the great power of the party and the masses."[42]

After the campaign, Duzhuang returned to work in the editorial department, but this attack on his probity clearly hurt his pride, and his enthusiasm for editorial work was never the same. Instead, he put his energy into a project of his own: translating the works of Charles Darwin. He worked late into the night on his translation, but this left him too tired to exert himself as before at his regular job. He knew that he was not putting his best effort into editing the journals—but his translations earned him several thousand yuan in royalties. This was important insurance in case things should get even worse at work.

In 1955, the "Campaign to Root Out Hidden Counterrevolutionaries" *(Sufan)* began to penetrate intellectual circles. In the agricultural academy and other education and cultural institutions, the campaign developed out of an attack on the writer Hu Feng who had made an appeal for greater intellectual autonomy. Hu's appeal was treated as a counterrevolutionary challenge to party authority, and soon a witchhunt spread through the ranks of intellectuals, looking for hidden counterrevolutionaries. Duzhuang and his colleagues were again gathered in small groups to study prepared materials on the "Hu Feng counterrevolutionary elements" and then to review their own political histories and respond to questions. At first, Duzhuang was not threatened: his name was listed in a *People's Daily* article on Democratic League members gathering to attack Hu Feng.[43] But Duzhuang's own relations with the U.S. Army during the war and with American journalists in the postwar era were known to the party from the "loyal and sincere study" campaign, and they immediately became the focus of intense questioning: had not Graham Peck worked for the U.S. Office of War Information (OWI)? Was not OWI an American intelligence agency? Had he not provided information to Peck? Had he not taken the journalist James Burke to gather information in the guerrilla areas? Was this not helping the Americans to spy on the party?

The questioning went on for an entire month. Nothing that Duzhuang could say would erase the suspicion that he had somehow been working for the Americans, that there was more to the story than he was admitting, and that he was hiding something and dissimulating. Finally, in exasperation, he burst out, "[T]here is nothing more to say!" and got up to leave. "This is resisting!" charged his interlocutors, and that was a serious matter. The official policy in all these campaigns promised "lenience for those who confess fully, unmerciful treatment for those who resist" *(tanbai congkuan, kangju congyan).* It was a mantra repeated in every political movement in China, and it served the purpose of inducing millions of people to confess fully—often to crimes they had never committed—in hopes (usually vain) of gaining a lenient sentence.

Duzhuang, however, would not confess. Finally, the committee handling his "historical problem" proposed a verdict of "no punishment." Duzhuang would not accept it. To him, this meant that there was a punishable problem, and he demanded that they specify what it was. When they could not, the verdict was changed to "an ordinary historical problem" *(yiban xing lishi wenti)*, referring to his service in the American AGAS (Air Ground Aid Service). Again, he refused to accept the verdict: he had contacted friends in the party before agreeing to work with the Americans, and they had approved. The United States was then an ally in the war against Japan. He suggested that they call it "an ordinary *revolutionary* history problem," but the party could not accept that.

In the end, no clear decision was reached. His "historical problem" remained unresolved. Duzhuang felt that at least his honor was intact. He had not agreed to any "counterrevolutionary" crime. But his wife found his behavior stubborn and unreasonable and feared that in the end the children would suffer: "Why do you always want to wear a red dress [of a new bride, i.e., a pure one]? In the end, you're the one to lose. The kids are still small. Just sign it! End the matter and satisfy them!" But he would not, and in the end the consequences of this obduracy was as others had warned: it left him with a "pigtail" that the party could grab the next time a political campaign came along. His family life had been unusually happy in the first years of the People's Republic, but in the Anti-Rightist Movement of 1957–58, politics would intervene to change everything.[44]

For the brothers of the Ye family, the early years of the People's Republic were most remarkable as a long-delayed period of normalcy, after years of war and revolution. Now in their thirties, they finally got a chance to have children and raise families. With nannies to help care for the children, and salaries adequate for a comfortable if modest lifestyle, these were good years for most, filled with happy memories. They were also years in which the nuclear family was firmly established as the dominant form in urban families, though conflicting norms on proper gender roles left some marriages deeply strained. Child-rearing practices varied from family to family, with party members living in exclusive compounds much more likely to entrust their young to the collective institutions of the state. Only gradually did politics enter the picture, as a slowly encroaching shadow that would darken the years to come.

⤳ *14*

Birthing Stories:
Rural Midwives in 1950s China

Gail Hershatter

IN 1996, WORKING with Chinese researcher Gao Xiaoxian, I set out to explore a curious historical wasteland—the first decade of rural socialist construction in the 1950s.[1] Studies of twentieth-century Chinese history usually talk about the 1950s as a series of campaigns and their aftermath. Yet we know little about the 1950s outside the center of political power, much less history at the margins—the relationship between state pronouncements and what people inside and outside state organizations understood to be happening then, or what they remember now, when they recall the early years of socialism half a century later. And one of the main sources with the potential to answer these questions—the individual and collective memories of China's farmers—is growing less accessible every year, as people age and die.

Among these rapidly disappearing rural memories, those of women have concerned us most. If farmers were about 80 percent of the total Chinese population in the 1950s, then women farmers were probably close to 40 percent.[2] In spite of their numbers, they were doubly marginalized, by virtue both of location and of gender. Written records tell us little about the responses of these women to state initiatives, the degree to which their daily lives were affected by 1950s policies, the levels—economic, social, psychological—at which change occurred. In order to understand something about rural women, we need to move beyond policy pronouncements. We usually think about China's twentieth century as divided almost perfectly in half by the 1949 revolution, or "liberation." But what happens to our notion of turning points in twentieth-century Chinese social and economic life when gender is placed at the center? Historian Joan Kelly once asked in a famous piece, "Did women have a Renaissance?" If she had been writing about China instead of Europe, she might have said, did women have a Chinese revolution? And if so, when? Exploring these questions, Gao Xiaoxian and I have collected life histories of approximately seventy women over the age of sixty, mainly in four villages in central and south Shaanxi province.[3]

This chapter reports on changes in childbirth practices in the very early years of the People's Republic. An exploration of this process offers insight about the intermingling of preliberation practices with postliberation state initiatives and the effects of both on the lives and attitudes of rural women. Documentary and archival sources are a crucial foundation for understanding change in the 1950s. But memories of individual childbirth practices, family relations, and the role of midwifery and other state initiatives in changing both are only accessible through the collection of oral narratives.

Midwives and the State

In June 1950, young Women's Federation workers visited the village of West Weiqu, in Chang'an county, just south of Xi'an.[4] Accompanied by two new-style midwives, they had come to survey health work among village women and children—a striking priority so early in the period of rural Communist Party state-building, before land reform had even begun in neighboring areas.[5]

Their initial experiences were not auspicious. Villagers were busy with the wheat harvest and a dam-building project. Most women were out in the fields and unavailable for meetings.[6] Because the surveyors were asking about children and who had delivered them, some villagers feared that the team intended to seize the children or to punish the midwives. The team had to move their work from West to East Weiqu, where one of their members had personal connections. Working through her social network, they located the six old-style midwives in the village and interviewed them one by one.[7]

Initially suspicious and frightened that the government would outlaw their work, these women gradually warmed up when the visitors explained that they were there to learn from them about midwifery. They described a fully elaborated set of techniques for assisting at difficult births, as well as a pharmacopia for the prevention and treatment of tetanus neonatorum *(siliufeng)*. Some of these methods—crude episiotomies, instructions on how to dismember a fetus if birthing it would kill the mother—were graphic reminders of the dangers of childbirth and the limitations of village facilities. Others—the ubiquity of tetanus neonatorum, which accounted for almost half of all infant deaths— were clearly a consequence of unsterile procedures. The total infant mortality rate was 38 percent (195 deaths),[8] apparently comparable to villages in other areas of China.[9]

All but eight of the village's 522 children had been birthed using these "old-style" methods.[10] Of the three women who had been delivered "new-style," one was the sister of a new-style midwife,[11] and the others, whose mothers-in-law were "very old" and therefore presumably unable to take charge, had learned about new-style birth from the local woman's representative.[12] These eight children were all alive and healthy, the report noted, and so villagers admired the new method. But they were also suspicious of it.

This report from the first months of party control in central Shaanxi anticipates many of the themes of women's health work throughout the collective period. Women's health was a state priority, safe childbirth was a key component of women's health, and good midwifery practices were central to making it possible.[13] Midwifery reform was one of the first issues through which rural Chinese encountered their new government.

Writing on this subject has portrayed a straightforward process wherein the state tried to bring scientific knowledge and practice to the countryside. Joshua Goldstein has described the campaign to train new-style midwives as an attempt by the party-state to "dislodge women's reproductive practices from local networks and institutions in order to restructure them within a new state system."[14] Opposing feudalism to science, he writes, "prenatal health care workers were mobilized to dismantle" previously existing practices.[15] And indeed, many of the 1950s articles he cites from the national publication *Xin Zhongguo funü* refer to

rural midwifery as "feudal, superstitious, backward," and old-style midwives as "feudal-minded, conceited and not interested in studying."[16]

In a slightly more positive assessment of the midwives, Delia Davin
suggests that the state was to supply the science, while the midwives
contributed elbow grease: "Many of the 'students' were village midwives who, though they had infected countless women with their un-
washed hands and long fingernails, had years of practical experience,
which when combined with a little theoretical knowledge, turned them
into useful medical workers."[17] There was no question which term was
dominant, however; ignorant midwives had to be retrained in scientific
methods, or they would pose a menace to women's health.

Both of these arguments have merit. The state did castigate the old-
style practitioners, and it did then retrain and use them. And yet
change in childbirth practices was not just a matter of a onetime encounter between the Communist state and feudal ignorance; rather, it
was a more extended and less clear-cut interaction, not fully captured
by campaign language and temporality. The state was continuing the
language and policies begun by its Nationalist predecessor, but was
committed to a far more extensive presence in rural areas. In encounters between state officials and midwives, the contrast with the confrontational tactics of land reform (and sometimes marriage reform) is
striking. Old-style midwives were not caricatured, attacked, or dis-
carded. Their techniques were investigated and reported in full. The
women themselves were offered additional training, incorporated
rather than denounced, and regarded as an important resource. Well
beyond the 1950s, most rural Shaanxi women gave birth at home,
many attended by old-style midwives who had undergone minimal retraining. Some midwives active before liberation even participated in
training the new, postliberation generation of midwives.

One can read this continuity in the practices and personnel of childbirth optimistically, arguing that it showed flexibility and pragmatism
on the part of various levels of the state, a willingness not to demonize
skilled old-style midwives, but rather to build on their skills while improving the quality of health care they delivered. A less optimistic conclusion might be that the state did not prioritize thoroughgoing attention to women's reproductive health, putting far more resources into
mobilizing women's labor (laodong) than into changing the conditions
of their labor and childbirth (shengchan). Gao Xiaoxian observes that in

Shaanxi, new-style childbirth did not become common until the 1970s, well after the 1950s push for collectivization and women's fieldwork. The revolution in reproduction proceeded on a much slower timeline than the revolution in production.[18] Amid the official denunciations of superstitious childbirth practices and feudal family relations, at the time when young women were being called forth into the fields, did their physical and social experience of childbirth undergo a parallel change? And if not, what are the implications for our understanding of revolution's scope?

Two States, One Policy

When it promoted the scientific modernization of childbirth practices, the party-state was continuing an effort begun by the Nationalists during the Nanjing decade. The Ministry of Health, founded by the new Nationalist government in 1928, immediately issued regulations that required midwives to undergo a two-year training course or its equivalent in order to be registered with the government. Old-style midwives were supposed to undergo two months of training and register as well.[19] The Ministry of Health established a National Midwifery Board that reorganized or opened midwifery schools in Beiping and Nanjing to train new midwives and retrain old ones. Several provinces, including Shaanxi, established their own midwifery schools. In 1935 the Commission on Medical Education, which included representatives from the government, proposed an expanded program for the training of village midwives.[20] Government regulations on midwifery, like many other initiatives undertaken by the Nationalists, had limited effect, especially in the countryside.[21]

In Republican China, the division between new- and old-style midwives was a profound one. The former tended to be from middle- or upper-class families and to work in urban areas, while the latter, who far outnumbered them, were primarily rural.[22] Charlotte Furth notes that "the twentieth-century public health reformer Marion Yang estimated in 1930 that there were 200,000 old-style midwives needing retraining."[23] Nationalist policy recognized that old-style midwives would necessarily continue to be important for many years to come, but their practices were sharply criticized by public health specialists. One wrote of the disastrous consequences of using cow dung to dress the umbilical cord in Fujian; another "lamented that because of their lack of education many older midwives failed to grasp the basic concepts of modern medicine, reverting to traditional methods soon after graduating from the course."[24] Marion Yang illustrated a 1928 article about midwifery training with a photo of a woman sitting in a basket, with the male basket carrier standing next to her. The caption was chilling: "Old type Chinese midwife (sitting in basket). Can only walk about on hands and knees. Has been seen to get up from this posture, wipe her hands on her clothes and put her fingers into the vagina without any further cleansing."[25] Old-style midwives were the oft-maligned other against which modern medical practice was defined; they were, however, the only resource available in most rural areas. And as Li Tingan noted in a 1935 study of rural health care, most villagers had little faith in new-style midwifery.[26]

The Communist Party continued both the criticism and retraining of old-style midwives, and the attempt to train new-style midwives.[27] The main difference between the Nationalists and the Communist Party on midwives was not ideological but practical: the Communist Party had a far more extensive and effective rural presence, and the scope of its efforts to reform rural midwifery accordingly affected many more people.

In May 1950, three Shaanxi work teams were dispatched to investigate rural maternal and child health by a coalition of state agencies. These teams were among the first contacts that rural people had with the new government, and the centerpiece of their work, and of similar campaigns that followed, was the reform of old-style midwives.[28] The work team members found that women usually died in childbirth from excessive bleeding or puerperal fever (chanrure), while 50 percent of newborns died from tetanus.[29] Two Shaanxi folk sayings summed up this situation: "We only see the bride, not the new mother" and "We only see the mother hold her child, but not the child walking."[30]

In the course of their three-week investigative trip, the work team reported, they had taught ten old-style midwives to wash their hands in boiled water, sterilize their scissors, and keep the scissors in a steamer during childbirth so that they would stay clean until the cord was cut. "One experience of this group is that the attitude toward old-style midwives should be unifying, educating, and gradually reforming them; one cannot mock, make fun of, or attack them."[31]

In August 1950, the Ministry of Health hosted a national conference of maternity and child health workers, beginning a campaign to eliminate puerperal fever and tetanus neonatorum.[32] In the decade that followed, rural China saw a substantial decrease in infant mortality, from a high of around three hundred per thousand; it may have been cut in half.[33] Elisabeth Croll observes that "[a] familiar slogan reflected the attention directed towards infant and child health: 'one pregnancy, one live birth; one live birth, one healthy child.' "[34] The chief cause of improvement in infant survival was the retraining of old-style midwives in a project coordinated by the Ministry of Health and the Women's Federation.[35] In 1959, looking back over a decade of health work, one author noted that the number of midwives had increased from 15,700 to 35,290, while the number of "assistant midwives" (apparently retrained midwives or those trained in a short course) had gone from 44,000 to 774,983.[36]

Old-Style Midwifery: Difficulties and Dangers

The old-style midwives who were interviewed by government agencies in 1950 provided a catalog of complicated births and draconian methods of dealing with them. In "well-circle labor" (*jingquan sheng*), when the birth canal was too narrow for the baby to descend, a midwife might push down on the woman's belly to push the baby out, use her legs to support the woman's back and pull her backward, or (more ominously) "chop the well rope with an axe or use an axe to hit the mouth of the well three times." If the child still did not emerge, the midwife would ask the older generation in the family which one they wanted to live, the mother or the child. If they wanted the mother to survive, she would then fashion a hook from a nail or use a firewood-trimming knife to pull the baby out or sometimes dismember it in utero with a knife or sickle.[37] In horizontal labor (*e'lao sheng*), if a hand or foot presented first and the midwife could not put it back in, she might prick it with a needle, cut it off with a knife, or sprinkle salt on it. (Villagers, the investigators reported, believed that if a pregnant woman went outside the door with salt in her hand, when she began to deliver the baby would reach out its hand to ask for salt.)[38] In "watermelon labor" (*xigua sheng*), the baby emerged still encased in the amniotic sac, and a midwife who did not know enough to break the sac might bury the baby alive.[39] In slow labor (*man sheng*), which might go on for several days, the midwife might forcibly separate the two parts of the pubic bone by breaking the symphysis pubis *(gufeng)*; then two assistants might try to pull the woman's legs as wide as possible while the midwife put some oil on her hand and tried to extract the baby. (Breaking the symphysis pubis was a procedure that would leave the mother permanently disabled.) If the buttocks presented first *(lianhua sheng)*, she would force the baby back in and try to pull out the legs instead. If the head began to protrude before the water broke *(dingbao sheng)*, she would break the water manually, then push the baby downward with her hands until it descended completely.[40] In the case of a retained placenta, old-style midwives tried to deliver it manually and then stanch the bleeding by having the woman drink a decoction of yellow wormwood water, ink, and children's urine to cool down her blood.[41]

If a woman gave birth in summertime, the old-style midwife might cut the cord with fire, in the belief that a baby's belly in summer was cold and that using fire would prevent future belly pain. In winter the belly was thought to be hot, so the cord was cut with scissors about eight inches away from the belly. The midwife then squeezed out the blood and flesh in the cord, tied it in a knot, passed it through a piece of oilpaper, covered it with a layer of cotton, and wrapped it in a cloth.[42]

In official literature, much criticism of old-style midwifery centered on unsanitary means of cutting the umbilical cord, which were said to lead to tetanus neonatorum in the baby and puerperal fever in the mother.[43] In the view of some old-style midwives, however, babies developed tetanus neonatorum if their mothers had become frightened or angry when pregnant, particularly if their anger was not expressed.[44] The disease would come on a few days after birth (hence the name) with crying, vomiting *(yongkou)*, and convulsions. It could be prevented by applying some "mouth-opening graupel" *(kaikouxian)* to the baby's mouth at birth; by burning incense on either side of the baby's mouth and cheeks; by treating the umbilicus with cure-all tablets *(wanyingding)* and pills to alleviate internal heat *(qingxinwan)*, or by having the baby take them by mouth; or by feeding the baby rat's testes dried in red orpiment powder.[45] In Liquan, a 1950 health survey reported, midwives would use a pottery shard to scratch the skin on the chest of a one-day-old. Then they would burn mugwort leaves *(aiye)* on a coin and bring the coin close to the infant's eyes, ears, mouth, and nose, raising bean-sized blisters.[46] If the baby developed tetanus neonatorum anyway, there were two accepted cures: to catch a live pigeon, tear the skin from its chest, and apply its still-warm skin to the umbilicus; or to feed the baby a dried rat fetus.[47] In spite of these methods, 84 of 522 babies in Weiqu village had died of tetanus neonatorum—43 percent of all infant deaths reported.[48]

As for postpartum mothers, bleeding and puerperal fever were common complications. More generally, government reports attributed women's postpartum health problems to poor care. In some areas, women were forbidden to sleep for a day and a night, or longer. Most were given only porridge for the first few days after birth, followed by noodles or dried pieces of steamed bread. In mountainous areas, nothing except corn was available, leading to weakness in women and their babies.[49]

In spite of these graphic descriptions of difficult and dangerous births, unsterile procedures, and poverty, early government reports were also forthright about the skills of many old-style midwives. A report on a Huayin county village mentioned midwife Hao née Chen, who at age seventy had been delivering children for more than forty years and was known throughout several counties for her skill with difficult births. Investigators noted that Hao had one of the dreaded S-shaped hooks, more than one *chi* (one-third of a meter) long, but that no one had ever seen her resort to using it. Rather, she used the method of rotating the baby *(huizhuan fa)* or cranium puncture *(toulu chuanci fa)*. "The only shortcoming," the report concluded, "is that she does not know about sterilization *(xiao du)*, and so women and infants are often at risk of illness."[50]

Village women interviewed about the 1950s in the 1990s corroborate this picture: the most skilled midwives often had been trained by their own mothers long before 1949, and received some supplemental training afterward. In Weinan county's Wang Family Village, a woman named Dang delivered babies both before and after liberation.[51] She had learned midwifery from *her* mother and much later took a training class in the township in the 1950s, learning to sing a midwife's song that summed up the basic procedures of new-style birth. ZQE, her daughter-in-law, recalls that when a family came to ask for Dang's services,

ZQE: Sometimes she would go in a big snowstorm or a rainstorm.
    She would use a walking stick, throw something on, and go.
GXX: Did your mother join in any training after liberation?

ZQE: Yes, she studied. The commune organized a training study
   class. She learned the midwife's song.
GXX: Did your mother ever encounter difficult births?
ZQE: Yes. There were posterior births. Even then my mother
   delivered them all. My mother never lost anyone in delivering babies. Sometimes when a doctor was doing a delivery
   and the baby wouldn't come down, they would call my
   mother. My mother would bring it down.[52]

New-Style Midwifery

By 1951, the slogan guiding women's health work in the Northwest
Region was "promote new-style midwifery, reform old midwives, train
new midwives."[53] A key component of state work on women's health
was the introduction of the new-style midwife, a freshly recruited and
trained agent of a new state, who was to symbolize and deliver the
benefits of modernity to rural women.

   In addition to emphasizing handwashing and sterilization, new-style
childbirth ideally entailed prenatal checkups, having the woman lie
down while in labor, and helping her to expel the umbilical cord and placenta without pulling or causing excessive blood loss. Each of these was
favorably compared to old-style practices.[54] One Shandong government
pamphlet outlined how old midwives should be retrained in courses of
about ten days. Topics included "Where children come from" (including
an introduction to the anatomy of female sexual organs); what to pay attention to during pregnancy; the advantages of new-style midwifery;
predelivery preparations; how to deliver a baby; what to do in the case of
difficulties; the postpartum month; and a final section on presentation of
children's diseases, vaccinations, how to propagandize new-style midwifery, and how to prepare work reports.[55] An appendix on "rules for
midwives" was divided into six things to do and six not to do: Do have
the woman deliver lying down, clip your fingernails and wash your
hands with soap or alcohol, boil the scissors, use mouth-to-mouth resus-
citation if the baby is not breathing, apply eyedrops, and vaccinate. Do
not have the woman sit on a *kang*, squat, stand, or sit to give birth; do
not use sorghum stalks or tile shards or teeth to cut the cord; do not
bathe the baby in a dirty basin; do not pull on the cord or placenta; if the
woman loses blood, do not let her move, have her lie down, and do not

put the hand into the vagina or tear the vaginal opening; and in the case of a difficult birth, do not act rashly *(luan dong shou)*.[56]

Although very few rural women appear to have had prenatal exams in the 1950s, the other procedures took hold wherever midwives were trained. ZXF had five children at home, two delivered by her mother-in-law during the very early years of collectivization and the rest by the brigade midwife. Her mother-in-law caught the baby, waited for the placenta, and only then cut the cord. The midwife's procedure was more elaborate: she examined the woman in labor, swabbed disinfectant on the pubic area, delivered the baby, cut the cord, wrapped the baby, and only then delivered the placenta.[57] As ZQL, trained as a midwife after 1949, recalls, with old-style delivery "people did not dare to pick up the baby and just put the baby on the ground. People did not dare to pick up the baby until the amniotic sac came down and the placenta came out. Now people pick up the baby first and then use forceps to take out the woman's placenta."[58] DFC, who gave birth to children both before and after 1949, remembers the main difference as one of position: in old-style childbirth, women "sat on the ground" (or perhaps squatted), while the new style required them to lie down.[59] She explains why the new style was better for the mother:

In the old society, midwives told people to sit on the ground. They were afraid that it would get the *kang* dirty. . . . Sitting down, people would get dizzy. They said that it was blood enchanting the heart *(xue mi xin)*. Watching the fresh blood flowing out, several basins' worth. That was the old society, sitting on the ground, watching the fresh blood and getting dizzy. . . . They didn't tell people to lie down. Ai, after all lying down is more comfortable. When I had that baby, she had me lie down, and after a while he was born. That way I didn't hurt from head to foot.[60]

Some women were reluctant to have any outsider present when they gave birth, even one who was trained in midwifery. One day ZQL, a young midwife-in-training, received an urgent message from her aunt. ZQL's cousin's wife, who had lost a baby the previous year, was in the middle of a difficult labor. ZQL ran to the house of her teacher, veteran midwife Liu Xihan, and the two women ran to the house of ZQL's cousin. Although her mother-in-law had summoned the midwives, ZQL's cousin was not happy to see them:

> ZQL: She said, "I'm suffering. You come to see me in labor. Do you think you are watching a game?" . . . We sat there for several hours but they didn't let us see the woman. I said, "You are wrong. You had us sitting here for several hours. Did the baby come out or not?" One of the baby's arms was hanging there.
>
> GXX: Aiyo, then what did you do?
>
> ZQL: Women were not allowed to lie on the *kang* in the old days. They sat on chairs. The midwife put her on the *kang* and put the arm back. Then it came out again. Again she put it back. The old woman said the baby would die. You know, I had been there for a long time but she didn't let us see her. . . .
>
> GXX: She didn't let you see her or her mother-in-law didn't let you see her?
>
> ZQL: The daughter-in-law didn't let us see her. I asked, "Did you see the head of the baby?" She said it was strange. After a while she said she was not sure whether it was the leg or arm that came out and it was already cold. I scolded her, . . . "If you were not my cousin's wife, I wouldn't have come here." The baby's arm came out and its head was inside. Finally we took it out. But it died after it came out. . . . We ran there. We sat there for several hours. She said, "What are you looking at? I am suffering." [Liu Xihan] said, "What are you talking about! I'm here for your own good. We are all women. What are we looking at? This is the new society. If it were the old society, I wouldn't have been here even if you invited me."[61]

Exposure to new-style midwifery did not mean that women would continue to use it or would disinfect scissors as new-style midwives did. LZL, for instance, who had five children between 1963 and 1973, delivered her first child in the Zhulinguan health station but her subsequent four (including one breech birth) at home with only her husband's assistance. Her encounter with new-style midwifery did not affect her own approach to disinfection, as she told us:

> GXX: When you gave birth, cutting the cord, did you know about it? What did you cut it with?

LZL: Scissors.

GXX: Did you disinfect the scissors?

LZL: Disinfect the scissors? Who gave a damn about that? You would just cut it and tie it.

GXX: You didn't wrap up the spot where the belly button was?

LZL: No . . . [62]

And even ZQL, who had been trained as a midwife before her marriage, saw her second child die of sepsis when he was born so quickly that the water had not yet boiled and her brother cut the cord with unsterilized scissors.[63]

Training and Collectivization

As collectivization went through its incremental stages in the Shaanxi countryside, midwifery stations *(jiesheng zhan)* were established in many townships *(xiang)*. As early as 1951, local health departments took primary responsibility for this work, with assistance from the Women's Federation.[64] In Danfeng county, for instance, a 1952 Women's Federation work report noted that during the previous year the health office had run two sets of training classes for eighty-five old-style midwives, and by the autumn of 1953, thirteen midwife stations were scattered around the county.[65] It appears that these stations were often a supervisory and training facility rather than a place where women gave birth. In Weibin township, Xianyang county, for instance, the forty midwives associated with three stations were actually scattered across twenty-seven villages.[66] Old-style midwives who had completed re-training were sent out to assist new-style midwives in deliveries, then organized into study groups that were supposed to meet once a week and stay in contact with health workers and Women's Federation cadres on a monthly basis.[67]

Official publications about women's health work reflected the environment of rural collectivization, in which women were being mobilized for fieldwork. In a 1954 Women's Federation pamphlet, for instance, new-style midwifery was necessary not only to relieve women's suffering but also to allow them to do even better at joining in the work of socialist production. The pamphlet introduced five models—some midwives, some midwifery stations—and each selection spoke of how the midwives overcame local suspicion and physical hardship, in a narrative formula honed to perfection by the production of labor model stories in other realms of endeavor. One midwife publicized new-style midwifery at the temple fair, ignoring the jeers of neighbors who said she was disgracing her ancestors by hauling around pictures of naked women. Unable to move around easily because of her bound feet, this same model midwife slid down into a shallow ravine and then clambered up to the other side to reach a woman in labor, braving a violent rainstorm to do so. When she received an award in January 1953 at the Northwest Region meeting for health work models, she explains that "I was so happy that I shed tears. If it were not for Chairman Mao and the Communist Party, how would I be where I am today? I will not forget this honor for the rest of my life."[68]

Here the specifics of childbirth recede into the greater theme of enthusiastic model women working for the collective good under the leadership of the party. Gone are the often disturbing details of the earlier government reports on midwifery practices. Nevertheless, several things are worth noting. First, all but one of the model midwives are older women who had considerable experience with old-style deliveries before liberation and only later received short-term training in new-style midwifery. When new and old midwives talk to each other in these stories, the language is one of mutual study and respect. Second, what is most important is not the ability of new-style midwives to deliver children safely—although that is also mentioned—but their willingness to ceaselessly communicate the advantages of new-style childbirth to their communities. This theme was elaborated in Women's Federation reports as early as 1951, when woman-work cadres cooperated with public health workers to explain new-style midwifery in literacy classes, posters, bamboo-clapper storytelling, street-corner plays, handbills, and wall newspapers. Visitors to public exhibits on women's health in county towns throughout central and south Shaanxi were said to number as many as several thousand.[69]

Collectivization altered the institutional supervision of childbirth. In Weibin, the township health office began propaganda about new-style midwifery in 1953, and the next year it broadened its educational effort to include menstrual hygiene and postpartum recovery. When collectivization began in 1955, the township midwifery stations made contact with the cooperatives, sending representatives down to the coops to inspect the work of local midwives and offer support for their work. Women whose fetuses showed transverse presentations were sent to the hospital. Within half a year, eight of eleven coops in the township were using new-style midwifery, which rose to account for 74 percent of all births. Midwives were paid in work-points, while postpartum women received fifty days' rest at half the average work-points they had earned in the three months before giving birth.[70]

When cooperatives were amalgamated into larger advanced producers' cooperatives, however, it became unclear who was supposed to run the midwifery stations. Contracts were no longer in force, and neither midwives nor postpartum women got paid for a year. In October 1956, the provincial Women's Federation Social Welfare Office delineated these problems in a report and promised to help straighten them out.[71] In 1957, county health officials spent time in each station, attempting to standardize work rules for the midwives, evaluate their performance, and determine who needed more training.[72]

By late 1956, Weinan county had applied the principles of central planning to midwifery, collecting statistics on the percentage of new-style births in each township and then setting higher target quotas for the coming year. By 1956, several townships were already reporting that 95 percent of all births were new style, though many others had not yet reached 50 percent.[73] County government documents in 1957 showed an awareness that in the final year of the First Five-Year Plan, work in women's and children's health needed to show achievements commensurate with those in production.[74] The practice of measuring the temporality of women's reproductive health by that of production campaigns continued into the Great Leap Forward, with its establishment of new birthing facilities *(chan yuan)*.

Beyond Campaign Time: Birthing Stories

The state focus on well-trained midwives should not be mistaken for a complete picture of rural childbirth.[75] Well into the 1950s, most rural Shaanxi babies continued to be delivered at home, sometimes by midwives but perhaps more frequently by mothers-in-law or with no assistance at all.

Mothers-in-law feature prominently in women's childbirth stories from before and after 1949, and their portrayal is not always positive.

Childbirth, in addition to its obvious potential for pain and danger, was a major turning point in the integration of young brides into the household of their in-laws. After marriage, many women in central and south Shaanxi made the transition to their marital homes gradually, returning to their natal homes often and sometimes staying for weeks. But it was taboo to give birth in the house of one's natal family. If a mother thought that her visiting daughter might go into labor, she would hurry to send her back to her mother-in-law's house.[76] Local belief held that "alive or dead, your own mother does not see it. . . . [I]f it was dead, she didn't see the pestilent energy. If it was alive she didn't see it either."[77] For both ritual and practical reasons, a first childbirth usually brought to an end the period of frequent visits to one's mother. It was also a moment, sometimes the first moment, when a mother-in-law was fully in charge of a young wife's well-being.

Many women recall the birth of their first child not only as painful and frightening but also as a moment that highlighted feelings of alienation from their mothers-in-law, their husbands, or both. FSF remembers: "When I gave birth to my second child, I had breakfast. It was raining. I felt the pain. But I did not say anything. My mother-in-law was hot-tempered. 'Are you really in labor?' I felt the contractions and wanted to go to the toilet. I was bleeding but I dared not say that. If you said something, she would say, 'How can you tell that to others. Aren't you ashamed? Having a child is just a natural phenomenon.' So I dared not say anything. I just walked here and there."[78] For FSF, who was selected for midwife training in 1954, these early experiences—a painful first labor, a postpartum infection, an unsympathetic mother-in-law, and a well-meaning but hapless husband—all contributed to her later determination to change the circumstances of childbirth for others:

> When I gave birth to my children, I sat on a small chair. . . . I myself knew how to deliver like that. Pull it out, go to the bed, take off the bamboo mat and sit on the grass. Put some ash on the grass and then put some rags on it. Just sit on that. I suffered too much. So I cannot sit for a long time even now. It was unbearable to use the ash at the end. What was worse, it festered for a month. . . . So when I did midwifery, they all said that I was careful. Because I myself experienced it. . . . I said I suffered a lot and would not let

you suffer that much. I could only walk by leaning against the wall for forty days. It was terrible for women who gave birth. So they all think I am a careful person. So I delivered babies for generations— three generations. I delivered most of the people here in T., except some who went to the hospitals.[79]

For QZF, her first two births in the late 1940s and just after liberation underscored her unhappiness with her husband and his family:

I was seventeen when I gave birth to my first baby. The day I went into labor, it was dark, and we were sleeping in the same bed. Nobody said anything. Before he went to cut wood, I got up to cook for him. . . . When I crouched by the pot, stirring, it was hurting so badly. At last I pushed myself to drain the rice quickly and started cooking it. When he got up to eat, I didn't say anything. He didn't know I was going into labor and I didn't say anything either.

Then he left. I was in labor. I was walking around and around the room and my stomach was hurting so badly. I was only seventeen! So I was turning around and around, walking around. When it was time to eat breakfast, I began to give birth.

My stomach was hurting unbelievably, but something was wrong and the baby wouldn't come down. The old woman [mother-in-law] was a vegetarian for religious reasons. On the first day and fifteenth day, she worshipped the spirits and ate vegetarian food. She wouldn't come to your room to see you, either. She wanted you to bind your feet. She had bound feet. She used a strip of cloth as wide as your palm, pretty long, to bind her feet. . . .

I sat on a short stool and pressed my rear end against it. . . . I couldn't sleep. What could I do? Heavens. It was unbearable when I sat down. At last, I walked in and out of the house. It hurt so badly . . . straight through to the afternoon. When I was a girl, I heard someone say that when you give birth to a baby, after you move around, you should sleep. Others said that you shouldn't sleep, that when you sleep, it would crawl onto your heart. I thought it over and said, whatever happens, dead or alive, I am going to sleep. I struggled to crawl onto my bed and stretched out to sleep. When I was lying on the bed, all at once I felt pressure two times. I pushed twice, and the baby came forward, rushed forward. *Dingding guangguang*, two pushes and the baby rolled down. After it came down, the old woman got some water in a wooden basin and put it down beside my bed. She gave me a pair of scissors. I cut the baby's umbilical cord myself and made a knot. I put a piece of old cotton on the top. I had prepared some pieces of cloth and bags ahead of time. After I washed the baby, I wrapped it in some cloth from a pair of pants. The placenta came out by itself. That's it. He had gone to cut firewood and had not come back yet. . . . Nowadays, between a husband and wife, if they feel something, they will talk about it. That's how the feeling between a husband and his wife should be. I didn't say anything and he didn't know, just like that. That's how it was when I gave birth to my first baby.

When I had my second baby, it was crop-watching season. We went under the kitchen stove and set up a bed, watching over the crops. . . . My stomach began to hurt again, so I crawled out of bed. People say, when carpenters bore a hole with a chisel, they beat out a rhythm. I also went to cut a bit of hair to put it there in advance. Finally, I got some fire to burn it and got the ashes and ground them up. I got up and boiled some water. I slept near the stove. I took some black sugar and poured the hot water in. I drank two mouthfuls. After I drank, my stomach began to hurt again. It was just like what happened before, when my water broke [the baby] moved back. I went to the bedroom, swept the floor, and stretched out on the floor. I lay there until the baby dropped, and only then got up. Think about it! It was just like that, I lay on the floor, and the baby dropped onto the floor. Then I pulled myself up to pick up the baby and wrap it up on the bed. That's how it was then. So considering the situation then, I had no choice. I thought it over, I was only twenty. At last, when the Marriage Law was announced, I simply proposed a divorce![80]

Government documents and the birthing stories of individual women cannot tell us how widespread this sort of family dynamic was and when it changed. When these same women describe the childbirth experiences of their own daughters-in-law, they speak of hospitals, high fees, and women who lead much softer work lives and thus sometimes have much harder first labors. The midwives among them talk, too, of recent complicated births that they have attended. In their villages, women no longer give birth alone, and brides often do not live in the same household with their mothers-in-law, much less under her authority. Still, in spite of QZF's narrative move—from lonely childbirth to Marriage Law to divorce in one quick phrase—it is difficult to imagine that these sorts of family relationships changed as quickly as midwifery practices. Childbirth was shaped not only by state campaigns but by the entire matrix of social relationships in which midwives and laboring women were enmeshed.[81] And as one final story suggests, these relationships extended beyond the visible connections of village society into the realm of the unseen spirit world.

Liu Xihan and the Ghosts of Childbirth's Danger

Liu Xihan was born in about 1906 in Xiguan village, in the southeastern corner of Shaanxi province. At the age of seven she began to help her mother with household tasks and midwifery. She married at fourteen and moved to Zhulinguan, where she worked at home as a weaver. Sometime before 1949 she began practice midwifery in Zhulinguan. After liberation she received additional training, and in February 1952 she became head of the Zhulinguan midwifery station run by the Women's Federation in one of thirteen stations being established around the county. Within three years she had eight people working under her direction. Of the forty-one children she had delivered by 1955, none developed tetanus neonatorum, nor did their mothers suffer from postpartum diseases.[82] Her reputation among villagers was high. DFC, a Zhulinguan villager, blames the 1953 death of her newborn son from sepsis on the fact that Liu Xihan was unable to attend the birth. Her next son, born the following year, was delivered by Liu and survived. Liu charged nothing for her services, although the town government paid for her instruments.[83]

Liu Xihan was a vocal advocate for new-style midwifery, even singing songs that explained its advantages.[84] She was a model citizen in other respects as well, persuading her husband and neighbors to sell surplus grain to the state in 1954. When a neighbor cursed her for promoting the unified purchase of grain ("Liu Xihan, you take my pot away. You take my quilt away. I'll hang myself in your doorway"), she continued her patient persuasion, reminding the old woman about food shortages in the old society. In every respect she seemed exemplary of the kind of new rural woman citizen cultivated by the party-state.[85]

And yet when village women remember Liu Xihan, who died in the late 1950s or early 1960s, their memories are more complex than the straightforward march toward safer childbirth (and unified grain purchase) featured in government publications and internal documents. Even as village women laud her skills of new-style midwifery, they also place Liu Xihan in a genealogy of midwives put at risk by powerful, dangerous forces present when a child was born. Childbirth, in their telling, was risky not only for the woman in labor but for those who attended her, and new-style midwifery did not remove the danger. The pollution of childbirth could affect the midwife or those who came in contact with her; one young midwife recalls that after she assisted Liu Xihan at a birth and brought some cucumbers home, no one would eat them, saying, "She is too dirty. Didn't you see what she went to do? . . . Later, everybody laughed at me and nobody ate the things I had touched. Then I started to hate it."[86] Another woman recalls that Liu Xihan's predecessor had also been a skilled old-style midwife, but frequent contact with the blood of childbirth made her go blind. It was for this reason, one woman told us, that she refused to learn midwifery herself when Liu Xihan offered to teach her: "No, my eyes are not good. I don't want to learn it. If I learn it, the blood will ruin my eyes. I won't learn."[87]

Even after liberation, even after the midwife station was founded and Liu Xihan became its head, even as sterile practices became more commonplace and tetanus neonatorum became less common, the perils of delivering children did not recede. Ultimately, people said, Liu Xihan had "died of midwifery" (*jiesheng gei sile, ba ming gei songle*). Called to attend a birth, she found herself delivering something malformed and odorous: "When she delivered the baby, she didn't know whether it was a baby or not. She was so scared that she got a fever that night. On the second day people sent a message to her son. The son went there and carried her back. It was in the afternoon. . . . By four in the afternoon, she breathed her last breath and died. Oh, that old woman, she was such a good midwife. As soon as someone called her, she would respond. She said, that person is suffering, as soon as she was called she would say I am going."[88] Nor was this the whole story behind Liu

Xihan's death. One day several months before her death, she confided a troubling episode to one of the village women, swearing her to secrecy. The listener remembers the story this way:

> That year, she came and said to me (I never dared tell anyone else), "Fengcun, I dare not say it. Please don't tell others. Otherwise the government will struggle against me." One night, a young man called her outside her window, "Aunt, come to deliver a baby for me." Just these words. She said, "OK, I am coming." She put on her clothes and carried the medicine box on her back.
>
> She said the young man carried the medicine box for her. Then they went to the east slope. When she came back, she forgot to bring her box. There was a cross written on it. When she came back, her husband said the next day, "Ya, where is your box?" She said the woman gave birth to a son. She asked the young man to bring her some water to wash her hands. The young man said, "Aunt, we had no water. And I have nothing to cook some food for you." "I don't want to eat. Just give me some water and let me wash my hands. I won't eat anything of yours. Let me wash my hands." The man said there was no water. So she wiped her hands on a stone and then went back home. She herself came back. She said she delivered a son for them. On the second day, my uncle said, "Where is your box?" She said, "I didn't take it with me last night." "Then why didn't I see your box? Where were you last night?" She told him. Her husband went to look for her box.
>
> It was on a tomb of a family. She wiped the blood on the tomb. She was so scared and only told me about it. She dared not tell others. If she told others, the state would struggle against her. She was so scared and dared not say so. This was superstitious. She delivered a baby for dead people. The old woman died not long after that.[89]

In this story several worlds brush up against each other, crossing boundaries that themselves are not clearly defined. The new-style midwife, full of the spirit of service shared by many midwives of her generation, goes off to deliver a baby. Afterward she is afraid, and her answers to her husband suggest that she is reluctant to discuss what she fears, even to admit that she has gone out. But there is the matter of the lost medical kit, and the place where her husband discovers it confirms that something is terribly wrong. She has unknowingly put her medical skill at the service of a spectral otherworld, has delivered a ghost baby, a frightening boundary violation in itself. Although she experiences this fear as an individual one, it draws upon a powerful collective fear of much longer standing, expressed in numerous Chinese stories of the supernatural with almost exactly this plot line.[90]

Yet she is afraid of something else as well—she worries that her fear will get her criticized for lingering superstition, she who has embraced science and propagated it so enthusiastically in the village. Here the world of science brushes up against an older set of beliefs in the person of the midwife, in an environment where only science can be spoken if one is to be progressive, useful, above reproach. So she keeps silent, or almost silent. And then, like a recurring nightmare, another monstrous birth comes her way, and this time it kills her.

The question is not whether contact with ghosts and monsters killed Liu Xihan, or even whether recurring trauma hastened her death. Whether she herself connected the two traumatic births cannot be known to us. What we do know is that women who remember her for her skill, her commitment to new-style childbirth, and her compassion also remember her death as caused by midwifery. She "died of midwifery," as our interviewee—herself an enthusiastic 1950s activist—put it.

For women who were of childbearing age in the early years of the People's Republic, the liminal and dangerous nature of childbirth was as real in the 1950s, and remains as real in 1990s memories, as the need to sterilize one's medical instruments. They certainly live partly by state temporality—they recount with feeling how campaigns changed their lives. But state temporality coexisted, perhaps even defined itself against, other temporalities that did not disappear with the advent of a new state regime. Knowledge, belief, and practice circulated in complex ways not captured by the state-as-conveyor-of-scientific-knowledge model. And this in turn suggests that a fully historicized understanding of rural childbirth and midwifery, and of the 1950s in rural China more generally, while it surely must include a full accounting of state campaigns, must entail as well an investigation of women's memories, or at least the memories they are willing and able to narrate.

✄ 15

Capitalists Choosing Communist China: The Liu Family of Shanghai, 1948–56

Sherman Cochran

IN THE WAKE of the Communist revolution of 1949, the overwhelming majority of China's elites who had the means to escape from China did not flee. In the early 1950s, many chose to return from abroad, including engineers and scientists (like the seventh son of the Ye family in Chapter 13, Joseph Esherick's chapter) and social scientists and literary figures (such as Lao She, who is mentioned in Chapter 9 by Perry Link). Even many officials who had been serving in the Nationalist government's diplomatic corps went home. Why did those who had the option of emigrating choose to stay or return? The motivations of all elite emigrants and returnees who faced this question are worth exploring because of their potential as leaders with access to power in the newly founded People's Republic. This chapter focuses on one portion of the elite, Chinese capitalists, and more specifically on one leading family, the Lius of Shanghai. With the coming of the revolution, why did they, as capitalists, choose to live in China under communism?

Those who have addressed the question of why Chinese capitalists stayed in China have generally explained the decision by attributing it to nationalism or transnationalism. Among the advocates of the nationalist interpretation, surely the most widely discussed is Mao Zedong. On December 25, 1947, at the height of the Chinese civil war, Mao envisioned "genuine national capitalists" as the ones who would contribute to the "new democratic national economy" of China after his Communist forces ousted Chiang Kai-shek's Nationalist government and took power.[1] Less than two years later, in 1949, when Mao claimed victory and established a new government, the Communist Party began to use Mao's terminology to separate capitalists into two groups: "national capitalists" *(minzu zibenjia)*, who were regarded as patriotic and were encouraged to stay as citizens of the People's Republic, and "comprador bureaucratic capitalists" *(maiban guanliao zibenjia)*, who were not eligible for citizenship because they were said to be in league with foreign imperialists and corrupt officials. Since then scholars in China have continued to make this distinction and have argued with each other about whether Chinese capitalists at all points in modern history deserve to be praised as nationalists or condemned as compradors and bureaucrats.[2]

Outside China, scholars have explained Chinese capitalists' decisions to stay or leave the country in 1949 by shifting attention from their nationalism to their transnationalism. In his aptly titled book *Emigrant Entrepreneurs*, Siu-lun Wong has analyzed the complex motivations driving Chinese industrialists to leave their cotton mills in Shanghai and move to Hong Kong during the Communist revolution of 1949, and he has noted that "it was not uncommon for the members of one family to go their separate ways," with one or more staying in China while the others went abroad.[3] Recently Parks Coble has endorsed Wong's point and added historical nuance to it. In Coble's view, Chinese capitalists made decisions to leave or stay in China in 1949 on the same basis as they had done at the beginning of the Sino-Japanese War of 1937–45 (which is the subject of Coble's book). "Businessmen responded in 1949 as many had in 1937 and 1938: disperse the family and resources, divide the risk," which meant, in 1949, that capitalist families kept some members at home in China and sent others abroad to Hong Kong, Southeast Asia, or the West, forming a transnational network for each family and family firm.[4]

Were the Chinese capitalists who chose to stay in China nationalists or transnationalists? Neither of these seemingly contradictory hypotheses has been tested in empirical research, and at best each rests on Chinese capitalists' retrospective reconstructions of their nationalism and undocumented references to their transnational "overseas connections."[5] The aim of this chapter is to evaluate nationalism, transnationalism, and other motivations of Chinese capitalists for staying in China mainly on the basis of an extraordinary family archive.[6] The private letters, memoirs, and other documents in this collection, all written by members of the Liu family, hold revealing clues about why they left, stayed in, or returned to China at the time of the Communist revolution in the late 1940s and early 1950s.

Leaving China

In 1948 and 1949, the head of the Liu family, Liu Hongsheng (1888–1956), changed his mind more than once about whether he and his family would live in China. By then he was in his sixties, and he had become one of China's leading industrialists, with major investments in manufacturing plants producing matches, woolens, cement, and briquettes.[7] As he brooded about whether to relocate his family and his vast assets, he was aggressively courted by both Chiang Kai-shek's Nationalist government and Mao Zedong's Communist forces, which waged battles against each other in the final stages of the Chinese civil war of 1946–49. Right up to the last year of this war, Liu remained aligned with Chiang and the Nationalists.

Disillusionment with the Nationalists

Even after the Communists mounted their decisive offensive in the fall of 1948 and the Nationalist forces began to retreat southward in China and then flee to Taiwan, Liu seemed prepared to continue to follow Chiang Kai-shek. Since the 1930s he had known Chiang as a fellow native-place associate from Ningbo, and he had held several positions in the Nationalist government. In 1932–34, he had been the director of the state-owned China Steam Navigation Company, and in 1936–37, he had served as head of the Chinese National Joint Production and Sales Union for Matches, a state-sponsored cartel. During the Sino-Japanese War, Liu had moved from coastal Shanghai to Chiang Kai-shek's wartime capital, Chongqing, in western China, where he had opened new industrial enterprises manufacturing woolens and matches and had presided over the government's cigarette and match monopoly, which was under the Ministry of Finance.[8] More recently, since returning to Shanghai at the end of the war in 1945, he had served as the government's chief director of the Chinese National Relief and Rehabilitation Administration and director of its Shanghai regional office. After thus following Chiang from Shanghai to Chongqing in the late 1930s and early 1940s and then back to Shanghai in the mid-1940s, why would not Liu follow him from Shanghai to Taiwan in 1948 and 1949?

In 1948, Liu took steps that seemed to commit him and his family irrevocably to a future in Taiwan. First he paid visits to Taiwan and the United States, and then he sent his fourth son (who had served as his right-hand man in Chongqing during the Sino-Japanese War) to Taiwan to open "a back way out." Before making the trip, Fourth Son collected gold, silver, and jewelry from his parents, brothers, and sisters and shipped these valuables to Taiwan on a boat belonging to the Zhongxing Navigation Company. Once there, he invested the family's wealth in large amounts of real estate and made preparations to open two new factories, a candy mill in Taipei and a chemical plant in Kaohsiung. Before returning to Shanghai, he left responsibility for managing this property in the hands of two of his brothers, American-educated Fifth Son and Japanese-educated Seventh Son, who took up residence in Taiwan at the time.[9]

Liu Hongsheng had barely made these substantial investments in Taiwan before he began to reconsider moving there. His doubts arose because of his experience with the Nationalist government's currency reform in Shanghai during the fall of 1948. Chiang Kai-shek introduced this reform as an attempt to halt runaway inflation and raise tax revenue, and in Shanghai it was carried out by Chiang's son, Chiang Ching-kuo. For two and one-half months between August 19 and October 31, 1948, Chiang Ching-kuo froze prices and appealed to Shanghai's capitalists to submit not only their old Chinese currency but also their gold, silver, and foreign currency in exchange for a new Chinese currency, the gold yuan.

Initially Chiang Ching-kuo tried to win Liu Hongsheng's support for the gold yuan reform by using a soft sell. He invited Liu to the Huizhong Hotel on Nanjing Road in Shanghai's Central District, addressed him as "uncle," and coaxed him into volunteering to turn over his gold, silver, and foreign currency for the sake of recovering stability and financing the war against communism. When Liu did not comply within the next day or two, Chiang took a hard line. He claimed to know what Liu's holdings were, and he threatened to punish him under martial law if his precious metals and foreign currency were not delivered to the Bank of China within three days. Meanwhile Chiang publicly attacked all of Shanghai's big, wealthy capitalists whom he referred to as "traitorous merchants." As he put it on the third day of his anticapitalist crusade, "Those who disturb the financial market are not the small merchants, but the big capitalists and big merchants." After his meetings with the Lius and other Shanghai capitalists, he concluded that they were friendly to his face, "but behind one's back there is no evil that they do not commit."[10]

Chiang's threats threw a scare into Liu Hongsheng, especially after the Nationalist government began carrying them out. Within the next few weeks, several uncooperative capitalists were arrested, with bail set for each one as high as U.S. $300,000 or even U.S. $1 million, and one of them was sentenced to death. According to Liu's fourth son, Liu Hongsheng was frightened into redeeming eight hundred gold bars, several thousand silver dollars, and U.S. $2.3 million in exchange for the new gold yuan currency at the Bank of China. Within the next few weeks the Lius and Shanghai's other capitalists were appalled by the outcome of the reform as the gold yuan currency became virtually worthless.[11]

On October 31, 1948, the Nationalist government admitted that the gold yuan reform had failed and revoked the price controls that had been introduced two and one-half months earlier. Chiang Ching-kuo publicly apologized to the people of Shanghai, although even then, as a parting shot at Chinese capitalists, he expressed the hope that the people would "not again allow traitorous merchant-speculators, bureaucratic politicians and ruffians and scoundrels to come and control Shanghai."[12]

Liu Hongsheng was deeply disturbed by the failure of the gold yuan reform and Chiang Ching-kuo's treatment of Chinese capitalists, and he was not alone. According to Lloyd Eastman, "Most people thereafter abandoned all hope for economic recovery; the failure of the reform seemed to demonstrate that the National Government was totally without resources to control the inflation."[13] Liu Hongsheng shared this view, and he ceased to envision any role for himself and his family members in Taiwan. Under the Nationalist government, he soberly told his children at a family meeting, "Taiwan would not be a safe place."[14]

Skepticism toward the Communists

If not following Chiang to Taiwan, would the Liu family remain in China under Communist rule? In early 1949, as the People's Liberation Army (PLA) swept southward from the northeast and descended on Shanghai, Liu Hongsheng and his family began to receive assurances from the Communist Party. If the Lius would stay in Shanghai, they were told, then after the PLA took over the city, their safety would be guaranteed and their factories would be protected. The Lius first heard this message within their own family meetings from Liu Hongsheng's sixth son.

Liu's sixth son insisted that all members of the family should remain in Shanghai and become committed to the Communist cause. He had been a party member since joining Mao at the Yan'an base area in 1938, more than ten years earlier, and he had secretly served as an underground agent in the fight against the Nationalists. (His party membership did not become public knowledge until the fall of the Gang of Four three decades later in the 1970s.)[15] Initially he seemed to stand alone as the only one proposing to keep the entire family together in Shanghai under Communist rule. Eventually in March 1949 he brought a classmate to a family meeting, explaining that this man was a Communist Party member who could speak authoritatively about the party's policies and plans.

Previously known to the family as Wang, this agent's real name was Dai De, and after Sixth Son revealed his identity, Dai explained in detail the party's policy of "promoting production, achieving economic prosperity, taking care of both state and private enterprises, and benefiting both employees and employers." He urged all of the Lius to stay in Shanghai, and he promised that the PLA would guarantee the Lius' safety and factories as soon as it took over the city. He followed up by visiting Fourth Son three times and urging him to work with the Communists to protect the Liu family's factories from sabotage by retreating Nationalist troops. During these last months before the PLA took over Shanghai, the Communists repeatedly urged the Lius to stay there in radio broadcasts to the city.[16]

Except for Sixth Son, the members of the Liu family were skeptical of the party's claims. Liu Hongsheng had met and chatted with Mao Zedong and Zhou Enlai twice each in Chongqing during the Sino-

Japanese War, and he had been favorably impressed with them as approachable and self-confident leaders, but he was still wary of the party and its policies toward capitalists. In the spring of 1949, after hearing Sixth Son and Dai De present the case in favor of Communist rule, he told his family, "The Communists will never be our real friends."[17]

Flight to Hong Kong

In the spring of 1949 on the eve of Communist takeover of Shanghai, Liu Hongsheng weighed his options. In light of the abysmal outcome of the Nationalist government's gold yuan reform, he ruled out emigration to Taiwan, and despite Sixth Son's assurances, he remained skeptical about keeping the entire family and all of its assets in Shanghai under Communist rule. As a third alternative, he proposed to move part of the family and its business to Hong Kong and leave the rest in Shanghai. According to Fourth Son, all family members except Sixth Son endorsed this decision, and they took as their motto one of Father's favorite English sayings, "Don't put all of your eggs in one basket."[18]

As Liu Hongsheng and his family deliberated over the decision whether to leave or stay, they came under close surveillance from Nationalist government officials who became suspicious of them for not leaving Shanghai sooner. In March 1949, Chiang Kai-shek ordered the Shanghai city government to organize the Committee for the Defense of Shanghai, and Liu Hongsheng was appointed to it. From then on, according to Fourth Son's memoirs, Liu Hongsheng was monitored closely by Chen Baotai, the head of the Shanghai Social Bureau. In May 1949, during the last days before the PLA reached Shanghai, Liu received a telephone call from Chen every hour of every day. Then on May 22, 1949, three days before the PLA's Third Field Army took over the city, Liu was ordered to attend an emergency meeting in Guangzhou with Chiang Kai-shek. Given no prior notice, he was picked up by Chen Baotai and three armed men who drove him to the airport and escorted him onto a private plane that was chartered for this flight. As recounted by Fourth Son, this sequence of events was "like a kidnapping" by the Nationalist secret police. Only after he was forced to fly out of Shanghai and was held against his will in Guangzhou did Liu escape from the Nationalists and flee to Hong Kong.[19]

In light of Liu Hongsheng's preparations for his trip to Hong Kong, it seems unlikely that he traveled from Shanghai to Guangzhou and Hong Kong as involuntarily as Fourth Son indicated in the account given above. As early as April 1949, more than a month before he was supposedly forced to fly from Shanghai to Guangzhou, he had corresponded with the Central Air Transportation Company about arranging his own flight between these two cities. In the same month, his top business associates from outside the family, two cousins named Cheng Nianpeng and Hua Erkang, had smuggled to Hong Kong foreign currency, finished products, and raw materials valued at U.S. $5 million. Then in early May, Cheng and Hua themselves had boarded a plane in Shanghai that was bound for Hong Kong. When workers from the Lius' Zhanghua Woolen Mills had tried to stop Cheng and Hua from leaving Shanghai, Liu Hongsheng had calmed down the crowd by promising that Cheng and Hua would not remain in Hong Kong for long. As it turned out, Liu joined his two business associates in Hong Kong only a few weeks later on May 24, 1949, and Cheng and Hua never returned to Shanghai.[20] Whether or not Liu Hongsheng was coerced by Chiang Kai-shek into leaving Shanghai, he seems to have severed his ties with the Nationalist government, and he did not visit Taiwan at this time or ever again.

Contingencies

Liu's decisions in May 1949 not to leave Shanghai for Taiwan under Nationalist rule and not to stay in Shanghai under Communist rule indicate the range of his options and the volatility of his situation. As Nara Dillon has pointed out in Chapter 4 of this volume, other Chinese capitalists also fled or contemplated fleeing from Shanghai at this time, and compared to the others, Liu had as much or more financial and cultural resources to secure a future for himself and his family anywhere in Asia or the West. Prior to 1949, he had spent twenty years educating his children abroad. In 1929, he had sent three of his sons to England, where they had earned degrees at Cambridge University in the 1930s, and subsequently he had given overseas educations to the rest of his twelve children except one, a son with severe learning disabilities. Besides sending three sons to England, he had educated one daughter there, and he had provided educations for three other sons and a daughter at colleges and universities in the United States and for two other sons and a daughter at colleges and universities in Japan. And yet even with his money, technology, Western- and Japanese-educated children, and other movable assets, Liu had great difficulty deciding where to go in 1949. His arrival in Hong Kong on May 24 still did not settle the issue, for he continued to wrestle with the question of whether he should stay in Hong Kong or return to China.

Returning to China

In November 1949, Liu Hongsheng was persuaded to return to Shanghai by members of his family and top leaders in the Communist Party. During his six months in Hong Kong, May–November 1949, he was torn between returning to them or remaining in Hong Kong, where his eighth son was due to arrive from the United States in mid-November. Caught in a tug of war, he had "his legs pulled apart" by the Shanghai group and the Hong Kong group until he finally reached a decision.[21]

Family Pressures

Despite the civil war, revolution, and turmoil, Liu Hongsheng's family in Shanghai never lost touch with him during his six months in Hong Kong. Fourth Son kept him fully informed of business matters, and as early as June 4, 1949, only two weeks after Liu Hongsheng had left Shanghai, Second Son appealed to him to come right back. "Father," he wrote in a letter to Hong Kong, "I have heard that you have decisively broken all ties with the [Nationalist] politicians in Guangdong province, and that makes me very happy. Your home is here in Shanghai." In the wake of the Communist takeover of Shanghai, Second Son acknowledged that the city had been through a crisis, but he maintained that it "had weathered the crisis without too much destruction," and he blamed the losses that did occur squarely on the Nationalists. "It's terribly painful to recall the wanton destruction of our property at the hands of the Nationalist troops before their retreat. Our rubber factory was a typical example." But according to Second Son, the wild and destructive Nationalist forces had now been replaced by well-disciplined Communist troops who were as good for Shanghai as the Nationalist troops had been bad. "There's no comparison between soldiers in that kind of [Nationalist] army and those in the PLA. They are two entirely different kinds of human beings."[22]

Within two short weeks since the PLA had marched into Shanghai, the new government had already won over the city's "common people" *(laobaixing)*. Second Son wrote to his father, "The city's common people have concluded that the new government is a good government because it is lenient, extremely clean, hard working, down to earth, patriotic, frugal. . . . It is perfect."[23] While reporting that the common people thought the new government was perfect, Second Son expressed his own opinion of the Communists in terms that were almost as uniformly positive. "I personally think that they have an extremely good chance of succeeding. There was a time when I had become very pessimistic due to all that had happened after we won the War of Resistance [against Japan in 1945], but now I have changed my mind. The new hope I've gained from the people's liberation government will give me courage to overcome all the difficulties and hardships that I may encounter on my future path."[24] Besides speaking for the common people and himself, Second Son also claimed that the most skeptical of Shanghai's anti-Communists had now come around to a favorable view of the new government: "Even those who had once pointed fingers at the Communists and were highly critical of them are now admitting that our country's destiny has never been in more capable hands than it is today. The people's government has brought hope that China will one day become a strong and prosperous nation. The road will be long, and there will be all kinds of difficulties and hardships for various individuals. But the direction is the right one."[25]

Now that the new government had favorably impressed the common people, the members of the Liu family, and even former anti-Communists, Second Son told his father that it was time for him to come home. "Your home is here in Shanghai. Only here will it be possible for you to do big things, and your ability will earn you more respect." In case Second Son's letter was not enough to persuade his father, he announced that he would come to Hong Kong in person as soon as he received permission from the new government to make the trip. "By then," he wrote, "I sincerely hope that you will be ready to return to Shanghai with me."[26]

As it turned out, Second Son did not make this trip from Shanghai to Hong Kong until five months later. In October 1949 (shortly after the founding of the People's Republic on October 1), he was sent by the Shanghai municipal government to bring his father home, but he failed to do so. According to Fourth Son (who did not make the trip to Hong Kong), "My father was somewhat influenced by the Nationalists' anti-Communist propaganda. Some friends also told him that the Communists might have been good at other things, but definitely not at economic matters. My father thought that this assessment sounded plausible. . . . He decided it was better for him to wait and see."[27] Father's decision frustrated Second Son, who returned to Shanghai alone.

Later in the same month, October 1949, Zhou Enlai, premier of the new national government at its capital in Beijing, dispatched emissaries to Hong Kong to convince Chinese capitalists to come back to China. These emissaries emphasized to Liu Hongsheng and other Chinese capitalists in Hong Kong that they had nothing to fear from the new government in China. As long as they were patriotic, they would be welcomed back, given protection for their families and property, and offered opportunities to serve as leaders.[28]

Zhou Enlai's emissaries apparently convinced Liu that he would find more promising business opportunities in Shanghai than he had discovered in Hong Kong. Liu's biggest Hong Kong venture was for buying wool in northwest China and selling it to carpet manufacturers in the United States, and after it fell through, he let his sons know that he was ready to return from Hong Kong to Shanghai.[29] In response, on November 1, 1949, Second Son paid his father another visit in Hong Kong. As soon as he arrived, Father explained to him why he had decided to go back (in words that were later repeated to the family in Shanghai): "I am an old man already over sixty. All of my enterprises are in China, so I'll go back and not stay abroad as a white Chinese [*bai Hua*, referring to Chinese at the time who were comparable to white Russian exiles from the Russian Revolution]. All of you are expecting me to return home. What's the point of my living alone in exile. I've decided to come home."[30] To avoid possible interference by agents of the Nationalist government, Liu Hongsheng and Second Son sneaked onto a steamship belonging to the British trading company Butterfield and Swire at midnight on November 2, 1949, and took it from Hong Kong to the north China port of Tianjin.[31] Greeted at the docks by newspaper reporters on November 3, Liu gave them three reasons why he and other Chinese capitalists would return to China from Hong

Kong: all of their enterprises were in Shanghai, all of the funds that they had taken to Hong Kong would soon be used up, and all of their fears that their property would be confiscated in China were now allayed. Others like himself, he predicted, would soon come back from Hong Kong, and he mentioned the example of Wu Yunchu, "the MSG King," who in fact did return to China soon thereafter.[32]

Catapulted into a Leadership Role

From the moment that Liu Hongsheng's ship docked in Tianjin on November 3, 1949, he found that officials in the new government made good on their promises to give him opportunities as a leader. On disembarking from the Butterfield and Swire ship, he was handed a telegram from Premier Zhou Enlai, inviting him and Second Son to Beijing. Proceeding directly to the capital, he had a two-and-one-half-hour lunch with Zhou on the same day, and he was assured by Zhou that he would have protection for his enterprises and other property and that he could retain the lifestyle to which he was accustomed. He was also urged to set an example for other Chinese industrialists and businessmen by cooperating with the new government.

When Liu heard Zhou say that he was a "national capitalist" as distinct from a "comprador bureaucratic capitalist," he was suspicious and expressed doubts about the term's applicability to himself. As he pointed out, he had previously held a post as a comprador for the Kailuan Mining Administration under British ownership, and he had served as an official managing the state-owned China Merchants Navigation Company under Chiang Kai-shek's Nationalist government. He accepted Zhou's designation only after he heard Zhou's explanation that the party used the term to express its approval of one group of capitalists (the "national" ones) and its disapproval of another group (the "comprador bureaucratic" ones). More confident, Liu then asked whether his Huadong Coal Mining Company would be returned to him along with his other enterprises, and he discovered that his new status did not automatically bring all of his property back into his hands. Zhou explained that Liu could have back all of his other enterprises because they were in light industry but not Huadong because it supplied coal to heavy industry, which, according to the new government's policy, was all under the ownership and management of the state. The most that Zhou could promise was that Liu would eventually be compensated for his loss of Huadong.[33]

The next day, November 4, 1949, on his return to Shanghai, Liu Hongsheng received another official welcome from Chen Yi, the city's new mayor. Over dinner in Chen's home, he was warmly received and encouraged to come directly to the mayor if he had any questions or difficulties. Almost overnight Liu found himself appointed to influential committees along with high-ranking Communists. On December 18, 1949, less than six weeks after his return to China, he became a member of the Shanghai Political Consultative Committee, which was chaired by Mayor Chen Yi and included Deputy Mayor Pan Hannian, the key liaison between the city's new political leaders and its capitalists (as Frederic Wakeman has shown in Chapter 2). Besides serving on this and other committees in Shanghai, Liu was appointed to organizations with responsibility for areas that extended beyond the city, such as the East China Military and Political Council, and he gave speeches on national and international issues as well as local ones.[34]

In his speeches (which were reprinted in newspapers), Liu Hongsheng endorsed the new government's leadership and proposed policies that entrepreneurs like himself should follow under Communist rule. On December 17, 1949, speaking as a member of the Shanghai People's Congress, he recalled that Shanghai had previously been "a semi-colonial city" in which Chinese people like himself in industry and commerce "were heavily oppressed by imperialism, feudalism, and bureaucratic capitalism. . . . We couldn't even breathe." But now "the liberation of Shanghai has opened up a free, glorious new world for industrialists, creating a new environment in which to shake off our chains." He admitted that even in this new world Chinese entrepreneurs faced many difficulties, and he urged them to prepare themselves by adopting the Communist Party's spirit of hard work and struggle. In this spirit, "we must eat bitterness at first so that we can enjoy happiness later."[35]

While urging his fellow Chinese entrepreneurs to take their inspiration from the party, Liu also made practical proposals for reforming Chinese industry to capture the export trade. In these proposals he anticipated the export strategy that was eventually adopted and ultimately helped to produce the "economic miracle" beginning in Hong Kong and Taiwan in the 1950s and 1960s and the People's Republic in the

1980s. In outlining his scheme, Liu cited the example of his own woolen mills, implying that the government should authorize him to put his principles into practice in this specific case. He proposed to carry out phase one by procuring wool from northwest China exactly as he had unsuccessfully tried to do when he was in Hong Kong a few months earlier. The only difference was that now he planned to manufacture it into woolen fabric in his Zhanghua Woolen Mill at Shanghai rather than exporting the raw wool abroad. In phase two, he would then export these woolens as finished products abroad, selling them primarily in the accessible markets of Asia, Africa, and Latin America and secondarily in the less-accessible markets of Europe and the United States, thus earning foreign exchange. In phase three, he would complete the cycle by using the foreign exchange to buy foreign-made producer goods, particularly chemicals that were needed to manufacture matches in his China Match Company at Shanghai.[36]

While giving these speeches publicly, Liu confided to his fourth son privately that he expected state planning agencies to carry out his ideas by giving government contracts to state-owned enterprises, not privately owned ones like his. Accordingly, he was pleasantly surprised when the Economic Planning Committee of the People's Republic ordered woolen uniforms for government officials from his mills rather than state-owned ones. He took this decision to mean that he was accepted as a capitalist under communism not only in theory but also in practice.[37]

Coming Home for Pragmatic Reasons

As shown here, Liu Hongsheng's rationale for choosing to live in China shifted after he returned home. Before leaving Hong Kong and even during his first days back in China, his reasons for returning were strikingly pragmatic and nonnationalistic. On the eve of his return to Shanghai from Hong Kong, he said that he was making the move because of his advanced age, his desire to be near his enterprises, and his Shanghai-based family members' expectations—considerations that seem to have been paramount in the minds of many Chinese capitalists at the time as they made their decisions whether to live in Shanghai or Hong Kong.[38] On his arrival in China, he cited for newspaper reporters slightly different but equally apolitical reasons for coming back: the location of his factories in Shanghai, the danger of exhausting his resources in Hong Kong, and the government's assurances that he could retain his property in the People's Republic. In his first meeting with Zhou Enlai, he was suspicious of ideological designations and questioned Zhou's characterization of him as a "national capitalist" until Zhou patiently explained that the term was used by the Chinese Communist Party to express approval of some capitalists as distinct from the rest.

These examples all suggest that Liu Hongsheng did not leave Hong Kong and return to China because he held the ideological orientation of a national capitalist (as opposed to a comprador bureaucratic capitalist) or because he was a nationalist (as distinct from a pragmatist). It was not until after he had returned to Shanghai and had become fully engaged in life and work in the People's Republic that he began to take strong nationalistic positions about the importance of bringing back to China all capitalists, especially his own sons.

Summoning the Family Home

If Liu Hongsheng became genuinely committed to the Communist cause after his return to China, then did his new orientation cause him to revise the survival strategy for his family? After his return to Shanghai, he had made ideologically charged speeches and other public pronouncements calling on all Chinese entrepreneurs to pledge allegiance to the People's Republic and devote their lives and work to it. But did he put these principles into practice by bringing his own family members home from Hong Kong and Taiwan to live and work in China? Within a surprisingly short time after his arrival in Shanghai, he did, in fact, send for his sons and urge them all to return home from abroad.

Instructing Sons to Come Home

In late 1949 and early 1950, while Liu Hongsheng was publicly endorsing the new Communist government in speeches, he privately endorsed it in letters to his eighth son in Hong Kong. This son, a recent graduate of Massachusetts Institute of Technology (class of 1947) and Harvard Business School (class of 1949), had traveled by ship from the United States, and on arrival in Hong Kong in mid-November 1949, he had expected to find that his father and possibly his whole family had fled there. Instead, he discovered that his father had departed for Shanghai and had left a message telling him to do the same.

Besides summoning Eighth Son to return to Shanghai, Liu Hongsheng also instructed him to bring with him Fifth Son and Seventh Son, who had been sent to Taiwan in the late 1940s and were the only other sons still abroad. These two brothers should immediately move from their current residences in Taiwan to Hong Kong and then come with Eighth Son to Shanghai, Father insisted, "so that we can all have a joyous family reunion together."[39]

In response, Eighth Son did not take his fifth and seventh brothers to Shanghai, but he did make the trip himself in early 1950. In Shanghai, he had a happy reunion with his mother, who had always favored him and had faithfully corresponded with him but had not seen him since his departure from China to America in 1945, nearly five years earlier. With his father and brothers, his relations were not so cordial, especially on the question of whether he should move permanently to China and live and work under communism. Father again offered him a position as a wool specialist in northwest China, and Eldest Son tried to interest him in an egg powder plant in central China. Second Son and Sixth Son did not show such high respect for his training. In fact, they questioned whether it had prepared him to take any job. His education at Harvard Business School had been "very reactionary," they told him, so he should begin his life in socialist China by undergoing "reeducation." Only Fourth Son advised him to return to Hong Kong, saying that he should follow the family's preliberation strategy of "not putting all their eggs (we brothers) in one basket." After spending two months in China, Eighth Son seized on Fourth Son's advice and took the train from Shanghai back to Hong Kong.

Defending China as a Free Country

After Eighth Son returned to Hong Kong, Liu Hongsheng continued to insist that he as well as Fifth Son and Seventh Son should come to live permanently in China, and he expressed mounting frustration with them for refusing to do so. He was particularly impatient with Eighth Son for arguing that life under communism would be intolerable because it would deprive him of his freedom. On March 28, 1950, he wrote to Eighth Son in Hong Kong:

I read your letter dated the 20th and learned that you are afraid our country lacks freedom of thought and you think it would be better to stay abroad. This attitude has resulted from egocentrism plus the influence of bogus international propaganda, so you do not know the truth, you vacillate, and you cannot make a decision. You are already thirty years old, and your viewpoint may be different from that of someone over sixty like myself, but we can arrive at the same view if we study the facts carefully.[40]

To bring Eighth Son around to "the same view" on the issue of freedom, Father challenged Eighth Son's assumption that freedom existed in the United States, Hong Kong, and preliberation Shanghai. "The so-called freedom [in these places], if examined realistically, is completely false," Father contended.

While in the United States, Father claimed, Eighth Son had become imbued with the wrong ideas about freedom because of his special circumstances in residence there. "You went abroad too early," he recalled with regret, referring to Eighth Son's first trip to the United States in 1937 at age sixteen. "There wasn't any older person in America to consult, so you had to deal with all matters exclusively on the basis of your own ideas. Gradually you have come to doubt your father's and your elder brothers' guidance. . . . You stayed in America for a long time and were influenced by American propaganda, so your prejudices have become deeply rooted and cannot be changed right away."[41] If Eighth Son would critically assess American propaganda and free himself from American prejudices, then he would be able to see that America lacked freedom, especially for Chinese and blacks. "In America," Father told his American-educated son, "both the Chinese and the black people have their residential areas restricted. They cannot freely choose where to live. When the Chinese enter U.S. territory, they are subjected to all kinds of abusive treatment that is heartbreaking."[42]

By comparison with the United States, Father noted, Hong Kong "may be a place that has more freedom," but any freedom there for Chinese was undercut by British colonial rule. Based on his recent experience, he observed, "In Hong Kong, our fellow countrymen who have taken up residence may think that they have all kinds of freedom in whoring, gambling, and excessive eating and drinking. But when it comes to conducting legitimate business—say, in international trade through shipping companies—the chairmen of the boards of directors and the chief executive officers must all be Englishmen or of some other foreign nationality."[43] Even vaunted Anglo-Saxon law did not give Chinese freedom in Hong Kong, Father explained to his son, because "the British laws used in the courtroom are designed to protect bad elements in the society for the sake of ensuring the continued prosperity of Hong Kong, so those Chinese who now consider Hong Kong to be a comfortable nest are as pitiful as I was before I traveled abroad and came to realize that I had lost my freedom [in preliberation Shanghai]."[44]

In preliberation Shanghai, Father admitted that he and other Chinese had grown up with the belief that they had freedom, and he had not realized that this belief was an illusion until 1927 when he was nearly forty years old. In old Shanghai, as he now remembered it,

> The speech and movements of high class Chinese living inside the foreign concessions were all controlled by the foreign police, but they themselves didn't realize it. I myself grew up in the foreign concessions, and at first I, too, was not conscious of the loss of freedom. But when I traveled to Europe and America in 1927, I saw that all the public parks in their countries allowed everyone to enter freely, and yet the public parks in Shanghai's foreign concessions still had a prominently posted public notice that read "Dogs and Chinese Not Admitted." I then suddenly woke up to the fact that Europeans and Americans have not treated the Chinese right.[45]

In both Shanghai and Hong Kong, Father charged, privileged Westerners and corrupt Chinese officials deprived the Chinese people of freedom. "You ought to know," he told Eighth Son,

> that Europeans and Americans occupied Shanghai and Hong Kong and amassed great fortunes under the protection of unequal treaties with all kinds of special privileges. The abnormal prosperity of Hong Kong and Shanghai is also attributable to Chinese officials' corruption and ineptitude and to the people's ignorance, lack of a world view, and obsession with comfort and pleasure. I'm sure you understand fully the indisputable fact that these people

have been blind to the widespread poverty and the declining standard of living throughout our country.[46]

Leaders who were blind to poverty and declining standards of living would never give the Chinese people a chance to experience genuine freedom, Father argued, and he concluded that the leaders of the People's Republic were succeeding in transforming China precisely because they did not have this blind spot.

"It's been over five months since I returned here to Shanghai," he reminded Eighth Son, writing in March 1950, "and I can see with my own eyes that Shanghai since liberation is much different than before." The revolutionaries, according to his observation, took away freedom only from those who deserved to lose it and not from anyone else. "The Communists conduct themselves with attentiveness and restraint. Everywhere they emphasize practicality, and they always seek to achieve a thorough understanding. There is no corruption and no show of personal favors. People are prohibited from concealing wrongdoing, and they do not dare break the law. Tax evaders and law breakers have lost their freedom, but law-abiding people do not feel any so-called 'lack of freedom.' "[47]

After making his case, Father once again gave assurances that he would find a suitable position for Eighth Son in China's woolen industry—as long as he was willing to embrace the principles and adopt the point of view that Father espoused. "If you agree with all the points I've made above, if you are willing to change your thinking, and if you resolutely decide to return to our country to serve in productive enterprises, I will be sure to shoulder the responsibility of finding you a suitable position either in the private sector or in a joint public-private enterprise in the northwest. You once learned to evaluate wool samples in an American woolen mill, and now you can put your ability to great use. I have high hopes for you."[48]

Father's impassioned arguments and expressions of high hopes for Eighth Son did not persuade him (or Fifth Son or Seventh Son) to move back to Shanghai. But Father's position showed that he had abandoned the family survival strategy of dispersing members overseas to divide the risk for their business and themselves. After teaching his sons in the late 1940s (and for decades before that) not to put all their eggs in one basket, now he insisted that they should all reunite in a single place and commit themselves to a single cause.

Liu Hongsheng's choice of language in these letters to his son indicates that his ideological commitments were not confined to his speeches and other public pronouncements. In November 1949, he had given almost purely apolitical reasons for his own return to Shanghai, but in the letter quoted above, dated March 28, 1950 (only five months later), he gave his son highly political reasons for coming home. On the basis of this evidence, it is difficult to say whether Father's rhetoric became politicized because he had undergone an ideological conversion or because he had become subject to censorship or self-censorship after his return to China. Whatever caused him to take this ideological turn, he subsequently turned still further, calling his family's attention to additional ideological reasons for staying in China and bringing its members home.

Embracing Nationalism during the Korean War

Although the letters and speeches quoted earlier contain critiques of foreign imperialism, Liu Hongsheng did not begin to take pride in China's achievements as a nation or urge his son to come home because of these achievements until China became involved in the Korean War against American-led UN troops in late 1950. Ever since he had been a schoolboy at St. John's Middle School and St. John's University (both founded in Shanghai by the American Episcopal Mission), he had been in awe of American power. Even after the fighting began in Korea, he was initially dubious about China's Resist America Aid Korea Campaign. In September and October 1950, when the Americans pushed North Korean troops out of South Korea and captured the North Korean capital of Pyongyang, he was afraid that they would drop an atomic bomb on his hometown of Shanghai.[49] But in December 1950, after the Chinese "Volunteer Army" crossed into North Korea and pushed the UN troops once again south of the thirty-eighth parallel, he took patriotic pride in this achievement and began to participate ardently in the Resist America Aid Korea Campaign.

Liu was not the only capitalist to make philanthropic donations to the war effort. (For other examples, see Chapter 4 by Nara Dillon). But among Shanghai's entrepreneurs, he took the lead. His enterprises gave funds to help cover the cost of acquiring airplanes and artillery, and he delivered speeches exhorting his employees and other entrepreneurs to make contributions too. In a substantive and symbolic gesture, he donated one thousand sets of woolen uniforms to troops at the front and personally wrote letters to another thousand veterans who had been wounded there. These patriotic actions inspired an editorial in the Shanghai newspaper *Wenhui bao* that hailed him as a model for all the Chinese people.[50]

Following Liu's lead, his second son also became personally involved in the Korean War. In the spring of 1951, Second Son served as a member of the First Chinese People's Delegation to Give Comfort in Korea. On its trip to Korea, he visited Chinese soldiers from the Volunteer Army on the front lines and talked with American prisoners of war in English, which he had learned as a student at Cambridge University in the 1930s. In 1952 he also served as a member of the second such delegation. Listening to Second Son's stories about Korea, Liu Hongsheng said that he was deeply moved by the bravery of the Chinese soldiers. In 1952 he told the family, "For the first time in my life, I am proud to be a Chinese [Zhongguoren]."[51]

Emerging from the Five-Anti Campaign as a National Leader

If the Korean War gave Liu Hongsheng new nationalistic reasons for staying in China and keeping his family there, then the Five-Anti Campaign added political reasons because it elevated him to a position of national leadership. First he became a representative from Shanghai to the People's Congress, and then he was designated as a member of the National Committee of the Chinese People's Political Consultative Conference. But he only acquired these high-ranking positions after paying a heavy price.

In the first months of 1952, the Lius and other capitalists in Shanghai and China's other major cities became targets of the party's Five-Anti Campaign, which was so named because it aimed to eliminate five kinds of wrongdoing: bribery, tax evasion, theft of state assets, cheating on labor or materials, and stealing state economic intelligence. Between January and May in 1952, thousands of capitalists in Shanghai were denounced by workers, fellow capitalists, and even members of their own families. While demonstrators paraded in the streets and shouted their

names over loudspeakers, capitalists had to open their factories and account books to inspection teams and, in many cases, were forced to
give confessions of their crimes. Some capitalists suffered more than
others from the Five-Anti Campaign, but even those who did not confess to any crimes seem to have felt socially violated and humiliated by
the experience.[52]

Liu Hongsheng, perhaps more than any other Chinese capitalist,
was in a position to be spared during the Five-Anti Campaign. Two
years before the campaign began, when the government had first introduced laws against tax evasion and other economic crimes, he had
immediately and publicly endorsed these new laws. "It is important for
merchants to have credibility," he had said, representing capitalists at a
meeting of the Shanghai Political Consultative Committee in 1950.
"Those who have evaded taxes have no credibility and are scum. We
should have nothing to do with them." Thus anticipating the Five-
Anti Campaign long before it began, he had advocated punishing vio-
lators of the new laws "severely and without concern for giving them
face."[53]

Even though Liu Hongsheng had taken the moral high ground and
had urged fellow capitalists to obey new laws against economic crimes
before the Five-Anti Campaign, he was not spared during the campaign. When party cadres made him their target in early 1952, he was
physically sickened by the experience. At age sixty-four, suffering from
a heart condition, he fell ill and stayed at home to recuperate. At the
height of the campaign, he expressed to his family the fear that the
campaign marked the end for capitalists in the People's Republic.
"Now that the Communist Party has put the country on the right
track," Fourth Son later recalled him telling his sons at his sickbed, "it
no longer needs the capitalist class as its friend. You boys go find your
own path and come up with your own way."[54]

And yet when the results of the Five-Anti investigations were announced, Liu Hongsheng and his family found that they had not only
survived but greatly benefited from the outcome. They were fully exonerated and declared to be "law-abiding." In fact, they were hailed as
model national capitalists, and they were rewarded with 2.5 million
yuan in special financing plus 2.8 million yuan in goods that had been
taken from other less-upright capitalists. Liu Hongsheng was invited
to go to Beijing to dine with Mao Zedong, and when he returned to

Shanghai, he assured his family that the party had not changed its favorable policy toward national capitalists, after all. More than ever, he told a Japanese journalist, he was enthusiastic about "taking the socialist path," as a representative to the National People's Congress and a member of the National Committee of Chinese People's Political Consultative Conference.[55]

Liu Hongsheng's vindication at the end of the Five-Anti Campaign gave him and his family an unblemished political record within China, but it still left unanswered lingering questions about his sons outside China. If the Lius were a model capitalist family, why had some of their sons not rejoined them in Shanghai? Were the sons abroad withholding family funds that had been smuggled out of China and rightfully belonged back in Shanghai? Should not Liu Hongsheng as a model national capitalist make sure that his entire family and all of his family's resources were devoted to the interests of the nation?

As shown earlier, since late 1949 Liu Hongsheng had tried to eliminate any doubt about his family's commitment to the People's Republic by ordering Eighth Son in Hong Kong to move to Shanghai and bring Fifth Son and Seventh Son along with him. By 1952, Father had no way to reach his fifth and seventh sons who were living in Taiwan under Nationalist rule, but he could and did take drastic action to force Eighth Son to return from Hong Kong.

Putting Eggs Involuntarily into One Basket

In July 1952 after the Five-Anti Campaign had ended, Sixth Son traveled from Shanghai to Hong Kong to persuade Eighth Son to come home with him. Ostensibly Sixth Son and his wife made the trip to attend her brother's wedding in Hong Kong. They had no difficulty securing permission to leave China because Sixth Son had been a member of the party since the 1930s, and he had demonstrated his unwavering loyalty to the new government of the People's Republic since it was founded in 1949.

After attending the wedding, a lavish affair held in Hong Kong's posh Peninsula Hotel, Sixth Son and Eighth Son met to discuss family matters. In age they were close—one was thirty-six years old and the other thirty-one—and between 1945 and 1947 while in their twenties, they had come to know each other particularly well while doing internships with businesses in the United States. Since they had not seen each other for more than two years, they brought each other up to date. Eighth Son proudly described his work as a sales engineer with the Swiss-owned Overseas Trading Company, offering proof that his brothers in Shanghai had been wrong when they had warned him that he would never find a job in Hong Kong. For his part, Sixth Son discussed the Liu family's life in China.

As the climax to his report on the family, Sixth Son dramatically revealed his most important news: Mother, age sixty-four, was gravely ill and wanted Eighth Son at her bedside. Both men knew that this news was particularly poignant for Eighth Son because his mother had doted on him during his childhood and had unfailingly corresponded with him throughout his two long sojourns in the United States, each for four years, 1937–41 and 1945–49.

Deeply concerned about his mother's health, Eighth Son packed his bags and joined his sixth brother and sister-in-law on their return trip to Shanghai, but they had barely crossed the Hong Kong–China border before Sixth Son confessed that he had lied. In Shenzhen at the Luohu Railway Station, as the brothers carried their bags from their Hong Kong train to their Shanghai-bound one, Sixth Son assured his brother that their mother was not ill, and he admitted that he had said so only to lure Eighth Son back to China. On hearing the truth, Eighth Son was stunned and dropped his suitcases, sending them crashing onto the station platform. At that moment and from then on, he was desperately eager to leave China, but he could not secure permission to do so for the next twenty-seven years. In 1979, he finally emigrated from the People's Republic, moving permanently to the United States.[56]

Conclusion

With Eighth Son back in the fold, Liu Hongsheng had another of his nine sons with him in Shanghai during the last years of his life. Between 1953 and 1956, he and his sons in China endorsed and carried out the government's policy of nationalizing private industry. As early as October 1953, Liu Hongsheng heard the party's call for the "transition to socialism" at the first meeting of China's National Federation of Industry and Commerce. According to Fourth Son, he immediately approved the idea of transforming the family's businesses into joint public-private enterprises *(gongsi heying)*, and the Liu family eventually completed this process in early 1956.[57]

Asked at the time about his loss of ownership and managerial authority, Liu Hongsheng said that he had no regrets. As he explained to Fourth Son, he felt grateful to the party for the nationalization of his enterprises because it had relieved him of his two greatest fears: bankruptcy in his lifetime and a fight within his family over his property after his death. In his last days, he said, he was comfortable living on a state pension of 5 percent of the value of his enterprises, which were assessed at 20 million yuan in 1956. On his deathbed, he told Fourth Son that all his children in China should divide his pension equally among themselves after his death, and then they should voluntarily return a portion to the state as a token of Liu Hongsheng's appreciation of the party. Soon after leaving these last instructions, he died of heart failure at age sixty-eight on October 1, 1956—the day that China celebrated the seventh anniversary of the founding of the People's Republic.[58]

It seems unlikely that Liu Hongsheng was quite as sanguine and serene in 1956 as he is portrayed above by Fourth Son, especially in light of all that he and his family had recently been through: the upheavals during the revolution, the humiliations during the Five-Anti Campaign, the losses of ownership and managerial authority over the family business during the transition to socialism. Nonetheless, the available evidence does suggest that Liu Hongsheng wanted all the members of his family to live in the People's Republic and that he was genuinely pleased to have so many of them with him there at the end of his life. His decision to return to China after the revolution, his efforts to persuade his sons to join him there from abroad, and his success at bringing home one son involuntarily all point directly to this conclusion.

Liu's strategy for his family's survival does not fit neatly into existing explanations for Chinese capitalists' decisions to stay or return to China during the Communist revolution of 1949. As shown here, his own motivations for returning from Hong Kong to China do not conform to Mao Zedong's conception of the national capitalist. On the day of Liu's arrival back in China, November 3, 1949, when he heard Zhou Enlai apply the term "national capitalist" to him, he initially doubted its relevance. Only after Zhou assured him that it indicated the party's approval of him did he accept it and use it to refer to himself. Moreover, he did not espouse nationalism before his return to China. Not until after he came back did he urge his sons to return to China for nationalistic reasons, and not until the early 1950s when China became involved in the Korean War did he declare, for the first time in his life, that he was proud to be a Chinese.

If Liu's decision to return to China cannot be explained by nationalism, neither can his decision to bring his family home be explained by transnationalism. Before the revolution, he had readily reached across national boundaries by sending his children abroad for their educations in England, the United States, and Japan, and he had preached the message that the family should be represented overseas and should not put all its eggs in one basket (i.e., China). As late as mid-1949, while residing for six months in Hong Kong and deciding whether to return to China, he undoubtedly considered whether to disperse his family and divide his family firm's risk (as he had done during the Sino-Japanese War of 1937–45). But soon after the founding of the People's Republic on October 1, 1949, he apparently concluded that this strategy would not be as viable as it had been in the past. Once he had returned to Shanghai in November 1949, he made every effort to bring all members of his family home to China, pleading with them in private correspondence and even duping one into returning.

The Lius' lack of nationalism and their withdrawal from transnational connections suggest that they stayed or returned to China above all to pursue new opportunities there as a family. By 1949, Father and Mother were in their sixties and wanted their children around them late in life, and Liu and his sons envisioned a prominent place for themselves as capitalists under communism. In early 1952, their doubts about whether they were indispensable surfaced during the Five-Anti Campaign. But even then they remained committed to the idea that the family should live and work together in the People's Republic, as evidenced by their successful effort to dragoon Eighth Son into coming home in the summer of 1952 after the Five-Anti Campaign had ended. Later, especially during the Anti-Rightist Movement of 1957, several members of the family came to regret their decisions to stay in China, and during the Cultural Revolution in the late 1960s, Second Son committed suicide. But during the early years of the People's Republic, all except Eighth Son gave every indication that they believed their own brand of capitalism was compatible with communism.

In the early 1950s, did the Lius and other Chinese who stayed or returned to China after the revolution set precedents for a kind of capitalism that would operate effectively under communism in the long run? Between the late 1950s and the late 1970s, Maoist campaigns seemed at the time to have purged all capitalists (if not all capitalist roaders) from China forever. But since the coming of the reforms in the late 1970s and the proposals for the admission of capitalists to the Communist Party in 2001 and 2002, it now seems possible that the Lius' belief in the compatibility of capitalism and communism in China might be vindicated after all.

Notes

1. The Early Years of the People's Republic of China

1. See, for example, *Tianjin jingji gaikuang* (Survey of Tianjin's economy) (Tianjin: Tianjin renmin chubanshe, 1984), 19.

2. Frederick C. Teiwes, "The Establishment and Consolidation of the New Regime, 1949–1957," in Roderick MacFarquhar, ed., *Cambridge History of China*, vol. 14, *The People's Republic, Part I: The Emergence of Revolutionary China, 1949–1965* (Cambridge: Cambridge University Press, 1987), 86–87.

3. Derk Bodde, *Peking Diary: A Year of Revolution* (New York: Schuman, 1950); and A. Doak Barnett, *China on the Eve of Communist Takeover* (New York: Praeger, 1963). Later works also documented how the Nationalist government had alienated intellectuals and businesspeople. See Suzanne Pepper, *Civil War in China: The Political Struggle, 1945–1949* (Lanham, Md.: Rowman and Littlefield, 1999 [1978]); and Lloyd E. Eastman, *Seeds of Destruction: Nationalist China in War and Revolution, 1937–1949* (Stanford: Stanford University Press, 1984).

4. See Maria Yen with Richard M. McCarthy, *The Umbrella Garden: A Picture of Student Life in Red China* (New York: Macmillan, 1954).

5. See, respectively, W. W. Rostow, *The Prospects for Communist China* (Cambridge, Mass.: Technology Press of Massachusetts Institute of Technology, 1954), 171; and Richard L. Walker, *China under Communism: The First Five Years* (New Haven: Yale University Press, 1955), 215.

6. Allen S. Whiting, *China Crosses the Yalu: The Decision to Enter the Korean War* (New York: Macmillan, 1960).

7. Robert Jay Lifton, *Thought Reform and the Psychology of Totalism: A Study of "Brainwashing" in China* (New York: Norton, 1961); and Allyn Rickett and Adele Rickett, *Prisoners of Liberation* (New York: Cameron Associates, 1957). See also the final chapters of A. Doak Barnett, *Communist China: The Early Years, 1949–55* (New York: Praeger, 1964).

8. An exception is C. K. Yang's set of studies on rural Guangdong, *A Chinese Village in Early Communist Transition* (Cambridge, Mass.: Massachusetts Institute of Technology Press, 1959) and *The Chinese Family in the Communist Revolution* (Cambridge, Mass.: Massachusetts Institute of Technology Press, 1959). Later works on rural China in the late 1940s and 1950s include William Hinton, *Fanshen: A Documentary of Revolution in a Chinese Village* (New York: Monthly Review Press, 1966); and Vivienne Shue, *Peasant China in Transition: The Dynamics of Development toward Socialism, 1949–1956* (Berkeley: University of California Press, 1980).

9. Joseph W. Esherick, Paul G. Pickowicz, and Andrew G. Walder, "The Chinese Cultural Revolution as History: An Introduction," in Joseph W. Esherick, Paul G. Pickowicz, and Andrew G. Walder, eds., *The Chinese Cultural Revolution as History* (Stanford: Stanford University Press, 2006).

10. Franz Schurmann, *Ideology and Organization in Communist China* (Berkeley: University of California Press, 1966).

11. Ezra F. Vogel, *Canton under Communism: Programs and Politics in a Provincial Capital, 1949–1968* (Cambridge, Mass.: Harvard University Press, 1969), 98–105. Later studies confirmed that regional identities and family allegiances remained potent during the early years of the People's Republic. See Dorothy J. Solinger, *Regional Government and Political Integration in Southwest China, 1949–1954: A Case Study* (Berkeley: University of California Press, 1977); and William L. Parish and Martin King Whyte, *Village and Family in Contemporary China* (Chicago: University of Chicago Press, 1978).

12. Kenneth Lieberthal, *Revolution and Tradition in Tientsin, 1949–1952* (Stanford: Stanford University Press, 1980).

13. Neil J. Diamant, *Revolutionizing the Family: Politics, Love, and Divorce in Urban and Rural China, 1949–1968* (Berkeley: University of California Press, 2000).

14. James Z. Gao, *The Communist Takeover of Hangzhou: The Transformation of City and Cadre, 1949–1954* (Honolulu: University of Hawaii Press, 2004); Eddy U, "The Making of *Zhishifenzi*: The Critical Impact of the Registration of Unemployed Intellectuals in the Early PRC," *China Quarterly* 173 (2003): 100–121.

15. On central policies and Mao, see *Jianguo yilai zhongyao wenxian xuanbian* (Selected important documents since the founding of the People's Republic of China) (Beijing: Zhongyang wenxian chubanshe, 1992–); and *Jianguo yilai Mao Zedong wengao* (Mao Zedong's manuscripts since the founding of the People's Republic of China) (Beijing: Zhongyang wenxian chubanshe, 1987–). For local military reports, see volumes from the *Zhongguo renmin jiefang jun lishi ziliao congshu* (Collection of historical materials on the People's Liberation Army) (Beijing: Jiefang jun chubanshe, 2002).

16. Chen Jian, *China's Road to the Korean War: The Making of the Sino-American Confrontation* (New York: Columbia University Press, 1994); and Chen Jian, *Mao's China and the Cold War* (Chapel Hill: University of North Carolina Press, 2001).

17. William C. Kirby, "Continuity and Change in Modern China: Economic Planning on the Mainland and on Taiwan, 1943–1958," *Australian Journal of Chinese Affairs* 24 (1990): 121–141. Recent works that cross the 1949 divide include Susan L. Glosser, *Chinese Visions of Family and State, 1915–1953* (Berkeley: University of California Press, 2003); Lü Xiaobo and Elizabeth J. Perry, eds., *Danwei: The Changing Chinese Workplace in Historical and Comparative Perspective* (Armonk, N.Y.:

M. E. Sharpe, 1997); and Mark W. Frazier, *The Making of the Chinese Industrial Workplace: State, Revolution, and Labor Management* (New York: Cambridge University Press, 2002).

18. "Emulating the Soviet Model, 1949–1957" is a section heading from the table of contents in MacFarquhar's *Cambridge History of China*, vol. 14, *The People's Republic, Part I.*

2. "Cleanup"

1. *Renmin ribao* (People's Daily), May 31, 1952, 1.

2. John Wilson Lewis, "Introduction: Order and Modernization in the Chinese City," in John Wilson Lewis, ed., *The City in Communist China* (Stanford: Stanford University Press, 1971), 2.

3. James Z. Gao, *The Communist Takeover of Hangzhou: The Transformation of City and Cadre, 1949–1954* (Honolulu: University of Hawaii Press, 2004), 11.

4. Bo Yibo's report was dated April 19, 1947. Other despoiled cities included Yuancheng, Handan, and Jiaozuo. Ibid., 15.

5. Ibid., 14.

6. Paraphrased from ibid., 14–15.

7. Ibid., 18–19.

8. Ibid., 17.

9. "Cuihui jiu jingcha jigou, baowei renmin zhengquan" (Smashing the old police organs, protecting the people's sovereignty), *Shanghai wenshi ziliao xuanji* 46 (1984): 104.

10. Ibid., 105.

11. Lewis, 2, 52.

12. Gao, 40. Li Zicheng overthrew the last Ming emperor but "lost the mandate" because his peasant troops could not accommodate themselves to the urban elites (and culture) of the capital.

13. *New York Times* (hereafter cited as NYT), April 19, 1949, 4.

14. There were four fundamental demands: (1) uncontested crossing of the Yangzi to establish bridgeheads at Jiangyin and Jinjiang, along with eight other places along a ninety-mile front west of Wuhu; (2) reorganization of all branches of the Nationalist Army into the People's Liberation Army; (3) eventual Communist occupation of all of China; and (4) Nanjing to serve only as a caretaker regime pending convocation of the Political Consultative Conference. Ibid.

15. NYT, April 20, 1949, 1.

16. Noel Barber, *The Fall of Shanghai* (New York: Coward, McCann and Geoghegan, 1979), 79–84.

17. NYT, April 21, 1949, 2:1.

18. E. R. Hooton, *The Greatest Tumult: The Chinese Civil War 1936–49* (London: Brassey's, 1991), 155.

19. NYT, April 21, 1949, 1; and April 24, 1949, 2.

20. NYT, April 25, 1949, 1.

21. NYT, April 24, 1949, 1.

22. Randall Gould, "Shanghai during the Takeover," *Annals of the American Academy of Political and Social Science* 277 (September 1951): 182–183, 193.

23. Mabel Waln Smith, *Springtime in Shanghai* (London: George G. Harrap and Co., 1957), 177.

24. NYT, April 25, 1949, 2.

25. Ibid.

26. NYT, April 27, 1949, 3.

27. Liu Feng, "Zai wei jingchaju li de douzheng" (The struggle in the collaborationist police force), *Wenshi ziliao xuanji (Shanghai jiefang sanshi zhounian zhuanji, shang)* (1979), 190–191. The total roster of twenty thousand included firemen, police, judicial police, and administration and general affairs personnel, plus the staff of twenty-eight precincts, two police stations, jails, police hospital, and police school. Lu Dagong, "Shanghai jingzheng daquan hui dao renmin shouli" (The authority of police administration in Shanghai returns to the hands of the people), *Shanghai wenshi ziliao xuanji* 37 (1981): 67–68.

28. Liu Feng, 178–179.

29. Wan Ren, "Guomindang Shanghai jingchaju li de dixia gongzuo" (Underground work in the police force of Guomindang Shanghai), *Shanghai wenshi ziliao xuanji* 44 (1983): 20.

30. Ibid.; Liu Feng, 180.

31. Liu Feng, 180.

32. Lu Dagong, 62.

33. Ibid., 62–63.

34. Wan Ren, 212–213.

35. Liu Feng, 191; "Cuihui jiu jingcha jigou," 107.

36. *Jiefang ribao* (Liberation Daily; hereafter cited as JFRB), Shanghai, June 3, 1949, in *Chinese Press Review* (hereafter cited as CPR) 904, June 3, 1949, 1–2.

37. Liu Feng, 191; "Cuihui jiu jingcha jigou," 106–107.

38. Lu Dagong, 63–65.

39. Gould, 183.

40. The PLA broke the Nationalists' defensive perimeter on May 23. Hooton, 157.

41. Percy Finch, *Shanghai and Beyond* (New York: Charles Scribner's Sons, 1953), 337–338; *China Daily*, February 12, 1987, 6.

42. Gao, 60.

43. Lynn Landman and Amos Landman, *Profile of Red China* (New York: Simon and Schuster, 1951), 18.

44. NYT, May 25, 1949, 1.

45. Lu Dagong, 63–64.

46. "Cuihui jiu jingcha jigou," 109–110, 112–113.

47. Lu Dagong, 65.

48. Ibid., 66–67; "Cuihui jiu jingcha jigou," 107.

49. "Cuihui jiu jingcha jigou," 108; one of the first discoveries Lu Dagong made after taking over the Shanghai police was nine bloody corpses of prominent political prisoners in the holding cell of the headquarters. He quickly moved to prevent other killings. Lu Dagong, 68–69.

50. Landman and Landman, 25.

51. Barber, 146–147; NYT, May 25, 1949, 1.

52. Robert Guillain, "China under the Red Flag," trans. L. F. Duchene, in Otto B. Van der Sprenkel, ed., *New China: Three Views* (London: Turnstile Press, 1950),

84; Paolo Rossi, *The Communist Conquest of Shanghai: A Warning to the West* (Denver: Twin Circle Publishing Company, 1970), 33.

53. Guillain, 84.

54. Interview with Sophie Souroujon, April 23, 2004.

55. Mariano Ezpeleta, *Red Shadows over Shanghai* (Quezon City: Zita Publishing Corporation, 1972), 185.

56. Gould, 184; interview with Joseph Chen, May 1970.

57. NYT, May 27, 1949, 4.

58. Finch, 339. See also Rossi, 14.

59. Guillain, 101.

60. The thousand or so Nationalists defending Broadway Mansions could have been subdued by the Communists in an hour if the latter had wanted to do so. But they decided not to because there were several hundred civilians in the buildings. Ezpeleta, 189.

61. NYT, May 26, 1949, 4; and May 25, 1949, 1.

62. Once they learned that the British-owned waterworks had also been taken, thousands of Shanghai residents pulled the plugs in their bathtubs. Now they felt that they could safely let their emergency reserve flow down the drain. NYT, May 28, 1949, 5.

63. Ibid.

64. *Dagong bao* estimated that only 20,000 Nationalists had escaped by sea, while 130,000 were left behind. An additional 330,000 Nationalist troops surrendered in Jiangsu and Zhejiang provinces. NYT, June 4, 1949, 4.

65. Lu Dagong, 69–70.

66. Gould, 184. See also Ezpeleta, 193.

67. "Cuihui jiu jingcha jigou," 113–115.

68. Lu Dagong, 70.

69. JFRB, June 9, 1949, in CPR 908, June 9, 1949, 9. Chen Yi had taken a degree in electrical engineering in France, where he also worked in the Michelin plant at Clermont-Ferrand. Barber, 161.

70. Henry Wei, *Courts and Police in Communist China to 1952*, Series 1, no. 1, 1952, of "Studies in Chinese Communism" (Lackland: Air Force Personnel and Training Research Center, December 1955), 48.

71. *Renmin ribao*, September 7, 1950, in Wei, 49, 51.

72. "Cuihui jiu jingcha jigou," 109.

73. *Shang bao* (Commerce News), Shanghai, June 7, 1949, in CPR 906, June 7, 1949, 10. Pan Hannian estimated that 70 to 80 percent of former Nationalist personnel continued to work in their jobs in Shanghai during the early years of the People's Republic of China (PRC). Marie-Claire Bergère and Wang Ju, "The Shanghai Federation of Industry and Commerce (SFIC) as an Instrument of the Chinese Communist Party United Front Policy (1949–1952)" (paper presented at the Conference on China's Mid-century Transitions, Harvard University, September 8–11, 1994), 5.

74. Pan Hannian had a reputation, as deputy mayor, of looking after *jiu renyuan* (old personnel), to whom he personally distributed maintenance allowances. Zhao Zukang, "Huiyi Pan Hannian tongzhi" (Recollecting Comrade Pan Hannian), *Shanghai wenshi ziliao xuanji* 42 (January 1983): 2–3.

75. Consular officials were concerned by "an ominous inability to establish contact with the incoming Communist officials. . . . Far from finding ourselves beset by a Gestapo, we could hardly locate officials of any sort." Gould, 184. The Russians closed their consulate on May 29 because the new regime had not officially recognized the Soviet Union. NYT, May 30, 1949, 1.

76. Guillain, 85–86.

77. *China Daily*, February 6, 1987, 6; *Robinhood* (tabloid), Shanghai, May 31, 1949, in CPR 901, May 29–31, 1949, 8.

78. *Dagong bao*, Shanghai, June 15, 1949, in CPR 912, June 15, 1949, 6.

79. Robert Loh and Humphrey Evans, *Escape from Red China* (New York: Coward-McCann, 1962), 149.

80. Finch, 340.

81. JFRB, May 28, 1949, in CPR 900, May 28, 1949, 2–3.

82. *Dagong bao*, May 26, 1949; *Shanghai renmin* (People of Shanghai), May 26, 1949; and JFRB, May 28, 1949, in CPR 899, May 25–27, 1949, 1, 3; and CPR 900, May 28, 1949, 2.

83. "Cuihui jiu jingcha jigou," 111–117.

84. Ezpeleta, 189, 194.

85. "Cuihui jiu jingcha jigou," 112.

86. John Gardner, "The *Wu-fan* Campaign in Shanghai: A Study in the Consolidation of Urban Control," in A. Doak Barnett, ed., *Chinese Communist Politics in Action* (Seattle: University of Washington Press, 1969), 477.

87. Matsumura Shiho, "Kenkoku shoki (1949–1952) ni okeru toshi jūmin no tōki kōsaku—Chūgoku tōshi jūmin no ryūdōsei to hensei genri" (The registration of urban residents during the initial establishment of the government [1949–1952]—the fluid nature and the principles of organization of China's urban residents) (unpublished paper, Tokyo, 2000), 12. The Communist Party was also much influenced by the passbook system introduced to them by Soviet advisers. A. Doak Barnett, *Communist China: The Early Years, 1949–55* (New York: Frederick A. Praeger, 1964), 645.

88. Gong Xikui, "Household Registration and the Caste-like Quality of Peasant Life," in Michael Dutton, ed., *Streetlife China* (Cambridge: Cambridge University Press, 1998), 81–82.

89. *Fei bao* (tabloid), Shanghai, June 8, 1949, in CPR 907, June 8, 1949, 9.

90. Lynn T. White III, "Deviance, Modernization, Rations, and Household Registers in Urban China," in Amy Auerbacher Wilson, Sidney Leonard Greenblatt, and Richard Whittingham Wilson, eds., *Deviance and Social Control in Chinese Society* (New York: Praeger, 1977), 155.

91. Ibid., 157–158.

92. *Shanghai News*, July 23, 1950, 2.

93. Gardner, 496.

94. This was intended to give the police time to check their original Nationalist identity cards before issuing new household certificates. JFRB, June 9, 1949, in CPR 908, June 9, 1949, 9.

95. *Dagong bao*, June 15, 1949, in CPR 912, June 15, 1949, 6–7.

96. JFRB, September 13, 1950, 2, 6.

97. White, 159.

98. JFRB, September 13, 1950, 2, 6.

99. Ibid.

100. Ibid.

101. Ibid.

102. Frederic Wakeman, "Licensing Leisure: The Chinese Nationalists' Attempt to Regulate Shanghai, 1927–49," *Journal of Asian Studies* 54.1 (February 1995): 19–42.

103. *Dagong bao*, May 29, 1949, in CPR 901, May 29–31, 1949, 14–15.

104. JFRB, June 16, 1949, in CPR 913, June 16, 1949, 10; JFRB, June 25, 1949, in CPR 922, June 29, 1949, 13.

105. See Wen-hsin Yeh, *The Alienated Academy: Culture and Politics in Republican China, 1919–1937* (Cambridge, Mass.: Council on East Asian Studies, Harvard University, 1990).

106. Gail Hershatter, "Regulating Sex in Shanghai: The Reform of Prostitution in 1920 and 1951," in Frederic Wakeman Jr. and Wen-hsin Yeh, eds., *Shanghai Sojourners* (Berkeley: Institute of East Asian Studies, University of California, 1992), 145–185; "Cuihui jiu jingcha jigou," 114; Christian Henriot, "'La Ferméture': The Abolishing of Prostitution in Shanghai, 1949–1958," *China Quarterly* 142 (June 1995): 467–486; Wei, 30; *Dagong bao*, June 27, 1949, in CPR 921, June 28, 1949, 9.

107. Guillain, 103; NYT, June 12, 1949, 26.

108. "Cuihui jiu jingcha jigou," 113.

109. JFRB, June 3, 1949, in CPR 904, June 3, 1949, 1–2; *Dagong bao*, June 8, 1949, in CPR 907, June 8, 1949, 2. Between May 2 and June 6, 1949, the general cost-of-living index more than doubled. With the year 1936 as a base of 100, the index was 42,373 on May 2 and 90,380 on June 6, according to Nanjing University statisticians. NYT, June 12, 1949, 26.

110. "Cuihui jiu jingcha jigou," 114; *Xinwen ribao* (News Daily), June 30, 1949, in CPR 923, June 30, 1949, 3.

111. Jerome Alan Cohen, *The Criminal Process in the People's Republic of China, 1949–1963, an Introduction* (Cambridge, Mass.: Harvard University Press, 1968), 10.

112. From 1949 to 1957, Shanghai sent more than one million people to live and work elsewhere. Barnett, *Communist China*, 662.

113. *Dagong bao*, December 17, 1949, in CPR 1043, December 17, 1949, 5; JFRB, January 18, 1950, 9–10. Most of the "loafers" were turned in by their neighbors. Cohen, 243.

114. JFRB, January 5, 1950, in CPR 1057, January 5, 1950, 10.

115. Mu, Fusheng (pseud.), *The Wilting of the Hundred Flowers: The Chinese Intelligentsia under Mao* (New York: Frederick A. Praeger, 1963), 178–180; Cohen, 240–241.

116. JFRB, September 14, 1950, 2.

117. Andre Bonnichon, *Law in Communist China* (The Hague: International Commission of Jurists, 1956), 4; Guillain, 91.

118. Peng said, at a meeting of the Administration Council on May 11, 1951, that there should be no hurry to establish "complete and detailed" codes, which were "neither mature nor urgently necessary." By 1955, there was yet no civil or criminal code enacted by the new regime. Wei, 10.

119. Ibid., 19. Only when the judicial reform of 1952–53 took place and the courts were purged of holdovers from the Nationalist government did the Communist Party feel confident about using the regular court system. Cohen, 9–10.

120. Bonnichon, 4, 6–7, 14–15; Guillain, 105–106.

121. Bonnichon, 8.

122. Ibid., 7.

123. *Shang bao*, June 16, 1949, in CPR 913, June 16, 1949, 7.

124. JFRB, June 18, 1949, in CPR 915, June 18–20, 1949, 7.

125. Wei, 12.

126. Ibid., 53.

127. Ibid., 50.

128. Ibid., 16.

129. JFRB, October 21, 1949, in CPR 996, October 21, 1949, 5.

130. JFRB, October 19, 1949, in CPR 994, October 19, 1949, 9.

131. "Cuihui jiu jingcha jigou," 113–116; *Dagong bao*, June 8, 1949, in CPR 907, June 8, 1949, 2; and JFRB, June 15, 1949, in CPR 912, June 15, 1949, 6.

132. "Cuihui jiu jingcha jigou," 113; JFRB, June 15, 1949, in CPR 912, June 15, 1949, 2.

133. *Dagong bao*, June 25, 1949, in CPR 921, June 28, 1949, 9, and *Dagong bao*, June 29, 1949, in CPR 922, June 29, 1949, 9. See also Guillain, 104.

134. *Dagong bao*, September 19, 1949, in CPR 974, September 20, 1949, 7–8.

135. JFRB, February 1, 1950, in CPR 1081, February 1, 1950, 8.

136. The Chinese press claimed that Nationalist secret service agents were using Shanghai as a liaison point to assemble stragglers in the Songjiang area to form an "advanced army of the National Defense Ministry in the Jiangsu Zhejiang border area." *Xinwen ribao*, August 20, 1949, in CPR 955, August 23, 1949, 7.

137. Otto Vander Sprenkel, "Part One," in Otto B. Vander Sprenkel, ed., *New China: Three Views* (London: Turnstile Press, 1950), 21; JFRB, January 18, 1950, 9.

138. JFRB, November 2, 1949, in CPR 1006, November 2, 1949, 9.

139. JFRB, September 15, 1949, in CPR 971, September 15, 1949, 7–8; *Dagong bao*, September 18, 1949, in CPR 972, 11; JFRB, October 18, 1949, in CPR 993, October 18, 1949, 6–7; JFRB, September 14, 1949, in CPR 970, September 14, 1949, 6.

140. JFRB, October 17, 1949, in CPR 992, October 16–17, 1949, 6–7.

141. "Cuihui jiu jingcha jigou," 117.

142. Ibid., 116–118; Zhu Baohe, ed., *Shanghai shi Baoshan xian zhi* (Baoshan county gazetteer) (Shanghai: Shanghai renmin chubanshe, 1992), 722.

143. *Dagong bao*, June 8, 1949, in CPR 907, June 8, 1949, 8.

144. JFRB, June 15, 1949, in CPR 912, June 15, 1949, 1.

145. See, for example, JFRB, June 24, 1949, in CPR 919, June 24, 1949, 7.

146. JFRB, July 1, 1949, in CPR 924, July 1, 1949, 8.

147. JFRB, June 29, 1949, in CPR 922, June 29, 1949, 7, and JFRB, June 30, 1949, in CPR 923, June 30, 1949, 7. Andrew Walder writes, "The ubiquitous theme of conspiracy has too long been discounted. . . . If we recognize the centrality of the theme of conspiracy and betrayal, we are led inevitably to a doctrinal source for the Cultural Revolution that is central to the political tradition that Maoists have long been understood to repudiate. For the theme of hidden conspiracy . . . is borrowed directly . . . from the Stalinist political culture of the era of mass liquidations and show trials." See Walder, "Cultural Revolution Radicalism: Variations on a Stalinist Theme," in William A. Joseph, Christine P. W. Wong, and David Zweig, eds., *New Perspectives on the Cultural Revolution* (Cambridge, Mass.: Council on East Asian Studies, Harvard University, 1991), 43.

148. JFRB, October 26, 1949, in CPR 1000, October 26, 1949, 10.

149. JFRB, November 23, 1949, in CPR 1023, November 23, 1949.

150. JFRB, October 16, 1949, in CPR 1000, October 26, 1949, 10.

151. JFRB, November 23, 1949, in CPR 1023, November 23, 1949.

152. *Dagong bao*, September 6, 1949, in CPR 964, September 3–6, 1949, 11.

153. JFRB, October 19, 1949, in CPR 1006, November 2, 1949, 9.

154. *Xinwen ribao*, November 24, 1949, in CPR 1024, November 24–25, 1949, 9.

155. *Dagong bao*, November 9, 1949, 2, in CPR 1012, November 9, 1949, 6.

156. JFRB, December 31, 1949, in CPR 1054, December 31, 1949, 5–6.

157. Chen Jian, *China's Road to the Korean War: The Making of the Sino-American Confrontation* (New York: Columbia University Press, 1994), 220.

158. U.S. Department of State, "The Hate America Campaign in Communist China" (Washington, D.C., 1953), 13–14.

159. Wei, 29.

160. *Zhonghua renmin gongheguo youguan gongan gongzuo fagui huibian, 1949.10–1956.6* (Collection of laws and regulations of the People's Republic of China concerning public security work, October 1949–June 1957) (Beijing: Qunzhong chubanshe, 1958), 2–7; Cohen, 299–302.

161. Gardner, 496.

162. Zhao Zukang, 3–4.

163. New China News Agency, Shanghai, June 17, 1951, 14; Wei, 39; Harriet C. Mills, "Thought Reform: Ideological Remolding in China," *Atlantic* 204.6 (December 1959): 76.

164. Zhang Jishun, "Shanghai *lilong*" (Neighborhood lanes), trans. Ma Xiaohe (unpublished paper, Center for Chinese Studies, University of California, Berkeley, 1994), 32–33.

165. Ibid., 32.

166. See, for the "constructivist approach," S. N. Eisenstadt, *Paradoxes of Democracy: Fragility, Continuity, and Change* (Baltimore: Johns Hopkins University Press, 1999), 33.

167. *Shanghai News*, December 27, 1951, 4.

168. Ibid.

169. Eisenstadt, 38.

170. Ibid., 40.

3. Masters of the Country?

1. Shen Han, "Huiyi Shanghai renmin baoandui" (Remembering the Shanghai People's Peace Preservation Corps), *Shanghai gongyun shiliao* 3 (1984): 16–20; Shanghai Municipal Archives (hereafter cited as SMA), C1-1-32.

2. Charles Hoffman, *The Chinese Worker* (Albany: State University of New York Press, 1974); William Brugger, *Democracy and Organization in the Chinese Industrial Enterprise, 1949–1953* (Cambridge: Cambridge University Press, 1976); Stephen Andors, *China's Industrial Revolution: Politics, Planning and Management, 1949 to the Present* (London: Martin Robinson, 1977); Andrew G. Walder, *Communist Neo-Traditionalism: Work and Authority in Chinese Industry* (Berkeley: University of California Press, 1986); Dorothy Kaple, *Dream of a Red Factory: The Legacy of High Stalinism in China* (Oxford: Oxford University Press, 1994); and Mark W. Frazier,

The Making of the Chinese Industrial Workplace: State, Revolution and Labor Management (Cambridge: Cambridge University Press, 2002). A work that does deal with activism outside the factory is Jackie Sheehan, *Chinese Workers: A New History* (London: Routledge, 1998), but Sheehan's treatment of the early years of the People's Republic is brief.

3. Shanghai zonggonghui mishuchu, ed., *Jiefanghou Shanghai gongyun ziliao* (Material on the post-liberation Shanghai labor movement) (Shanghai: Laodong chubanshe, 1950), 149–156. In a speech in 1950 at a national conference of labor bureau directors, Minister of Labor Li Lisan gave an even higher figure, stating that in the fifteen biggest Chinese cities, from June to December 1949, a total of 7,021 labor disputes had taken place—of which 4,436 were in Shanghai. SMA, C1-2-250. The reason for the discrepancy between Li's figures and those compiled by the union is unclear, but Li may have been referring to a wider range of conflicts that went beyond what the union classified as "major disturbances."

4. Elizabeth J. Perry, *Shanghai on Strike: The Politics of Chinese Labor* (Stanford: Stanford University Press, 1993).

5. In the entire year of 1919, Shanghai experienced only 59 strikes, 33 of which were connected with May Fourth. In 1925, Shanghai witnessed 175 strikes, 100 of which were in conjunction with May Thirtieth. These figures are drawn from Shanghai Bureau of Social Affairs, ed., *Strikes and Lockouts in Shanghai, 1918–1932* (Shanghai: City Government of Shanghai, 1933), and *Shehui yuekan* (Society Monthly), a publication of the Shanghai Bureau of Social Affairs, for subsequent years.

6. "Shanghai shi zonggonghui chou siqi bu sanyue lai de gongzuo zongjie" (Summary of work for the past three months by the Shanghai municipal federation of trade unions preparatory private enterprise department), 1949, in SMA.

7. Ibid.

8. "Guanyu geji gonghui taolun he chuanda 'Shenqi shijian de jiaoxun' de tongzhi" (Notice concerning the discussion and distribution of "lessons of the Shen Seven incident" for all levels of the union), *Shanghai gongyun ziliao* 1 (March 15, 1950): 9–20.

9. This case is described in SMA, C1-2-41.

10. The following case appeared in *Jiefang ribao* (Liberation Daily), April 9, 1951, and was reprinted in *Tewu pohuai gongchang de zuixing* (Crimes of secret agents destroying factories) (Shanghai: Huadong renmin chubanshe, 1951), 8–13.

11. Elizabeth J. Perry, *Patrolling the Revolution: Worker Militias, Citizenship and State-Building in Modern China* (Lanham: Rowman and Littlefield, 2006), chapter 3.

12. *Shanghai shi laodong ju gongzuo baogao* (Work report of the Shanghai Labor Bureau), 1952; courtesy of SFTU.

13. The Dadong case is drawn from Zhang Jinping, "Dadong yanchang shijian de zhenxiang" (The truth about the Dadong Tobacco Factory affair), n.d.; courtesy of SFTU.

14. The collection *Tewu pohuai gongchang de zuixing* (1951) provides information on ten major cases of "secret agent" agitation in Shanghai factories; in seven of the ten cases, former militiamen are depicted as having played key roles in instigating the conflicts.

15. SMA, C1-2-240.

16. Zou Pei and Liu Zhen, *Zhongguo gongren yundong shihua* (Historical tales of the Chinese labor movement) (Beijing: Zhongguo gongren chubanshe, 1993), 1: 217–218.

17. Zhongguo renmin zhengzhi xieshang huiyi Shanghai shi weiyuanhui wenshi ziliao weiyuan hui and Shanghai zhengxie zhi you she, eds., *Guanghui licheng* (Glorious course) (Shanghai: Shanghai shi zhengxie wenshi ziliao bianji bu, 1996), 255; Shen Han, 16–20; Zhu Hua, *Shanghai yibai nian* (Shanghai century) (Shanghai: Shanghai renmin chubanshe, 1999), 290.

18. Shanghai di yi mianfang zhichang gongren yundong shi bianxiezu, ed., *Shanghai Di yi mianfang zhichang gongren yundong shi* (History of the labor movement in the Shanghai Number One Cotton Spinning and Weaving Mill) (Beijing: Zhong gong dang shi chubanshe, 1997), 163–177.

19. SMA, C1-2-163; Li Jiaqi, ed., *Shanghai gongyun zhi* (Shanghai labor movement gazetteer) (Shanghai: Shanghai shehui kexue yuan chubanshe, 1997), 430.

20. SMA, Q6-31-566.

21. SMA, C1-1-16; Zhang Jinping, "Baiwan zhigong touru baowei da Shanghai de zhandou" (A million workers join the battle to defend greater Shanghai), in Jiang Zhizhong, ed., *Jingbei da Shanghai* (Guarding greater Shanghai) (Shanghai: Shanghai yuandong chubanshe, 1994), 181.

22. Zhang Qi, "Ji Shanghai renmin baoandui" (A record of the Shanghai People's Peace Preservation Corps), in Shanghai renmin jiefang jun Shanghai jingbeiqu, Zhong gong Shanghai shiwei dang shi ziliao zhengji weiyuanhui, eds., *Shanghai zhanyi* (The battle of Shanghai) (Shanghai: Xuelin chubanshe, 1989), 219.

23. Paul Harper, "The Party and the Unions in Communist China," *China Quarterly* 37 (January–March 1969): 84–119.

24. SMA, C-2-499.

25. "Shanghai zonggonghui jiucha bu guanyu jiefang qianhou zhigong douzheng qingkuang de baogao" (Report of the picket department of the Shanghai Federation of Trade Unions concerning the struggle situation of workers before and after liberation), in SMA, ed., *Shanghai jiefang* (The liberation of Shanghai) (Beijing: Dang'an chubanshe, 1989), 142.

26. David Michael Finkenstein, *Washington's Taiwan Dilemma, 1949–1950* (Fairfax, Va.: George Mason University, 1993), 292–294; and Robert Accinelli, *Crisis and Commitment: U.S. Policy toward Taiwan, 1950–1955* (Chapel Hill: University of North Carolina Press, 1996), 16, 272.

27. SMA, B120-1-69; Jiang Yi, *Chen Yi zai Shanghai* (Chen Yi in Shanghai) (Beijing: Zhong gong dang shi chubanshe, 1992), 92–95. See Dangdai Zhongguo congshu bianji bu, ed., *Dangdai Zhongguo minbing* (Militias in contemporary China) (Beijing: Zhongguo shehui kexue chubanshe, 1989), 343.

28. Zhang Jinping, "Baiwan zhigong touru," 182.

29. *Shanghai gongyun shi ziliao* 13 (February 28, 1951): 25–26.

30. Zhang Jinping, "Baiwan zhigong touru," 183–184; SMA, C1-1-54.

31. Zhang Jinping, "Baiwan zhigong touru," 184.

32. Ibid., 187–189; SMA, C1-1-60.

33. Li Jiaqi, *Shanghai gongyun zhi*, 419.

34. Zhang Jinping, "Baiwan zhigong touru," 189.

35. SMA, Q0-4(5)-25.

36. SMA, C1-1-54, C1-2-397, C1-2-489.

37. SMA, C1-2-363.

38. SMA, C1-2-491.

39. SMA, C1-2-458.

40. Between January 11 and February 22, 1951, among the 3,341 counterrevolutionaries registered at Shanghai's privately owned factories were 1,643 former Industry Defense Corps members. SMA, C1-2-483 and Q6-31-265.

41. SMA, C1-2-458.

42. SMA, B127-1-1186.

43. Tang Chunliang, *Li Lisan zhuan* (Biography of Li Lisan) (Harbin: Heilongjiang renmin chubanshe, 1989), 150.

44. Elizabeth J. Perry, "Labor's Love Lost: Worker Militancy in Communist China," *International Labor and Working-Class History* 50 (Fall 1996): 64–76.

45. SMA, C1-2-397.

46. SMA, C1-2-487.

47. SMA, Q6-31-566.

48. SMA, C1-2-680.

49. Li Sishen and Liu Zhikun, *Li Lisan zhi mi* (The riddle of Li Lisan) (Beijing: Renmin chubanshe, 2005), chapter 11.

50. SMA, C1-2-680.

51. SMA, C1-2-646.

52. Li Jiaqi, *Shanghai gongyun zhi*, 432.

53. Frederick C. Teiwes, *Politics at Mao's Court: Gao Gang and Party Factionalism in the Early 1950s* (Armonk, N.Y.: M. E. Sharpe, 1990), 184–185.

54. SMA, B54-4; Elizabeth J. Perry, "Shanghai's 1957 Strike Wave," *China Quarterly* 137 (March 1994): 1–27.

55. Perry, *Patrolling the Revolution*, chapter 5.

56. *Renmin ribao* (People's Daily), September 22, 1949.

57. Li Sishen and Liu Zhikun, chapter 10.

58. Tang Chunliang, 153.

59. Harper, 96. See also Sheehan, chapter 1.

60. Li Jiaqi, "Wushi niandai chu pipan gonghui de 'jingjizhuyi,' 'gongtuanzhuyi,' jiqi zai Shanghai de yingxiang" (The early 1950s critique of "economism" and "syndicalism" and its influence on Shanghai), *Shanghai gongyun shi* 6 (1986): 1–7; Tang Chunliang, 144–154.

61. Robert E. Bedeski, *State-Building in Modern China: The Kuomintang in the Prewar Period* (Berkeley: University of California Institute of East Asian Studies, 1981); Bruce J. Dickson, *Democratization in China and Taiwan: The Adaptability of Leninist Parties* (Oxford: Oxford University Press, 1997); William C. Kirby, "The Chinese Party-State under Dictatorship and Democracy on the Mainland and on Taiwan," in William C. Kirby, ed., *Realms of Freedom in Modern China* (Stanford: Stanford University Press, 2004), 113–138.

4. New Democracy and the Demise of Private Charity in Shanghai

1. For example, Joseph W. Esherick, "Ten Theses on the Chinese Revolution," and Paul A. Cohen, "Reflections on a Watershed Date: The 1949 Divide in Chinese History," in Jeffrey N. Wasserstrom, ed., *Twentieth Century China: New Approaches* (New York: Routledge, 2003).

2. William P. Kirby, "Continuity and Change in Modern China: Economic Planning on the Mainland and on Taiwan, 1943–1958," *Australian Journal of Chinese Affairs* 24 (1990): 121–141; Susan Glosser, *Chinese Visions of Family and State, 1915–1953* (Berkeley: University of California Press, 2001); Gail Hershatter, *Dangerous Pleasures: Prostitution and Modernity in Twentieth Century Shanghai* (Berkeley: University of California Press, 1997); Mark Frazier, *The Making of the Chinese Industrial Workplace: State, Revolution and Labor Management* (Cambridge: Cambridge University Press, 2002); and Elizabeth J. Perry and Lu Xiaobo, eds., *Danwei: The Changing Chinese Workplace in Historical and Comparative Perspective* (Armonk, N.Y.: M. E. Sharpe, 1997).

3. Mao Tse-tung, *On New Democracy* (Peking: Foreign Languages Press, 1967), 7–10.

4. Lu Zhiren, "Nanmin gongzuo" (Refugee work), in Zhong gong Shanghai dang shi ziliao zhengji weiyuanhui, ed., *Kangzhan chuqi de nanmin gongzuo* (Refugee work at the beginning of the war of resistance) (Shanghai: Shanghai xinwen chubanju, 1993), 7; and Patricia Stranahan, "Radicalization of Refugees: Communist Party Activity in Wartime Shanghai's Displaced Person's Camps," *Modern China* 26.2 (2000): 176.

5. Zhong gong daibiaotuan zhu Hu banshichu jinianguan, ed., *Zhongguo jiefangqu jiuji zonghui zai Shanghai* (The Chinese Liberated Areas Relief Commission's central office in Shanghai) (Shanghai: Xuelin chubanshe, 1996), 2; Dong Biwu, "Zhu Zhongguo fuli hui chengli ershi zhounian" (Celebrating the China Welfare Foundation's twentieth anniversary), in *Dong Biwu xuanji* (Selected works of Dong Biwu) (Beijing: Renmin chubanshe, 1985), 475.

6. Tony Saich, *The Rise to Power of the Chinese Communist Party: Documents and Analysis* (Armonk, N.Y.: M. E. Sharpe, 1996), 1236–1237.

7. Kenneth Lieberthal, "Mao vs. Liu? Policy towards Industry and Commerce, 1946–1949," *China Quarterly* 47 (July–September 1971): 519.

8. Saich, 1201.

9. Zhu Hua, *Shanghai yibai nian* (Shanghai century) (Shanghai: Shanghai renmin chubanshe, 1999), 291.

10. *Shanghai shi zhengquan xitong, difang junshi xitong, tongyi zhanxian xitong, qunzhong tuanti xitong zuzhi shi ziliao* (Materials on the organizational history of the Shanghai municipal political system, local military system, United Front system, and mass association system) (Shanghai: Shanghai renmin chubanshe, 1991), 504–505; and Ma Yili and Liu Hanbang, eds., *Shanghai shehui tuanti gailan* (Directory of Shanghai's social organizations) (Shanghai: Shanghai renmin chubanshe, 1993), 8.

11. Xiong Yuezhi, ed., *Shanghai tongshi: Minguo zhengzhi* (General history of Shanghai: Republican politics) (Shanghai: Shanghai renmin chubanshe, 1999), 7:444; *Shanghai shi zhengquan xitong*, 504–505.

12. Zhu Hua, 270.

13. Li Jiaqi, ed., *Shanghai gongyun zhi* (Shanghai labor movement gazetteer) (Shanghai: Shanghai shehui kexue yuan chubanshe, 1997), 13.

14. The obvious exception to this policy was organizations affiliated with the Nationalists, including militia and underground operatives, which the Communists moved against immediately. Heterodox religious sects such as the Yiguandao were also banned. See Zou Ronggeng, "Zongshu" (Summary), in Zhong gong

Shanghai shiwei dang shi yanjiushi, eds., *Shanghai jiefang chuqi* (The early days of the liberation of Shanghai) (Shanghai: Zhong gong dang shi chubanshe, 1999); Ma Yili and Liu Hanbang, 8; and Liu Songbin, *Zhongguo gongchandang dui da chengshi de jieguan, 1945–1952* (The Chinese Communist Party's takeover of major cities, 1945–1952) (Beijing: Beijing tushuguan chubanshe, 1997), 7.

15. Zhang Yongnian, "Jieguan Shanghai shi qu zhengquan jigou huigu" (Remembering the takeover of Shanghai's political organizations), in Shi Hongxi, ed., *Jieguan Shanghai qinli ji* (Personal memoirs of the takeover of Shanghai) (Shanghai: Shanghai shi zhengxie wenshi ziliao bianji bu, 1997), 122; and Shanghai Municipal Archives (hereafter cited as SMA), B168-1-796, B168-1-797, B168-1-798.

16. Ma Yili and Liu Hanbang, 8.

17. *Jiefang ribao* (Liberation Daily; hereafter cited as JFRB), October 10, 1950.

18. "Monism" refers to a political regime in which the only intermediate bodies allowed to exist between state and society are a limited number of state-sponsored mass associations, typically labor unions, peasant associations, women's federations, youth leagues, and sometimes business federations. Vladimir Lenin famously referred to these associations as the "transmission belts" between the party and the people. Juan J. Linz, "Totalitarian and Authoritarian Regimes," in Fred I. Greenstein and Nelson Polsby, eds., *Handbook of Political Science* (Reading, Mass.: Addison-Wesley, 1975), 3:277. For treatment of the elite in the Russian Revolution, see Sheila Fitzpatrick, *The Russian Revolution 1917–1932* (Oxford: Oxford University Press, 1982), 70–74; Richard Sakwa, *Soviet Communists in Power: A Study of Moscow during the Civil War, 1918–21* (London: Macmillan Press, 1988), 14–22; and Dmitri Volkogonov, *Lenin: A New Biography* (New York: Free Press, 1994), 375. My thanks to Douglas Stiffler for pointing me to this latter reference.

19. SMA, B168-1-501, 7.

20. Ibid., 5.

21. Ibid., 10–12.

22. The Nationalists issued regulations in 1946 to establish a Social Welfare Association in every city, county, and province, composed of private charities. See *Shehui yuekan* 1.3 (1946): 87–88.

23. *Renmin ribao* (People's Daily), May 5, 1950.

24. Dong Biwu, 288–289.

25. Ibid., 287.

26. JFRB, October 7, 1950.

27. Zhao Puchu, "Kangzhan chuqi de Shanghai nanmin gongzuo" (Refugee work in Shanghai at the beginning of the War of Resistance), in *Kangzhan chuqi de nanmin gongzuo*, 26; Wang Yaoshan, "Daixu" (Preface), in *Kangzhan chuqi de nanmin gongzuo*, 5.

28. JFRB, October 6, 1950.

29. JFRB, October 10, 1950.

30. Ibid.

31. Ibid.

32. SMA, Q118-1-7, 84–86.

33. SMA, B168-1-796, 19.

34. Xu Xiaoqun, *Chinese Professionals and the Republican State: The Rise of Professional Associations in Shanghai 1912–1937* (Cambridge: Cambridge University Press, 2001), 100–102.

35. Ma Yili and Liu Hanbang, 9.

36. Julia C. Strauss, "Paternalist Terror: The Campaign to Suppress Counter-revolutionaries and Regime Consolidation in the People's Republic of China, 1950–1953," *Comparative Studies in Society and History* 44 (January 2002): 80–105; Qian Daming, "Shanghai jiefang chuqi de zhenya fangeming yundong" (The Campaign to Suppress Counterrevolutionaries in the early days of the liberation of Shanghai), in Li Zhuanhua, ed., *Shanghai jiefang chuqi de shehui gaizao* (Social reform in the early days of the liberation of Shanghai) (Beijing: Zhong gong dang shi chubanshe, 1999), 72.

37. Qian Daming, 73–76.

38. JFRB, December 31, 1950.

39. JFRB, January 19, 1951.

40. Ma Yili and Liu Hanbang, 9.

41. JFRB, February 22, 1950.

42. JFRB, March 28, 1951.

43. SMA, B168-1-509.

44. SMA, B168-1-240, 20.

45. JFRB, November 21, 1950.

46. Shanghai shi bianzhi weiyuanhui bangongshi, ed., *Shanghai dangzheng jigou yange 1949–1986* (Development of Shanghai's party and government organizations) (Shanghai: Shanghai renmin chubanshe, 1988), 17.

47. Shanghai zonggonghui, *Liangnian lai de Shanghai gongren yundong* (The Shanghai labor movement during the past two years) (Shanghai: Shanghai zonggonghui, 1951), 9.

48. Bo Yibo, *Ruogan zhongda juece yu shijian de huigu* (Remembering some major policy decisions and events) (Beijing: Zhong gong zhongyang dangxiao chubanshe, 1991), 1:139–140.

49. Zhu Hua, 320; John Gardner, "The Wu-fan Campaign in Shanghai: A Study of the Consolidation of Urban Control," in A. Doak Barnett, ed., *Chinese Communist Politics in Action* (Seattle: University of Washington Press, 1969), 503, 505.

50. SMA, B168-1-240, 20.

51. Ibid., 23.

52. Zhu Hua, 321.

53. Bo Yibo, 1:164.

54. Gardner, 510–513.

55. Bo Yibo, 1:170–172.

56. SMA, B168-1-240, 20–21, 23, 31.

57. Bo Yibo, 1:168–169.

58. Ibid., 1:170.

59. Zhong gong Shanghai shi zuzhi bu, *Zhongguo gongchandang Shanghai shi zuzhi shi ziliao* (Sources on the history of the Chinese Communist Party's Shanghai municipal organization) (Shanghai: Shanghai renmin chubanshe, 1991), 419.

60. Lyman P. Van Slyke, *Enemies and Friends: The United Front in Chinese Communist History* (Stanford: Stanford University Press, 1967), 232–233.

61. Bo Yibo, 1:174–175.

62. Gardner, 520; and Robert Loh and Humphrey Evans, *Escape from Red China* (New York: Coward-McCann, 1962), 100.

63. Lynn T. White III, *Policies of Chaos: The Organizational Causes of Violence in China's Cultural Revolution* (Princeton: Princeton University Press, 1989), 71–75.

64. SMA, B168-1-240, 24.

65. Ibid., 27–28.

66. Ibid., 26.

67. Ibid., 26–28.

68. SMA, B168-1-506, 23.

69. Ma Yili and Liu Hanbang, 10.

70. SMA, B168-1-805, 9.

71. SMA, Q118-2-25; Xiong Yuezhi, ed., *Lao Shanghai: Ming ren, ming shi, ming wu* (Old Shanghai: Famous people, famous events, famous things) (Shanghai: Shanghai renmin chubanshe, 1997), 350.

72. Ma Yili and Liu Hanbang, 10.

73. SMA, B168-1-805, 5.

74. Ma Yili and Liu Hanbang, 11.

75. SMA, B168-1-506, 26–27; and Human Rights Watch/Asia, *Death by Default: A Policy of Fatal Neglect in China's State Orphanages* (New York: Human Rights Watch, 1996), 118.

76. SMA, B168-1-817, 28. These procedures included filing a petition to disband with the Bureau of Civil Affairs and publishing legal notices in the newspapers.

77. *Shanghai weisheng 1949–1983* (Public health in Shanghai, 1949–1983) (Shanghai: Shanghai kexue jishu chubanshe, 1986), 677.

78. SMA, B168-1-817, 27.

79. Frederick C. Teiwes, *Politics at Mao's Court: Party Factionalism in the Early 1950s* (Armonk, N.Y.: M. E. Sharpe, 1990), 121.

80. Zhu Hua, 325.

81. Roderick MacFarquhar, *Origins of the Cultural Revolution: Contradictions among the People 1956–1957* (New York: Columbia University Press, 1974), 1: 19–20.

82. Ibid., 1:21–22.

83. Zhu Hua, 329.

84. Human Rights Watch/Asia, 118.

85. *Shanghai weisheng*, 677.

86. SMA, B168-1-817, 27.

87. Roderick MacFarquhar, *The Hundred Flowers Campaign and the Chinese Intellectuals* (New York: Praeger, 1960), 202.

88. Ibid., 273; and Frederick C. Teiwes, *Politics and Purges in China: Rectification and the Decline of Party Norms, 1950–1965* (White Plains, N.Y.: M. E. Sharpe, 1979), 268.

89. This interpretation agrees with Kenneth Lieberthal's argument that the Three-Anti and Five-Anti campaigns constituted a second revolution. See Kenneth G. Lieberthal, *Revolution and Tradition in Tientsin, 1949–1952* (Stanford: Stanford University Press, 1980).

5. From Resisting Communists to Resisting America

1. All information about Li Huaguo is from 511th Military Intelligence Service Co., Interrogation Report No. KG 1342, November 1952; Allied Translator and

Interpreter Service (hereafter cited as ATIS) Interrogation Reports, File 950054, Box 336; Intelligence Document File Publications ("950000" File) 1947–62; Assistant Chief of Staff, G-2 (Intelligence); Records of the Army Staff, 1903–92, Record Group 319; National Archives at College Park, Md. (hereafter cited as NACP).

2. He Changfeng et al., eds., *Guizhou dangdai shi* (Contemporary history of Guizhou) (Chongqing: Xinan shifan daxue chubanshe, 1995), 22.

3. Over two-thirds of the more than twenty-one thousand Chinese prisoners chose Taiwan over mainland China. See Philip West with Li Zhihua, "Interior Stories of the Chinese POWs in the Korean War," in Philip West and Ji-moon Suh, eds., *Remembering the "Forgotten War": The Korean War through Literature and Art* (Armonk, N.Y.: M. E. Sharpe, 2001), 152–186.

4. Cheng and Selden call the early 1950s the "honeymoon years of the People's Republic." Tiejun Cheng and Mark Selden, "The Origins and Consequences of China's Hukou System," *China Quarterly* 139 (September 1994): 646.

5. Joseph W. Esherick, "War and Revolution: Chinese Society during the 1940s," *Twentieth Century China* 27.1 (November 2001): 26.

6. James Z. Gao, *The Communist Takeover of Hangzhou: The Transformation of City and Cadre, 1949–1954* (Honolulu: University of Hawaii Press, 2004).

7. Julia C. Strauss, "Paternalist Terror: The Campaign to Suppress Counter-revolutionaries and Regime Consolidation in the People's Republic of China, 1950–1953," *Comparative Studies in Society and History* 44 (January 2002): 80–105.

8. Fang Shixin, "Yi jinjun da xinan de Guizhou ganbu dui" (Remembering the Guizhou Cadre Team advancing to the great southwest), in Zou xiang da xinan bianweihui, ed., *Zou xiang da xinan* (Heading for the great southwest) (Chengdu: Sichuan kexue jishu chubanshe, 1989), 25. Thanks to James Gao for sharing this source.

9. Ibid., 26–27.

10. He Changfeng et al., 6

11. Fang Shixin, 29; He Changfeng et al., 3.

12. Deng Xiaoping, "Guizhou xinqu gongzuo de celüe" (Tactics in newly liberated areas of Guizhou), in *Deng Xiaoping wenxuan, 1938–1965* (Selected writings of Deng Xiaoping) (Beijing: Renmin chubanshe, 1989), 142–144.

13. "Zhongyang zhuanfa Guizhou xinqu gongzuo celüe wenti dianbao de piyu" (Remarks on party central's transmission of a telegram about tactical questions in newly liberated areas of Guizhou), in *Jianguo yilai Mao Zedong wengao* (Mao Zedong's manuscripts since the founding of the People's Republic of China; hereafter cited as MWG) (Beijing: Zhongyang wenxian chubanshe, 1987), 1:143–144.

14. Xu Yunbei, "Huigu Guizhou jiefang chuqi de douzheng" (Remembering the initial stage of liberating Guizhou), *Guizhou wenshi ziliao xuanji* 14 (1983): 4; Pan Yan, "Huiyi Guizhou jiaofei douzheng" (Remembering the bandit suppression struggle in Guizhou), in Hebei wenshi ziliao bianjibu, ed., *Jindai Zhongguo tufei shilu* (Records of bandits in modern China) (Shijiazhuang: Qunzhong chubanshe, 1992), 2:551.

15. Guizhou sheng Cengong xian zhi bianzuan weiyuanhui, ed., *Cengong xian zhi* (Cengong county gazetteer) (Guiyang: Guizhou renmin chubanshe, 1993), 884.

16. Guizhou sheng Zhenyuan xian zhi bianzuan weiyuanhui, ed., *Zhenyuan xian zhi* (Zhenyuan county gazetteer) (Guiyang: Guizhou renmin chubanshe, 1992),

579; Ge Renjing, " 'Maoke' jiuqin ji" (The capture of the "cat"), in *Jindai Zhongguo tufei shilu*, 2:631–633.

17. Ren Xiwen, "Jianku de zhandou—huiyi 1949 nian zhi 1950 nian gongliang zhengshou gongzuo de licheng" (Arduous battle—remembering the course of grain tax collection from 1949 to 1950), in Zou xiang da xinan bianweihui, 636.

18. Ibid., 637.

19. G. William Skinner, "Aftermath of Communist Liberation in the Chengtu Plain," *Pacific Affairs* 24.1 (March 1951): 64.

20. "Deng Xiaoping guanyu xinan qingkuang he gongzuo fangzhen gei Liu Shaoqi, Zhong gong zhongyang de baogao" (Deng Xiaoping's report to Liu Shaoqi and party center on the situation in the southwest and work policy), in Zhongguo renmin jiefang jun lishi ziliao congshu bianshen weiyuanhui, ed., *Jiaofei douzheng: Xinan diqu* (Bandit eradication struggle: Southwest region) (Beijing: Jiefang jun chubanshe, 2002), 93.

21. Dorothy J. Solinger, *Regional Government and Political Integration in Southwest China, 1949–1954: A Case Study* (Berkeley: University of California Press, 1977), 71.

22. ATIS Interrogation Report No. KG 0797, October 24, 1951; Interrogation Reports KG 0779–KG 0902, File 461.01, Box 60; General Correspondence, 1951; Assistant Chief of Staff, G-2, Theater Intelligence Division; Records of the U.S. Army Military District of Washington, 1942–91, Record Group 554, Entry 17A (General Headquarters, Far East Command, Supreme Command for Allied Powers, and United Nations Command); NACP.

23. Solinger, 79.

24. Zhou Chunyuan, He Changfeng, and Zhang Xiangguang, *Guizhou jindai shi* (Modern history of Guizhou) (Guiyang: Guizhou renmin chubanshe, 1987), 369.

25. Pan Yan, "Huiyi Guizhou jiaofei douzheng" (1992), 2:550–551; Pan Yan, "Huigu Guizhou jiaofei douzheng" (Recalling the bandit suppression struggle in Guizhou), *Guizhou wenshi ziliao xuanji* 11 (1982): 11.

26. Yang Yong, "Huigu Guizhou jiefang" (Recalling the liberation of Guizhou), *Guizhou wenshi ziliao xuanji* 11 (1982): 4.

27. Pan Yan, "Huiyi Guizhou jiaofei douzheng" (1992), 552.

28. He Changfeng et al., 20.

29. Zou xiang da xinan bianweihui, 2; He Changfeng et al., 20.

30. "Zhong gong Guizhou shengwei guanyu zhaokai ge fenqu silingyuan, diwei shuji huiyi de baogao" (Guizhou Communist Party committee report on a meeting convening commanders and district party secretaries), in *Xinan qu tudi gaige yundong ziliao huibian* (Document collection on the land reform movement in the southwest) (Chongqing: Zhong gong zhongyang xinan ju nongcun gongzuo bu, 1954), 1:403. I thank Michael Schoenhals for sharing this collection.

31. "Chuanxi jun qu guanyu jixun renmin ziwei wuzhuang gugan xiang xinan jun qu de baogao" (Report from the West Sichuan Military Region to the Southwest Military Region on assembling backbones for people's self-defense corps), in *Xinan qu tudi gaige yundong ziliao huibian*, 1:546.

32. *Cengong xian zhi*, 884–885.

33. Ge Renjing, 2:631–633.

34. Wang Jue, "Liming zhi chu hua Zhenyuan" (Talks on Zhenyuan at first daybreak), *Zhenyuan wenshi ziliao* 4 (1990): 5.

35. Yang Yong, 5.

36. *Jiaofei douzheng: Xinan diqu*, 93.

37. The following account is from 511th Military Intelligence Service Co., Interrogation Report No. KG 1293, September 19, 1952; ATIS Interrogation Reports, File 950054, Box 336; Intelligence Document File Publications ("950000" File) 1947–62; Assistant Chief of Staff, G-2 (Intelligence); RG 319; NACP.

38. Military Intelligence Service Group/Far East, Interrogation Report No. KG 1224, July 31, 1952; ATIS Interrogation Reports, File 950054, Box 335; Intelligence Document File Publications ("950000" File) 1947–62; Assistant Chief of Staff, G-2 (Intelligence); RG 319; NACP.

39. 511th Military Intelligence Service Co., Interrogation Report No. KG 1193, June 30, 1952; ATIS Interrogation Reports, File 950054, Box 335; Intelligence Document File Publications ("950000" File) 1947–62; Assistant Chief of Staff, G-2 (Intelligence); RG 319; NACP.

40. 511th Military Intelligence Service Co., Interrogation Report No. KG 1409, December 6, 1952; ATIS Interrogation Reports, File 950054, Box 337; Intelligence Document File Publications ("950000" File) 1947–62; Assistant Chief of Staff, G-2 (Intelligence); RG 319; NACP.

41. Solinger, 85.

42. 511th Military Intelligence Service Co., Interrogation Report No. KG 1353, November 13, 1952; ATIS Interrogation Reports, File 950054, Box 336; Intelligence Document File Publications ("950000" File) 1947–62; Assistant Chief of Staff, G-2 (Intelligence); RG 319; NACP.

43. Deng Xiaoping, "Guanyu Xinan shaoshu minzu wenti" (On the minority nationality question in the southwest), in *Deng Xiaoping wenxuan, 1938–1965*, 165.

44. Yang Yong, 5.

45. 511th Military Intelligence Service Co., Interrogation Report No. KG 1293, September 19, 1952; RG 319; NACP.

46. Deng Xiaoping, "Kefu muqian Xinan dang nei de bu liang qingxiang" (Overcome the present harmful tendencies in the party in the southwest), in *Deng Xiaoping wenxuan, 1938–1965*, 159.

47. Deng Delin, "Jianguo chuqi Guizhou jiaofei douzheng zhong de tiebi hewei" (Iron encirclement in the Guizhou bandit suppression struggle during the early period of the People's Republic), *Guizhou shehui kexue* 6 (1999): 104.

48. Deng Lifeng, *Xin Zhongguo junshi huodong jishi, 1949–1959* (Record of military activities in new China, 1949–1959) (Beijing: Zhong gong dang shi ziliao chubanshe, 1989), 164.

49. Liu Lang, *Liu xue dao tianming* (Bleeding until dawn) (Hong Kong: Yazhou chubanshe), 10.

50. ATIS Interrogation Report No. KG 0695, September 4, 1951; Interrogation Reports KG 0641–KG 0778, File 461.01, Box 59; General Correspondence, 1951; Assistant Chief of Staff, G-2; RG 554, Entry 17A; NACP.

51. Military Intelligence Service Group/Far East, Interrogation Report No. KG 0922, January 5, 1952; ATIS Interrogation Reports, File 950054, Box 332; Intelligence Document File Publications ("950000" File) 1947–62; Assistant Chief of Staff, G-2 (Intelligence); RG 319; NACP.

52. Skinner, 66, 68.

53. 511th Military Intelligence Service Co., Interrogation Report No. KG 1293, September 19, 1952; RG 319; NACP.

54. ATIS Interrogation Report No. KG 0831, November 2, 1951; Interrogation Reports KG 0779–KG 0902, File 461.01, Box 60; General Correspondence, 1951; Assistant Chief of Staff, G-2; RG 554, Entry 17A; NACP; and Military Intelligence Service Group/Far East, Interrogation Report No. KG 1067, April 14, 1952; ATIS Interrogation Reports, File 950054, Box 333; Intelligence Document File Publications ("950000" File) 1947–62; Assistant Chief of Staff, G-2 (Intelligence); RG 319; NACP.

55. ATIS Interrogation Report No. KG 0572, September 14, 1951; Interrogation Reports KG 0480–KG 0640, File 461.01, Box 58; General Correspondence, 1951; Assistant Chief of Staff, G-2; RG 554, Entry 17A; NACP.

56. Strauss, 83.

57. "Guanyu xinan ju zonghe baogao de fudian he piyu" (Retransmittal and remarks on the Southwest Bureau's composite report), in MWG, 1:661–662.

58. "Zhong gong zhongyang Xinan ju guanyu zhenya fangeming huodong de gongzuo qingkuang he jinhou jihua de baogao" (Report from the Southwest Bureau on the work situation and plan for the future in suppressing counterrevolutionary activities), in *Xinan qu tudi gaige yundong ziliao huibian*, 1:377–378.

59. "Zhongyang guanyu Xinan ju zhenya fangeming huodong baogao de piyu he fudian" (Party central's remarks and retransmittal of the Southwest Bureau's report on suppressing counterrevolutionary activities), in MWG, 1:663–664.

60. "Guanyu dui fangeming fenzi bixu da de wen da de zhun da de hen de dianbao" (Telegram on how we must hit counterrevolutionaries firmly, precisely, and ruthlessly), in MWG (Beijing: Zhongyang wenxian chubanshe, 1988), 2:36–37.

61. *Zhenyuan xian zhi*, 579; and Ge Renjing, 631–633.

62. *Cengong xian zhi*, 884.

63. ATIS Interrogation Report No. KG 0554, n.d.; Interrogation Reports KG 0480–KG 0640, File 461.01, Box 58; General Correspondence, 1951; Assistant Chief of Staff, G-2; RG 554, Entry 17A; NACP.

64. ATIS Interrogation Report No. KG 0831, November 2, 1951; RG 554, Entry 17A; NACP.

65. 511th Military Intelligence Service Co., Interrogation Report No. KG 1293, September 19, 1952; RG 319; NACP.

66. Strauss mentions a possible low of 700,000 or 800,000 and a high of 2 million killed in the campaign against counterrevolutionaries; Strauss, 87. Jurgen Domes puts the number at over 3 million in *The Internal Politics of China, 1949–1972*, trans. Rudiger Machetzki (New York: Praeger, 1973), 52. Meisner estimates that 2 million people were executed during the first three years of the People's Republic. Maurice Meisner, *Mao's China and After: A History of the People's Republic*, 3rd ed. (New York: Free Press, 1999), 72. And Richard L. Walker provides the staggering figure of 14 million deaths in *China under Communism: The First Five Years* (New Haven: Yale University Press, 1955), 219.

67. ATIS Interrogation Report No. KG 0710, October 6, 1951; Interrogation Reports KG 0641–KG 0778, File 461.01, Box 59; General Correspondence, 1951; Assistant Chief of Staff, G-2; RG 554, Entry 17A; NACP.

68. ATIS Interrogation Report No. KG 0201, August 2, 1951; Interrogation Reports KG 0155–KG 0318, File 461.01, Box 56; General Correspondence, 1951; Assistant Chief of Staff, G-2; RG 554, Entry 17A; NACP.

69. *Xinqian ribao* (New Guizhou Daily), December 20, 1950, 1.

70. Ibid. Shortly after this announcement, greeting teams began meeting with PLA bandit suppression troops and presenting them with gifts such as cigarettes and silk banners; *Xinqian ribao*, December 29, 1950, 2.

71. Wang Jue, 6.

72. Ibid., 7–8.

73. Tian Xinghua, *Zou xiang guangming: Xiangxi feishou sishi nian gaizao jishi* (Heading for the light: Forty years of reforming bandit chieftains in west Hunan) (Beijing: Haichao chubanshe, 1993), 191.

74. Ibid., 198.

75. ATIS Interrogation Report No. KT 1397, September 17, 1951; Interrogation Reports KT 1377–KT 1750, File 461.01, Box 65; General Correspondence, 1951; Assistant Chief of Staff, G-2; RG 554, Entry 17A; NACP.

76. The official report of Chen's achievement claimed that he "routed 3 enemy advances, personally threw 207 grenades, wounding countless enemy soldiers and killing 67." See Tian Xinghua, 203.

77. Da Ying, *Zhiyuanjun zhanfu jishi* (Chronicle of Chinese People's Volunteer prisoners of war) (Beijing: Kunlun chubanshe, 1987); Neil J. Diamant, "Between Martyrdom and Mischief: The Political and Social Predicament of CCP War Widows and Veterans, 1949–1966," in Diana Lary and Stephen MacKinnon, eds., *Scars of War: The Impact of Warfare on Modern China* (Vancouver: UBC Press, 2001), 162–185.

78. Walker's *China under Communism* is an example of the totalitarian school's take on early 1950s China.

79. Neil J. Diamant, *Revolutionizing the Family: Politics, Love, and Divorce in Urban and Rural China, 1949–1968* (Berkeley: University of California Press, 2000), 11, 47.

80. Meisner, 72–73.

81. Military Intelligence Service Group/Far East, Interrogation Report No. KG 1224, July 31, 1952; RG 319; NACP.

82. Strauss, 99.

6. The Chinese Communist "Liberation" of Tibet, 1949–51

1. See, for example, Zhongyang dang'anguan, ed., *Zhong gong zhongyang wenjian xuanji* (Selected documents of the Chinese Communist Party central committee; hereafter cited as ZYWJ) (Beijing: Zhong gong zhongyang dangxiao chubanshe, 1989), 1:111; and Zhong gong zhongyang tongzhan bu, ed., *Minzu wenti wenxian huibian* (Collected documents on the nationality issue; hereafter cited as MZWT) (Beijing: Zhong gong zhongyang dangxiao chubanshe, 1991), 31–32, 123–124.

2. ZYWJ, 1:62–63.

3. MZWT, 177–180.

4. Zhongguo gongnong hongjun di si fangmianjun zhanshi bianji weiyuanhui, ed., *Zhongguo gongnong hongjun di si fangmianjun zhanshi ziliao xuanbian, changzheng shiqi* (Selected materials on the history of the Fourth Front Army of the Chinese Red Army, Long March period) (Beijing: Jiefang jun chubanshe, 1992), 150–152.

5. Jin Chongji et al., *Zhu De zhuan* (Biography of Zhu De) (Beijing: Zhongyang wenxian chubanshe, 1993), 372–373.

6. MZWT, 288.

7. Edgar Snow, *Red Star over China* (New York: Grove Weidenfeld, 1968), 444.

8. Shi Zhe, *Zai lishi juren shenbian: Shi Zhe huiyi lu* (At the side of historical giants: Shi Zhe's memoirs) (Beijing: Zhong gong zhongyang dang xiao chubanshe, 1998), 342–343.

9. MZWT, 265–267.

10. MZWT, 348.

11. Zhong gong zhongyang wenxian yanjiu shi, ed., *Jianguo yilai zhongyao wenxian xuanbian* (Selected important documents since the founding of the People's Republic) (Beijing: Zhongyang wenxian chubanshe, 1991), 1:24.

12. Shi Zhe, 339–340.

13. Zhong gong zhongyang wenxian yanjiu shi, Zhongyang dang'anguan, eds., *Jianguo yilai Liu Shaoqi wengao* (Liu Shaoqi's manuscripts since the formation of the People's Republic; hereafter cited as LWG) (Beijing: Zhongyang wenxian chubanshe, 1998), 1:2.

14. Melvyn Goldstein, *A History of Modern Tibet: The Demise of the Lamaist State* (Berkeley: University of California Press, 1989), 613–614.

15. *Renmin ribao* (People's Daily; hereafter cited as RMRB), September 2, 1949.

16. Zhong gong zhongyang wenxian yanjiu shi, Zhong gong Xizang zizhiqu weiyuanhui, and Zhongguo Zang xue yanjiu zhongxin, eds., *Mao Zedong Xizang gongzuo wenxuan* (Selected works of Mao Zedong on Tibetan affairs; hereafter cited as MXZWX) (Beijing: Zhongyang wenxian chubanshe, 2001), 1.

17. MXZWX, 4–5.

18. MXZWX, 7–8.

19. *Jianguo yilai Mao Zedong wengao* (Mao Zedong's manuscripts since the founding of the People's Republic of China; hereafter cited as MWG) (Beijing: Zhongyang wenxian chubanshe, 1987), 1:208–209.

20. Xizang zizhiqu dang shi ziliao zhengji weiyuanhui and Xizang junqu dang shi ziliao zhengji lingdao xiaozu, eds., *Heping jiefang Xizang* (Peaceful liberation of Tibet; hereafter cited as HPJF) (Lhasa: Xizang renmin chubanshe, 1995), 49.

21. MWG, 1:226–227.

22. HPJF, 59–60.

23. MWG, 1:208.

24. MWG, 1:226.

25. HPJF, 60.

26. Ji Youquan, *Bai xue: Jiefang Xizang jishi* (White snow: A factual record of the liberation of Tibet) (Beijing: Zhongguo wuzi chubanshe, 1993), 32–33.

27. MXZWX, 38–39.

28. Zhong gong zhongyang wenxian yanjiu shi, Zhongguo renmin jiefang jun junshi kexue yuan, eds., *Deng Xiaoping junshi wenji* (Collection of Deng Xiaoping's military papers) (Beijing: Junshi kexue chubanshe and zhongyang wenxian chubanshe, 2004), 2:281–282.

29. HPJF, 51.

30. HPJF, 55.

31. HPJF, 59.

32. HPJF, 59.

33. MWG, 1:1.

34. LWG, 1:2; and HPJF, 59–60.

35. MXZWX, 9–10; and Xizang zizhi qu dang shi ziliao zhengji weiyuanhui, ed., *Zhong gong Xizang dang shi dashi ji* (Important events in Chinese Communist Party history in Tibet, 1949–1994; hereafter cited as DSJ) (Lhasa: Xizang renmin chubanshe, 1995), 6.

36. The selection of the Tenth Panchen Lama was supported and endorsed by the Nationalist government but was not confirmed by the Dalai Lama.

37. HPJF, 252.

38. MXZWX, 3.

39. RMRB, January 21, 1950.

40. HPJF, 67.

41. HPJF, 68.

42. HPJF, 68.

43. Goldstein, 623–624.

44. Ibid., 626.

45. U.S. Department of State, *Foreign Relations of the United States, East Asia and the Pacific, 1950* (Washington, D.C.: GPO, 1976), 6:275–276.

46. Zhai Qiang, *The Dragon, the Lion, and the Eagle: Chinese-British-American Relations, 1949–1958* (Kent, Ohio: Kent State University Press, 1994), 49–50.

47. RMRB, January 21, 1950.

48. Tsepon W. D. Shakabpa, *Tibet: A Political History* (New Haven: Yale University Press, 1967), 300.

49. DSJ, 9; and HPJF, 20–21.

50. DSJ, 10.

51. HPJF, 75–76.

52. HPJF, 77–78; Dangdai Zhongguo congshu bianji bu, ed., *Dangdai Zhongguo de Xizang* (Tibet in contemporary China; hereafter cited as DDXZ) (Beijing: Zhongguo shehui kexue chubanshe, 1991), 136.

53. MXZWX, 16.

54. MXZWX, 20–21; and DSJ, 12.

55. Goldstein, 738–739.

56. Ji Youquan, 121–122.

57. DSJ, 13.

58. Goldstein, 685–686.

59. Ibid., 645.

60. MXZWX, 15.

61. DSJ, 9; and HPJF, 20–21.

62. Shakabpa, 299.

63. Zhong gong zhongyang wenxian yanjiu shi, ed., *Zhou Enlai nianpu, 1949–1976* (Zhou Enlai chronology, 1949–1976) (Zhong gong zhongyang wenxian chubanshe, 1997), 1:61, 65.

64. Xizang zizhiqu dang shi bangongshi, ed., *Zhou Enlai yu Xizang* (Zhou Enlai and Tibet) (Beijing: Zhongguo Zang xue chubanshe, 1998), 6–7.

65. DSJ, 9–10.

66. Ji Youquan, 143–144.

67. MWG, 1:475–477.

68. DSJ, 15.

69. DSJ, 16.

70. DSJ, 16–17.

71. DSJ, 17.

72. Goldstein, chapter 18; see also Dangdai Zhongguo congshu bianji bu, *Dangdai Zhongguo jundui de junshi gongzuo* (Military affairs of the contemporary Chinese army) (Beijing: Zhongguo shehui kexue chubanshe, 1989), 1:212–215.

73. Goldstein, 687.

74. MWG, 1:549.

75. DDXZ, 156; and *Deng Xiaoping junshi wenji*, 2:309.

76. DDXZ, 149–150.

77. Goldstein, 699–702.

78. Ibid., 707–708.

79. Zhai Qiang, 58–62.

80. Indian note, October 26, 1950, in Margaret Carlyle, ed., *Documents on International Affairs, 1949–1950* (London: Oxford University Press, 1953), 550–551.

81. Indian notes, October 31, 1950, in ibid., 552–554.

82. MWG, 1:549

83. MXZWX, 33.

84. MXZWX, 34–35.

85. HPJF, 176–178; see also Carlyle, 554–556.

86. B. N. Mullik, *My Years with Nehru: The Chinese Betrayal* (Bombay: Allied Publishers, 1971), 80.

87. HPJF, 213–214; see also Goldstein, 742–743.

88. HPJF, 119; and *Zhou Enlai yu Xizang*, 11–12.

89. Tsering Shakya, *The Dragon in the Land of Snow* (New York: Columbia University Press, 1999), 62.

90. Ibid., 64.

91. DDXZ, 164; and Shakya, 69.

92. For the text of the "Seventeen-Point Agreement," see Shakya, 449–452.

93. This is different from Goldstein's account that the first secret agreement contained eight points. Goldstein, 770.

94. HPJF, 129–130.

95. HPJF, 130.

96. DDXZ, 188–189.

97. Ya Hanzhang, "Recalling Escorting the Panchen Lama Back to Tibet," in Zhang Yuxin, ed., *Heping jiefang Xizang 50 zhounian jinian wenji* (Collected papers in commemoration of the fiftieth anniversary of Tibet's peaceful liberation; hereafter cited as *50 zhounian*) (Beijing: Zhongguo Zang xue chubanshe, 2001), 332–333.

98. Goldstein, 757–758; see also HPJF, 218–219.

99. DSJ, 30–31.

100. Shakya, 85.

101. HPJF, 269.

102. HPJF, 219.

103. HPJF, 219; and *50 zhounian*, 320.

104. MXZWX, 38–39.

105. MXZWX, 56.

106. HPJF, 207.

107. *Zhou Enlai nianpu, 1949–1976*, 1:36.

7. Big Brother Is Watching

1. *Dalian renmin ribao* (Dalian People's Daily), May 9–10, 1955.

2. Zhang Yufen, *Dalian aiguozhuyi jiaoyu jidi xunzong* (Education for building the base of nationalism in Dalian) (Dalian: Liaoning shifan daxue chubanshe, 1995), 69–71.

3. Bo Wanlie, "Su jun zhu Jinxian de qingkuang" (The situation of Soviet troops stationed in Jinxian), in Dalian shi shizhi bangongshi, ed., *Sulian hongjun zai Dalian* (The Soviet Red Army in Dalian; hereafter cited as SHJZDL) (Dalian: Dongbei caijing daxue yinshuachang, 1995), 215.

4. Xia Zhenduo, "Sulian hongjun zai Dalian shi nian sumiao" (Sketch of the Soviet Red Army's ten years in Dalian), *Dalian chunqiu* 771 (1995): 30. By 1955, at the time of the Soviet army pullout, the number had decreased to 120,000 troops.

5. Dieter Heinzig, *The Soviet Union and Communist China 1945–1950: The Arduous Road to the Alliance* (Armonk, N.Y.: M. E. Sharpe, 2004), 51–125, 348, 415.

6. The Nationalists had already appointed a mayor for Dalian by September 1945. Shen Yi, the appointee, never served a day in office in Dalian.

7. Paul Paddock, *China Diary: Crisis Diplomacy in Dairen* (Ames: Iowa State University Press, 1977), 38–39.

8. SHJZDL, 17–18.

9. Odd Arne Westad, ed., *Brothers in Arms: The Rise and Fall of the Sino-Soviet Alliance, 1945–1963* (Stanford: Stanford University Press, 1998). See also Odd Arne Westad, *Cold War and Revolution: Soviet-American Rivalry and the Origins of the Chinese Civil War, 1944–46* (New York: Columbia University Press, 1993); and James Reardon-Anderson, *Yenan and the Great Powers: The Origins of Chinese Communist Foreign Policy, 1944–1946* (New York: Columbia University Press, 1980).

10. Lüda was the name given to the area encompassing Dalian, Lüshun, Jinzhou, and the rest of the former Japanese colonial territory known as the Guandong Leased Territory.

11. Qu Xiaofan, *Jindai dongbei chengshi de lishi bianqian* (The historical change of modern cities in northeast China) (Changchun: Dongbei shifandaxue chubanshe, 2001), 325.

12. Dalian shi gongan ju shizhi yanjiushi bian, ed., *Dalian gongan shi xuanbian* (Collected accounts of the history of the Dalian police force) (Dalian: Dalian beihai yinshua gongsi, 1985), 1:277.

13. "Da hanjian Zhang Benzheng" (Big traitor Zhang Benzheng), *Dalian chunqiu* 74.4 (1994): 34–36.

14. Han Guang, "Lüda ba nian" (Eight years in Lüda), in SHJZDL, 65.

15. Han Guang, "Guanyu Dalian jiefang chuqi dang ruogan qingkuang de shuoming" (Explaining several situations regarding the party in Dalian during the initial period of liberation), *Dalian chunqiu* 83.1 (1996): 8.

16. Dong Xizheng, "Su jun zai Lüshun de shi nian" (Ten years of the Soviet army in Lüshun), *Dalian dangshi* 53.1 (1991): 16.

17. Bo Wanlie, 208–215.

18. Wang Qiren, "Chuli yu Su jun dangju guanxi de jige yuanze" (Some principles in dealing with the Soviet military authorities), in SHJZDL, 105.

19. Bo Wanlie, 213.

20. "Zhong gong Dalian qu dangwei guanyu san nian lai Zhong-Su guanxi de zongjie baogao" (The Chinese Communist Party Commitee, Dalian area summary report of three years of Sino-Soviet relations), in SHJZDL, 307–310.

21. "Zhang Wentian zai Dongbei ju zuzhi bu zhaokai de Dalian ganbu huiyi-shang de jianghua" (Zhang Wentian's speech given at a meeting of cadres from Dalian called by the Northeast Bureau), in SHJZDL, 288–290.

22. Bo Wanlie, 213–214.

23. Tan Songping, "Jieguan Daguanchang jingchashu yu jianli Zhongshan qu wei" (Recovering the colonial Daguangchang district police office and establishing the Zhongshan district police), in Zhong gong Dalian shi Zhongshan qu wei dang shi bangongshi, ed., *Zhongshan chunxiao* (Zhongshan's dawn of spring) (Dalian: Dalian haiyun xueyuan chubanshe, 1992), 5–6.

24. Liu Yunguang, "Wo suo liaojie de Su jun" (My understanding of the Soviet army), in Dalian shi shizhi bangongshi, ed., *Chengshi de jieguan yu shehui gaizao, Dalian juan* (Urban takeover and social reform, Dalian volume) (Dalian: Dalian chubanshe, 1998), 189. The "Red Building" was an overcrowded compound built by a Japanese firm to house temporary Chinese laborers who came to Dalian sea-sonally to work on the docks.

25. Repatriation of Dalian's sizable Japanese population occurred in three main waves, the largest lasting from December 1946 to April 1947, when 180,000 Japa-nese were sent back to Japan. See Dalian gang shi bianweihui bian, *Dalian gang shi* (A history of the port of Dalian) (Dalian: Dalian chubanshe, 1995), 242–244.

26. Han Guang, "Lüda ba nian," 64.

27. Ding Qun, "Liu Shunyuan yu 'Lüda shijian'" (Liu Shunyuan and the "Lüda Incident"), *Xinhua wenzhai* 5 (1996): 142.

28. See Zhao Jichang, "JinChaJi bianqu zhu Dalian de banshi jigou" (Shanxi-Chahar-Hebei border region's administrative body stationed in Dalian), *Dalian dang shi ziliao tongxun* 6 (September 1983): 23–32.

29. Suzanne Pepper, *Civil War in China: The Political Struggle, 1945–1949* (Lanham, Md.: Rowan and Littlefield, 1999 [1978]), 331. Pepper quotes Mao's fa-mous March 5, 1949, statement that "the period of 'from the city to the village' and of the city leading the village has now begun."

30. Liu Chengong and Wang Yanjing, *Ershi shiji Dalian gongren yundong shi* (The history of the Dalian workers' movement in the twentieth century) (Shenyang: Liaoning renmin chubanshe, 2001), 446–447.

31. Tang Yunchao, "Jiefang chuqi de Dalian gongren yundong" (The workers' movement in early post-liberation Dalian), in Zhong gong Dalian shiwei dang shi ziliao zhengji bangongshi, ed., *Jiefang chuqi de Dalian* (Early post-liberation Dalian) (Dalian: Dalian ribaoshe yinshuachang, 1985), 18.

32. Tang Yunchao, "Chongfan gongyun zhanxian" (Returning to the battle lines of the workers' movement), in *Chengshi de jieguan yu shehui gaizao*, 157–161.

33. The Soviets took over the main Japanese heavy industries in Dalian in Au-gust 1945, which became Sino-Soviet "Joint Enterprises" in 1947. They included Dalian's shipbuilding facilities, an oil refinery, a power station, and salt-making fa-cilities, totaling over thirty factories and enterprises in all. Zhu Li, "Jinian Su jun jiefang Dalian 52 zhou nian" (Commemorating the fifty-second anniversary of the Soviet army's liberation of Dalian), *Xigang wenshi ziliao* 4 (1997): 135.

34. Tang Yunchao, "Riben touxiang hou Su jun zai Dalian de qingkuang" (The situation of the Soviet military in Dalian after the surrender of Japan), in SHJZDL, 86.

35. "Ba Shen yu Du Ping tanhua jiyao, September 17, 1947" (A summary of the talks between Ba Shen and Du Ping on September 17, 1947), in SHJZDL, 279–280.

36. Set up in April 1947, this was the visible "civilian government for the area," which followed the stipulations of the Yalta agreement. The Soviet military authorities, headquartered in Lüshun, also had their own office for handling civilian administration, referred to in Chinese sources as the Minzheng ju (Civil Administration Office). All of the policies and public statements made by the party-controlled Guandong government had to first be approved by the Minzheng ju.

37. Liu Shunyuan, "Zhong gong Dalian dang zuzhi yu zhu lian Su jun guanxi" (The party organization and its relations to the Soviet army stationed in Dalian), in SHJZDL, 76–77.

38. Wang Shiming, "Lüshun jiefang chuqi yu Su jun guanxi de huigu" (Looking back at relations with the Soviet army in early post-liberation Lüshun), in SHJZDL, 114–115.

39. "Ba Shen yu Du Ping," 278–279.

40. "Guanyu Lian gong yu Zhong gong tongzhi zai wancheng gonggu Guandong Sulian haijun junshi genjudi gongtong renwu zhong de gongzuo guanxi wenti de jidian yijian" (Some opinions regarding the issues of mutual responsibility in completing the task of strengthening Chinese Communist Party–Soviet Party relations in the Guandong Soviet naval base area), issued by the Guandong Party Committee on March 15, 1948, in SHJZDL, 292–299.

41. Ding Qun, 142.

42. "Ba Shen yu Du Ping," 278–279.

43. "Guandong muqian xingshi yu dang de renwu" (The current situation in Guandong and the party's responsibility), in SHJZDL, 284–285.

44. Ding Qun, 139.

45. "Ba Shen yu Du Ping," 278–279.

46. Pepper, 377–381.

47. Liu was appointed vice party secretary of Shandong, while Tang went on to organize unions in Harbin. Liu Shunyuan, 76–77.

48. "Guandong muqian," 284.

49. Liang Enbao, ed., *Lüshun chenguang 1945–1956* (Dawn in Lüshun: 1945–1956) (Lüshun: Lüshun dang shi chubanshe, 1993), 55

50. "Guandong muqian," 284–286.

51. "Zhang Wentian zai Dongbei ju zuzhi bu zhaokai de Dalian ganbu huiyi shang de jianghua" (Zhang Wentian's speech given at a meeting of cadres from Dalian called by the Northeast Bureau), in SHJZDL, 288–290.

52. Han Guang, "Lüda ba nian," 63–64.

53. "Han Guang, Yuan Shouhua yu 'Ba Shen' tongzhi, 'Anteluobofu' tongzhi tanhua jilue" (Records of a discussion between Han Guang, Yuan Shouhua, comrade "Ba Shen" and comrade "Anteluobofu"), March 16, 1948, in SHJZDL, 300–306.

54. See Pepper, 377–381.

55. "Wu Xiuquan zai Dongbei ju zuzhi bu zhaodai de Dalian ganbu huiyi shang de jianghua" (Wu Xiuquan's speech given at a meeting of cadres from Dalian called by the Northeast Bureau), in SHJZDL, 288–290.

56. "Guanyu Lian gong yu Zhong gong tongzhi zai wancheng gonggu Guandong Sulian haijun junshi genjudi gongtong renwu zhong de gongzuo guanxi wenti de jidian yijian" (Some opinions regarding the issues of mutual responsibility in completing the task of strengthening party–Soviet Party relations in the Guandong Soviet naval base area), issued by the Guandong Party Committee on March 15, 1948, in SHJZDL, 292–299.

57. Han Guang, "Lüda ba nian," 59.

58. SHJZDL, 293–294.

59. SHJZDL, 296.

60. Chen Qiying, "Dalian: Xin Zhongguo de mofan dushi" (Dalian: New China's model city), *Lüyou zazhi* 23.11 (November 1949): 1–8.

61. Zhi Cheng, "Canguan Zhong Su youyiguan tan weida de Zhong Su youyi" (Visiting the Sino-Soviet friendship hall and discussing our great Sino-Soviet friendship), *Minzhu qingnian* 80 (November 5, 1949): 9.

62. Li Zongying, Liu Shiwei, and Liao Bingxiong, eds., *Dongbei xing* (Travels through the northeast) (Hong Kong: Dagong bao chubanshe, 1950), 52–53.

63. The 1950 Sino-Soviet Friendship Treaty, signed in Moscow on February 14, 1950, ended Soviet military control of Guandong and stipulated Soviet withdrawal from Dalian by the end of 1952.

64. Bo Wanlie, 211–215.

65. Dalian gongan ju, ed., *Dalian gongan lishi changbian* (Historical chronicles of the Dalian police) (Dalian: Dalian yinshua gongye zongchang, 1987), 141–152.

66. Liu Ying, "Dalian Zhong-Su youhao xiehui" (The Dalian Sino-Soviet Friendship Association), in *Chengshi de jieguan yu shehui gaizao*, 294–303. See also Klaus H. Pringsheim, "The Sino-Soviet Friendship Association (October 1949–October 1951)" (master's thesis, Columbia University, 1959).

67. "Shi youxie yi nian ban gongzuo zongjie" (A summary of one and a half years of Sino-Soviet Friendship Association work in Dalian), *Youyi* 3.8 (October 15, 1948): 18–21.

68. Liu Ying, 294–303.

69. Gui Fang, "Jieshao Siergou qu youxie fenhui" (Introduction to the Siergou district chapter of the Sino-Soviet Friendship Association), *Youyi* 3.5 (September 1, 1948): 13.

70. "Shahekou qu youxie gongzuo yu shejiao gongzuo jiehe" (Combining Friendship Association work and social education in Shahekou district), *Youyi* 3.1 (July 1, 1948): 15.

71. "Shi youxie yi nian ban gongzuo zongjie" (A summary of one and a half years of Sino-Soviet Friendship Association work in Dalian), *Youyi* 3.8 (October 15, 1948): 19.

72. Gui Fang, 13.

73. See "Qiu ming en ren" (Life saving benefactor), *Dalian renmin ribao*, June 6, 1955. See also Wang Xianglan, "Qin shen de jingli gaosu le wo shenme" (What my own experience tells me), *Dalian renmin ribao*, May 28, 1955.

74. "Wo ai Su jun shushu" (I love my Soviet army uncle), *Dalian renmin ribao*, June 6, 1955. See also Yan Shouming, "Zuo Sulian mama zui xihuan de ren" (I want to be the one my Soviet mom likes best), *Dalian renmin ribao*, May 28, 1955; and Li Feng, " 'Lina' (Xu Guiying) he ta de mama" ("Lina" [Xu Guiying] and her mom), in *Zhong-Su youyi de gushi* (Stories of Sino-Soviet friendship) (Shenyang: Liaoning renmin chubanshe, 1955), 69–73.

75. "Wo ai Su jun shushu."

76. Yan Shouming.

77. Zhang Pei, *Dalian fangwen gaiyao* (An outline of a visit to Dalian) (Dongbei xinhua shudian, 1949), 74–75.

8. The Call of the Oases

1. Major works on the Communist takeover include Ezra F. Vogel, *Canton under Communism: Programs and Politics in a Provincial Capital, 1949–1968* (Cambridge, Mass.: Harvard University Press, 1969); Kenneth G. Lieberthal, *Revolution and Tradition in Tientsin, 1949–1952* (Stanford: Stanford University Press, 1980); Steven Levine, *Anvil of Victory: The Communist Revolution in Manchuria, 1945–1948* (New York: Columbia University Press, 1987); and James Z. Gao, *The Communist Takeover of Hangzhou: The Transformation of City and Cadre, 1949–1954* (Honolulu: University of Hawaii Press, 2004).

2. Justin Jon Rudelson, *Oasis Identities: Uyghur Nationalism along China's Silk Road* (New York: Columbia University Press, 1993), 42.

3. Ibid., 41. See also Thomas Hoppe, "Observation on Uyghur Land in Turpan Country, Xinjiang—A Preliminary Report on Fieldwork in Summer, 1985," *Central Asiatic Journal* 31.3–4 (1987): 224–251.

4. Huang Jianhua, *Guomindang zhengfu de Xinjiang zhengce shulun* (On policies of the Nationalist government toward Xinjiang) (Beijing: Minzu chubanshe, 2003), 9.

5. Zhang Dajun, *Xinjiang fengbao qishi nian* (Seventy years of storms in Xinjiang) (Taibei: Lanxi chubanshe, 1980), 3264.

6. Donald H. McMillen, *Chinese Communist Power and Policy in Xinjiang, 1949–1977* (Boulder: Westview, 1979), 25. In 1885, the Qing court provided *xiang yin* (military pay) of 3.65 million taels of silver, and it dropped to 2.24 million taels in 1904. Nonetheless, Xinjiang's military expenses were about 1.9 million taels a year. The surplus funds could help Xinjiang balance its government budget. The Nationalist government's financial support was paid in paper currency. In the 1940s, because the paper currency was seriously devalued, the local governments had to "resort to local sources to resolve financial issues by themselves." See Huang Jianhua, 239.

7. Huang Zhaohong, *Wushi huiyi* (Reminiscences at age fifty) (Changsha: Yuelu chubanshe, 1999), 290–291, 296–297.

8. Jin Zhaoxian, "Guomindang tongzhi Xinjiang de fangfa yanjiu" (On the Nationalist approach to ruling Xinjiang), *Xinjiang wenshi ziliao xuan* 2 (1995): 70.

9. Lin Zhengyan, "Sheng Shicai xiao zhuan" (A brief biography of Sheng Shicai), *Zhuanji wenxue* 55.2 (1990): 1.

10. Rudelson, 7. The term "Uyghur" was not used to define the Turkic Muslim dwellers until the 1930s. Dru C. Gladney, "The Ethnogenesis of the Uighur," *Central Asian Survey* 9.1 (1990): 1–28.

11. Yang Zhengxi, "Guanyu zhaopin Musilin shibing de dianbao" (Telegram on recruitment of Muslim soldiers) and "Jinzhi zhengfu renming ahong de mingling" (An order prohibiting government appointment of imams), in Chen Huisheng and Chen Chao, *Minguo Xinjiang shi* (Republican history of Xinjiang) (Urumqi: Xinjiang renmin chubanshe, 1999), 89.

12. Zhang Zhizhong, *Zhang Zhizhong huiyi lu* (The memoirs of Zhang Zhizhong) (Beijing: Wenshi ziliao chubanshe, 1985), 541.

13. "Xinjiang zongdu Yang Zhengxi de baogao" (Report of the governor of Xinjiang Yang Zhengxi) (September 6, 1917), in Zhongyang yanjiu yuan jindai shi yanjiusuo, ed., *Zhong E guanxi shiliao: Xinjiang juan* (Historical materials on Sino-Russian relations: Xinjiang) (Taibei: Zhongyang yanjiu yuan jindai shi yanjiusuo, 1983), 6.

14. Interview, Abdurahim Amin, Beijing, December 2003.

15. Burhan Shahidi, *Xinjiang wushi nian* (Fifty years in Xinjiang) (Beijing: Wenshi ziliao chubanshe, 1984), 152.

16. Andrew D. W. Forbes, *Warlords and Muslim in Chinese Central Asia: A Political History of Republican Xinjiang, 1911–1949* (Cambridge: Cambridge University Press, 1986), 217.

17. Xinjiang Uyghur Autonomous Region Archives (hereafter cited as XUARA), 14/3/64. Emin was vice-chairman of the provincial government.

18. XUARA, 14/3/64.

19. For detailed discussion of Abasoff's case, see David D. Wang, *Under the Soviet Shadow: The Yining Incident: Ethnic Conflict and International Rivalry in Xinjiang, 1944–1949* (Hong Kong: Chinese University Press, 1999), 353–360.

20. Saifudin Azizi, *Saifudin huiyi lu* (Memoirs of Saifudin) (Beijing: Huaxia chubanshe, 1993), 514.

21. Allen Whiting and Sheng Shih-ts'ai, *Sinkang: Pawn or Pivot?* (East Lansing: Michigan State University Press, 1958), 117–118. Whiting writes that he got the information from "a reliable source." Yet Tao Zhiyue's memoir does not mention whether he had such a conversation with the Soviet consul-general.

22. See Dieter Heinzig, *The Soviet Union and Communist China 1945–1950: The Arduous Road to the Alliance* (Armonk, N.Y.: M. E. Sharpe, 2004), chapter 3.

23. Ibid., 385.

24. Yuan Dejin and Liu Zhenhua, *Xibei jiefang zhanzheng jishi* (The true record of the liberation war in the northwest) (Beijing: Renmin chubanshe, 2003), 508–514.

25. *Qunzhong ribao* (Masses Daily), July 17, 1949.

26. Yuan Dejin and Liu Zhenhua, 542.

27. Ibid., 594.

28. Du Pengcheng, *Zhanzheng riji, 1947–1949* (War diary, 1947–1949) (Beijing: Jiefang jun wenyi chubanshe, 1998), 518.

29. The Minutes of Stalin's Meeting with the Delegation of the Chinese Communist Party headed by Liu Shaoqi (June 27, 1949), Presidential Archives of the Russian Federation (PARF), 45/1/328.

30. Yuan Dejin and Liu Zhenhua, 568–670.

31. Zhang Zhizhong, 784.

32. Huang Jianhua, 191.

33. Zhang Zhizhong, 788.

34. Tao Zhiyue, *Tao Zhiyue zishu* (A self-account of Tao Zhiyue) (Changsha: Hunan renmin chubanshe, 1989), 105–106.

35. XUARA, 14/3/64.

36. Wang, 360.

37. Burhan Shahidi, 356–357.

38. Zhong gong Xinjiang Weiwuer zizhiqu weiyuanhui dang shi gongzuo weiyuanhui, Zhongguo renmin jiefang jun Xinjiang junqu zhengzhi bu, eds., *Xin-*

jiang heping jiefang (The peaceful liberation of Xinjiang) (Urumqi: Xinjiang renmin chubanshe, 1990), 5.

39. See *Gansu ribao* (Gansu Daily), May 19, 1949; *Dagong bao*, May 20, 1949; *Xibei ribao* (Northwest Daily), July 20, 1949; and *Heping ribao* (Peace Daily), July 22, 1949.

40. *Gansu ribao*, September 14–15, 1949.

41. XUARA, 2/5/901.

42. Xinjiang shehui kexue yuan lishi yanjiusuo, ed., *Xinjiang jian shi* (A brief history of Xinjiang) (Urumqi: Xinjiang renmin chubanshe, 1987), 3:498.

43. Lou Shuren, Ma Chengxiang, and the Nationalist intelligence agency left Dihua on September 24; Ye Cheng did not leave until the morning of September 25. Afterward, the Pan-Turkish leaders, including vice-chairman of the Xinjiang provincial government Mehmed Emin and Isa Yusuf Alptekin, fled for India.

44. XUARA, 175/1/1.

45. XUARA, 14/3/64.

46. XUARA, 14/3/64.

47. Xibei yanjiuhui, *Xinjiang jiaotong jieshao* (Introduction to Xinjiang's transportation) (reprinted by PLA First Front Army, September 7, 1949), 1.

48. Ibid., 4.

49. Ibid.

50. Interview, Abdurahim Amin, Beijing, December 2003.

51. Ibid. According to Amin's memory, there were only two paved roads, known as the *da shizi* (big cross), in Dihua, totaling less than 0.8 mile by 1949.

52. XUARA, 175/2/65.

53. Fan Yinkai, *Xinjiang jianshe bingtuan shi* (A history of the Xinjiang production corps) (Urumqi: Xinjiang kexue jishu chubanshe, 1997), 166

54. Interview, Gulisiati Tursun, Urumqi, January 2004.

55. Li Fusheng, ed., *Xinjiang bingtuan tunken shubian shi* (History of the Xinjiang corps in farming and defending the frontier) (Urumqi: Xinjiang keji weisheng chubanshe, 1997), 148.

56. XUARA, 175/2/5.

57. For case reports, see *Neibu cankao* (Internal reference), 1954, held at the Universities Service Centre for China Studies, Chinese University of Hong Kong.

58. Li Xuejun and Li Minjie, *Xibei dajue zhan* (Decisive battle in the northwest) (Zhengzhou: Henan renmin chubanshe, 1999), 551–553.

59. XUARA, 175/2/42.

60. XUARA, M1/1/9.

61. Li Kaiquan, "Gansu nübing fangtanlu" (Interviews of Gansu women soldiers), in Xinjiang jianshe bingtuan lishi bianzuan weiyuanhui, ed., *Xinjiang jianshe bingtuan lishi ziliao xuanbian* (Selected historical materials on the Xinjiang production corps) (Urumqi: Xinjiang renmin chubanshe, 2003), 13:238.

62. Ibid., 13:239–244.

63. Yuan Guoxiang, ed., *Ershi shiji Xinjiang tupian jishi* (Pictorial records of twentieth century Xinjiang) (Urumqi: Xinjiang meishu sheying chubanshe, 1999), 2:83–91.

64. Xinjiang Military District Archives (hereafter cited as XMDA), 13/7.

65. Liao Yiwu, "Nü bing de nüer—Liu Sixiang" (Daughter of a woman soldier—Liu Sixiang), in *Zhongguo diceng fangtanlu* (Talks with lower-class Chinese) (Taibei: Maitian chubanshe, 2002), 7.

66. XMDA, 13/18.

67. *Xin Hunan ribao* (New Hunan Daily), February 10, 1951.

68. Li Kaiquan, 13:239.

69. XMDA, 13/42.

70. Liao Yiwu, 7–8.

71. XMDA, 13/15.

72. Interview of Wei Yuying and other women soldiers by Li Kaiquan, Shihezi, 2003.

73. XMDA, 13/23; 13/27.

74. This document stipulates that each woman could bring as many as three children to Xinjiang. XMDA, 13/42.

75. XMDA, 13/71.

76. Liao Yiwu, 10.

77. XMDA, 13/80.

78. XMDA, 13/75.

79. XMDA, 13/96.

80. Li Fusheng, 221.

81. By the end of 1952, the Xinjiang Military District had recruited 13,644 female students. Another 12,892 women came to Xinjiang by other arrangements. XMDA, 13/97.

82. For example, Shandong planned to recruit 7,000 women. It sent fourteen recruiting teams to the villages in Wendeng and Laiyang counties, requiring each team to recruit about 450 women. XMDA, 13/58. In 1955, Shanghai sent 1,200 ex-prostitutes aged eighteen to thirty-five, who had received education through physical labor, to Xinjiang to join the PLA farms. *Neibu cankao* 162 (May 26, 1955): 388.

83. Rudelson, 17.

84. "On Correcting Mistaken Ideas in the Party" (December 1929), in *Selected Works of Mao Tse-tung* (Beijing: Foreign Languages Press, 1963), 1:106.

85. Li Fusheng, 290–293.

86. Li Sheng, *Zhongguo Xinjiang: Lishi yu xianzhuang* (China's Xinjiang: History and current conditions) (Urumqi: Xinjiang renmin chubanshe, 2003), 5–6.

87. Another contingency was that the senior leaders of the Yili regime, including Abmet Jan Kasim, Ishakjan Monhakiyev, Abdul Kerim Abasoff, and Luo Zi, were killed in a plane crash on their way to Beijing.

88. Discussing frontier as an open-ended process, Leonard Thompson and Howard Lamar write that ongoing social and cultural processes may continue after political hegemony is established on a frontier. Leonard Thompson and Howard Lamar, eds., *The Frontier in History: North America and Southern Africa Compared* (New Haven: Yale University Press, 1981), 7, 310–311.

9. The Crocodile Bird

1. The mistake arises from reading fourth-tone *xiàng* (face, looks) as first-tone *xiāng* (mutual). This is about as literate as translating "comedy" as *laixi* (come-plays) on grounds that the word "come" appears in the word "comedy."

2. Lin Peirui (Perry Link), "Xiangsheng yuyan yishu zatan" (Random talk on the language and art of *xiangsheng*), in *Banyang suibi* (Notes of a semi-foreigner) (Taibei: Sanmin chubanshe, 1999), 243–264; Perry Link, "The Genie and the Lamp: Revolutionary Xiangsheng," in Bonnie S. McDougall, ed., *Popular Chinese Literature and Performing Arts in the People's Republic of China 1949–79* (Berkeley: University of California Press, 1984), 83–111.

3. Hou Baolin and Guo Qiru, "Xiju zatan" (Random talk on plays), in Quanmei chubanshe, ed., *Zhongguo xiangsheng jinghua* (The best of Chinese *xiangsheng*) (Taibei: Quanmei chubanshe, n.d.), 3:95.

4. Wu Xiaoling, professor of Chinese in the Chinese Academy of Social Sciences.

5. Performed by Sun Yukui and Hui Wanhua and recorded in 1953 by Luo Changpei. See Perry Link, "The Mum Sparrow: Non-Vegetarian Xiangsheng in Action," *CHINOPERL Papers* 16 (1992): 1–27.

6. Wang Jue, Wang Jingshou, and Teng Tianxiang's *Zhongguo xiangsheng shi* (History of Chinese *xiangsheng*) (Beijing: Yanshan chubanshe, 1995) is one of the best general histories. Gu Yewen's *Xiangsheng jieshao* (Introduction to *xiangsheng*) (Shanghai: Wenyi chubanshe, 1952) was a precursor.

7. Wang, Wang, and Teng, 233.

8. Yu Shide, "Wo zhe ban beizi" (This half of my life), *Heilongjiang wenshi ziliao* 15 (December 1984), cited at www.mapai.org. See also Wang, Wang, and Teng, 222ff.

9. *Quyi* (July 1982): 11–12.

10. Yu Shide.

11. Lao She's "Xiang xiangsheng xiaozu daoxi" (Congratulating the *xiangsheng* Small Group), "Jieshao Beijing xiangsheng gaijin xiaozu" (An introduction to the Beijing Small Group for the improvement of *xiangsheng*), and "Tan xiangsheng de gaizao" (On *xiangsheng* reform), in *Lao She quyi wenxuan* (Anthology of Lao She's *quyi*) (Beijing: Zhongguo quyi chubanshe, 1982), 186, 188, 190–191. Also Wang, Wang, and Teng, 231.

12. Wang, Wang, and Teng, 228; and Yu Shide.

13. Lao She, "Jieshao Beijing xiangsheng gaijin xiaozu," 188.

14. Lao She, "Tan xiangsheng de gaizao," 190–191.

15. Wang, Wang, and Teng, 221, 223.

16. Ibid., 226.

17. A photograph of Bob Hope cheering U.S. troops in Korea is available at www.olive-drab.com/gallery/description_0021.phpCNN.com. A photograph of Chang Baokun cheering Chinese troops in Korea appears before page one in *Chang Baokun xiangsheng xuan* (Anthology of Chang Baokun's *xiangsheng*) (Tianjin: Baihua wenyi chubanshe, 1981).

18. Collected in Xi Xiangyuan and Sun Yukui, eds., *Zhi laohu* (Paper tiger) (Beijing: Sanlian shudian, 1950).

19. Ibid., 7.

20. Ibid., 24–25.

21. Ibid., 4.

22. Ibid., 12.

23. Lao She, "Jieshao Beijing xiangsheng gaijin xiaozu," 189.

24. Partially reprinted in Gu Yewen, 88–89.

25. Zhongguo quyi yanjiuhui, *Xiangsheng dianhua xuanji* (Anthology of *xiangsheng* cushions) (Beijing: Zuojia chubanshe, 1958), 1–3.

26. Zhongguo quyi yanjiuhui, ed., *Xiangsheng chuangzuo xuanji* (Anthology of *xiangsheng* works) (Beijing: Zuojia chubanshe, 1957), 185–192.

27. According to Wang, Wang, and Teng, 233.

28. These examples are from "Shiyue geming songzan" (In praise of the October Revolution), *Shuoshuo changchang* 23 (November 1951) and "Zhong-Su guanxi shi shuoben" (The History of Sino-Soviet Relations) *Shuoshuo changchang* 3 (1950).

29. These generalizations are clear from He's autobiography *He Chi zizhuan* (Autobiography of He Chi) (Beijing: Zhongguo minjian wenyi chubanshe, 1989). See also Xue Baokun, *Zhongguo de xiangsheng* (China's *xiangsheng*) (Beijing: Renmin chubanshe, 1985), 135ff.

30. Wu Xiaoling, "Luetan xiangsheng de chuangzuo wenti" (Brief discussion of the problem of creating *xiangsheng*), *Beijing wenyi* 8 (1955): 20–21.

31. Quoted in Marja Kaikkonen, *Laughable Propaganda: Modern Xiangsheng as Didactic Entertainment*, East Asian Monographs, no. 1 (Stockholm: Institute of Oriental Languages, 1990), 122.

32. Lao She, "Tan xiangsheng de gaizao," 191–192.

33. Xi Xiangyuan, Liu Baorui, and Guo Quanbao, "Xixing manji" (Notes on travel to the West), in *Xiangsheng chuangzuo xuanji*, 12–22.

34. Ibid., 18–19.

35. Chen Yongquan and Zhang Shanzeng, "Daoyun liangshi de ren" (Grain thief), *Beijing wenyi* 8 (1955): 11–14.

36. Xia Yutian, "Nü duizhang" (Female team leader), in *Xin xiangsheng ji* (New *xiangsheng* collection) (Shanghai: Shanghai wenhua chubanshe, 1965), 28–29.

37. "Gei 'Dui duilian' ti de yijian" (Opinions on "Matching Couplets"), in Gu Yewen, 109.

38. I am indebted to James Z. Gao for this example. For more on Zhang Yiming, see Gao's book *The Communist Takeover of Hangzhou: The Transformation of City and Cadre, 1949–1954* (Honolulu: University of Hawaii Press, 2004), 232–233, 305n.58.

39. Chen Sitong, "Dui xiangsheng gaige gongzuo de yijian" (Opinions on *xiangsheng* reform work), in Shanghai wenhua chubanshe, ed., *Xiangsheng luncong* (Collected commentaries on *xiangsheng*) (Shanghai: Shanghai wenhua chubanshe, 1957), 102.

40. *Xiangsheng chuangzuo xuanji*, 4–5.

41. Ibid., 13–14.

42. *Hou Baolin xiangsheng xuan* (Selection of Hou Baolin's *xiangsheng*) (Beijing: Renmin wenxue chubanshe, 1980), 12–22.

43. Ibid., 1–11.

44. Lang Defeng, Chen Wenhai, Jiang Qingkui, Jia Hongbin, Hou Bozhao, and Li Peiji, "Ye xing ji" (Traveling at night), in *Xiangsheng chuangzuo xuanji*, 217–226.

45. Xue Baokun, 139.

46. Wu Xiaoling, "Luetan xiangsheng de chuangzuo wenti," 20.

47. He Chi tells us in his autobiography that soldiers were using these three phrases at the time to describe irresponsible work in their midst. *He Chi zizhuan*, 250. The text of "Buying Monkeys" appears in *Xiangsheng chuangzuo xuanji*, 88–105.

48. *Xiangsheng chuangzuo xuanji*, 97–99.

49. *He Chi zizhuan*, 250–251; also He Chi, "Cong 'mai hour' tan qi: Dui biaoxian renmin neibu maodun de xiangsheng chuangzuo de yixie kanfa" (On "Buying

Monkeys": Some thoughts on *xiangsheng* that portrays contradictions among the people), *Quyi* 3 (1980): 25.

50. Wang, Wang, and Teng, 238–239.

51. *Xiangsheng chuangzuo xuanji*, 202–203.

52. Wang, Wang, and Teng, 240.

53. Ibid., 240–241.

54. *He Chi zizhuan*, 264.

55. *Shuoshuo changchang* 2 (1952): 9–13.

56. *Shuoshuo changchang* 19 (1951): 51; and *Shuoshuo changchang* 2 (1952): 4–8.

57. "Mao Zedong sixiang" (Mao Zedong thought) appears, for example, in Lao She, "Wenyi zuojia ye yao zengchan jieyue" (Authors and artists should also increase production and practice economy), *Shuoshuo changchang* 4.6 (1951): 9. "Yi xiaocuo" appears in Xi Xiangyuan and Sun Yukui, 26.

58. *He Chi zizhuan*, 283–288.

59. He Chi, "Cong 'mai hour' tan qi," 26.

60. Ibid., 24.

61. *Shuoshuo changchang* 10 (1951): 10.

10. *"The Very First Lesson"*

1. Cuthbert M. O'Gara, *The Surrender to Secularism* (St. Louis, Mo.: Cardinal Mindszenty Foundation, 1989 [1967]), 11.

2. Mao Tse-tung, *Selected Works of Mao Tse-tung* (Peking: Foreign Languages Press, 1967), 5:34.

3. There is nothing to indicate that Jia Lanpo intended this double meaning. Yang Haoning (art) and Jia Lanpo (text), *Women de zuxian 1: Women wushiwan nian de zuxian* (Our ancestors 1: Our ancestors 500,000 years ago) (Tianjin?: Zhishi shudian, 1951), preface (n.p.).

4. It was published in Frederick Engels (Engesi), *Makesizhuyi de renzhong youlai shuo* (The Marxist theory of human origins) (Shanghai: Chunchao shuju, 1928). I have not been able to find any extant copies of this book or of a 1930 translation of Engels's essay. The earliest I have found is Frederick Engels (Engesi), *Cong yuan dao ren* (From ape to human), trans. Cao Baohua and Yu Guangyuan (Shijiazhuang: Jiefang she, 1948).

5. Lin Yaohua, *Cong yuan dao ren de yanjiu* (Research on from ape to human) (Beijing: Gengyun chubanshe, 1951).

6. The most thorough source on small study groups remains Martin King Whyte's *Small Groups and Political Rituals in China* (Berkeley: University of California Press, 1974).

7. A. Doak Barnett, *Communist China: The Early Years, 1949–55* (New York: Praeger, 1964), 101.

8. Robert Jay Lifton, *Thought Reform and the Psychology of Totalism: A Study of "Brainwashing" in China* (New York: Norton, 1969 [1961]), 257.

9. Since perfectly good English translations of this work already exist and the Chinese does not differ significantly in meaning, I have borrowed this from Frederick Engels, *The Part Played by Labor in the Transition from Ape to Man* (New York: International Publishers, 1950), 9 (italics in original). For the Chinese, see Engesi, *Cong yuan dao ren*, 4.

10. Engesi, *Cong yuan dao ren*, 6–8.

11. Ibid., 11; and Engels, *The Part Played*, 14.

12. Xue Hongda, ed., *Cong yuan dao ren* (From ape to human) (Shanghai: Huadong shudian, 1950), 34.

13. Jia Zuzhang, *Cong yuan dao ren* (From ape to human) (Shanghai?: Kaiming shudian, 1950), 30.

14. Yang Haoning and Jia Lanpo, *Women de zuxian 1*, 17.

15. Pei Wenzhong, *Renlei de qiyuan he fazhan* (Human origins and development) (Beijing: Zhongguo qingnian chubanshe, 1956), 11.

16. Yang Haoning and Jia Lanpo, *Women de zuxian 1*, 17; Jia Lanpo and Liu Xianting, *Cong yu dao ren* (From fish to human) (Tianjin: Zhishi shudian, 1951), preface (n.p.); Yang Ye, *Women de zuxian* (Our ancestors) (Hankou: Wuhan gongren chubanshe, 1952), 35–37.

17. Yang Ye, 35–36.

18. Guliefu (Gurev), *Renlei shi zenyang zhangcheng de* (How humans developed), trans. Chen Yingxin (Shanghai: Kaiming shudian, 1950 [1946]).

19. See, among others, Wang Shan, *Laodong chuangzao renlei* (Labor created humanity) (Shanghai: Shanghai qunzhong chubanshe, 1951), 1; and Guo Yishi, *Renlei shi cong nali lai de* (Where humans came from) (Beijing: Tongsu duwu chubanshe, 1955), 1. Sources that discuss Buddhist creation stories are far rarer, but Wang Shan's is one.

20. M. Ilin and E. A. Segal, *How Man Became a Giant*, trans. Beatrice Kinkead (London: Routledge, 1942), 19. For Chinese examples, see, among others, Yang Ye, 7; Jia Zuzhang, 2–3.

21. Yang Haoning (art) and Jia Lanpo (text), *Women de zuxian 2: Women ershiwan nian de zuxian* (Our ancestors 2: Our ancestors 200,000 years ago) (Tianjin?: Zhishi shudian, 1951), 47.

22. Huang Weirong, *Zhongguo yuanren* (Peking Man) (Shanghai: Shaonian ertong chubanshe, 1954), 1–2; and Wu Rukang, *Renlei de qiyuan he fazhan* (Human origins and development) (Beijing: Kexue puji chubanshe, 1965), 5. A pundit might suggest that it was Nüwa's labor that created humanity.

23. Puliexueciji (M. S. Plisetskii), *Relei shi zenyang shengchan he fazhan de* (How humans were produced and developed), trans. Bi Li (Shanghai: Zhonghua shuju, 1951), 17–21.

24. Wang Xiaoshi, *Cong yuan dao ren: Tongsu jianghua* (From ape to human: A simple account) (Shanghai: Xinya shudian, 1950), 61. Other examples abound.

25. Yang Haoning and Jia Lanpo, *Women de zuxian 2*, preface (n.p.). For a later example, see Dong Shuangqiu, *Ren shi zenyang lai de* (How people came to be) (Changsha: Hunan renmin chubanshe, 1957), 2.

26. There were about three million Catholics and fewer than one million Protestants in China in 1949. Richard Madsen, *China's Catholics: Tragedy and Hope in an Emerging Civil Society* (Berkeley: University of California Press, 1998), 137.

27. Laurence Schneider, *Biology and Revolution in Twentieth-Century China* (Lanham, Md.: Rowman and Littlefield, 2003), 280.

28. The infamous Lysenkoist attacks on Mendelian genetics did not prevent this lionization of Darwin. I discuss the subject in detail in Sigrid Schmalzer, "The People's Peking Man: Popular Paleoanthropology in Twentieth-Century China" (Ph.D. diss., University of California, San Diego, 2004).

29. Karl Marx, "Marx to Engels, 19 December 1860," in E. J. Hobsbawm et al., eds., *Karl Marx, Frederick Engels: Collected Works* (Moscow: Progress Publishers, 1985), 41:232.

30. Karl Marx, "Marx to Ferdinand Lasalle, 16 January 1861," in *Karl Marx, Frederick Engels,* 41:247.

31. Karl Marx and Frederick Engels, *Selected Correspondence* (Moscow: Progress Publishers, 1975), 120.

32. Fang Qie, *Cong yuan dao ren toushi: Laodong zenyang chuangzao le renlei benshen he shijie* (A penetrating look at from ape to human: How labor created humanity itself and the world) (Shanghai: Shanghai bianyi she, 1950), 8.

33. Puliexueciji, 56.

34. Guliefu (Gurev), *Renlei shi zenyang zhangcheng de* (How humans developed) (Beijing: Zhongguo qingnian chubanshe, 1953), 18.

35. Pei Wenzhong and Jia Lanpo, *Laodong chuangzao le ren* (Labor created humanity) (Beijing: Zhonghua quanguo kexue jishu puji xiehui, 1954), 1–2.

36. Wu Rukang, 11. A very similar statement could still be seen in 2005 near the gorilla house at the Beijing zoo.

37. Mao Tse-tung, "On New Democracy," in *Selected Works of Mao Tse-tung* (Peking: Foreign Languages Press, 1965), 2:381.

38. As one example of four found, see Wang Shan, preface (n.p.).

39. Mao Tse-tung, "On New Democracy," 380.

40. See John Tong, "The Church from 1949 to 1990," in Edmond Tang and Jean-Paul Wiest, eds., *The Catholic Church in Modern China: Perspectives* (Maryknoll, N.Y.: Orbis Books, 1993), 8–9.

41. Li Qingbo, *Renlei qiyuan wenti* (The question of human origins) (Shanghai: Xinsheng chubanshe, 1951), 23.

42. For example, the author raised the question of why some apes remained apes and did not evolve into humans when the forests disappeared. Li Qingbo, 30.

43. Tong, 10–11.

44. Peter Bowler, *Theories of Human Evolution: A Century of Debate, 1844–1944* (Baltimore: Johns Hopkins University Press, 1984), 168, 207–208. See also Arthur Keith, *Concerning Man's Origin* (New York: G. P. Putnam's Sons, 1928), 27.

45. Gregory Guldin, *The Saga of Anthropology in China: From Malinowski to Mao* (Armonk, N.Y.: M. E. Sharpe, 1994), 66, 68, 100.

46. Lu Yudao in Liu Xian, *Cong yuan dao ren fazhan shi* (A history of development from ape to human) (Shanghai: Zhongguo kexue tushu yiqi gongsi, 1950), preface 2.

47. Han Wenli, "Jian ping Liu Xian zhu *Cong yuan dao ren fazhan shi*" (A brief criticism of Liu Xian's *A history of development from ape to human*), *Renmin ribao* (People's Daily), June 17, 1951, 6.

48. "Shanghai zhishi jie gai guanche 'baijia zhengming' wenti" (Shanghai intellectual circles take a turn at the question of "One hundred schools contending"), *Guangming ribao* (Guangming Daily), May 1, 1957, 2.

49. For a different reading of Liu's book, see Schneider, 152–153.

50. Maurice Meisner, *Li Ta-chao and the Origins of Chinese Marxism* (Cambridge, Mass.: Harvard University Press, 1967).

51. Han Wenli, 6.

52. See the 1950 republishing of Zhu Xi's 1940 book, *Women de zuxian* (Our ancestors) (Shanghai: Wenhua shenghuo chubanshe, 1950 [1940]).

53. A review in a *Wenhui bao* supplement criticized a picture book—Tu Jingzong and Chen Guangyu, *Laodong chuangzao ren* (Labor created humanity) (Shanghai: Shanghai wenhua shudian, 1951?)—for, among other faults, attributing the social organization of labor and its fruits to apes. See Zhou Long, "Ping *Laodong chuangzao ren*" (Criticizing *Labor Created Humanity*), *Wenhui bao fu kan*, June 19, 1951.

54. "Shanghai zhishi jie gai guanche 'baijia zhengming' wenti," 2.

55. Liu was not as unfortunate as many other intellectuals who were killed during the Cultural Revolution. After the Cultural Revolution, he was even able to participate in the restructuring of the discipline of anthropology under Deng Xiaoping's more permissive administration. Interview data, 2002.

56. Bowler, 75.

57. Ales Hrdlicka was an early exception who maintained that Neanderthals were ancestors of modern humans. See his "The Neanderthal Phase of Man," *Journal of the Royal Anthropological Institute of Great Britain and Ireland* 57 (1927): 249–274.

58. See, for example, Franz Weidenreich, *Apes, Giants, and Man* (Chicago: University of Chicago Press, 1946); and Franz Weidenreich, "Some Problems Dealing with Ancient Man," *American Anthropologist* 42.3 (1940): 380–383.

59. Ernst Mayr, "Taxonomic Categories in Fossil Hominids," *Cold Spring Harbor Symposia on Quantitative Biology* 15 (1950): 109–118.

60. On the single species model and race politics in the postwar context, see Robert N. Proctor, "Three Roots of Human Recency: Molecular Anthropology, the Refigured Acheulean, and the UNESCO Response to Auschwitz," *Current Anthropology* 44.2 (2003): 213–239.

61. For example, Yang Zhongjian's personal library, stored at the Institute for Vertebrate Paleontology and Paleoanthropology in Beijing, contains materials he received from the American Museum of Natural History in the 1950s.

62. Pei Wenzhong, *Ziran fazhan jian shi* (A short history of natural development) (Beijing: Lianying shudian, 1950), 58. This sentiment was echoed in Cheng Mingshi and Fang Shiming, *Cong yuan dao ren tongsu hua shi* (A simple history of from ape to human in pictures) (Shanghai: Ren shi jian chubanshe, 1951), 42. Yang Ye (Yang Ye, 12) leaned toward seeing Peking Man as an ancestor but insisted that more evidence was needed to be certain. For examples of phylogenetic trees showing Peking Man as an offshoot, see Xue Hongda, 3; Pei Wenzhong, *Ziran fazhan*, 45; and Wang Xiaoshi, 24.

63. Zhu Xi, *Women de zuxian* (1950), 163.

64. Jia Lanpo, *Zhongguo yuanren* (Peking Man) (Shanghai: Longmen lianhe shuju, 1950), 135–137.

65. Cheng Wanfu and Qin Jueshi, eds., *Zhongguo yuanren: Women wushiwan nian de zuxian* (Peking Man: Our ancestors 500,000 years ago) (Nanjing: Minfeng yinshuguan, 1953), 14–28.

66. Yang Ye, 10; Fang Shaoqing (pen name for Fang Zongxi), *Gu yuan zenyang biancheng ren* (How ancient apes became human) (Beijing: Zhongguo qingnian chubanshe, 1958), 48.

67. On the "Western origins" theory in the Republican era, see Fa-ti Fan, "How Did the Chinese Become Native? Science and the Search for National Origins in

the May Fourth Era," in Kai-wing Chow, Tze-ki Hon, Hung-yok Ip, and Don C. Price, eds., *Nation, Modernity, and the Restructuring of the Field of Cultural Production in China: Beyond the May Fourth Paradigm* (forthcoming).

68. Yang Ye, 6.

69. On the usefulness of Peking Man for national identity in contemporary China, see Barry Sautman, "Peking Man and the Politics of Paleoanthropological Nationalism in China," *Journal of Asian Studies* 60.1 (2001): 95–124. I expand on Sautman's thesis and offer a critique of it in my doctoral dissertation; see Schmalzer.

70. Zhongguo lishi yanjiu hui, *Gaoji zhongxue Zhongguo lishi* (Upper secondary school Chinese history), vol. 1 (Beijing: Xinhua chubanshe, 1950); and Qian Huabei renmin zhengfu jiaoyu bu, *Gaoji xiaoxue lishi keben* (Upper elementary school history textbook), vol. 1 (Beijing: Renmin jiaoyu chubanshe, 1951 [1950]).

71. For example, Zhongguo lishi yanjiu hui, 1:5. Such statements followed the approach set out by Xu Xusheng, *Zhongguo gushi de chuanshuo shidai* (The legendary era of Chinese ancient history), rev. and enlarged ed. (Beijing: Kexue chubanshe, 1960 [1943]).

72. Yang Ye, 25–28. See also Jia Lanpo, *Zhongguo yuanren* (Peking Man) (Beijing: Zhonghua shuju, 1962), 24.

73. Fang Qie, *Cong yuan dao ren*, 70–71. Official handbooks for history teachers specifically prescribed such usage of the *Book of Rites* to illustrate the transition from primitive communism to slave society. Joseph R. Levenson, "The Place of Confucius in Communist China," in Albert Feuerwerker, ed., *History in Communist China* (Cambridge, Mass.: MIT Press, 1968), 60.

74. Fang Qie, *Cong yuan dao ren*, 79.

75. There have been many books written about the search for the missing fossils. A book published in Hong Kong in 1952 refuted the recent claims from the mainland and suggested that the fossils had been taken from China by the Soviets. See Wei Juxian, *Beijing ren de xialuo* (The whereabouts of Peking Man) (Hong Kong: Shuowenshe, 1952). A recent work on the subject is Li Mingsheng and Yue Nan, *Xunzhao "Beijing ren"* (The search for "Peking Man") (Beijing: Huaxia chubanshe, 2000). The English-language book on the subject best known in China is Harry L. Shapiro, *Peking Man* (New York: Simon and Schuster, 1974). Shapiro was a physical anthropologist at the American Museum of Natural History and thus had a personal interest in solving the mystery.

76. See Cheng Te-k'un, "Archaeology in Communist China," in *History in Communist China*, 53.

77. Zhoukoudian Peking Man Site Exhibition Hall Guest Book, April 19, 1956 (hereafter cited as Zhoukoudian Guest Book). Unfortunately, 1956 appears to have been the only year such a guest book was kept. Later books allowed for names and dates but no comments.

78. Zhoukoudian Guest Book, June 29, 1956.

79. Wang Suihan, "Guo hen, jia chou" (Nation's vengefulness, family's enmity)," *Dianying wenxue* 5 (1961): 18–33.

80. The article specifically says, "Even if the Peking Man fossils really cannot be found, this still will not be considered too great a loss, because all the large museums around the world already have casts." Ji Zhi, " 'Beijing ren' tougu xialuo bu ming" (The whereabouts of Peking Man are not clear), *Kexue zhishi* 1.2 (1946): 42.

81. Interview with the author, October 8, 2002.

82. Fang Qie, *Cong yuan dao ren*, 7–8. Charles Carroll, *The Negro a Beast* (St. Louis, Mo.: American Book and Bible House, 1900).

83. Weidenreich, *Apes, Giants, and Man*, 24.

84. Jia Lanpo, *Zhongguo yuanren* (1950), preface, 2–3.

85. Jia Lanpo, "You renleixue de guandian kan Mei diguozhuyi de qinlue shouduan" (A look at American imperialist methods of aggression from the viewpoint of anthropology), *Kexue dazhong* 5 (1952): 110.

86. Fang Qie, *Zhonghua minzu de ernü* (Sons and daughters of the Chinese nationality) (Shanghai: Shanghai bianyi chubanshe, 1951), 3–6.

87. For scholarship on policy toward minority nationalities in the People's Republic of China, see June Teufel Dreyer, *China's Forty Millions: Minority Nationalities and National Integration in the People's Republic of China* (Cambridge, Mass.: Harvard University Press, 1976); and Ralph Litzinger, *Other Chinas: The Yao and the Politics of National Belonging* (Durham, N.C.: Duke University Press, 2000).

88. See, for example, Lin Yaohua, 149; Huang Weirong, 33; Pei Wenzhong and Jia Lanpo, *Laodong chuangzao le ren*, 16; Pei Wenzhong, *Renlei de qiyuan*, 11; Wu Rukang, 73.

89. Shanghai kexue jiaoyu dianying zhipianchang (Shanghai science education film studios), *Zhongguo yuanren* (Peking Man) (1959).

90. Huang Weirong, 35.

91. I am not claiming that censorship and political harassment do not occur in such societies but that such practices are generally opposed and are to a significant extent proscribed by law.

92. See, for example, Zhu Xi, *Women de zuxian* (1950), 146; Jia Lanpo, *Zhongguo yuanren* (1950), 11–16; Huang Weirong, 29–32; Fang Shaoqing, 91–92.

93. Barnett; Lifton; Franz Schurmann, *Ideology and Organization in Communist China* (Berkeley: University of California Press, 1966); Whyte.

94. Zhoukoudian Guest Book, June 22?, 1956.

11. Acting Like Revolutionaries

1. For short biographies of Sang Hu, Huang Zuolin, and Huang Shaofen, see *Zhongguo dabaike quanshu: Dianying* (The China encyclopedia: Film) (Beijing: Zhongguo dabaike quanshu chubanshe, 1991), 338, 197, 195. Hereafter cited as ZGDBK.

2. See Wei Shaochang, ed., *Shi Hui tan yishu* (Shi Hui on art) (Shanghai: Shanghai wenyi chubanshe, 1982). This volume includes a useful essay by Ye Ming titled "Yi Shi Hui" (Remembering Shi Hui), 527–538.

3. ZGDBK, 238.

4. See Edward Gunn, *Unwelcome Muse: Chinese Literature in Shanghai and Peking, 1937–1945* (New York: Columbia University Press, 1980), 111–150.

5. For a discussion of *Ye dian*, see Paul G. Pickowicz, "Sinifying and Popularizing Foreign Culture: From Maxim Gorky's *The Lower Depths* to Huang Zuolin's *Ye dian*," *Modern Chinese Literature* 7.2 (Fall 1993): 7–31.

6. "1949 ying tan jian shiji" (Events in the film world in 1949), *Qingqing dianying* (hereafter cited as QQDY) 18.1 (January 15, 1950).

7. QQDY 18.1 (January 15, 1950).

8. See *Zhongguo dianyingjia lie zhuan* (Biographies of Chinese filmmakers; hereafter cited as ZGDYJLZ) (Beijing: Zhongguo dianying chubanshe, 1982), 2:9, for a discussion of Yu Ling's activities.

9. "Xiju dianying lianhe qilai" (The worlds of theater and film unite), QQDY 17.15 (August 1, 1949).

10. QQDY 18.1 (January 15, 1950).

11. QQDY 17.16 (August 15, 1949).

12. "Quan Shanghai dianying yuan diaocha biao" (An investigation chart on movie theaters in Shanghai), QQDY 17.19 (October 1, 1949).

13. Shanghai Municipal Archives (hereafter cited as SMA), B172-1-35.

14. See Zhiwei Xiao, "Purging China of Western Cultural Influence: The Case of the Anti-Hollywood Campaign in Shanghai, 1949–51," forthcoming.

15. Ibid.

16. QQDY 18.1 (January 15, 1950).

17. QQDY 18.1 (January 15, 1950).

18. QQDY 18.1 (January 15, 1950).

19. Lao She, *Huoche ji* (Train record) (Shanghai: Shanghai zazhi gongsi, 1941), 101–195.

20. The screenplay is in Lao She, *Wo zhei yi beizi* (This life of mine) (Beijing: Jiefang jun wenyi chubanshe, 2001), 120–199.

21. Ibid., 199–200.

22. *Zhongguo yishu yingpian bianmu* (A catalogue of Chinese art films; hereafter cited as ZGYYB) (Beijing: Wenhua yishu chubanshe, 1981), 1:55–56.

23. SMA, B172-1-35.

24. Lao She, *Wo zhei yi beizi*, 200.

25. For a post-Mao reevaluation of this important artist, see Wei Xiangtao, *Yi ke yingxing de chenfu: Shangguan Yunzhu zhuan* (Grieving for a movie star: A biography of Shangguan Yunzhu) (Beijing: Zhongguo dianying chubanshe, 1986). Interviewees insist that Shangguan's Cultural Revolution suicide was related to a pre–Cultural Revolution intimate relationship with Mao Zedong. Wei Xiangtao (110–113) describes a private meeting between Mao and Shangguan set up by Shanghai Mayor Chen Yi on January 10, 1956, at which Mao admitted to being a fan of the famous actress.

26. SMA, B172-1-35.

27. SMA, B172-1-35.

28. Li Yuangang, "Dui *Taiping chun* de ji dian yijian" (A critique of *Taiping chun*), *Wenhui bao* (Wenhui Daily), June 24, 1950.

29. Mei Duo, "Ping *Taiping chun*" (Criticizing *Taiping chun*), *Wenhui bao*, June 24, 1950.

30. Sang Hu, "Guanyu *Taiping chun*" (On *Taiping chun*), *Dazhong dianying* 1.2 (1950): 14.

31. Shi Hui, "Jiefang yinian lai de Shanghai ying ju jie" (The Shanghai film and theater worlds in the year since liberation), QQDY 18.13 (July 1, 1950).

32. For an extended discussion of the meaning of the term *fanshen*, see William Hinton, *Fanshen: A Documentary of Revolution in a Chinese Village* (Berkeley: University of California Press, 1997).

33. SMA, B172-1-35.

34. Allyn Rickett and Adele Rickett, *Prisoners of Liberation* (San Francisco: China Books, 1981).

35. Sigrid Schmalzer, "The People's Peking Man: Popular Paleoanthropology in Twentieth-Century China" (Ph.D. diss., University of California, San Diego, 2004).

36. "Sixiang wenti" (Ideological problems), *Dazhong dianying* 1.7 (1950).

37. Ibid.

38. SMA, B172-1-35.

39. Mao Dun, *Fushi* (Corruption) (Shanghai: Hua xia shudian, 1949). The screenplay is in Ke Ling, *Ke Ling dianying juben xuanji* (An anthology of Ke Ling's screenplays) (Beijing: Zhongguo dianying chubanshe, 1980), 125–210.

40. Shi Bangshu, "*Fushi* de 'pai hou pai' zhi" (Before and after the filming of *Fushi*), *Dazhong dianying* 1.13 (1950).

41. See Chen Xihe, "*Jiejie meimei zhanqilai* de choubei jingguo" (Preparations for making *Jiejie meimei zhanqilai*), and Su Chun, "Shanghai minzhu fulian tongzhi tan *Jiejie meimei zhanqilai*" (Comrades from the democratic Women's Association discuss *Jiejie meimei zhanqilai*), *Dazhong dianying* 16 (February 1951), 26–29.

42. Gail Hershatter, *Dangerous Pleasures: Prostitution and Modernity in Twentieth-Century Shanghai* (Berkeley: University of California Press, 1997).

43. See Emily Honig, "Pride and Prejudice: Subei People in Contemporary Shanghai," in Perry Link, Richard Madsen, and Paul G. Pickowicz, eds., *Unofficial China: Popular Culture and Thought in the People's Republic* (Boulder: Westview Press, 1989), 142.

44. SMA, B172-1-35.

45. Yao Fangcao, "Li Linyun de chouhen" (The hatred of Li Linyun), *Dazhong dianying* 16 (February 1951): 30.

46. For a typical positive review, see Tian Yin, "Zhu fu xin sheng de jiemeimen" (Celebrating the rebirth of women), *Xinmin bao* (New People's Daily), February 17, 1951.

47. QQDY 18.20 (December 15, 1950).

48. For a collection of critical articles on *Wu Xun zhuan*, see *Guanyu yingpian "Wu Xun zhuan" de pipan* (Concerning critical opinions of the film *Wu Xun zhuan*), 2 vols. (Beijing: Zhongyang dianying ju, 1951).

49. For discussions of the Wu Xun campaign, see Jay Leyda, *Dianying: An Account of Films and the Film Audience in China* (Cambridge, Mass.: MIT Press, 1972), 197–198; and Paul Clark, *Chinese Cinema: Culture and Politics since 1949* (Cambridge: Cambridge University Press, 1987), 45–50.

50. SMA, B172-1-35.

51. See Jeremy Brown, "Staging Xiaojinzhuang: The City in the Countryside, 1974–1976," in Joseph W. Esherick, Paul G. Pickowicz, and Andrew G. Walder, eds., *The Chinese Cultural Revolution as History* (Stanford: Stanford University Press, 2006), 153–184.

52. For a brief discussion of the criticisms of this film, see Clark, 51.

53. Zhao Han, "Ping *Guan lianzhang*" (A critique of *Guan lianzhang*), *Dazhong dianying* 20 (April 10, 1951): 24–25.

54. ZGYYB, 1:97.

55. Wei Shaochang, 536.

56. ZGDYJLZ, 2:76–77, a watered-down version of the article prepared by Ye Ming for Wei Shaochang's book on Shi Hui, offers a typical account of his death that avoids use of the term "suicide." Shi Hui's rightist designation was reversed in

1979. Official sources still fail to identify Shi Hui as the screenwriter of *Wu hai ye hang*. See ZGYYB, 1:284–285.

57. See ZGDBK, 24–25, 196; and ZGDYJLZ, 2:245.

12. Creating "New China's First New-Style Regular University," 1949–50

1. *Renmin ribao* (People's Daily), October 3, 1950, 2.

2. Liu Shaoqi, "Zai Zhongguo renmin daxue kaixue dianli shang de jianghua" (Speech at the opening ceremony of Renda), in Zhong gong zhongyang wenxian yanjiushi Liu Shaoqi yanjiuzu, ed., *Liu Shaoqi lun jiaoyu* (Liu Shaoqi on education) (Beijing: Jiaoyu kexue chubanshe, 1998), 91.

3. On the takeover and transformation of higher education institutions by the Chinese Communists, see Suzanne Pepper, *Radicalism and Education Reform in 20th-Century China: The Search for an Ideal Development Model* (Cambridge: Cambridge University Press, 1996), 164–191; Ruth Hayhoe, *Chinese Universities, 1895–1995: A Century of Cultural Conflict* (New York: Garland Publishing, 1996), 73–90; and Immanuel C. Y. Hsu, "The Reorganisation of Higher Education in Communist China, 1949–61," *China Quarterly* 19 (July–September 1964): 128–160.

4. Michael David-Fox, *Revolution of the Mind: Higher Learning among the Bolsheviks, 1918–1929* (Ithaca: Cornell University Press, 1997), 3–4; Sheila Fitzpatrick, *The Commissariat of Enlightenment: Soviet Organization of Education and the Arts under Lunacharsky, October 1917–1921* (Cambridge: Cambridge University Press, 1970), 4–5, 49–51; and Fitzpatrick, *Education and Social Mobility in the Soviet Union, 1921–1934* (Cambridge: Cambridge University Press, 1979), 79–80.

5. As Hong Yung Lee has argued, the regime had to make a choice in the 1950s between social advancement for the revolutionary cadres and advancement for the well-educated and technically proficient. Hong Yung Lee, *From Revolutionary Cadres to Party Technocrats in Socialist China* (Berkeley: University of California Press, 1991), 387–389.

6. On the treaty negotiations, see Dieter Heinzig, *The Soviet Union and Communist China 1945–1950: The Arduous Road to the Alliance* (Armonk, N.Y.: M. E. Sharpe, 2004), 263–384.

7. "Liu Shaoqi's letter to Joseph Stalin, July 6, 1949," Arkhiv Prezidenta Rossiiskoi Federatsii (Archive of the President of the Russian Federation; hereafter cited as APRF) 45/1/328/51–55, trans. in Andrei Ledovsky, "The Moscow Visit of a Delegation of the Communist Party of China in June to August 1949 (Part 2)," *Far Eastern Affairs* 5 (1996): 86–87.

8. Xu Zehao, *Wang Jiaxiang zhuan* (Biography of Wang Jiaxiang) (Beijing: Dangdai Zhongguo chubanshe, 1996), 458–463; Zhong gong zhongyang wenxian yanjiushi, *Liu Shaoqi zhuan* (Biography of Liu Shaoqi) (Beijing: Zhongyang wenxian chubanshe, 1998), 2:650; "Mao Zedong's Telegram to Liu Shaoqi to Be Handed to Joseph Stalin," APRF 45/1/328/137–140, trans. in Andrei Ledovsky, "The Moscow Visit of a Delegation of the Communist Party of China in June to August 1949 (Part I)," *Far Eastern Affairs* 4 (1996): 89–91; and Li Xin, "Zhongguo renmin daxue de choubei" (Planning for the establishment of Renda) (unpublished manuscript, n.d.).

9. There was suspicion among the Chinese that he was an intelligence agent. One interviewee remembered that the Soviet teachers at the university seemed to leave the room whenever Filippov entered. Interview with Xu Bin, October 17, 2000.

10. Douglas A. Stiffler, "Building Socialism at Chinese People's University: Chinese Cadres and Soviet Experts in the People's Republic of China, 1949–57" (Ph.D. diss., University of California, San Diego, 2002), 50–62.

11. P. I. Fesenko and V. F. Filippov, "Doklad o khode raboty po organizatsii novogo universiteta v Pekine" (Report on the progress of work on the organization of a new university in Beijing), October 13, 1949, Rossiiskii Tsentr Khraneniia i Izucheniia Dokumentov Noveishei Istorii (Russian Center for the Storage and Investigation of the Documents of Contemporary History; hereafter cited as RTsKhIDNI) 16/137/142, 304.

12. Ibid., 313–319. On student activism on university campuses in Beijing during 1945–49, see Suzanne Pepper, *Civil War in China: The Political Struggle, 1945–1949* (Berkeley: University of California Press, 1978), especially 42–93; and James Yick, *Making Urban Revolution in China: The CCP-GMD Struggle for Beiping-Tianjin, 1945–1949* (Armonk, N.Y.: M. E. Sharpe, 1995), 80–136.

13. Fesenko and Filippov, 313.

14. Ibid., 311–312.

15. Wu Yuzhang (1878–1966), from Sichuan, had served as an aide to Sun Yatsen and was one of the celebrated "five elders" of the Chinese revolution. In Yan'an, he served as head of the Lu Xun Literature and Arts Academy and Yan'an University. In the civil war period, Wu served as head of North China United University. Wu is also noted for his role in the reform of the Chinese language. See Donald W. Klein and Anne B. Clark, *Biographic Dictionary of Chinese Communism 1921–1965* (Cambridge, Mass.: Harvard University Press, 1971), 2:959–965; and Zhongguo renmin daxue gaodeng jiaoyu yanjiushi, xiaoshi bianxie zu, ed., *Zhongguo renmin daxue renwu zhuan* (Biographies of Renda personages) (Beijing: Zhongguo renmin daxue, 1993), 1:1–16.

16. Hu Xikui (1896–1970), a native of Xiaogan county, Hubei, joined the Communist Party in Nanjing in 1925 and studied at Sun Yat-sen University in Moscow from November 1926 to the summer of 1928. Hu became known as an underground party leader in occupied areas of north China. He served as provincial party secretary in Rehe, north of the Great Wall, where he earned Mao's favor by pursuing violent land reform struggles. In spring and summer 1949, Hu Xikui and his patron Liu Lantao were in charge of the political thought retraining camp rather grandiloquently named North China People's Revolutionary University. See *Zhongguo renmin daxue renwu zhuan*, 1:52–64; and "Hu Xikui zhuan lue" (Biographical sketch of Hu Xikui), in Zhong gong Hubei sheng Xiaogan diwei, Xiaogan shiwei dang shi ziliao zhengbian weiyuanhui bangongshi, eds., *Hu Xikui jinian wenji* (Collection of essays commemorating Hu Xikui) (Beijing: Zhongguo renmin daxue chubanshe, 1986), 167–220.

17. Cheng Fangwu (1897–1984), a Hunanese, was a luminary of the May Fourth–era literary movement. He joined the party while a student in France in 1928 and was subsequently dispatched to Germany, where he worked on a translation of *The Communist Manifesto*. From 1937 to 1949, Cheng led a series of party training schools in Yan'an and north China that were the forerunners of Renda. See *Zhongguo renmin daxue renwu zhuan*, 1:17–31; Yu Piao and Li Hongcheng,

Cheng Fangwu zhuan (Biography of Cheng Fangwu) (Beijing: Dangdai Zhongguo chubanshe, 1997); and Cheng Fangwu, *Zhanhuo zhongde daxue—cong Shaanbei gongxue dao renmin daxue de huigu* (A university in the fires of war: From the North Shaanxi Academy to Renda) (Beijing: Renmin jiaoyu chubanshe, 1982).

18. "Zhongguo renmin daxue jiankuang (waibin canguan jieshao gao)" (A brief introduction to Renda: Introductory draft for consultation by foreign guests), Renda Archives 197A, 9.

19. Xu Weili, "Huainian women de guoji pengyou he laoshi" (Remembering fondly our international friend and teacher), *Renmin daxue zhoukan* 61 (November 7, 1952): 3.

20. Cheng Fangwu, "Zhongguo renmin daxue de jiaoyanshi gongzuo" (The work of teaching-research sections at Renda), *Renmin jiaoyu* (April 1951): 11.

21. For Renda's departmental structure and Soviet expert assignments, see appendices A–C in Stiffler, 482–491.

22. *Liu Shaoqi lun jiaoyu*, 91.

23. Bolshevik domination of higher education institutions was finally achieved in the Cultural Revolution period beginning in 1928. See the essays by Sheila Fitzpatrick, "The Cultural Revolution as Class War" and by George M. Enteen, "Marxist Historians during the Cultural Revolution: A Case Study of Professional Infighting," in Sheila Fitzpatrick, ed., *The Cultural Revolution in Russia, 1928–1931* (Bloomington: Indiana University Press, 1978).

24. Soviet advisers' reports on Renda are found in the Soviet archives in Moscow. See Letter from V. Filippov to E. F. Kovalev (February 27, 1950), RTsKhIDNI 17/137/405, 49–53; "Otchet o rabote po organizatsii narodnogo universiteta Kitaia v g. Pekine" (Report on the work of organizing Renda in Beijing), (May 2, 1950), RTsKhIDNI 17/137/405, 62–64; and "Doklad o rabote gruppi Sovetskikh prepodavatelei v vyshikh uchebnikh zavedeniia g. Pekina" (Report on the work of the group of Soviet teachers in the higher education institutions of the city of Beijing), (December 18, 1950), RTsKhIDNI 17/137/723, 1–22.

25. Two reports from the rector of the university were translated from Chinese to Russian and are included with the Soviet archival documents. See "Doklad Rektora v TsKh KPK" (Report of the rector to the Central Committee [CC] of the Chinese Community Party [CCP]), (n.d., included with Filippov's letter of May 2, 1950), RTsKhIDNI 17/137/405, 65–72; and "Doklad Rektora narodnogo universiteta Kitaia TsKh KPK v Marte 1950 g," (March 1950 Report of the rector of Renda to the CC of the CCP), (March 28, 1950), 73–90.

26. Letter from V. Filippov to E. F. Kovalev (December 25, 1949), RTsKhIDNI 17/137/405, 4–5.

27. This would not be the case after the death of Stalin, however, when the Soviet education expert Kudriavtsev urged the opposite approach, that is, seeking out and making use of "old" specialists from the pre-1949 intelligentsia. See "Benxiao Sulian guwen Gudeliaozuofu tongzhi lixiao guiguo qian qubie jianghua" (The farewell speech of this school's Soviet expert, comrade Kudriavtsev before his departure and return to his country), Renda Archives 141A, 25.

28. Zhongguo renmin daxue gaodeng jiaoyanshi, xiaoshi bianxie zu, ed., *Zhongguo renmin daxue dashiji (1937 nian 7 yue–1992 nian 2 yue)* (Important events in the history of Renda, July 1937–February 1992) (Beijing: Zhongguo renmin daxue chubanshe, 1992), 92–94.

29. Ibid., 91.

30. Letter from V. Filippov to E. F. Kovalev (February 27, 1950), 49–53.

31. Ibid., 49.

32. Ibid., 50.

33. "Table 4: Social and Political Backgrounds of Students of the Russian Brigade, 1949–50," in Stiffler, 137–138.

34. Letter from V. Filippov to E. F. Kovalev (February 27, 1950), 51.

35. Ibid., 51–52.

36. Ibid., 52–53.

37. Letter from V. Filippov to E. F. Kovalev (December 15, 1949), RTsKhIDNI 17/137/405, 2–3.

38. Ibid.

39. "Zhongguo renmin daxue benke diyi xueqi ji diyiqi xunlianban de jiaoyu fangzhen he jihua (caoan)" (Draft educational policy and plan for the first semester of the regular course and the first session of the training classes at Renda) (November 12, 1949), Renda Archives 2A, 39.

40. Ibid.; and "Plan organizatsii narodnogo universiteta kitaia. Uchebniie plany na pervyi semestr dlia universitetov i kursov" (Plan of organization of Renda. Teaching plans for the first semester of the regular course division and the short courses) (December 25, 1949), RTsKhIDNI 17/137/405, 9.

41. "Doklad Rektora narodnogo universiteta Kitaia TsKh KPK v Marte 1950 g," 74.

42. "Table 5: Social and Political Backgrounds of First Group of 1,565 Students Recruited for Regular-Class Division at Chinese People's University, January–February, 1950," in Stiffler, 143–144.

43. "Table 6: Summary of the Students of Chinese People's University (March 24, 1950)" and Tables 7–9, in ibid., 145–146, 153–154.

44. Letter from V. Filippov to E. F. Kovalev (February 27, 1950), 51–52.

45. Ibid., 53.

46. Ibid., 52.

47. "Otchet o rabote po organizatsii narodnogo universiteta Kitaia v g. Pekine," 62–64.

48. "Doklad o rabote gruppi Sovetskikh prepodavatelei v vyshikh uchebnikh zavedeniia g. Pekina," 1–22.

49. Ibid., 5.

50. "Zhongguo renmin daxue benke diyi xueqi ji diyiqi shunlianbande jiaoyu fangzhen he jihua (caoan)," 39.

51. "Zhongguo renmin daxue xiaoshi (chugao)" (Draft history of Renda), Renda Archives 220A, 17.

52. "Doklad Rektora v TsKh KPK," 65.

53. "Doklad Rektora narodnogo universiteta Kitaia TsKh KPK v Marte 1950 g," 74.

54. "Doklad Rektora v TsKh KPK," 66.

55. Ibid., 69–70.

56. Ibid., 66.

57. Ibid., 66–67.

58. Yang Huilian, a "young intellectual" student from Harbin, stressed that students from relatively prosperous backgrounds were satisfied with living conditions

and food at the university. Interview with Yang Huilian, Beijing, September 17, 2000.

59. "Doklad Rektora narodnogo universiteta Kitaia TsKh KPK v Marte 1950 g.," 75.

60. "Doklad Rektora v TsKh KPK," 68.

61. Ibid., 70.

62. Ibid., 69.

63. See Rudolph Wagner, *Inside a Service Trade: Studies in Contemporary Chinese Prose* (Cambridge, Mass.: Harvard University Press, 1992), for the journalistic and literary theme of tensions between "young intellectuals" and older party cadres in the early and mid-1950s.

64. "Doklad Rektora v TsKh KPK," 69.

65. Ibid.

66. On the abandonment of worker-peasant short courses in favor of academic "regularization," see Pepper, *Radicalism and Education Reform in 20th-Century China*, 189–190.

13. The Ye Family in New China

1. *Ye shi zupu* (Ye family genealogy), 6th ed. (n.p.: 1944), juan 9–12. The larger history of the Ye family will be treated in a book now in preparation.

2. On the nuclear family in twentieth-century China, see Susan L. Glosser, *Chinese Visions of Family and State, 1915–1953* (Berkeley: University of California, 2003); William L. Parish and Martin King Whyte, *Village and Family in Contemporary China* (Chicago: University of Chicago Press, 1978), 131–138; and Martin King Whyte and William L. Parish, *Urban Life in Contemporary China* (Chicago: University of Chicago Press, 1984), 152–159.

3. Kenneth G. Lieberthal, *Revolution and Tradition in Tientsin, 1949–1952* (Stanford: Stanford University Press, 1980), 42–51; and Ye Duyi, *Sui jiusi qi yu weihui—bashi huiyi* (Despite nine deaths, I still have no regrets: Memoirs at age eighty) (Beijing: Qunyan chubanshe, 1994), 60–61.

4. Ye Yun interview, 2001. On Liu in Tianjin, see Lieberthal, 42–51.

5. Interviews with Ye Duzheng, September 1994 and May 1995.

6. On the Democratic League, see Carsun Chang, *Third Force in China* (New York: Bookman Associates, 1952); and Roger B. Jeans, ed., *Roads Not Taken: The Struggle of Opposition Parties in Twentieth-Century China* (Boulder: Westview Press, 1992).

7. Ye Duyi, *Sui jiusi*, 61; for the composition of the Political Consultative Conference, see *Renmin ribao* (People's Daily; hereafter cited as RMRB), September 22, 1949.

8. On the committee, see *Zhongguo gongchandang lishi da cidian: Shehui zhuyi shiqi* (Historical dictionary of the Chinese Communist Party: Socialist period) (Beijing: Zhongguo zhongyang dangxiao, 1991), 4; on membership; see RMRB, October 22, 1949; on officers, see RMRB, September 16, 1950.

9. Ye Duyi, *Sui jiusi*, 69.

10. Frederick C. Teiwes, "Establishment and Consolidation of the New Regime," in Roderick MacFarquhar and John K. Fairbank, eds., *The Cambridge History of China*, vol. 14; *The People's Republic of China, Part I: The Emergence of Revolutionary China, 1949–1965* (Cambridge: Cambridge University Press, 1987), 77.

11. RMRB, March 14, 1951.

12. RMRB, October 13, 1951.

13. Ye Yun interview, August 2001; Ye Duyi interview, January 1995; and Ye Duzhuang, untitled 1991 mss., 88–90.

14. Ye Duzhuang, 1991, 94–96.

15. On *xiangsheng*, see Chapter 9 by Perry Link in this volume.

16. Ye Lizhong interview, February 1995.

17. Hong Yung Lee, *From Revoslutionary Cadres to Party Technocrats in Socialist China* (Berkeley: University of California Press, 1991), 35, 49.

18. Ye Fang interviews, spring 1995.

19. Ye Duzhuang, 1991, 107–116; and Ye Durou interview, March 1995.

20. Fang Shi married a party comrade during the war at age twenty-three, but their first surviving child came only in 1950.

21. Chen Cheng interview, February 1995.

22. Interviews with Ye Fang, 1995; Ye Xinxin, July 1997; Ye Lin, July 1997; Ye Dabao, August 2001; Ye Binbin, August 2001; and Ye Yangyang, August 2001.

23. Sun Song diary *(Meishu riji)*, 1955, 8–11, 25–28, 54, 80. In some entries these amounts are given in ten thousands of yuan, the official unit of currency—the much-inflated values of the 1940s having continued until the wan (ten thousand) multiplier was eliminated in the mid-1950s.

24. Ye Duzhuang, *Guoyan yunyan* (Mist and clouds before my eyes), 1992 mss., 103–117; and Ye Liang interview, July 2002.

25. Fang Shi interview, September 2001.

26. Fang Shi interview, 1995.

27. On women in modern China, see Wang Zheng, *Women in the Chinese Enlightenment: Oral and Textual Histories* (Berkeley: University of California Press, 1999); Elisabeth Croll, *Changing Identities of Chinese Women: Rhetoric, Experience, and Self-perception in the Twentieth Century* (Hong Kong: Hong Kong University Press, 1995); Kay Ann Johnson, *Women, the Family, and Peasant Revolution in China* (Chicago: University of Chicago Press, 1983); and Margery Wolf, *Revolution Postponed: Women in Revolutionary China* (Stanford: Stanford University Press, 1985).

28. See also Jung Chang, *Wild Swans: Three Daughters of China* (New York: Anchor Books, 1991), 138–159, 180–181, 197–201.

29. Fang Shi interview, 1995.

30. Ye Duzhuang, *Guoyan yunyan*, 108–110, 112–113.

31. Ye Binbin interview, August 2001. Lin Ying's complaints fill her memoir *Kanke de daolu* (Bumpy road) (Beijing: Tongfang wenhua guan, n.d. [1994 preface]).

32. RMRB, January 15, 1950; RMRB, February 18, 1950.

33. Ye Duyi interview, January 1995.

34. Ye Duyi, *Sui jiusi*, 63–64.

35. Ibid., 70–72; and RMRB, November 12, 1950.

36. Sheldon H. Harris, *Factories of Death: Japanese Biological Warfare, 1932–45, and the American Cover-up* (New York: Routledge, 1994). On the veracity of the charges, see Katherine Weatherby, "Deceiving the Deceivers: Moscow, Beijing, Pyongyang, and the Allegations of Bacteriological Weapons Use in Korea," *Cold War International History Project Bulletin* 11 (1998): 176–184; and Milton Leitenberg, "New Russian Evidence on the Korean War Biological Warfare Allegations: Background and Analysis," *Cold War International History Project Bulletin* 11 (1998): 185–199. See also Ruth Ro-

gaski, "Nature, Annihilation, and Modernity: China's Korean War Germ-Warfare Experience Reconsidered," *Journal of Asian Studies* 61.2 (May 2002): 381–415.

37. Fang Shi interviews, 1995; and September 2001. RMRB, May 17, 1952, carries the New China News Agency (NCNA) account. See also reproductions of written confessions from the two airmen, dated April 8, 1952, and April 14, 1952, in RMRB, May 6, 1952.

38. Fang Shi interviews, 1995; and September 2001.

39. Personnel document dated July 6, 1949; "Lishi zizhuan" (Historical autobiography), n.d. (1951?); "Ye Duzhuang zai da xuexi zhong buchong cailiao zhi er" (Ye Duzhuang's second group of supplementary materials for big study), September 1951, all from Ye Duzhuang dossier, Chinese Academy of Agricultural Sciences Archives.

40. See Chapter 5 by Jeremy Brown in this volume.

41. RMRB, November 12, 1950.

42. Quotations from undated fragment in cadre appraisal section of Ye Duzhuang dossier. In the dossier the "corrupt" funds are listed in the old inflated currency, yielding the impressive sum of 456,500 yuan.

43. RMRB, June 17, 1955.

44. Ye Duzhuang memoirs, *"Jiefang yihou"* (After liberation), 24, 36–49; and *"Yuzhong ji"* (Prison record), 1993 mss., 37. Regrettably, Ye Duzhuang's dossier contains no materials on the Sufan Campaign.

14. Birthing Stories

1. This research, carried out from 1996 to 2006, was funded by a grant from the Luce Foundation's U.S.-China Cooperative Research Program, with additional assistance from the Pacific Rim Research Program of the University of California. My most profound thanks go to my research partner Gao Xiaoxian, Research Office director of the Shaanxi Provincial Women's Federation and general secretary of the Shaanxi Research Association for Women and Family, and to Wang Guohong and Zhao Chen for their assistance on two different fieldwork trips.

2. This is a shameless approximation. See Judith Banister, *China's Changing Population* (Stanford: Stanford University Press, 1987), 329, for urban population totals and urban population as a percentage of the total population, which rose from 10.6 percent in 1949 to 18.4 percent in 1959. Banister (25) gives the overall sex ratio provided by the 1953 census as 107.6; the rural sex ratio was likely more skewed in favor of males.

3. These villages are far from the main Communist wartime base area: Village B is in the cotton-growing belt of Guanzhong in central Shaanxi; Village T is in the southwest tea and rice region of the province, close to Sichuan; Village Z is in Shaanxi's southeastern mountains near Henan and Hubei provinces; and Village G is in the northern part of central Shaanxi (Weibei), on the edge of a dramatic gorge.

4. This undated document is filed by the Shaanxi Provincial Archives with documents from the year 1950. "Fuying weisheng gongzuo diaocha gongzuo" (Investigation work on women and children's health work), Fulian Archives 178–106–002, n.d. (1950?). Newpaper accounts corroborate a drive to survey women's health conditions in April and May 1950; see *Qunzhong ribao* (Masses Daily), June 27, 1950, 2.

5. This survey of women and child health took place even before the land reform, which was promulgated nationally in June 1950. As Jeremy Brown's chapter (Chapter 5) on southwest China and James Gao's chapter (Chapter 8) on Xinjiang suggest, consolidation of even rudimentary state control was a protracted process in many parts of China, and so it is striking that this type of health work was made a priority so early in the process of social transformation. In Weinan Special District, just northeast of Chang'an county, widespread land reform did not even begin until October 1950. See Weinan diqu nongye hezuo shi bianweihui, ed., *Weinan diqu nongye hezuo shiliao* (Historical materials on agricultural cooperation in Weinan district) (Xi'an: Shaanxi renmin chubanshe, 1993), 7–8. The first Women's Congress in Weinan county, however, had been held in May 1950, founding the county-level Women's Federation. See Weinan xian zhi bianji weiyuanhui, ed., *Weinan xian zhi* (Weinan county gazetteer) (Shaanxi: Sanqin chubanshe, 1987), 491. If Chang'an county was following a similar timetable, and if the surveyors were working for the Women's Federation, then a survey of women's and children's health and childbirth practices was one of the first actions undertaken by the new organization.

6. Women routinely participated in fieldwork during the busy season in Guanzhong, in spite of normative constraints on work outside of domestic space. See Gail Hershatter, "Local Meanings of Gender and Work in Rural Shaanxi in the 1950s," in Gail Henderson and Barbara Entwisle, eds., *Re-Drawing Boundaries: Work, Household, and Gender in China* (Berkeley: University of California Press, 2000), 79–96.

7. "Fuying weisheng gongzuo diaocha gongzuo," 1–2, 9.

8. Of 522 children born in the village, 62 percent had survived. Of the infant deaths, 84 (43 percent) were attributed to tetanus neonatorum and 111 to unspecified other causes. It is unclear how long a period is represented by the total of 522 births. Of these 522 births, 278 male and 243 female were "normal" (*pingchan*), and 1 male birth was "difficult" (*nanchan*). See ibid. A provincial-level report from the same period says that of 522 births in the village, 514 were old-style deliveries, and that of these, 314 died—a radically different total that raises questions about the accuracy of counting in all such reports. See "Shaanxi sheng 1950 nian fuying weisheng diaocha zongjie" (Summary of an investigation of women and children's health in Shaanxi province in 1950), Shaanxi Provincial Archives Minzheng ting files 198–113, 1950, 29–34.

9. In 1928, national infant mortality was estimated at 250 per 1,000 live births, with many of the deaths attributed to tetanus neonatorum. See Marion Yang, "Midwifery Training in China," *China Medical Journal* 42 (1928): 769, also cited in Ka-che Yip, *Health and National Reconstruction in Nationalist China: The Development of Modern Health Services, 1928–1937* (Ann Arbor: Association for Asian Studies, 1995), 10. The death rate in rural areas was likely higher. A 1951 government survey done by the Central Women's and Children's Health team estimated that of more than 830,000 children born each year in the northwest (Shaanxi, Gansu, Ningxia, Qinghai, and Xinjiang), the mortality rate was 285 per 1,000, or more than 238,000 children per year. *Qunzhong ribao*, December 1, 1951, 3.

10. This survey gives the number of children born recently in the village as 521 or 522, at two different points in the report. Of these, 8 had been delivered by the new-style method (6 to one mother and 1 each to two others).

11. It appears that this new-style midwife must have been trained before the Communists arrived in 1949, since she had already delivered her sister's six children by 1950.

12. "Fuying weisheng gongzuo diaocha gongzuo," 2.

13. See, for instance, *Qunzhong ribao,* June 27, 1950, 2.

14. Joshua Goldstein, "Scissors, Surveys, and Psycho-Prophylactics: Prenatal Health Care Campaigns and State Building in China, 1949–1954," *Journal of Historical Sociology* 11.2 (June 1998): 154.

15. Ibid., 156.

16. Ibid., 163, 162.

17. Delia Davin, "Women in the Countryside of China," in Margery Wolf and Roxane Witke, eds., *Women in Chinese Society* (Stanford: Stanford University Press, 1975), 257; Delia Davin, *Woman-Work: Women and the Party in Revolutionary China* (Oxford: Oxford University Press, 1976), 131–132.

18. Gao Xiaoxian, personal communication, October 2000.

19. Yip, 58–59; see also Yang, "Midwifery Training in China" (1928), 774–775; and "Editorial: Midwifery Training in Peking," *China Medical Journal* 42 (1928): 782–784.

20. Yip, 165–172. Shaanxi established a midwifery school in 1934, recruiting thirty unmarried woman between the ages of eighteen and twenty-five per year to study for three years, including a one-year practicum. The school had little influence on rural health practices. See Qin Yan and Yue Long, *Zouchu fengbi: Shaanbei funü hunyin yu shengyu 1900–1949* (Leaving isolation behind: Marriage and childbirth among women in north Shaanxi, 1900–1949) (Xi'an: Shaanxi renmin chubanshe, 1997), 190.

21. Yip, 59.

22. Ibid., 167, summarizes a survey in Nanchang, Jiangxi, on this point.

23. Marion Yang, "Control of Practicing Midwives in China," *Chinese Medical Journal* 44.5 (1930): 428–431, cited in Charlotte Furth, *A Flourishing Yin: Gender in China's Medical History, 960–1665* (Berkeley: University of California Press, 1999), 298 n. 68. In an earlier article, Yang estimated their number at four hundred thousand. Yang, "Midwifery Training in China" (1928), 774.

24. Yip, 10, 167.

25. Yang, "Midwifery Training in China" (1928): illustration 768–769. Yang, 769, cited a maternal mortality rate of 15 per 1,000 births in China and an infant mortality rate of 250 to 300 per 1,000.

26. Li Tingan, *Zhongguo xiangcun weisheng wenti* (Problems of rural health in China) (Shanghai: Shangwu yinshuguan, 1935), 25, notes that in Dingxian, 90.7 percent of births were delivered by old-style midwives, 10 percent by new-style midwives, and 0.3 percent with no assistance at all, in spite of a long-running rural health program. For a brief catalog of common birth complications, causes of postpartum infection, and the need for trained midwives, see 65–68.

27. The need for women's health work and midwife reform is documented in *Shaan-Gan-Ning bianqu funü yundong wenxian ziliao (xuji)* (Documentary material on the Shaan-Gan-Ning Border Region women's movement [cont.]) (n.p.: Shaanxi sheng fulian, 1985), 165–166 and 356; see also Qin Yan and Yue Long, 179–205. On the women's health campaign that began in the Shaan-Gan-Ning base area in April 1944, see *Shaan-Gan-Ning bianqu funü yundong dashi jishu* (Record of major

events in the Shaan-Gan-Ning Border Region women's movement) (n.p.: Shaan-Gan-Ning sanshengqu fulian, 1987), 166–170.

28. The teams visited Baoji, Lantian, and the Xi'an suburbs. *Qunzhong ribao*, June 27, 1950, 2.

29. Ibid.

30. *Qunzhong ribao*, December 1, 1951, 3.

31. *Qunzhong ribao*, June 27, 1950, 2.

32. Kahti Lim, "Obstetrics and Gynecology in Past Ten Years," *Chinese Medical Journal* 79.5 (November 1959): 375.

33. Banister, 82–83; she discounts as excessively optimistic many of the mid-1950s rural survey results.

34. Elisabeth Croll, *From Heaven to Earth: Images and Experiences of Development in China* (New York: Routledge, 1994), 183.

35. Goldstein, 153.

36. Lim, 375; on the second statistic, see also Zhu Futang, "Jianguo shinian lai ertong baojian shiye de chengjiu" (Achievements in the enterprise of children's health in the past ten years since the founding of the People's Republic), *Zhonghua erke zazhi* 10.5 (October 1, 1959): 367.

37. "Fuying weisheng gongzuo diaocha gongzuo," 3–4; for a similar case, see "Shaanxi sheng 1950 nian fuying weisheng diaocha zongjie."

38. "Fuying weisheng gongzuo diaocha gongzuo," 4.

39. Ibid., 4.

40. Ibid., 5.

41. Ibid. More graphic descriptions are found in "Shaanxi sheng 1950 nian fuying weisheng diaocha zongjie" and in "Shaanxi sheng 51 nian fuyou weisheng cailiao" (Material on women's and children's health in Shaanxi province in 1951), Fulian Archives 178-112-006, March–December 1951. On similar criticisms of midwives in medical texts from the Song and Qing periods, see Yi-Li Wu, "Reproducing Women: Constructions of Female Health and Illness in Qing China," draft ms., chapter 6, cited with permission.

42. "Fuying weisheng gongzuo diaocha gongzuo," 5–6.

43. On criticisms of old-style midwives in Shaanbei, see Qin Yan and Yue Long, 191–194. Similar criticisms appear in a 1951 Women's Federation survey; see "Shaanxi sheng 51 nian fuyou weisheng cailiao."

44. "Fuying weisheng gongzuo diaocha gongzuo," 7.

45. Ibid., 7.

46. "Shaanxi sheng 1950 nian fuying weisheng diaocha zongjie," 29–34.

47. "Fuying weisheng gongzuo diaocha gongzuo," 7.

48. Ibid., 8.

49. "Shaanxi sheng 1950 nian fuying weisheng diaocha zongjie," 29–34.

50. Ibid.

51. Wang Family Village is about sixty kilometers (thirty-seven miles) northeast of Xi'an.

52. Gao Xiaoxian and Gail Hershatter, interview with ZQE, August 5, 1996, tape 2 transcript, 16. Daughters-in-law conventionally refer to their mothers-in-law as "mother."

53. *Qunzhong ribao*, December 1, 1951, 3.

54. For a summary of such comparisons, drawing on birth customs in Shaanbei, see Qin Yan and Yue Long, 191–194. A 1951 Shaanxi survey deplored the situation in which women had no set place to give birth, instead squatting in outhouses, corrals, or corners. "Shaanxi sheng 51 nian fuyou weisheng cailiao."

55. Lu Xia, *Gaizao jiu chanpo jingyan jieshao* (Introduction to the experience of reforming old midwives) (Jinan: Shandong renmin chubanshe, 1951), 8.

56. Ibid., 18–19.

57. Wang Guohong, interview with ZXF, July 6, 1997, transcript, 3–5.

58. Gao and Hershatter, interview with ZQL, July 31, 1999, transcript, 23.

59. The 1970s and 1980s birthing movement in the United States, which questioned the authority of doctors and helped popularize the work of midwives, advocated exactly the opposite, "liberating" women from their prone position and instructing them to move around and to squat so that gravity could assist them.

60. Gao and Hershatter, interview with DFC, July 28, 1999, part 5 transcript, 20.

61. Gao and Hershatter, interview with ZQL, July 31, 1999, transcript, 23.

62. Gao and Hershatter, interview with LZL, July 29, 1999, transcript, 9–10.

63. Gao and Hershatter, interview with ZQL, July 31, 1999, transcript, 22.

64. "Shaanxi sheng 51 nian fuyou weisheng cailiao."

65. "Danfeng xian funü gongzuo yinian lai de zongjie" (Danfeng county summary of woman-work in the past year), Danfeng County Archives (Fulian reports), September 27, 1952; and "Danfeng xian yinian lai de funü gongzuo zongjie baogao" (Danfeng county summary of woman-work in the past year), Danfeng County Archives (Fulian reports), October 30, 1953.

66. "Xianyang xian Weibin xiang yinian lai fuyou weisheng gongzuo qingkuang" (Conditions of women's and children's health work in the past year in Xianyang county, Weibin township), Fulian Archives 178-153-081, October 22, 1956. As early as 1951, Women's Federation cadres took responsibility for the political retraining of old-style midwives. "Shaanxi sheng 51 nian fuyou weisheng cailiao."

67. The actual level of contact with government agencies, and the thoroughness of retraining, is difficult to ascertain in the enthusiastic planning sections of these early work reports. See, for instance, "Shaanxi sheng 51 nian fuyou weisheng cailiao."

68. Shaanxi sheng fulian fuli bu, *Fuying weisheng gongzuo jingyan jieshao* (Introduction to the experience of work on women's and children's health) (n.p.: September 1954), 1–3.

69. "Shaanxi sheng 51 nian fuyou weisheng cailiao."

70. "Xianyang xian Weibin xiang yinian lai fuyou weisheng gongzuo qingkuang."

71. Ibid.

72. "Weinan xian renmin weiyuanhui 1957 nian 1–6 yuefen fuyou weisheng gongzuo jihua" (Weinan county people's committee work plan for women's and children's health, January–June, 1957) (n.d.), Weinan County Archives, Record 6 (author's numbering).

73. Ibid.

74. Ibid.

75. Here I disagree somewhat with Goldstein (177), whose argument renders the state more unified and its reach more consistent than seems warranted. At the same time, "women" are cast as autonomous subjects unimplicated in either state making or feudal patriarchy.

76. Gao and Hershatter, interview with LZR, March 26, 2001, transcript, 59.

77. The taboo on having one's mother attend one's birth apparently also extended to uxorilocally married women who lived with their mothers. Gao and Hershatter, interview with DFC, July 28, 1999, part 5 transcript, 22.

78. Gao and Hershatter, interview with FSF, July 7, 1997, transcript, 5.

79. Ibid., 1.

80. Gao and Hershatter, interview with QZF, July 6, 1997, transcript, 17.

81. On reproductive culture in reform-era rural China, see Li Yinhe, *Shengyu yu Zhongguo cunluo wenhua* (Reproduction and Chinese village culture) (Hong Kong: Oxford University Press, 1993); and Gao Xiaoxian, "Pinkun diqu funü yunchanqi baojian fuwu fenxi" (An analysis of health care services for pregnancy and childbirth in poor districts), *Funü yanjiu* 4 (2002): 59–62.

82. "Danfeng xian di si qu Zhulinguan xiang Liu Xihan mofan danxing cailiao" (Single material about the model Liu Xihan, Zhulinguan township, fourth district, Danfeng county), Danfeng County Archives, February 21, 1955. On the number of stations around the county, see "Danfeng xian yinian lai de funü gongzuo zongjie baogao" (Danfeng county summary of woman-work in the past year), Danfeng County Archives (Fulian reports), October 30, 1953.

83. Gao and Hershatter, interview with DFC, July 28, 1999, part 1 transcript, 4.

84. "Danfeng xian di si qu Zhulinguan xiang Liu Xihan mofan danxing cailiao"; Gao and Hershatter, interview with DFC, July 28, 1999, part 5 transcript, 20.

85. "Danfeng xian di si qu Zhulinguan xiang Liu Xihan mofan danxing cailiao."

86. Gao and Hershatter, interview with ZQL, July 31, 1999, transcript, 22. On beliefs about the pollution of postpartum discharge, see also Emily Ahern [Martin], "The Power and Pollution of Chinese Women," in *Women in Chinese Society*, 193–214.

87. Gao and Hershatter, interview with DFC, July 28, 1999, part 5 transcript, 20. Yi-Li Wu traces the classical Chinese medical discourse of the Ghost Fetus, a false pregnancy thought to result from intercourse with ghosts or frustrated female sexuality. Yi-Li Wu, "Ghost Fetuses, False Pregnancies, and the Parameters of Medical Uncertainty in Classical Chinese Gynecology," *Nan Nü* 4.2 (2002): 170–206, esp. 188–195.

88. Gao and Hershatter, interview with DFC, July 28, 1999, part 5 transcript, 20.

89. Ibid., 20–21.

90. Yu Hua incorporates a version of this theme, in which a midwife delivers a ghost baby and subsequently dies, into his short story "World Like Mist"; see Yu Hua, *The Past and the Punishments*, trans. Andrew F. Jones (Honolulu: University of Hawaii, 1996), esp. 87–93, 104, 109–110. Profound thanks to Andrew Jones for reminding me why Liu Xihan's story sounded so familiar. On the recurring theme of "a fertile union between human male and female ghost" in seventeenth-century Chinese fiction, see Judith Zeitlin, *The Phantom Heroine: Ghosts and Gender in Seventeenth-Century Chinese Literature* (Honolulu: University of Hawaii Press, 2007), chapter 1.

15. Capitalists Choosing Communist China

1. Mao Tse-tung (Mao Zedong), *The Selected Works of Mao Tse-tung* (Peking: Foreign Languages Press, 1969), 4:167–169.

2. For recent examples of historical writing and helpful historiographical analysis, see Tim Wright, ed., *The Chinese Economy in the Early Twentieth Century: Recent Studies* (New York: St. Martin's, 1992); and Tim Wright, "The Spiritual Heritage of Chinese Capitalism," in Jonathan Unger, ed., *Using the Past to Serve the Present* (Armonk, N.Y.: M. E. Sharpe, 1993), 205–238.

3. Siu-lun Wong, *Emigrant Entrepreneurs: Shanghai Industrialists in Hong Kong* (Hong Kong: Oxford University Press, 1988), 28.

4. Parks M. Coble, *Chinese Capitalists in Japan's New Order: The Occupied Lower Yangzi, 1937–1945* (Berkeley: University of California Press, 2003), 213.

5. For brief references to the examples of the Rong and Guo families, see Wong, 28–31; and Lynn T. White III, "Leadership in Shanghai, 1955–69," in Robert A. Scalapino, ed., *Elites in the People's Republic of China* (Seattle: University of Washington Press, 1972), 306.

6. The Liu family archive is held by the Center for Research on Chinese Business History at the Economics Institute of the Shanghai Academy of Social Sciences. It was deposited there as part of the Liu Hongsheng Papers in 1958, two years after Liu's death, by his fourth son, Liu Nianzhi. Some of the Liu family letters have been published in Shanghai shehui kexueyuan jingji yanjiusuo, ed., *Liu Hongsheng qiye shiliao* (Historical materials on Liu Hongsheng's enterprises), 3 vols. (Shanghai: Shanghai renmin chubanshe, 1981). In the notes to this chapter where I have referred to letters that have been published, I have given the appropriate page numbers in these volumes (hereafter cited as LHS). Where I have referred to unpublished letters, I have given their location as the Liu Papers.

7. Sherman Cochran, *Encountering Chinese Networks: Western, Japanese, and Chinese Corporations in China, 1880–1937* (Berkeley: University of California Press, 2000), chapter 7; Coble, 182–194.

8. Father to Mother, August 15, 1945, and Father to Liu Jisheng, August 15, 1945, Liu Papers; Cochran, 167–174; Coble, 187–189; Howard L. Boorman and Richard C. Howard, eds., *Biographical Dictionary of Republican China* (New York: Columbia University Press, 1968), 2:399.

9. Eighth Son to Father and Mother, February 9, 1948; Eighth Son to his brothers, June 19, 1948; and Eighth Son to Eldest Son, August 16, 1948—all in Liu Papers; Liu Nianzhi, *Shiyejia, Liu Hongsheng chuanlu—huiyi wode fuqin* (A biography of the industrialist Liu Hongsheng—reminiscences of my father) (Beijing: Wenshi ziliao chubanshe, 1982), 110.

10. Quotations in this paragraph are from Lloyd E. Eastman, *Seeds of Destruction: Nationalist China in War and Revolution, 1937–1949* (Stanford: Stanford University Press, 1984), 182–183.

11. Liu Nianzhi, 108–109.

12. Quoted by Eastman, 192.

13. Ibid., 196–197.

14. Liu Nianzhi, 110–111.

15. Ibid., 98.

16. Ibid., 112–113.

17. Ibid., 111.

18. Ibid., 112–113.

19. Ibid., 114–115.

20. Zhang Dehua to Father, April 28, 1949, Liu Papers; Liu Nianzhi, 111–112.

21. Liu Nianzhi, 116.

22. Second Son to Father, June 4, 1949, LHS, 3:455–456.

23. Ibid.

24. Ibid.

25. Ibid.

26. Ibid.

27. Liu Nianzhi, 115–116.

28. Ibid. In this passage, Liu does not identify Zhou's emissaries by name. They might have been Pan Zongyao and Zhang Huinong, who were the two emissaries that Zhou Enlai sent to Hong Kong to persuade the banker Chen Guangfu and other leading financiers and capitalists to return to China in 1950. See Chen Guangfu, *Chen Guangfu riji* (Diary of Chen Guangfu) (Shanghai: Shiji chuban jituan, Shanghai shudian chubanshe, 2002), 249–251. I am grateful to Dr. Pui Tak Lee for this reference.

29. Eighth Son to Eldest Son, August 16, 1948, Liu Papers; Father to Hu Yigeng, July 14, 19, 25, and 27, 1949, LHS, 3:368–372; and Fifth Son and Seventh Son to Father, August 25, 1949, LHS, 3:454.

30. Liu Nianzhi, 116.

31. Ibid., 115–116.

32. *Wenhui bao* (Wenhui Daily), November 5, 1949.

33. Liu Nianzhi, 116–117.

34. *Wenhui bao*, December 18, 1949.

35. *Wenhui bao*, December 17, 1949.

36. Ibid.; and *Wenhui bao*, February 8, 1950.

37. Liu Nianzhi, 118–123.

38. For other examples, see Wong, 31–32.

39. Father to Eighth Son, December 17, 1949, LHS, 3:456–457.

40. Ibid., 3:457–458.

41. Ibid.

42. Ibid.

43. Ibid.

44. Ibid.

45. Ibid. On the controversial sign that is mentioned in this quotation, see Robert A. Bickers and Jeffrey N. Wasserstrom, "Shanghai's 'Dogs and Chinese Not Admitted' Sign: Legend, History, and Contemporary Symbol," *China Quarterly* 142 (June 1995): 444–466.

46. Father to Eighth Son, March 28, 1950, LHS, 3:457–458.

47. Ibid.

48. Ibid.

49. Liu Nianzhi, 120.

50. *Wenhui bao*, January 16, 1951.

51. Liu Nianzhi, 120–121.

52. John Gardner, "The *Wu-fan* Campaign in Shanghai: A Study in the Consolidation of Urban Control," in A. Doak Barnett, ed., *Chinese Communist Politics in Action* (Seattle: University of Washington Press, 1969), 477–539.

53. *Wenhui bao*, September 5, 1950; and December 2, 1950. Quotations are from the latter.

54. Liu Nianzhi, 120.

55. Watanabe Takujuro, "Shihonka no jiko kaizō" (Self-reform among capitalists), in Nihon hōritsuka hō-Chu daihyōdan, Kokusai hōritsuka renraku kyōkai, eds., *Chūgoku no hō to shakai* (Law and society in China) (Tokyo: Shin dokushosha, 1960), 164–166.

56. Liu Hongsheng was not unique in his concerted efforts to bring Eighth Son home in 1949 and the early 1950s. For another example of a sexagenarian father summoning his son from Hong Kong back to Shanghai to manage family enterprises in 1949 and the early 1950s, see Wong, 34.

57. Liu Nianzhi, 123–125.

58. Ibid., 125–126.

Contributors

JEREMY BROWN is a Ph.D. Candidate and Associate in History at the University of California, San Diego. His dissertation focuses on crossing the rural-urban divide during the Mao period. His publications include a chapter about a model village staged by Jiang Qing in *The Chinese Cultural Revolution as History* (2006).

CHEN JIAN is Michael J. Zak Professor of History for U.S.-China Relations and Director of the China and Asia-Pacific Studies Program at Cornell Univesity. Among his many publications are *China's Road to the Korean War: The Making of the Chinese-American Confrontation* (1994), *Chinese Communist Foreign Policy and the Cold War in Asia* (1996, coeditor), and *Mao's China and the Cold War* (2001).

SHERMAN COCHRAN is the Hu Shih Professor of Chinese History at Cornell University. His research has been mainly on Chinese business history, and his most recent book is *Chinese Medicine Men: Consumer Culture in China and Southeast Asia* (2006).

NARA DILLON is Assistant Professor of Political Studies and Asian Studies at Bard College in Annandale-on-Hudson, New York. She is coeditor, with Jean Oi, of *At the Crossroads of Empires: Middlemen, Social Networks, and Statebuilding in Republican Shanghai* (forthcoming). She is also working on a book titled *The Paradox of the Welfare State: The Politics of Privilege in Revolutionary Shanghai*.

JOSEPH W. ESHERICK is Professor of History and Hwei-Chi and Julia Hsiu Professor of Chinese Studies at the University of California, San Diego. He is the author of *Reform and Revolution in China: The 1911 Revolution in Hunan and Hubei* (1976) and *Origins of the Boxer Uprising* (1986), and is writing a book on the Ye family and modern China.

JAMES Z. GAO is Associate Professor of History at the University of Maryland at College Park. He is the author of *The Communist Takeover of Hangzhou: The Transformation of City and Cadre, 1949–1954* (2004) and several articles on modern China. His current research is on "Shanghai Market: Rice Consumers, Merchants, and the State, 1866–1955."

GAIL HERSHATTER is Professor of History at the University of California, Santa Cruz. Her books include *The Workers of Tianjin, 1900–1949* (1986), *Personal Voices: Chinese Women in the 1980s* (with Emily Honig, 1988), *Dangerous Pleasures: Prostitution and Modernity in Twentieth-Century Shanghai* (1997), and *Women in China's Long Twentieth Century* (2007). Her current project is "The Gender of Memory: Rural Women and China's Collective Past."

CHRISTIAN A. HESS is Research Councils UK Academic Fellow in Asian History at the University of Warwick. He recently completed his Ph.D. in modern Chinese history at the University of California, San Diego. He is currently revising his dissertation, which focuses on the impact of the Japanese wartime empire and subsequent Soviet occupation of Dalian on the process of reframing the city as part of the People's Republic of China.

PERRY LINK is Professor of East Asian Studies at Princeton University. His books and articles span the fields of modern Chinese language, literature, popular culture, and political values. He is the author of *The Uses of Literature: Life in the Socialist Chinese Literary System* (2000) and is now writing on how rhythms, conceptual metaphors, and political formality in contemporary Chinese language tend to influence how people see things in daily life.

ELIZABETH J. PERRY is Henry Rosovsky Professor of Government and faculty associate of the Fairbank Center for East Asian Research at Harvard University. She is currently working on a study of the early Chinese Communist labor movement and its political influence, tentatively titled *Anyuan: Mining China's Revolutionary Tradition*.

PAUL G. PICKOWICZ is Distinguished Professor of History and Chinese Studies at the University of California, San Diego. He is the author of *Marxist Literary Thought in China* (1981), coauthor of *Chinese Village, Socialist State* (1991) and *Revolution, Resistance, and Reform in Village China* (2005), and coeditor of *Unofficial China* (1989), *New Chinese Cinemas* (1994), *Popular China* (2002), *The Chinese Cultural Revolution as History* (2006), and *From Underground to Independent: Alternative Film Culture in Contemporary China* (2006). He is the inaugural holder of the UC San Diego Modern Chinese History Endowed Chair.

SIGRID SCHMALZER is Assistant Professor of History at the University of Massachusetts, Amherst. Her research focuses on intersections between scientific and popular cultures in twentieth-century China, with publications including "Breeding a Better China" (*Geographical Review*) and "Fishing and Fishers in Penghu, Taiwan" (*East Asian History*). Her first book, forthcoming from the University of Chicago Press, is titled *The People's Peking Man: Popular Science and Human Identity in Twentieth-Century China*.

DOUGLAS A. STIFFLER is Assistant Professor of History at Juniata College in Huntingdon, Pennsylvania. His areas of research interest include higher education in the People's Republic of China, Sino-Soviet relations, and China in the cold war. He is working on a book on the "honeymoon years" of the Sino-Soviet relationship in the 1950s.

FREDERIC WAKEMAN JR. was the Haas Professor of Asian Studies at the University of California, Berkeley. His most recent book is *Spymaster: Dai Li and the Chinese Secret Service* (2003). Before his death in September 2006, he completed a draft of *Red Star over Shanghai*, a study of security work in Shanghai during the 1940s and early 1950s.

Index